Colonialisn  Development

In this comparative-historical analysis of Spanish America, James Mahoney offers a new theory of colonialism and postcolonial development. The book explores why certain kinds of societies are subject to certain kinds of colonialism and why these forms of colonialism give rise to countries with differing levels of economic prosperity and social well-being. Mahoney contends that differences in the extent of colonialism are best explained by the potentially evolving fit between the institutions of the colonizing nation and those of the colonized society. Moreover, he shows how institutions forged under colonialism bring countries to relative levels of development that may prove remarkably enduring in the postcolonial period. The argument is sure to stir discussion and debate, both among experts on Spanish America who believe that development is not tightly bound by the colonial past and among scholars of colonialism who suggest that the institutional identity of the colonizing nation is of little consequence.

James Mahoney is Fitzgerald professor of economic history and a professor of political science and sociology at Northwestern University. He is the author of *The Legacies of Liberalism: Path Dependence and Political Regimes in Central America* (2001), which received the Barrington Moore Jr. Prize of the Comparative and Historical Section of the American Sociological Association. He is also coeditor of *Comparative Historical Analysis in the Social Sciences* (2003), which received the Giovanni Sartori Book Award of the Qualitative Methods Section of the American Political Science Association. Mahoney is a past president of the Section on Qualitative and Multi-Method Research of the American Political Science Association and Chair-Elect of the Section on Comparative and Historical Sociology of the American Sociological Association.

Cambridge Studies in Comparative Politics

Other Books in the Series

Continued after the Index

Advance Praise for *Colonialism and Postcolonial Development*

Colonialism and Postcolonial Development

Spanish America in Comparative Perspective

JAMES MAHONEY

Northwestern University

CAMBRIDGE
UNIVERSITY PRESS

CAMBRIDGE UNIVERSITY PRESS
Cambridge, New York, Melbourne, Madrid, Cape Town, Singapore,
São Paulo, Delhi, Dubai, Tokyo

Cambridge University Press
32 Avenue of the Americas, New York, NY 10013-2473, USA

www.cambridge.org
Information on this title: www.cambridge.org/9780521133289

First published 2010

Printed in the United States of America

A catalog record for this publication is available from the British Library.

Library of Congress Cataloging in Publication data

Mahoney, James, 1968–
Colonialism and postcolonial development : Spanish America in comparative
perspective / James Mahoney.
p.   cm. – (Cambridge studies in comparative politics)
Includes bibliographical references and index.
ISBN 978-0-521-11634-3 (hardback) – ISBN 978-0-521-13328-9 (pbk.)
1. Spain – Colonies – America – Administration.   2. Latin America – Colonization.
3. Postcolonialism – Latin America.   4. Comparative government – Latin America.
5. Latin America – Foreign relations – Spain.   6. Spain – Foreign relations –
Latin America.   I. Title.
F1410.M274   2010
325′.346098 – dc22   2009022864

ISBN 978-0-521-11634-3 Hardback
ISBN 978-0-521-13328-9 Paperback

*Dedicated to my mother, Maureen Mahoney,
and to the memory of my father, Elmer Lee Mahoney*

Contents

Tables, Figures, and Maps

Tables

Figures

xi

Maps

Preface

Comparative-historical analysis achieves its potential when it generates new theoretical insights of broad utility *and* novel understandings of particular cases. Focused on questions of colonialism and postcolonial development, this book seeks to realize the dual promise of comparative-historical analysis. It offers a general theory for explaining variations in colonialism and long-run development among non-European countries. And it uses this theory, along with other analytical principles, to work out a new explanation of colonial and postcolonial experiences specifically for fifteen mainland countries of Spanish America.

The book's argument takes issue with certain assumptions embedded in leading geographical and institutional explanations of development, offering alternative and more historically oriented frames of reference in their place. It insists that to explain forms of colonialism, one must look at the *interaction* between the potentially evolving political-economic institutions of the colonizing nation and the societal institutions in the colonized territory, which also may change over time. And to make sense of the consequences of colonialism for development, the book argues, one must pay special attention to the collective actors that are born out of colonialism and whose capacities will vary depending on the kinds and extent of colonial institutions that were implanted. When applied to Spanish America, the approach yields a new account of why certain territories were subjected to more or less colonialism across different eras and why these alternative colonial experiences gave rise to new nations with contrasting levels of economic and social development.

The ideas in this book have been germinating for nearly as long as I have been engaging social science questions. When I was an undergraduate student at the University of Minnesota, the lectures of August Nimtz introduced me to the power of arguments attributing developmental paths to modes of colonial domination. Concurrently, classes with Kathryn Sikkink piqued my interest in Latin America and pointed me to Guillermo O'Donnell's work on modernization and authoritarianism, which suggested the possibility of long-run continuities in relative levels of economic and social development. These experiences, I can now see, planted in my mind the basic insight that

xiii

variations in colonialism might explain why Latin American countries today exhibit strikingly different levels of socioeconomic development.

Yet I did not begin any actual work on colonial legacies and long-run development for many years. More than anything else, political events in the world conspired to direct my research elsewhere. While I was at Minnesota, the revolutionary movements in Latin America charged my emotions and captivated my imagination; I wrote my senior honors thesis on the causes of social revolutions in Central America and the Caribbean. Then, when I pursued graduate study at the University of California, Berkeley, the "third wave" of democratization swept across the globe, refocusing my scholarly energies toward issues of democracy and authoritarianism. I wrote a Ph.D. dissertation on the historical roots of contrasting political regimes in Central America, which became the foundation for my first book, *The Legacies of Liberalism: Path Dependence and Political Regimes in Central America* (2001).

During the summer of 2000, I finally started this research on colonialism and development. Meanwhile, as it turned out, the second Gulf War and the subsequent U.S. occupation of Iraq meant that I was soon again working in line with world events. Across the social sciences, exciting new research aimed at explaining colonialism and postcolonial development was taking place. As I read this burgeoning literature, I came to see more clearly the methodological differences between the comparative-historical approach that I was employing and the cross-national regression techniques that were often used in other work. Though it may have delayed this project a bit, I could not resist writing articles aimed at explicating these differences. For those who know my writings on methodology, it will come as no surprise to hear that I believe comparative-historical analysis offers an especially powerful approach for explaining why particular cases experience specific outcomes (as opposed to estimating the average effects of causes). In this book, though, my purpose is not to advocate on behalf of comparative-historical research by abstractly spelling out its distinctive methodological features. Insofar as the book makes a case for comparative-historical analysis, it tries to do so by showing that the approach can anchor a valid explanation of processes of colonialism and postcolonial development in Spanish America as they have actually occurred historically.

I had the topic and method worked out early; it remained for me to do the research and write the book. I greatly underestimated just how difficult that would be, especially establishing a historical grasp over fifteen different Spanish American countries across very long periods of time. It took years of reading books and articles before I felt comfortable writing case narratives that were simultaneously sensitive to historical realities and consistent with an overarching theoretical argument. In fact, however, it was very fortunate that the historiography had become so voluminous over the last two or three decades; otherwise, I would not have had enough basic information to make the arguments here. Moreover, my reading of histories and my quest to establish a command over many cases soon became a labor of love. It instilled great purpose into my work over the last several years.

As an unanticipated result of this effort, I often came away from the books and articles that I was reading with profound admiration for the historians who produced them. Through their mastery of times and places, exceeding my own for every country covered in this book, the best historians make original interpretations that change the way we think about both individual cases and general processes. My own goals in writing this book are, of course, quite different from what most historians set out to achieve. I do not try to offer a novel argument using fresh archival material or by assembling already-discovered primary sources in new ways. Rather, throughout the book, I rely on historians' works themselves as my sources of information, drawing especially on points of consensus and, whenever possible, accounts about which there is little controversy. Precisely because this book builds so thoroughly on preexisting evidence and established interpretations of individual cases, the basic facts discussed below will not be much in the way of "news" to the relevant specialists. Instead, my ambition is to use systematic comparisons, new theoretical ideas, and the explicit assessment of alternative causal arguments to arrange mostly uncontested facts into a new and valid explanation. Comparative-historical analysis is that mode of research in which investigators contribute to historical understanding on the basis of broad comparisons and the conscious engagement of theory with fine-grained evidence. When comparative-historical analysts are successful, their findings can complement those of the historians on whose research they inevitably depend.

Most of the work for this book was completed in the solitude of my offices at Brown University (before fall 2005) and Northwestern University (after fall 2005). But it was in contact with students and colleagues that I was inspired to do much of my best thinking. Let me therefore acknowledge the people whose support and suggestions helped me to move this project from conception to completion.

I would first of all like to recognize the talented graduate students who collaborated with me in their roles as research assistants or as coauthors on papers and articles related to this project. My heartfelt thanks go to Jennifer Darrah, Diego Finchelstein, Carlos Freytes, Aaron Katz, Matthew Lange, Jennifer Rosen, Celso Villegas, and Matthias vom Hau. This group knows probably better than anyone else the research that went into this book and the feelings of excitement and occasional dismay that it brought to me. I also received very helpful comments from the following students: Jennifer Cyr, Christopher R. Day, Jesse Dillon Savage, Andrew Kelly, Armando Lara-Millan, Erin Metz McDonnell, Elizabeth Onasch, Madeline Otis, and Robert Rapoport. In thanking these individuals, I need to acknowledge the support provided by the National Science Foundation. In 2001, when Joane Nagel and Patricia White worked as the NSF Sociology Program directors, I received a Career Award grant that provided financial support for travel and research over a five-year period. Without this grant, I would never have been able to follow through on this study.

Many colleagues in history, political science, and sociology commented on draft chapters and related papers. In most cases I heeded their good advice, but sometimes I may not have been able to address their concerns. Let me therefore thank the following individuals without implying their agreement with all aspects of my argument: Jeremy Adelman, Ruth Berins Collier, Miguel Centeno, John Coatsworth, Frank Dobbin, Susan Eckstein, Marion Fourcade-Gourinchas, John Gerring, Gary Goertz, Jeffrey Herbst, José Itzigsohn, Steven Levitsky, Mara Loveman, Shannon O'Neil, Charles C. Ragin, James Robinson, Ben Ross Schneider, Kenneth Shadlen, Thomas Skidmore, Richard Snyder, Hillel Soifer, and the late Charles Tilly. I also received helpful feedback during presentations of this material at Arizona State University, Brown University, Cornell University, the University of Florida, Harvard University, New York University, Northwestern University, the University of Notre Dame, the University of Pennsylvania, and Princeton University. Although I cannot individually thank all of the professors and graduate students who asked questions or made suggestions at these presentations, I can at least point out that they profoundly shaped my thinking.

I was fortunate to receive extensive and vital feedback on the first nearly full draft of the book at a workshop in November 2007 at the University of Washington. This workshop was Margaret Levi's magnificent "Seattle Seminar," in which prospective authors of the Cambridge Studies in Comparative Politics series are invited to have their draft manuscripts discussed over a two-day period. I benefited enormously from the event, and especially from the comments of Maureen Eger, Robert Fishman, Anthony Gill, Stephen E. Hansen, Edgar Kiser, Margaret Levi, Steven Pfaff, Audrey Sacks, and Rebecca Szper. At about that time, Ben Ross Schneider also gave the whole manuscript an extremely close reading that rescued me from many errors and pointed me in promising new directions. After I revised the manuscript in light of these comments, it was finally ready for review. At Cambridge University Press, Lewis Bateman served as a wonderfully supportive editor and arranged for referee reports from which I benefited. The very talented Nancy Trotic did a magnificent job with the copyediting. For help in making the maps, I am grateful to David Cox and Erin Kimball.

My career trajectory has taken me from graduate school in political science at Berkeley to the faculty of the Sociology Department at Brown University to my current joint position in the departments of Political Science and Sociology at Northwestern University. At each stop, I have acquired one or two prominent supporters who helped me in ways that I cannot begin to measure. For believing in me, let me thank David Collier, Peter Evans, Dietrich Rueschemeyer, and Kathleen Thelen. I also need to thank my close colleagues Bruce Carruthers, Edward Gibson, Patrick Heller, Ann Shola Orloff, and Monica Prasad for encouraging me with this project and all my efforts on matters comparative and historical. Although Theda Skocpol was neither my mentor nor my colleague, she is one of my intellectual heroes, and I hope that readers will appreciate just how deeply her ideas have influenced this book.

Finally, of course, let me thank my family. My wife, Sharon Kamra, deserves my gratitude above all, for she had to live with the preoccupied professor. Sharon has a full-time career as a project director, but it was her expert management of our household that enabled me to attend to my research and still spend lots of time engaged with our wonderful children, Maya and Alexander. My mother has been a constant source of encouragement and love for my family; she is, to me, the most dependable person in the world. The memory of my father also continues to inspire me, for he was nothing if not the world's most committed perfectionist. As I now complete this book, I can see some of my mom's work ethic in myself. And I needed it, because – for better or worse – I also inherited some of my dad's yearning to try to get things just right.

1

Explaining Levels of Colonialism and Postcolonial Development

Much of the developing world was dragged into the modern era by colonialism. However one judges it, this is a historical legacy with which all scholars interested in the political economy of development, especially political economy over the long duration, must come to terms.

– Atul Kohli

Comparative historical analysis serves as an ideal strategy for mediating between theory and history. Provided that it is not mechanically applied, it can prompt both theoretical extensions and reformulations, on the one hand, and new ways of looking at concrete historical cases, on the other.

– Theda Skocpol

Colonialism was a great force of change in the modern era. From the Americas to the Asian and African continents, colonial expansion brought Europeans and their institutions around the world. It stirred nationalist sentiments and intensified competition within the European core; and the colonies provided an outlet for citizens who sought or were compelled to pursue a new life overseas. By disseminating people and institutions, moreover, colonialism forever changed the structure of trade and production within what had been an almost exclusively European commercial system. Nothing less than a genuinely worldwide system of states and trade was born out of colonialism. In the judgment of Karl Marx and Friedrich Engels, "the colonization of America, trade with the colonies, the increase in the means of exchange and in commodities generally, gave to commerce, to navigation, to industry, an impulse never before known."[1]

But the consequences of colonialism were, of course, felt most deeply in those territories and by those people subjected to this intervention. Preexisting societies were traumatically rearranged and sometimes destroyed. This was as true for precolonial societies renowned as great civilizations – such as the Aztec and Inca empires in the Americas – as it was for less well remembered precolonial chiefdoms and hunter-gatherer groups. The institutions established during colonialism, furthermore, exhibited over-time effects, whether directly through their own persistence or indirectly through the actors and processes that they brought into being. Colonial authorities and settlers almost invariably imposed administrative and political boundaries that subsequently became the basis – or at least the critical starting point – for demarking the borders of new nation-states. Within those borders, colonialism wrought economic arrangements and state machineries that structured productive activity and that affected the level of prosperity for the societies that remained. Colonial powers also introduced new cultural distinctions and modes of interest representation upon which subsequent social-stratification systems and political regimes were built.

In modern world history, colonialism is marked by a state's successful claim to sovereignty over a foreign land. Under a colonial arrangement, major actors in the interstate system at least implicitly recognize the colonizing state's patrimony over the occupied territory; and this recognition is founded in part upon the colonizing state's proven ability to implant settlers, maintain governance structures, and extract resources in the territory.[2] This definition makes colonialism a more thoroughgoing form of territorial control than what is conventionally thought of as imperialism or, for that matter, economic and political dependency. While imperialism and dependency entail asymmetrical relationships between states, they do not inherently involve a loss of sovereignty or even the insertion of governance structures under the control of a metropolis. Colonialism is set apart from these other kinds of interstate domination above all because it renders subordinate (or makes obsolete) all prior political entities that could once lay claim to – and perhaps back up through coercive means, if necessary – final authority over territorial inhabitants. So thoroughgoing is colonial domination that other international actors must treat the metropolis as the de facto political representative of the occupied land.

Though delimited in these ways, the intersocietal relationships that qualify as colonialism are nevertheless numerous and varied. According to David B. Abernethy, modern European colonialism was carried out by eight different countries and encompassed the territories of what became 125 different nation-states at one time or another.[3] Most of western Europe was sooner or later engaged in colonial projects, and most areas in the rest of the world became objects of these projects.

The undeniable, paramount importance of colonialism beckons social scientists to study the causes and consequences of this historical process. But what is the most fruitful way for researchers to proceed with their explanatory investigations? One worthy approach is to explore why colonialism occurred in certain places and at certain times;[4] another is to generalize broadly about the effects of colonialism for Europe, for the non-European regions, or for the world system as a whole.[5] Yet some scholars – especially comparatively and historically oriented social scientists – will always be drawn to questions about the sources of alternative modes of colonialism and their legacies for nation-states. Why did similar or different forms of colonialism arise within the borders of what are now sovereign states? What were the long-run consequences of particular kinds of colonialism for the national citizens of those states? Answering these questions, as this book seeks to do, requires treating territories corresponding to modern nation-states as the basic units of analysis, including during historical episodes prior to their appearance as sovereign entities.

In this introductory chapter, I develop a historical-institutional framework for studying colonialism and postcolonial development. The framework offers both principles for the causal analysis of particular cases and a general theory consisting of propositions to be applied broadly to former colonial cases.[6] The *principles of analysis* are developed in critical dialogue with the two currently dominant orientations for explaining national development: geographic and institutional perspectives. Concerning the geographic perspectives, I argue that they too often assume that features of the natural environment directly affect development; these approaches fail to give appropriate weight to mediating institutions. And they provide little guidance for theorizing the time-variant effects of geography and the ways in which geographic effects depend on the arrangement of already-existing institutions. The reigning institutional perspectives, for their part, are much too prone to treat institutions as devices that merely coordinate behavior, rather than as power-implicating instruments that unevenly distribute resources and constitute collective actors. Moreover, existing institutional work on colonialism in particular has suffered from vague conceptions of institutions and overly generalized understandings of their effects that cannot make sense of basic historical facts about particular cases. In response to the limitations of both geographic and institutional perspectives, I formulate alternative principles to be used in historically grounded, case-oriented explanation.

The *general theory* lays out orienting hypotheses that are intended to apply broadly across cases. These hypotheses seek to explain variations in both (1) levels of colonialism, which refer to the extent of settlement and institutional implantation in colonized territories, and (2) levels of postcolonial economic and social development, which capture national differences in prosperity and human well-being. To account for variations in levels of colonialism, the theory highlights the interaction between the institutions of the colonizing nation and the institutions of the precolonial society. Contrasts in the political-economic institutions of the European colonizers are hypothesized as essential for grasping why these nations often pursue quite distinct modes of colonialism in similar precolonial societies. Likewise, variations in the institutional complexity of precolonial societies are crucial for understanding why European colonizers with similar political economies follow contrasting modes of colonization. Thus, to explain levels of colonialism, I examine the "fit" between the institutions of the colonizing nation and those of the colonized territory.

To explain levels of postcolonial economic and social development, the general theory calls attention to the interaction between a territory's level of colonialism and the political economy of the colonizing European nation. The long-run consequences of a given level of colonialism vary across colonizers with different political economies. Extensive colonialism featuring heavy settlement and institution building is not expected always or usually to leave behind rich and egalitarian new countries (as some analysts suggest). Nor is extensive colonialism predicted to produce impoverished and conflict-ridden states (as others suggest). Rather, the effect of a given level of colonialism for long-run development depends on the political-economic institutions of the colonizing power.

In the core chapters of this book, both the principles of analysis and the general theory are employed in the analysis of Spanish America. My approach throughout is to start with the general theory but supplement it with ideas anticipated by the principles of analysis. In this chapter, I do not yet summarize the findings that are derived from this comparative-historical analysis; that summary is found in the concluding chapter. However, I do advance reasons why a close focus on the Spanish American countries makes good methodological sense.

The discussion so far merely anticipates arguments that need to be developed at length. I begin this task in the next section by addressing conceptual issues concerning the final outcome under investigation: relative levels of development.

RELATIVE LEVELS OF DEVELOPMENT

Why are some countries more developed than others? This basic question, posed again and again by thoughtful analysts, is an inquiry about *relative* levels of development. It asks why some nations have relatively higher (or lower) positions within the overall hierarchy of development. In a world system in which countries exhibit enormously different economic and social conditions, identifying the causes of relative levels of development must be regarded as one of the most fundamental tasks of the social sciences.

When treated as a theoretical construct, *development* may be defined, following Amartya Sen, as "the expansion of the 'capabilities' of people to lead the kind of lives they value – and have reason to value."[7] Under this definition, development is the process through which individuals are empowered to meet their objectively justifiable interests. Tangible improvements in wealth and social welfare are the crucial, though not the exclusive, components of development. Growth of the economy and real income, especially at lower and middle levels of prosperity, expands capabilities by providing access to basic goods and services that all people have reason to value. Advances in education and health enable individuals to lead longer, more informed, and enjoyable lives – things that human beings inherently and rightly seek. And both economic and social enhancements provide opportunities for individuals to engage in collective activities that are intrinsically

Table 1.1. Approximate levels of economic development for the Spanish American countries, late nineteenth century to present

Higher level	Intermediate level	Lower level
1. Argentina	5. Mexico	9. Paraguay
2. Uruguay	6. Costa Rica	10. Guatemala
3. Chile	7. Colombia	11. El Salvador
4. Venezuela	8. Peru	12. Ecuador
		13. Nicaragua
		14. Bolivia
		15. Honduras

worthy and often essential for securing other kinds of freedoms, including political democracy.[8]

Though not the only aspects of development, the expansion of wealth and human welfare – what I call economic and social development – are thus among its most important ones. They will be the focus of this book. I will inquire specifically about the causes of relative levels of economic and social development among the mainland Spanish American countries (see Tables 1.1 and 1.2) and, to a lesser degree, among the countries colonized by Britain and Portugal (see Chapter 7). The national differences in relative levels of development presented in Tables 1.1 and 1.2 will be described further and substantiated at length in light of the available data. The focus for now, however, is more general: understanding relative levels of development as an object of explanation.

The Stability of Relative Levels of Development

Relative levels of development – unlike absolute levels – tend to persist over time. Countries that now feature higher levels of wealth (or better

Table 1.2. Approximate levels of social development for the Spanish American countries, late nineteenth century to present

Higher level	Intermediate level	Lower level
1. Uruguay	5. Paraguay	9. Ecuador
2. Argentina	6. Colombia	10. Peru
3. Costa Rica	7. Venezuela	11. Honduras
4. Chile	8. Mexico	12. El Salvador
		13. Nicaragua
		14. Bolivia
		15. Guatemala

performance on health, education, and other social indicators) usually have been among the wealthier (or healthier, more educated, and so on) nations for many decades or even centuries. Similarly, countries that are now relatively poor have usually been relatively poor for a long time, often for as long as they have been countries. To be sure, there are some exceptions, such as the once-peripheral case of South Korea, which achieved a comparatively high level of development during the second half of the twentieth century.[9] But the *majority* of countries tend to fall into relatively stable positions within the global hierarchy of development.

Social scientists have long explored puzzles related to the persistence of relative levels of national development. Much of this work takes its cue from efforts to explain why certain countries – especially those in western Europe – emerged at the top of the development hierarchy in the first place. The question, "Why Europe?" (i.e., why Europe or a particular region in Europe was the birthplace of capitalist commercialization and industrialization) originally preoccupied the classical theorists and subsequently many of the most insightful scholars of macrohistorical inquiry.[10] Contemporary analysts have progressed to the point of identifying historical sources of variations in socioeconomic development among the European countries themselves, as well as other advanced capitalist nations.[11] What is more, whole paradigms of scholarship have explored the inability of less-developed countries to catch up with or replicate the developmental experiences of Europe.[12] From this work, we now know much about why nations in Africa, Asia, and Latin America have not been able to sustain high growth over extended periods of time. Likewise, we now have plausible theories to explain why a few extraordinary cases have been able to break with the pattern and achieve significant improvements in their relative level of development.

What tends to be missing, however, are well-developed theories about the origins of varying levels of development among the "non-European" countries. We still know precious little about why countries in Africa, Asia, and Latin America exhibit higher or lower levels of socioeconomic development relative to one another. Why, for example, is Uruguay so much wealthier than Bolivia? Why is Botswana a model of development in Africa whereas Sierra Leone is not? Can we identify the "original" sources of relative levels of development in such diverse countries as Uruguay, Bolivia, Botswana, and Sierra Leone using a single set of explanatory principles and a general theoretical framework? This book proposes that we can.

Rates versus Relative Levels of Development

Stability marks relative levels of national development because differences in *rates* of growth and social progress for countries are *not* stable. Episodes of *sustained* high (or low) growth rates are rare in the contemporary world economy. Likewise, dramatic improvements in social welfare (e.g., literacy, life expectancy, and education) are often held hostage by uneven growth rates – for although long-run social development is not simply a derivative of economic growth, it is shaped by such growth.[13]

Evidence for the instability of rates of economic growth is not merely impressionistic. In one important study, William Easterly and colleagues find that the correlation for national growth rates across decades ranges from 0.1 to 0.3, and hence that the performance of countries in one decade only weakly predicts performance in the next decade. These authors conclude, "With a few famous exceptions, the same countries do not do well period after period; countries are 'success stories' one period and disappointments the next."[14] In his review of the "new growth" literature, Jonathan Temple likewise warns against using growth rates as a basis for estimating long-run performance: "Frequently countries have done well for short periods, only for growth to collapse later on."[15]

A concern with *relative levels* of development differs in basic ways from a focus on *rates* of development. Whereas rates highlight variations in performance during specified intervals of time, relative levels cast the spotlight on differences that tend to endure across any given period. Precisely because relative levels of development are so persistent, one must explain them historically: their origins rest at some point *before* countries stabilize their positions in the hierarchy of development. By contrast, the causes driving rates of development are typically far less historically rooted, and they may include such short-range factors as natural disasters, business cycles, and public policies.

Nevertheless, changes do occur even for relative levels of economic development, and recent work on global inequality allows us to generalize about these changes. Most notably, richer countries tend to grow faster than poorer countries, producing national-level income divergence in the world economy.[16] Specifically, at least in the post–World War II era, upper-middle-income nations have had the highest growth rates, and lower-income nations have had the lowest. As a result, the global trend has been toward income divergence, even though there has been some convergence among the set of wealthy nations. To be sure, this trend assumes that countries are not weighted for population[17] and that control variables are not introduced that mediate the effect of the initial level of economic development.[18] Within these constraints, wealthier countries grow at higher rates than poorer countries, thereby following a pattern of divergence that has existed at least since the Industrial Revolution.

One implication of this research is that it is useful to distinguish between, on the one hand, the lower-income and middle-income countries of the world and, on the other hand, the upper-middle-income and higher-income countries. The latter group is simply pulling away from the former. However, among the lower- and middle-income countries, neither sustained convergence nor divergence appears to be taking place. Rather, when treated as a single population, the lower- and middle-income countries have been stable in their relative levels of development.

This last point is of essential importance, because the vast majority of former European colonies in Africa, Asia, and Latin America are now lower- or middle-income countries – the population that has exhibited the most stability in relative levels of development. Contemporary differences in levels of development among these countries are *not* primarily the result of diverging rates of growth or social progress since independence. Rather, the bulk of their differences can be attributed to the fact that they *started out* with different levels of development. If one wishes to explain why they have contrasting relative levels of development today, therefore, the main task is to locate the *causes of their initial differences*. This task requires one to pursue historical analysis and avoid dwelling on the ups and downs that may have occurred in more contemporary periods.

The Infrequency of Sustained Progress

A country will experience a significant change in its relative level of development only when the variables that affect rates of growth (or rates of social progress) assume atypical values for prolonged periods of time. This means that we can learn about the sources of stability in relative levels of development by elucidating why it is so rare for countries to maintain certain values on key variables (or combinations of variables) over the long run. To address this issue, however, we need to locate those specific variables that actually affect rates of progress.

Interestingly, the econometric new growth literature is not particularly useful for pinpointing factors that cause trajectories of high or low growth rates. Although well over fifty variables have been found to be significantly associated with growth, the effects of most of them are fragile.[19] Slight changes in the control variables or indicators of the regression model overturn conclusions about their impact. In addition, those variables that are robustly related to growth rates are small in number and closely tied to the phenomenon of development itself. For example, one important sensitivity analysis found that only four variables – initial level of gross domestic product (GDP) per capita, investment spending, population growth rate, and formal education – are positively correlated with growth across different model specifications. As Ross Levine and David Renelt note in reporting this finding, these factors are in part measures or symptoms of development itself; or, as Douglass C. North and Robert P. Thomas put it in reaching similar findings, "The factors we have listed (innovation, economies of scale, education, capital accumulation, etc.) are not causes of growth; they *are* growth."[20]

Comparative-historical studies that analyze a small number of countries have arguably been more successful at explaining exceptional economic performance among the less developed countries. Various works on the "developmental state" – a research program pioneered by scholars such as Alice Amsden, Peter B. Evans, Dietrich Rueschemeyer, and Robert Wade – suggest that sustained growth is driven by a state apparatus with centralized power, corporate coherence and autonomy, and dense social ties to key domestic groups, especially capitalists.[21] Likewise, more "society-centered" analyses – formulated by scholars such as Joel S. Migdal, Robert Putnam, and Amartya Sen – argue that sustained development requires the removal of patron-client relations and other hierarchical forms of domination.[22] Together, these literatures help make sense of the economic "miracles" in Korea and Taiwan and cases of great social progress such as Kerala, India.[23] They also suggest that a prolonged development failure (e.g., movement from a relatively high per capita income to a relatively low per capita income) would be precipitated by the disintegration of existing state machineries and the degeneration of positive-sum social arrangements into zero-sum conflict.

With these insights at hand, we can begin to understand why so few countries have managed to achieve sustained high rates of growth and social progress. Most basically, a developmental state and a society lacking rigid hierarchical bonds of dependence are extremely difficult to construct. In all developing countries, powerful actors derive resources from institutional arrangements that promote inequalities. To dislodge these institutions and actors, a fundamental transformation of the basic distribution of power within society is often required. Historically, such transformations have occurred largely in conjunction with foreign interventions, land reforms, revolutions, or wars that unseat dominant economic actors.[24] Other possible conditions are copious international economic aid, an auspicious global trade environment, low levels of foreign direct investment, a delayed transition to mass politics, and powerful legitimating ideologies addressing external threats.[25] Whatever the exact recipe for developmental states and egalitarian societies, the ingredients are not often present or found in the right quantities and sequence.

In sum, the stability of relative levels of national development is a function of the rarity of those conditions that promote sustained high (or low) rates of development. Once countries arrive at their particular relative levels of development, they generally stay more or less at those levels unless something exceptional happens. If one wishes to explain differences in levels of development, therefore, one should *not* center explanatory attention on processes that take place after a country has already settled into a given level of development. The real explanatory challenge is, instead, identifying the *historical origins* of the initial levels of development.

We have now developed an understanding of what it is that this book ultimately seeks to explain. It is time to examine the ways in which different kinds of explanatory factors will or will not enter the analysis.

EXISTING PERSPECTIVES AND THEIR LIMITATIONS:
NEW PRINCIPLES FOR CASE ANALYSIS

Competing theoretical perspectives emphasizing either geography or institutions strongly influence contemporary debates about the origins of development. These perspectives propose fundamentally different kinds of causes, directing attention either to physical features of the landscape or to socially constructed rules that guide behavior. Despite these differences, both perspectives as currently formulated share certain problematic ahistorical assumptions about how to explain levels of development. As a corrective, this section critiques these limitations and formulates alternatives.

Geographical Explanations

The idea that geographical endowments can explain levels of development is not new. Niccolò Machiavelli, Charles de Secondat Montesquieu, and Arnold J. Toynbee all embraced this orientation.[26] In our times, the hypothesis is associated with brilliant scholars such as Jared Diamond, David Landes, and Jeffrey D. Sachs.[27] Their work has established beyond any reasonable doubt that several features of geography are correlated with contemporary levels of national development. Even the simple variable of distance from the equator performs reasonably well as a predictor of current levels of GDP per capita: countries that are more distant from the equator tend to be richer. Yet for the purposes of actually *explaining* levels of development, as opposed to identifying features that are correlated with development, we must ask questions about *how* geography affects development, *when* geography affects development, and *what specific features* of geography affect development. For each of these questions, the existing literature provides insights, but these insights need to be enriched by a more historically contextualized approach if adequate explanation is to be achieved.

Many geographical features are virtually permanent, preceding in time all other potentially relevant causal factors. As such, geographical determinants can often be treated as fully exogenous causes – the "immovable movers" in a causal argument. One still needs to inquire, however, whether even enduring geographic features *directly* shape levels of development or whether their effects work primarily or exclusively through intermediary causal processes. In recent years, several economists have addressed this issue by exploring the effect of geographic variables, such as distance from the equator, while controlling for institutional variables (e.g., the extent of rule of law). The title of an article by Dani Rodrik, Arvind Subramanian, and Francesco Trebbi suggests the major findings: "Institutions Rule: The Primacy of Institutions over Geography and Integration in Economic Development." Rodrik and collaborators conclude that "the quality of institutions trumps everything else. Once institutions are controlled for . . . geography has at best weak direct effects."[28] Even stronger conclusions appear in William Easterly and Ross Levine's essay "Tropics, Germs, and Crops: How Endowments Influence Economic Development." These authors find that geographical endowments "do not explain economic development beyond the ability of endowments to explain institutional development."[29] Geographical effects simply disappear once controls for institutional variables are introduced. The key overall implication is that geography appears to shape levels of development *indirectly*, by working through institutional variables. Scholars of long-run development therefore need to ask about the ways in which particular natural endowments promote or hinder specific kinds of institution building.

Geographical features may be relatively timeless, but their effects on institution building are not. The same geographical features can have very different – even opposite – effects on institutional development, depending on the historical epoch in which they are situated. One reason why historical context makes a difference is, of course, changing technology. For instance, John Luke Gallup, Jeffrey D. Sachs, and Andrew D. Mellinger point out:

In early civilizations, when transport and communications were too costly to support much inter-regional and inter-national trade (and virtually any oceanic trade), geographical advantage came overwhelmingly from agricultural productivity rather than from access to markets. Therefore, early civilizations almost invariably emerged in highly fertile river valleys such as the Nile, Indus, Tigris, Euphrates, Yellow, and Yangtze rivers. These civilizations produced high-density populations that in later eras were actually disadvantaged by their remoteness from international trade.[30]

As technology advanced to favor oceanic commerce, the isolation of river valleys became disadvantageous to sustaining high levels of economic productivity. Similar technology-related arguments have been formulated to explain why tropical areas tended to perform well before 1500, whereas temperate areas have been favored in more recent periods.[31]

The consequences of geography for institution building also vary depending on the actor that pursues institution building. Actors who seek overseas trade, for example, may value strategic port locations in a way that overland traders do not. And changes in a given actor may lead it to react to the same geography in distinct ways. For instance, whereas soils capable of sustaining productive family farms may have been of interest to late-eighteenth-century Spanish colonial settlers in the Americas, this kind of geographical feature was not of particular note to the Spanish conquistadors who first occupied the Americas in the sixteenth century. When attempting to understand how geography shapes institution building, therefore, one must pay attention to the orientation of the institution builder.

From various literatures, we can begin to draw certain tentative conclusions about the implications of specific geographical features – natural resources, soils, climates, disease environments, and physical location – for institutional creation. Starting with natural resources, we may note that analyses of the "Dutch disease" suggest that countries with abundant resources – hard-rock minerals, timber, and especially petroleum – grow at slower rates than their resource-poor counterparts.[32] Some of these arguments maintain that an institutional mechanism is the culprit: resource abundance fosters rent-seeking states that engage in corruption and poor economic management.[33] These arguments are relevant to the present study because colonial authorities and settlers were often attracted to regions rich in scarce natural resources. One can reasonably hypothesize that the extent of these resources affected the ways in which colonizers pursued settlement and organized the colonial state. This is true even though the specific resources of interest likely differed across time and across colonizers.

Regional differences in climate and soil are associated with varying potentials for pursuing profitable agriculture, which in turn can influence institution building. More tropical environments, for example, pose difficulties for crop production due to a host of ecological maladies – poor soils, pest problems, lack of water, and unfavorable temperatures and seasons. On average, more temperate regions achieve significantly greater yields for staples such as cereals, maize, roots, and vegetables.[34] In work on Latin America, these differences have been called upon to explain the higher levels of development in the more temperate Southern Cone region of Argentina, Chile, and Uruguay. For instance, John Luke Gallup, Alejandro Gaviria, and Eduardo Lora find that in Latin America, "the four tropical zones have the lowest GDP per capita, clustered around $5,000 (in 1995 dollars), except for the highlands at $4,343. The three temperate regions in the Southern Cone . . . have much higher income, averaging from $7,500 to $10,000."[35] In a similar vein, Stanley L. Engerman and Kenneth L. Sokoloff argue that contrasting kinds of soil and climate are associated with different potentials for economies of scale. They emphasize "the suitability of the climate and soils for the cultivation of sugar and other highly valued commodities that embodied economies of production in the use of slaves."[36] Regions with climate and soils appropriate for export plantation agriculture, they argue, are especially likely to be subject to a mode of institution building that promotes inequality and inhibits socioeconomic progress.

Undeniably, there is an association between temperate zones and greater development and between tropical zones and lesser development in many regions of the world, Latin America included. Likewise, there is no gainsaying that variables related to other aspects of climate are correlated with development in Latin America and elsewhere. But are these relationships causal in nature? It is the position of this book that they are not: geographic conditions are strongly associated with an antecedent factor, and this antecedent factor – much more than geographically determined agrarian potential itself – gives rise to the institutions that drive levels of development. The association between geography and institution building is thus a by-product of a more fundamental historical cause.

The more fundamental cause in question is the institutional organization of precolonial societies. The varying institutional forms that these societies assumed were not equally distributed across different geographic settings. Rather, precolonial societal institutions were correlated with geography. Ironically, given their agrarian characteristics, prosperous precolonial societies with highly differentiated institutions tended to be located in tropical regions that did not feature optimal conditions for agriculture, especially European crops. Smaller, poorer precolonial societies with less differentiated institutions, by contrast, were often located in those regions with the best (from a European perspective) geographic conditions. In turn, I contend, differences in the organization of indigenous societies shaped the extent and form of European institution building during colonialism *independently* of geographical conditions. This argument is supported by statistical models that simultaneously control for precolonial population size and a large range of geographic variables related to agricultural productivity; these models find little or no effect for geography on institutions.[37] Moreover, the historical evidence presented below shows that socioeconomic development in colonial regions did not depend primarily on agricultural potential. Countries that had similar agricultural endowments (e.g., Nicaragua and Costa Rica) sometimes turned out quite differently; likewise, countries with quite different agricultural settings (e.g., Colombia and Paraguay) sometimes ended up with broadly similar levels of socioeconomic development.

Tropical and temperate areas vary in their so-called disease climates, and some scholars hypothesize that this variation drives contrasts in institutional effectiveness. Daron Acemoglu, Simon Johnson, and James A. Robinson use data from Philip D. Curtin's work on soldiers, bishops, and sailors stationed in different colonies to measure the potential risks of mortality for colonial settlers.[38] In many colonial situations, Europeans were especially vulnerable to death from malaria and yellow fever, diseases that were not usually fatal for the indigenous population. Europeans had access to information about the propensity of these diseases and may have taken it into consideration when making decisions about where (and whether) to settle. Given this, Acemoglu, Johnson, and Robinson hypothesize that the mortality environment was a key cause of the extent of European settlement, and that, in turn, the degree of European settlement had powerful effects on the kinds of institutions that were established in the colonies.

Yet as an empirical matter, there are a great many exceptions to the argument that European colonists chose not to settle in high-mortality environments.[39] Most notably, during the first two centuries of Spanish colonialism in the Americas, Europeans lived mainly in tropical areas, such as Peru and Mexico, that featured high-mortality environments. Territories with more favorable disease climates were comparatively unoccupied by the Spanish. In their most recent work, Acemoglu, Johnson, and Robinson stress precolonial urbanization and population density as the fundamental causes of variations in colonial institutional establishment.[40] In this newer work, mortality environment is relegated to the status of an indirect effect.

Finally, we may note that geography affects access to markets, which can shape the capacity of a territory to engage in trade. The most obvious reason is the cost of transporting goods to potential consumers, which is influenced by spatial proximity to markets, local landscape, and the presence of a sea or navigable river. For would-be institution builders, these kinds of factors figured as prominent considerations. Since the earliest conquest civilizations were founded, geographies that allow access to markets have been chosen as sites of settlement and institutional establishment. Even today, certain geographic features that deny access to markets, such as being a landlocked country, are associated with lower levels of development. Hence, we would be wise to pay attention to the effects of geography on market accessibility. But we should also be aware that these effects might vary across time depending on the types of commerce and specific organizations of interregional economies. The kind of geography that provides superior access to commercial opportunities is likely to change in conjunction with new technology and the evolution of economic organization.

Any adequate explanation of long-run development needs to be attuned to the effects of geographic variables. Yet these effects are indirect, exerting themselves only or primarily through mediating institutions. Consequently, in the analysis below, I will take geography quite seriously, but I will do so with the goal of understanding how it shapes the establishment of colonial institutions, rather than by trying to make a direct link between geography and development. And in analyzing the impact of geography on colonial institutions, I will avoid any mono-causal geographic determinism; other factors, including demographics, preexisting institutions, and changes associated with world-historical time, also shape institutional outcomes.

Institutional Perspectives: The Advantages of a Distributional Approach

Most work on levels of national development now emphasizes institutional variables as partially or fully explaining these levels. And despite other differences between institutionalists associated with alternative schools, most scholars define institutions in broadly similar ways.[41] They see institutions as rules or generalizable procedures that provide a guide for behavior and that promote predictable patterns of interaction (whether consensual or conflictual).[42] To have effect, these rules and procedures assume the form of ideas, memory traces, or "schemas" that exist in people's minds as knowledge about how to behave. When written down and codified, institutions are "formal"; otherwise, they exist informally – sometimes unconsciously – as information carried by individuals. Consensus thus exists that, minimally, institutions (1) consist of formal or informal rules, (2) offer a guide to behavior, and (3) are consciously or unconsciously known by individuals in a given population.

The real differences among alternative institutional approaches concern the hypothesized *consequences* of institutions, not their definition. To put these differences into sharp relief, two ideal-typical orientations can be delineated. One approach sees institutions as *coordinating devices* that solve collective action problems and that help individuals realize mutual gains. This is a common orientation among scholars who take free-rider problems as the norm and see institutions as generating cooperation by imposing humanly made constraints on self-interested individuals.[43] The alternative approach views institutions as *distributional instruments* that allocate resources unevenly and thereby help constitute asymmetrical collective actors. This orientation puts considerations of power front and center by emphasizing distributional conflict among aggregate actors as a basic driving force in history.[44]

My purpose in drawing this contrast is not to suggest that all institutions or any given institution must either promote coordination or exhibit distributional consequences. But nor is it to stake out neutral ground and argue that the two approaches need to be combined in a coequal synthesis. Rather, I want to take sides and insist that institutions are first and foremost distributional instruments and only secondarily coordinating mechanisms. Conceptions of institutions as constraints that generate cooperation, I argue, need to be subsumed within a power-distributional approach if institutional effects are to be correctly modeled. Three sets of considerations suggest why this argument must be made.

In the first place, many institutions do not solve collective action problems and deliver public benefits, but all institutions do have distributional effects. Institutions invariably shape distributional outcomes because human behavior cannot be regulated in ways that affect all equally. Individuals and groups inevitably enter into social interactions with different endowments of resources, and these differences ensure that any given set of rules for patterning their action will have unequal implications for subsequent resource allocations, no matter how justly the institutions are designed. Even institutions that are expressly designed to promote fairness and democracy, such as one vote per person in elections, differentially benefit individuals depending on their resources (e.g., levels of education or wealth). Likewise, seemingly neutral institutions – such as language or the rules that govern day-to-day codes of appropriateness – privilege some actors (e.g., those with better cultural skills) more than others. Moreover, of course, many institutions are created with the very purpose of distributing resources to particular kinds of individuals. The reward systems built into economic institutions such as job markets are a case in point, but the same is true of countless other social and political institutions: their intended function is to reward (or punish) individuals with particular characteristics. The uneven distributional consequences of institutions are undeniable and are precisely why institutional upholders normally must use the threat of sanctions to achieve compliance among those whose behavior they regulate.[45]

The view of institutions as generating mutual gains is challenged by the fact that many institutions – especially outside of the marketplace – are inefficient.[46] Myriad reasons account for this inefficiency (e.g., poor information, the short time horizons of actors, and lock-in via path dependence), but the most basic one is related to the distributional consequences of institutions. In the words of Jack Knight, "Institutions may or may not be socially efficient: it depends on whether or not the institutional form that distributionally favors the actors capable of asserting their strategic advantage is socially efficient."[47] Actors are not motivated to modify socially inefficient institutions so long as those institutions deliver disproportionate benefits to them. To achieve self-gain, in fact, actors may seek to destroy institutions that sustain public goods and that promote coordination by replacing them with ones that *reduce* coordination and collective benefits. They will succeed if they have sufficient resources to do so.

In the second place, a distributional approach directs attention to issues of conflict and power – issues that are essential for valid explanation but that remain hidden so long as institutions are characterized as coordinating devices. Institutional forms, rooted in their unequal allocations, always embody an objectively identifiable conflict. In many cases, to be sure, the conflict is only latent. Perhaps the power of one group relative to others is so great that the disadvantaged actors must passively acquiesce in the face of an inescapable status quo. Or perhaps institutions have, over time, become reified and thus viewed as inherent features of the world. Even when not taken as such inevitabilities, most institutions will tend toward stability because they disproportionately distribute resources to actors who are already powerful, reinforcing their position and better enabling them to uphold the arrangements from which they already gain. This is one reason why abrupt institutional change, unlike gradual change, is difficult and often requires transformations in the relative balance of power between advantaged and disadvantaged actors.[48] And when such change does occur, it may well take a shape that is unforeseen and unintended. As Knight emphasizes:

Social institutions are the by-product of strategic conflict over substantive social outcomes. By this I mean that social actors produce social institutions in the process of seeking distributional advantage in the conflict over substantive benefits. In some cases they create institutional rules consciously, and in other cases the rules emerge as unintended consequences of the pursuit of strategic advantage.[49]

When employing an institutional approach, therefore, it is essential to treat institutions as the objects of contestation among actors differentially implicated in their resource allocations. Only this perspective can capture the prominent role that power and conflict play in actual patterns of institutional formation and change.

In the third place, a distributional approach to institutions has advantages over a coordinating approach because it allows one to properly situate the coordinating effects of institutions as *outcomes* of distributional processes. From this perspective, institutions coordinate behavior among individuals *because of* their distributional effects. Individuals are commonly advantaged or disadvantaged by multiple institutions that reinforce one another. A shared position as privileged (or not) within institutional complexes provides a basis for subjective identification and coordinated collective action.[50] The existence of institutions that place whole groups of people in objectively similar positions with respect to the allocation of resources is, in fact, what allows us to talk meaningfully about collective actors such as states, classes, and ethnic groups. The behavior of these collective actors, in turn, is what gives institutional complexes their causal efficacy. The challenge for analysts of institutions is thus to identify the collective actors that are born out of institutional resource allocations. For these collective actors (perhaps in conflict with one another) are likely to be the forces that carry forward the effects of institutions on outcomes of interest, including new institutional arrangements.

Colonial Institutions as Long-Run Causes

Having introduced the basic orientation to institutions that is used in this book, let us now look at work on specifically the colonial-institutional causes of levels of development. Here it is instructive to center the discussion on two enormously influential articles by Acemoglu, Johnson, and Robinson.[51] This focus is appropriate because these authors propose a "general theory" of colonialism and development – that is, a broadly conceived argument that seeks to elucidate causal patterns applicable to all former European colonies. Many other works on colonialism and development, by contrast, do not formulate general theories. Some are primarily interpretive rather than explanatory, such as D. K. Fieldhouse's magisterial *The Colonial Empires: A Comparative Survey from the Eighteenth Century*; and some focus on one particular region, such as Crawford Young's *The African Colonial State in Comparative Perspective*. Still other excellent books derive major lessons about colonialism and development from comparative case studies, such as Atul Kohli's *State-Directed Development: Political Power and Industrialization in the Global Periphery* and Jonathan Krieckhaus's *Dictating Development: How Europe Shaped the Global Periphery*.[52] The insights of these rich works will be drawn upon in this analysis. But for the purpose of showcasing what is distinctive about the general arguments proposed here, a contrast with Acemoglu, Johnson, and Robinson's theory is most enlightening.

Building on North's celebrated work on economic growth, Acemoglu, Johnson, and Robinson see institutions that guarantee property rights as the fundamental cause of long-run development. Property rights induce development by promoting markets (i.e., opportunities to exchange commodities and services), and the authors measure them as protection against the risk of expropriation. When the risk of expropriation is low, economic actors have greater incentives to invest and exchange, and their self-interested behavior becomes coordinated in predictable, market-oriented ways. Interestingly, however, the *specific* institutions that guarantee or constitute property rights are themselves not well defined in this argument. These institutions are called "the institutions of private property" and are contrasted with "extractive institutions," but they are never actually specified concretely.[53] Adam Przeworski makes the point forcefully: "As invoked by this literature, the concept of 'secure property rights' is just a muddle."[54] What is more, Acemoglu, Johnson, and Robinson assume that European colonizers are effectively marked by identical institutions, all sharing functional property rights. This is why they insist that "it is not the identity of the colonizer . . . that matters" when evaluating the effect of colonialism on long-run development.[55] This is also why they believe that when Europeans pursue "settler colonialism," they invariably establish effective property rights, and that it is only when Europeans do not physically settle a colonial territory that extractive institutions predominate.

If we are to develop a compelling theory of colonialism and development, however, it will not do to pretend that all European colonizers are institutionally identical in their possession of property rights. In actuality, the degree to which European colonizers are marked by capitalist institutions and property rights varies a great deal. As Acemoglu, Johnson, and Robinson themselves make clear in other work not focused on colonialism, one can readily distinguish European powers after 1500 according to the extent to which royal power was checked and commercial interests were politically influential.[56] These kinds of institutional differences are obviously potentially consequential because they may shape the nature of the institutions that the colonizing powers bring to their colonies. Most basically, European colonizers that are not characterized by effective market institutions are unlikely to implant capitalist institutions in their colonies, even when they pursue large-scale settlement.

Nor does it suffice to leave undefined the concrete colonial institutions that actually drive long-run development (or to speak of them vaguely as "property rights" and "extractive institutions"). As one critic of Acemoglu, Johnson, and Robinson pointedly asks, "Is the dichotomy between extractive institutions and private property enough to explain the diversity of situations found in the developing world?"[57] Problems with the sweeping generalizations in Acemoglu, Johnson, and Robinson's work are disguised by the reporting of results in an article-length format that only superficially engages the historiography. "Its references to history are broad and lacking in details about actual 'historical facts'; in their interpretations [they] include very few historical data, sequence analysis or detailed contextual studies." As a result, they "take for granted the existence of a reality which, in many cases, has been challenged by historical studies."[58] Clearly, however, to explain development outcomes, any historical-institutional theory of colonialism worthy of the name must be compatible with the empirical records of the individual countries when analyzed in some detail.

What is needed, then, is a truly historically grounded analysis of the concrete colonial institutions that shape long-run development. While the best way to identify and describe such institutions is through the close appraisal of real cases, we can nevertheless make some general remarks about fruitful directions to be pursued. For one thing, in line with our distributional approach, institutions that produce hierarchical forms of domination are nearly always of great importance. Laws that regulate access to labor and land, as well as cultural institutions that control access to social status, have these effects.[59] Thus, attention must turn to colonial rules for securing indigenous labor, for assigning land rights, and for designating local political power holders. These institutions often connect ethnoracial categories to patterns of resource allocation; they can make ethnic identities into highly enduring axes of contention for the people designated by the identities. The consequence for development may be especially grave when a large portion of the overall society is excluded, on the basis of their ethnoracial identity, from the fruits of economic prosperity.

In terms of state institutions, we need to look at those rules and associated patterns of action that promote (or block) "the perception of investment opportunities and their transformation into actual investments" – what Albert O. Hirschman calls simply "entrepreneurship."[60] These state institutions might be referred to as "property rights," if one wishes, but they involve primarily rules that *coordinate investment*, not primarily rules that protect against the risk of expropriation, the latter being what is measured by Acemoglu, Johnson, and Robinson.[61] Emphasizing investment opportunities helps us better understand why familiar market institutions such as trade quotas, production regulations, and price controls affect development. These can stifle entrepreneurship without raising any risk of expropriation. Moreover, a focus on investment opportunities helps us see more clearly how commercial opportunities (or commercial obstructions) are *constitutive of actors* with certain kinds of interests. For the most important long-run effect of state institutions that regulate the market is not to constrain the choices of individuals with unchanging preferences. Rather, the critical consequence is the very creation of powerful collective actors oriented toward certain outcomes and not others. Most crucially, institutions fostering investment opportunities bring into being commercial classes, even in situations of colonial rule. When trade opportunities are enhanced, actors with adequate capital and connections to markets may be converted into the equivalent of a colonial bourgeoisie. Alternatively, hefty constraints on the colonial market may foster monopolistic elites with vested interests in commercial obstructions. And the extent to which either a colonial bourgeoisie or a market-obstructing elite is constituted can have consequences for development long after the colonial institutions that originally brought them into being have ceased to exist.

In sum, a historically grounded institutional theory of colonialism and development needs to examine how specific institutions and institutional complexes put whole groups of individuals in similar positions vis-à-vis the flow of resources. From these common positions, collective actors are born. These actors may then become critical forces in shaping productive activity and development outcomes, even long after the demise of the original institutions from which they were first assembled.

A GENERAL THEORY OF COLONIALISM AND DEVELOPMENT

The general theory presented in this section outlines hypotheses for explaining variations in both levels of colonialism and levels of postcolonial development. The hypotheses are developed through a chain of reasoning focused around four arguments. First, in distinct contrast to other recent work on colonialism and development, I hold that the institutional composition of the European colonizers – in particular, the institutions that constitute their political economies – needs to be a center of attention. Second, I suggest that in order to conceptualize how territories differentially experience institution building during colonialism, we must analyze their contrasting levels of colonialism. Third, to identify the origins of differing levels of colonialism, I emphasize the institutional organization of the indigenous population at the onset of colonialism. Finally, for understanding the causal consequences of differing levels of colonialism for long-run development, I stress above all else the ways in which colonial institutions constitute particular elite economic actors and define societal ethnic cleavages.

These arguments fit together nicely to form a single overarching theory of colonialism and development. But to see exactly how, it is essential to elaborate each argument in turn.

Mercantilist versus Liberal Colonizers

The European nations that engaged in overseas colonialism during the modern era – Belgium, Britain, France, Germany, Italy, the Netherlands, Portugal, and Spain – were not institutionally identical. And their institutional differences affected the ways in which they pursued colonialism, with large consequences for long-run development. For our purposes now, we will do best if we generalize about macro-institutional differences and similarities among the European colonizers and leave the details to the case analyses in subsequent chapters. To make these generalizations, it is instructive to examine the overall political economies of the colonizing European powers.

From Adam Smith and Karl Marx to Douglass North and Immanuel Wallerstein, scholars have distinguished alternative kinds of political-economic systems by asking basic questions about state activity in the economic realm. Among these animating questions are the following: (1) To what extent is the state oriented toward maximizing immediate consumption versus investing in long-run accumulation? (2) How heavily does the state regulate economic activity? (3) Does the state support an official system of socioeconomic stratification? By treating these questions as typological dimensions, we can distinguish two ideal-typical political economies that characterized European colonizers: mercantilist and liberal (see Table 1.3).

Under a *mercantilist* political economy, state authorities seek national economic self-sufficiency and organize productive activity to ensure favorable trade balances and the accumulation of precious metals.[62] They are centrally concerned with maximizing wealth generation in the short run to meet their hefty immediate consumption imperatives. The key institutions they wield are a series of restrictions on trade, on property ownership, and on economic and political participation. These "statist" regulations have major distributional consequences, providing rents to certain groups and denying privileges to others.[63] The principal beneficiaries are an aligned set of political and economic elites, the latter including monopolistic merchants and wealthy landed classes. These elites sit atop and actively uphold a rigidly hierarchical society in which the vast majority cannot advance.

By contrast, under a *liberal* political economy, state authorities allow economic actors to control and use surplus capital for the purpose of

Table 1.3. Types of political economies

	Mercantilist	Liberal
Accumulation Orientation	Promotion of economic self-sufficiency; short-run consumption	Promotion of international comparative advantages; long-run investment
State Regulation	More restrictions on trade, ownership, and economic participation	Fewer restrictions on trade, ownership, and economic participation
Stratification System	Status-group hierarchy; patrimonial state-economic elite	Market-based class stratification; capitalist elite

stimulating comparative international advantages and long-run accumulation. Entrepreneurial investments that seek to upgrade technology and achieve competitiveness in open markets are characteristic and encouraged. To provide the appropriate incentives, moreover, a liberal state works to ensure law and order and to protect trade and production for profit; it avoids the most severe restrictions limiting and regulating commercial interests.[64] And the market is the main tool for shaping stratification; institutions that explicitly privilege status groups and impose hierarchical relations of dependence are discouraged. Nevertheless, the stratification that results from market institutions can entail as much inequality as under mercantilist arrangements, or more.

These definitions are not the only ways in which the terms *mercantilist* and *liberal* have been employed, to be sure. *Mercantilism* is sometimes used as an encompassing description of non–laissez-faire economic policy in Europe from the fifteenth century through the nineteenth. With this broad definition, what I call mercantilism could be thought of as "classical mercantilism," and what I call liberalism could be recast as "enlightened mercantilism." Yet this approach runs the risk of stretching the concept of mercantilism to include virtually all modern political-economic systems. For its part, the idea of a liberal political economy is similar in meaning to "capitalist political economy." Capitalism, however, is often understood as a mode of production defined by free wage labor, and possibly also industrialism, which is not my main concern in differentiating European colonizers. In addition, by some definitions, mercantilism is itself a type of capitalist production, which makes it impossible to contrast mercantilism to capitalism. For these reasons, I adopt the labels *mercantilist* and *liberal political economies* and define them as in Table 1.3.

Mercantilism as a political economy characterized European colonizers primarily during the first two centuries of colonialism, from the fifteenth century through the seventeenth, when Spain and Portugal took sovereignty over the bulk of the New World. Thereafter, all European nations rapidly or gradually moved toward liberal political economies, especially as British hegemony replaced Spanish dominance in the European states system and as worldwide capitalism gained momentum. Even Spain and Portugal evolved toward liberalism during the course of their overseas colonial projects. Such evolution underscores how, analytically speaking, the key issue is not *which* European nation pursues colonialism, but rather *the kind of political economy* of that European nation at the time of its colonial project. One cannot adequately "control" for the identity of a European colonizer simply by recognizing its national identity (e.g., Spain or Britain); rather, one needs to be attentive to the actual institutional features of the European nation, which may change over time.[65]

Distinguishing mercantilist and liberal political economies in European history is nothing new; the contrast, perhaps under different labels, has long been an implicit or explicit point of reference in macropolitical inquiry. What is new is the contention that these different political economies are essential for explaining the causes and consequences of colonialism. To develop this argument further, we need to introduce the concept of level of colonialism.

Level of Colonialism

Level of colonialism refers to the extent to which a colonizing power installs economic, political, and sociocultural institutions in a colonized territory. The concept is intended to capture the relative degree to which a colonizing nation imposes – often in significantly modified ways, obviously – features of itself on a colonized territory. Such a focus is warranted because, as J. A. Hobson wisely noted, the most basic test of colonialism is "the power of colonists to transplant the civilization they represent to the new natural and social environment in which they find themselves."[66] Colonization inherently entails settlement and institutional transplantation, and differences in the extent to which such processes occur reflect fundamental differences in colonialism itself. When generalizing about the overall level of colonialism in a given territory, it is relevant to consider a broad range of institutions and their associated organizations, including political arrangements (e.g., forms of government, policing units, and courts), modes of economic activity (e.g., labor systems, trade policies, and types of agriculture), and sociocultural conventions (e.g., religious doctrines, entertainment venues, and family structure). Although these diverse institutions define level of colonialism in general, for explanatory purposes we will pull out those that are especially consequential for postcolonial levels of economic and social development.

The concept of level of colonialism can be related to other efforts by scholars to distinguish forms of colonialism. Some analysts, for example, have focused on the extent of European settlement that accompanies colonialism. This measure is correlated with level of colonialism: more settlement usually means more institutional implantation. Other scholars have distinguished between direct and indirect forms of colonialism,[67] between settler and extractive colonialism,[68] and between center and peripheral colonialism.[69] Although such distinctions may be useful for particular colonial situations, they cannot always be extended across the full range of European colonizers. The contrast between direct and indirect colonialism applies reasonably well to the British colonies, where this difference was formally codified, but it is awkward for the Spanish colonies in the Americas, which tend to blur the two categories. Likewise, settler and extractive colonialism were not mutually exclusive modes in Spanish America. Conversely, the idea of center versus periphery works well for the Spanish colonies, where a single colonial system existed, but it is problematic to use when classifying the disparate British colonies, which were spread around the globe and colonized at different world-historical times. In short, while other distinctions are useful

and indeed will appear in the analysis below, for the purposes of building
a general theory, the concept of level of colonialism has the advantage of
allowing systematic comparison across the full range of colonial experiences.

Causes of Levels of Colonialism

In any given colonized territory, the causes of level of colonialism are rooted
in the interaction of a particular type of European society and a particular type of precolonial society. As we have seen, European societies can
be classified as mercantilist or liberal, according to their dominant political
economy. But how shall we characterize the indigenous societies that these
mercantilist and liberal powers colonize? For explanatory purposes, I suggest, they are best compared and categorized according to their own level
of *institutional complexity*. A focus on institutional complexity is fruitful
because it calls attention to those features of indigenous societies that European powers consider most relevant when making decisions about how to
pursue colonialism. The institutional complexity of the precolonial society
powerfully shapes the extent to which colonizers believe it is feasible and
desirable to impose their institutions and people.

A precolonial society's politics, economics, and culture are all relevant
when judging level of institutional complexity. As Table 1.4 suggests, the
least complex societies include what anthropologists traditionally called
bands and tribes, or what are often referred to as hunting-gathering, herd-
ing, and horticultural societies.[70] Politically, these are pre-state societies,
with decentralized and nonbureaucratic decision-making institutions. Economically, they lack a significant division of labor and organize production
into relatively nonspecialized activities – mainly hunting, gathering, fishing,

Table 1.4. Types of precolonial societies

	Lower complexity	Intermediate complexity	Higher complexity
Political Institutions	Decentralized and nonbureaucratic	Centralized but nonbureaucratic	Centralized and bureaucratic
Economic Institutions	No significant division of labor; no slavery; no intensive agriculture	Some division of labor; limited or no slavery; semi-intensive agriculture	Significant division of labor; large-scale slavery; intensive agriculture
Sociocultural Institutions	Single ethnicity and language; kin-based relations; religion not a central basis for rule	Single ethnicity and language; class- and residence-based relations; religion used for rule	Multiple ethnicities and languages; class- and residence-based relations; religion used for rule

and perhaps semi-sedentary agriculture. Socioculturally, they are marked by a small population with a homogenous ethnicity and a single language; kin-based relationships; frequent mobility; and the absence of formal religion, central authority, and systematic labor exploitation.

By contrast, precolonial societies that have a high level of institutional complexity have been described as "proto-states," "states," "historical bureaucratic societies," or "advanced civilizations."[71] Political institutions in these societies are marked by centralized authority and multiple layers of patrimonial-bureaucratic governance. In the economic sphere, they organize intensive agricultural production with an advanced division of labor, normally based at least in part on slavery. Their sociocultural institutions stratify large populations in the thousands and sometimes millions across ethnic, class, and residence divides. In addition, sociocultural institutions – including religion – are used to generate political legitimacy and rationalize inequalities.

Finally, precolonial societies with intermediate levels of institutional complexity are classified as "chiefdoms" or "advanced horticultural societies" in the social science literature.[72] They feature centralized but nonbureaucratic authority structures in the political realm; some division of labor, settled agriculture, and tribute collection in the economic realm; and ethnic and language homogeneity alongside class and residence stratification in the sociocultural realm. Individual chiefdoms often encompass several thousand people, but never as many as one hundred thousand.

The level of institutional complexity of a society is causally consequential because it affects the prospects of specifically *economic accumulation* for European colonizers. To be sure, diverse factors lead European nations to choose to colonize particular territories at particular times, including nationalism, population growth, religion, and the politics of the day.[73] Among the factors that influence the *onset* of colonialism, economic considerations arguably play a secondary role. Once European nations choose to impose colonialism in a given territory, however, the *extent* to which they do so is shaped primarily by economic considerations. Even if political authorities and settlers show appalling ignorance of the societies that they colonize, they still do notice and pay very careful attention to the size and institutional complexity of these societies. It is these societal features that allow them to assess the immediate or potential economic returns that extensive colonialism might bring. Unless extraordinary circumstances apply, European colonizers do not pursue extensive colonial institution building in the absence of such economic returns.

Taken together, knowledge of the political economy of a colonizing nation and knowledge of the institutional complexity of a precolonial society provide a basis for predicting level of colonialism. As Figure 1.1 suggests, mercantilist and liberal colonial powers pursue different levels of colonialism in territories marked by similar levels of institutional complexity.

COLONIZER INSTITUTIONS

		Mercantilist	Liberal
Higher Complexity		Higher Level of Colonialism	Lower Level of Colonialism
Lower Complexity		Lower Level of Colonialism	Higher Level of Colonialism

PRECOLONIAL INSTITUTIONS (label at left, spanning both rows)

FIGURE 1.1. Predicted Levels of Colonialism

Mercantilist powers pursue higher levels of colonialism in comparatively more complex precolonial regions. They do so because more complex indigenous societies provide them with excellent opportunities for economic gain. Especially because of their orientation toward consumption and immediate accumulation, mercantilist powers are drawn toward extensive colonialism in large, densely settled precolonial societies that feature a tribute-collecting state and a hierarchically structured economy with coercive labor. In these societies, authorities and settlers can seize existing state-led surplus-extraction networks and employ already-developed coercive labor systems for the purpose of rapid resource extraction. In effect, the political economy of complex indigenous societies is familiar to mercantilist colonizers and (broadly) congruent with their own patterns of economic allocation found at home.[74] Hence, in colonial areas with a complex indigenous society, we expect to see significant mercantilist activity, including the growth of a large settler population and the introduction of institutionalized ways of life from the metropolis.

When mercantilist powers encounter regions with comparatively less complex indigenous societies, they engage in lower levels of colonialism. Hunter-gatherer and semi-sedentary societies provide fewer opportunities for exploiting indigenous labor and for seizing existing tribute-extraction networks. The problem with these societies is not only that resource extraction requires the introduction of completely new patterns of authority and production. Rather, it is also that less complex societies tend to more actively resist incorporation into coercive economic structures and hierarchical stratification systems. Given that mercantilists are not oriented toward economic activities that require a long-run investment, therefore, they may be predisposed to ignore (relatively speaking) their colonial possessions with less complex indigenous societies.

Conversely, liberal economic powers pursue lower levels of colonialism in more complex precolonial regions and higher levels of colonialism in less complex regions. More complex precolonial regions feature entrenched precapitalist institutions, and these institutions make it difficult for liberal colonizers to achieve market-based accumulation. A patrimonial state, entrenched precommercial agriculture, and multiple ethnicities within a densely populated polity – all of these are viewed as obstacles to efficient production and accumulation. Again, the problem is not only that the basic economic start-up costs of attempting to fundamentally transform a large and complex indigenous society are prohibitively high; it is also that the indigenous population may actively resist the colonial imposition of unfamiliar forms of economic activity. When confronted with a complex civilization that cannot easily be dislodged, then, liberal colonizers implant only a limited range of institutions and a small number of settlers.

Precolonial regions with hunter-gatherer or semi-sedentary societies, for their part, can be more readily displaced or destroyed to make way for the introduction of liberal institutions that facilitate long-run accumulation for the European nation and its settler population. Like their mercantilist counterparts, certainly, liberal colonizers view less complex indigenous societies as obstacles to be removed; they are not attracted to territories with these societies because their populations can be profitably exploited. Instead, liberal colonizers are drawn to these regions because they can be completely overwritten with new institutions. In sparsely populated areas with less complex indigenous societies, the preexisting order can be almost entirely eliminated, allowing for the installation of institutions that replicate and even improve upon those in the metropolis. Hence, liberal powers may heavily settle and significantly impose institutions in their colonial possessions with less complex indigenous societies.

Consequences of Levels of Colonialism

Level of colonialism is important in its own right as an outcome to be explained. But in this study, level of colonialism is also of interest as a cause of postcolonial development. Two variables in particular – level of colonialism and the political economy of the colonizer – jointly produce postcolonial levels of socioeconomic development (see Figure 1.2). Level of mercantilist colonialism is *negatively* related to postcolonial development, whereas level of liberal colonialism is *positively* related to postcolonial development. To understand why these relationships make good analytic sense, something more needs to be said about the specific institutions and actors that accompany the mercantilist and liberal modes of colonialism.

Within their most important colonial possessions, mercantilist powers impose restrictions on economic participation and grant exclusive rights to privileged merchants. They also construct or uphold coercive labor systems

COLONIZER INSTITUTIONS

		Mercantilist	Liberal
LEVEL OF COLONIALISM	**Higher**	Lower Level of Development	Higher Level of Development
	Lower	Higher Level of Development	Lower Level of Development

FIGURE 1.2. Predicted Levels of Postcolonial Development

and sociocultural conventions that define different and unequal ethnoracial categories. As a consequence, higher levels of mercantilist colonialism leave behind powerful commercial actors who enjoy and seek to preserve monopoly rights while stifling those who might stimulate investment and profits through exchange in open markets. The monopolistic colonial merchants are, furthermore, likely to be closely aligned with landed interests who control dependent labor – actors who are also not oriented or positioned to promote long-run economic development. Powerful coalitions of antimarket actors can thereby be expected to come into being and operate as roadblocks to development once the artificial colonial supports are torn down. Meanwhile, the labor and cultural institutions of extensive mercantilist colonialism subject the indigenous population (or perhaps an imported worker population) to systematic deprivation and ensure its long-run poverty. Insofar as this group represents a substantial percentage of the total population, which is the norm under extensive mercantilist colonialism, the social performance of the territory as a whole is greatly compromised.

Less extensive mercantilist colonialism is hardly innocuous and certainly does not allow a territory to fully escape these calamities. But it does spare the territory from the most deleterious effects of colonialism. Thus, if a mercantilist power chooses to mostly ignore a colonial area, powerful coalitions of monopolistic merchants and landed classes will be truncated or absent. And labor-exploiting institutions will be less extensive, with the possibility that indigenous people might be actively incorporated into society on something other than a completely subservient basis. Most importantly, because mercantilist institutions and actors are weaker, the postcolonial society can still be relatively easily reconfigured with new institutions and actors. The "advantage" of lower levels of mercantilist colonialism is, therefore, not linked to anything positive that colonialism brings. Rather, the damage done by colonialism is not so extensive as to completely close out future possibilities for successful development.

In liberal colonialism, the hypothesized pattern is just the opposite: higher levels of colonialism are associated with higher levels of postcolonial development. When liberal colonial authorities heavily colonize an area, they create institutions that resemble those found in the metropolis. They lay down coherent administrative, juridical, and police institutions that provide the basic infrastructure for functioning markets. These institutions empower a local bourgeoisie from the settler population that is capable of promoting autonomous economic development and also expanding the very state institutions that constituted it in the first place. A virtuous circle can thus ensue, one in which effective state institutions and investment-oriented elites reinforce each other, driving the economy toward ever-higher levels of development. Still, there is no cause for a celebration of extensive liberal colonialism. For it does not extend anything approaching full and equal citizenship rights to all people. And while it does ultimately tend to produce more homogenous societies with less deeply implanted ethnic hierarchies, it does so through processes that are socially devastating in the short run – namely, the physical isolation and/or elimination of the indigenous population.

Unmitigated underdevelopment is the outcome expected when low levels of colonialism are pursued by a liberal colonizer. Less extensive liberal colonialism introduces problematic governance institutions that define subordinate groups according to race, region, or religion. For when liberals indirectly and incompletely rule their colonial territories, they empower only a small group of elite allies and subordinate all others. While this is an economical means of controlling large populations, it places most people in a position of dependency and creates a polarized society in which elites appeal to ethnicity, ideology, or territorial homeland to bolster their rule or their claim to power. Indeed, the same indirect-governance institutions that demarcate subordinate groups usually also define politically privileged patrons who are charged with imposing order and sustaining legitimacy. By ensuring that loyal supporters hold monopolies over valued commodities, limited liberal colonialism breeds politically privileged rent-seeking economic elites quite incapable of orchestrating postcolonial development.

Models of Colonialism and Development

Now, finally, all of the pieces of the general theoretical argument can fall into place. We can summarize the basic argument with three-variable models for mercantilist and liberal colonialism, presented in Figure 1.3. In the models, the association between precolonial level of institutional complexity (variable 1) and postcolonial level of development (variable 3) is ultimately negative for both mercantilist and liberal colonizers. However, the directions

a. Mercantilist Colonialism

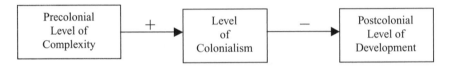

b. Liberal Colonialism

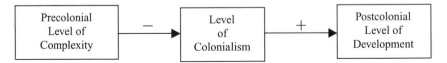

FIGURE 1.3. Models of Mercantilist and Liberal Colonialism

of the colonial causal processes (variable 2) that mediate this relationship are inverted. Thus, for the mercantilist colonies, the absence of precolonial complexity is an advantage because it leads to *less extensive* colonialism, which in turn has comparatively positive effects on long-run development. By contrast, for the liberal colonies, the absence of precolonial complexity is an advantage because it produces *more extensive* colonialism, which has comparatively positive effects for postcolonial development.

With these models, we can see why colonialism triggered a "great reversal" in levels of economic development.[75] Precolonial territories that were in some sense the most economically advanced – that is, state-like societies – tended to become the least economically developed postcolonial nations under both mercantilist and liberal colonialism (though via very different colonial processes). By contrast, the least economically developed precolonial societies – that is, nonsedentary and semi-sedentary societies – tended to become the wealthiest postcolonial countries, irrespective of the particular colonizer.

Although it is not acknowledged in the literature, there was in fact no great reversal for *social* development. The more institutionally complex and "wealthier" precolonial societies were *not* the most socially developed ones. Rather, they had lower levels of social development.[76] Colonialism reinforced this poor social performance by leaving behind large subordinate ethnic populations. By contrast, individuals living in territories marked by less institutional complexity (e.g., hunter-gatherer bands) enjoyed, on average, healthier and longer lives during precolonial periods. The inhabitants of these territories after colonialism were also better off, not only because they lived in richer postcolonial societies, but also because these societies had less rigid, more egalitarian stratification systems.

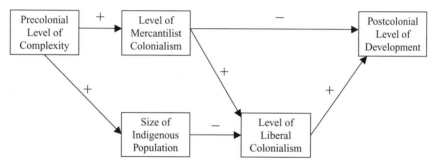

FIGURE 1.4. A Model of Mercantilist-Liberal Colonialism

Lastly, the general theory can be extended to accommodate more complex colonial situations. Figure 1.4 offers an elaborated model in which a territory is first colonized by a mercantilist power and subsequently by a liberal one. This "mercantilist-liberal" model is appropriate here because, as we shall see, Spain evolved from a classically mercantilist power in the sixteenth and seventeenth centuries to a more liberal (or "enlightened mercantilist") power toward the end of the eighteenth century. The mercantilist-liberal model thus best captures the overall colonial experience in Spanish America.

In this model, the initial step is the link between precolonial level of complexity and level of mercantilist colonialism (following the basic mercantilist model). The next major step concerns the determinants of level of liberal colonialism. Since there is no longer any precolonial society in the aftermath of mercantilist colonialism, the model hypothesizes that the size of the remaining indigenous population (which is positively related to precolonial level of complexity) and the extent of mercantilist colonialism itself together shape level of liberal colonialism. The size of the indigenous population in effect substitutes for the complexity of the precolonial society, and thus it is expected to be negatively related to level of liberal colonialism. Level of mercantilist colonialism, however, is hypothesized to be positively related to level of liberal colonialism. The assumption here is that liberal colonizers will be more likely to settle and implant institutions in areas where extensive European colonial settlement has already occurred, even if that original settlement was directed by a mercantilist power. The final key step in the model holds that level of postcolonial development is the product of *both* level of mercantilist colonialism and level of liberal colonialism.

Clearly, the mercantilist-liberal model yields more complicated and less exact predictions than do models in which only a single type of colonizer is involved. Level of liberal colonialism, in particular, is affected by two countervailing forces (size of indigenous population and level of mercantilist colonialism), which can cancel each other out. Likewise, for explaining the final outcome of postcolonial development, levels of both mercantilist and liberal colonialism are crucial, but they work in opposite directions. Consequently, when conducting the causal analysis of particular cases, we will sometimes have to supplement this version of the general model with additional variables – including geographical ones – as suggested in the earlier discussion of principles for case analysis. The implication is, again, that the general model is an essential starting point, but it needs to be augmented with additional insights for adequate historical explanation to be achieved.

A FOCUS ON SPANISH AMERICA

The principles of analysis and general theory developed in this chapter could be used to explain levels of colonialism and levels of postcolonial development among any or all territories that experienced European overseas colonialism. And the argument could be tested in a variety of ways. One obvious approach would be to pursue a large-N statistical analysis, drawing on the full range of cases from around the world and identifying quantifiable proxies to stand for the major explanatory factors and other relevant control variables emphasized here. But that is not the main kind of empirical test that I employ in this book. Instead, I use a comparative-historical methodology that draws on evidence from countries located in a single region and colonized by a single European nation. Although broader comparisons with British and Portuguese colonialism are made (see Chapter 7), the bulk of the analysis focuses closely on the fifteen mainland countries of the Americas that were colonized by Spain. Why is this focus appropriate?

One set of reasons for selecting the countries of Spanish America concerns the advantages of working with a relatively small number of cases.[77] The Spanish American region is not so large and heterogeneous as to prohibit historically grounded research. And the close analysis of individual cases allows for the matching of conceptual definitions with fine-grained evidence. Concepts can be measured within the overall context of each case, thereby avoiding certain simple measurement errors that sometimes arise in research focused on large numbers of cases.[78] This is especially true given that the argument at hand draws on "thick" concepts – such as precolonial societal complexity, level of colonialism, and postcolonial economic development – that are not always adequately captured by quantitative proxies such as precolonial population density, number of colonial settlers, and GDP per capita.

More importantly, comparative case-study research allows for the simultaneous assessment of general causal factors that operate across all cases and more specific causal factors that assume significance in only certain cases (or individual cases). By conjoining both kinds of causes, the comparative-historical researcher can pursue "complete" explanations – that is, explanations that identify combinations of nontrivial causes that are jointly sufficient for outcomes.[79] Certainly, a large-N, statistical model could be used to test the importance of the general causal variables emphasized here, including their hypothesized interactions. And if the theory is correct, these statistical tests should explain some portion of the variation in levels of colonialism and long-run development (provided that appropriate indicators are found and measurement error is not too large a problem). But a statistical model could not uncover variables that may be of particular relevance to select cases; all case-specific causes would be relegated to the error term. By contrast, each of the country analyses in this book draws on the theoretical principles formulated above to supplement the general argument and to arrive at a causal account that is valid even when confronted with historical details and the particularities stressed in histories of the individual case.

These considerations suggest some reasons for analyzing a relatively small number of cases using a comparative-historical methodology; they do not tell us why specifically the fifteen Spanish American countries should be examined. The answer to this question involves recognizing that the degree to which valid causal inference can be achieved depends heavily on the kinds of similarities and differences present among the cases under analysis. The Spanish American cases share certain crucial similarities and contrast in other basic ways to offer great leverage for causal inference. For one thing, similar colonial experiences among these cases allow for the elimination of many temporal and contextual variations that otherwise would have to be addressed. These territories were all colonized by Spain at roughly the same time and achieved independence more or less together, allowing us to control for key changes associated with world-historical time. Indeed, the three major Spanish American countries that are not featured in this book – Panama, Cuba, and the Dominican Republic – are excluded in part because they lack these core similarities.[80] Likewise, Spanish monarchs applied certain institutional arrangements to all of their New World colonies, such as the Catholic religion and the encomienda system of labor exploitation, even as they did so to differing degrees. Hence, we can zero in on the *extent* to which similar kinds of colonial institutions were developed and worry less about having to control for broad differences in *types* of colonial institutions.

Still other reasons for focusing on the fifteen mainland Spanish American countries draw our attention to differences across cases. One crucial point concerns variation in the institutional identity of Spain: before 1700, Spain approximated the ideal type of a mercantilist colonizer; by the late 1700s, however, it more closely corresponded to the liberal type. By looking at Spanish America, therefore, we can evaluate hypotheses about both mercantilist *and* liberal colonialism. And we can do so using the same territorial units, thereby controlling for many other kinds of differences that might otherwise need consideration. We can explore, for example, whether regions that were heavily colonized during the mercantilist phase but marginally colonized during the liberal phase experienced lower levels of postcolonial development (as the mercantilist-liberal model predicts). Analogously, we can see empirically if regions that were marginally colonized during the mercantilist phase but heavily colonized during the liberal phase follow the prediction of higher levels of postcolonial development.

Cases within Spanish America, finally, capture the full spectrum of theoretically important variation across precolonial, colonial, and postcolonial phases. Precolonial societies exhibit institutional complexity ranging from hunter-gatherer bands to large-scale bureaucratic civilizations. Colonial Spanish America includes both "center" territories that featured huge, European-like cities and "peripheral" territories that were almost uninhabited by settlers. Postcolonial levels of development within Spanish America differ to an extent that is nearly equal to what exists in the full universe of non-OECD countries (see Chapter 6). Thus, in selecting the Spanish American cases, one chooses a population of cases whose range of differences on key variables approximates the degree of variation for most formerly colonized countries.

The Analysis to Come

In the following chapters, the principles of analysis and the general theory developed in this introduction are put to work in the in-depth analysis of fifteen Spanish American countries (and more briefly for British and Portuguese colonial cases). The evidence is gathered mostly from secondary sources – books, articles, and monographs by historians and area and country experts. For the Spanish American cases, each country receives sustained analysis in its own right; and each country is evaluated in light of an extensive reading of the historiography. At the same time, systematic comparisons are always explicitly made across the cases. Indeed, causal arguments are formally summarized using qualitative comparative methods at the conclusion of key substantive chapters.

The investigation begins, in Chapter 2, with the evolution of Spain and its colonial empire in the Americas during the course of some three centuries. In the core chapters, Chapters 3 and 4, attention turns to, respectively, the Habsburg colonial empire (1500–1700) and the Bourbon colonial empire (1700–1808). These chapters elucidate the causes and consequences of levels of colonialism during episodes of mercantilist colonialism and liberal colonialism, respectively. Postcolonial developmental trajectories are the subject of Chapters 5 and 6, including the ways in which nineteenth-century processes of war fighting affected development in certain special cases. Chapter 7 evaluates the theoretical framework in light of comparative evidence from British and Portuguese colonialism. Finally, the book concludes with a summary of findings and a consideration of their larger implications.

2

Spain and Its Colonial Empire in the Americas

The history of the nineteenth and twentieth centuries . . . has been, in essence, the struggle between the Hapsburg heritage of economic and political traditional society, regional autonomy, and Christian ideals and the Bourbon legacy of liberal economics, centralized authority, and "enlightened" thought.
– Miles L. Wortman

Basic changes took place in Spain's institutional organization and policy orientation during the more than three centuries it held sovereignty over territories in the Americas. From the early sixteenth century until the end of the seventeenth, Spain was a great mercantilist empire, the most powerful of its kind in the world. Organized fundamentally to wage war and conquer territory, the Habsburg Empire was always in desperate need of resources, and it imposed classically mercantilist policies at home and abroad to generate them. The monarchy regulated production through guilds, restricted trade, and hoarded precious metals. And it upheld order with a stratification system that arranged citizens into a hierarchy of caste groups all ultimately beneath the king.

The rise of the Bourbon monarchy in the eighteenth century did not all at once and altogether transform Spain from a nation organized by classically mercantilist institutions to one that was enlightened and liberal. Yet during the first half of the eighteenth century, Bourbon monarchs did pursue reforms at home that centralized authority, furthered the bureaucratization of the state, and cut into the overwhelming political power of landed and ecclesiastical elites. Then, under the thirty-year reign of Charles III (1759–88), liberalizing reforms were implemented: assaults on the church, the reduction of corporate privileges, the loosening of commercial restrictions, and eventually the declaration of "free trade" within the Spanish Empire. While these reforms did not erase the elite stratification system, the guilds, and the monopolies, they did make Spain into a nation predicated on an uneasy (and soon unsustainable) balance of mercantilist and liberal ideas, actors, and institutions.

Undeniably, the reforms in Spain during the late eighteenth century had large consequences for the evolution of colonialism in the Americas. They influenced the kinds of territories in the New World where the Spanish preferred to live. And they transformed the types of institutions that the Crown and the settlers brought to the New World. These changes, in turn, helped to reverse the effects of levels of Spanish colonialism on long-run development. In the following chapters, we will consider these implications at length. But for now, in this chapter, we shall explore more carefully the characteristics of Spain and its colonial empire during the two historical periods.

THE MERCANTILIST PHASE, 1492–1700

Mercantilism predominated from Spain's first contact with the New World until the fall of the Habsburg monarchy in 1700. In the Americas, these years saw the conquest of the most complex indigenous societies, permanent Spanish settlement, and the implantation of sometimes radically new institutions. We can prepare ourselves for explaining the different ways in which Spain colonized distinct New World territories by considering here, sequentially, the basic institutions and orientation of Habsburg Spain, the political organization of its territories in the New World, and the settlers who carried the Spanish institutions across the sea and into the Americas.

The Habsburg Monarchy

Spain is the name we use to designate the political entity that formed out of the alliance of the kingdoms of Castile and Aragon after the celebrated marriage of Isabella and Ferdinand.[1] In 1492, the year of Columbus, this union of Catholic kings completed the reconquest of Islamic Granada and expelled the Jews, poising it to turn to more worldly affairs and make its bid for political dominance in Europe.

Holy Roman Emperor Charles V (1516–56) already inherited vast territories scattered throughout the continent. When he ascended to the throne of Castile, making him King Charles I of Castile, he could lay claim to the prized Low Countries, Franche-Comté, the Duchy of Burgundy, Naples, Sicily, Sardinia, and of course the newly discovered possessions in America. This was a formidable empire, to be sure, but it lacked centralized control, and holding on to it while pursuing further expansion fostered continuous crisis and ultimately proved impossible for the Habsburg monarchs.[2] "The struggle with France in the 1520s, the offensive and defensive operations against the Turks in the 1530s, and then, in the 1540s and 1550s, the hopeless task of quelling heresy and revolt in Germany, imposed a constant strain on Imperial finances."[3] By 1588, when England crushed the Invincible Armada, the end of Spain's hegemony within Europe was at hand. For, as J. H. Elliott concludes, "The late 1580s and the 1590s seem in retrospect the critical years [of Spain's decline]: the years of major reverses in Spain's north European policies, of another official 'bankruptcy' in 1597, of the death of the old king himself in 1598, and of the famine and plague which swept through Castile and Andalusia at the end of the century."[4] Spain remained a major power into the seventeenth century, but it never again seriously threatened to conquer the world.

Empire building required staunch mercantilist policy, which made Spain a conquering power but ironically jeopardized long-run accumulation in the Castilian economy.[5] According to Robert S. Smith, Castilian economic thinking was marked by "the absence of even theoretical interest in laissez faire and simple competition."[6] Beginning with Ferdinand and Isabella, the Crown protected the wool industry at the expense of all else. This left Spain thoroughly dependent on costly manufactured imports (linen cloth, dry goods, and paper products) and increasingly food (fish, corn, and wheat) from the Low Countries, Italy, France, and England. Such policy was maintained because the heavy taxes on wool exports provided immediate capital, which was always desperately needed, whereas advancing agriculture would have required a long-run commitment.[7] Agriculture could not but stay backward under this crushing system of taxes and monarchical protections. Nor could a competitive textile industry ever take root under the prevailing policies. As John Lynch points out, "Throughout the sixteenth century Spanish industry was shackled by regulations... At a time when industry in the rest of Europe was beginning to escape from guild control, that of Castile was put into a corporate straightjacket."[8] Absent any kind of manufacturing and industrial breakthrough, Spain was soon relegated to the semiperiphery of the capitalist world economy.[9]

The sixteenth century was thus the height of mercantilism in Spain, even as liberalism started to sprout in other parts of Europe. During this century, the great merchant guilds (*consulados*) were formed in the major Spanish port cities. After 1543, the Guild of the Merchants of Seville monopolized trade between Spain and America, at least until the Consulado of Cádiz used its superior location to win its own monopoly control in the mid-seventeenth century.[10] Dozens of new artisan guilds (shoemakers, hatters, butchers, locksmiths) also formed in the major cities in the mid-sixteenth century.[11] The Crown further controlled the economy by prohibiting the export of precious metals, confining the shipment of merchandise to Spanish ships, and imposing weighty customs duties.[12]

Nor did Spanish society deviate far from the mercantilist ideal of a rigid and hierarchically organized estate system.[13] At the top of the hierarchy were a small number of tightly linked families who made up the political-economic elite: dukes, marquises, counts, and other high-ranking titled nobility. Though less than 2 percent of the population, this tiny stratum controlled much of the kingdom's land and, along with knights, hidalgos, and other lesser nobility, monopolized political authority within Castile. Cardinals and archbishops of the dioceses must also be included among this rarefied elite, for the church had its own vast territories and commanded considerable influence over all important political affairs and sociocultural events. At the bottom was the so-called common estate, a mostly rural class that labored on the properties of the nobility and accounted for some 90 percent of Castile's population.[14]

After 1492, of course, the New World territories were brought under the proto-bureaucratic structure of Castile. Ferdinand and Isabella initially created the House of Trade as a mercantile tribunal to oversee monopoly trade with America, including the licensing and registration of all ships and merchandise bound for the New World.[15] Soon the House of Trade became part of the Council of the Indies, the overarching bureaucratic organ charged with running all American affairs on behalf of the monarchy. The Council controlled migration flows and recommended major political officials, including the viceroys – those highest-ranking Spanish officials in the New World who embodied the authority of the monarch himself. Despite all of these responsibilities, however, Council ministers usually had no experience in the New World and could not directly oversee territories that required two to three months for one-way travel through the monopolistic fleet systems (the *flota* for Mexico and the *galeones* for Peru).

The Organization of Colonial Rule

Colonial political-administrative organization in the Americas before 1700 was disorganized, often changing, and incomplete and inconsistent in its application. But it is still quite possible and useful to describe its basic forms.[16] Most simply, the Habsburg colonial territory was composed of two large viceroyalties (see Maps 2.1 and 2.2). In 1535, Charles I ordered the creation of the Viceroyalty of New Spain, which encompassed the nations of modern Mexico and Central America, as well as portions of the United States and Venezuela. Then, in 1542, the Crown established the Viceroyalty of Peru, which encompassed Panama and all of the Spanish possessions in South America except part of Venezuela. These viceroyalties were subdivided into a series of *audiencias*, which were originally designated as courts of justice but actually became critical political bodies in charge of myriad governance tasks.[17] The audiencias were further split into governorships (*gobiernos*) or provinces (*provincias*), as well as smaller political jurisdictions such as principal mayoralties (*alcaldías mayores*) and *corregimientos*. Finally, of course, Spanish settlers lived in towns of varying sizes, which had their own political councils (*cabildos, ayuntamientos*).

Already by the seventeenth century, we begin to see the contemporary countries of Spanish America in these political units. As Table 2.1 summarizes,

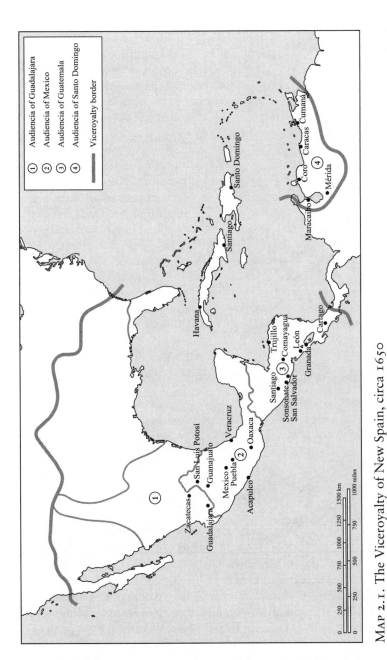

MAP 2.1. The Viceroyalty of New Spain, circa 1650

Sources: Mark A. Burkholder and Lyman L. Johnson, *Colonial Latin America,* 4th ed. (New York: Oxford University Press, 2001), 82; Carolyn Hall and Héctor Pérez Brignoli, *Historical Atlas of Central America* (Norman: University of Oklahoma Press, 2003), 33; Cathryn L. Lombardi and John V. Lombardi (with K. Lynn Stoner), *Latin American History: A Teaching Atlas* (Madison: University of Wisconsin Press, 1983), 28.

MAP 2.2. The Viceroyalty of Peru, circa 1650
Sources: Mark A. Burkholder and Lyman L. Johnson, *Colonial Latin America*, 4th ed. (New York: Oxford University Press, 2001), 82; Cathryn L. Lombardi and John V. Lombardi (with K. Lynn Stoner), *Latin American History: A Teaching Atlas* (Madison: University of Wisconsin Press, 1983), 29; Nicolás Sánchez-Albornoz, *The Population of Latin America: A History*, trans. W. A. R. Richardson (Berkeley: University of California Press, 1974), 81.

Table 2.1. Political-administrative location of modern countries within the
Spanish Empire, circa 1650

Modern country	Approximate political-administrative location circa 1650	Notes
Argentina	Governorships of Tucumán and the River Plate within the Audiencia of Charcas	The Cuyo region is part of the Audiencia of Chile.
Bolivia	Upper Peru within the Audiencia of Charcas	
Chile	Audiencia of Chile	Northern Chile is part of the Audiencia of Charcas.
Colombia	Audiencia of Santa Fe de Bogotá	
Costa Rica	Governorship of Costa Rica within the Audiencia of Guatemala	The Nicoya region is part of the Governorship of Nicaragua.
Ecuador	Audiencia of Quito	
El Salvador	Principal mayoralties in the Governorship of Guatemala within the Audiencia of Guatemala	
Guatemala	Governorship of Guatemala within the Audiencia of Guatemala	
Honduras	Governorship of Honduras within the Audiencia of Guatemala	
Mexico	Audiencias of Mexico and Guadalajara	The Chiapas region is part of the Audiencia of Guatemala. Much of the Audiencia of Guadalajara becomes part of the United States.
Nicaragua	Governorship of Nicaragua within the Audiencia of Guatemala	
Paraguay	Governorship of Paraguay within the Audiencia of Charcas	
Peru	Audiencia of Lima	
Uruguay	Governorship of the River Plate within the Audiencia of Charcas	
Venezuela	South American part of the Audiencia of Santo Domingo	

the modern state territories started to acquire political significance because they roughly overlapped with the audiencias, governorships, and principal mayoralties of the Spanish Empire. As we analyze colonial Spanish America, therefore, we will be able to gather and use data that more or less apply to the future countries by focusing on colonial political jurisdictions. In proceeding this way, however, we shall not make the mistake of assuming that the modern countries actually existed or that their emergence was a teleological inevitability, destined to occur irrespective of intervening events during the eighteenth and nineteenth centuries.

New World territories occupied by Spain were – or at least were treated as – part of Castilian society.[18] One might thus argue, as does Ricardo Levene, that the New World territories were not fundamentally distinct from other possessions in Europe that came under Castilian sovereignty. As Levene puts it in the title of his book, "las Indias no eran colonias" (the Indies were not colonies).[19] Yet such a position makes little sense by any conventional definition of colonialism or colonies. Unlike the Low Countries or Naples, the Americas were (to Europeans) a distant, unfamiliar, and indeed entirely new set of lands. Spaniards regarded their inhabitants as inferior in ways that legitimated brutal oppression and large-scale exploitation – practices far beyond what was deemed appropriate or feasible for people hailing from the European continent. To rule the New World, moreover, Castilian kings established brand-new administrative bodies and staffed them with personnel charged with extracting resources as thoroughly and quickly as possible. And Spain sent large numbers of its own people as settlers partly for the purpose of implanting its values and modes of behavior in what it saw as alien and pagan lands. Although other European powers sought their own influence on the fringes of Spain's New World empire, they too were forced to accept Spanish hegemony as the de facto reality. Let us thus harbor no illusions that the Spanish relationship to the New World was something other than colonialism.

The Colonial Population

Spanish colonialism moved hundreds of thousands of people to the New World, and it was through these people that institutions were transplanted into the Americas. That arrivals from Spain would carry with them knowledge of Spanish institutions and then might install some of these institutions directly or in modified form hardly needs belaboring. This is especially true when we recognize that the settlers were not an atypical group somehow hostile or immune to the dominant ways of Spain.

Historical works suggest that two hundred thousand or more emigrants traveled to the New World during the sixteenth century, and possibly nearly that many during the first half of the seventeenth century.[20] It is therefore not unreasonable to believe that well over half a million passengers were carried from Spain to the New World during the Habsburg phase of colonialism (Spain's population in the late fifteenth century was about 5.3 million). Some portion of these travelers returned home, but a hefty majority did not. Bureaucratic oversight of this migration was handled at first by the House of Trade, the royal agency in Seville that also controlled commerce and navigation, and later (after 1546) by the Council of the Indies in Madrid. Migration was voluntary; no one was forced to move. Early on, in fact, when the Crown experimented with creating agricultural colonies in the Caribbean, the king granted all of his subject people the right to live in the New World and encouraged them to move by paying for their voyage and promising them land and agricultural inputs upon arrival. By the mid-sixteenth century, however, the Crown limited New World travel to peninsular Spaniards (in the case of women, they also had to be married) and ceased providing incentives to migrate; licenses were in fact now required.[21] Still, it seems wrong to conclude, as does one set of commentators, that these state restrictions dramatically reduced the outflow of people.[22] In fact, before the eighteenth century, enforced legal controls on the movement of Catholic Spaniards to the New World were never so substantial as to represent serious impediments for those who were determined to come.[23] It was commonplace and easy for Catholic Spaniards – even sometimes single women – to bypass the legal obstacles. Substantial numbers of foreigners also slipped through the cracks. The real challenges and risks for peninsular Catholic males were economic, for individuals had to finance their voyage in one way or another and then stake out a new life in a faraway world. But these considerations did not prevent large numbers of people of modest means from undertaking the voyage (sometimes as indentured servants).

The migrants hailed overwhelmingly from the Andalusia, Extremadura, León, and New and Old Castile regions of Spain.[24] These were places with towns and cities that had good access to news from the New World. This facility of communication probably explains why people left these locations at high rates better than do socioeconomic factors, such as the prosperity of the local economy.[25] The travelers had remarkably different class and estate origins: they included educated bureaucrats, merchants (wealthy or not), ecclesiastics, artisans, peasants, major and marginal hidalgos, and sailors and servants. We should not imagine that they were a fully representative sample of Spanish society; on some dimensions, they certainly were not. For instance, few women and children initially made the trip; by the 1560s, still only about 30 percent were women, who settled in Mexico City and Lima in large numbers at that time.[26] Overall, however, we can confidently conclude that the emigrants who arrived in the New World were not people drawn primarily from any one class or caste, much less people who escaped the influence of the mercantilist political economy of the sixteenth and seventeenth centuries. These were people who were part and parcel of mercantilist Spain, and they, in their own autonomous ways, would aid the Habsburg monarchy in transplanting its institutions into the Americas.

No revolution occurred when Bourbon monarchs replaced the Habsburgs. But under the Bourbons, Spain did witness the introduction of more "enlightened" policies and institutions. Moreover, these reforms were often most completely *implemented* in the American colonies. The effect of the Bourbon reforms was thus to leave Spanish America with a colonial heritage that combined mercantilism and liberalism.

Bourbon Reforms

By the time the first Bourbon king, Philip V (1701–46), ascended the throne, Spain had become a more or less unitary state and was no longer in possession of dependencies around Europe; the empire was basically reduced to modern Spain and its American colonies.[27] The economy at home was still overwhelmingly agricultural, backward compared to that of England, and rigidly stratified into hierarchical groups. In the early eighteenth century, the first words of Enlightenment thought were spoken, though they could barely be heard, and they certainly lacked anything like a consolidated bourgeois class to give them real voice.[28] One of the few portents of the liberal changes to come occurred when the War of the Spanish Succession (1700–1713) forced Philip V to grant his ally England some access to trade in the New World, thereby temporarily breaking the Spanish commercial monopoly.

Even though at first nearly everything remained the same under the Bourbons, there was one conspicuous transformation: state modernization. The first half century of their rule witnessed real administrative changes that professionalized and modernized the absolutist state and that increased its power vis-à-vis regional governments and landed aristocrats.[29] Under a new intendant system, these more professional provincial officials were appointed to oversee public administration, finance, and military and judicial affairs. Centralization was then pushed further by the capable and reform-minded King Charles III (1759–88), who among other things extended the power of the state's ministries at the expense of the nobility.[30] "When, therefore, Charles III began to implement the reforming projects which were being prepared he had a central agency, at once more efficient and manageable, that afforded far greater possibilities of control over colonial affairs than had ever been available to the Habsburgs."[31] Yet how effective was he at using this more centralized state to transform reigning economic institutions? The answers are different for Spain and the New World, and also for different territories within the New World.

State proposals and legal actions after 1759 for modernizing Spain itself were ambitiously liberal, but they were often not implemented, leaving the country a contradictory amalgam of mercantilist and liberal institutions.[32]

For instance, the Crown issued legislation promoting greater freedom of trade for textiles and grain. But the textile protections were soon reinstated when Spanish industries failed to compete, and while free trade in grain was staunchly maintained by Charles III, this effort was reversed in the early nineteenth century.[33] More successfully, the monarchy abolished the trade monopolies of Cádiz and Seville, which crucially boosted commercial growth in Catalonia and helped stimulate the formation of bourgeois merchants in Barcelona. While Cádiz's traditional merchant actors still wielded influence over trade, the center of economic gravity had shifted to Catalonia and Barcelona, regions where Enlightenment ideas had taken hold. Other guilds and monopolies were likewise weakened, including to some degree the powerful *mesta* that represented the sheepholders, even as the country overall remained fettered by privileged associations.[34] As for the nobility, its size was reduced and its political leverage loosened with state centralization, but its inherited and acquired privileges (including certain seignorial rights), its estates, and its social standing persisted largely intact.[35] Concerning the church, the government of Charles III was unambiguously antipapal, and it famously issued a royal decree expelling the Jesuits from Spain and the colonies in 1767. Still, in other ways, the Bourbon reforms did not undercut ecclesiastical power. While the monarchy promulgated legislation curtailing the privilege of *fuero*, which provided clerics with various judicial protections and immunities, it was not successful in fully abolishing it.[36]

It was in the colonial New World – not Spain proper – where the Crown's reforms had their most demonstrable and far-reaching impacts. In the realm of administration, reform efforts began in earnest in the 1750s, when the Crown prohibited the sale of audiencia seats and appointed to the administrative courts educated officials committed to bureaucratic norms. The measures were a resounding success in Mexico City and Lima: the audiencias were transformed from governmental organs dominated by Creoles and "native sons" to ones run mostly by peninsulars and Creoles from peripheral parts of the empire.[37] In both government and the courts, furthermore, the Bourbons installed more predictable career trajectories, so that promotions and advancement better reflected seniority and merit, as opposed to wealth and patrimonialism.[38] This was accomplished partly through the introduction of the intendant system, a reform that, especially in commercially oriented urban areas of the New World, helped fight corruption among local officials (*corregidores* and *alcaldes mayores*) by installing more professional administrators, who then monitored local government, promoted economic growth, oversaw public works, collected revenue, and regulated ecclesiastical institutions.[39]

What is more, the Bourbons initiated reforms that liberalized economic policy.[40] The declaration of "free trade" – begun in the 1760s and extended to most colonial areas by the 1770s – ended the monopoly of Cádiz, lowered tariffs, and allowed broad participation by the colonies in trade with each other and with Spain (though rarely with other parts of Europe).[41] Especially targeted for reform were laws that previously restricted trade almost entirely to the American ports of Veracruz, Cartagena, Portobelo, Havana, and Callao and that allowed only the flota and galeones ships to sail prescribed routes at stipulated intervals. The fleet systems had become so dilapidated and so burdened by regulations and fees that they made their voyages unpredictably and increasingly infrequently by the end of the seventeenth century. Meanwhile, contraband trade flourished to the point that the New World was thoroughly dependent on English and Dutch smugglers for the provision of both basic and luxury goods. The changes under Charles III sought to rectify these problems. The old fleets were superseded by "register" (i.e., individually licensed) and free-trade ships that responded to supply and demand. They were permitted to move with fewer constraints, visit a much wider range of ports, and transport goods from one part of the empire to another without having to engage in smuggling or meet impossibly stringent regulations. Bourbon policies also encroached on the powerful merchant monopolies of Lima and Mexico City, as well as certain trading companies (e.g., the Caracas Company) that had been more recently established. Reforms put the administration of commerce taxes in the hands of royal officials rather than the consulados, as had historically been the case; and the Bourbons encouraged new merchants from ports not linked to the guilds to partake in the rewards of the more open trade regime.

Bureaucratic and liberal economic reforms initiated by Bourbon monarchs were, in short, a significant institutional reorientation. And their consequences were rather immediately felt: they stimulated nothing short of an explosion of trade. From 1782 to 1796, the value of colonial goods exported to Spain increased tenfold, while the value of imported goods arriving in the colonies increased fourfold.[42] Many of the exports were now livestock and agricultural products – hides, cacao, tobacco, wheat, yerba, coffee, and sugar – that were produced in previously remote parts of the empire. While Habsburg "bullionist" economic policies had discouraged agrarian exports from the Americas,[43] the Bourbons actively promoted commercial agriculture. Such a fundamental reorientation lay behind the rise of peripheral areas in the Americas that had suffocated under mercantilist regulations. This peripheral rise was, in turn, part of a broader "reversal of fortunes" in Spanish America during the period from 1750 to 1850.[44] The reasons for the colonial reversal – as well as exceptions to it – will be examined on a case-by-case basis in the analysis to come. For now, suffice it to stress that one critical factor explaining economic successes and failures in the Americas during the Bourbon period involves precisely the extent to which people and institutions were introduced into particular territories. For while the Bourbons sought to apply their reforms across the whole empire, the reality is that Bourbon colonialism – like Habsburg colonialism before it – laid down institutional changes quite unevenly in the New World.

MAP 2.3. Colonial Spanish America, circa 1780
Sources: Mark A. Burkholder and Lyman L. Johnson, *Colonial Latin America*, 4th ed. (New York: Oxford University Press, 2001), 257; Cathryn L. Lombardi and John V. Lombardi (with K. Lynn Stoner), *Latin American History: A Teaching Atlas* (Madison: University of Wisconsin Press, 1983), 31–2.

Political Reorganization and Settlement Patterns

Bourbon administrative reforms also entailed a basic restructuring of the viceroyalties in ways that allowed previously peripheral areas to become political and bureaucratic centers (see Map 2.3). The Viceroyalty of New

Granada was created in 1739 (after an earlier aborted effort), and it encompassed more or less modern Colombia, Ecuador, and Venezuela. Then, in 1776, the Bourbons established the Viceroyalty of the River Plate, which included the lands of roughly modern Argentina, Bolivia, Paraguay, and Uruguay (and a slice of northern Chile). Hence, the old Viceroyalty of New Spain remained intact, while the old Viceroyalty of Peru was reduced to modern Peru and most of Chile. Commercial areas within the new viceroyalties enjoyed greater autonomy and political clout. Notably, Caracas was made the capital of a captaincy general in 1777 and then home to an audiencia in 1786; and Buenos Aires housed its own audiencia after 1783.

Disappointingly little is known about Spanish migration to the New World during the eighteenth century. Writing in 1985, Magnus Mörner believed that the only existing estimate of total net migration, which was 52,500 persons, was "merely a conjecture without any real basis."[45] More recently, David Eltis estimated that 193,000 Spaniards left for the New World from 1700 to 1760, but his methods are dubious.[46] The distinguished historians Mark A. Burkholder and Lyman L. Johnson suggest that the Spanish migrants who arrived after 1700 (especially after the 1760s) often made their way to once-peripheral areas of the empire. They estimate the total net migration during the eighteenth century at forty to fifty thousand for the peripheral colonies (excluding Mexico and Peru).[47] As we shall see in Chapter 4 by looking at individual cases, several previously marginal cities were indisputably key destinations for Spanish arrivals during the eighteenth century. And some previously major colonial cities stagnated or declined during this same period. While a portion of this demographic change is due to intracolonial migration among the existing settlers, as opposed to migration across the Atlantic, the outcome is the same: Spaniards were populating new areas in considerable numbers, especially after the reforms of the 1760s and 1770s.

Whatever their exact numbers, the eighteenth-century Spanish migrants were surely oriented more toward liberal ideas than were their counterparts from the previous two centuries. This is obviously true for the professional bureaucrats who arrived in the region with the express purpose of enforcing Charles III's reforms. But it also holds for other actors, who were drawn to travel across the Atlantic in order to pursue the opportunities that arose from market reforms. Most notable here are the merchants who arrived in the port cities of once-peripheral areas: "The loosening of commercial restrictions after 1765 and the more important administrative and territorial reforms attracted Spanish merchants to the peripheral ports and capital cities. Peninsulars dominated the merchant elites of Buenos Aires, Caracas, Santiago, and Havana."[48]

Some of these merchants were Catalans linked to the emerging bourgeoisie and the nascent capitalist economy of Barcelona.[49] They embraced liberal economic thought and carried their ideas from Spain to the colonies. Non-elite migrants were often Galicians, Asturians, and Basques who traveled to the New World as artisans or unskilled workers. These individuals sought to make a fortune in America, or at least lead a prosperous life, through whatever opportunities presented themselves.[50] And in the late eighteenth century, these opportunities were more commercially oriented than they had been during all previous periods. Non-elite settlers acting on their own interests therefore might also contribute to the construction of more liberal institutions in the Americas.

CONCLUSION

Spain evolved during the eighteenth century from the epitome of a classically mercantilist political economy to an enlightened-mercantilist political economy that was increasingly subject to liberal influences. This transition was particularly salient in the New World, where royal policy aimed at modernizing bureaucracy and stimulating trade reflected the emergent Spanish liberalism. The implication of this transition is that colonialism in the Americas entailed a dual legacy – a mercantilist-liberal one. The liberal advance occurred only during the late colonial period and was built on top of more than two centuries of mercantilist colonialism. But it will not serve us to pretend that this liberal heritage was inconsequential any more than it would be appropriate to assume that the liberal phase made the prior mercantilist phase irrelevant. We need to take both periods of colonialism seriously.

Taking both phases seriously entails two overarching tasks. First, it means identifying and explaining variations in the extent to which Spanish colonizers established institutions during each phase and across each territory that would become a country in Spanish America. Second, it means understanding how different combinations of mercantilist and liberal institutions led particular countries to arrive at specific positions in the world hierarchy of development. These tasks are pursued in the next two chapters.

3

Mercantilist Colonialism

In simple terms, Spanish settlers were drawn initially to areas where there were minerals or large Indian populations from whom tribute could be extracted.
– Linda A. Newson

The poorer the region was as a colony, the richer and more developed it is today.
– Andre Gunder Frank

The classically mercantilist phase (1492–1700) of Spanish colonialism saw the uprooting of indigenous societies; the physical settlement of the region by Europeans; and the installation of new political, economic, and sociocultural institutions. These processes occurred in each of the territories that would become the modern countries of Spanish America. Yet the extent to which the Spanish reorganized indigenous people, developed settlements, and installed institutions varied across these territories. Such variations, in turn, affected the degree to which entrenched mercantilist actors came into being, with large subsequent implications for national development.

It is useful, I suggest, to categorize the territories corresponding to the modern countries of Spanish America according to three types of mercantilist colonies: centers, peripheries, and semiperipheries (see Table 3.1). The mercantilist colonial centers of Mexico, Peru, and Bolivia were the principal areas of Spanish settlement and activity, featuring the most important colonial administrations, the most intensive and far-reaching systems of labor exploitation, and the greatest expressions of Spanish sociocultural life (including Catholic religion). Each colonial center was represented by one city – Mexico City, Lima, and Potosí, respectively – that especially concentrated Spanish people and institutions and that served as a heartland of the overall colonial project, even though huge parts of Mexico, Peru, and Bolivia were not colonized at all.

In stark contrast to the centers, the colonial peripheries in their entirety were backwater territories within the Spanish Empire – they were unimportant to the Crown for political administration, for economic production and wealth generation, and for the extension of sociocultural mores into the New World. In the seventeenth century, the leading Spanish cities

Table 3.1. Types of Spanish colonial territories, circa 1650

Colonial centers	Colonial peripheries	Colonial semiperipheries
Mexico	Uruguay	Guatemala
Peru	Argentina	Colombia
Bolivia	Chile	Ecuador
	Paraguay	
	Venezuela	
	El Salvador	
	Honduras	
	Nicaragua	
	Costa Rica	

in the peripheries were impoverished frontier settlements, such as Buenos Aires (Argentina), Santiago (Chile), Cartago (Costa Rica), Sonsonate (El Salvador), Comayagua (Honduras), León (Nicaragua), Asunción (Paraguay), and Caracas (Venezuela). Finally, the colonial semiperipheries stood between the centers and peripheries in their level of Spanish settlement and institutional implantation. Santiago (Guatemala), Bogotá (Colombia), and Quito (Ecuador) were among the largest cities in mid-seventeenth-century colonial Spanish America, but in comparison to Mexico City, Lima, and Potosí, they contained fewer Spanish residents, fewer high-ranking political and religious officials, and fewer indigenous people who were subject to exploitative labor institutions. Still, as we shall see, in their institutional legacies these mercantilist semiperipheries bore a stronger resemblance to the colonial centers than to the colonial peripheries.

One key task of this chapter is to explain why particular territories became particular types of colonies. It has already been established that I take the mercantilist political-economic composition of colonizing Spain to be an essential part of the explanation. The present challenge is to account for different outcomes within the region while Spanish institutional identity remains constant (i.e., classically mercantilist throughout the sixteenth and seventeenth centuries). On this matter, the historical literature on Spanish colonialism points the way in suggesting as causes the kinds of precolonial indigenous societies and the extent of exploitable precious resources, especially gold and silver, that were present in each territory when the Spanish arrived. From this starting point, I use comparative evidence to identify the relative causal roles played by precolonial populations and precious minerals in driving varying levels of Spanish settlement and institution building. As will become clear, of the two general causes – indigenous societal organization and precious minerals – I find the former to be the more important one for the specific purpose of explaining why territories became colonial centers, semiperipheries, or peripheries (as opposed to, for example, explaining the extent to which Spain settled and built institutions in the New World *as a whole*).

Indigenous societal size and organization strongly influenced the extent to which colonizers could extract surplus labor from native populations. It was specifically those territories where precolonial societies were organized as populous states that colonizers readily imposed political domination and then advanced accumulation on the back of indigenous labor. As Linda A. Newson argues, Spaniards were attracted to indigenous people living under state-like authority for two essential reasons:

First, these Indians [in the state-like societies] produced surpluses and they had been subject to tribute payments and labor drafts in the pre-Columbian period, so that although the Spanish modified the systems by which they were exacted, such demands were not considered extraordinary. Second, the hierarchical structure of these societies permitted the Spanish to control and exploit large Indian populations through a relatively small number of native leaders.[1]

The contrast with less complex societies is stark:

The control and exploitation of essentially egalitarian tribes who subsisted on the products of shifting cultivation supplemented by hunting, fishing, and gathering could not be effected so easily by means of the same institutions. These Indians had not paid tribute or provided labor for extracommunal purposes in pre-Columbian times, so that no organizational structure existed for their exaction and the task was made even more difficult by the lack of effective leadership . . . The nomadic hunters, fishers, and gatherers provided even less in terms of surpluses and sources of labor, and they were more difficult to control than tribes, so that little effort was made to bring them under Spanish control.[2]

Between the state societies and the tribes/hunter-gatherers were various kinds of settled agricultural chiefdoms. Although some such chiefdoms were quite populous and offered good opportunities for labor extraction, they still lacked the centralized political organizations that would have enabled the Spanish to readily control and exploit their populations as they did with the indigenous states. Hence, these chiefdoms were not the focus of Spanish colonizing efforts.

Even as the institutional complexity of the precolonial societies figures centrally in the causal analysis below, the role of geographical variables is not overlooked. The extent to which regions contained significant pockets of exploitable precious minerals emerges as a prominent factor shaping Spanish settlement and institution building. Likewise, the spatial proximity of territories to the two great indigenous civilizations of the Americas – the Aztec and Inca empires – influenced Spanish decisions about where to establish residence and lay down institutions. Nevertheless, the presence of a complex indigenous society is the only factor that was *necessary* for the creation of a colonial center before the eighteenth century.

The analysis in this chapter does not stop with the sources of Spanish institution building. It works toward the explanation of differences in postcolonial development by considering the colonial actors who were created out of mercantilist settlement and who would later shape and limit the possibilities for development during the Bourbon colonial phase. Two kinds of collective actors are especially important here.

First, colonial institutions wrought subordinate ethnic populations of different sizes and capacities. Explaining the creation of these populations requires paying attention to the extent to which Spanish institutions *exploited* indigenous people and sometimes also Africans. Formally speaking, exploitation occurs when one group's material well-being depends on systematically appropriating the fruits of the labor of another group.[3] Exploitation needs to be distinguished from oppression, which involves harsh treatment of varying kinds but is not designed primarily to facilitate the extraction of surplus.[4] In Spanish America, both exploitation (e.g., slavery and the encomienda) and oppression (e.g., forced religious conversion and extermination campaigns) were common during the mercantilist phase, but it was especially the former that led to the construction of large, systematically marginalized, and yet enduring indigenous populations. Where such populations were created, long-run social development was nearly always compromised, even when a postcolonial nation managed to achieve a significant measure of economic prosperity.

Consideration must also be given to those elite actors who were originally constituted during this first phase of Spanish colonialism and whose economic interests and behavior later stood as hindrances to development. Above all, these actors included wealthy merchants who profited under Spanish trade regulations that allotted monopoly control over legal commerce. These privileged and protected merchants used their substantial resources for lavish consumption rather than entrepreneurial investments that might stimulate production and growth in the New World. Usually tied to the merchants in symbiotic economic relationships (and often consanguineous ones as well) were large agricultural estate owners, whose existence depended upon and was a response to colonial institutions regulating land and labor. Landed elites obstructed development by focusing production toward local markets and by reproducing impoverished workers whose feeble purchasing power provided scant internal markets for manufactured goods. The alliances between merchants and estate owners were the great mercantilist coalitions of the Habsburg colonial era.

Other powerful collective actors were constituted by monarchical policy, and they were sometimes linked to the merchant-landed elite. Most notably, high-ranking religious authorities were empowered by stipulations mandating the spread of Christianity, and wealthy mine owners were brought into being in part through monopolistic regulations governing the extraction of precious minerals. But the role of the church and these miners in steering the economy was indirect and, as we shall see, mainly a function of the power of the merchants and large estate owners. Hence, the main focus in this chapter will be on the institutional constitution of the merchants and landed elites. Affiliated but secondary elite actors will receive less attention.

There was variation in the degree to which Spanish institutions created new collectivities in the form of disadvantaged ethnic populations and elite mercantilist groups across colonial centers, semiperipheries, and peripheries. These actors were most fully constituted in the colonial centers, though they were also strongly present in the semiperipheries. By contrast, in the colonial peripheries, the limited extent of Spanish institutional establishment led to weakly constituted merchant-landed elites and comparatively smaller exploited native populations. As a result, the colonial peripheries – though initially the most marginal and poorest regions within the Spanish Empire – were better equipped to experience socioeconomic development in the years after independence.

Arguments now have been previewed; it remains for them to be developed in light of the historical evidence. In what follows, I do this by considering similarities and differences among the cases across (1) the organization of the precolonial populations; (2) the extent of Habsburg colonization; and (3) the degree to which colonial institutions constituted subordinate ethnic populations and elite mercantilist actors. The last of these areas – the institutional creation of subordinate and elite actors – is relevant because these were the collective forces who shaped development outcomes later in the colonial period. In the next chapter, therefore, we will have to revisit them and their long-term historical roles. But in this chapter, we need to understand how they were brought into being in the first place.

THE COLONIAL CENTERS

We begin our case analyses by exploring the creation of the three colonial centers: Mexico, Peru, and Bolivia. These areas were colonial centers because the Spanish heavily settled certain strategic cities – above all, Mexico City, Lima, and Potosí – and implanted in them numerous and deeply rooted institutions. For each case, it makes sense to first consider the nature of the precolonial populations, which included the most complex and state-like societies in all of the Americas. Then we can look at the ways in which colonial policies and institutions transformed these societies while simultaneously empowering Spanish mercantilist actors.

Mexico

Precolonial Societies. From its capital city, Tenochtitlán, the Aztec imperial state indirectly controlled the densely settled peasant communities of central Mexico (see Map 3.1).[5] At the time of Cortés's first contact in 1519, this empire had reached its height, encompassing over a million people in

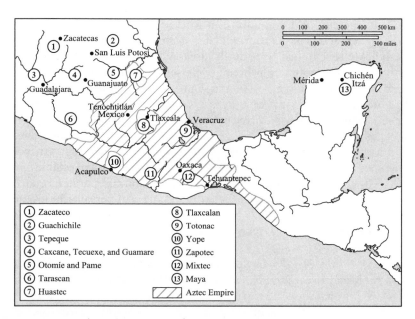

① Zacateco		⑧ Tlaxcalan	
② Guachichile		⑨ Totonac	
③ Tepeque		⑩ Yope	
④ Caxcane, Tecuexe, and Guamare		⑪ Zapotec	
⑤ Otomíe and Pame		⑫ Mixtec	
⑥ Tarascan		⑬ Maya	
⑦ Huastec		Aztec Empire	

MAP 3.1. Precolonial Societies of Mexico
Sources: P. J. Bakewell, *Silver Mining and Society in Colonial Mexico: Zacatecas, 1546–1700* (Cambridge: Cambridge University Press, 1971), 266; Alan Knight, *Mexico: From the Beginning to the Spanish Conquest* (Cambridge: Cambridge University Press, 2002), 133; Cathryn L. Lombardi and John V. Lombardi (with K. Lynn Stoner), *Latin American History: A Teaching Atlas* (Madison: University of Wisconsin Press, 1983), 16; Richard F. Townsend, *The Aztecs*, rev. ed. (New York: Thames & Hudson, 2000).

the Valley of Mexico and several million more in the surrounding areas. The population was ethnically diverse, including perhaps twenty different groups (e.g., Huastecs, Totonacs, Mixtecs, and Zapotecs) loosely tied together by a dominant language (Nahuatl) and shared cultural practices.[6] At the head was King Montezuma II, who ruled in conjunction with a cousin and deputy emperor (*cihuacoatl*) and other hereditary nobles and religious authorities. These potentates relied on an elaborate tributary system to sustain lavish consumption and costly militarization projects. Tribute mostly took the form of the extraction of agricultural surplus (e.g., maize and beans) from peasant producers, and it was collected on a regularly scheduled basis by caciques before being transferred to the rulers via meritocratic nobles. The peasantry also supplied the human effort and lives for large-scale warfare and the Aztecs' magnificent temples, causeways, and canals. The entire system was politically fragile and ultimately held together by repression, including, famously, the prolific use of human sacrifice.

There were other indigenous societies of varying complexity. To the west, the Tarascans had their powerful, tribute-collecting confederation-state with a base in the city of Tzintzuntzan in Michoacán.[7] The Tarascans fiercely resisted encroachment, defeating Aztec armies in crucial battles, though they quickly succumbed to Spanish diseases and conquest. Further to the north, where the population became sparser, various chiefdom and tribal societies were present (e.g., Guamares, Pames, Guachichiles, and Zacatecos). Many of these northern people lived a semi-sedentary lifestyle or perhaps were organized into decentralized confederations that harvested corn, beans, and squash.[8] The Spanish referred to them all as Chichimecs (literally, at the time, "sons of dogs").[9] Smaller societies within the core Aztec area sometimes retained autonomy, such as the kingdom of Metztitlán and the highland people of Tlaxcala – the latter of whom allied with Cortés and the invading Spanish. To the southeast, the Aztec Empire ended at roughly the present-day border of Mexico and Guatemala; the Yucatán peninsula was home to Maya people, who also escaped Aztec control.[10]

The Fall of the Aztecs. When word of an impressive agricultural civilization in central Mexico reached Spanish settlers in the Caribbean, Hernán Cortés organized his unauthorized expedition to explore the area. From April 1519 to August 1521, Cortés and his supporters were able to march from Veracruz to Tenochtitlán, capture Montezuma II, and bring down the Aztec Empire.[11] As Inga Clendinnen suggests, the fall of the Aztecs "poses a painful question: How was it that a motley bunch of Spanish adventurers, never numbering much more than four hundred or so, was able to defeat an Amerindian military power on its home ground in the space of two years?"[12] Painful as it may be, the question needs an answer if we are to understand why Mexico became a colonial center. For if the Aztecs had been able to defend themselves at all successfully, the heartland of the Spanish Empire might not have been located in central Mexico.

The great irony of the Aztec Empire is that the same complex sociopolitical structure that was its signal achievement explains why a few hundred European soldiers were able to speedily bring about its demise. The structural vulnerabilities were twofold. In the first place, the very concentration of power meant that the entire empire could be destabilized if the leadership in Tenochtitlán was defeated. When Cortés kidnapped Montezuma in November 1519, the citizens of Tenochtitlán ceased to abide by the rule of the Aztec leader, and the empire started to grind to a halt. As Hugh Thomas writes:

The crisis was great, for the Emperor was essential to the direction of Mexican society. The Emperor was not just "he who commands", but also the "heart of the city", a "quetzal feather", "a great silk cotton tree", and a "wall, a barricade", in whose shade people took refuge... he was supposed to speak on behalf of the gods... His task was not only to govern the Mexica [Aztecs] but, so it was supposed, to keep alive the universe itself. Now he was, physically, in the hands of a wholly unpredictable group of visitors about whom no one knew anything.[13]

Collapse was imminent once Montezuma was mortally wounded. To be sure, the Spanish were temporarily forced from the capital, and, starting with Montezuma's brother Cuitláhuac, new, restorative leaders mobilized opposition forces. But alternative leaders could never effectively govern and were soon reduced to making a last stand at Tenochtitlán. Meanwhile, the vast population of the empire outside of Tenochtitlán sensed the changing political winds and openly resisted their old masters.

This last observation suggests the second critical vulnerability of the Aztecs: they only indirectly ruled the subject peoples whom they exploited, and they hardly controlled all people, even within central Mexico. It was relatively easy for a small force of outside invaders to make fast allies of resentful or opportunistic ethnic groups.[14] On his original march to Tenochtitlán, Cortés established alliances with, first, the Totonacs near Veracruz and then (after several fierce battles) with the mighty Tlaxcala. Later, when the Spanish were forced from Tenochtitlán, the Tlaxcala rebuffed Cuitláhuac's overture for friendship and instead reaffirmed ties with Cortés. This alliance allowed the Spanish to lead a brutal campaign during which obsequious indigenous leaders in the east and around the lakes near Tenochtitlán were intimidated into submission and made to pledge loyalty to the Spanish Crown. When Cortés returned to defeat Cuitláhuac, he therefore did so with tens of thousands of allies, who helped him burn down Tenochtitlán and seize the reins of the great empire once and for all.

In their engagements with the Aztecs and other indigenous people, the Spanish had decisive military advantages: steel swords, horses, tactical knowledge, and superior missile weapons.[15] Yet when we compare the fate of the Aztecs to that of other (less centralized and less institutionally differentiated) indigenous societies in Mexico, the structural vulnerabilities stressed here, as opposed to the military prowess of the Spanish, emerge decisively as the critical explanatory factors. Francisco de Montejo's fortified campaign to conquer the less complex Maya chiefdoms of the Yucatán, for example, failed miserably, despite the same military advantages. As Nancy M. Farriss points out:

It took a full two decades to conquer Yucatan, in contrast with a bare two years to subdue the Aztecs. The Maya had no overarching imperial structure that could be toppled with one swift blow to the center. Yucatan was divided into at least sixteen autonomous provinces with varying degrees of internal unity. Each of the provinces, and sometimes subunits within them, had to be negotiated with, and failing that, conquered separately.[16]

The same basic points can be made about the indigenous societies in what is now northern Mexico and the southwestern United States: they lacked the political centralization of the Aztecs, and the well-armed Spanish had to stage a decades-long war after 1550 before they could pacify these countless political entities.[17] By contrast, after making short work of the Aztecs, the

Spanish also easily controlled the complex Tarascan state of Michoacán simply by making its inexperienced *cazonci* (king), Tzintzicha Tangaxoan, their subservient vassal and later executing him.[18] Variation in the pace of conquest during the sixteenth century was thus driven by differences in the institutional complexity of indigenous societies.

Spanish Settlement. Central Mexico, the heartland of the former indigenous states, was the primary location of Spanish settlement in North America. From 1493 to 1600, the region received almost a third of all arriving Spanish settlers, a far higher proportion than in any other part of the empire, including Peru.[19] Starting from just 2,000 to 3,000 persons in 1521, the Spanish population in Mexico grew to 60,000 in 1568 and to more than 125,000 by 1646.[20] The bulk of these people lived in the inner sections of the four central provinces of the Audiencia of Mexico: Mexico, Puebla, Oaxaca, and Michoacán.[21] In particular, the Spanish lived overwhelmingly within concentrated pockets in the Valley of Mexico, especially the capital city of Mexico. Built on top of the island of Tenochtitlán, and with a Spanish population of fifteen thousand households by 1630,[22] Mexico City was the center within the center. As Richard Boyer points out, Mexico City became the magnet for all expressions of encroaching Spanish colonialism:

The merchants and artisans, the viceregal and archdiocesan courts, the royal bureaucrats and city aldermen, and the religious corporations made Mexico City the undisputed locus of wealth, power, and influence in the viceroyalty. The powerful and the rich were at home there, but all other types came too. Immigrants from Europe made Mexico City their first destination. Indians and castas came from the countryside and from other towns to settle in rustic faubourgs on swampy land at the fringe of the European core ... The influx of Indian migrants, remarkable because it occurred during the demographic collapse of native people throughout the colony, underscores the continuous destruction of Indian society as well as the attraction of Mexico City.[23]

Mexico City was further linked to all other important population centers in New Spain and was the hub of an international trading network that reached east to Spain, west to the Philippines, and south to Peru.[24] This was the destination for many thousands of black slaves, who served as domestics, personal servants, blacksmiths, dyers, and meatcutters.[25] And Mexico City was home to an archdiocese and the headquarters of the secular clergy – those priests who were administratively under royal authority and who collected the tithe (a 10 percent tax on agricultural production) and other ecclesiastical fees and levies.[26]

Throughout the Audiencia of Mexico, Spanish settlement gravitated toward former indigenous towns. Puebla de los Angeles became the second most important colonial town, with a few thousand Spanish settlers in the seventeenth century.[27] Though Puebla's founders wanted to create a settlement of industrious farmers who did not depend on indigenous labor (and thereby protect the native Tlaxcala people, who were so crucial as allies during the conquest), the economy that developed – which was "the best grain-producing district in New Spain in the sixteenth century" and notable for its textile industries – relied thoroughly on indigenous tribute and labor.[28] Farther to the south, where Aztec control had been only partially institutionalized, the town of Antequera (now called Oaxaca) and the surrounding region featured a smaller Spanish population, perhaps several hundred residents in the early seventeenth century, with only a few merchants, who prospered from the trade of cotton clothing woven by indigenous women.[29] In the Tabasco, Chiapas, and Yucatán regions, where the Aztec Empire had not taken hold at all, there were no large Spanish settlements to speak of; the major reason was the difficulty of securing tribute from the indigenous populations.[30] On the coasts, Veracruz and Acapulco functioned as the audiencia's main Atlantic and Pacific ports, respectively (the latter crucial in the illegal trade). Very few people chose to live in either town, however: when ships were not in port, the towns were deserted. The native populations around Veracruz and Acapulco were small to begin with, but they practically vanished after the arrival of the Spanish, forcing the merchants (who themselves lived in Mexico City) to rely on black slaves to perform the dock work.[31]

Spanish settlement was sparse, too, throughout the entire Audiencia of Guadalajara (also known as the Audiencia of New Galicia), which was established in 1548 with Guadalajara as its capital after 1560 (see Map 2.1). The audiencia was peripheral during the mercantilist phase, illustrating nicely how the institutions of the indigenous population drove patterns of Spanish occupation. For northern Mexico housed the most important mineral deposits of New Spain, including the rich silver mines of Zacatecas. Yet because it was home to nomadic and chiefdom indigenous groups, the Spanish could not live here without triggering fierce resistance, much less use the local population as a reliable labor force.[32] Once authorities and settlers found that they could extract the minerals without intensive colonization, they harbored no illusions about populating the north.

Such was the case even though Mexican silver production steadily increased from 1550 until 1700 and indeed until the end of the colonial period,[33] eventually making New Spain the most important source of bullion in the empire.[34] When Zacatecas's silver production was booming during the seventeenth century, the town remained an isolated mining village, with a Spanish population of only about five hundred households.[35] Other northern mining towns, such as San Luis Potosí (in the Audiencia of Mexico), were even smaller. The audiencia capital at Guadalajara was likewise a modest town that could be ignored by the viceroys in Mexico City as long as the mines were productive.[36] In short, in the northern parts of Mexico, where the Aztec state ended and less complex indigenous societies were the norm, the Spanish did not pursue large-scale settlement or extensive institution building before the eighteenth century, even in the most lucrative areas. It was instead the capital of the Aztec Empire, whose mineral wealth the conquerors found to be disappointingly small, where colonial institutions and people were concentrated.

Nor, finally, should we suppose that the Spanish settled and implanted institutions according to the agricultural potential of different regions. Certainly, the lands around Mexico City were fertile and attracted early estate owners, who were actually mostly livestock ranchers. By the seventeenth century, these cattle barons had diversified their estates to include wheat and other food production, thereby creating haciendas in the basin around Mexico City and in the temperate valleys of Puebla.[37] Yet in the more sparsely populated southern lowland areas (e.g., Veracruz), the Spanish did not settle, even though sugarcane and other cash crops were profitably harvested on plantations with African slave labor.[38] Besides, as the work of François Chevalier made so clear, great estates proliferated to the north when roads linked the capital with the mining towns.[39]

European grain spread to the irrigated highlands south of Puebla (Atlixco, Tepeaca) and north of Mexico City (Tlalnepantla and Huehuetoca), and then on from there, pushing back the Chichimeca frontier (San Juan del Río, Querétaro). By the end of the sixteenth century, wheat and maize gilded the black soil of the Bajío and were harvested around Morelia and Guadalajara in the west and Oaxaca in the south.[40]

Successful haciendas producing both indigenous crops and European staples were thus hardly concentrated in central Mexico.

The Fate of the Indigenous Population. To the settlers, the real economic spoils of the Aztec Empire were found with its people. They provided the labor power – readily harnessed through modification of existing tribute institutions – that could generate wealth for Spanish residents in what was, after all, an overwhelmingly agricultural economy. This was true despite the fact that during the sixteenth century, the size of this labor pool shrank dramatically. The indigenous population of central Mexico fell from perhaps 10 million in 1519 to 6 million in 1550, to 2 million in 1585, finally reaching a nadir of possibly 1 million in the early seventeenth century.[41] This amounts to a decline of around 90 percent in less than a century. It is possible that the chiefdom societies of Yucatán suffered even greater relative population losses.[42] By contrast, the less complex societies of the northern frontier appear to have survived at higher rates, sometimes maintaining a majority of their people during this period.[43] Consensus exists in the broadest terms over the causation of the demographic collapse. To quote Alan Knight:

Although war, maltreatment and, it has been suggested, an erosion of the very will to live all contributed to this catastrophic decline in Indian population, disease was clearly the crucial factor. It could strike down populations in regions – like Oaxaca – where fighting and social dislocation had been much less severe than in the

Valley of Mexico. And it lingered endemically, preventing any swift demographic revival.[44]

The killer diseases included smallpox, measles, influenza, and yellow fever, and they struck across several intervals during the sixteenth and early seventeenth centuries, with truly horrific effects.[45]

Through what methods and with what consequences did the Spanish extract surplus from this depleted though still large population? Although slavery was sometimes employed, especially during the first decades of Spanish settlement,[46] the key early instrument was the *encomienda*, a legal institution that empowered individual conquistadors to seize tribute and labor from a designated number of indigenous people (theoretically in exchange for protection and religious salvation). Encomiendas were applied early in the Valley of Mexico by the original conquistadors; some thirty encomenderos controlled an estimated 180,000 tributaries in the mid-1530s.[47] Thereafter, the size of the typical encomienda dwindled to a few hundred indigenous people, though the institution remained a source of great wealth for select families. While Spanish frontiersmen who settled in Yucatán and other more remote parts enjoyed encomienda grants, in general, as the complexity of the native society declined, so too did the ability of the Spanish to enforce systematic tribute demands.[48] Where they were imposed or even attempted, nevertheless, encomiendas had the effect of homogenizing indigenous people into an undifferentiated group by identifying tributaries primarily with their town location, not with their traditional ethnic community, as the Aztecs had done.[49] This is one example of a more general process of ethnic homogenization, aptly described by Irene Silverblatt: "Spanish practices ... imposed broad, universal classifications on their subjects: all natives of the 'New World' were 'Indian' subjects of Spain; all Spaniards, regardless of social distinctions, were privileged colonists."[50]

Also propelling ethnic homogeneity among formerly diverse peoples were efforts, starting in the mid-sixteenth century, to spatially concentrate the native population into towns – known as *congregaciones* – that were strictly segregated from the Spanish dwellings.[51] This policy of congregación was applied unevenly, and with varying levels of success;[52] its early-seventeenth-century incarnation, for example, moved about forty thousand to eighty thousand indigenous people.[53] Even when incompletely instituted, however, the policy created many fully vacated territories in places where diseases had already caused the decline of the indigenous population, which allowed the Crown to distribute the unoccupied lands to settlers through royal grants (*mercedes*). Haciendas were thereby born. "Insofar as it did effect change," writes Charles Gibson of the congregación policy, "its tendency was to concentrate even further the surviving native population, to make this population more accessible to controls by hacendados and others, and to render lands formerly occupied by Indians available to Spaniards."[54]

In the indigenous towns created, native people were subject to high rates of taxation and religious conversion, but they were still in charge of land-tenure management.[55] For although the Spanish laws fluctuated over time and were not fairly enforced, the Crown generally protected rights to communal lands around the native towns.[56]

The tendency of surplus extraction in Mexico to constitute indigenous people as an undifferentiated, impoverished, segregated, and self-governing group continued despite various institutional reformulations. After much vacillation, the Crown passed the New Laws of 1542 in an effort to restrict the encomienda to a single lifetime and ultimately end personal service by indigenous people. By the close of the sixteenth century, the spirit of these laws was enforced to the point that the encomienda was a mostly defunct institution.[57] Even so, the monarchy remained sensitive to the labor needs of the settlers, and it therefore created the new institution of *repartimiento*, whereby native people were compelled to work on Spanish estates on a rotational basis at fixed wages. Repartimiento labor peaked from 1570 until 1630, and it involved two departures from the encomiendas: the use of wages rather than nonsalaried vassalage, and the use of labor on Spanish property rather than the confiscation of commodities produced on indigenous lands.[58] The repartimiento system melded well with both the policy of congregaciones and the rise of hacienda agriculture; the former provided locations from which to draft the labor, and the latter provided destinations for the workers. Still, native people's rights to landholdings and self-government continued to be generally protected such that, within their exploited communities, they retained parts of their cultures, even if this went unnoticed by the Spanish.

Nor did the subsequent transition to wage labor in many parts of Mexico substantially alter the situation of indigenous people. The repartimiento system paved the way for wage labor by introducing labor contracts and by forcing landlords to negotiate wages for voluntary and temporary workers during harvests. By the late seventeenth century, wages and debt peonage were the key instruments through which indigenous labor was secured on the haciendas, especially in the densely populated Valley of Mexico, but also to a considerable extent in the northern territories of New Galicia (though there were exceptions, such as Yucatán, where forced labor and even encomiendas persisted throughout the seventeenth century).[59] In the northern mining districts, wage labor took hold even earlier – from the mid-sixteenth century.[60] Lacking access to a usable and affordable labor force, northern Spanish miners had to turn to wages right away to attract indigenous workers from central Mexico. Northern Mexico's labor market was therefore always mostly migratory and – speaking quite broadly – "capitalist." In the mines of Zacatecas, for example, a couple of thousand indigenous wage laborers and a much smaller number of repartimiento Indians and black slaves performed most of the work.[61]

Although diverse methods of exploitation were in play across time and across space, the overall result was quite straightforward: Spanish institutions transformed the vast majority of the Mexican population into a separate, subject people condemned to live under very low levels of economic and social development.

The Mercantilist Elite. By the end of the seventeenth century, an elite group of merchants and estate-owning settlers had come into being. Although their historical role as obstacles to economic progress occurred during the late colonial period, they were forged under Habsburg colonialism, as an inevitable outgrowth of precisely Mexico's centrality during this time. Let us therefore briefly examine their institutional creation.

First of all there were the great merchants, the wealthiest individuals in all of New Spain, residing in the fanciest neighborhoods of Mexico City. Their privileges and resources – and thus their very existence – derived squarely from economic regulations imposed by the Crown. Large wholesale merchants especially benefited from the flota system of transatlantic contact that ensured monopoly rights for the consulados of Seville and Mexico City (the latter created in 1592). As Louisa Schell Hoberman suggests, the whole system was designed in ways that helped Mexico City's merchants accumulate income from the mineral economy: they supplied the mines with key merchandise (iron, steel, and livestock); they purchased the silver that was extracted and processed at the mines; they were influential at the mint in Mexico City that coined silver; and they circulated the refined silver throughout the New World and the international economy.[62] Not only did they run the official colonial trade, they also controlled the lucrative contraband exchange.[63] Great merchants could and did invest their substantial profits in urban real estate, hacienda agriculture, and manufacturing industries. Their wealth also bought them political power. They occupied or owned leading offices in the royal and ecclesiastical treasuries, offices that were sold by the Crown in the seventeenth century.[64] They even routinely provided legal and illegal loans to public officials, including the viceroy himself.[65]

In rural Mexico, however, it was the owners of large livestock and agricultural estates – the hacendados – who held political sway, purchasing *regimientos* (town-council seats) from the Crown.[66] These landed elites were empowered by the evolving labor institutions that regulated the indigenous workforce and by the land policies that had triggered the formation of the large privately owned estates. They of course enjoyed the greatest leverage on their estates (in practice through a resident *mayordomo*), expecting and receiving deference from workers and support when needed in local disputes. This power often extended to nearby indigenous communities from which the labor force might be extracted. Preeminent at the local level, the landlords were also tied in various ways to high-ranking colonial authorities. The hacendados monopolized municipal offices in Mexico City and most other towns. Furthermore, "through marriage, business, friendship, and kinship, links were forged with the royal bureaucracy that gave the landowners access to the seats of political power. High court judges, retainers of the viceroys, and other Spanish bureaucrats married the daughters of the landowning class and thus acquired both property and family connections."[67] Rich mine owners from the north became hacendados themselves, using their connections to judges and governors to buy huge food-producing estates in New Galicia.[68] Loans distributed by the church – which could be secured only with land – further had the effect of linking urban investors to landed segments of the elite.[69] With the hacendados, then, we find the numerically largest part of the Spanish elite and a group that overlapped with all the rest of Mexico's most powerful actors.

Peru

Precolonial Societies. The other most expansive indigenous civilization of the early sixteenth century – the Inca Empire, or Tawantinsuyu – encompassed territory from contemporary Ecuador to northern Chile and perhaps 10 million inhabitants who spoke dozens of languages, including above all Quechua (see Map 3.2).[70] The sacred center of the empire was Cuzco, which contained some 100,000 to 150,000 people, along with numerous impressive stone palaces, plazas, and religious compounds. Beyond Cuzco and eastern Peru, the Incas had only recently conquered much of what they called the "Four Parts" of Tawantinsuyu. For example, territories that reached into Bolivia, Chile, and western Peru were taken only in the 1460s, and much of the empire north of Lima came under Inca possession after 1470. The Incas seized and pacified these territories by mobilizing tens of thousands of soldiers – a feat that was facilitated by their far-reaching network of roads, outposts, and storage facilities. Within conquered communities, production remained organized around kinship groups (*ayllus*) that farmed on communal lands. Community leaders (*kurakas*) collected tribute for themselves and on behalf of Inca provincial governors. To meet the tribute demands, which were paid in the form of labor (not in kind), peasants worked on lands designated for the government. They also crucially provided periodic corvée services known as *mit'a* (or *mita*).[71] Mita obligations often demanded that individuals migrate from their ayllus to Cuzco and elsewhere to perform myriad tasks – such as cloth weaving, road construction, mining, and army service – for their Inca masters.

At the top of the hierarchy was the supreme ruler – the Sapa Inca – who traced his ancestry to the Sun god, Itil, and who along with his principal wife was advised by other elite figures in Cuzco's aristocracy. Though power was concentrated at the top, the Sapa Inca depended very much on his governors and captains to collect tribute and bring laborers to Cuzco, and these officials in turn worked through the kurakas at the community level. Under

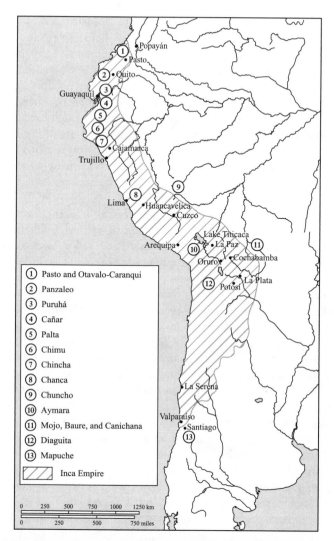

MAP 3.2. Precolonial Societies of Peru, Bolivia, and Ecuador
Sources: Kenneth J. Andrien, *Andean Worlds: Indigenous History, Culture, and Consciousness under Spanish Rule, 1532–1825* (Albuquerque: University of New Mexico Press, 2001), 16; Cathryn L. Lombardi and John V. Lombardi (with K. Lynn Stoner), *Latin American History: A Teaching Atlas* (Madison: University of Wisconsin Press, 1983), 11, 20; Linda A. Newson, *Life and Death in Early Colonial Ecuador* (Norman: University of Oklahoma Press, 1995), 29.

Inca rule, some communities were significantly transformed by centralized institutions, whereas others continued much as before; perhaps a majority of the inhabitants of the Inca Empire never actually saw an Inca. In the central highlands, for example, the Incas thoroughly absorbed the dozens of agricultural chiefdoms and confederations that had occupied this area in the fourteenth century. But in the valleys of coastal Peru, where numerous complex kingdoms had existed before Tawantinsuyu, the Inca influence was less visible.[72] The Incas never controlled substantial parts of Peru, including eastern parts of the tropical Amazon – home to the mysterious Mojos and Chunchos, hunter-gatherer tribes that apparently effectively resisted centralizing encroachment.[73]

The Fall of the Incas. The Incas were as vulnerable as the Aztecs to swift overthrow and control by a small contingent of Spanish soldiers who possessed superior weapons, horses, and better tactical knowledge.[74] For the Incas' underlying structural vulnerabilities were the same as the Aztecs': they controlled a complex, state-like polity susceptible to both sudden collapse at the top and rapid disintegration from within.

We can emphasize these realities even while acknowledging that the Spanish arrived at an auspicious time to take advantage of the Incas' weaknesses. When Francisco Pizarro's brigade of fewer than two hundred men showed up in late 1532, the bloody civil war over the succession between Huayna Capac's two most powerful sons – Atahualpa and Huáscar – had yet to conclude. Although the timing was serendipitous for the Spaniards, the stunning outcome of the encounter between Pizarro and Atahualpa suggests that Old World soldiers would have easily overrun the Incas even if they had arrived ten years earlier. Pizarro's small group not only captured Atahualpa and killed at least fifteen hundred Inca soldiers, they did so without suffering a single fatality.[75]

The other great vulnerability of the Inca Empire was its hugely diverse and often tacitly disloyal population; most Inca communities were Inca only because the Cuzco authorities had coercively incorporated them as subject people. The Spanish made strategic alliances with these discontented people, who sensed the changing balance of power and sought to situate themselves within it.[76] As they traveled across Peru, the Spanish invaders encountered resistance, but they were assisted by native supporters and by the roads and outposts that the Incas had created and used for their own conquering purposes. By the 1540s, the greatest threat to Spanish hegemony was no longer neo-Inca rebellions but rather the Spaniards' own internal strife, which bred a destructive civil war among the conquerors (who of course involved indigenous people centrally in their infighting) and between the conquerors and the Crown, a conflict not to be resolved until after midcentury.[77]

The Creation of a Colonial Center. News of Pizarro's feat soon "set off a virtual 'gold rush' to Peru that threatened to depopulate the Caribbean Islands and other less lucrative parts of the colonies."[78] In 1536, when the great Manco Inca revolt at Cuzco occurred, there was a Spanish population of perhaps two thousand in Peru. By the mid-1540s, this had increased to four to five thousand, and then to eight thousand by 1555.[79] Already in 1535, Pizarro had founded the coastal city of Lima, then known as the City of Kings, near an important indigenous town (Pachacamac), in an effort to offer Spanish settlers a capital with a Europe-like climate and maritime communication.[80] The fact that the desert coastal region around Lima was occupied by long-standing kingdoms that offered excellent possibilities for tribute extraction made Lima an especially viable choice.[81] Once founded, Lima displaced Cuzco as the most popular destination for Spanish immigrants and became a magnet for Indian immigrants from the northern and central highlands and other parts of the central coast. In 1610, Lima's population (including the surrounding area) was an estimated twenty-five thousand, about half Spaniards; by the 1680s, the number was eighty thousand, with possibly as many as thirty thousand Spaniards.[82] The urban area also featured a large African population, estimated at twenty thousand in 1640.[83] Peru was made a viceroyalty and Lima home to an audiencia in 1543; Lima claimed an archbishopric and a powerful and independent-minded town council. By the mid-sixteenth century, James Lockhart reports, the capital was replete with Spanish social institutions:

Lima, which was then, as it always afterward remained, the center of the Spanish presence, was a quite imposing city, full of the large, sometimes palatial Spanish style houses of the encomenderos, with artisans' and merchants' shops lining the square and central streets. Around the city lay a garden area where intensive Spanish irrigation agriculture was carried on, mainly by black slaves, to supply the local market. Encomenderos from the highlands, leaving employees behind to care for their interests, spent much of their time in the capital. Lima was the Peruvian headquarters of merchant firms, based ultimately in Seville, which traded along the route from Seville to Panama, Lima, Arequipa, and the highlands, importing goods and sending back silver.[84]

Wherever the Inca Empire had predominated, the Spanish usually forged numerous and deep footholds. Hundreds of Spanish families arrived at Cuzco after the initial conquest, erecting cathedrals from the palaces of the supreme Inca leaders, and many indigenous families remained or returned here as well. In the early seventeenth century, Cuzco boasted a Spanish population of more than three thousand, and its large surrounding indigenous population produced many of the coca leaves consumed throughout the Andes. In what is now southern Peru, the town of Arequipa was founded in 1540 in a fertile and sparsely populated area. Arequipa became home to encomenderos who invested in profitable wine estates, then had trouble overcoming a series of devastating earthquakes and suffered economic decline when in 1572 Arica became the official port for moving silver.[85] Between Cuzco and Lima, the Spanish occupied the economically stable town of Huamanga (Ayacucho) in the densely populated highlands, and near here they established large encomiendas and later textile factories drawing laborers from the sizable surrounding indigenous communities.[86] Overall, Spanish population growth occurred in many parts of Peru: the territory contained approximately seventeen thousand Spanish households in 1630, making Lima the second most populous audiencia, after Mexico.[87]

While the concentrated population and complex institutions of the Inca Empire explain rather well why Habsburg Spain brought its people in abundance to Peru, exploitable precious resources in this territory (and even more in the neighboring Audiencia of Charcas, discussed later) were critical to ensuring that the Viceroyalty of Peru did not become completely subordinate to New Spain. At first, Spaniards retrieved their gold and silver by plundering the Incas. Later, deposits of gold and silver were discovered in remote places – especially silver in frigid Castrovirreyna, where a minuscule European population resided with their forced laborers at the beginning of the seventeenth century.[88] Most important were deposits of the extremely rare mercury ore, which was used after 1573 for the patio process of amalgamation in processing Potosí's silver. The famous mine of Santa Bárbara, about three miles from Huancavelica, became one of the principal sources of mercury in the world after its discovery in 1563.[89] For the Crown, Huancavelica and Potosí were the two poles that upheld the entire viceroyalty, and their importance entitled miners from both cities to substantial mita labor drafts.[90] Even so, like the other mineral regions of Peru, Huancavelica was a poor location for the Spanish to live, given the lack of opportunity for profitably exploiting local indigenous labor through tribute collection. The area thus never became more than an isolated boomtown with a few hundred Spanish settlers, a couple hundred African slaves, and a few thousand permanent indigenous residents.

The Fate of the Indigenous Population. The huge numbers of exploitable indigenous people attracted Spaniards to Peru. But, as in Mexico, this indigenous population shrank rapidly as colonial settlement proceeded. By one estimate, Peru's pre-Spanish population of 9 million fell to slightly over 1 million by 1580 and then declined to six hundred thousand by 1620.[91] Some of the Peruvian population migrated or was forcibly relocated to the mines of Potosí, though this portion of the total decline must have been minimal, since most of the Potosí workers came from within Charcas itself.[92] As in Mexico, diseases, dislocation, and Spanish abuses explain nearly all of the demographic catastrophe. Nearly 100 percent of the dense native populations of central coastal Peru were destroyed, with the implication that

Lima's population was eventually composed almost completely of migrants – including thousands of African slaves.[93] By contrast, as Noble David Cook indicates, the people living in the highlands fared a little better:

By 1620, Indian Peru was highland Peru, especially from Cajamarca to Lake Titicaca. In this vast region, the culture and language of the native inhabitants were not destroyed but only transformed during the early colonial era. The Indian population of the highland region fell from 1.045 million to 585,000 in the half century following 1570. In the same period, the coastal population collapsed from 250,000 to 87,000. Although under severe pressure, the highland Indian was able to survive the shock of the Old World invasion.[94]

Though the changes did not occur all at once, the highland indigenous population itself was radically transformed during the Habsburg colonial period. Before the late sixteenth century, indigenous institutions in the communities often endured while Spanish institutions were being erected. This was true because, beginning with the first encomiendas in Peru granted by Pizarro, the Spanish duplicated the practices of the Incan state.[95] Encomenderos assumed the tribute-collecting positions that had been occupied by Inca representatives, allowing the kurakas to keep their traditional roles and act as crucial intermediaries, often in alliance with the Spanish. According to Karen Spalding, "the kuraka who accepted the Spanish encomendero as his local overlord often built up a relationship with him reminiscent of the ties of ceremony, reciprocal gifts, and feasting that linked the local elite to the representative of the Inca state."[96] Alliances with the kurakas and their use as intermediaries are not too surprising when we recognize broad similarities between the conquering Spanish and the Incas:

Like the Incas, the Spanish derived their great wealth from institutions that tapped the labor of a colonially fashioned peasantry; like the Incas, they attempted to shape Andean senses of self and position – with varying degrees of success – by expanding imperial religion. Like their Inca counterparts, Spanish instruments of government built on systems of indirect rule; and, taking advantage of internal ranks dividing conquered people, they promoted local elites (*kurakas*) to middlemen in imperial administration.[97]

Alarmed by the collapse of the indigenous population, however, and enticed by the possibilities that mineral wealth in Huancavelica and Potosí had engendered, the Spanish Crown by the 1570s moved to break with Inca precedents and sweep away crucial indigenous conventions. Two fundamental reforms carried out by the famous administration of Viceroy Francisco de Toledo (1569–81) effected these changes. First, Toledo reconfigured the Inca mita, which came to refer to any system of forced labor.[98] Under the new colonial mita, Spanish authorities forced kurakas in the vast lands reaching from Cuzco to southern Bolivia to make available for labor services up to one-seventh of their tributary population. Of course, systems of forced labor had long been part and parcel of life in the Andes; the mita, after all, had been invented by the Incas. Yet in the hands of the Spanish, the institution forced draftees (*mitayos*) to endure particularly harsh exploitation and face often-bleak prospects of returning to stable community life after the work. Especially brutal for the mitayos were the Spanish regimes of forced labor in the mines (*mita de minas*). Here, indigenous people were subjected to often mortally dangerous work, the stuff of the Black Legend of Spanish colonialism. Even forms of mita that did not lead to the mines (*mita de plaza*) entailed prolonged absences to carry out hard labor on farms, in textile mills, and for public works (especially in Lima). Worse than the absences per se for community survival were the disruptions to agricultural production. For when and if mitayos might return to their community could not be known under the Spanish system, jeopardizing the reciprocal interchanges of labor upon which subsistence economies had been built. As Steve J. Stern concludes, "By injecting new risks and uncertainties into local work relationships, the colonial mita induced a *collective* deterioration which undermined the efficacy of traditional institutions as a reliable source of labor."[99]

Toledo's other major innovation was a huge resettlement program intended to concentrate the rapidly diminishing indigenous population in large Spanish-style towns known in Peru as *reducciones*. The viceroy "organized the reducciones into 614 administrative districts, or repartimientos, each headed by a kuraka and an appointed town council of Andean elders. The repartimientos were grouped into eight larger provinces and placed under the control of a Spanish corregidor de indios."[100] Altogether, it is possible that more than 1.5 million people were relocated, often to the mining centers and the agricultural valleys of the sierra in Peru and Bolivia.[101] What the Spanish Crown hoped to achieve with these measures was straightforward: it sought to standardize tribute collection (formally now implemented as a head tax on tributaries), better regulate the mita, stabilize the size of the indigenous population, facilitate religious conversion, and control uprisings. Yet the implementation was riddled with contradictions. For one thing, the reducciones actually stimulated mass migration rather than permanently settling people. This was because the reducciones became the sites where Spanish authorities could most readily impose the dreaded mita. Individuals were therefore often better off leaving their traditional ayllu and becoming migrants – known as *forasteros*[102] – which freed them from labor drafts and had the effect of creating a highly mobile society. Furthermore, by moving people to new lands, the reducciones exacerbated population declines, especially when indigenous people were brought to the disease-fomenting lowland regions.[103] In addition, rather than preserving modes of indigenous leadership, the reducciones undermined the traditional role of the kuraka and replaced it with a new and highly corrupt governance structure. Whereas in the past the authority of the kurakas had depended on their ability to fulfill vital community functions, such legitimacy was now rooted in the colonial state's sanctioning of privileged power holders responsible for "siphoning off surplus for the Spaniards."[104] The irony is that both the officially appointed indigenous town representatives and the Spanish corregidores who oversaw them were so deeply involved in their own modes of corruption that the new leadership structure simply gave them more opportunities for personal aggrandizement.[105]

For all of these reasons, the reducciones were ultimately a failure at achieving the specific Spanish goals. Yet they were hardly without consequences. For in combination with the mita and tribute-collection policies, the reducciones helped to convert the Inca Empire's heterogeneous highland population into a more homogenous and visibly impoverished ethnic group – a people that the Spanish here also called Indians and understood to be an inferior and servile race.[106] Partially incorporated into Spanish commercial and economic channels, but also spatially set off from the Spanish cities, Peru's indigenous highland population consisted of hundreds of thousands of people facing dire health and economic conditions at the end of the seventeenth century.

The Mercantilist Elite. Economic elites in Peru plainly depended upon indigenous and African labor in the ways suggested above. And labor exploitation was, in turn, obviously dependent on the institutions created and supported by the colonial state. For it was the colonial state that upheld the coercive labor system as well as the various taxes, guilds, and protections from which the elite profited.

Lima's merchants – the individuals who made money by importing and selling Spanish and contraband merchandise in exchange for New World silver and gold – were the system's greatest beneficiaries.[107] As Lima grew and used its strategic location to become the center of trade within the viceroyalty, the Crown required that all imports and exports be channeled through the city, thereby giving the merchants a virtual monopoly over commerce and trade.[108] According to L. A. Clayton, they "controlled the movement of goods and silver throughout the viceroyalty, acted essentially as brokers for the mine owners in the interior, were wholesalers for the host of small retailers in Peru and generated much commerce for the merchant fleet."[109] After 1613, their consulado collaborated with the Sevillan monopoly in Spain, including by restricting the flow of goods into the Peruvian market to ensure scarcity and high prices.[110] Merchants also prospered from illegal intracolonial trade with New Spain, such as the exchange of New World silver, wine, mercury, and cacao for luxury commodities from the Far East that arrived first in the Mexican market.[111] While great wealth flowed from monopolistic rights in these various ways, merchants did not initially enjoy the social status or political influence of encomenderos or landlords. This fact may help explain why they spent notoriously on charity, especially the church.[112]

Estate ownership was another basic source of power. Some of Peru's upper-landed-class families could trace their estates back to encomiendas held during the first decades of colonialism.[113] Yet since encomiendas did not involve actual ownership of indigenous territories, families acquired such lands only when haciendas spread in coastal valleys and later in the highlands during the mid- to late sixteenth and early seventeenth centuries. Land grants sponsored by viceroys, governors, and town councils were critical institutions stimulating the spread of these estates. Investment capital supplied by clerical organizations also promoted haciendas by allowing Spanish settlers to purchase land from kurakas and the Crown.[114] Once constituted, Peru's landed elite enjoyed many of the same political privileges as their counterparts in Mexico – including, often, ownership of the highest administrative offices, such as the royal treasury and the Audiencia of Lima.[115] Yet they ultimately depended quite heavily on Potosí's wealth, given that nearly all of the agricultural estates (with the partial exception of the sugar plantations) had as their primary markets regional population centers that existed on the back of the mineral riches. Without Potosí's silver, the Peruvian landed elite would have devolved (and in fact eventually did so) into owners of backward-looking food-producing estates that lacked dynamism and that were unprepared and unable to be competitive in more open markets.

Bolivia

Precolonial Societies. The Spanish referred to Bolivia as Upper Peru, and when they first encountered it, the Incas were masters of the native Aymara kingdoms in the altiplano reaching from Lake Titicaca to Potosí (see Map 3.2).[116] The Aymaras and other populations nearby (e.g., the Uru people) totaled at least several hundred thousand and perhaps one million.[117] In their kingdoms, the Aymaras lived in ayllus, practiced sedentary agriculture, and traded various handicrafts and foods (e.g., corn, potatoes, quinoa, fruits, and meats) across highland and lowland areas. Traditionally, each ayllu paid tribute to a regional kuraka, who in turn was accountable to the higher nobles and kings. The arrival of the Incas did not substantially disrupt these norms, but the Incas modified arrangements to serve their own purposes: the Aymaras dispensed tribute to the Incas, delivered sacred objects and young nobles to Cuzco, and supplied labor for the construction of roads and the provision of warehouses controlled by the Inca state.

Beyond the highlands, indigenous societies with less complexity dotted the landscape. In the savannahs of northeastern Bolivia, for example, several chiefdoms (e.g., Baures, Cayuvavas, Movimas, Canichanas, and Itonamas) adapted to the floodplains and pursued year-round settled agriculture. Although fully sedentary and possessing farming plantations, these dispersed settlements lacked centralized governments and sophisticated tribute networks; they were consequently nearly unconquerable, for both the Incas and the Spanish.[118] Still less complex groups lived in the vast tropical lowlands of eastern Bolivia, surviving the sandy plains and harsh seasonal variations of the Gran Chaco through hunting and gathering.[119]

Spanish Colonization. When the first Spaniards arrived – about one hundred soldiers who showed up in 1535 – the Aymara communities greeted them peacefully, because the soldiers were accompanied by a large contingent of indigenous troops associated with the Huáscar faction of the Incas, whom the Aymaras had historically supported.[120] The Spanish soon became abusive, however, and discontented Aymara factions launched rebellions, infuriating Francisco Pizarro and leading him to respond harshly. Once major contingents of the Aymaras were brutally defeated, Pizarro appointed two of his brothers to rule the region.

With little delay, the Pizarros established settlements in the southern altiplano, including one at La Plata (then also known as Chuquisaca, or sometimes just Charcas; now called Sucre). Densely settled by the Aymaras, La Plata provided the Spanish with a ready labor force and a core of soldiers. When settlers chanced upon rich veins of silver at nearby Potosí, La Plata suddenly became the link between Peru and lands further to the south. In 1552 a bishopric was established, and in 1558 the city became home to the independent Audiencia of Charcas, with executive and judicial authority. By 1630, La Plata's Spanish population was more than a thousand.[121] In the mid-sixteenth century, the Spanish also founded the city of La Paz at the site of a leading indigenous town in the heart of Aymara territory. La Paz was an agricultural and commercial center, with industries producing textiles, wine, and chocolate. But silver was not plentiful, and population data suggest that the city was inhabited by only a few hundred Spanish in the mid-seventeenth century.[122] In between La Plata and La Paz, the Spanish founded the mining city of Oruro, which for at least part of the seventeenth century was more populous than La Paz.[123]

Although La Plata, La Paz, and Oruro were notable urban areas, the mining city of Potosí is the real reason that Upper Peru warrants the classificatory status of colonial center. The Spanish rushed to settle Potosí's dry and cold highland valley following the discovery in the late 1540s of ore close to the surface of a minor peak known as Cerro Rico (rich hill). At first, miners relied on indigenous wind ovens to extract silver, and many of the workers and technicians were *yanaconas* – indigenous men who had been displaced by the conquest or otherwise were not tied to an ayllu and who worked in exchange for wages.[124] The early rush to Potosí also brought tribute-paying encomienda workers, individuals who were not free. In consequence, as Peter Bakewell notes, "by 1550 two fundamental types of Indian labor operated at Potosí – yanacona and encomienda . . . the distinction is undeniable, and denotes the start of a dual system of labor [i.e., wage labor and coerced labor] that was to persist in one form or another through the colonial era."[125]

Potosí also became the site of major colonial institutional innovations when depression hit in the 1560s after the surface ore was exhausted and the existing laborers proved inadequate for shaft mining. To rectify the situation, Viceroy Toledo brought the modern amalgamation refining process and the mita labor draft to the city in 1573.[126] Silver production at Potosí shot up, such that the city soon accounted for the large majority of all Peruvian silver.[127] Remarkably, in fact, "in the years 1575–1600 Potosí produced perhaps half of all Spanish American silver."[128] By 1577, the city was populated by two thousand Spanish households, many of which contained Spanish women and children. Over the next three decades, the Spanish population grew larger, though estimates of exactly how much larger vary widely, ranging from several thousand to several tens of thousands.[129] The resident indigenous population of Potosí was also very large; the city was probably inhabited by well over one hundred thousand people in the early seventeenth century, making it the most populated city in the New World and about equal to London at the time.[130] Although marked by the raucous living typical of a mining district, Potosí housed an impressive parish church and several other lesser churches, an active town council and government office, a royal treasury, a mint, a vibrant public plaza, and the most lavish market in the Americas. The Spanish population was entertained by bullfights, the lighting of bonfires, and elaborate religious processions. To sustain all of this population and activity, lengthy trains of llamas supplied the city at great cost with textiles, wine, and food from throughout the viceroyalty.[131]

Potosí's wealth fueled the settlement of still other remote parts of Upper Peru, securing Bolivia's status as a center within the empire. The Spanish founded Cochabamba in 1571 because its large indigenous population possessed the agricultural labor power needed to feed Potosí's population and service its mines.[132] Even the Chaco region, where the indigenous population was sparse and hostile, saw the intrusion of expeditions from Paraguay, which brought about the creation of Santa Cruz de la Sierra in 1561. According to no less an authority than Herbert Klein:

With the final settlement of the frontiers and the interior towns, the growth of the silver mining industry, and the integration of the older Indian agricultural market with the new Spanish one, Upper Peru became one of the wealthiest centers of the new Spanish empire in America. Its dense populations of settled Indians provided a seemingly inexhaustible labor force, while its mines were quickly recognized as the principal source of silver in the Americas, if not in the entire world at this time.[133]

The Fate of the Indigenous Population. Transforming Upper Peru into an early Spanish colonial center entailed a thoroughgoing uprooting of the native population. Tens of thousands of indigenous people were concentrated in the barren lands of Potosí, having migrated or been forcibly transferred from communities across the Bolivian and Peruvian highlands. The mita draftees – roughly 13,500 of them each year – were brought to Potosí to perform arduous mining and refining work for a period of one year.[134] The Crown, the viceroy, the president of the Audiencia of Charcas, and the corregidor of Potosí all had their hands in – and regularly clashed over – the specific organization of the mita.[135] But encomenderos and especially town kurakas were the individuals who physically oversaw the gathering and delivery of the mitayos. With population declines, it became increasingly apparent that the kurakas could not meet their obligations, and in time the Spanish permitted payments in silver in exchange for the missing mitayos, though it became harder for the kurakas to make these payments as time went on.[136] In the mines of Potosí, a majority of indigenous workers were actually wage laborers (*mingas*), so that it is wrong to portray the economy as built entirely on forced mita labor.[137] Moreover, outside of mining, wage labor characterized many other tasks (e.g., craftwork, freighting, and charcoal production) performed by the thousands of indigenous people who lived in Potosí but did not work in the mines. Nevertheless, in comparison to Mexico, there was greater reliance on forced labor in Upper Peru. As D. A. Brading and Harry E. Cross put it, "To pass from Mexico to Peru is to enter a vale of tears."[138] Only the coerced labor used in the mining regions around Mexico City – where, as in the Bolivian altiplano, a dense indigenous population resided – even approximated the horrible mita drafts of Potosí in the late sixteenth and seventeenth centuries.[139]

Other institutions besides the mita facilitated labor exploitation. In the initial decades after conquest, for instance, encomiendas that were passed down from generation to generation were used to secure agricultural tribute.[140] By the seventeenth century, the Spanish were extracting surplus from the mobile forces of landless laborers who arrived at haciendas and towns seeking wages.[141] As in Peru, these migrating forasteros were the ironic product of Spanish relocation policies intended to group indigenous people into reducciones, where they would be converted into Christians and exploited through tribute payments and mita contributions. Forasteros often found their way to Spanish estates around La Plata, La Paz, and especially Cochabamba, as well as the mineral regions of Potosí and Oruro. In fact, by the late seventeenth century, Oruro contained tens of thousands of indigenous people, many of whom worked in the silver mines for wages. In the early eighteenth century, Oruro was producing nearly a third as much silver as Potosí, even though its authorities never succeeded in their bid to reallocate a portion of Potosí's coerced workers to their region.[142]

While the policies of the Spaniards in Bolivia broke apart preexisting indigenous identities and often lifestyles, their germs drove much of the numerical decline of this population. Beginning in the 1570s, a series of smallpox, measles, and influenza epidemics struck the area. The concentration of the indigenous population into urban centers, especially Potosí, exacerbated the effects of these diseases.[143] Although good data on the extent of population loss are not available for Upper Peru, one can extrapolate from

Cook's work on Peru and estimate a population decline of about 50 percent from 1570 to 1620 for Upper Peru (however, Nicolás Sánchez-Albornoz suggests a more extensive loss).[144] If at all valid, this depopulation rate compares favorably with that of many parts of Mexico, suggesting that the highland population of the Inca Empire may have survived at higher rates than did the Aztecs in central Mexico. Regardless, Bolivia retained well over a hundred thousand indigenous persons – concentrated in the highlands – in the seventeenth century, making it one of the more densely settled parts of the Spanish Empire.

The Mercantilist Elite. Azogueros, as the owners of silver mines and refineries in Potosí were known, oversaw a huge portion of the total economic output in the New World. During the seventeenth century, however, their numbers and influence declined in step with the falling profitability of silver mining.[145] Greater wealth in fact belonged to the merchant community, which in Upper Peru meant especially silver merchants and moneylenders. "In Potosí as in other mining towns of the Andes and Mexico," Bakewell points out, "the *mercaderes de plata* [silver merchants] tended to accumulate more wealth than the men directly occupied in mining silver ore and turning it into metal."[146] Some of the merchants' wealth came from control over the production and delivery of silver. Great profits also flowed from financing the mines and refineries. Indeed, by the early seventeenth century, "the azogueros found themselves dependent upon silver merchants and money lenders for operating capital."[147] Moreover, the merchant elite's access to capital enabled them to invest in other growing sectors of the economy, including hacienda agriculture. Even the Crown ultimately relied on them to finance most sectors of the nonsubsistence colonial economy.[148] In turn, the merchants reaped the benefits of the Crown's monopoly system governing trade, mercury dispersion, land grants, and silver minting and transport; in each instance, the merchants were granted privileges or exclusive rights in exchange for making the monopolistic economic structures function roughly as intended. They could therefore most readily tap into the profits that were to be had from the closed colonial economy.

Links were strong between the merchants and large landowners – the latter of whom were also part of Bolivia's elite, though they probably enjoyed less economic power than their counterparts in Mexico and Peru. Landed elites, of course, controlled Bolivia's haciendas, which produced corn, wheat, potatoes, fruits, and other staples and which had proliferated during the mining boom at the expense of native communities throughout the highlands and valleys (especially around Cochabamba, La Plata, and Tarija).[149] By the second half of the seventeenth century, however, the large estates had mostly stopped expanding, and "they absorbed only about a third of the Indian labor force in the entire region of Charcas."[150] Thus, the economic troubles and the turn inward for the landed elite of Bolivia appear to have started at a very early stage.

At the end of the Habsburg period, then, the Bolivian dominant class was led by colonial merchants who were closely linked to both landed and mineral interests. In time, the decline of the mines would weaken both the merchant and mineral components of the elite, leaving the landed upper class as the clearly dominant fraction. These changes were part of the larger colonial marginalization and economic impoverishment of Upper Peru – processes that unfolded later, under Bourbon rule.

THE COLONIAL PERIPHERIES

From the heartlands of the empire, we turn now to the colonial peripheries – those territories in the Americas that were only perfunctorily settled and colonized under Habsburg Spain. In looking at these cases, we shall see that the Crown was not moved to devote people and resources to regions that lacked good opportunities for mercantilist accumulation via mineral extraction or tribute collection. Likewise, Spanish settlers themselves generally avoided areas that did not promise quick enrichment. Given their mostly overlooked status, the colonial peripheries were never going to have powerful mercantilist coalitions nor be built on oppressive ethnic hierarchies that were at all equivalent to those of the colonial centers. Instead, the Spanish elite in these areas was nugatory within the empire, indigenous people became mestizos at high rates, and the settlers who did stay had to look to commodities other than precious metals to stimulate any growth.

The Southern Fringe: Uruguay, Argentina, and Chile

Precolonial Societies. Before first contact with the Spanish, the Inca Empire had extended into portions of the Southern Cone, encompassing northern Chile and a slice of northwestern Argentina.[151] However, in the vast territories south and east of the Inca Empire – in most of Chile and Argentina and all of Uruguay – complex indigenous societies were *not* present (see Map 3.3). The perhaps one million individuals in these areas beyond the Inca Empire subsisted mostly as hunter-gatherers, though some practiced slash-and-burn agriculture and lived a more settled life.

In Uruguay, the Charrúa pursued a nonsedentary lifestyle; several dozen individuals established temporary settlements according to seasonal variations in vegetation and the location of animals. Men hunted animals with bows and arrows, while women gathered berries, roots, and other food. Leaders and shamans possessed exotic objects that symbolized their rank, and groups distinguished themselves from one another by dress, tattoos, and body ornamentation.[152] This kind of hunter-gatherer society was common throughout the precolonial Southern Cone, and it was the only form of human organization in precolonial Uruguay.

In central and southern Argentina, tens or even hundreds of thousands of individuals sharing language families could be found. Most of these people

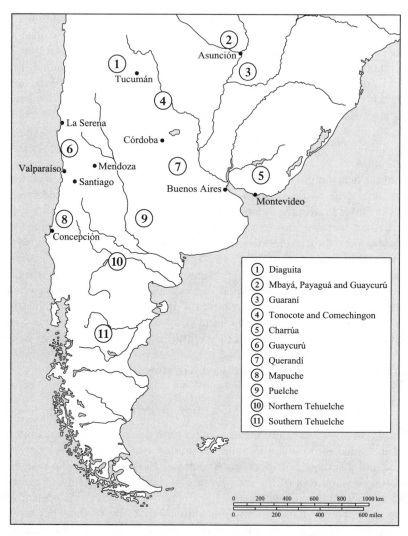

MAP 3.3. Precolonial Societies of Uruguay, Argentina, Chile, and Paraguay
Sources: John M. Cooper, "The Southern Hunters," in Julian H. Stew-
ard, ed., *Handbook of South American Indians*, vol. 1, *The Marginal
Tribes* (Washington, DC: U.S. Government Printing Office, 1946), 15; Jorge
Hidalgo, "The Indians of Southern South America in the Middle of the
Sixteenth Century," in Leslie Bethell, ed., *The Cambridge History of Latin
America*, vol. 1, *Colonial Latin America* (Cambridge: Cambridge University
Press, 1984), 93.

are now classified as belonging to the Querandí ethnic group (located in the lands between Buenos Aires and Córdoba), the Puelche ethnic group (south of Buenos Aires to the Negro River), and the Tehuelche ethnic group (still further south).[153] The Querandí organized themselves into small bands and subsisted from hunting, fishing, and gathering; it is possible that they also practiced primitive agriculture. A German missionary from the first Spanish expedition to encounter the Querandí described them as follows: "These Querandíes do not have fixed residences, they roam the territory like gypsies. When they travel in summer (usually over distances of 30 leagues), if they don't find water or thistles, they find and kill deer or wild beasts and drink the blood; if they didn't, they would die of thirst."[154] Farther south, individuals roamed in small bands, and seasonal agriculture definitely was not a supplement to hunting and gathering. For example, "the *Puelche* had no agriculture, and originally no domesticated animals, except the dog."[155] Likewise, "the Tehuelche lived a precarious and simple life in material terms, keeping warm against the cruel Patagonian winds with skin capes and makeshift skin lean-tos . . . The Tehuelche traveled by foot in small family bands, following seasonal movements of the guanaco [llama] and the rhea [ostrich]. Their seasonal hunting and gathering pattern was punctuated by trading fairs with Pampas groups to the east."[156]

More densely settled areas were in Chile, where five hundred thousand or more Mapuche people resided between the Itata and Cruces rivers south of contemporary Santiago; just to the north were the Picunche.[157] Despite their considerable population, the Mapuche "had not undergone an agricultural revolution and, therefore, were not fully organized into sedentary productive communities."[158] Rather, they lived in disconnected and temporary settlements; their economy was based on gathering, fishing, and hunting, though they did practice slash-and-burn agriculture (not irrigated or fertilized), including potato, corn, squash, and bean farming. Given the large number of Mapuche people, it is appropriate to ask, as does José Bengoa, "How was it possible to sustain this population in the absence of a fully developed system of agriculture?"[159] The answer is the rich ecology of the region, which offered an abundant supply of game and fish and many opportunities for gathering edible plants, including the pine nuts (*piñones*) that, when ground into flour, were a Mapuche staple. At the same time, it is not fantastic to believe that the Mapuche would have soon organized themselves as a fully sedentary agricultural society if the Spanish had not arrived when they did.

Uruguay. Uruguayan territory – known to European colonists as the Banda Oriental (i.e., the "eastern bank" of the Uruguay River) – was little transformed by colonialism before the mid-eighteenth century.[160] Beginning in 1516, exploratory expeditions entered the Río de la Plata in quest of precious metals and rich agricultural societies. Instead, what they found on the eastern bank were the Charrúas and other inhospitable hunter-gatherer societies. Settlers from a different kind of colonizing nation might have prized this sparsely populated territory, for it was marked by "fertile and undulating lands, a temperate climate, numerous rivers and streams, good ports on nearly all sides, and indigenous tribes in a state of natural savagery." But mercantilist Spanish conquerors saw only "a land that was without cultivation; there was no gold, nor silver, nor emeralds; the trees bore no nourishing fruit, nor was it possible to extract from them rubber or essences, as in the tropics... The aboriginal tribes that populated these lands lacked agriculture, domesticated animals, [and] woven fabrics... Under these conditions, the territory was of absolutely no interest to the Spanish."[161]

The Banda Oriental was little inhabited during the seventeenth century. In the interior, the Charrúas mastered horsemanship and fiercely resisted enslavement or relocation by the Spanish. Not until after independence did settlers fully conquer the Charrúas. The tiny Spanish population of the area – perhaps several hundred individuals in the mid-seventeenth century – was located along the coastal region, which at some point to the north became Portuguese territory; many of the early settlers of Uruguay were actually Portuguese. With the introduction of cattle in the early 1600s, the landscape of the region was forever changed. The Banda Oriental became a gigantic grazing pasture and slaughter ground for thousands upon thousands of cattle.[162] Before the eighteenth century, these animals were considered Crown property and could be legally killed or transported only with payment to the town council of Buenos Aires. This helps explain why many of the early cattlemen of the region hailed from Buenos Aires; and it accounts for the unease and the sense that Buenos Aires was unfairly privileged among the gaucho residents of the Banda Oriental, whose survival depended on cattle.

In 1680, the Portuguese founded Colonia del Sacramento (Nova Colônia do Sacramento) in western Uruguay, just thirty miles across the River Plate from Buenos Aires.[163] From this fortified port town, Portuguese, English, and Dutch traders brought slaves, tobacco, wine, and textiles into the supposedly closed Spanish market. Colonia also provided an easy point of access for outsiders to indiscriminately kill cattle and steal their hides. Though Spain's response was gradual in coming, due to Portugal's power vis-à-vis Spain in the late seventeenth century, it ultimately involved the containment of Colonia and the construction of a Spanish military fort at present-day Montevideo. San Felipe de Montevideo was founded in 1726 with a population of about one hundred people, who were imported from Buenos Aires and the Canary Islands. Despite such a modest start, the city would eventually lead the impressive development of Uruguay. But none of this happened under the Habsburgs.

Argentina. Early Spanish adventurers seeking a great Indian kingdom also found southern Argentina difficult and undesirable for settlement. Though

Pedro de Mendoza's outing was larger and better armed than those led by Cortés and Pizarro, it simply could not survive in the rolling plains of Argentina, where less complex groups of indigenous people roamed. The expedition succumbed to malnutrition, disease, and, especially, relentless attacks by the Querandí.[164]

When they did finally settle in Argentina, the Spanish confined their occupation to an arc reaching from the mines of Potosí to Buenos Aires; vast territories in southern and northeastern Argentina remained uninhabited by Europeans. Within the arc of settlement, the extent of colonial institutional establishment varied in close relation to the size and complexity of the indigenous population. In the northwestern Tucumán jurisdiction, where more complex indigenous societies were located, the Spanish established more extensive institutions after arriving from the highlands of Bolivia. By contrast, in the River Plate jurisdiction around Buenos Aires, where the indigenous societies were less complex, the Spanish pursued limited colonial activities. The distinction between these two areas was eventually formalized when Tucumán and the River Plate became separate governorships within the Viceroyalty of Peru.[165]

The Governorship of Tucumán was really a region of Upper Peru, given that it was within the Audiencia of Charcas and that its principal function was providing labor and exports to help run the Potosí mineral economy. Many small colonial towns were founded here – Santiago del Estero, San Miguel del Tucumán, Salta, Jujuy, and La Rioja, each with a few hundred Spanish settlers in the mid-seventeenth century. The one large city was the capital of Córdoba (established in 1573), which was home to more than two thousand Spaniards at the end of the seventeenth century.[166]

Sedentary indigenous groups living in the Governorship of Tucumán were handled much the same as other ethnic groups on the southern edges of the Inca Empire: they were subject to systems of forced labor, including encomiendas and the mita. Jorge Comadrán Ruiz's data for 1596 show that in La Rioja, where the complex Diaguita society was located, twenty thousand individuals were in encomiendas; in Córdoba, where the somewhat less complex Comechingone people lived, the number was twelve thousand; in Santiago del Estero, home to the semi-sedentary Tonocote society, Spaniards held an estimated eight thousand people in this arrangement.[167] When the demographic collapse of the indigenous population of Argentina eroded the base for encomiendas, the governor ordered labor drafts; reducciones were also orchestrated, in order to concentrate workers.[168]

More settled and economically vibrant than the rest of the Southern Cone, the Governorship of Tucumán could be argued to have been a semiperiphery of the Habsburg Empire. Merchant-encomenderos here exported cotton and low-grade textiles for Potosí; and modest quantities of wheat, corn, cattle, and cattle-derived products were sent to both Potosí and Chile (northwestern towns such as Mendoza were at the time actually part of the Audiencia of

Chile).[169] Córdoba, as already mentioned, did have a fairly large population. On the other hand, Viceroy Toledo viewed the region as nothing more than a source of livestock for the mining population, which is what it indeed largely was. Tucumán was always subordinate to the Audiencia of Charcas, which in turn was subordinate to the Viceroyalty of Peru.[170] And neither the governor nor the wealthiest elites of Córdoba were influential vis-à-vis the Lima authorities; they were treated as underlings who controlled a part of the empire best known for its mules.

In contrast to the interior of Argentina, the littoral around Buenos Aires was clearly a periphery in the empire; Spanish authorities left it isolated before the late seventeenth century. "When the reality came to show the failure of hopes [of riches in the region], interest was lost in the Rio de la Plata... The Spanish government stopped paying attention to these territories[,] ... bringing a miserable life to the province."[171] The region suffered mightily from Spain's fixation with the mines in Upper Peru: "So long as Potosí predominated and was the main attraction in the economic activity of South America, the inhabitants of the Plata and at the key port of Buenos Aires were at the mercy of the interior – an ironic trend considering the subsequent historical role of the port and its hegemony over the interior."[172]

Although forts and short-lived settlements had previously been established at Buenos Aires, the city was permanently occupied only in 1580, when sixty-six male settlers made enough peace with the surrounding indigenous people to survive in the plains region.[173] In 1622, the entire European population of Buenos Aires, Santa Fe, and Corrientes was about 1,600; in 1684, this large region had around 4,550 European residents.[174] Portuguese merchants really controlled trade in the region, establishing ties to business interests in Córdoba of the Tucumán province.[175] These "foreign" merchants were wealthier than the Spanish settlers, the latter group depending almost completely on the cattle industry held as a monopoly by the town council of Buenos Aires. The Portuguese demanded silver from Potosí in exchange for their imported products (e.g., linens, silks, swords, horseshoes, wine, spices, and slaves).[176] From this demand commenced the siphoning of silver from Upper Peru and its transport via Córdoba to finance contraband trade in the River Plate.

Under the mercantilist rules, all trade through Buenos Aires was supposed to occur in registered Spanish vessels that were part of the fleet system whose voyages were strictly regulated by the Crown. The Habsburg authorities, moreover, prohibited commercial intercourse between the port and the rest of the empire. They outright banned participation by Buenos Aires in the exchange of silver and slaves. Absurdly enough, settlers in Buenos Aires were required to use Lima as a port for trading with Spain. In 1622, the Crown established a customs house at Córdoba (later moved to Jujuy) to thwart the transport of silver and to force Buenos Aires to export locally produced cattle goods.[177] It is possible that these measures slowed the contraband trade and the flow of silver into the region in the mid-seventeenth century.[178] Concomitantly, there was a drop in the quantity of European goods entering the region. The River Plate economy therefore remained depressed until the late seventeenth century. Indeed, the area felt more like an experimental settler community than a fully established colonial town: houses were made of mud rather than brick, no large cathedrals or religious establishments were present, encomiendas went unfilled, and significant economic activity was confined to brief episodes when ships were in port. Governors and settlers in the region complained bitterly about the Crown's unwillingness to come to their aid in the face of shortages of goods, high prices, conflict with foreign merchants, poor communications with Córdoba, and attacks by the Querandí. Yet, given the perceived lack of immediately profitable resources in the area, the Crown chose to maintain trade policies that suffocated commerce and development in the River Plate.

Chile. From a strictly geographical perspective, Chile was in many ways an ideal area for settlement and might have appeared destined to become an important part of the empire. Ecologically, its fertile central valley was admirably suited for growing wheat, grapes, olives, and other Spanish staples. Its temperate climate, gentle breezes, and rolling hills stood in stark contrast to the disease-fomenting coastal environment near Lima. Although Chile was not overwhelmingly mineral-rich like Potosí, gold could be mined near several coastal towns, from La Serena in the north to Osorno in the south. Moreover, the native Mapuche were a sufficiently abundant population for the extraction of labor. The early Spanish settlers of the region were duly impressed.[179]

And yet one can reasonably conclude, following Simon Collier and William F. Sater, that Chile "was [among] the most remote of all the Spanish possessions."[180] How is this possible? Why did such a promising region become a periphery? The short answer is that the Mapuches were not a complex society. The case of Chile quite nicely underscores the importance of the *organization* of the preexisting indigenous population (as opposed to its size alone) in explaining the level of Spanish colonialism. The Spanish did not center their colonial activities in this region because its large indigenous population lacked the kinds of institutions that would have permitted profitable mercantilist exploitation, even though in other respects the region was superb.

Only in the north of Chile were the Spanish able to readily establish tribute-collecting and military-recruitment systems. Encomiendas were possible here because the indigenous groups had been previously incorporated into the bureaucratic and coercive structures of the Inca Empire. But in central and southern Chile, the Mapuche effectively resisted the Spanish, just as they had done with the Incas. Resistance occurred in many areas of the empire where less sedentary people lived, but nowhere did it attain the levels seen in Chile:

The most distinctive feature of the Spanish conquest of Chile was the never-ending war with the Araucanians [Mapuche]. In Chile alone of all the Spanish colonies in the New World the pattern of settlement was dramatically reversed. Instead of a quick military victory followed by a period of constructive advance, the Spaniards found themselves embroiled in a costly conflict that continued at intervals for more than two centuries and threatened at times to destroy them.[181]

When in 1541 Pedro de Valdivia selected the Mapocho Valley for the location of Santiago, the ten thousand or so native inhabitants revolted. Then, when the Spanish sought to control regions to the south in the Mapuche heartland, the two-century-long war was launched. The Mapuche were certainly fierce resisters, but we need to realize that their sociopolitical organization is what allowed them to sustain recalcitrance. As Brian Loveman points out, "their very dispersion and lack of centralized political structure made virtually impossible either a definitive 'victory' or the administration of a Spanish conquest on a scale like that of Peru."[182] Beyond this, the large size of the Mapuche population is certainly also important to explaining why these people played the historical role that they did.

Although there were periodic truces, warfare predominated in sixteenth- and seventeenth-century Chile.[183] After Valdivia was killed in the fighting in 1550, the region headed toward ruin, with indigenous assaults routing newly founded settlements and forcing their abandonment. Revolts in the last years of the sixteenth century overran several Spanish towns, killing perhaps 20 to 25 percent of the Spanish population. After that, Spain actively intervened to defeat the Mapuche. The Crown authorized the royal treasury of Peru to provide special defense funds:

In 1600 the king of Spain established a permanent military subsidy, or *situado*, for Chile, and war in Chile became a permanent, institutionalized business of the Lima merchants and shippers until almost the end of the seventeenth century. The *situado*, a symbol of the poverty of the Chilean colony, also freed the encomenderos from most financial and military obligations of the war. Conquest and pacification thus became largely a public venture instead of a private semi-feudal imitation of the Spanish reconquest of their homeland from the Moors.[184]

Initially, this situado provided for fifteen hundred soldiers, a number that was later increased to two thousand. This creation of a permanent armed force was almost without precedent, even in the center of the empire. Despite the substantial resources, however, the war continued through the seventeenth century, with a huge indigenous uprising in 1655 once more destroying many Spanish settlements and causing an exodus from areas south of the Maule River.

Chile therefore evolved into a military garrison whose central purpose in the Habsburg Empire was to secure Peru from hostile attacks emanating from the south. Spanish immigrants to the area were by and large men appointed for military service. In some cases, the soldiers chose to settle permanently in Santiago, which housed its own audiencia after 1567 (further empowered in 1609) and its own bishopric seat. Yet at the end of the sixteenth century, Santiago's population was only an estimated five hundred to seven hundred Spaniards and some two thousand mestizos and indigenous people (often children).[185] The city contained a mere 170 houses, mostly one-story adobe and mud buildings. Curfews were sounded at nightfall to call home the rugged frontier residents who chose or were obligated to live in this perilous region. In 1647, an earthquake destroyed most of the city's buildings, forcing the settlers to start over once more. Other Spanish towns in Chile – such as La Serena, Chillán, and Concepción – were smaller still, though like Santiago composed of soldiers and poor frontier residents. Throughout colonial Chile, rates of miscegenation were high, and mestizos (especially mestizas) were often counted as Spanish.[186] Warfare and miscegenation (as well as diseases) gradually reduced the once-large indigenous population of Chile – and it was this reduction, as much as anything else, that enabled the Spanish to begin to stabilize the territory starting in the late seventeenth century.

If the Mapuche had been controllable early on, Chile likely would have evolved into a more important region, perhaps sharing similarities with both Ecuador and Colombia (semiperiphery cases that we will consider below). For, as in Ecuador, there was a dense population to exploit in the interest of furnishing agricultural and manufactured products to the bloated Potosí market. And surely such activity would have commenced had it been feasible. At the same time, like Colombia, the region had many scattered mines that would have appealed to the Spaniards' avarice had they been able to mobilize the Mapuche for labor services. As it was, gold production declined to virtually nothing after the mid-sixteenth century, and the returns from newfound copper and silver deposits in the seventeenth century amounted to very little. Hence, despite the fact that Chile was at least the fifth best endowed territory in terms of valuable minerals (after Bolivia, Mexico, Peru, and Colombia), this wealth did not materialize until after independence.[187]

The economy, such as it was, encouraged governors and settlers to devote much energy to hunting down indigenous people to serve in encomiendas or to be sold as slaves. Indigenous people were always needed to work on the estates (of varying sizes) that produced agricultural and livestock exports for Peru (e.g., tallow, hides, wine, apples, and olives).[188] Indigenous people were also sought as workers in the wineries, tanneries, and mills. Such labor exploitation took on an especially horrific form in Chile. For in the wake of the indigenous revolts in the late sixteenth century, the Council of the Indies authorized and even encouraged the legal enslavement of rebellious Indians in Chile. What is more, political authorities here quite openly worked to kill nonsedentary indigenous people presumed inappropriate for coerced labor.

The economic elites were landed potentates who dominated town administration and merchants who ran the import-export business with Peru. Yet the military situation was so dire that the agrarian economy and its landlord class could never blossom. The merchants were protected by the monopoly system, and their profits were in some ways enhanced by the danger of moving goods to and from this territory. Yet "the merchants of Chile were subject to continual instability... The cause was a struggle with the merchants of Lima, who imposed on them low prices for tallow and wheat. In the seventeenth century, noticeably, there were many merchants who were legally dispossessed or went bankrupt."[189] Indeed, while the port of Valparaíso had potential as a commercial center, no Spanish fleet came to the coasts of Chile; merchandise shipped from Valparaíso could reach Spain only by way of Peru.[190]

In terms of its crucial institutional features, then, we must conclude that Chile ended up like Uruguay and the littoral of Argentina: the territory lacked arrangements that could sustain powerful merchants, entrenched landed elites who controlled huge pools of dependent labor, and an economically and politically significant church. Moreover, despite the presence of an initially large indigenous population, the Spanish could not transform the Mapuche into a sedentary and spatially concentrated population that might then be subject to orderly exploitation.

Other South American Peripheries: Paraguay and Venezuela

Paraguay. Asunción, Paraguay, lies a thousand miles from the mouth of the River Plate; to reach it in 1537, Spanish soldiers left over from Mendoza's ill-fated expedition had to plod through tropical wilderness occupied by roaming, hostile indigenous groups. Near Asunción, however, they encountered the Guaraní, a more hospitable, semi-agricultural people. The Guaraní inhabited territory east of the Paraguay River to the Atlantic coast, especially around Asunción (see Map 3.3).[191] They probably numbered at least three hundred thousand, organized into hundreds of separate and autonomous settlements. More complex than surrounding groups, the Guaraní often lived for two or three years at a given place before relocating, and they used slash-and-burn techniques to pursue small-scale farming (of, e.g., maize, sweet potatoes, and squash) on land surrounding their villages. Their society was stratified: Caciques represented each patrilineal family (*tevií*), and shamans oversaw religious festivities to pay tribute to Tupa, the supreme deity. Yet Guaraní cultivation was relatively primitive, lacking real irrigation and relying on shifting of agricultural plots over time. Indeed, the Guaraní continued to depend on hunting and gathering for much or most of their subsistence. Thus, like the Mapuche of Chile, the Guaraní were a populous but still semi-sedentary society.

West of the Paraguay River, in the Gran Chaco region, nomadic indigenous groups who lived from hunting, fishing, and gathering were the norm. Altogether, they encompassed an estimated 180,000 individuals in the early sixteenth century.[192] Chaco bands such as the Payaguá, who canoed and wandered along the banks of the Paraguay River, fought regularly with the Guaraní. When the Spanish arrived in the Asunción region, therefore, they were able to befriend the Guaraní by presenting themselves as allies in the historic struggle against the Payaguá and other raiders. In exchange, Guaraní leaders treated the Spanish as caciques and provided them with food, knowledge of the region, and women. Although this early episode of Spanish-Guaraní cooperation is sometimes celebrated as idyllic, important segments of the Guaraní population were in fact always discontented, leading revolts already in the early and mid-1540s.[193]

Unsurprisingly, the small Spanish population at Asunción soon tried to apply forced-labor programs to their Guaraní "allies." In 1556, the city governor introduced an encomienda system (the *encomienda mitaya*), dividing up about twenty thousand indigenous people among 320 Spanish conquistadors.[194] Other indigenous people were made personal servants through what became known as the *yanaconazgo* or the *encomienda originaria*.[195] Nevertheless, the Guaraní were unaccustomed to systematically providing labor services or tribute to any centralized political authority. As the Spanish tried to impose their methods of exploitation in this setting where no preexisting expropriation institutions could be harnessed, they soon found that their repression and their germs caused massive population collapse.[196] "The available labour had already become quite scarce in about 1600 and there were repeated complaints about a shortage."[197] By 1674, the total population of the province of Paraguay was only thirty-nine thousand people, of whom about half were Guaraní, meaning that the indigenous population declined by more than 90 percent in the first century and a half of Spanish colonialism. Large-scale systems of labor exploitation could thus not take root here. By 1674, fewer than four thousand Guaraní were held in encomiendas.[198]

Spanish land was mostly subsistence farms that produced both native foods (e.g., maize, sweet potatoes, manioc, groundnuts, and beans) and European foods (e.g., wheat, rice, barley, sugarcane, and citrus fruits). Never impressive in scale, these agricultural activities did not generate a powerful landed elite:

Arable farming remained small-scale throughout the colonial period. It was practised on holdings of no more than a few or, at most, a few tens of hectares. In the latter instance, the farmer often had available additional labour, besides that of the family.

There did not develop, as in other parts of the Spanish colonial empire, a dualistic system with large market-oriented, relatively modern and capitalistically organised Spanish arable farms (*haciendas*), on the one hand, and small, more traditionally organised, indigenous subsistence holdings on the other. Nor did the growing of more commercial crops, such as sugar cane and cotton, lead in Paraguay to the creation of large plantations. These crops were usually grown mainly to supply the needs of the family and, only if there were small surpluses, were these sold.[199]

Larger in scale was the production of yerba tea leaves (which grew wild here), used to make the maté beverage, the consumption of which spread rapidly in the mid-seventeenth century.[200] Yerba exports began passing through Santa Fe (Argentina), and from there they eventually reached Peru.[201] Most of the Spanish population in Paraguay was in some way involved in the production, transport, or trade of yerba, though indigenous people carried out the backbreaking work. And it was merchants from Argentina – not Paraguayans – who financed the yerba trade and who therefore reaped the lion's share of its profits.[202] Poverty-stricken Paraguay itself never developed any significant merchant class at all.

The overall marginality of Paraguay within the empire is well revealed by the trajectory of its premier city, Asunción. Although in 1541 the entire Spanish population of the Plata region, approximately eight hundred individuals, was briefly concentrated in this city,[203] the Spanish population subsequently grew very slowly. In fact, due to extensive miscegenation, the small population that did live here was mostly mestizo.[204] These residents lived in simple houses made of clay, straw, and palm leaves. Public buildings were likewise made of clay and timber, not brick. "In about 1700, even a building like the cathedral still had walls of adobe and a roof of straw and palms supported on hardwood beams...The advantage of the simple construction method was that houses and other buildings could be relatively quickly rebuilt, which was important, because floods, caused by high river levels or torrential rainfall, sometimes washed them away and the tooth of time did its work quickly."[205] Even the wealthiest residents remained rugged frontiersmen, impossibly far removed from the elite lifestyles practiced in Potosí and Lima.

Other Spanish towns founded near Asunción in the second half of the sixteenth century were simply military forts designed to keep out the encroaching Portuguese. Most lands further west of Asunción, in the Gran Chaco, remained uninhabited by the Spanish until the nineteenth century. The hunter-gatherer societies of these areas (e.g., the Payaguá, Guató, Guaycurú, and Mbayá peoples) effectively resisted incorporation into the encomienda system and dissuaded the Spanish from seriously pursuing territorial advancement.

While the cathedrals in Asunción were small adobe chapels, the communal farming missions of rural Paraguay initially flourished and were more

remarkable. Beginning in the early seventeenth century, the Jesuits established a series of these missions that together housed tens of thousands
of Guaraní people in what is now northeastern Paraguay and southwest
Brazil.[206] The missions worked to Christianize their inhabitants while pro-
tecting them from the most abusive forms of forced labor. Spanish authorities supported the Jesuits in part to prevent the Portuguese from advancing
westward. Indeed, from the perspective of the Crown, "the missions were
not effective rivals of the New World colonists for control of the Indians.
They were granted jurisdiction in remote areas and gathered together Indians who were not accessible to the colonists."[207] However, the defenseless
missions soon fell victim to attacks and slave raids led by *bandeirantes* from
São Paulo. In consequence, beginning in the 1630s, the Jesuits relocated to
southeast Paraguay and northeast Argentina, where they could escape Portuguese assaults. From there, some thirty missions continued to function in
relative isolation until the Jesuits were forced to leave in 1767, after which
time the missions lost their closed character, saw the gradual decline of communal farming, and deteriorated economically into small and impoverished
enclaves.[208]

Venezuela. When Columbus's third voyage took him to the north coast of
South America, present-day Venezuela (then known as Tierra Firme) was
occupied by a range of diverse indigenous groups, including several sedentary
chiefdoms (see Map 3.4).[209] These farming communities were the Jirajara
and Caquetio peoples of northwestern Venezuela; several Caribe chiefdoms
(e.g., the Pariagoto, Cumanagoto, Chaima, Palenque, and Guarine peoples)
living farther to the east on the north coast; and the Timoto-Cuica society in
the Andean region of western Venezuela. Numerous hunter-gatherer groups
also roamed the vast Venezuelan llanos, as did some semi-sedentary societies,
such as the Otomac. Although the evidence is still rather fragmentary, the
chroniclers describe the Jirajara and Caquetio societies as having permanent
towns, irrigated crops, and loose political federations that sometimes united
to fight major wars. Likewise, the Caribe groups farther to the east featured
"a rather advanced type of horticulture" in which a large number of plants
and trees were cultivated (maize, manioc, sweet potatoes, ají, chili peppers,
pineapples, and other fruits).[210] And the Timoto-Cuica people are usually
portrayed as the most complex of all, exhibiting well-laid-out villages surrounded by agricultural estates with terraced fields, irrigation ditches, and
water-storage tanks. The size of individual indigenous communities is not
known, but altogether the pre-Columbian population of Venezuela has been
estimated at one million.[211]

Spanish incursions were at first pearl hunts and slave raids along the coast,
the latter of which brought indigenous people to the Caribbean to perform
plantation labor.[212] By the 1530s, officially sanctioned Spanish expeditions
led by German captains in quest of El Dorado (literally, "the Golden One,"

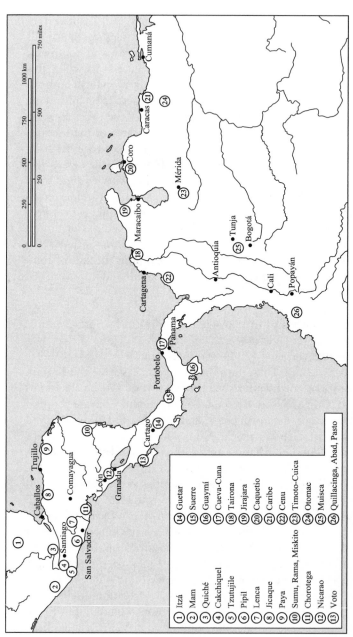

MAP 3.4. Precolonial Societies of Central America, Colombia, and Venezuela

Sources: Carolyn Hall and Héctor Pérez Brignoli, *Historical Atlas of Central America* (Norman: University of Oklahoma Press, 2003), 61, 65; Mary W. Helms, "The Indians of the Caribbean and Circum-Caribbean at the End of the Fifteenth Century," in Leslie Bethell, ed., *The Cambridge History of Latin America*, vol. 1, *Colonial Latin America* (Cambridge: Cambridge University Press, 1984), 38–9; Julian H. Steward, ed., *Handbook of South American Indians*, vol. 4, *The Circum-Caribbean Tribes* (Washington, DC: U.S. Government Printing Office, 1948).

90

meaning "the Golden Indian") had touched the interior of Venezuela and parts of eastern Colombia.[213] Slave raiders and explorers quickly discovered that the indigenous groups of the region could not be easily exploited, despite the fact that they often practiced agriculture. John V. Lombardi offers the reason: "In no part of Venezuela were there large concentrations of urbanized Indians living under centralized political control."[214] Instead, even the most complex societies were organized as semi-autonomous communities lacking central political leadership and tribute-collecting authorities. The Spanish therefore could not control Venezuela's indigenous people simply by manipulating or assassinating the elite and assuming the reins of an existing empire. Rather, they had to try to pacify one community after another. It is not surprising, therefore, that a recurrent theme in all major histories of the settlement period in Venezuela is the fierce resistance of indigenous people who would not allow themselves to be subject to colonial rule. This resistance made systematic exploitation through conventional instruments nearly impossible.[215] The cultural demise of these peoples came about through other means: because they were not concentrated into large indigenous towns (as in the colonial centers), ethnic groups were simply folded into the population at large, and their cultural distinctiveness slowly dissolved.

A lack of abundant precious minerals clinched Venezuela's status as a backwater territory. Although gold mining was pursued in several places, "the exploitation of these gold mines was in general very modest, and in many cases yielded little or no profit."[216] Once reserves of easily captured slaves were exhausted, therefore, the region lost value to the Crown and allure for colonial settlers. The first Spanish towns (e.g., Coro and Cumaná) were basically military outposts from which the slave raids were launched. In the second half of the sixteenth century, additional precarious settlements were established, often in areas with small amounts of gold or copper: Barquisimeto and Carora in the Segovia Highlands, Trujillo in the Andes region, and Valencia and Caracas in the central coastal range.[217] Population data for these settlements are notoriously hard to come by. Some probably attracted hundreds of Spanish settlers in the early seventeenth century, such that all of Venezuela may have housed a few thousand Spaniards.[218]

Caracas emerged as the premier city in colonial Venezuela because it was able to achieve a reasonable level of political stability and because it was well endowed for the production of wheat and cacao, the latter of which became the major export of Venezuela before coffee flourished in the nineteenth century. Settlers successfully pacified the most powerful Caribe indigenous groups, such as the Teques, with the help of a smallpox epidemic. The temperate climate of elevated Caracas then proved favorable for wheat production, which offered export opportunities in the late sixteenth century, due to a shortage of flour in Spain. About half of the wheat was sold in the Cartagena market and consumed by sailors from the Portobelo fleet on their return voyage to Spain. With the cereal profits, Caracas was transformed from a military outpost to a town with some two-story buildings, a municipal government (*cabildo*), craftsmen (who probably also farmed), and encomienda labor.[219]

Cacao was practically a staple in Mexico, and its exportation from Caracas after 1630 linked Venezuela much more to New Spain than to Peru. In exchange for cacao and some sugar and tobacco, Venezuelan traders received manufactured goods and slaves (both African and African American), the latter arriving legally or illegally in large numbers from the mid-seventeenth century to the late eighteenth century (peaking in the second half of the eighteenth century).[220] Yet,

although Venezuelan landowners complained constantly about the shortage of labor and the need for more black slaves, they apparently did not enjoy enough prosperity to pay the high prices required to attract slavers to the Venezuelan coast. In part the Venezuelan market was too small to be worth the risk, and in part the scarcity of money in the Venezuelan economy made quick and efficient contraband trade with foreign slave traders complicated.[221]

Any economic takeoff in Venezuela would thus have to await an influx of investment capital. For toward the end of the seventeenth century, the region was still just a series of outposts for a small number of Spaniards on the fringe of the colonial empire.

The Peripheries of Central America: El Salvador, Honduras, Nicaragua, and Costa Rica

Precolonial Societies. Precolonial Central America was home to many populous societies whose inhabitants engaged in advanced agriculture and made tribute payments to ruling noble classes or individual chiefs. The large size and political complexity of these native societies are not controversial facts among specialists on the period, but they may be surprising to other Latin Americanists, who sometimes assume that most of Central America was sparsely populated at the time of the Spanish conquest. As one authority notes, "Without exception, the sources who knew Central America during the Conquest period consistently reported large and densely settled populations... It remained for scholars of the present century to assert that Central America was sparsely inhabited."[222]

Pipil societies occupied most of western and central El Salvador (see Map 3.4). The Pipil people spoke Nahuatl, the language of the Aztecs, and their 350,000 people were organized into state-like polities. In central El Salvador, a ruling elite based in the capital of Cuscatlán oversaw some fifty subject settlements; in the western region, a smaller polity based in Izalco controlled perhaps a dozen. These were militaristic states with standing armies whose members were recruited through conscription. In addition to warfare, Pipil society revolved around advanced agriculture in which irrigation was practiced; a wide range of both native and non-native plants were cultivated in orchards and hedgerows. The surpluses that were generated allowed ruling nobilities in Cuscatlán and Izalco to collect cacao, cotton, maize, beans, and chiles as tribute.[223]

In eastern El Salvador and central Honduras, the Lenca people were organized into classical chiefdoms not unlike those in Venezuela.[224] Similarly, along the Honduras-Nicaragua border to the south, the Chorotega had formed a chiefdom society.[225] Together, these societies contained hundreds of thousands of people.[226] The Lenca and Chorotega were each arranged into separate and partially autonomous communities of varying sizes, with the largest towns containing several thousand individuals. Caciques controlled these population centers in the absence of overarching political authority. Sustenance was achieved mostly through small-scale communal agriculture (e.g., maize, beans, and manioc); irrigation techniques do not appear to have been widely developed.

In western Nicaragua and northwestern Costa Rica, another relatively complex Nahuatl-speaking society was present, this one known to the Spanish as the Nicaraos, named after a cacique. Unlike the Pipil of El Salvador, however, the Nicaraos are currently understood to have been organized as a "maximal chiefdom," not a proto-state.[227] The Nicaraos probably had "a relatively weak tribute system based on voluntary payments such as one would expect in a chiefdom."[228] And they lacked the system of law, centralized government, and professional ruling class that we associate with a state. Still, Nicarao society was densely populated, with at least one hundred thousand people living in a relatively small area; and it engaged in advanced agriculture, slavery, and market trade, using cacao as money.

Various other classical chiefdoms were present in western Nicaragua and throughout Costa Rica. Unlike the Pipil and Nicarao, who resembled the Aztecs in many ways, the precolonial groups to the south often showed cultural similarities to Colombian and Caribbean native societies. They varied in size, from several hundred individuals to many thousands, but when added together they were quite populous: at the time of the conquest, perhaps a million people lived in the chiefdoms of Nicaragua, and many hundreds of thousands in Costa Rica and Panama as well.[229] Communities normally produced enough to have significant agricultural surpluses, engage in extensive trade with neighbors, and support wealthy chiefs. Individual societies were nevertheless separated from one another to the point that the Spanish were not able to control the region even when the largest groups were defeated. The precise locations of these largest chiefdoms are not known for certain, but some were in northwest Costa Rica (e.g., a pocket of the Nicoyas around Guanacaste) and some in the Central Valley of Costa Rica (e.g., the Garabito and Guarco).[230] As a general rule, the more complex indigenous societies of Central America were located closer to the Pacific Ocean.

Many Central American societies at the time of the Spanish conquest were not fully sedentary, especially toward the Atlantic coast.[231] In Honduras, the north coast was home to the Jicaque and Paya indigenous people, both of whom sometimes practiced shifting agriculture but also relied heavily on collecting wild fruits and vegetables; fishing; and hunting animals such as white-tailed deer, rabbits, and birds. Likewise, in eastern Honduras and Nicaragua, the Sumu practiced slash-and-burn agriculture in conjunction with hunting and gathering. The Rama of southeastern Nicaragua and the Suerre of eastern Costa Rica, both located near the Atlantic coast, probably supplemented a seafood diet with agriculture. All of these groups lived in smaller villages or tribes with no permanent political authorities. Conflict among groupings was the norm, which prepared them to mount powerful opposition to the European encroachers when the time came.

El Salvador. When conquistador Pedro de Alvarado and his followers crushed the Pipil state at Cuscatlán in 1524, the territory of modern El Salvador – originally but one region (known as San Salvador) within the province of Guatemala – was opened up for settlement, excluding the eastern parts where the less controllable Lenca resided.[232] Encomenderos from Guatemala were excited by the area's dense population, while merchants from there were lured by the potential profits from cacao, which had been extensively harvested, collected as tribute, and used as money in the Pipil polity. Spanish settlers founded a town at Sonsonate near the port of Acajutla – in the center of indigenous activity – and soon actively sought and competed for the surplus labor of the local population. The encomenderos oversaw the direct extraction via tribute obligations using preexisting Pipil networks; the merchants controlled the pricing and shipment of products.[233]

Despite the fact that El Salvador's indigenous people were accustomed to providing tribute and an agricultural commodity (cacao) that was in great demand in Mexico, the region never advanced beyond the status of a colonial periphery. In the late sixteenth century, in fact, when cacao exports were peaking, the town of Sonsonate still had only a few hundred settlers.[234] It attracted almost no new settlers from the Caribbean or from Mexico (in dramatic contrast to Peru). And it was never a focus of concern for high-ranking officials. Settlers and officials simply bypassed this area, even though it had once housed an indigenous state.

What missing ingredient(s) would have enabled El Salvador to become a focus of colonialism? One answer is, of course, gold and silver, which figured so prominently in mercantilist Spain's extraction designs. Except for tiny amounts near San Miguel, there were no precious minerals in El Salvador. Cacao was a valuable agricultural commodity in the New World, to be sure, but mercantilist colonialism was never at all oriented toward profit generation via open intracolonial trade among the New World territories. No agricultural product could substitute for precious minerals in meeting the Habsburg Crown's accumulation needs.

Beyond this, El Salvador lacked an indigenous empire on the scale of the Aztec and Inca empires. The states at Cuscatlán and Izalco, though certainly quite complex in their institutions, did not contain populations so numerous that they could weather the Spanish invasion and still provide enough workers for profitable exploitation. Consequently, after the ineluctable population losses, so few people were left that established institutions could no longer function as instruments of surplus extraction for the Spanish. For instance, the impressive Pipil societies, which had once numbered more than three hundred thousand persons, were soon reduced by diseases and repression to only tens of thousands.[235] The disappearance of these populations triggered the decline of cacao production and made the area unprofitable. Encomenderos who initially had access to huge numbers of workers tried to supplement their labor forces with recruits imported from Chiapas, Quetzaltenango, and Verapaz.[236] But they were too far from the core of the Aztec Empire to have access to truly expansive pools of labor. Eventually, they simply had to give up on the region when its concentrated populations vanished.

Nor did the export of indigo (a blue dye) in the seventeenth century provide any solution. Indigo grew wild in El Salvador, and it was exchanged in the pre-Columbian period, but the indigenous population did not extensively cultivate it or collect it as tribute. The Spanish could not therefore simply modify an existing system of cultivation and tribute collection. Instead, they had to establish new commercial indigo estates (both small and large) in areas where cacao had not already depleted the soil, especially around the districts of San Salvador, San Vicente, San Miguel, and to a lesser extent Santa Ana. Labor shortages during harvest season were again a serious problem. African slaves were an option, but prices were high in Guatemala, and authorities feared revolts. "Thus the indigo growers, when they did have the capital and the opportunity to buy negro slaves, often encountered indifference or even hostility from the authorities in Santiago, who felt that the slave population was already dangerously large."[237] Moreover, Spain's ongoing economic crisis depressed what demand there was for nonmineral exports and led the Crown to almost totally neglect minor colonial areas – which meant not sending its fleet to the port of Trujillo in the Gulf of Honduras, where pirate activity was common. Indigo estate owners thus had to transport their product to Veracruz in the Gulf of Mexico with costly mule trains. To make matters worse, the Veracruz town council taxed the product, and Guatemalan merchants with ties to the trading houses in Cádiz also took their cut.[238]

By the late seventeenth century, consequently, urban Spanish settlements such as Sonsonate, San Miguel, and San Salvador, which had once held some promise at the height of the export booms, remained impoverished towns with only a couple hundred Spanish households.[239] Encomenderos and merchants who had briefly played a visible role were now gone, never having entrenched themselves in this corner of the colonial empire.

Honduras. Honduras initially seemed to offer its own combination of resources attractive to Spanish colonizers. Its fairly dense indigenous population captured the attention of early-sixteenth-century slave raiders from the Caribbean and Panama, and gold strikes stirred rumors of great wealth. Within New Spain, Honduras acquired high status early on: Hernán Cortés led an expedition into the area; Spanish interests from Guatemala and Panama fought for control of it; the ports of Trujillo and Caballos received the annual flota from Seville; and for a brief period in the mid-1540s, the towns of Gracias a Dios and Comayagua competed to become the seat of a new audiencia with jurisdiction over the full isthmus territory extending from Chiapas to Panama.[240]

But Honduras's resources were only a mirage. Soon after contact with European germs and slave raids, the indigenous population collapsed almost entirely.[241] Linda A. Newson estimates that by 1550, the population of western and central Honduras – where the Lenca and other chiefdom societies were located – fell from six hundred thousand to thirty-two thousand, a nearly 95 percent decline.[242] Epidemics again did most of the work, but slaving, famines, and abuse also contributed. The collapse in more eastern parts was less dramatic, but these areas were home to hunter-gatherer and semi-sedentary inhabitants who could not be controlled by the Spanish. Any sedentary indigenous communities that remained in Honduras after 1550 were jealously guarded by miners and landowners who resented efforts by slavers to steal their labor force.[243]

The promise of great mineral wealth also proved vaporous. True, Spanish explorers did extract gold and silver around Olancho and the Guayape River.[244] In the 1540s, perhaps as many as one thousand black slaves were imported to work in that area, and for more than a decade the mines were profitable. Soon, however, the readily extractable minerals were exhausted. In 1580, silver strikes in Guascarán and Tegucigalpa rekindled hopes. The Crown tried to do its part by reducing the one-fifth *quinto* tax to only one-tenth and supplying mercury to process the silver. But it could not resolve chronic labor shortages in these sparsely populated areas – and for a time the Crown made things worse by prohibiting settlers from using indigenous labor in the mines.

A further basic problem was the high cost of extracting silver in the Honduran landscape, with its veins of intermittent and uneven quality, extraordinarily hard volcanic rock, and high water tables. These conditions allowed for small-scale prospecting and provided a livelihood for some "folk miners" who worked alone. But they were not suitable for the kind of large-scale extraction operation that interested the Crown. Mining areas consequently became corrupt and lawless as a tiny elite that controlled the few profitable operations manipulated local governments in order to avoid the royal orders regulating registration, taxes, and labor safety. Overall, as Murdo MacLeod concludes, "during most of the seventeenth century [mining] was a poverty-stricken industry... ignored by central authorities in Spain and Guatemala, and unable to solve the problems presented by the terrain and the local rock formations... The mines of Tegucigalpa occupied a poor, unimportant section of depressed Central America, overshadowed by Guatemala, San Salvador, and even Nicaragua."[245]

Settlement here followed the rise and fall of economic activity. In 1536, Governor Pedro de Alvarado established Gracias a Dios as the provincial capital because of its proximity to the initial gold strikes. After 1548, when the audiencia seat was transferred to Santiago de Guatemala, the Gracias a Dios region stagnated, and Comayagua became the permanent provincial capital.[246] Silver discoveries after midcentury shifted the center of Spanish activity, such as it was, to the central highlands around Tegucigalpa. Yet settlement was never significant. Perhaps two dozen officials and a few hundred colonial settlers lived in Comayagua and Tegucigalpa in the mid-seventeenth century. Other Spanish towns – Gracias a Dios, San Pedro, and Choluteca – were even smaller, each containing fewer than a hundred Spaniards.[247]

We must conclude, then, that Honduras was a colonial backwater region of little concern to Spanish authorities. Even the most developed areas around Tegucigalpa were still lawless frontier towns. To Spain, the region had failed as a mineral enclave and now stood as nothing but a rural outpost dotted with livestock and a small, increasingly ladino population.

Nicaragua. Colonization in Nicaragua involved at first plundering the region through slaving and then utterly neglecting it once its population had crashed. The process started when expeditions from Panama sponsored by Governor Pedrarias Dávila (Pedro Arias de Ávila) hastily explored western areas where the densely populated Nicarao and Chorotega chiefdoms were located. In 1524, in a race with competing conquistadors moving south from Mexico, Pedrarias's men founded Granada (on Lake Nicaragua, in the middle of a populous indigenous province) and León (originally on Lake Managua, next to the indigenous town of Jalteba). From the beginning, they rivaled each other for influence.[248] From 1524 to the 1540s, the Spanish from these towns led repeated expeditions to capture indigenous people or convince friendly caciques to turn over their existing slaves. People so acquired were then shipped to Panama or Peru.[249] By 1548, the indigenous population of western Nicaragua "had fallen to 46,372 from an estimated aboriginal population of 609,262, a decline of 92.4 percent."[250] The total number of slaves that were taken from Nicaragua is not known, though some analysts put the figure in the hundreds of thousands.[251]

When the New Laws were enforced in the 1550s, depopulation rates had already decreased the profitability of the slave trade. Most Spaniards themselves had already left for more promising areas. Those who remained still tried to use the encomienda to extract foodstuffs and personal services from indigenous people. With the population collapse, however, the institution was also of declining impact.[252]

Beyond León and Granada, the other early Spanish settlements of note were Nueva Segovia (in northern Nicaragua) and Realejo (on the Pacific coast). Gold deposits were discovered in the Segovia Mountains in 1527, causing a brief rush to the area. The amount smelted was small, however, and after the mid-1530s virtually nothing was heard from the mining industry in Nicaragua until the eighteenth century.[253] The port town of Realejo was active in shipbuilding and contributed soldiers, slaves, and agricultural supplies for the Peruvian conquest. However, the relocation of León after 1610 caused many of Realejo's merchants to move there; after that, Realejo stagnated. In most other parts of Nicaragua, including eastern parts where less complex indigenous groups resided, the Spanish were unable or unwilling to physically settle, despite the occasional efforts by Franciscan and Mercedarian friars to convert the local inhabitants. The weak Spanish presence in the east allowed English pirates to establish footholds along the Mosquito Coast. In the seventeenth century, buccaneers used these bases to sack León, Granada, and other towns.[254]

Small-scale exports from Nicaragua never amounted to near enough to sustain any wealthy merchants or a powerful landed class. Cacao production in western Nicaragua in the mid-seventeenth century seemed promising, but "it declined as the result of devastating pirate attacks, excessive Spanish duties, the closing of Río San Juan commerce, and the consequent increasing cost of land carriage. Most of the abandoned cacao estates then reverted to cattle."[255] After 1600, indigo was produced in and exported from western Nicaragua. The quantities hardly approached those of El Salvador, however.[256] In the absence of a significant export, the closest thing to an elite in Nicaragua were the Granada-based families who used the Río San Juan to send locally produced foodstuffs and livestock products around Central America.

By the end of the seventeenth century, the province of Nicaragua was essentially a deserted cattle run. Perhaps twenty thousand indigenous people remained in the western zone. The largest colonial towns – León, Granada, and Nueva Segovia – recorded only about two hundred Spanish households each, and even most of these residents lived in the countryside as subsistence farmers and ranchers.[257]

Costa Rica. "Costa Rica was the governorship most forgotten, marginal, and backward of the four components of the Captaincy General of Guatemala, and as such one of the regions most abandoned by the Crown," writes Elizabeth Fonseca.[258] She notes that the general causes are the same as what we have found elsewhere: "In the first place we can point out the lack of an indigenous population as one of the fundamental causes of the marginality... The absence of precious minerals and mines was another cause of the little interest aroused by the province."[259]

Spanish activity in the region dates to early-sixteenth-century slaving operations in Nicoya (then part of Nicaragua), though Europeans did not successfully settle the interior of Costa Rica until Juan Vázquez de Coronado and his mostly Guatemalan entourage founded Cartago, the capital of the Governorship of Costa Rica after 1565.[260] When Vázquez de Coronado's men originally occupied the Central Valley, the indigenous chiefdoms of the Garabito and Guarco were still densely populated. Spanish invaders openly wondered whether this population would survive long enough to support significant tribute collection. The question was soon answered: "The pandemic of 1576–81... reduced the Indian populations of highland Costa Rica to a very few, and from then on the area was to become chronically starved for labor."[261] By the early seventeenth century, only about eight thousand indigenous people were under Spanish control as tribute payers in the Central Valley; the other area of some Spanish settlement was the town of Esparza in the Pacific lowlands, and here perhaps two or three thousand indigenous people were incorporated as tributaries.[262] In the southern region of Talamanca and on the Atlantic coast, the resistance of less complex indigenous groups was sufficient to inhibit Spanish settlement beyond the occasional missionary expedition.

The Costa Rican economy functioned mainly as a way station for goods produced in Nicaragua and Honduras to reach Panama. Mules and other livestock products were transported through Costa Rica to be traded at Portobelo. In time, some residents of Cartago entered this trade for themselves, breeding the mules and slaughtering the cattle for their tallow and hides. In addition, Costa Ricans began to produce basic foodstuffs for the sailors and merchants coming and going in Panama. "At the end of the sixteenth century, Costa Rica exported to Panama wheat flour, biscuits, sweets, garlic, anís, and mules."[263] But the collapse of the Portobelo fairs in the early seventeenth century spelled the end of even this modest commerce.

Cacao was harvested in the Matina Valley along the hot and sickly Caribbean coast, and some early settlers smuggled the product to British traders and their agents.[264] Wealthier residents from Cartago were eager to invest in the industry, but labor shortages were the ever-present obstacle: the dwindling Voto indigenous people simply would not be usurped to serve as a plantation labor force. Small numbers of African slaves were used, but they generally proved too costly.[265] Worse, cacao was Costa Rica's most readily taxable commodity, and duties were collected on its transport, whether by sea to Portobelo or by land to Nicaragua. When one also factors in the heavy costs of periodic pirate attacks on both ships and the cacao plantations themselves, it is easy to see why, in Costa Rica, "few people were earning more than a meager living from cacao."[266]

By the end of the seventeenth century, Costa Rica's indigenous population had largely disappeared, reduced to scattered towns of only a few hundred people as a result of disease, maltreatment, miscegenation, and cultural assimilation. The Spanish population was likewise tiny; "there were only two stable Spanish settlements: Cartago and Espíritu Santo de Esparza." In fact, Esparza barely existed, having become virtually uninhabited in the early seventeenth century.[267] For its part, the entire jurisdiction of Cartago was populated in 1699 by only a little more than two thousand persons (including all indigenous people, slaves, Spanish, and ladinos/mestizos).[268] Indeed, "in 1675, the city of Cartago did not have even forty households, since nearly all the Spanish worked and lived in the countryside."[269]

THE COLONIAL SEMIPERIPHERIES

Guatemala, Colombia, and Ecuador were the Habsburg semiperipheries – those regions marked by intermediate levels of settlement and institutionalization. The major cities of Santiago, Bogotá, and Quito concentrated many thousands of Spanish settlers, far more than in the peripheries, but still not the tens of thousands of people who lived in the urban areas of the colonial centers. Within these cities and in the countryside, lucrative trade monopolies, large agricultural estates, and sometimes mining operations provided the seeds for mercantilist coalitions to grow and even thrive, something that did not occur in the peripheries. But unlike in the colonial centers, the reigning merchants of these semiperipheries were not the leading commercial actors of the whole empire; and the landlords and miners here lacked the economic and political prominence of their counterparts in the centers.

To explain why these three cases became semiperipheries rather than full-blown centers or isolated backwaters, the complexity of the indigenous societies is again one very relevant consideration. But it is, again, only part of the story. Guatemala and Ecuador had populous and state-like indigenous societies, yet these territories did not become colonial centers. They were disadvantaged by their considerable distance from the capitals of the Aztec and Inca empires, the places where any mercantilist colonization effort would have to be focused. And they could not make up for this disadvantage with precious minerals, because these were largely absent in Guatemala and Ecuador. Colombia had more significant deposits of precious metals, but its indigenous population (though containing state-like formations) was too small to lure Spanish colonists, especially given the area's geographic isolation from the Aztec and Inca headquarters. Guatemala, Ecuador, and Colombia thus had some of the ingredients necessary for substantial colonization, but they lacked others, at least in part, and they thus remained at the semiperiphery of the empire.

Guatemala

Precolonial Societies. When Cortés arrived in the Yucatán, the region of contemporary Guatemala was densely populated by perhaps 2 million indigenous people, often Mayas.[270] Maya civilization had long since passed its height (classic Maya civilization is dated at roughly A.D. 300 to A.D. 900), but many groups had reestablished state-like political organization, probably in the aftermath of Toltec invasions from Mexico. Several disunited Maya kingdoms, including the Quichés, Cakchiqueles, Tzutujiles, Mames, and Petén Itzás, populated Guatemala in the early sixteenth century (see Map 3.4). Interspersed within these kingdoms were various chiefdom societies; in some cases, the kingdoms were but a collection of loosely connected chiefdoms.[271]

The largest polities were agrarian states ruled by militaristic leaders who extracted surplus and labor from commoners and orchestrated warfare to expand their territorial influence.[272] Peasant commoners and slaves devoted much of their lives to military service and to slash-and-burn agriculture, especially the cultivation of food staples such as corn, chiles, and beans. They treated the office-holding elite as sacred and linked them to the gods through participation in rituals, including human sacrifice. Although in important respects the large Maya states resembled the Aztec state, they were less bureaucratic and controlled fewer people and more limited territory. In the case of the powerful Quichés, for example, the capital city at Utatlán was inhabited by many thousands of people, but it was not the great spectacle that was Tenochtitlán.

Spanish Colonization. Colonial settlement patterns were driven by possibilities for exploiting the indigenous population. Tribute considerations were paramount, because precious metals were not present here, except for very small amounts around Huehuetenango.[273] Where small and less complex indigenous societies existed, Spanish soldiers were unable to subdue the population and establish effective control. Vast parts of Guatemala remained unoccupied by the Spanish decades after the formal conquest was complete.[274] Settlers mainly populated only the region east of Lake Atitlán, where their erstwhile allies the Cakchiqueles lived. Following a series of mishaps related to its construction, the capital of Santiago was founded in 1543 at the site of present-day Antigua (where it remained until 1773).[275] At the end of the sixteenth century, Santiago was inhabited by some 3,700 Spanish people, a number that increased to 5,600 by 1650.[276] The population of Greater Santiago grew from 12,000 to at least 30,000 between 1620 and 1700, far larger than in any other part of Central America.[277] In fact, within Central America, "the only city that truly grew during the seventeenth century was Guatemala [Santiago], seat of the regional government, of the

Audienca, of higher education, of the grand monasteries, of the principal bishopric, and the center of economic power within the kingdom."[278]

Santiago's political position and economic role thus made Guatemala a semiperiphery region. Early on, Santiago's residents successfully lobbied for the seat of the regional audiencia (it had been located briefly in Honduras), ensuring that the province would be the political center of at least Central America.[279] Nevertheless, governors and audiencia presidents in Santiago oversaw staffs composed of only around thirty royal officials.[280] The Santiago town council was also a small institution, even more so once its seats had to be purchased at high prices from the Crown beginning in the late sixteenth century.[281] The province's economy depended on the export of agricultural commodities to Mexico, especially cacao and later indigo. It also profited from illegal trade with Peru, which ran through the port at Realejo.[282]

In terms of its overall political and economic positioning within the colonial empire, Guatemala was essentially a diminished version of Mexico and Peru. Given the area's highland indigenous societies, whose people were descendants of the original great civilization of Mesoamerica but no longer part of a single expansive empire – as was the case in Mexico and Peru – this outcome might be expected. Nevertheless, we recall that the region of modern El Salvador also contained a state-like indigenous society, and it was the center of cacao and indigo production, Central America's most important agricultural exports before the eighteenth century. One might suppose, then, that El Salvador, not the area around Santiago de Guatemala, should have become the leading colonial area in Central America, an outcome certainly favored by many of the Spanish who resided in Sonsonate and San Miguel. Yet Guatemala had a decisive advantage: it was more proximate to and had better access to Mexico City, the inevitable heartland of the Spanish colonial empire. El Salvador was on the southwestern end of the great indigenous states of Central America and lacked access to the Atlantic Ocean. By contrast, Santiago de Guatemala was more strategically placed in the midst of the former Maya societies, within range of key markets in Mexico by both land and sea. It was thus Santiago that was positioned to forge the political and economic ties necessary to win the audiencia and gain the status of a colonial semiperiphery, not the fledgling towns of El Salvador. Having political power within the empire, in turn, allowed the Guatemalan elite to control the Salvadoran economy. El Salvador may have been the location of agricultural production for export, but it was the politically powerful merchants from Santiago who siphoned off most of the wealth to be had from these exports.

The Fate of the Indigenous Population. Spanish settlers in Santiago and in the cacao-producing districts near the Pacific coast employed encomiendas to collect corn, beans, and cacao from indigenous people and to obtain their labor services for public works and domestic upkeep.[283] Encomenderos sometimes worked through existing Maya networks, but they imposed higher obligations than had traditionally been the case.[284] The goods received were often sold by intermediaries when prices were high.[285] As a result, during the sixteenth century, "the encomienda constituted the principal source of wealth for the Spanish in Guatemala."[286] The best quantitative data on this institution come from an assessment prepared in the mid-sixteenth century by Alonso López de Cerrato, the audiencia president who some believe worked to enforce the New Laws restricting the use of encomiendas. Cerrato's data show that seventy-nine encomenderos controlled nearly twenty-four thousand indigenous people in southern Guatemala.[287] Demographic historians George Lovell, Christopher Lutz, and William Swezey extrapolate from Cerrato's assessment to estimate that at least eighty-five thousand indigenous people were potential tributaries, and probably a majority of them were actually incorporated into encomiendas.[288] Whatever the exact number, exploitation through the encomienda was widespread.

Efforts to secure tributaries were, obviously, complicated by the rapid decline of the indigenous population. Again using Cerrato's data, Lovell and colleagues estimate that within the first twenty-five years of Spanish settlement, the indigenous population declined by around 75 percent, to a total of 428,000 (excluding El Petén).[289] By 1600, perhaps fewer than 150,000 indigenous people remained.[290] With this population decline, authorities imposed restrictions on the harshest forms of the encomienda. However, the congregación policy of concentrating the indigenous population took hold. According to one estimate, "by the early 1570s there were three hundred of these Indian towns with a total of 40,000 to 45,000 inhabitants."[291] The use of repartimientos to conscript indigenous people to serve on public works and to labor for individual Spaniards in need of services also accelerated.[292] As in Mexico, the Crown increasingly sought to control tribute collection for itself, and programs of forced labor were no longer the main basis of wealth for individual Spanish elites. Debt peonage was probably quite common.[293]

These various institutions concentrated the indigenous population and made it into a homogenous and subservient race in the minds of most Spanish settlers. In vast territories outside of Santiago (e.g., the Verapaz and the western highlands), where the population was almost entirely indigenous, people lived in largely self-governing peasant communities with rights to communal lands. The communities might provide laborers for Spanish-style haciendas, and they might be subject to intrusions from Spanish religious authorities, but they also were subsistence farming villages that enjoyed relative freedom from direct colonial supervision and resource claims by Spanish elites.[294] On the one hand, these communities helped sustain Guatemala's very large indigenous population and practically ensured that the postcolonial nation would be mostly indigenous. On the other hand, they also meant that indigenous people normally lived under conditions of abject poverty and in isolation from the rest of colonial society. The combination of these facts put Guatemala on a path toward extremely low levels of social development.

The Mercantilist Elite. Although relatively impoverished, Guatemala's economy sustained merchant-landed elite actors not unlike those found in the center territories. And these elites became obstructions to late colonial economic development just as much as their counterparts in Mexico and Peru. Let us briefly examine them as they existed under the Habsburgs, to complete our understanding of the contribution of this early phase of colonialism to long-run development.

"The large merchants were the fundamental sector of the oligarchy of Santiago of Guatemala," conclude Jorge Luján Muñoz and Horacio Cabezas Carcache.[295] These merchants had already taken root by the end of the sixteenth century, controlling the trade that was the basis of the Guatemalan economy.[296] Stephen Webre emphasizes how the trade was both legal and illegal, and how it connected Guatemala to both Mexico and Peru:

City merchants exported a number of regional products including cacao and dyestuffs, principally indigo, to New Spain ... In addition to the trade with New Spain, Guatemalan merchants also handled a lucrative commerce with Peru ... [Most important] was Guatemala's role as a transshipment point for quantities of Castilian, Mexican, and Chinese manufactured goods bound for El Callao ...

... In the seventeenth century, therefore, the city of Guatemala and its ports (principally El Realejo but also to a lesser extent Iztapa and Acajutla) became the hub of a very considerable intercolonial trading network, partly legal and partly not, that linked the Philippines through Acapulco, Spain through Veracruz, and the manufacturing centers of Mexico all with the markets of Peru.[297]

The merchants collected hefty profits from the legal export commodities upon their required pass through Santiago. Alternatively, if the exports were contraband headed for Callao, the merchants illegally took their share. For both kinds of trade, they exercised near-monopoly rights, which went largely unchallenged in the region. In fact, commercial interests, not landed interests, owned most of the seats on the town council of Santiago, which was uncharacteristic of colonial Spanish America. Merchants recently arrived from Spain (peninsulars), especially, controlled this political body numerically.[298]

Santiago's merchants were far richer and more powerful than the region's leading group of hacendados.[299] The latter used indigenous labor to grow fruits, vegetables, sugarcane, and especially wheat in the valleys of Jilotepeque, Canales, Sacatepéquez, and Mixco. Other landed settlers took tribute from indigenous communities near Amatitlán, where traditional crops such as corn, beans, cacao, and chiles were grown.[300] As in all the other important colonial regions, agriculture was mostly oriented toward local markets and fostered little internal purchasing power or demand for imported goods. As a consequence, Spanish agrarian estates were often obstacles to export-oriented agriculture. The same was obviously true of the various farms that were held on common lands by native communities and that functioned mostly outside the Spanish cash economy.

In short, at the conclusion of the Habsburg period, Guatemala had inherited a visible mercantilist elite. Santiago's large merchants were especially impressive as a political and economic dominant class. Through their extensive trade networks, these merchants enjoyed ties to actors throughout the Americas. In terms of their linkages to producing classes, however, they were reliant on Salvadoran growers, not on any landholding class within Guatemala itself. The hacendados within Guatemala were in fact mostly ladinos who controlled relatively unprofitable estates that were often underdeveloped and not particularly large by Spanish American standards of the time. The contribution of landed elites to economic prosperity in Guatemala was thus quite secondary next to that of the merchants.

Colombia

Precolonial Societies. State-like polities, tribute-collecting chiefdoms, and simple agricultural and semi-sedentary groups – all of these were present in the complicated political landscape of precolonial Colombia with its 3 million inhabitants.[301] Chibcha-speaking Muisca people were the largest group; about 1 million of them lived in some ten thousand square miles in the eastern highlands (see Map 3.4).[302] The Muiscas were really two loosely knit, tribute-collecting kingdoms – the Zaque of Tunja and the Zipa of Bogotá – together with other smaller and mostly independent chiefdoms. They supported hierarchically ordered societies with permanent military and religious authorities and centralized collection of tribute (e.g., potatoes and maize). But the Muiscas were not overlords of great urban centers, impressive networks of roads, elaborate bureaucratic structures, or strikingly advanced agriculture. Muiscas might have been on the verge of developing a unified empire, but at the onset of Spanish colonialism, they were smaller states, more like the Mayas than the Aztecs.

Dozens of other chiefdoms collected tribute and pursued settled agriculture in Colombia, scattered about and decentralized in a way that also resembles precolonial Central America. Among them were both hierarchically organized chiefdoms with permanent political authorities, such as the Guanes, the Chitateros, and the Sondaguas to the north of the Muisca, and less hierarchical ones without ruling chiefs, such as the Panches and Pijaos to the south.[303] It was the latter societies that proved especially difficult for the Spanish to control. Toward the coast, the Tairona people lived in densely populated and nucleated villages, cultivated various foods and even cotton using irrigated agriculture, and constructed buildings and roadways with stone.[304] Near the coast, too, were Caribe chiefdoms that grew maize and yucca and that may have engaged in tribute collection.[305] Southern regions near Ecuador, along the Inca frontier, were populated by still more sedentary chiefdom societies, such as the Quillacingas, Pastos, and Abads.[306] And roaming throughout Colombia were various bands that did not pursue any permanent agriculture at all.[307]

Colonial Settlement. Spanish population centers took root in the mid-1530s; their size corresponded closely with the size and complexity of the indigenous population.[308] The largest and most important one was Santa Fe de Bogotá, created when Gonzalo Jiménez's troubled expedition marched through the Muisca territory, terrifying the independent chiefdoms, killing the Zaque and Zipa lords, and looting treasure wherever it could be found (often in tombs). Not long after Jiménez invaded the Muiscas, other expeditions – led by Sebastián de Belalcázar and the German explorer Nicolaus Federmann – arrived in this cool highland area, which Jiménez named New Granada. The Spanish population at Bogotá was perhaps only six hundred in 1570, but it grew to two thousand by 1630.[309] By the middle of the seventeenth century, Bogotá was a political center with its own audiencia[310] and was home to an active religious community, Spanish festivals and entertainment, and a huge market at which goods of all sorts were exchanged.[311]

Other settlements of note were created to harness native labor, to defend imperial interests, or to exploit natural resources. The town of Tunja, constructed just about where the Zaque lord had ruled, provided about as many indigenous tributaries as did Bogotá.[312] Along the hot tropical coast, Cartagena housed the region's main port and urban center; the town also became a significant ecclesiastical center and home to military forces placed to ward off pirate attacks.[313] To the west and south of the former Muisca lands, ephemeral Spanish towns developed and then disappeared in tandem with the rise and fall of gold production. Mid-sixteenth-century settlers were already mining gold in quite a few western settlements – Popayán, Almaguer, Santa Fe de Antioquia, Tocaima, Ibagué, Mariquita, La Victoria, and La Palma – with the commercial town of Cali providing the region's treasury office and gold-smelting house.[314] "Indian communities in these regions were rarely comparable to the Chibchas [Muiscas] in their social and economic complexity; however, they had relatively large populations, well-organized agricultural systems and, most important, traditions of gold mining and gold working, all of which the Spanish were eager to exploit."[315] The resulting towns were tiny, shifting camps where placer mining was pursued; the indigenous population was often quite hostile.[316] In the late seventeenth century, new discoveries of gold triggered the founding of still more towns in the highlands of Rionegro and the Valley of the Osos; the number of settlements in the west remained high.

An intermediate level of Spanish settlement and institutional formation thus occurred in Colombia – an outcome that can be usefully contrasted to the peripheralization of Chile and Venezuela. In some respects, Chile was at least as likely as Colombia to have become a site of semiperipheral institutionalization. Chile not only possessed deposits of precious minerals nearly equivalent to those of Colombia, it also was located near the viceroyalty capital of Lima, putting it within range of a great center of Spanish life. By contrast, Colombia was isolated along the north coast, quite distant from the major colonial activity in both Mexico and Peru. Colombia became a semiperiphery and Chile did not because of differences in the organization of their indigenous populations. In Chile, the resistance of the semi-sedentary Mapuche people made heavy Spanish settlement all but impossible; but in Colombia, sedentary and tribute-collecting chiefdoms provided a sometimes controllable and exploitable population for the Spanish. Moreover, because territorial control could be more readily established in Colombia, it was possible to profitably use African slaves for labor when gold was found in sparsely inhabited parts. Here, comparisons with Venezuela become instructive. Venezuela's indigenous population was organized into chiefdoms much like Colombia's; the same groups sometimes lived in both territories. But Venezuela was of comparatively little interest to the Spanish. The reason is clearly that Venezuela did not contain important deposits of minerals. Had its geography been richer in minerals, the region almost certainly would have experienced a Colombia-like pattern of colonization. Or, conversely, had Colombia lacked its gold deposits, it would never have become anything but a colonial periphery (in that respect like El Salvador, which had a small indigenous state but no mineral wealth). It was the *combination* of gold and a reasonably large and complex indigenous population that enabled Colombia (for better or, more likely, for worse) to avoid complete peripheralization.

The Fate of the Indigenous Population. Much as in other parts of the empire, the precolonial societies of Colombia were undermined by Spanish diseases, exploitation, and abuse. The pattern was especially similar to that in Central America: densely populated chiefdoms were unable to sustain their numbers for very long after the Spanish arrival. The dwindling populations then became intertwined with the Spanish population, driving high rates of miscegenation.[317]

Of course, the specific situation of the indigenous population varied from region to region. Variations were linked to differences in the virulence of European diseases across highland and lowland areas, as well as differences in levels of Spanish settlement. Rates of survival were higher in the cooler highland societies – where the Spanish tended not to settle – such as the Sierra Nevadas region around Santa Marta, home of the Tairona people.[318] But in the disease-ridden lowland areas, sickness and abuse nearly completely destroyed the indigenous populations, including on the Caribbean coast and in the gold-mining regions around the Cauca Valley. In the eastern highlands, home of the Muisca people, diseases were less virulent, leaving a labor force that the Spanish could exploit for a longer time. Nevertheless, Bogotá suffered repeated smallpox epidemics in the sixteenth century and then typhus outbreaks in the seventeenth – catastrophes that took huge tolls. Finally, in remote lowland areas that the Spanish ignored, the native communities managed to survive, though in reduced numbers.

From the tribute records left behind by royal inspectors, scholars "are able to conclude that, in the period comprising 1558–1564, an indigenous population existed whose base was 300,000 tributaries."[319] Relocation programs sought to concentrate this large tributary population into nucleated villages. But the population was collapsing, and with it the encomienda base.[320] According to Julián B. Ruiz Rivera's data, for example, approximately thirty-eight thousand tributaries were distributed in all of Bogotá and Tunja during the years 1595–1602; the number was only twenty thousand by 1636–1640.[321] To make matters worse (for the Spanish), the relocation programs failed to effectively concentrate the collapsing population, despite repeated efforts.[322] The result was that the Muisca people and other chiefdoms became scattered communities lacking much of their previous cultural identity. And encomienda labor became a scarce and highly sought-after commodity – even more so once gold mining brought settlers to the west, which stimulated the agricultural economy in the east.

Africans were eventually imported to supplement or substitute for the insufficient indigenous population.[323] Teams of black slaves were the primary workforce at the key mines in Zaragoza and Remedios in the district of Antioquia. Moreover, according to an estimate by Germán Colmenares, African labor accounted for a large majority of the workforce at most of the mines where the gold rushes took place between 1590 and 1640; only about 25 percent of total gold production was in areas that relied primarily on indigenous labor.[324] Imports of African slaves declined with the initial exhaustion of gold, only to rebound when new deposits were uncovered in the Chocó and Cauca.[325] With the conspicuous decline in its settled indigenous population, Colombia's mineral economy became ever more reliant on African slave labor.

The Mercantilist Elite. Elite actors who would later pose significant problems for development were a legacy of Habsburg colonialism. Who exactly were these actors in the Colombian context? They were not, interestingly enough, elites whose wealth derived primarily from the ownership of mines. Although miners had enough money to buy slaves and pay the fees and bribes to the corregidores necessary to receive indigenous labor, they usually controlled small operations and could not amass huge fortunes. One key reason is that mineral deposits were scattered over wide areas or found in small veins in which refractory ores were present. Colombian placer mining lent itself to independent prospectors (*mazamorreros*) who worked with very small teams of laborers and quickly moved on when a location was exhausted.[326] While wealthy investors might own three or four dozen black slaves, they did not control huge companies stationed at a single location, for Colombia's geography did not permit deep-shaft vein mining (unlike at Potosí and Zacatecas).

Landed elites were to be a much larger obstacle to later development. These were the original encomenderos and others who invested in arable farming and cattle ranching in various regions – on the coast around Cartagena, in the countryside surrounding Bogotá and Tunja, near Santa Fe de Antioquia, and around Popayán and Pasto toward Quito. Their estates generated food, luxury crops (e.g., wine, tobacco, and sugar), and inputs for basic manufactures (e.g., wool and cotton).[327] They depended heavily on the mining economy to stimulate urban market demand. The church, too, may well have been a key landowner during this period, but the rural properties it controlled are not clearly identified in the literature.[328]

But the biggest problem was to be the wholesale merchants who operated out of Cartagena and were connected to political authorities in Bogotá. They were the ones who really profited from the mineral economy. As Colmenares makes clear, "Gold was, in New Granada, a product whose benefits remained in the hands of the commercial merchants. Certainly, gold stimulated commerce, but only in one direction: that of Cartagena and of the fleet that arrived every year from Seville."[329] The large merchants also benefited from contraband trade and their relations with British merchants in the Caribbean, with Portuguese slavers returning from Africa, and with other marauders who roamed the seas. Large wholesalers and retailers, further, supplied smaller itinerant traders who brought food and goods of all kinds to the distant mining towns in exchange for gold. This activity gave the merchants control over the supply lines to most urban points, which in turn enabled them to smuggle much of the gold produced in Colombia to foreigners who did not collect the royal quinto.[330] Corruption at all levels made it difficult for the Crown to prevent the siphoning of gold into foreign hands. "The Spanish crown tried repeatedly to prevent colonial contact with foreigners, but officials ordered to restrict intercourse often engaged in it themselves."[331] With the wealth they legally and illegally accumulated, Colombia's merchants financed various other enterprises, including rural estates and mining operations. Hence, once again, we find that merchants were first among the elite class, and they were surely the actors who profited the most from the institutional order of Spanish colonialism as it was laid down in New Granada.

Ecuador

Precolonial Societies. When the Europeans arrived, most of Ecuador's 1.6 million people were located in the sierra region. These highlanders lived in countless agricultural communities that were integrated into larger polities headed by tribute-collecting chiefs.[332] Although state-like forms of organization were long established elsewhere in the Andes, in densely settled Ecuador they were introduced relatively late, possibly because the climate here allowed for year-round agricultural production; thus, state organization was not necessary to sustain surpluses.[333] Only when the Incas captured the region in the late fifteenth century did the chiefdoms become part of a state empire. They were incorporated into the Inca system to degrees that varied along a north-south axis. Otavalo-Caranqui and Pasto peoples in the north (see Map 3.2) were brought in late and quite incompletely. By contrast, more southern groups – such as the Palta, the Cañar, and to some extent the Puruhá – were integrated to the point that their institutions bore a strong Inca stamp: hierarchical political structures built around decimal organization, mita labor, the vertical archipelago system, the use of roads and warehouses, the Quechua language, and the worship of the sun. Around modern-day Quito, the Panzaleo people straddled the line between areas of greater and lesser consolidation of the Inca state.[334]

Ecological zones other than the sierra were much less populated. Along the coast, fewer than a hundred thousand individuals lived in bands and small chiefdoms; they practiced shifting agriculture (except toward the south, where more permanent fields were present). To the east of the sierra in the forest-covered Oriente, a range of diverse small groups survived in part from hunting and gathering and in part from shifting cultivation. These societies were not important to the Spanish Crown and its settlers, though epidemics and missionaries still reduced their populations and disrupted their cultures.[335]

Spanish Colonization. Colonists set their sights on the densely settled sierra. But settlement proceeded slowly, and not until the end of the sixteenth century did Ecuador acquire a semiperipheral status.[336] Founded in 1534, Quito was home to the early encomenderos, who argued to the Crown that the area's active town council, large religious community, and distance from Lima necessitated the creation of a new audiencia. They got their way in 1563 when the Audiencia of Quito was born.[337] The audiencia's boundaries were, of course, never firmly established, but it was understood to encompass parts of what is now northern and eastern Peru and territory along the Amazon reaching far across Brazil. In 1580, however, the capital city of Quito contained only four hundred Spanish households.[338] Meanwhile, the other settlements of the audiencia – such as the coastal town of Guayaquil (founded in 1538) and the towns of Cuenca (1557) and Loja

(1548) – had no more than one hundred households each.[339] The Spanish did not subdue Esmeraldas in the northwest until the nineteenth century.[340] And the huge Amazon basin remained uninhabited by the Spanish until the Jesuits and other missionaries managed to congregate some indigenous people into a series of small villages in the mid-seventeenth century.[341] Altogether, the late-sixteenth-century audiencia had fewer than nine hundred Spanish households.[342]

Though part of this region had once been within the Inca Empire, the Audiencia of Quito was never poised to become a colonial center, because the territory included neither the capital of this great empire (as Peru did) nor enormous deposits of precious minerals (such as Bolivia had). On the first point, let us recall that a key justification for having a separate audiencia at Quito was precisely its distance from the dominant audiencia at Lima. Quito was like Santiago in Guatemala: part of a great indigenous civilization meriting its own audiencia, but not so close to the heartland of that civilization as to achieve center status for itself. On the second point, it is true that gold and some silver were mined in various parts of the Cuenca and Loja provinces (e.g., at Zamura and Chachapoyas) during the sixteenth century. However, the return was always modest, and the mineral industry in Ecuador soon evaporated.[343] As in Honduras, the problem here was partly geological: hard volcanic rock covered most of the mineral-rich strata. In addition, as John Leddy Phelan notes, the minerals were "located in isolated and almost inaccessible sites on the eastern slopes of the cordillera . . . [in] the territory of a small, belligerent Indian population. They were not the docile tribes of the high Sierra, previously subjugated by the Incas, but primitive folk fiercely determined to maintain their freedom from the intruders." Still, as Phelan continues, "if the mines had been lucrative, the Spaniards would have had the incentive to crush Indian resistance, as they did in the Chichimeca country in north-central Mexico."[344]

One might wonder why Ecuador did not remain an ignored periphery – perhaps like Honduras, another densely settled region with disappointing mineral wealth. The comparison is especially apt if we recall that encomenderos in Honduras sought to control the capital of an audiencia extending throughout Central America. In contrast to their Honduran counterparts, however, the encomenderos of Ecuador enjoyed a critical resource advantage: the indigenous people were part of such a populous empire that they could retain a semblance of their communities in the face of demographic disaster.[345] In Honduras, elite settlers very quickly found themselves unable to profitably exploit an indigenous population whose numbers and institutions had completely collapsed. But in Ecuador, the indigenous societies that had once been part of the Inca Empire – though reduced and disrupted during the sixteenth century, to be sure – remained sufficiently intact for colonial settlers to mobilize workers and derive profits within the mercantilist system.

Fabric production was the key to these profits. Quito's role as the leading site of textile manufacturing in the Viceroyalty of Peru came naturally, not only because of the Andean valleys' excellent grazing pasture for sheep, but also because the Incas had previously demanded labor services in the form of weaving.[346] Colonial settlers were therefore able to modify existing practices and draft indigenous people as mitayos or entice them to work in cloth factories (*obrajes*) as "volunteers" who were secured through debt-peonage arrangements. In the late 1600s, perhaps two hundred legal and illegal obrajes were in operation producing an indigo-dyed fabric (*paño azul*). These sweatshops – the largest of which were located on communal indigenous lands – likely employed at least thirty thousand workers.[347] Woolen cloth, blankets, hats, sacks, and wadding were shipped throughout the Viceroyalty of Peru. Although textile trade stood in violation of basic mercantilist principles, it occurred because the Spanish Crown was unwilling to enforce its official restrictive policies on the obrajes. Such royal indifference was likely related to the large profits that Spanish officials reaped by licensing the legal obrajes and demanding payments from the illegal ones, as well as to the lack of concerted opposition among Andalusian merchants, who were not positioned to meet the New World demand for cheap textiles.[348]

With Ecuador's niche in textiles reasonably secure (its main competitor at the time was actually Chinese contraband), the Spanish population grew larger. By 1630, the Audiencia of Quito had more than five thousand Spanish households, around three thousand in Quito itself.[349] The city emerged as a leading religious center, with a bishop and impressive churches, the latter funded in part by rich merchants who "bequeathed substantial portions of their estates to the Church."[350] Comparatively speaking, "the diocese of Quito shared with the archbishopric of Mexico fourth place among all American sees in terms of wealth (as reflected by the stipends of their prelates), following Lima, Puebla, and Chuquisaca."[351] Though never an economic powerhouse, Quito was home to residents who amassed small fortunes from fabric manufacturing and to elites who accumulated wealth elsewhere in the viceroyalty but preferred to live here. The audiencia gave some political standing to the region, and the cabildo provided a local forum for elites to voice their concerns.[352] Overall, then, a great deal had changed since 1580: "The peaceful and prosperous city that housed the bishopric seat and the Audiencia tribunal was converted in the first decades of the seventeenth century into a noisy urban center with a variety of ethnic groups and castes, with innumerable convents and religious orders, grand houses, plazas, fountains and magnificent churches, notable for their beauty and prosperity in all of colonial America."[353]

Other areas of Ecuador – including, importantly, coastal Guayaquil – had a very different colonial experience: that of peripheralization. Guayaquil functioned as the transshipment port for goods to and from Cuenca and

Quito, yet its local economy in the seventeenth century really depended on shipbuilding and repair.[354] Early Spanish settlers overexploited the lowland indigenous population, which was already highly vulnerable to the spread of infectious diseases, such that its numbers collapsed from a precolonial total of more than 350,000 to around 3,500 by the end of the sixteenth century – one of the worst depopulation rates anywhere in the Spanish Empire.[355] Soon, residents around Guayaquil began producing and illegally exporting cacao. But during the seventeenth century, these exports were modest, and the town remained remote, barren, and poor.[356] Modernizing developments in Guayaquil had to await the Bourbon phase of Spanish colonialism.

The Fate of the Indigenous Population. Systematic exploitation was the reality of colonialism for indigenous people in Ecuador. Encomenderos, officials, and priests extracted basic goods – maize, cotton, wheat, and chickens – from nearly all communities. And indigenous people in the sierra were required to make cash payments even greater than those levied in Mexico. Unofficial extractions of tribute were also common, especially in the Quito province, where the Spanish were concentrated. To make everything much worse, by the 1570s, "all highland communities were subject to forced labor under the mita. The quota levied was set at one-fifth, which is the highest proportion exacted anywhere in the Spanish Empire."[357] Individuals subjected to the mita might perform any one of several possible tasks, including factory work, labor on plantations and haciendas, public works, and mining. To avoid such obligations, some indigenous people left their villages, becoming migrating forasteros. The Spanish Crown indirectly encouraged fugitivism by granting forasteros exemption from the mita. There was no contradiction here, for the resulting migrants were resettled into new communities and subject to tribute demands by the Crown itself.[358] Toledo's program of reducciones was part of this larger process of congregating the indigenous population into areas where they could be most easily exploited by Spanish officials.

The effects of forced labor and migration, however, were not uniform across territories: "[the] impact on native communities varied with the tasks to which mitayos were assigned, the periods for which they were employed, and whether they were required to change their residence or work in regions to which they were not acclimatized."[359] Labor in Ecuador's textile obrajes was notoriously harsh,[360] but the mills were often located on native lands, and thus the work was less disruptive to subsistence patterns and family life. Obraje workers typically were also farmers who could fall back on subsistence for survival. By contrast, service in mining or long-term public works projects frequently entailed travel across long distances and removal from established ways of life. These differences seem to explain the somewhat greater levels of depopulation in the southern sierra compared to the northern sierra.

Ecuador's indigenous population had declined to perhaps 250,000 persons at the end of the sixteenth century, a reduction of 85 percent from precolonial times.[361] In addition to Spanish warfare and abuses, European diseases were, as usual, a culprit in this decline.[362] Of course, particular regions were subject to various degrees of population loss. Notably, the indigenous population of the sierra appears to have stabilized by the early seventeenth century, such that contemporary observers even assumed (probably erroneously) that demographic growth was occurring. Even if early stabilization was driven by migration from other regions rather than a real leveling off of the death rate, it still afforded elites in Quito a more reliable labor base than was present in other regions.[363] Mortality rates were truly terrible along the coast, where the population was nearly eliminated; parts of the Oriente region also saw devastatingly high depopulation rates. At the conclusion of the mercantilist phase, in sum, Ecuador was left with a comparatively large and often hyper-exploited indigenous population concentrated in the highlands, precisely those areas where the Inca Empire had once had its strongest footholds. Areas where the Incas had not penetrated – including Guayaquil – saw the indigenous population mostly disappear.

The Mercantilist Elite. The considerable developmental problems that would beset Ecuador later in the colonial period were rooted in actors founded through Habsburg institutions. Again, these actors were above all merchants and the landed upper class.

Under the textile economy, wealthy individuals who formed trading companies or loaned capital to those seeking to pursue long-distance trade reaped great economic rewards.[364] "The appeal of commerce relegated other branches of the economy to a secondary position, giving the economy a warped appearance. Investment in exchange was still more attractive than investment in production."[365] Merchants acquired their profits by exporting cheap textiles in bulk to markets as far north as Popayán and as far south as Potosí. The trade was thoroughly dependent on colonial institutions: the product itself would not have been fabricated without coerced labor in the mills, and the huge market at Potosí was artificially contrived through the institutions that built the mining economy. Finally, of course, the mercantilist system protected Quito's position by shutting out would-be rival European producers, especially England. With the money generated from protected trade, the merchants imported a wide variety of goods – including fine European fabrics that were not made in the local sweatshops but were viewed as essential to refined living.

Landed encomenderos have received a good deal more attention than merchants in the historiography of colonial Ecuador. The encomenderos, after all, originally founded the obrajes.[366] Sometimes they created textile mills on common lands that were controlled by indigenous communities; these *obrajes de comunidad* then became a primary means of collecting tribute from the dwindling villages. Royal administrators appointed by the Crown imposed myriad fees on the obrajes de comunidad, ensuring themselves a piece of the action.[367] In other cases, "encomenderos were able to found private obrajes within the territorial limits of their encomiendas which gave them direct control over the Indians working in their obrajes."[368] Spanish officials were also sure to extort payments from the private obrajes, which in time became more profitable than the obrajes de comunidad.[369] In the towns, encomenderos ran the cabildos as a counterbalance to the power of the audiencia.[370] Many encomenderos were sooner or later also hacienda owners, growing maize and cereals and raising animals in the fertile Quito Basin. Food and livestock from the haciendas were sometimes exported to Peru and Colombia, but most of it was intended for the city of Quito. Sheep farms dotted the still heavily populated regions of Riobamba and Latacunga; the wool they produced was the raw material for the obrajes.[371] Broadly speaking, the landed estates of Ecuador were medium-size farms;[372] it is therefore possible that because of the importance of obraje ownership in Ecuador, traditional haciendas were for a time a less salient component of the elite's wealth and power than in the center and semiperipheral cases. But as soon as the textile regime came under threat, during the next phase of colonialism, all segments of the elite fell back onto the ownership of large food-producing estates.

CONCLUSION

Under the Habsburgs, Spanish settlers and authorities pursued greater or lesser levels of colonialism in the Americas largely in response to, above all else, the complexity of the indigenous societies they encountered. Indigenous societies with highly differentiated institutions were always a great attraction, for they permitted the collection of tribute and the exploitation of labor. Less complex societies, with their pre-state inhabitants, were difficult to conquer and nearly impossible to mobilize for resource extraction. The Spanish therefore settled and imposed conventions most thoroughly in those regions where indigenous states were located; they were content to leave comparatively alone the colonial possessions where hunter-gatherer bands roamed and, in some cases, those occupied by settled chiefdoms as well.

While the presence of a preexisting state polity was necessary for a territory to become a full-blown center region of the Habsburg colonial system, it was not sufficient. Other, more geographically based causes combined with it to produce particular levels of colonialism. Of these auxiliary causes, especially crucial were the presence of significant mineral wealth and even simple geographical proximity to the Aztec or Inca civilizations. Levels of colonialism during the mercantilist phase were thus driven by a threefold *combination* of causes: complexity of the indigenous population, extent of mineral wealth, and proximity to one of the two great indigenous empires.

The causal logic underpinning this argument can be stated more formally with the notation of set-theoretic analysis.[373] As Table 3.2 suggests, each of

Table 3.2. Determinants of center, semiperipheral, and peripheral colonies: Mercantilist era

Country	(A) Complex indigenous society	(B) Significant mineral wealth	(C) Near empire capital	A & (B v C)	(Y) Colonial center
Argentina	0.0	0.0	0.0	0.0	0.0
Bolivia	1.0	1.0	0.5	1.0	1.0
Chile	0.0	0.5	0.5	0.0	0.0
Colombia	1.0	0.5	0.0	0.5	0.5
Costa Rica	0.5	0.0	0.0	0.0	0.0
Ecuador	1.0	0.0	0.5	0.5	0.5
El Salvador	1.0	0.0	0.0	0.0	0.0
Guatemala	1.0	0.0	0.5	0.5	0.5
Honduras	0.5	0.0	0.0	0.0	0.0
Mexico	1.0	1.0	1.0	1.0	1.0
Nicaragua	0.5	0.0	0.0	0.0	0.0
Paraguay	0.0	0.0	0.0	0.0	0.0
Peru	1.0	1.0	1.0	1.0	1.0
Uruguay	0.0	0.0	0.0	0.0	0.0
Venezuela	0.5	0.0	0.0	0.0	0.0

Note: 1.0 = full or nearly full membership; 0.5 = partial membership; 0.0 = little or no membership. The "&" symbol stands for the logical AND, and the "v" symbol stands for the logical OR.

the three causes may be coded into simple three-value sets: the value of 0.0 is used when cases have little or no membership in the category representing a given causal factor; 0.5 is used when cases have partial membership in the category; and 1.0 is used when cases have full or nearly full membership in the category. The first three columns – (A), (B), and (C) – report the case scores for the three causes: complex indigenous society, significant mineral wealth, and proximity to the capital of the Aztec or Inca Empire. The last column, (Y), codes cases according to whether they were colonial centers (1.0), semiperipheries (0.5), or peripheries (0.0). The scores for no single causal factor are perfectly matched with the outcome scores. In the cases of Costa Rica, Honduras, Nicaragua, and Venezuela, for example, values for the complexity of the indigenous society fail to match values for the outcome; these territories had indigenous societies of an intermediate complexity but nevertheless became colonial peripheries instead of semiperipheries. Likewise, scores for the complexity of the indigenous society do not match the outcome scores for Ecuador, El Salvador, and Guatemala; these territories had highly complex indigenous societies but nevertheless did not become colonial centers.

The fourth column reports the set-theoretic score that is produced by the combination of a complex indigenous society and either significant mineral wealth or proximity to a great empire; this is represented by the expression $A \& (B \text{ v } C)$, where the "$\&$" symbol stands for the logical AND and the "v" sign stands for the logical OR.[374] As the scores for this column show, there is a perfect matching between this combination and the extent to which territories were members of the category of colonial center. Logically speaking, the combination is a sufficient cause of colonial-center status. Societies that became colonial centers featured a complex indigenous society and also either contained significant mineral wealth or were close to the Aztec or Inca Empire. In Mexico and Peru, all three of these conditions were fully present; in Bolivia, only the empire-proximity factor was not fully present (though the case still receives a 1.0 on the outcome, because mineral wealth substitutes for proximity to an empire). Societies that became colonial peripheries either had indigenous polities of low levels of complexity or completely lacked significant mineral wealth and were not close to the Aztec or Inca Empire. Three peripheral societies – Argentina, Paraguay, and Uruguay – receive 0.0 scores for all causal factors, such that their status as peripheries is overdetermined (i.e., even if they had had a completely different score on any one causal factor, they still would have become peripheries). For Chile, peripheral status was driven by the low level of complexity of the Mapuche, indigenous people who prevented the Spanish from exploiting a densely settled region that was close to the Inca Empire and that also contained an intermediate level of mineral wealth. For Costa Rica, El Salvador, Honduras, Nicaragua, and Venezuela, where at least reasonably complex indigenous societies were present, peripheral status resulted from the absence of both significant mineral wealth and proximity to the Inca or Aztec Empire. Finally, the semiperipheral regions possessed indigenous societies of high complexity and either featured some mineral wealth (Colombia) or were reasonably close to the Aztec or Inca Empire (Guatemala and Ecuador). There were thus different causal paths for the semiperipheries, as represented by their different values on the three causal factors.

The formalization of these causal logics is obviously no substitute for the analysis presented above. But it does allow us to reach summary conclusions and reflect broadly on the general model of mercantilist colonialism (as presented in Chapter 1). We may conclude, for example, that only one cause – complex indigenous population – was individually necessary for becoming a colonial center.[375] Mineral wealth and proximity to the Aztec or Inca capital were "important," but they could substitute for each other, and neither of them was individually necessary for a territory to become a colonial center.

Formalizing the results allows us to state explicitly certain counterfactuals concerning the institutional legacy of Spanish mercantilist colonialism in the Americas. If Costa Rica, El Salvador, Honduras, Nicaragua, and Venezuela

Table 3.3. Relationship between mercantilist colonialism and levels of development

Country	(X) Colonial center	(Y_1) Higher level of economic development	(Y_2) Higher level of social development
Argentina	0.0	1.0	1.0
Bolivia	1.0	0.0	0.0
Chile	0.0	1.0	1.0
Colombia	0.5	0.5	0.5
Costa Rica	0.0	0.5	1.0
Ecuador	0.5	0.0	0.0
El Salvador	0.0	0.0	0.0
Guatemala	0.5	0.0	0.0
Honduras	0.0	0.0	0.0
Mexico	1.0	0.5	0.5
Nicaragua	0.0	0.0	0.0
Paraguay	0.0	0.0	0.5
Peru	1.0	0.5	0.0
Uruguay	0.0	1.0	1.0
Venezuela	0.0	1.0	0.5

Note: 1.0 = full or nearly full membership; 0.5 = partial membership; 0.0 = little or no membership.

had contained more significant mineral wealth, for instance, these territories would have developed mercantilist coalitions analogous to those in semiperipheral Ecuador, Guatemala, and Colombia. And if Ecuador, Guatemala, and Colombia had featured indigenous societies with a low level of complexity, they would not have developed their significant merchant-landed classes. As it turned out historically, however, powerful mercantilist coalitions and large subordinate ethnic populations were constructed in only Bolivia, Colombia, Ecuador, Guatemala, Mexico, and Peru. In these six cases, the legacy of the first part of Spanish colonialism entailed entrenched obstacles to future economic and social progress. The peripheral cases of Argentina, Chile, Costa Rica, El Salvador, Honduras, Nicaragua, Paraguay, Uruguay, and Venezuela were spared major obstacles. From an institutional perspective, these peripheral regions were the ones with the better prospects for long-run development.

To what extent did the mercantilist phase of Spanish colonialism determine future developmental success or failure? Can we match each territory's colonial position (center, semiperiphery, periphery) with its postcolonial levels of economic and social development (lower, intermediate, higher)? The general model for mercantilist colonialism anticipates an inverted matching, in which more extensive colonialism produces lower levels of development. As Table 3.3 shows, there is some inverse relationship, but it is far from perfect. Several of the peripheral colonial territories (i.e., El Salvador, Honduras, Nicaragua, and Paraguay) ended up with low, not high, levels of economic or social development. And Mexico and Peru achieved an intermediate level of economic development – not a low one, as the inverse relationship would suggest. Hence, patterns of mercantilist colonialism by themselves at best partially explain future development outcomes.

Nevertheless, a striking pattern is present in the data: only mercantilist peripheries (i.e., Argentina, Chile, Costa Rica, Uruguay, and Venezuela) achieved a high level of postcolonial economic or social development. Peripheral status during the mercantilist phase was necessary, though not sufficient, for future developmental success. Or, said differently, the status of center or semiperiphery appears to have been sufficient for *not* achieving a high level of development. The mercantilist phase is therefore an essential part of the story of long-run outcomes in Spanish American countries.

More explanatory work remains to be done, obviously. We must understand what happened during the second phase of Spanish colonialism – the liberal phase – that allowed some mercantilist peripheries to achieve higher levels of development than others. Likewise, we must identify factors that explain why some mercantilist centers and semiperipheries fared better than others in the aftermath of colonialism. Once we have explored these matters, we will be in a position to understand how the mercantilist and liberal phases together explain development outcomes in Spanish America.

4

Liberal Colonialism

During the late colonial period the population and economies of the once-stagnant peripheral colonies in Spanish America grew rapidly . . . The economic expansion of the periphery during the last hundred years of the empire equaled the rapid growth experienced during the early stages of the mining boom in Peru and New Spain.
– Mark A. Burkholder and Lyman L. Johnson

During the late colonial reorientation the Atlantic seaboard areas experienced growth and consolidation, since they profited most from navigational improvements and were best placed for the bulk exports to Europe which were becoming increasingly viable. Some former fringe areas now took on many of the characteristics of centrality and even displaced the old central areas to an extent . . . We must not think, however, that the mercantile communities of Mexico City and Lima faded away under the onslaught . . . Although the established commercial centers lost their exclusive status, they seem to have maintained a certain dominance, and such diminution as occurred seems to have been more in percentile terms than absolute.
– James Lockhart and Stuart B. Schwartz

The liberal phase of Spanish colonialism (1700–1808) was a major departure from the mercantilist era. Especially under the late Bourbon monarchy, institutional development and colonial settlement were redirected to several territories that had been peripheral under the Habsburgs, while some former colonial centers and semiperipheries became marginal peripheries. Moreover, there was a transformation in the *kinds* of institutions and settlers brought to the New World. Whereas the Habsburgs had imposed classically mercantilist institutions and actors, the Bourbon reformers introduced more liberal ones. Included in the "enlightened" package were bureaucratic reformulations to forge a more capable colonial state and liberalizing economic reforms to stimulate export production. Where most thoroughly implanted, these changes brought into being a new class of commercial actors with greater political autonomy and an orientation toward generating wealth via exchange in open markets.

The categories of colonial center, periphery, and semiperiphery remain fruitful for situating territories during the liberal phase (see Table 4.1). Argentina was the prototypical liberal colonial center: a periphery during the Habsburg phase, this territory rose on the back of a commercial network

Table 4.1. Types of Spanish colonial territories, circa 1780

Colonial centers	Colonial semiperipheries	Colonial peripheries
Argentina	Colombia	Bolivia
Mexico	Peru	Chile
	Uruguay	Costa Rica
	Venezuela	Ecuador
		El Salvador
		Guatemala
		Honduras
		Nicaragua
		Paraguay

centered in Buenos Aires to become a major late colonial player in the Americas. Uruguay and Venezuela were also rising peripheries, though they offered fewer commercial opportunities than Argentina and hence became colonial semiperipheries rather than centers. Mexico was the other colonial center, holding on to its core position because the Bourbons remained attracted to an already-existing colonial heartland that featured still-impressive mineral wealth. The same was true to a lesser degree for Colombia and Peru, semiperipheries with comparatively less-extensive mineral resources. The majority of territories – Bolivia, Chile, Costa Rica, Ecuador, El Salvador, Guatemala, Honduras, Nicaragua, and Paraguay – were simply peripheral during this period. Lacking good possibilities for wealth accumulation through either trading or mineral extraction, they were ignored as sites of settlement and liberal institutional implantation.

Spain's evolution from a mercantilist to a more liberal state thus caused many territories to switch their position within the colonial ordering of center, semiperiphery, and periphery. But, as is plainly evident, not all territories changed positions. Mexico retained center status during both phases. Likewise, six territories (Chile, Costa Rica, El Salvador, Honduras, Nicaragua, and Paraguay) were peripheral for the entire colonial period. Overall, while colonial status during the Habsburg period is inversely related to colonial status during the Bourbon period, it is only *weakly* so, with many exceptions. Other variables also shaped levels of colonialism during the Bourbon phase.

There were in fact two different causal paths to the position of colonial center or semiperiphery during the late Bourbon period. One path – exemplified by Argentina but also applicable to Uruguay and Venezuela – was that of the *rising periphery*, or a marginal territory that rather suddenly became important in the Spanish system during the late eighteenth century. Here the combination of a sparse indigenous population and a strategic commercial port brought settlers and liberal institutions into relatively wide-open territories. The second path – exemplified by Mexico but applicable to Peru and Colombia as well – was that of the *mercantilist carryover*, or a territory that was important during the mercantilist period and continued to attract substantial liberal colonialism. Such areas remained prominent in the designs of the Spanish Crown because of their large Spanish populations and the existence of at least moderate mineral wealth.

In short, then, two sets of variables were at work in inducing Spanish attention to particular regions during the liberal phase of colonialism. In one path, the combination of a sparse indigenous population and a strategic commercial port brought people and new institutions to territories. In another path, the combination of a previous high level of colonialism and significant new mineral wealth sustained extensive colonial settlement and institution building. Territories that did not feature the conditions for either of these paths became peripheries during the liberal phase.

New elite actors were brought into being to a much greater extent in the liberal cores (i.e., centers and semiperipheries) than in the territories that received little attention under the Bourbons. The rising peripheries (Argentina, Uruguay, and Venezuela), in particular, were endowed with significant liberal institutions without having previously acquired substantial mercantilist ones. These were therefore areas where liberal actors were incubated in the absence of direct interference from consolidated and potent mercantilist elites. When new, more liberal merchants arrived here, they neither merged with landed interests nor themselves participated in labor-repressive agricultural systems. And they were less dependent on Spanish restrictions and monopolies than were previous generations of traders. In the relatively virgin lands of these rising peripheries, something closer to a market-oriented commercial class was born. Distorted though it was, this class was the best approximation to a classic bourgeoisie that could gestate within colonial Spanish America. And it was this class that steered the emergent agricultural export economies of these territories, positioning them to become the richest nations in Spanish America once independence was achieved.

We can best appreciate the bourgeois orientation of the merchants in the rising peripheries when we compare them to the commercial classes that appeared in the mercantilist carryovers (Mexico, Peru, and Colombia) during the late colonial period. The mercantilist carryovers experienced a dual colonial heritage; they were recipients of significant institutions during both the Habsburg and Bourbon phases of colonialism. The very considerable mercantilist institutions from the first phase left in their wake entrenched economic interests capable of disrupting market-oriented commerce. Bourbon reformers sought to uproot or work around these interests, but they were not entirely successful. Late colonial merchants in these territories remained oriented toward accumulation via the channels of monopoly associated with mineral economies, channels that remained intact. They were not risk-taking entrepreneurs who looked to commercial agriculture as a central mode of accumulation; instead, they remained tied to landed elites oriented toward production for local markets. Thus, the mercantilist-carryover regions faced obstacles from the first phase of colonialism that prohibited them from entry into the club of the richest nations of nineteenth- and twentieth-century Latin America.

In the Bourbon peripheries, regions that were ignored by the Crown and settlers alike, liberal institutions and bourgeois commercial interests never took hold at all. This fate was especially damning for those territories – Bolivia, Ecuador, and Guatemala – that had been leading mercantilist colonies but now descended into obscurity. These *fallen-core* regions were left with elite commercial actors whose orientation was quite antithetical to successful participation in open international markets. The commercial classes were either completely fused with labor-repressive landed elites or so accustomed to profits via monopoly channels that they could not compete when their privileges came under assault. The consequence for the fallen cores was a failure to integrate with world markets and the onset of severe economic underdevelopment.

The remaining Bourbon peripheries – Chile, Costa Rica, El Salvador, Honduras, Nicaragua, and Paraguay – had been peripheral during the Habsburg period. These *sustained peripheries* saw the imposition of neither substantial mercantilist nor substantial liberal institutions. Their postcolonial trajectories of development were, as a result, underdetermined by Spanish colonialism and very much open to processes and occurrences after independence. We must therefore look to postcolonial nineteenth-century events to explain outcomes in the sustained peripheries.

In addition to calling central attention to elite merchant actors, we shall in this chapter pick up the story of the main subordinate group created during the mercantilist phase: indigenous people. We will see that their reality as an exploited ethnic group continued under new, perhaps more market-oriented arrangements. But we can now link that exploitation to long-run development outcomes. Hierarchical ethnic stratification left particularly pronounced effects in the realm of social development. Indeed, only if a country's indigenous population was small at the time of independence would that country ever experience a higher level of social development; the presence of even a modestly large indigenous population at the time of independence nearly *guaranteed* that a Spanish American country would not perform comparatively well in the area of social development. Of course, by shaping the absolute resources available within a nation, level of economic development also affected social performance. And, as we will learn, the overall causal package for achieving social development involved the combination of a small indigenous population *and* an at least average level of economic development.

These are previews of the arguments to be presented in this chapter. What we need to do now is develop them for each of the cases. I will first discuss the three rising peripheries (Argentina, Uruguay, and Venezuela) and then the three mercantilist carryovers (Mexico, Peru, and Colombia). After that, we will turn our attention to the liberal peripheries, moving from the three fallen-core areas (Bolivia, Ecuador, and Guatemala) to a discussion of the six sustained peripheries (Chile, Paraguay, El Salvador, Honduras, Nicaragua, and Costa Rica). The last section of the chapter formally summarizes the argument about the onset of differing levels of liberal colonialism and also draws key conclusions about the effects of colonialism on final developmental outcomes.

THE RISING PERIPHERIES

Under Bourbon colonialism, attention was directed to the rising peripheries because they featured geographically strategic ports connected to potential inland markets not fettered by deeply entrenched indigenous institutions or mercantilist economies. The liberal institutions that were then created by the end of the colonial period shaped elite and subordinate actors in ways generally conducive to regionally high levels of development. The logic of this process was most apparent in Argentina, while Uruguay was a diminished version of the Argentine pattern. By contrast, the case of Venezuela raises special issues, best discussed and understood through comparisons and contrasts with the Argentine and Uruguayan cases.

Argentina

The territory corresponding to modern Argentina, as we saw in Chapter 3, did not undergo a singular colonial experience during the Habsburg phase. Rather, during the seventeenth century, the littoral of the Governorship of the River Plate was an isolated periphery, while the interior region of the Governorship of Tucumán was a semiperiphery linked to the Potosí economy through its encomienda-based livestock and agricultural economy. Now, during the late eighteenth century, Buenos Aires rather suddenly became a full-blown colonial center and the leading economy of South America, tied to both Peru and Europe. Meanwhile, the interior towns of the northwest remained semiperipheral, but increasingly more linked to Buenos Aires than to a fading Potosí.

The Creation of a Colonial Center. The available demographic data illustrate the turnabout in Buenos Aires quite clearly. The city grew from 11,600 persons in 1744 to 26,100 in 1778, and by 1810 the number was 42,250.[1] Two-thirds or more of this population was European, with many new arrivals from Spain. Slaves of African descent, purchased by the city's elite to work as servants, made up most of the rest; indigenous people were only about 5 percent of the *porteño* population.[2] In the interior, by contrast, while population growth occurred, it was driven by the recovery of indigenous people and the expansion of a scattered rural population, not by concentrated urbanization. The Spanish population at Córdoba was about 2,500 in the late eighteenth century, while the totals for Salta and Tucumán were 1,900 and 1,300, respectively. Other towns, such as Santiago del Estero, La Rioja, and Jujuy, had Spanish populations of less than five hundred. In all towns except Buenos Aires, there were at least as many Africans as Europeans. And while thousands of Spanish people were dispersed in the vast countryside of the interior, they were surpassed in number by indigenous people (with the exception of the countryside around Córdoba).[3]

If these population trends suggest a new centrality for the River Plate (though not the interior), then why and how did this happen? Most basically, the River Plate drew colonial attention because it was an obvious location of activity for profit-oriented merchants. "Though not a natural or convenient port . . . Buenos Aires was the gateway to the important cart and mule trades of the Interior."[4] Moreover, as Aldo Ferrer points out:

> The geographical location of the Río de la Plata made it the best route of access to the heart of the Spanish colonial empire south of Peru. The distance from Buenos Aires to Potosí could be reached from Lima only after four months of travel over 2,500 kilometers of mountain trails. Therefore, the price of imported merchandise in Potosí varied according to whether it arrived via Lima or Buenos Aires. In Potosí a length of cloth coming from Lima cost six or seven times more than one coming from Buenos Aires.[5]

Besides, shipping Potosí's silver and other interior goods out of an Atlantic port at Buenos Aires made good sense. Everyone was aware of these advantages; the huge contraband trade and its infuriating consequences for Spain were hardly royal secrets. The reality is that Portuguese, British, and Dutch smuggling forced the hand of the Crown. "Faced with the prospect of being commercially eliminated by Britain and anxious to promote a revival of her own manufactures, Spain had to follow in the wake of her rivals and develop more liberal economic relations with her own colonies."[6] The Bourbons overrode the objections of Lima merchants and instituted the "free-trade" policies (discussed in Chapter 2) in 1778.

Weakly implanted mercantilist economic institutions were in no time replaced with more liberal ones. The new economic rules allowed Buenos Aires to engage in commerce directly with Spain and with all other parts of Spanish America (though not legally with other European countries, of course). In addition, "the old trading licenses were abolished, along with many of the old taxes – *palmeo, tonelada, San Telmo, extranjería, visitas.* Only the *alcabala* and the *almojarifazgo* survived, the rates for both being reduced in most cases from 6 percent to 3 percent."[7] Buenos Aires became the official port through which Potosí silver was shipped; it was also the main South American point for receiving articles from Europe. And new trade policies permitted the open exchange of slaves, which helps explain the large African population of Buenos Aires. Beyond this, the Crown actively worked to augment growth in the region by modernizing production methods for the livestock industry.[8]

Political and administrative institutions reinforced the economic changes. The creation of the Viceroyalty of the River Plate transferred Lima's control of the mines to Argentine hands.[9] The viceroy of the River Plate was now the most important political official in South America. Furthermore, the new intendant system of administration mostly did away with the confusing arrangement of *gobiernos, corregimientos,* and *alcaldías mayores.*[10] The intendant officials were high-status, well-salaried, royal appointees from Spain who were chosen for their competence and integrity. With their creation, moribund financial institutions – primitive accounting, inefficient procedures for collecting customs duties, and unsupervised financial officials – were reformed. Though these changes did not implant a fully rationalized and bureaucratic system, because family connections and low salaries often made the bureaucrats dependent on the merchants, the reforms did centralize treasury matters under the authority of more competent administrators, create a more efficient tribunal of accounts, and establish checks on the worst forms of corruption.[11] They were an important step toward the creation of a functioning legal system.

Liberal Elites and Economic Development. Whether they intended it or not, Bourbon reformers created a new class of powerful merchants when they introduced their policies into the River Plate. These merchants were in some ways similar to those who had developed in the colonial centers under the Habsburgs, but they also showed striking dissimilarities, especially in the extent to which they were fused with a labor-exploiting landed class. Explicating these differences is essential to explaining the remarkable economic rise of Buenos Aires in the late colonial period.

Like the great merchants of Lima and Mexico City, those of Buenos Aires were often *peninsulares.* But in sharp contrast to their counterparts, the *porteño* wholesalers hailed overwhelmingly from the northern and Basque regions of Spain – precisely those locations where a politically autonomous Spanish bourgeoisie had taken root in the late eighteenth century.[12] They came to Buenos Aires to make money as intermediaries, working between the Spanish trading houses and the local suppliers who controlled the town markets in the interior. Unlike the merchants in Mexico, Peru, and Bolivia, very few traders in Buenos Aires were agents of Cádiz-based firms or dependent on any single Spanish port. The contraband trade, which remained commonplace in the River Plate despite the efforts of the Bourbons, in fact linked the Buenos Aires merchants broadly to Europe.

Yet *porteño* merchants were not a dynamic bourgeoisie, much less industrially oriented in any way.[13] They were still products of colonialism, originally quite dependent on the mercantilist sectors of the economy. For nearly all commercial trade was at first fueled by Potosí's silver. According to John Lynch, Tulio Halperín-Donghi, and other authorities, precious metals represented 80 percent or more of the value of all exports leaving the River Plate in the late eighteenth century.[14] Only with the revenue generated from silver and gold exports could merchants purchase textiles and hardware from Europe and then use their connections to local traders to distribute these goods in the interior and in Buenos Aires itself.[15]

More distinctive was the fact that the River Plate merchants never became fused with a landed elite. Buenos Aires commercial interests simply did not often invest in land ownership. In general, as Susan Migden Socolow writes,

the merchants were urban men with urban interests. The open range, the herds of wild cattle, the hostile Indian population, the vague boundaries of *estancias*, and the low value given to ranch lands, held little interest for merchants looking for investments which either brought large profit or were directly related to the commerce of the city... Owning rural land was neither a good nor prestigious investment, and therefore attracted little capital.

As a consequence, "ranching lands... did not attract significant investment by merchants during the time of the Viceroyalty. Only fourteen merchants of the city were active ranchers."[16]

Although increasing in size, the landed class of Argentina also varied considerably from what we have seen in Spanish America to this point. Most basically, labor-repressive agriculture was not the foundation of its wealth accumulation. For this landed class consisted mostly of the *estancieros* (ranch owners), who spread along the pampas – first toward the Salado River and later toward the west and southwest. Increasingly in the late eighteenth and early nineteenth centuries, they supplied cattle hides for consumers in Europe and salted meat for slaves in Brazil and Cuba, as well as sending mules to the traditional market in Peru. To call this group an elite is almost misleading, for, unlike the great hacendado classes of Mexico and Peru, the Argentinean landowners were uneducated Creoles who controlled estates of quite varied sizes; large estates did not dominate. These ranchers did frequently purchase black slaves, though rarely in large quantities; they always depended heavily on seasonal wage labor provided by fairly well-compensated gaucho peons.[17] As for their political power, we can refer to the title of an article by Carlos A. Mayo: "Landed but Not Powerful: The Colonial Estancieros of Buenos Aires."[18] Mayo reaches the conclusion in his title by showing that with few exceptions, the estancieros did not control the cabildos of the rural areas where they resided. Instead, as in Buenos Aires itself, merchant interests were the politically dominant class.[19]

Together, the merchants and estancieros were the leading actors in what was by the early nineteenth century an agrarian-capitalist system. This economy was "capitalist" in the specific sense that it featured, on the one hand, commercial actors who were responsive to local and international market demand and, on the other, producing sectors that competed with one another for profits and were forced to be efficient or face dissolution. Argentinean wholesalers worked with both European import-export houses and local merchants to ensure the supply of profitable staples. They infused capital into those sectors of the economy in which comparative advantage lay. The merchants' role in dispensing loans to producers of key export products was especially crucial, for the economy still lacked modern financial institutions, such as banks.[20] For their part, the estancieros were not propped up by the state or guaranteed a profit; they had to prove themselves efficient in a market setting. In a context where land was plentiful, uncompetitive estancieros saw their cattle liquidated, while their more profitable rivals enjoyed cattle capitalization. "On the estancias of Buenos Aires," Samuel Amaral argues, "resources were allocated according to the signs posted by markets, not according to privileges conceded by any authority. Transactions conducted within and outside the firm, the estancia, were guided by market prices. That was the rise of capitalism on the Argentine pampas."[21]

By creating the original institutions that fostered this capitalist system, the Bourbon reforms had launched a remarkable period of economic prosperity in Argentina. As Jonathan Brown remarks, "a golden age began in 1776," and this epoch unfolded across multiple stages of agrarian exportation until the early twentieth century.[22] No one agrarian export was the key to wealth during the golden age. In fact, *none* of the leading exports of this economy "could be considered strategic in any way, and they seldom enjoyed a dominant position in any significant market."[23] British, American, French, and Belgian markets were the main outlets, but their relative importance shifted significantly over time, including for particular products. In the early nineteenth century, the leading commodity was cattle hides, shipped at first to Britain in exchange for woolens and cottons and later to France and the United States as their markets grew. Hides generally represented more than 50 percent of the value of all Buenos Aires' exports from the 1820s until the 1850s.[24] After midcentury, the economy moved toward wool exportation, with the Belgian market at first driving demand. In 1872, wool exports made up more than 40 percent of the total, while hides had declined to about 20 percent.[25] Then, toward the end of the century, when wool markets started to tighten, cereals became the main staple of the agrarian economy. In the first decades of the twentieth century, wheat and maize exports generated two to three times more foreign exchange than did wool, and beef exports (live cattle and frozen meat) accounted for nearly as much as wool.[26]

But we need not dwell on the changing staple products, land-use patterns, and modes of labor that *sustained* over-time development in Argentina; the argument presented here is that, already by the early nineteenth century, Argentina was at the top of the economic hierarchy within Spanish America. According to John H. Coatsworth, Argentina's GDP per capita in

1800 was about twice the size of Mexico's and larger still relative to that of Peru and Chile.[27] At this time, Argentina was in fact slightly richer (measured by GDP per capita) than the United States![28] To be sure, Argentina experienced impressive growth rates during the late nineteenth and early twentieth centuries. But so did most of Spanish America: the golden age of development in Argentina overlapped with the remarkable twenty-five-fold increase in world trade in Latin America that occurred from approximately the middle of the nineteenth century to the beginning of World War I.[29] What differentiated Argentina from other countries in the region was not growth during this general period of booming primary-product exports and outward expansion. Rather, it was the fact that Argentina entered this period with a higher level of economic development – an advantage that the country then sustained throughout the rest of its history.

The relative economic success of Argentina was thus established in the late colonial period. If the historiography generally has not spotlighted this early takeoff, it is because too much attention has been directed at economic processes that took place later in the nineteenth century – especially when wool and then wheat became the country's key exports. As one set of historians puts it, "In general, the historiography on Argentine agrarian regions has suggested that the moment of great transformations occurred in the second half of the nineteenth century and that these changes implied a basic and radical break with previous conditions."[30] Yet by the mid-nineteenth century, Argentina had already enjoyed a half century as the region's most prosperous and thriving area; mid-nineteenth-century developments had little to do with shaping Argentina's *relative* level of economic development within Spanish America. The root causes of Argentina's relative prosperity rest with the institutions and economic actors that came into being in the late eighteenth century: politically dominant free-trade merchants not tied to landed elites, state officials not oriented toward monopolistic regulation, and market-responsive landed elites not dependent on subordinate indigenous labor. This perspective allows us to explain perfectly well why Argentina was able to rise to the top of the region in the first place. And once it had achieved this relative success, by the end of the colonial period, Argentina did not grow at a faster rate than the rest of Latin America.[31] Scholars who attribute Argentine success to the production of wool, cereals, and/or beef therefore simply fail to appreciate that these exports did not *cause* Argentina to pull ahead of the rest of the region. Argentina's relative success vis-à-vis the rest of Latin America was initiated much earlier, specifically during the late colonial period.

The Indigenous Population and Social Development. Excellent commercial opportunities brought Spanish merchants and other settlers to the River Plate. Yet these opportunities were perceived as excellent only because the region housed neither a complex indigenous society nor an entrenched and protected Spanish elite. Liberal colonizers encountered in the River Plate instead a comparatively open territory that was, to a greater extent than most regions of the empire, theirs for the taking.[32] This reality, too, helps explain why Buenos Aires became a center of colonial activity during the Bourbon reform period.

By the beginning of the eighteenth century, the remaining indigenous people (e.g., the Pehuenches, Tehuelches, and Puelches) who still inhabited the prairies and hills of the pampas and Patagonia had congregated themselves into various small chiefdoms, now often under the influence of Mapuche people from Chile. These groups became herders and developed an active network of trade in cattle, horses, and livestock products. They also formed confederations to protect their villages in the face of encroaching frontier settlers and to lead the occasional raid against the Spanish interlopers. Colonial settlers had long since given up trying to control this population for the purposes of large-scale exploitation; their main objective now was to pacify or eliminate the indigenous peoples such that frontier settlement and agrarian capitalism could proceed without obstruction. Colonial governors created military forts and militia forces to ward off Indian attacks and initiate offensives as they cleared the land for estancias and farms.[33]

Argentina's social hierarchy was still rigid and unequal in the late colonial period, for, as Halperín-Donghi notes, Argentina was "a society less reformed than its economy."[34] Nevertheless, because Buenos Aires had been a Habsburg periphery, it carried little of the mercantilist baggage that so notably blocked social progress in the interior and in the mercantilist centers of Spanish America.[35] Two basic processes were in play to promote the littoral to one of the highest tiers of social development in postcolonial Spanish America. In the first place, ethnic divisions, while never as sharp here as in the interior – not to mention in Mexico, and especially in Peru – were becoming even less prominent. "In the Littoral, the division between Spaniards and half-castes did not have the importance that it retained in the interior. Spaniards formed the bulk of the population, there were scarcely any Indians, at least in the towns, and almost all the Negroes were marked off from the rest by the institution of slavery."[36] Throughout the viceroyalty, indigenous persons who adopted aspects of European culture were classified as mestizos, while individuals of mixed indigenous-European heritage were often considered, by themselves and others, as *blancos* (whites).[37] By the late colonial period, little more than 10 percent of the littoral population and about 30 percent of the full Argentine population was considered indigenous; the respective percentages for the African population are quite similar.[38] Regarding this African population, although legal slavery continued into the 1820s, the number of slaves declined substantially after 1813, when the children of slaves were granted freedom. Moreover, because slavery was more an urban than a rural phenomenon in Argentina, African Argentines were rather easily integrated into the economy and culture.

Miscegenation was rapid in Buenos Aires, and a distinctively black population declined dramatically during the nineteenth century.[39] The absence of visibly large indigenous and African populations enabled postcolonial political leaders to imagine the nation as ethnically homogenous and European, a portrayal that later facilitated the extension of rights and entitlements to a broad spectrum of citizens.

In the second place, economic development itself had large implications for social progress. During the late eighteenth and early nineteenth centuries, growth provided new resources for doctors and basic health care, and even sometimes for teachers and schools not linked to the church. To be sure, these resources were not equally accessible to all individuals; class and ethnicity mattered. This was especially true in the interior, where social progress was less extensive. But in Buenos Aires, the spillover effects of economic development on social development were extensive and broadly felt. The wealth of this city triggered the decline of a relatively poor primary sector of the economy and the rise of a relatively large tertiary sector, marked by comparatively high-wage occupations in transport, trade, and services.[40] Although data on the health and education of this population are not available, it is eminently reasonable to imagine that the *porteños* were healthier and more educated than the typical person living in Spanish America.[41] It is perhaps not surprising that under these conditions, Buenos Aires became the home of liberal thought in Spanish America, so much so that Halperín-Donghi considers Argentina "a country born liberal."[42]

After the mid-nineteenth century, the arrival of hundreds of thousands of immigrants gave more credibility to the myth that the population was entirely European. Starting with liberal elites in late-nineteenth-century Argentina, intellectuals have long proclaimed this migration to be the main source of progress and civilization in the nation. Connections between migration and development are rendered superficially plausible by the fact that the nineteenth-century immigrants usually hailed from Italy (mostly northern Italy), a capitalist western European nation. Yet we need to keep in mind a simple truth: the surge of European immigrants occurred well *after* Argentina had established itself as the most developed part of Spanish America. "Although independent Argentina at once moved to encourage more general immigration," J. D. Gould points out, "the unstable political regime worked in the opposite direction, and it was not until more settled conditions were reflected in the adoption of the Constitution of 1853 that the way was effectively opened for mass immigration."[43] The numbers and demographic characteristics of the Italian and other European migrants to Argentina are items of great interest in the historiography. But the important point for us is simply that these migration flows did not become heavy until the 1880s.[44] Argentina's economic opportunities and social progress caused people to choose to settle here, especially in the littoral region – not the other way around.

We need to tie up one loose end before leaving the Argentine case. The discussions in this chapter and the previous one have emphasized the contrast in colonial experiences between the interior region and the littoral region. Such an emphasis is important because these differences manifested themselves in contrasting levels of development. For, as we have seen, Argentina's rise to the top of the Latin American hierarchy was driven by the growth of Buenos Aires and the surrounding area, not by any dynamism in the region corresponding to the old Governorship of Tucumán. Drawing upon data on urbanization and economic activity for the early and mid-nineteenth century, Carlos Newland reaches the following conclusion:

The littoral region...had a relatively modern economic structure, similar to that of the United States or Canada, a relatively small primary sector for the time, an important pastoral sector, and a substantial tertiary sector. It also had a relatively high and growing degree of urbanization...The interior region...was similar to other Latin American countries in terms of the distribution of its labor force by economic activity. It had a large primary sector, mainly devoted to agricultural activities. The degree of urbanization in the Interior was not only low but also seems to have diminished over the period.[45]

To the extent that the interior later became significantly developed, it was carried along by Buenos Aires. This had to be the case, because the interior, a semiperipheral colonial region lacking the full-blown liberal institutions of Buenos Aires, could not on its own progress at a high rate in the late eighteenth and early nineteenth centuries. While it makes sense to view Argentina overall as dominantly a colonial periphery during the Habsburg period and a colonial center during the Bourbon period, we need not deny important regional variations, particularly differences between the interior and the littoral. The framework employed here is flexible enough to make sense of these regional variations without losing sight of the general pattern that marked the country as a whole.

Uruguay

Colonial settlement and the creation of new market institutions at the end of the eighteenth century elevated Montevideo and the surrounding territory to the status of colonial semiperiphery. Although liberal institutions in Montevideo were less thoroughly implanted than in Buenos Aires, the interior of the Eastern Bank was relatively unfettered by mercantilist institutions from the Habsburg period. As a result, Uruguay experienced an overall colonial heritage that was, just as in Argentina, tilted in the direction of economic liberalism.

Uruguay Becomes a Semiperiphery. Montevideo was exposed to the same set of liberalizing reforms that brought development to Buenos Aires – freedom to trade directly with Spain and other colonial ports, the abolition of many licenses and taxes, and administrative modernization. Moreover, to the extent that restrictions on trade remained, the Montevideo port was privileged by the Spanish.[46] For one thing, merchant ships were often required to pass through Montevideo before arriving at Buenos Aires or other destinations. Furthermore, the Crown probably set royal fees at lower levels for Montevideo than for Buenos Aires.[47] And, critically, after 1791 Montevideo was given a monopoly over the trade of black slaves destined to labor in La Plata, Chile, and Peru. These changes helped beget a very prosperous late colonial city. Yet in comparison to Buenos Aires, Montevideo's population was much smaller, and its trade "never exceeded a quarter of that passing through Buenos Aires."[48] Worse still, Uruguay was quite politically subordinate within the new viceroyalty. Why did this happen? What prevented Montevideo from carrying the Eastern Bank to the status of full-blown colonial center, as Buenos Aires did for Argentina?

The core reason is that the port at Montevideo offered fewer commercial opportunities. True, Montevideo did have some real geographical advantages. "Compared with the harbour of Buenos Aires, that of Montevideo was deeper, more accessible, more sheltered and better situated in relation to Europe."[49] Yet greatly outweighing this was the fact that beyond Montevideo, the Eastern Bank was either mostly deserted or dangerously infiltrated by the rival Portuguese. Montevideo was isolated from its hinterland and disconnected from the contraband trade that brought silver to the River Plate[50] – in striking contrast to Buenos Aires, which was historically linked to South American silver through commercial networks stretching to Potosí. It was thus only natural that the Bourbons would select Buenos Aires as the port to handle the silver trade, for it had long illegally played this role. And it was only natural, too, that they would choose the city (Buenos Aires) that was more distant from the Portuguese and better connected to the interior as the main location for receiving imports from the Old World.

As these points suggest, the founding of Montevideo had hardly brought an end to the troubles with Portugal on the Eastern Bank. "Uruguay was a battleground over which the tide of empire flowed in the continuing struggle between Spain and Portugal, more narrowly between the Spanish Platine center at Buenos Aires and the giant Portuguese colony of Brazil... The buffer territory of the Banda Oriental was a natural scene of conflict."[51] In the course of this struggle, possession of the town of Colonia shifted between the two crowns during the mid-eighteenth century before it finally came under permanent Spanish control in 1777. Many northern settlements – often initially military guard posts – were created by the Bourbons as defense lines against Portuguese intruders who occupied land, stole cattle, and smuggled goods. In the southwest, settlers spontaneously created small towns, some of which survived (e.g., Trinidad, Dolores, and Rosario).[52] With the Portuguese threat, however, any settlements and developments in the interior necessarily took a militaristic form. Nearly a quarter of the Eastern Bank population consisted of soldiers.[53]

Though home to its own governorship after 1749, Montevideo long remained a fortified citadel primarily oriented toward warding off European encroachments. Only when the Bourbons implanted their free-trade institutions did this change. The population living in the Montevideo jurisdiction increased from less than 1,000 in 1750 to 6,368 in 1787 and then to 9,359 in 1805. Individuals identified as Spaniards always made up more than half of this total; most of the rest were African slaves.[54] "The demographic growth of Montevideo ... was primarily a consequence of the development of its port, a natural gift, favored by successive privileges conceded by the Crown and nourished by production from the prairie."[55] The new arrivals were sailors, traders, soldiers, and craftsmen who sought to take advantage of the port activity. Demographic growth, in turn, brought colonial modernization to the city: the creation of a system of roads, large public buildings, a hospital, the Church of Matriz, a system for potable water, and bustling markets filled with all the vendors and activities one would expect in a thriving community in the late colonial empire.[56]

Liberal Elites and Economic Development. Given Montevideo's status as a colonial entrepôt, it is not surprising that the richest actors in colonial Uruguay depended on commerce rather than production. Like the elite of Argentina, Uruguay's elite was a port-based merchant class. Merchants made their money primarily through the import-export business and secondarily through the supply of credit and through investments in urban and rural property.[57] They were tied to different ports in Spain, with several linked to traders in Catalonia.[58] Although not as wealthy as their Buenos Aires counterparts, the Montevideo wholesalers and retailers amassed considerable fortunes, an unknown portion of which came illegally via contraband items hidden from royal authorities (including slaves, alcohol, and tobacco). And although similar in most ways to the wholesalers of Buenos Aires, the Montevideo merchants were somewhat more likely to acquire land and own estancias, though their main income still came from trade.

They inherited an export economy dependent almost entirely on livestock products – mostly dried hides, but also some other cattle derivatives (e.g., fat, tallow, beef jerky, and candles). Uruguay's hide exports roughly equaled or possibly exceeded those of Buenos Aires in the period after 1778.[59] In exchange for the hides, which were sent mostly to Cádiz and Barcelona, the merchants imported not only European goods, but also slaves, sugar, rum, yerba, and tobacco from Brazil and Cuba. The distribution of these latter tropical products connected the merchants with the interior of Argentina and fueled a rivalry between the two ports.[60]

Cattle estancias administered by absentee landlords and often financed by the merchants were the sites of production. These estates had spread rapidly in response to the Bourbon trade reforms of 1778.[61] In comparison to the estancias near Buenos Aires, the Eastern Bank ranches were probably larger on average and possibly marked by greater land concentration, due to the fact that this region was the true heart of colonial cattle ranching.[62] The workers were chiefly wage-earning gauchos, some of whom roamed on horseback in the classic way, without a home, and some of whom were small farmers at the same time. Gaucho labor was supplemented by slaves and squatters who worked on a more permanent basis.[63]

No precise estimate is available for the wealth of the Uruguayan economy at the end of the colonial period, but the territory was surely already at the upper end of the regional hierarchy. According to Coatsworth, for example, the evidence indicates that Uruguay had "already achieved a level of income per capita well above the rest of Latin America by the end of the colonial period."[64] This is consistent with data on exports and imports that show a thriving economy. The number of hides exported annually ranged from about one hundred thousand to six hundred thousand during the period from 1780 to 1810.[65] Huge quantities of African slaves and other tropical imports were also brought through the region. Furthermore, the population growth and development in Montevideo itself stimulated substantial internal demand for European industrial products.[66] On top of this, contraband continued to generate huge revenues, though they are hard to estimate.[67] Montevideo's commerce thus made Uruguay a comparatively rich colonial region.

The Indigenous Population and Social Development. Uruguay was also well situated to enjoy high levels of social development. The prosperity of the area certainly contributed to this outcome, but ethnic homogeneity and the absence of mercantilist status markers also mattered heavily.

Indigenous people represented only 10 percent of the late-eighteenth-century population, and they were confined to the Eastern Bank's most northern regions.[68] Numerous confrontations with frontier settlers – which often amounted to extermination campaigns by the settlers – had driven them here in the preceding decades. The indigenous uprisings near Montevideo had been brutally defeated by the early 1750s, and the area south of the Río Negro was also violently cleared out around this time. Thereafter, Montevideo and surrounding parts lacked any significant indigenous population. In the interior, roaming gauchos intermingled with indigenous people, such that the Uruguayan hinterland was actually quite ethnically mixed, though individuals not living in identifiably indigenous communities were construed as white. Over time, the remaining indigenous communities in the north gradually lost their cultural distinctiveness and became classified as Charrúas. This was also true of the Guaranís, who arrived here from Paraguay after the expulsion of the Jesuits in 1767.[69]

More conspicuous during the late colonial period was the African slave population, which composed at least a quarter of the population in

Montevideo.[70] During the early and mid-nineteenth century, however, they were gradually folded into the larger population. Two observations make sense of this occurrence. First, even before the great surge of migration at the end of the nineteenth century, tens of thousands of Europeans arrived in Montevideo and other urban centers, and they partly obscured the visible African minority.[71] Second, people with some African background often could and did identify themselves as white. This was possible because the Eastern Bank never depended on plantation agriculture. In fact, rigid status classification was not part of the colonial equation here. As Julio Millot and Magdalena Bertino point out, "The lack of noble titles, estates, and guild organizations that characterized the Eastern Bank was [a] trait of modernity."[72] Without an ossified sociocultural hierarchy, residents could imagine an ethnically homogenous nation made up mostly of hardworking city dwellers and individualistic gauchos. To the extent that such imagery had elements of truth, it boded well for human development by reflecting a socioeconomic structure that was more egalitarian than in most parts of Latin America. And to the extent that such imagery was an exaggeration, it still favored postcolonial social development by promoting the idea that all citizens of the Uruguayan nation should be entitled to some of the fruits of its economic prosperity.

Venezuela

In Argentina and Uruguay, economic growth commenced in the late eighteenth century when Bourbon reforms stimulated the emergence of market-oriented merchants and estancieros and transformed previously ignored port towns into wealthy trading cities. By contrast, in colonial Venezuela, export-led growth began decades earlier and at first had a decidedly mercantilist cast. By the mid-eighteenth century, Venezuela featured a mono-crop slave economy overseen by a powerful monopolistic trading company. To accommodate this reality, the discussion of Venezuela must pay attention to its differences from, as well as its similarities to, the River Plate colonies.

Bourbon Mercantilism. Contraband is really what brought the first royal attention to Venezuela. Its source was the cacao trade, exports of which now went not only to Mexico but also to Europe, where elite consumers had finally acquired a taste for chocolate. With the Spanish Crown still mostly ignoring Venezuela, however, the Dutch controlled much of the revenue stream. "Nothing could be worse than the existing state of affairs, in which the wealth of the colony served only to enrich the Dutch and other foreigners."[73] Bourbon reformers responded by accepting the advice of Basque merchants and founding the Caracas Company, which started formal business with the province in 1730.[74]

The Caracas Company (Real Compañia Guipuzcoana de Caracas) was a private stock company that enjoyed monopolistic privileges within the still thoroughly mercantilist trade system: it was authorized to dispatch ships; it was granted control over pricing; it oversaw all commerce between Venezuela and Spain; and it assumed a role in policing contraband.[75] The Caracas Company made considerable profits (some from its own contraband), and it oversaw substantial increases in the acreage dedicated to cacao in the mid-eighteenth century. But resistance to the company from cacao planters and merchants was intense; they even led a failed revolt against it in 1749 (León's rebellion). Especially resented were the company's artificially low prices, which stood as a considerable reduction from what Dutch merchants had been paying (in fact, many planters still relied on foreign contraband to get by).[76]

Meanwhile, the number of black slaves also increased under company tutelage. During the eighteenth century, an estimated seventy thousand slaves were imported to the region, with a peak during the period from 1750 to 1780.[77] Slave settlements became common in northern areas near the plantations.[78] "In total, the Venezuelan territory absorbed 121,168 black slaves from 1500–1800, a figure equivalent to 12 percent of the legal importation to the Spanish colonies during the same period."[79] Solidifying a plantation economy in which Africans provided the bulk of the workforce was thus one of the company's most important (and notorious) achievements.

Given this history, it is not surprising that the landed elites of Venezuela differed markedly from the estancieros of the River Plate. In their relations with producers, the Venezuelan planters bore more obvious similarities to the labor-repressive hacendados of Mexico and Peru. However, whereas the hacendados were typically merged with a powerful, monopolistic merchant class, Venezuela's slave-owning planters resented both the Caracas Company and the local merchants (they probably actually preferred the company).[80] When the Caracas Company finally lost monopoly privileges and was dissolved in the early 1780s, therefore, the planters remained as the leading sector of the elite, while a vacuum existed in the merchant sector.

In sum, although Venezuela was a colonial periphery before 1700, with the creation of the Caracas Company and the growth of plantation agriculture, it inherited *mercantilist* economic institutions in the eighteenth century, even under Bourbon rule. The actors wrought by these institutions – especially labor-repressive planters – presented a major obstacle to development.

The Emergence of a Liberal Semiperiphery. A distinctive corporate colony until the 1770s, Venezuela soon became a liberal trading colony, rivaled only by Cuba in its level of agrarian exports and economic importance among the nonmineral Spanish territories in the Americas. The late colonial efflorescence of Venezuela was centered in the province of Caracas and was made possible by the strategic location of the port of La Guaira, which handled almost 90 percent of Venezuela's trade with Spain.[81] A day's travel from the city of Caracas, La Guaira was also near the rich Tuy and Aragua valleys, where the bulk of the province's cacao, coffee, indigo, and tobacco were produced. Activity at this port city increased dramatically when the economy moved from slow growth via mono-crop agriculture to rapid growth via diversified agriculture:

By 1784–5 cacao accounted for 65% of total exports, down from 85–90% in the mid-1770s. Indigo in the interim had come into the picture and took up some 15% of the total value... In the 10 years after 1785, cacao's share dropped to 55% in an expanding economy, whilst indigo's increased to around 40%. Coffee and cotton made their first major incursions into the export lists.[82]

By the end of the colonial period, cacao accounted for slightly less than half of all exports, indigo about 30 percent, and coffee about 20 percent.[83] Given that the absolute volume of cacao exportation did not decline but increased during this time, the diversification signaled a large gain in total export output.

It was not the free-trade reforms of 1778 that immediately heralded the economic good times. In Venezuela, these reforms did not take effect until 1789, several years *after* the export expansion had begun. Nevertheless, it *was* other Bourbon reforms in economic regulations that triggered the change. The abolition of the privileges of the Caracas Company, for one thing, ensured the failure of this organization and finally allowed autonomous merchants to compete with one another and to legally trade products other than cacao.[84] Venezuela was further granted several special trade exemptions that promoted its growth. The most important was the right to legally trade with non-Spanish territories in the Caribbean – which included French and Dutch possessions at first, and after 1783 also British possessions, as well as the nascent United States. By the end of the colonial period, more than one-third of Venezuelan exports were destined for these non-Spanish territories. In addition, during intervals of war, Venezuela received the right to trade directly with Spain's European allies. "The combination of free-trade periods with the specific regulations governing the province from 1777 onwards probably gave Caracas a unique position in the empire, a *de facto* freedom to trade regularly with markets outside the empire."[85]

Administrative reforms also increased Venezuela's stature in the empire. In 1776, the intendant system was installed, followed the next year by the new captaincy general in Caracas. In 1786 the Audiencia of Caracas merged the six provinces of Venezuela, and in 1803 Caracas became the seat of an archbishop.[86] All of this secured for Caracas greater independence from Bogotá and Santo Domingo, while simultaneously consolidating its control over what had been highly autonomous provinces. Population growth further accompanied Venezuela's enhanced political position and rising economic fortunes, though the region was never a magnet for Spanish arrivals. The city of Caracas, the colony's only metropolitan center, grew from fewer than 20,000 people in the 1770s to more than 40,000 at the end of the colonial period.[87] Of these 40,000, perhaps 12,000 were Spanish. The province of Caracas more generally grew from about 330,000 in 1785–7 to about 427,000 in 1800–9.[88] About one hundred Spaniards a year were arriving in Venezuela in the late colonial period, often merchants or administrative and religious officials. Several thousand Europeans also arrived illegally from the Canary Islands and Spanish Hispaniola, but even their numbers were not sufficient for Venezuela to rise from semiperiphery to center status.[89]

No numerical estimate exists to summarize the size of the Venezuelan economy at the end of the late colonial period. But historians agree that the export surge briefly brought the Caracas province to a relatively high level of development within the Americas. P. Michael McKinley's characterization is as follows: "By the tail-end of the eighteenth century, Caracas was emerging for the first time as a significant member of the Spanish Empire... An economic flowering unparalleled in the region's long history brought Caracas temporarily out of the relative obscurity in which it had lain."[90] This temporary economic prosperity was driven by Spanish merchants who arrived in Venezuela after the dismantling of the Caracas Company. Several dozen large and medium-size traders competed with one another to purchase cacao, indigo, and coffee and to sell imports such as textiles, wines, and flour.[91] In contrast to the situation that prevailed under the Caracas Company, the merchants' market-based prices and improved infrastructure (warehouses and more ships) fostered local production and fueled exports. According to McKinley, the merchants forged a "competitive commercial structure."[92]

Still, Venezuela's prosperity was brief, and it never took the Caracas province to the top of the development hierarchy in late colonial Spanish America. By the mid-nineteenth century, Venezuela was probably an average-level economic performer in the region. The country moved to a high level of economic development only in the mid-twentieth century, and only because of the oil boom (developments that will be discussed in Chapter 6).

Reasons for Venezuela's Intermediate Level of Development. Why did Venezuela not sustain its growth and become a leading economy of Spanish America in the nineteenth century, like Argentina and Uruguay? With Venezuela situated near the equator, one might be tempted to argue that it lacked the natural endowment for producing profitable export commodities that the River Plate colonies possessed. Yet Venezuela's soil was suited for the production of some of the most valued agricultural exports in the region, including not only cacao and indigo, but also coffee, the market for which took off after the 1830s. Venezuela had geographical potential, as shown by the territory's late-eighteenth-century efflorescence, but its economy was marred by numerous defects that did not exist in Argentina and Uruguay. These defects can be seen in light of the colonial past we have covered and through contrasts with Argentina and Uruguay.

Fundamental economic problems were rooted in the relative balance of power between merchants and planters. Unlike in Argentina and Uruguay, this balance was strongly tilted in favor of the planters:

The commercial sector of the caraqueño economy was less imposing than many of its counterparts elsewhere in the empire. Merchants in Caracas, unlike merchants in other colonies, were not the final arbiters of the economy or even necessarily its strongest brokers. It was not just that the comparatively smaller economy of the province precluded commercial activity on the scale of, say, Buenos Aires, or Veracruz and Mexico City. The commercial branch of our economy was an altogether weaker entity, even when considered solely in the provincial context.

This worked to the advantage of the political balance inside Caracas. The large merchants of the province, in light of the limitations placed on their pursuits, turned to agricultural holdings to establish a broader base for their wealth. In the process they drew closer to the *hacendado* elite of the colony.[93]

Thus, although the merchants introduced a competitive structure into Venezuela, they never amassed huge fortunes from their efforts. Their economic limitations led them, unlike their counterparts in the River Plate, to invest in agriculture and to enter into the privileged landed strata through marriage, thereby fusing themselves with a richer and more established class of labor-repressive landlords.

Such a class configuration, obviously quite different from that of Argentina and Uruguay, did not prepare the independent nation of Venezuela to achieve a high level of development in the nineteenth century. Problems were ever present on both the capital and labor sides of the equation. In terms of capital, in the absence of a class of powerful, commercially oriented traders, Venezuela was less able than Argentina and Uruguay to redirect investment and production to profitable sectors as opportunities in the world economy presented themselves. When the international market shifted in favor of coffee in the 1830s, planters abruptly sought to convert their cacao estates and other landholdings to the more profitable crop. However, the credit necessary for them to do so was not forthcoming from the small merchant class. Instead, financing came mostly as short-term loans borrowed at highly disadvantageous rates from European sources. This situation proved inadequate for achieving economic development. Brief downturns in market prices caused foreclosures, bankruptcies, and the evaporation of additional credit. High market prices certainly stimulated production, but they also produced the very debt responsible for the difficulties when prices went briefly awry.[94] In short, one fundamental limitation was that there was no blossoming bourgeoisie free of connections to a landed class that could spearhead economic development in Venezuela.

Equally consequential, the repressive labor system inherited from the colonial period posed obstacles for economic progress. As with plantation economies throughout Spanish America, the one in Venezuela was stifled by labor shortages. By 1800, the indigenous population had fallen to less than 15 percent of the total population.[95] Meanwhile, slave imports into Venezuela diminished significantly in the 1780s and were eliminated for good not long after independence.[96] Planters turned to repressive laws to tie their increasingly free workers to the estates. But competition among planters and the lack of an adequate rural police force meant that nonslave workers often escaped to work for wages on a neighboring estate or followed other economic pursuits.[97] To make matters worse, labor repression hardly stimulated the internal market: enslavement, low wages, and limited mobility deflated rural purchasing power. Not surprisingly, then, the countryside became backward and a hindrance to progress.

African slavery also shaped Venezuela's long-run trajectory of social development. It did so by fostering ethnic stratification, especially between whites on the one hand and blacks and *pardos* (individuals of mixed race) on the other. Since the colonial period, these racial categories have overlapped considerably with economic opportunities and life chances. The denial of opportunities to individuals not identified as white has forced these people – who make up much of Venezuela's population – to endure lower levels of education and health, with shorter life spans, than people considered white. This reality goes a long way toward explaining why Venezuela did not achieve the level of social development reached in Argentina and Uruguay, societies where ethnic distinctions melted away to a far greater extent.

THE MERCANTILIST CARRYOVERS

Important in Spanish colonial designs during the Habsburg phase, Mexico, Peru, and Colombia remained prominent in the colonial project during the Bourbon phase as well. These countries avoided peripheralization not because they featured a particularly attractive set of conditions for commercial agriculture – though they all did contain relatively strategic port areas. Instead, they merited continued colonial attention mostly because they housed many Spanish people and institutions and because they possessed mineral economies whose wealth potential was too great for the Crown and settlers to ignore. These mercantilist carryovers were, accordingly, recipients of many late Bourbon institutions and became hybrid colonies – an often-contradictory composite of mercantilist and liberal institutions. Their long-run economic and social performance was shaped by these opposing institutional tendencies and the actors they left behind.

Mexico

A Sustained Center. A massive indigenous population did not diminish Spanish interest in Mexico during the reform period of the Bourbons. Instead, the territory remained at the very center of the Spanish colonial project. Population growth for all groups was considerable. "In broad terms the Mexican population grew from an estimated 3,336,000 persons in 1742 to some 6,122,000 persons in 1810. Nearly all the races which inhabited the colony multiplied at the same rate."[98] For the majority of the population – the indigenous people – an overall recovery from epidemic disease explains this growth rather well. For example, the spectacular rise of Guadalajara, the capital of New Galicia, from a desolate town to a flourishing city was driven by the huge increase in the rural population in the countryside.[99] But for the Spanish population, a portion of the increase was due to peasant migrants who arrived from northern Spain, especially Basques and the Montañeses of Santander.[100]

Spanish migrants were attracted to Mexico City because, as John E. Kicza points out, the city remained the heart of the colonial project in New Spain and the New World:

Mexico City was the headquarters of colonial government and ecclesiastical administration, the dominant commercial center of Middle America, an important manufacturing site, by far the largest city in the Americas at the time, and the residence of the greatest part of New Spain's elite. In the last century before the achievement of independence, it dwarfed all other cities in the Americas in the completeness and intricacy of its social composition and in the scale and diversity of its business institutions.[101]

From a population of 112,000 in 1772, Mexico City grew to 169,000 persons in 1810. In the early nineteenth century, approximately half of this population was Spanish, with indigenous people and *castas* (people of mixed race) making up fairly equal portions of the rest.[102] Yet if we look beyond Mexico City and its surrounding area, a striking new demographic pattern becomes visible. Previously marginal towns in the north and west (e.g., Guanajuato and Guadalajara) became prosperous growth centers, whereas towns that had thrived during the Habsburg period now declined (e.g., Puebla). Indeed, "northern New Spain had 26 percent of the viceroyalty's population in 1742 and 38 percent by 1810."[103] Alan Knight underscores the link between these population trends and the economic dynamism associated with mining:

Migration . . . favored regions of dynamic growth like the Bajío, as against relatively declining zones, like Puebla and its hinterland. Between 1742 and 1793 – a half century of mining growth – the population of the Guanajuato intendancy increased one and a half times; the city of Guanajuato itself (closely followed by Querétaro) reached 55,000, easily outstripping New York or Boston. Guadalajara, similarly benefiting from the mining boom and the growth of the centre-west, sometimes increased its population by as much as 10 percent in a single year; by the end of the colonial period it had reached perhaps 40,000, equaling Philadelphia.[104]

The new Spanish settlement trends were partly driven by the size of the indigenous population at the regional level; Spanish immigrants now often settled in areas with a sparse indigenous population and avoided places with a dense indigenous population. There was thus a reversal of migration patterns, with areas lacking indigenous people becoming the new magnets. However, Mexico *as a whole* had a dense indigenous population, and thus we would expect this territory in general to have experienced overall low levels of settlement. The question thus arises: Why did Mexico remain an important site for Spanish migration and activity during the Bourbon period?

The answer has two essential components, both suggested by the discussion so far. First, the very fact that Mexico was already a center region – replete with rich Spanish life and functioning Spanish economic institutions, above all else in Mexico City – certainly encouraged continued high levels of colonialism, despite any obstacles posed by the existence of precapitalist native formations. "In accord with long Iberian tradition, large cities were perceived as the centers of cultured and civilized life...All sectors of Hispanic colonial society aspired to [locate] oneself and one's family in an important city." In New Spain, "the advantages enjoyed by Mexico City against the other metropoles" were not only its size and cultural prominence, but also its perceived employment opportunities.[105] Here we need to bear in mind that peninsular newcomers after 1750 were mostly economically disadvantaged, and Mexico City offered comparatively good prospects for them to work as shopkeepers, bureaucrats, artisans, or professionals.[106]

Second, outside of Mexico City, the Crown retained its interest in Mexico because of minerals, which promoted the colonization of some new areas during the Bourbon phase and generated essential wealth for the continued vitality of Mexico City. Growth in the mineral economy occurred in spurts during the eighteenth century, with several crests and subsequent declines, but the overall trend was a significant upward one, including a boom after 1776.[107] Guanajuato became the leading mining region, with its Valenciana mine employing more than three thousand workers, and much of the rest of its population working in occupations related to the silver business. The full intendancy of Guanajuato grew to four hundred thousand people on the back of great mineral wealth. Some older and declining mining regions, including Zacatecas, were now forced to undergo major financial and technological changes to try to remain productive. These areas were never large population centers, and they remained on the periphery of Spanish settlement.[108]

To sum up, Spanish settlement and institutional development in Mexico were driven mostly by the prior importance of this territory and its continued mineral prosperity. While at the regional level Spanish settlers showed a preference for northern peripheral locations that were not heavily populated by indigenous people, the territory as a whole was clearly at the center of the late colonial Spanish Empire.

The Limits of Bourbon Reform. Observers of Mexico have long commented on the fact that the country is distinctive in Latin America (in Knight's words, "particularly distinct, peculiarly peculiar"), in part because of its colonial period.[109] From the perspective of this book, such distinctiveness is rooted in Mexico's status as the sole country that was both a mercantilist center and a liberal center. Mexico experienced full-blown versions of both Habsburg and Bourbon colonialism; it was an amalgam of these two contradictory heritages. The limitations and ultimate legacies of the Bourbon reform for the country as a whole are best seen from this perspective.[110]

Starting with political reforms, we can note that Bourbon reformers had some success in overhauling Habsburg administrative institutions. With the advent of the intendant system in the 1780s, salaried and trained officials (though quite underpaid) now usually controlled the new administrative districts. And the previously dominant local interests ("native sons" and Creoles) of the audiencias at Mexico and Guadalajara and of the cabildo at Mexico City were mostly replaced with peninsular Spaniards.[111] Even the town councils of the countryside saw peninsular merchants dislodge older elite families.[112] These changes allowed the Bourbons to substantially increase taxation, a fact that turned many Creoles against the colonial state.[113] New peninsular administrators had these successes because they were not necessarily in direct competition with the dominant socioeconomic class, which remained fundamentally merchant-landed and mineral-landed. Subdelegates from intendancies, however, were more allied with the Mexican hacendados, a situation that blocked successful reform. In the south and east, for example, the subdelegates simply ignored royal orders prohibiting the forced monopoly sale of goods to indigenous communities. And in central Mexico, the intendants actively colluded with landlords to extort extra tribute from indigenous communities.[114] The overall point is that while Bourbon political reforms weakened the direct political influence of older elite families, they did not fundamentally shift the political system to one in which neutral bureaucrats carried out policy autonomously from dominant socioeconomic interests.

The basic problem of laying down new institutions and actors without removing the preexisting ones also hampered the Bourbon effort to modernize the economy. Liberalizing economic reforms did occur, and in quite significant ways: the Cádiz monopoly was ended, Mexico City also lost its monopoly, and new consulados were established at both Veracruz and Guadalajara.[115] Strategically located as the port of passage for silver exports, Veracruz was especially able to take advantage of the reforms.

Veracruz, previously a mere point of transit, soon housed a group of merchants who dispatched their wares directly to the north. They bypassed the Mexico City almaceneros [warehouse owners] and dealt directly with provincial traders. Moreover, a new breed of traveling dealers, who bought at Veracruz and sold wherever they found a market, sprang into existence. The lines of credit also changed. The Veracruz merchants obtained their imports from Spanish shippers who, financed in many cases by foreign trading houses, did not expect immediate cash payment.[116]

With the appearance of the Veracruz merchants' guild, "Mexico City's merchants' guild found itself pressed to adopt the more progressive attitude of the Veracruz organization." However, "the old merchants were loath to allow commercial initiative to pass to the new element" at Veracruz.[117] In fact, Mexico City's merchants still benefited from and remained committed to the quite restricted trading structure in which profits flowed from cooperation with the heavily taxing Crown and its long-standing monopoly channels. Though investment in the domestic economy was never outright discouraged, this group sought and received its wealth by selling European manufactures that were financed by minerals. It profited under a crippling system in which these imported goods might be assessed 35–40 percent in various taxes (duties, alcabalas, and fees) and in which silver that otherwise might have fueled domestic development was systematically transferred to Spain.[118]

With the Bourbon reforms, two competing groups of merchants suddenly now existed: the more market-oriented traders of Veracruz and the traditional monopolists at Mexico City. Given the thrust of the Bourbon project, Veracruz must have seemed on the cusp of overtaking Mexico City as the premier center of commerce in New Spain and perhaps thus ushering in a dynamic agricultural economy. Yet "the Veracruz merchants could supplant those of the capital only if they were able either to assume control over large-scale acquisition of European finished goods or to take over distribution of them to the provinces. They succeeded in doing neither."[119] Mexico City merchants blocked the rise of Veracruz and its traders by stationing their own business associates (often relatives with substantial silver coinage) at Veracruz to purchase directly from the arriving ships. The distribution of the goods shipped to Veracruz consequently remained mostly in the hands of the Mexico City traders. These traders also sent their agents to Spain to secure merchandise for shipment to the capital, undercutting Veracruz as an importer of European manufactures. Meanwhile, the consulado at Mexico City continued to dominate the highly lucrative Manila contraband trade running through Acapulco. Liberal reforms therefore did cause an emergent bourgeoisie to appear at Veracruz. But its development was fundamentally stunted by the mercantile class at Mexico City.

Nor did the Bourbon reform trigger the formation of a rural class equivalent to the market-oriented estancieros of the River Plate. With very few regional exceptions (e.g., Oaxaca), the Mexican elite – including its richest members in Mexico City – was simultaneously a merchant and a landed class.[120] If not tied to commerce, wealthy Mexican landlords were mine owners or representatives of the church, the latter organization continuing to be a major landowner and lending institution throughout this period.[121] In most of Mexico, hacienda agriculture geared toward food production remained preeminent, even though the high rate of hacienda sales and estate transfers in the eighteenth century suggests that landowning yielded at best unstable profits.[122] The great estates were sensitive to market demand, as evidenced by the rise of cereal (especially wheat) farming in New Galicia in response to the growth of urban areas during the eighteenth century. Nevertheless, agricultural production was almost always destined for consumers *within* Mexico. Notwithstanding cochineal exports (and modest sugar exports), Mexico's foreign exchange was overwhelmingly generated by mineral exports. The Mexican agricultural economy was thoroughly inward-looking, and it prospered only because of an expanding market created by population growth.[123]

Another key contrast with Argentina concerns the situation of rural workers. The estancias (of varying sizes) of late colonial Argentina used the fairly well-compensated seasonal labor of migrating gauchos; Mexico's landlords, by contrast, depended on low-wage and indebted workers with little mobility. Haciendas commonly maintained large resident workforces (e.g., perhaps two hundred workers), and they also often drew seasonal laborers from nearby indigenous communities. Debt peonage and quasi-coercive labor were widely practiced in Oaxaca and the more sparsely populated northern territories. In western and central Mexico, a wage-labor system closer to that of Argentina did take hold by the late eighteenth century.[124] Yet the economic situation of the average wage-earning hacienda worker in late colonial Mexico was almost surely worse than that of the Argentine gaucho. A key cause of the spread of wage labor in Mexico was demographic: population growth fostered a labor surplus, and market forces compelled individuals to live or work on the haciendas. But this same labor surplus also ensured exceptionally low wages and sustained rural poverty in Mexico. According to historian Eric Van Young, "It is possible to speak of an ever-increasing impoverishment among the mass of rural inhabitants during the last century of Spanish domination."[125] In fact, rural impoverishment was rooted not only in declining real wages, but also in declining access to land, credit, and goods, which was brought on by the same population pressures that helped to spread wage labor.

Consequences for Economic Development. Mexico's starting position as an average-level economic performer in Spanish America was sealed during the late colonial period. In 1800, Mexico was already well behind the export-driven economies of the River Plate on any per capita measurement of economic development. According to Coatsworth's well-known estimates, for instance, Mexico's GDP per capita in 1800 was only half that of Argentina. Analogously, while in absolute terms Mexico exported four times as much as Argentina, in per capita terms its export sector was about one-fifth the size of Argentina's.[126] It is further relevant that while the economy was buoyed by substantial mineral exports right up until Hidalgo's Revolt (1810–11), it is likely that growth had already stagnated during the late Bourbon period as mineral profits were increasingly siphoned off by both the Crown and the

Mexico City merchants and were not reinvested locally in export enterprises or industry.[127]

We may say that, structurally speaking, Mexico could not become a highly developed economy because, first, its local markets were insufficient to sustain such development on their own and, second, its export sector was not competitive in international trade. Concerning the first factor, even with substantial population growth, the low-wage and quasi-coercive agricultural economy allowed for neither economic dynamism nor the kind of consumer purchasing power necessary to trigger growth via production for the domestic market. There were simply no mechanisms for any economic surpluses to find their way into the hands of the direct producers; there were, rather, institutions and actors blocking such transfers. Likewise, profits from production were not put toward investment in new industries, since so few opportunities for such investment existed in this low-income, low-skill, high-tax, and high-debt economy. Nor were the cloth-producing obrajes – concentrated in central Mexico, the Bajío, and Puebla and hopelessly dependent on acquiring ever-cheaper labor – capable of sustaining themselves in any kind of competitive market.[128] If robust development was to commence in Mexico, it would have had to occur significantly via markets abroad.

This brings us to Mexico's inability to become competitive in international trade. We have already explored how and why colonial actors failed to fully capitalize on the new possibilities for trade of the late eighteenth century. Then, after 1810, the mineral economy utterly collapsed, exposing all of the vulnerabilities of the Mexican economy. Historians have devoted much effort to identifying the causes of stagnant or perhaps negative growth in Mexico during the period from roughly 1810 to 1850.[129] Much of this research is animated by the question of why Mexico did not achieve growth rates similar to those of the United States in the first half of the nineteenth century. But whatever the utility of such comparisons, if our frame of analysis is within Spanish America, this period in Mexican history does not stand out as critical, for colonialism had already left Mexico well behind the River Plate countries. For a time, certainly, the violence of the independence wars contributed to especially poor performance in Mexico, which temporarily put the country even further behind. But the consequences of this political turmoil for poor growth in the decades after 1810 in Mexico are easily exaggerated.[130] Moreover, Mexico experienced strong growth during the second half of the nineteenth century – so strong that it actually gained a little ground in comparison to Argentina from 1800 to 1900.[131]

But there was another important difference between Mexico and Argentina in the decades that followed independence. Whereas Mexico remained dependent on mineral exports and stalled in the pursuit of commercial agricultural production, Argentina quickly turned from minerals to alternative exports in the aftermath of independence. Why was Argentina so much more successful at developing an agrarian-export economy?

Explanations involving geography and natural endowments come to mind. Coatsworth's analysis of the 1810–50 stagnation in Mexico emphasizes the high overland-transportation costs resulting from the distance between Mexico City and the sea.[132] True enough, land-transportation problems made Mexican commodities less competitive than those of Argentina. But it was no accident of geography that economic activity was centered around Mexico City and not in areas where transportation was easier. These problems of distance were in fact a consequence of the patterns of colonial settlement and institution building that have been explained here. If Mexico had been a periphery during the Habsburg period, then economic activity under the Bourbons might well have been centered near the seacoast, not in the inaccessible highland valleys, and one would have argued that Mexico's *advantage* – like Argentina's – lay in its strategic port location!

Nor was Argentina's success relative to Mexico driven simply by a better export endowment. Argentina's exports were a series of different livestock products and later wheat and maize, none of which were in any sense strategic. In fact, what seems remarkable about Argentina was its ability to shift easily from one export to another in response to evolving market conditions. Mexico had regions that were certainly capable of producing livestock, maize, coffee, and wheat and even somewhat strategic products such as dyestuffs.[133] And, as Coatsworth notes, "railroad technology developed in the 1830s and could easily have been imported by 1840" to overcome overland-transport problems.[134] What really mattered in the Mexican case was that mid-nineteenth-century economic activity was never significantly geared toward capitalizing on the export of any of these agricultural products.[135] Economic actors fixated instead on reviving the collapsed mineral economy and pursuing growth via agricultural production for local markets. There were virtually no efforts at modernizing agriculture or improving infrastructure; a basic reorganization of the economy toward agro-exportation was not pursued. This makes perfect sense when we recognize the kind of dominant socioeconomic class that was implanted during the colonial period. Mexico's landed merchants and landed miners were not the right actors for innovating or for redirecting production in ways that might stimulate agricultural exports.

The Indigenous Population and Social Development. Mexico's trajectory of economic development left much to be desired, but its performance in the area of social development was even worse from a regional-comparative perspective. In explaining why, two sets of considerations are relevant. First, the economic development that did exist hardly boosted well-being for the average citizen. Even if the late colonial Mexican economy itself was not outright impoverished, the vast majority of its people were. Wealth could not trickle down into producers' hands. Rural workers suffered a meager and declining standard of living as landlords cut wages and discontinued in-kind remuneration in response to labor surpluses. Facing newly heightened risks, too, were the mine workers, who lost out when the shares system of payment was eliminated in favor of the depreciating daily wage.[136] In the towns and cities, the real wages of textile workers fell, and artisans became indebted to merchant-financiers.[137] There were simply few winners in the late colonial economy of Mexico.

The second relevant factor concerns indigenous people in particular. Sixty percent of the population was still indigenous, a category defined in part by phenotype but also increasingly by cultural characteristics (language, dress, and lifestyle).[138] In northern Mexico, the percentage of indigenous people was much lower than in most areas, while in southern regions they were present in large majorities: "Indians dominated the ethnic composition of provinces such as Oaxaca, Puebla, Veracruz, Yucatán, Tlaxcala, and Mexico, where its population corresponded to 88, 74, 74, 72, 72, and 66 percent, respectively, of the total." Overall, "the prolonged Spanish presence had modified very little the ancient prehispanic pattern of the distribution of the population."[139]

How did specifically this population fare under the Bourbons? On the one hand, the eighteenth century unambiguously saw an improvement: the numbers of indigenous people finally recovered, and even grew – and being able to stay alive is surely requisite for any kind of human development. Furthermore, the most rigid caste barriers began to erode. For example, in the cities, it became harder to maintain the separation between mestizo and Indian; in the countryside, the same thing happened when indigenous people left for hacienda work.[140]

Despite these trends, however, nothing in the data remotely suggests that indigenous people in the aggregate experienced anything but a very low level of human development. Here we should bring into focus the typical situation for indigenous people: "A large part of the Indian populations that inhabited the center, the west, and the south lived in towns and communities that had preserved the communal land system and a great deal of social and cultural cohesion . . . Their social and cultural structure expressed a profound connection to the land, little changed by the presence of Europeans." These "voluntarily isolated and autosufficient communities . . . that nevertheless maintained frequent contact with their oppressors" were still mostly protected by the courts as corporate entities, enabling inhabitants to maintain components of their culture.[141] But in the Spanish system, the communities were also areas of great poverty and deprivation. The basic problem was a day-to-day lack of resources; but on top of this, disease epidemics and weather-induced crop failures periodically struck, with tragic consequences. And to the extent that there were forces working to transform indigenous communities, they did not improve conditions, either. Encroaching landlords, new administrative systems, and population increases in the late colonial period – these threatened the landholdings, reciprocity norms, and corporate structure upon which the social cohesion of communities rested.[142] Such pressures were a sign of things to come under postcolonial liberal reform. Nevertheless, already in the early nineteenth century, it was clear that the heroic perseverance of indigenous people as the majority of the population despite their three-hundred-year encounter with the Spanish ensured that the new Mexican nation would at first be marked by low levels of performance on social indicators.

Peru

Severed from Bolivia and the River Plate in 1776, the Viceroyalty of Peru lost economic and political importance within the Spanish Empire and was thus relegated to the semiperiphery. The territory no longer held monopoly control of South American bullion and European imports, both of which now ran legally through Buenos Aires. And the Bourbon Crown's imperial planning was occupied more and more by the rising and newly prosperous Viceroyalty of the River Plate. On the other hand, Lima still housed a substantial Spanish population and served as the administrative capital of the Andes, and the territory was still buoyed by its mineral economy. If Peru was reduced to a semiperipheral player in the empire, it nevertheless strongly felt the effects of the liberal institutional changes sweeping the region in the late colonial period. Its overall heritage was, accordingly, a dual Habsburg-Bourbon colonial experience broadly similar to that of Mexico.

The Semiperipheral Colony. Various facts suggest that Peru was no longer a center colonial region. For one, population expansion here began much later than in Mexico. In fact, the indigenous population shrank all the way up to 1730, when only an estimated 613,000 native people remained in Lower Peru and Upper Peru (Bolivia) combined. By comparison, the indigenous population of New Spain in 1742 was 2.4 million.[143] After 1750, the indigenous population of Peru finally started to grow, totaling around 750,000 at the end of the century, though it was still less than a quarter of Mexico's. Spaniards in Peru numbered about 150,000 in the late 1700s; by contrast, New Spain had roughly one million Spaniards in 1810. Significant though less dramatic differences in size also marked the cities of the two territories – for example, Mexico City had about the same number of Spanish citizens as Lima, Arequipa, and Cuzco combined. The Spanish population of 25,000 in the Lima intendancy (about 20,000 in the city of Lima itself) at the end of the eighteenth century was no larger than in 1680, due in part to the great earthquakes of 1687 and 1746. Finally, "peninsular immigration to Peru was even smaller than to New Spain. With fewer opportunities in trade and in civil, military, and ecclesiastical positions, the attractions were limited."[144]

In Peru as much as anywhere, Bourbon administrative reforms were successful in dislodging the elite individuals who owned and occupied the highest political offices. At the Audiencia of Lima, nearly all the Creole elites were transferred or were obligated to retire and then replaced with *peninsulares*. After 1784, when the intendant system was imposed, subdelegates replaced the corregidores, who had previously overseen the indigenous communities and supervised town councils. Cuzco's new audiencia, created in 1787 in the aftermath of the Tupac Amaru revolt, was also filled with *peninsulares*.[145]

If the Bourbons toppled the merchant elite from the pinnacle of political power, does this also mean that they succeeded with other reforms, including those that ran counter to this group's economic interests? The answer is mixed. For one thing, at the local level, the new subdelegates of the intendancy system functioned autonomously, and, as in Mexico, they continued to exploit the indigenous population using the same methods that the corregidores used (e.g., the sale of goods at monopoly prices, excessive tribute collection), despite Bourbon legislation to the contrary. Not surprisingly, they often worked in concert with landlords in these endeavors.[146] What is more, the Bourbon vision of reform in Peru was itself inherently circumscribed in ways that encouraged institutional persistence. For the Bourbons remained focused on bolstering the mineral economy and their share of the taxes thereby generated. They could do this because, despite the loss of all output from Upper Peru after 1777, silver mining in Peru did not collapse. Instead, led by the mines at Cerro de Pasco, Peru's silver industry mostly prospered until the end of the eighteenth century (though mercury production at Huancavelica declined after 1770, which limited production increases). By the 1780s, in fact, Cerro de Pasco yielded more silver than Potosí.[147] Royal revenues were derived by confiscating a portion of this output via the mining fees and by taxing the commerce that silver ultimately financed. Late colonial administrative reorganizations further assisted the financial situation of the Crown by augmenting the rate and enforcement of these taxes.[148] With the mineral economy doing so well, it is not surprising that the Bourbons saw silver exports as Peru's best and nearly exclusive way to help the monarchy's ever-troubled finances.

The Trajectory of Economic Development. Bourbon administrators imagined that economic liberalization would stimulate the economy of the Viceroyalty of Peru. But they were wrong. Late colonial growth beyond the mineral sector was not possible given the institutions and actors that carried over from the Habsburg period. The organization of the commercial sector and that of the agricultural sector were both obstacles, and they need to be discussed in turn.

Predictably, wholesale merchants from the consulado at Lima complained bitterly about free trade and the loss of Upper Peru and the River Plate from the viceroyalty.[149] Their concerns were not unfounded. As Patricia H. Marks notes, the Bourbon reformers intended to weaken the Lima merchants: "It is clear that the Bourbon reformers attempted to diminish the wealth and power of the *limeño* elite."[150] Fiscal policies were the Crown's weapon of choice: taxes to disrupt the profitable trade in sugar and wheat between Callao and Chile, extra levies on goods shipped from Lima or Callao to Buenos Aires and Arica, and special fees to oversee the provision of imported goods.[151] The Bourbons went so far as to promote new merchants based in Spain, including one particular trading house, Cinco Gremios Mayores de Madrid, at the direct expense of the Lima consulado. These various maneuvers "severely affected the large *Limeño* wholesaler who over the course of the early colonial period had been the principal beneficiary of Lima's monopoly trade... *Limeño* businessmen had... to share their domestic market with a new and substantial group of peninsular merchants."[152] New commercial actors also gained a foothold at Arequipa when the port of Arica was opened for trade with Spain and the rest of the Americas.[153] According to Alexander von Humboldt, smaller-scale merchants prospered in Bourbon Peru, and commercial wealth became more evenly distributed.[154] From all of this, one strand of the historiography leaves the impression that the old merchant class – the "mercantile splendor" of Lima – was swept away.[155]

While there is no gainsaying that metropolitan merchants were active in the export of specie and the import of Spanish manufactures, the Bourbon reforms never stimulated an autonomous class of investors oriented toward profit through exchange in competitive international markets. New merchants were often simply folded into Lima's established mercantile circles and its consulado, which continued to control trade in Peru. Indeed, some of these "new" merchants were established families from the traditional Lima merchant class who had merely adapted to the new environment and used the monopolistic channels that still existed.[156] Thus, there were really no late colonial merchants poised to invest aggressively in long-term projects, even in the thriving silver mines.[157] Rather, the new traders prospered much as had their predecessors: through short-term accumulation associated with control over the import trade and influence over the distributors who sold in localities. They especially financed the local traders who supplied goods and loans to miners. This was the natural market, for it was the miners with their bullion who had purchasing power in the late colonial economy. To achieve long-term security, the Lima merchants also bought land in the countryside and real estate in Lima. But neither could these investments spur economic progress, given the organization of rural production.

Despite the mines, late colonial Peru was still an agricultural society dominated by food production on indigenous lands and Spanish estates. Hundreds of haciendas of varying sizes surrounded the mining regions and the roads connecting Lima to Cuzco and Arequipa. In central and southern Peru, indigenous communities farmed expansive communal lands.[158] Whatever the specific form of landholding, production was almost always destined for local consumption, either in the village itself or in the nearest urban center. Despite the fact that merchants were often also landowners, there was never an aspiration to modernize production on the estates. Cultivation techniques remained much the same as they had been in the seventeenth century, and on indigenous lands, food production often looked similar to that of the pre-Columbian period.[159] Internal demand was depressed, because of the impoverished and permanently indebted producing class. On the indigenous estates, in fact, communities still had to meet heavy tribute obligations, leading caciques to rent out land to roaming forasteros or hire out their residents at the haciendas and the obrajes. The purchasing power of the mestizos and Spaniards who farmed their own small estates or worked as hacienda employees was not much better.[160] All in all, the capital-starved domestic market reinforced primitive modes of agrarian production in the countryside.

As for the export sector of the economy, coastal plantations did profitably produce commodities for markets in the Americas; they were sent not only to Lima and the highland cities but also to Buenos Aires and ports in Guatemala. But the export products of Peru were almost never shipped to Spain.[161] In some cases, including wine from the vineyards of Arequipa, the commodity stood no chance of competing with European producers. In other cases, Peruvian producers were unable to keep up with New World competitors; for example, sugar from the north-coast plantations lost out to exports from Brazil and the Caribbean. Likewise, in the livestock industry, Peru could not compete with the strategically located River Plate.[162]

Nonmineral exports capable of stimulating high growth were thus not forthcoming in late colonial Peru. The local actors who controlled the capital generated by the mineral economy – the new and old merchants – were not oriented toward investment in a dynamic agro-export sector. There was no investor class to forge nonmineral linkages between Peru and European markets. In addition, geographic factors mattered a great deal. The problem was not primarily a mismatch between the primary products sought in Europe and the agricultural endowment of Peru: "As contemporary observers never tired of pointing out, Peru was capable of producing excellent coffee and an enormous range of other agricultural goods."[163] Rather, the problem was the Pacific coast location of the port of Callao in relation to Atlantic markets in Europe. Although Callao was strategic for markets in Central and South America, and was indeed "the best port on the west coast of the continent,"[164] the costs of shipping to any point in Europe were considerable. When the Bourbons recognized and eliminated the absurd practice of privileging Callao as South America's nearly exclusive legal port, therefore, Peruvian producers of sugar, cacao, tobacco, and cotton were quickly undercut by rivals with easy access to the Atlantic Ocean. As John R. Fisher argues, Peru had prospered greatly under the Habsburg institutions, but it could not do the same under more liberal arrangements:

Lima's relative prosperity in the past had rested upon her monopoly privileges and upon her sovereignty over Upper Peru . . . Deprived of Lima's commercial monopoly and of the mineral wealth of Potosí, Peru rapidly emerged as a casualty of imperial rationalization and reform, since she was unable to compete economically with other parts of the empire . . . When, in time of European war, disruption of communications with Spain was added to the perennial problems of low domestic demand, shortage of capital and labour, difficulty of internal communication and geographical isolation, continuing economic decline was inevitable.[165]

At the end of the late colonial period, Peru had assumed its position as an intermediate-level economic developer within the region: the territory was probably wealthier on a per capita basis than Ecuador, Bolivia, and Central America, but not nearly as wealthy as Argentina and Uruguay.[166] The economy spiraled into crisis when mineral production first stagnated and then utterly collapsed following the wars of independence.[167] The crisis was probably as grave as in Mexico before 1850. To make matters worse, Peru's recovery between 1850 and 1900 was only partial. Although guano exports boomed during most of these years, the resultant huge profits did not translate into long-lasting development.[168] At the end of the nineteenth century, Peru was probably poorer than Mexico.

The Trajectory of Social Development. The health and education situation for the typical resident in Peru during the late colonial and early independence periods was at least as bad as the rather appalling situation described earlier for individuals living in Mexico. Like Mexico, Peru, as a Habsburg colonial center, had inherited all of the corporatist and hierarchical cultural institutions from the first phase of colonial rule. While the Bourbons sought to pull back or limit the extent of titled nobility, aristocratic privilege, and ecclesiastical power in Peru, the effort was for the most part unsuccessful. Most telling was the fact that individuals were still classified into rigid caste groups, with the vast majority of people occupying categories such as *indio* (Indian), *esclavo* (slave), *negro* (black), and mestizo – which carried great social stigma, closed off opportunities in the economy and government, and limited life chances.

In Peru, as Charles F. Walker writes about the late colonial period, "the lines dividing Indians and non-Indians were more sharply drawn than in the other center of colonial Spanish America, Mexico, and intermediate groups, although important, were comparatively less significant."[169] What accounts for this difference? Why was the cultural separation between indigenous and Spanish people greater in Peru than in Mexico? The relevant factor was not population density per se. Concentrated in large majorities across the central and southern highlands, Peru's indigenous people composed about

60 percent of the total late colonial population – roughly the same proportion as in Mexico.[170] More important was the distribution of this population. The ancient Inca capital at Cuzco, the heartland of the indigenous peoples, was physically separated from the colonial capital at coastal Lima. With few exceptions, as Florencia E. Mallon notes, this separation yielded "a dualistic or bipolar pattern – Indian highlands, versus a white, Black and mestizo coast."[171] By contrast, in Mexico, the colonial state was built in the very center of the Aztec Empire, and political authorities were physically close to the indigenous communities of the Central Valley. The mining sectors in the two territories reinforced this difference. In Mexico, wage labor was established early on in the key northern mineral regions, with the effect of integrating indigenous people into the Spanish socioeconomic system. But in Peru, the mita system continued to mobilize draftees, thus maintaining a rigid division between indigenous and Spanish workers. Tribute collection from the indigenous communities of highland Peru in the late colonial period likewise appears to have been more intense than was the case in Mexico. Notably, the historiography on Mexico suggests that tribute was waning in the late eighteenth century, while histories of Peru emphasize how the Bourbons oversaw a substantial increase in the head tax.[172] Lastly, the fact that the mita and the head tax were reinstated and widely employed in Peru after independence under new names (i.e., *servicio a la república* and *contribución indígena*) suggests more intense exploitation and a wider ethnic split than in Mexico.

These differences help explain why late colonial Peru was the source of the most important indigenous revolts during the colonial period. In Peru, the greater spatial separation (in comparison to Mexico) between the indigenous and the Spanish communities afforded indigenous residents the autonomy and the capacity to act against colonial exploitation. Although the Bourbons surely sought to keep control over the native communities via the intendant system, the physical presence of the Lima-based colonial state remained very marginal in the highland communities where most indigenous people lived. As a result, indigenous communities not only were especially likely to view Bourbon administrators as outside encroachers, they also could organize and actually do something in response. This capacity was what underlay the highland revolts and unrest during 1726–37 and 1751–6, as well as the Great Rebellion of 1780–1, led by Tupac Amaru II. To be sure, in each case these revolts were triggered most immediately by reforms that put increased financial pressure on the indigenous communities.[173] But what is remarkable is that the Peruvian communities had the structural capability to strike out as they did when exploitation peaked and their grievances became most intense.

Yet there is an irony to these capacities for collective action. The very self-containment and separation necessary for them were rooted in a bifurcated system that left indigenous communities highly marginalized. To a greater extent than in Mexico, highland Peruvian indigenous communities were physically divorced from the Spanish colonial economy and the Spanish settlers who had historically exploited them. While such spatial and cultural distance enabled the communities to retain many traditional characteristics, these same conditions left them in a subordinated position, one in which their residents faced a precarious existence and diminished life chances. This is the main reason that Peru started out with a very low level of social development, despite its intermediate level of economic performance.

Colombia

Colombia remained a semiperiphery during the liberal phase, the one territory that held this status throughout the colonial epoch. Bourbon reforms were launched here early in the eighteenth century, soon to create the impressively large Viceroyalty of New Granada, with its capital at Bogotá. Yet the Bourbons repeatedly failed to lay down new administrative structures at the local level, and they had only marginal luck at stimulating an export economy. They did not fully overcome the Habsburg legacy.

The Semiperipheral Colony. Spanish authorities and settlers made Colombia a Bourbon semiperiphery for the same basic reasons as they did Peru: it possessed enough mineral wealth and enough of a Spanish population to continue to merit imperial attention. In absolute monetary terms, Colombia's gold exports were not nearly as large as Peru's silver exports. But gold was profitable, and it constituted fully 70 percent of Colombia's total exports during the late eighteenth century.[174] To the Crown, certainly, the nearly exclusive purpose of the Colombian economy was to provide bullion.

Bullion brought little progress to Colombia, however. The two main gold-producing regions of the eighteenth century – the Pacific west and Antioquia – practiced low-intensity mining and were desolate settlement areas little changed from the prior century. Gold-bearing ores were sold on site to local merchants who traded in various imported goods. And when the ore was transported to foundries to be converted into ingots, it might change hands again and stimulate expenditures before being taxed and exported to Spain. Nevertheless, the miners of Popayán, Cali, and Antioquia did not usually reinvest profits. Most of the internal wealth was actually siphoned off by the wholesale merchants in Cartagena and the trading houses in Spain. They controlled the imports and financed the local distributors.[175]

Although mainly a source of bullion, Colombia also merited monarchical attention because of its strategic role in imperial matters. Its northern coast was situated in the threatened Caribbean, and traders here were heavily involved in smuggling. Bogotá was temporarily elevated to the status of viceroyalty capital in 1717 precisely to protect Spanish commerce and defend the empire from British incursions. The decision was reinstated in 1738 shortly before Spain went to war with England. On paper, this viceroyalty encompassed most of what is now Colombia, Venezuela, Ecuador, and Panama. In practice, of course, the viceroy had almost no actual command over geographically distant political districts such as Caracas and Quito. Even within Colombia itself, colonial authority was extremely uneven, as the territory remained a mosaic of isolated regions separated by long distances and difficult terrain. Spanish migration to New Granada overall was not high in the late eighteenth century, and residents remained highly dispersed, with no particularly large cities: "Bogotá, the viceregal capital and New Granada's leading city in the late eighteenth century, had a mere 20,000 or so inhabitants; the only city of comparable size was Cartagena de Indias, New Granada's major port."[176] The monarchy no doubt would have liked to better integrate and control these areas, but it was so preoccupied on so many different fronts that it could not consider devoting the extraordinary resources necessary for real control in this second-tier colonial territory.

The Limits of Bourbon Reform. Even without a firm grip over much of the Viceroyalty of New Granada, the Bourbons were not dissuaded from trying to increase revenue collection. Authorities imposed notably high sales taxes and used monopolies to artificially elevate prices for tobacco and *aguardiente* (cane alcohol). In Quito and several towns in Colombia, the taxes and monopolies triggered the urban riots of the 1760s. Then, beginning in 1778 and culminating in the spring of 1781, rural protesters joined the urban opposition, leading the anti-tax Comunero rebellion, which put Bogotá in jeopardy and frightened colonial elites.[177] The Comunero rebellion played into the hands of the archbishop and his allies, who successfully opposed the creation of an intendancy system in New Granada. But "without an intendancy system, structural reform of New Granada's government proved impossible."[178] The viceroyalty remained decentralized and organizationally confusing, with each region acting as its own autonomous domain. Administrators in Bogotá lacked delegates to supervise activity in the vaguely defined authority spheres – audiencias, provinces, and corregimientos – that carried over from the Habsburgs.

What about economic reforms? Were the Bourbons successful at breaking the Habsburg institutions governing the economy? Commercial reforms were at first similar to those in Venezuela. Free-trade laws went into effect in 1778, but war thwarted the entry of Spanish ships into Cartagena. "When Cartagena's trade was finally unblocked, it was not by commerce with Spain, but by permission to trade with foreigners. In March 1781, the crown allowed merchants in Cartagena de Indias to trade with ports of allied and neutral powers, thereby allowing contacts with North American ports and with the French and Dutch colonies in the Caribbean."[179] In Caracas (Venezuela), as we saw, markets in the Caribbean and the United States stimulated export production and were a boon for trade; the same was true for commerce between Caracas and Spain when peace finally allowed this trade to begin.

In Colombia, however, liberalizing reforms failed to give rise to equally impressive legal trade, leaving the region behind Venezuela at the conclusion of the colonial period. Initially, it is true, their effect was to increase commercial trade with foreigners in the Caribbean and, after 1785, with Spain itself. Cotton, tobacco, cacao, and cascarilla together amounted to 20 percent of total legal exports to Barcelona and Cádiz in the late eighteenth century (bullion represented 73 percent).[180] In addition, illegal commerce thrived in New Granada, with communities of smugglers on the Caribbean coast exchanging gold, cacao, livestock, and hides for textiles, wine, and various foodstuffs.[181] However, the overall impact of commercial agriculture on the economy was slight: the vast majority of agricultural production was intended for local markets, and export agriculture had little relevance to most Colombian farmers and landowners. A final contrast with late-eighteenth-century Venezuela clinches the point: although smaller than Colombia, Venezuela exported nearly three times as much in commercial goods; and although lacking mineral wealth, Venezuela imported more from Spain.[182] In short, as the foremost authority on eighteenth-century Colombia concludes, "Bourbon economic policy did not...succeed in making New Granada a markedly more export-oriented economy, geared to supplying metropolitan Spain with a larger, more diverse range of its resources."[183]

If Colombia did not become a "markedly more export-oriented economy," what are the major reasons why? We can first take up considerations related to geography.[184] A good deal of the population was located in the interior, and distance and unfavorable terrain imposed costs that made it very challenging for interior producers to compete in the markets abroad. On the other hand, Colombia had some geographic factors working in its favor. For one, the port at Cartagena was relatively close to Spain and historically linked to the metropolis through the system of fleets. In addition, the territory was richly endowed: livestock, cotton, tobacco, dyewoods, cacao, and indigo all could be produced locally and exported from the coastal region. Crucially, several of these goods were produced in the Cartagena province or along the coastal region itself, minimizing transportation costs. Given these advantages, we can appreciate why eighteenth-century commentators were already lamenting Colombia's failure to exploit untapped natural resources.[185]

More fundamentally, it was colonial institutions and the actors they empowered that served as a brake on Colombia's economy. The tobacco monopoly effectively stifled this promising export by levying considerable taxes and prohibiting many regions and farmers from growing the crop.[186] Cacao production was also hindered by fees on exports from Maracaibo shipped through Caracas.[187] And the special privileges of neutral trade initially granted to both Colombia and Venezuela were soon denied to

Colombia as the Crown cracked down on contraband, which of course was often financed with the Colombian gold that the monarchy so badly needed for itself. More generally, while the viceroys and other actors did encourage export products such as dyewoods, "these aims frequently were subordinated to, and sometimes conflicted with, the long-established priorities of producing bullion, defending its shipment to Spain, and preventing its leakage from the system through contraband trade."[188] Resources would have had to be dedicated to infrastructure development and loans to export producers in order to develop an economy in which nonmineral exports played a leading role. So long as gold offered such easy profits, this investment was not forthcoming from those actors most capable of making it.

Here we come to the decisive nail in the coffin of the possibility of a late colonial commercial boom: the merchant class at Cartagena. Most Spanish traders who arrived at Cartagena expected and received gold for their goods. Likewise, since the Habsburg period, the Cartagena wholesalers had traditionally viewed gold as the way to finance the imports from which they so handsomely profited. When new merchants arrived from Cádiz and Catalonia, consequently, they tended to fall into established patterns and look to specie as the singular basis of wealth. Late-eighteenth-century merchants were apparently not often closely tied to landed elites, and in this respect they were actually similar to the commercial actors who arrived at the River Plate to handle South American silver exportation in the late eighteenth century. But Colombia's merchants "contributed little to developing the territory's resources, for their connections with the colonial economy that lay beyond Cartagena were always tenuous, and their commitment to domestic development correspondingly slight."[189] Very much *unlike* their counterparts at Buenos Aires, the new merchants of Cartagena were an enclave community, largely disconnected from the interior of New Granada, and not oriented toward channeling profits into the promotion of export agriculture. They were content to leave the interior of Colombia to low-priced food producers whose sights were set on only the most local markets.

Despite its mineral wealth and scatterings of other exports, therefore, Colombia would achieve no better than an intermediate level of economic development within the hierarchy of late colonial and nineteenth-century Spanish America. Although Cartagena and the political capital at Bogotá connected Colombia to the world economy more significantly than was the case in truly isolated pockets of the empire, Colombia nevertheless had not received the kinds of institutions and actors needed for growth via agricultural exportation in this world economy.

Ethnicity and Social Development. A regionally intermediate level of long-run social development was also part of Colombia's fate. One reason is that middling economic performance tends to favor middling social development. But it is also relevant to consider the pattern of ethnic stratification that had crystallized during the eighteenth century. For, as the case of Peru so well illustrates, average economic performance does not lead to average social performance when the majority of the population is a spatially and economically marginalized ethnic group.

Colombian society featured an expansive category of "mixed race" that effectively broke down a dichotomous social structure and enabled the territory to escape the low levels of social development found in Andean regions to the south. Miscegenation during the eighteenth century moved many indigenous people into the category of mestizo, and in Colombia this category entitled them to the de facto right to participate in rural life as wage-earning hacienda residents or smallholding peasant producers.[190] With the rise of mestizos, the language of the Muiscas virtually disappeared, and populous indigenous communities became relatively rare.[191]

At the end of the eighteenth century, the only areas in which Indians were still a local majority were in the province of Pasto, in the Llanos of Casanare, and in frontier areas along the Pacific and Caribbean coasts where Indians had successfully resisted, or evaded, white encroachments. Elsewhere, Indians had become a minority in their own land, outnumbered by whites and mestizos.[192]

Quite obviously, the reduction of the indigenous peoples to a mere 20 percent of the total population stands in striking contrast to the Andean territories.

Similarly, the declining importance of slavery allowed many individuals of African descent to enter the category of mixed race (*mulato* or *zambo*). Slaves were still concentrated near plantations in the coastal region and in the western Chocó region. By the end of the eighteenth century, however, locally born slaves were sufficient to meet labor demands in the Chocó, and nonslave *mazamorreros* were already the main workers in the mines of Antioquia. Slaves were only 8 percent of the total population of Colombia in 1778–80 and 2.3 percent in 1835 (slavery was abolished in 1852).[193] Free blacks, to be sure, faced harsh discrimination and were systematically denied opportunities. In the Chocó, for instance, white-supremacist views were common, and "black farmers were not welcome near the Spanish communities or mines."[194] However, African Colombians were not very concentrated spatially. Even in the Chocó region, "a few families might cluster together, but black villages did not develop except for a few isolated *palenques* [runaway-slave settlements]."[195] Spatial proximity between Afro-Colombians, whites, and mestizos, in turn, led to substantial racial mixing. And as this occurred, it became harder and harder to distinguish between free blacks and individuals of mixed heritage.

Meanwhile, as indigenous and African people increasingly entered into mixed racial categories, white people became less separated socioculturally from these mixed races. This needs little empirical substantiation for the poorer whites who worked with mestizos and mulattos on the estates or in the mining zones. More interesting is the possibility that the Colombian white elite was also increasingly less removed from the other strata. The wealthiest individuals in Colombia – the peninsular Spaniards who made up the merchant elite in Cartagena – were, so to speak, "new money" and not part of a nobility from the prior colonial epoch. They were too oriented toward Spain and too detached from Colombian society to stand out as a visible aristocracy above everyone else. By contrast, the political elite at Bogotá included Creole nobles who traced their ancestry back to the conquistadors and who wanted to retain social distance in the eighteenth century. They still invested heavily in the status symbols of the times: churches and religious institutions, dowries, well-staffed households, education, elegant dress, landed estates, and service and contributions to the colonial government and the Crown.[196] Yet they lacked great wealth and aristocratic titles, and they never controlled government in New Granada in the way that Creole elites did in Mexico and Peru before the reforms of the late eighteenth century.[197] Given this, when Bogotá failed to grow significantly during the eighteenth century, we can only assume that the self-identified Colombian nobility also stagnated. Besides, we know for certain that authority and power in Colombia were divided among several cities and regions, each with its own small and not overwhelmingly rich group of elite actors. The division between the haves and the have-nots was considerable in each domain. But Colombia was not another Mexico or Peru when it came to the existence of a singular and integrated dominant class. This elite fragmentation probably also contributed to relatively higher social status for regular citizens in Colombia.

THE FALLEN CORES

If the rising peripheries inherited the most favorable balance of colonial institutions (i.e., significant liberal institutions without substantial prior mercantilist institutions), then the fallen cores were bequeathed just the opposite: deeply implanted mercantilist actors who were not counterweighted or over-ridden by subsequently installed liberal institutions. The once-important colonial regions corresponding to Bolivia, Ecuador, and Guatemala – each with its own still quite dense indigenous population – were now ignored by the Bourbon Crown and settlers except insofar as these actors could plunder any remaining and easily extractable resources. This kind of limited liberal colonialism only exacerbated the problematic institutional arrangements previously introduced during the Habsburg period.

Bolivia

Bolivia was a center region under the Habsburgs because of Potosí's extraordinary mineral wealth and the territory's large indigenous populations, from which the Spanish could mobilize workers. When Potosí's silver output declined dramatically in the late seventeenth century, the raison d'être for this colonial center suddenly evaporated. The Crown no longer had an interest in directing special administrative attention to Upper Peru, and Spanish settlers no longer found the barren land of Potosí a desirable place to live. Upper Peru thus descended to the periphery of the empire. With its fall, Bolivia provides an intriguing natural experiment: a region that was heavily colonized by a mercantilist power and then mostly ignored by a liberal power. As we shall see, the combination was a recipe for developmental disaster.

Descent to the Periphery. Mineral production at Potosí experienced a deep recession from the 1680s to the 1730s due to a combination of factors, including the exhaustion of near-surface high-quality deposits, declining silver prices in the world market, the Crown's enforcement of the royal quinto (unlike in Mexico, where the *diezmo*, or one-tenth tax, was used), the high cost of transporting mercury from Arica to Potosí, and the tendency of miners to accept cash payment from indigenous communities instead of mita draftees.[198] In the early eighteenth century, the value of silver output at Potosí was less than 20 percent of what it had been a century earlier. Likewise, output at Oruro experienced a precipitous decline in the one-hundred-year period after 1650. Mineral production in Upper Peru finally revived in the second half of the eighteenth century, due mostly to an upsurge in the value of silver in the world market. But the recovery failed to bring Potosí's yield even close to what it had been during the late sixteenth and early seventeenth centuries.[199] "Compared with the spectacular growth of Mexico's silver mines in the late eighteenth century," Brooke Larson writes, "Potosí's slow recovery was unimpressive to the Bourbons... Silver mining at Potosí was not particularly profitable in the late eighteenth century, and it no longer attracted entrepreneurs in possession of capital or courage."[200] In fact, at the height of the recovery, Potosí did not even produce the majority of Peruvian silver, while other areas such as Oruro never recovered at all.[201]

Colonial attention and settlement went into dramatic reversal in step with this economic decline. Populations crashed at nearly all urban centers. According to Herbert S. Klein:

It was among whites that the depression in silver production had its greatest impact. At least one hundred thousand Spanish-speaking whites migrated out of the mine centers and away from the region seeking their fortune in more economically dynamic areas of the empire. In this century-long depression, both Oruro and Potosí lost over half of their respective populations, with Potosí falling to just thirty thousand persons and Oruro to some twenty thousand by the middle of the eighteenth century. In fact, every city either lost population or stagnated in the depression period.[202]

Nor was the Spanish Crown itself much interested in mobilizing resources to Upper Peru. The monarchy let the mita decay, despite Potosí's great dependence on it. Production techniques at Potosí became antiquated, as modernization efforts from above were sporadic and never successful – a marked contrast to Bourbon policy in various mineral regions of Mexico.[203] The state also remained aloof when ambitious proposals were put forward to stimulate nonmineral sectors of the economy.[204] Finally, the intendant system that was installed here along with Bolivia's incorporation into the new Viceroyalty of the River Plate was marred by corruption and royal indifference.[205]

The simple truth is that Upper Peru had little to offer either settlers or the Crown once its mineral economy ceased to provide easy and reliable wealth. A booming colony, the territory busted when the mines failed. The once-large Spanish population of the area migrated out, not to be replaced by any new modernizing actors.

The Colonial Roots of Economic Underdevelopment. In explaining economic underdevelopment in Bolivia, it is fruitful to examine the failure of commercial agriculture – not only because commercial agriculture was vital to economic success in late colonial Spanish America, but also because it allows us to see how *both* the absence of liberal actors *and* the lingering strength of mercantilist ones inhibited development.

Some of the best land for commercial agriculture in Bolivia was to the east, in the tropical lowland areas that formed the intendancy of Santa Cruz de la Sierra – a region that remained mostly unoccupied by the Spanish. As recent history confirms, the climate and soil here are well suited for export agriculture. Francisco de Viedma, the imaginative intendant of the late eighteenth century, was rather farsighted in believing that

the possibilities for commercial agriculture were endless: cacao plantations would displace imports from Caracas and Guayaquil; coca fields would rival the established cocales of the yungas east of La Paz; rice paddies, cotton fields, and sugar plantations would substitute jungle crops for coastal imports. Alto Peru's tropical frontier would be turned into the central source for all the specialized agricultural commodities traditionally imported from distant lands.[206]

In the late Bourbon period, of course, the area was still home to indigenous groups who had previously been relocated via reducciones and Jesuit mission communities, including the Mojos and Chiquitos. But these groups were not so large that they could not be pushed aside, ignored, or, in Viedma's optimistic vision, incorporated into the commercial economy.

If neither geography nor demography foreclosed growth, what did? The answer rests with the configuration of economic actors forged through colonialism. Critically, market-oriented merchants from Barcelona and other areas of Spain never located themselves here – in no small part because of the absence of easy access to a port. When, therefore, Viedma proposed to stimulate commercial agriculture by building a road to link Cochabamba with the mission communities of the northeast, he had no investor class to back him. He encountered, instead, reactions ranging from indifference to resistance. The opposition of merchants at La Plata was notable. This group controlled the Santa Cruz route, and to them, "monopoly and privilege were considered the principles of economic advantage, no matter how many proposals set forth the ideals of unregulated trade and technological innovation. The precepts of mercantilist thought posited a static economy, in which one port's gain was another's loss."[207] Merchants in La Paz also sought to undermine Viedma's proposal, for it threatened their exclusive control of the coca trade. Skepticism about investing "scarce capital into enterprises that offered no guarantee of success" was indeed common among merchants and landlords, actors who embraced the assumption that demand was inelastic and was changeable only by the dictates of royal authority. They "were content to invest in a variety of local enterprises and leave the commercial conquest of the tropics to the fertile imaginations of 'progressive' reformers. It would take another two hundred years for Viedma's plan to be realized."[208]

Nor was there much hope for economic takeoff in the other regions of Upper Peru. For who would spur this prosperity? Certainly, it would not be the indigenous communities, which were still heavily exploited and shut out from the most profitable opportunities in the colonial economy (although they did, of course, produce for local markets). Meanwhile, landlords faced a deteriorating economic situation during the crisis. In response to labor shortages, they increasingly moved toward sharecropping arrangements.[209] Although sharecropping allowed some hacienda workers to engage in their own surplus production and escape debt peonage, neither this production nor that which occurred on land designated for the estate owner was intended for any markets other than the nearest urban center. Landlords and small producers alike looked to meet only the limited consumption demands of the poor rural society of which they were a part.

Mine owners (*azogueros*) and merchants from the Habsburg era were hardly the solution, either. The azogueros were completely dependent on the Crown for mita laborers and on outside financiers for credit. Their numbers and influence had already declined during the seventeenth century, and the economic troubles of the eighteenth century exacerbated this trend. Never an actor oriented toward long-run investment in risky enterprise, the azogueros were by the end of the colonial period thoroughly under the thumb of the colonial state and incapable of financing themselves, much less other entrepreneurial activities.[210]

This returns us, finally, to the merchant community, traditionally led by the *aviadores* (silver merchants) who controlled the mineral trade and supplied credit to the azogueros. Their profits had always come at the expense of the royal treasury. With the crisis of production, the Bourbons finally moved against them, at first by supporting the creation of a credit institution known as the Azogueros' Company, which took silver exchange out of private hands. Then, in 1779, the Crown created the Royal Bank of San Carlos to provide loans and inputs for miners. Inadequate though it was for reviving the mineral boom, the new banking institution removed a leading source of wealth for the aviadores. "As the Royal Bank came to monopolize the exchange of unminted silver and a good part of the supply of mining provisions, merchants no longer felt any attraction to provide loans to *azogueros*, as they had during the first half of the century."[211] Problems for the aviadores were compounded by the fact that the merchants at Buenos Aires were now reaping most of the profits from the import business associated with the silver trade. Never predisposed toward investment outside of their monopolistic channels, large silver merchants were undercut by the end of the colonial period. Merchant power devolved to the local level, where traders were tightly linked to and intermeshed with Bolivia's landlord class.

By the late colonial period, then, the Bolivian economy was being pushed ever more in the direction of subsistence. One of Bolivia's fundamental shortcomings was that it was an isolated territory that had been ignored during the late colonial period. But the problem was also that it had inherited powerful economic actors – now represented by backward-looking landed elites linked in complex relations of dependency with local merchants and indigenous communities – from an earlier colonial epoch, actors who obstructed the growth opportunities that did exist.

The Indigenous Population and Social Underdevelopment. The story of human well-being in Bolivia, as elsewhere in Spanish America, is intimately linked to ethnic stratification. People defined as indigenous totaled nearly five hundred thousand in the 1780s and eight hundred thousand in 1827.[212] The exact size of the non-indigenous population at these times is not known, but the number of Spanish people altogether was not large. We can infer this simply by considering data on the population of the urban areas, where many or most Spanish people would have lived. By the early nineteenth century, Potosí, Oruro, and La Plata were largely deserted, the three towns together containing perhaps thirty thousand people. The most substantial urban settlement was La Paz, but its population was only forty thousand at the end of the colonial period. Even if these urban populations were *entirely* Spanish people, the hundreds of thousands of rural indigenous people still constituted the vast majority of the total population.

Bolivian society was sharply bifurcated between Spaniards and Indians; the intermediary category of mestizo (*cholo* in Bolivia) made little headway toward breaking down the racial division. Colonial authorities and elite settlers were simply very reluctant to accept people of mixed heritage as non-indigenous.[213] The obvious explanation for this reluctance is that Bolivia's mestizo population posed severe problems for forced-labor and tribute-collection programs. To assign individuals of mixed race a measure of dignity and social standing significantly higher than that of indigenous people would pose unacceptable risks to the rural extraction system. It would allow people denigrated as Indians to escape their obligations by appealing to membership in a more favorable intermediary category. Thus, the perseverance of mercantilist practices into the late colonial period inhibited elites from pursuing anything but the most reactionary approach to racial inclusion. In turn, racial exclusion undercut social mobility for nonwhite people and left Bolivia rigidly stratified.

Since the average level of well-being in Bolivia depended mostly on the welfare of indigenous people, let us look a bit more closely at their late colonial experience. Mostly descendants of the Aymaras, indigenous people usually still lived in their own communities, concentrated especially in the La Paz province south and east of Lake Titicaca. They retained possession of substantial communal land in exchange for tribute and mita obligations. On the Aymara lands, native languages and practices prevailed. Each individual family typically controlled several small plots subject to rules on their use that were not entirely different from those of three hundred years earlier. The ayllu also still existed (though in modified form), with each one governed by its own elected leaders and with groups of ayllus represented by hereditary kurakas. "The fundamental tension within the aboriginal sector was that which pitted rich against poor, a division ordinary enough, but that now acquired a particularly unsavory appearance due to the sharp social contrasts of the time brought on by demographic compression and general economic contraction."[214] During the Bourbon period, the Crown began to apply head taxes to resident forasteros in the communities, which had the effect of diminishing migration, stabilizing communities, and increasing royal revenues. The mita still exacted a painful toll, and hacienda labor was often the only option during times of dearth. But the encroachment of the mita and hacienda institutions was of declining intensity during the eighteenth century.[215]

Yet little was well for this population, of course. The maladies facing indigenous peasant communities included both everyday problems (e.g., water shortages, inadequate diets based on quinoa and potatoes, and limited access to public works and services) and periodic crises (e.g., drought, crop failures, and hyperexploitation by the Spanish to make up for missing revenue). While such crises brought starvation and the most intense suffering to Bolivia, the everyday problems were enough by themselves to ensure deprivation and to make the new Bolivian country that emerged in the nineteenth century among the least socially developed regions of Spanish America.

Ecuador

We find at work in Ecuador the same basic causal processes as in Bolivia: the country descended to the status of colonial periphery due to an absence of possibilities for accumulation through minerals or trade, the problematic imposition of weak liberal institutions on top of strong existing mercantilist ones, and the onset of long-run economic and social underdevelopment. But in Ecuador, this pattern was played out within what had been a prosperous textile-based economy, not a mineral-dependent economy like Bolivia's. Colonial trends distinctive to Ecuador therefore need to be highlighted – including the rise of coastal Guayaquil, which had been spared the introduction of mercantilist institutions under the Habsburgs and now attracted much attention from the Bourbons.

Crisis and Peripheralization. Thoroughly dependent on the sale of cloth in markets in Lima and New Granada, Ecuador's entire economy was thrown into deep crisis when textile manufacturing collapsed during the eighteenth century. The highland textile industry plummeted to the point that it generated zero or even negative profits by the second half of the eighteenth century. In terms of output, Robson Brines Tyrer estimates a decline of at least 50 percent and perhaps as much as 75 percent from 1700 to 1800. His data also show "a considerable decline in the number of obrajes and the number of Indians employed in cloth production."[216] Once the profits for the region's *paño azul* (indigo-dyed fabric) disappeared, Quito's wealthy merchants were no longer able to procure silver, which sapped Ecuador of the capital necessary to keep all other components of the highland economy afloat.

These basic facts are not in dispute among historians; nor are the general causes of Ecuador's depression much debated anymore. The obvious immediate source of falling profits was the introduction of cheap, high-quality European cloth into the colonial market. In the early eighteenth century, "French traders began flooding the Pacific markets with European cloth. In effect, this inundation of European imports ended the period of Spanish mercantile protection most responsible for the growth of the *Quiteño* cloth manufactories."[217] Although the Bourbon monarchy eventually stemmed these illegal French imports, its own easing of trade restrictions permitted European textiles to make headway in the mid-eighteenth century. Matters only deteriorated with the proclamation of free trade, around which time English textiles put further pressure on Ecuadorian producers. "In short," as Kenneth J. Andrien concludes, "by liberalizing trade restrictions and allowing the introduction of high-quality imports, the crown effectively ended the traditional oligopolistic arrangement responsible for the prosperity of Quito's mills."[218]

People left in great numbers from the sierra provinces where the obrajes had once flourished. Many north-central provinces had negative population growth rates; the overall population of the Audiencia of Quito stagnated.[219] Urban areas with large numbers of Spanish families also experienced declines. Both the city and the corregimiento of Quito, where most people were classified as "non-Indian," saw population decreases in the late colonial period.[220] The diminishing Spanish population signaled Ecuador's transformation into a colonial backwater within the Bourbon empire.

An Exception: Guayaquil. There was a regional exception to the trends described so far. The coastal city of Guayaquil experienced no crisis and no depopulation; rather, it underwent an economic and demographic boom during the late colonial era. While it makes sense to regard Ecuador as a whole as moving from semiperiphery to periphery during this period, the region of Guayaquil is best understood as following the opposite trajectory: periphery to semiperiphery.

Bourbon colonial attention quite naturally turned away from the land-locked highlands to coastal Guayaquil, as the city featured a port location ideal for shipping cacao and other tropical goods that could be produced on neighboring plantations.

The reform of Spanish commercial policy from the 1770s began an unprecedented escalation in coastal plantation agriculture... Although estates on the fertile coastal plain produced copious amounts of tobacco, hardwoods, and sugar, the cultivation and export of cacao became the most lucrative regional economic activity. The crown further encouraged this export boom in 1779 by halving the port taxes (*almojari-fazgos*) on all goods leaving Guayaquil and on all shipments of cacao entering other American ports. As a result, from the 1790s the province and port of Guayaquil could participate directly in both colonial and global markets for cacao, which ensured regional prosperity until the rapid decline in world prices for the crop by the 1840s.[221]

As the export sector expanded, the Guayaquil province became the fastest-growing part of the audiencia. Indigenous forasteros migrated here from the north-central highlands; the size of the Spanish population also increased. "Internal migration and newcomers from Spain pushed the number of Euro-peans from 2,300 in 1765 to just under 5,500 in 1790... Most of them settled in the city of Guayaquil (where they formed over 25 percent of the residents) or in parishes involved in the export economy."[222] Guayaquil was transformed into an urban center, with residents working in the arti-san, craft, and commercial sectors. Although the city was not as large as Quito, it was gaining ground, and its exports made it a consequential part of the audiencia.

Guayaquil's port location was the basis for its economic rise. This becomes quite clear when one compares Guayaquil with the intendancy of Santa Cruz in Bolivia – another region that, as we saw, was suitable for agro-export production (including cacao) and also not fettered by an entrenched colonial order or settled indigenous population. Guayaquil succeeded where Santa Cruz failed because, with its coastal location, export products could be profitably shipped to distant markets without having to incur the substantial land-transportation costs that Santa Cruz's goods inevitably did. Yet even though geography was critical in this basic way, Guayaquil still faced some of the same obstacles as Santa Cruz. Calling attention to these problems is important if we wish to understand why Guayaquil could not carry the rest of Ecuador to a higher level of economic development. Here, contrasts between Guayaquil within Ecuador and Montevideo within Uruguay are enlightening.

Ecuador's prior status as a colonial semiperiphery left roadblocks that thwarted the possibility that Guayaquil might lead an economic takeoff in the way that Montevideo did for Uruguay. In Uruguay and the rest of the River Plate, new traders and merchants could succeed because they did not have to contend with a previously established mercantilist coalition. This was a fortuitous legacy of peripheral status during the mercantilist era. Uruguay's nascent bourgeoisie could look outward to a still relatively wide-open hinterland that was mainly organized around wage-labor ranching estates and that lacked conspicuously present indigenous settlements. But things were quite different in Ecuador. Once-prosperous merchants suffered mightily under the new liberal regime, and they stood strongly opposed to the market-oriented adjustments that allowed for the economic expansion of Guayaquil.[223] Besides, the crisis conditions they faced robbed them of the capital needed to control the Guayaquil trade. The leading economic role in Guayaquil consequently fell to large merchant houses from Lima and New Spain, which ended up marketing Guayaquil's exports, overseeing imports from Europe, and controlling most of the profits.[224] Emerging local commercial actors were too weak to compete with these powerful preexisting forces:

Guayaquil's planters and merchants faced considerable disadvantages in controlling the sale and marketing of regional exports. Coastal elites lacked the large capital resources and access to credit abroad needed to sell their exports in the most lucrative retail markets in Spain and the Indies. As a result, they could never hope to compete with the larger metropolitan and colonial merchant houses... Consequently, the coastal export economy prospered, but it lacked the potential to generate large profits capable of transforming the coast into a dynamic, diversified, and more independent economic center in the Pacific basin.[225]

Economic dynamism could not be extended beyond the coastal region. For the interior of Ecuador lacked the purchasing power and the potential for revenue generation needed for long-run growth. It featured, instead, the impoverished remnants of what had been a heavily penetrated colonial region under the Habsburgs. Historically exploited and culturally separated, the vast indigenous communities could not provide the needed internal market for European imports. Nor could markets expand in a context of impoverished Spanish consumers, whose better-off members had always depended on royal restrictions for wealth and who still relied heavily on surplus extraction from indigenous people. Whereas Montevideo's merchants could look west to promising markets, foreign merchants in Guayaquil saw little potential when they looked east at the crisis-ridden and impoverished interior. Instead, they saw Guayaquil for what it was: an isolated and disconnected pocket within an otherwise unsalvageable (from the perspective of economic growth) Kingdom of Quito.

Economic and Social Underdevelopment. To complete our explanation of the onset of long-run poverty in Ecuador, we need to consider explicitly the late colonial actors whose positions and behaviors underpinned this outcome. Mercantilist actors centered in Quito – who were forged under Habsburg regulations – were reconfigured during the Bourbon era. Under the liberalizing reforms, many of the *obrajeros* (textile mill owners) went bankrupt, though some of the larger, privately owned mills were capable of maintaining profits (it was the *obrajes de comunidad* that were especially unable to compete).[226] Quito's leading merchants sometimes tried their hand at the textile business by purchasing rural obrajes to support their commercial enterprises in the face of dwindling income. However, given the deterioration of demand in Peru for the Quito product, these new merchant-producers were not successful, either. Long accustomed to easy wealth via state regulation, they failed to adapt to the newly competitive textile environment and became but another obstacle to economic development. Ecuador's notably powerful church also suffered greatly – for it, too, was strongly tied to the obraje economy, both as a financier and as a leading mill owner. The church was no more able to reinvent itself in the new economic climate than were the conservative merchants.

With other options closed off, control over land and rural labor represented the increasingly exclusive fallback for economic security in late colonial Ecuador. Wealthy citizens often still owned one or two textile workshops or engaged in commercial activities, but they relied ever more heavily on their large landed estates for material well-being.[227] In terms of their contribution to the economy, however, these large estates yielded only basic foodstuffs for small, state-regulated local markets. They were never designed to be – and could not be – efficient competitors in deregulated markets beyond the nearest towns that they supplied.[228]

Indigenous people, still mostly concentrated in the north-central sierra despite migration, made up the bulk of the workforce on these haciendas. Around Quito and Latacunga, in fact, more than 60 percent of indigenous people were registered as *conciertos* – that is, resident hacienda workers.[229] In some other highland places, the majority of indigenous people continued to live in subsistence-producing villages, but sizable numbers were nevertheless employed on Spanish estates. Work as a concierto had certain advantages, given prevailing colonial institutions. The permanent estate workers were exempted from tribute obligations, offered a small plot of land to cultivate, and paid a wage (though meager and insufficient, leading to debt peonage). By contrast, in the villages, indigenous people lacked access to monetary income, faced heavy taxation when money did circulate, and were still subject to forced labor, including sometimes the mita.

Severe deprivation was thus unquestionably the late colonial situation for indigenous people, even though historians debate the specific impact of the crash of the obrajes.[230] To make things worse, under the Bourbon order, large increases in taxation and tribute collection fell especially heavily on native communities.[231] These policies were in fact the trigger for the rebellions in Ecuador during the late eighteenth century.[232] When independence came, the tribute practices remained in full effect.[233] Ecuador, with its dense indigenous population and economic poverty, therefore naturally found itself at the bottom of the regional hierarchy of social development in the early nineteenth century.

Guatemala

Guatemala also failed to develop the institutions and actors necessary to avoid underdevelopment. Nevertheless, the region did briefly spawn a promising indigo industry, and its place as an underperformer within Spanish America was less overdetermined than one might suppose, given its current position in the regional hierarchy. Surprising as it may seem now, late colonial Guatemala had certain similarities to the rising peripheries of South America. And one can better appreciate the sources of Guatemala's long-run economic underdevelopment in the context of these similarities.

Recovery and Crisis. Indigo exports were the backbone of Guatemala's economy during the eighteenth century. Although indigo was harvested mostly in the hot Pacific lowlands of El Salvador, it was financed by Guatemalan merchants and transported to the Guatemalan capital to be taxed. From there, it was delivered to the Caribbean coast and shipped to Cádiz via the port of Santo Tomás, only to be reexported to the textile-producing countries of England and Holland. Production surged after 1760, when annual output was roughly double the average for the previous fifty years; contraband trade running from the Atlantic side also thrived.[234] Legal and illegal exportation in turn allowed merchants to import a stream of goods from Europe, China, and South America. With indigo commanding a leading place in the world market – Central American indigo was considered the best-quality dye that could be purchased – Guatemala generally prospered.[235]

The Guatemalan indigo boom bears some notable similarities to Venezuela's experience with cacao during the mid-eighteenth century. Guatemala even had certain advantages that Venezuela lacked. The structure of indigo production in the Audiencia of Guatemala – very much *unlike* cacao production in Venezuela – featured a substantial role for small-scale peasant producers. These farmers, mostly Salvadoran ladinos of modest means, likely accounted for a majority of all production, and they certainly produced the great majority of the highest-quality indigo for which Guatemala was renowned and which was so vital to its ability to compete in the world market.[236] Small indigo producers may not have been exactly equivalent to the wage-earning gaucho workers of the River Plate, but as a producing class, they probably resembled the gauchos more than they did the enslaved African workers who carried out the cacao harvesting in Venezuela.

Yet despite this comparatively advantageous labor structure, Guatemala was unable to achieve even the intermediate economic prosperity that Venezuela captured by the end of the colonial period. Venezuela diversified its exports in the late eighteenth century and continued to grow into the nineteenth. But Guatemala remained a mono-crop economy, stagnating in the late eighteenth century and collapsing into utter crisis by the end of the colonial period. Guatemala could not keep up with Venezuela's new indigo exports; nor could the audiencia move to other potential exports, such as cotton and coffee. Consequently, when the price for indigo declined and wars interrupted trade, the region rather suddenly "faced severe economic turmoil... and the economy came crashing down."[237] Indebted small producers were reduced to subsistence farming or turned to haciendas as wage earners, while merchants suffered in the absence of the trade revenue that sustained their import and financing businesses. At the time of independence, Guatemala was thus only tenuously linked to the newly available markets where Venezuela had strong footholds.

The Causes of Stagnation. To explain these developments, we need to refer back to relevant actors from the Habsburg period while also taking note of the absence of significant institutional transformation under the Bourbons. Paying attention to Guatemala's merchant class brings both sets of considerations nicely into focus.

Although many of Guatemala's richest merchants were new migrants,[238] "they were Spanish mercantilists in their fundamental outlook," and quite out of step with the Bourbon changes percolating elsewhere.[239] They were dependent on traditional trading houses in Cádiz, and they were part and parcel of the monopolistic trading system created under the Habsburgs. Throughout all of Central America, they were the main source of loans and cash and the principal buyers and distributors of goods. Spanish reformers therefore found themselves "confronted with a monopoly – an undesirable weed in an atmosphere of liberalized commerce – which already had taken deep root and was in full flower before the implementation in America of laws enacted to increase production and trade."[240] To be sure, the reformers (e.g., appointed captains general) tried to dislodge them. They encouraged new traders by opening alternative ports. To eliminate merchants' control over pricing, they transferred the location of the indigo fair and moved to impose government-fixed prices on the sale of indigo. In all such endeavors, however, the Crown proved miserably unsuccessful. Commercial traffic remained centered at the old port of Santo Tomás and was still very much controlled by the Cádiz merchants. As Troy S. Floyd points out, diverting the commercial stream toward new ports

> would have required that the government encourage merchants in Barcelona or northern Spain to enter the Salvadoran indigo trade and to trade directly with Honduras and Nicaragua...The fact that no such attempts were made suggests that Bourbon commercial reforms were too narrowly conceived and did not take into account the deep entrenchment of commercial interests established before reform efforts in America were attempted.[241]

Nor could efforts to control the indigo fair and set pricing succeed without a more intensive effort. The Bourbon financing scheme was far too underfunded to provide the capital needed for harvest. Besides, merchants simply ignored the royal orders. In no time at all, the colonial government conceded and returned control of the sale and pricing of indigo to the merchants, who then organized their own guild to thwart any further attacks.[242]

Of course, Guatemalan merchants were not so potent that the Bourbon monarchy would have failed to overpower them if it had been willing to devote enough resources to the effort. But the monarchy was unwilling to move decisively against them – in contrast, in this instance, to what had occurred with the merchants of Venezuela, where Bourbon policies did ruin the Caracas Company. For in contrast to Venezuela, which had held economic promise, the Audiencia of Guatemala seemed to offer very little and thus was not worth the effort. The economic problems were numerous. Although the port at Santo Tomás was the best corridor for shipping El Salvador's indigo, its use still required a difficult overland journey, across treacherous terrain.[243] The impoverished and disconnected Central American population provided an unintegrated and unpromising market for European imports. And the huge difficulties of extracting silver within the audiencia only continued during this century.[244] Worse, the area was subject to periodic natural calamities, as was most obviously apparent when earthquakes forced authorities to move the capital from Santiago to Guatemala City. Santiago had already stopped growing during the previous century.[245] In 1782, after the move, the new capital's population fell to about thirteen thousand, with only 3,338 people classified as of European descent.[246]

Imperial neglect, in turn, meant that no rising bourgeoisie was present to counter the traditional merchant class. Left unchecked, the merchant monopoly maneuvered in ways that bred market failure and the crisis of the late eighteenth century. When Guatemalan indigo faced heightened international competition, the merchants simply squeezed Salvadoran producers with lower prices while maintaining their own artificially high profits. And to compensate for declining interest rates, they paid less for the best-quality indigo, which diluted overall indigo quality.[247] The consequence was that Guatemala lost its comparative advantage. Meanwhile, taxes here remained especially high under the Bourbons, which placed a further burden on producers.[248] The overall result was bankruptcy for large and small indigo producers alike and economic crisis for the region.

It obviously follows that life chances and social well-being were very poor for the vast majority of individuals in this part of the empire. And ethnic stratification only exacerbated these tendencies. Ladinoization had occurred in urban areas and around the regions associated with commercial agriculture (e.g., southern Guatemala).[249] But western Guatemala, where the Maya states had been centered, remained almost entirely indigenous (and significant pockets of indigenous people were located in the north and east as well).[250] Overall, Guatemala's 270,000 indigenous people made up two-thirds of the total population at the end of the eighteenth century, with the Quiché group (which was now defined to include Cakchiquel, Quiché, and several other non-Mam linguistic communities) representing most of the total.[251] Native groups retained communal rights to lands, but they frequently lost the fruits of their labor to the Spanish officials, friars, and local merchants who inhabited the western indigenous highlands.[252] As in many other parts of Spanish America, this was an ethnic-stratification system that left most people at the bottom and fostered much social hardship.

THE SUSTAINED PERIPHERIES

Finally, it is time to examine the sustained peripheries – those countries whose history was marked by low-intensity colonialism during both the Habsburg and Bourbon periods. As we shall see, these regions were not "advantaged" by the Bourbons in any of the ways that the rising peripheries were. Yet these places had not been disadvantaged under the Habsburgs, as the fallen cores had. They thus endured the least significant colonial imprinting in the region, which left long-run outcomes much more open in these countries than elsewhere. The paths of postcolonial development in the sustained peripheries, in fact, depended heavily on what specifically happened in the decades immediately following independence. We must therefore finish the analysis of these cases in the next chapter, looking at a time when postcolonial processes at last differentiated these countries into higher and lower levels of development.

Chile

Chile was a relatively marginal territory under the Bourbons, even though it attracted a fair number of settlers during the eighteenth century. This colonial marginality was rooted, most simply, in Chile's inability to generate considerable wealth through either minerals or agricultural exports.

Gold production in northern zones did increase during the mid-eighteenth century. However, "although mining was Chile's most dynamic activity, most mines were small. Large-scale mining...simply did not exist."[253] Overall mineral output remained modest in comparison to that of Colombia, not to mention late colonial Mexico and Peru.[254] Nor were there any prominent nonmineral sources of prosperity. Unlike Peru, Chile lacked almost entirely an internal market of its own, ensuring that Valparaíso was a far less economically important port than Callao. It is true that Chile's northern region supplied some wheat to the Lima market; for some historians, this exportation signaled an important transformation.[255] But from a comparative perspective, wheat production was very limited before the mid-nineteenth century, and it certainly did not yet connect the territory to any distant markets. As Arnold J. Bauer points out, the export economy of late colonial Chile looked much as it had before: "Between 1750 and 1850 few changes occurred in the external markets of Chilean agriculture. Its isolated geographic position and scarcity of the population on the Pacific coasts...made it difficult to increase exportation."[256]

Nor did the free-trade reforms of 1778 have much impact. The Chilean market was already oversupplied with imported goods, and in the absence of successful export commerce, the situation remained the same when the reforms went into effect.[257] Indeed, with high military expenditures and a poor import/export ratio, Chile found itself deeply indebted and facing serious economic problems at the end of the eighteenth century.[258] Commercial actors looked almost exclusively to local markets as the basis for recovery. In fact, to handle the trade deficit, "the merchants of Santiago advised decreasing trade to Europe."[259]

No liberal actors consolidated themselves here and overturned the prevailing social and economic relations. According to several analysts, about twenty-four thousand immigrants came to Chile between 1701 and 1810, including Basque traders.[260] And the overall Chilean population increased steadily during the Bourbon period; Santiago itself grew to a good-size city of perhaps thirty-two thousand people by the end of the eighteenth century.[261] Despite these population trends, however, Bourbon transformation was not evident in other, more important areas: local elites continued to dominate the cabildo and the audiencia; the practices of the heavily taxed trade running through the Cádiz monopoly remained unaltered; and the structure of production and the leading class groups of society were intact. This last point carries the implication that traditional merchants were still tightly connected to – even fused with – the landed elites of the central valley. The merchants continued to import goods for hacendados in exchange for a few easily transported items. Further, "the alliance between the landlords of the central valley and the merchants was not limited to this symbiotic relationship;

there was also extensive intermarriage between the two groups."[262] It was not until 1810, when legislation moved things in a more market-oriented direction, that this fusion started to break down.[263]

Meanwhile, changes *were* occurring in the ethnic composition of society. "The Indian population, which must have represented 40 to 50 percent of the total population in 1700, was reduced to less than 10 percent" by the end of the eighteenth century.[264] Although the south remained a colonial frontier, still controlled by hostile indigenous societies until the late nineteenth century, inhabitants of the more populous central-valley region converted into mestizos. These mestizos were often service tenants (*inquilinos*) who paid off land rents with their labor. According to Brian Loveman:

If *inquilinaje* in Chile bore some resemblance to *colono* or service-tenant labor systems in other Latin American nations, its origins and the predominantly mestizo composition of its work force distinguished it from the harsher arrangements involving Indian labor in Peru, Bolivia, and Ecuador. Even when economic conditions worsened, Chilean *inquilinos* as a class did not experience systematic cultural and ethnic repression on the scale of the rural labor forces in the Andes, nor did debt peonage typically restrict their mobility.[265]

The absence of ethnic bifurcation meant that life conditions for Chilean workers were surely better than for workers in the Andes. At the time of independence, nevertheless, Chile was still a very poor region within the empire, lacking entirely the economic dynamism it would have needed in order to rise to the upper echelons of social development in Spanish America.

Paraguay

"As the colonial era drew toward its end, few in Madrid would have been able to locate Paraguay on a map of the empire."[266] The territory still had no gold, silver, or other easily exploitable precious resource. Its most important urban area, Asunción, was an unimpressive town trapped in an interior with difficult access to Europe and other parts of the empire.

The poor state of the few roads and the almost utter absence of bridges made travel and the transport of goods and ideas a torturous process. Travel, even at the pace of an oxcart, became impossible during frequent rains, and a Paraguayan living more than fifty miles from the capital was locked in dismal isolation. In such circumstances, what change came to Paraguay came creeping on all fours.[267]

Worse still, there was hardly anyone with sufficient resources to purchase goods, even if merchants could have brought them from the capital to the hinterland. For this was an overwhelmingly rural society, composed of isolated producers living on small, almost self-sufficient farms and ranches. They had no money or influence with which to attract traders from distant parts.[268]

Colonial attention and liberal institutional development would have surely required the appearance of a significant export product in Paraguay. Wild yerba leaves for maté tea – whose production did increase somewhat in the late colonial period – could not fit this bill; the South American yerba market was not large, and there was never a European market for the tea. Besides, the merchants at Buenos Aires and the Spanish Crown itself controlled the yerba profits, not any Paraguayan trader class.[269] The other possible exports included cotton, tobacco, and cattle. But these also never took off, partly because of problematic ecological conditions and geographic isolation, partly because yerba absorbed all of Paraguay's small local labor force, and partly because there was no concerted effort by the Crown to try to stimulate production of the more profitable commodities, except tobacco.[270] We must remember, too, that the Spanish authorities in Paraguay faced recurrent threats. They were challenged not only by hostile indigenous groups, especially nomadic tribes of the Chaco, but also by the meddling Portuguese contrabandists.[271] These realities forced residents to serve extended tours of military duty – yet another obstacle to settlement, political stability, and growth.

Paraguay was therefore comparatively ignored throughout the colonial period. This is not to imply, obviously, that two hundred and fifty years of colonialism left no mark. The colonial mark was imprinted quite deeply on indigenous people – an estimated forty thousand of them now living in special villages from which they were still routinely exploited (including those who resided on enclaves left behind by the Jesuit missions) and the remaining twenty thousand hunter-gatherers, who faced intense oppression from encroaching frontiersmen.[272] Yet in comparison to many other parts of the empire, Paraguay in the late colonial period could not be said to have a large indigenous population – in terms of sheer numbers, visibility, or economic contribution. Taken as a whole, Paraguay was too marginal during the colonial period for Spanish institutions and their concomitant actors to be treated as the leading culprits in Paraguay's eventual status as one of Spanish America's poorer countries.

El Salvador

More than most areas, El Salvador during the second half of the eighteenth century was the site of production for agrarian exportation. Indigo harvested in the provinces of San Salvador and Sonsonate constituted almost all of Central America's late colonial exports to Cádiz.[273] Despite this, the intendancy of San Salvador, which was created under Charles III, remained unimportant for the duration of Bourbon rule. Spanish settlers did not migrate here, and liberal colonial institutions were not laid down. David Browning's description is apt: "Though the main towns boasted stone churches and paved streets, they were in fact little more than overgrown villages offering a simple and often primitive life and few urban amenities."[274] In 1807, when El Salvador's population was estimated to be two hundred thousand, only fifty-six hundred Spanish people were living here.[275]

Why was El Salvador's export production not associated with more extensive Bourbon colonialism? The answer is related to the marketing of indigo, which ran through the Guatemalan merchants at the port of Santo Tomás. These merchants, we have seen, siphoned off most of the profits from indigo. Any fortunes to be acquired in Central America thus required control over commerce in Guatemala, not production in El Salvador. Production was in fact led by small and medium-size ladino growers, who were responsible for some two-thirds of all indigo harvested and an even higher proportion of the best-quality product.[276] The Bourbons were inadequate in their defense of these growers, leaving them at the mercy of the Guatemalan merchants for capital and transportation. Their fate became tragic when the market for indigo declined at the end of the colonial period. "Most producers were mortgaged to the Guatemalan merchants, who advanced loans for production. Once the recession set in, the merchants seized the indigo holdings for nonpayment of debts."[277] Indebted Salvadoran export producers then returned to growing basic foodstuffs and livestock, often on land that they no longer owned.[278]

Still, El Salvador did not inherit from the colonial period ossified institutions that outright prevented economic development in the decades after independence. Haciendas were present in the central and western regions, with San Salvador being their core market, but they occupied only one-third of the total area of El Salvador. They were not particularly large or labor-intensive; small producers were common everywhere, including as renters on hacienda land.[279] Local merchants existed, but the capital-rich, monopolistic ones all hailed from Guatemala. El Salvador thus appears to have been a very poor region that was not especially constrained later on by the type of colonial institutions and actors that it had acquired.

Although today El Salvador is a nation of mostly ladino citizens, in the late eighteenth century it was a territory evenly divided between ladinos/mulattos and indigenous people; Spanish citizens represented only a tiny fraction of the total. Indigenous communities controlled one-third of Salvadoran land and visibly embraced their own modes of dress, language, and lifestyle.[280] The late colonial period thus featured, as Aldo A. Lauria-Santiago reports,

the existence of communal and ethnic autonomy of both Indians and Ladino peasant communities throughout El Salvador... By the late eighteenth century, a distinctive colonial institution – the Indian community – emerged side by side with an emerging Ladino peasantry with its own communal forms of land use and organization. As the Ladino population increased and some Indian towns became fully Ladino, many Indian communities grew and expanded their landholdings.[281]

The ladino population typically viewed the indigenous population with contempt. Therefore, even if El Salvador had achieved more economic prosperity during the late colonial period, it is likely that much of the population would still not have risen from situations of extreme poverty. Given the absence of both wealth and ethnic homogeneity, the outcome of poor social development was sealed for postcolonial El Salvador.

Honduras

If the puzzle of El Salvador is why it was marginal in the colonial period despite much agrarian production for export, then for Honduras the challenge is identifying exactly what was missing that prevented significant exportation under the Bourbons. Answers can be found by considering, in turn, mineral production and agrarian production.

Silver and gold mining continued modestly in the old, established regions, and several new fields were developed during the eighteenth century, mainly within the jurisdiction of Tegucigalpa. According to Linda Newson, "At the end of the eighteenth century about 100,000 pesos of silver was being smelted or amalgamated annually, but this is a considerable underestimate of the amount of silver mined, because much of it was smelted illegally and smuggled across to the Caribbean coast for sale to the English."[282] It is reasonable to ask why royal attention did not follow this mineral wealth, all the more so given that Spain had interests in countering the British presence on the Mosquito Coast. Critical here was the small size of the indigenous population, viewed by the settlers as an insurmountable obstacle to successful mining. In 1804, Honduras's estimated total population of 127,600 included only about 35,000 indigenous people, mainly descendents of the Lencas, who lived mostly in eastern parts that were not under Spanish control.[283] True, since the mid-seventeenth century, indigenous workers had been made available to miners under the repartimiento. But mine owners nevertheless found it exceedingly difficult to obtain adequate labor. And the profitability of the mines was not sufficient for them to pay the high wages needed to attract alternative (noncoerced) workers. These miners also lacked the capital to take serious investment risks in this chancy industry.[284] Honduras's eighteenth-century mining industry thus sputtered and mostly failed for want of the conditions found in more important colonial areas.

In the right context, this factor – the sparseness of the indigenous population – might have attracted liberal colonization and stimulated agrarian export production, as occurred in the rising peripheries. One can imagine how this might have unfolded. Perhaps settlers could have specialized in products derived from livestock – for which the grasslands of Olancho were well suited – and exported them through the ports at Trujillo and Omoa, both of which were declared free in 1784.[285] After all, Honduran ranchers had long raised cattle and sold them to Guatemalan merchants at annual fairs; why not therefore export hides overseas in exchange for textiles, as Argentina and Uruguay did? The root problem in this regard was that the Honduran ports were not strategic in the way that the ports at Buenos Aires and Montevideo were. The River Plate had to be protected and privileged by the Crown, because it was the best location for shipping silver. But the ports at Honduras served no similarly vital purpose for the Crown; Spain would have liked to secure them from the British, but this was not economically feasible. Furthermore, compared to even the Guatemalan port at Santo Tomás, those at Trujillo and Omoa were not well linked to an interior where goods could be sold profitably. Transportation between the Honduran coast and the heartlands of the audiencia was greatly complicated by distance and difficult terrain.[286] Besides, the Honduran cattle producers were constrained by the Guatemalan merchant monopoly in many of the same ways that Salvadoran indigo producers were. In sum, any attractiveness that Honduras held as a site of liberal colonialism deriving from its sparse population was undercut by the absence of possibilities for merchants to make this region a base for market-oriented accumulation.

Lastly, with its abject poverty, Honduras was not to be a site of social progress. It is quite possible that, had the economic resources materialized, social development would have followed. For this was not a society deeply stratified by ethnicity and class privilege. In western and central Honduras, the ladino-indigenous distinction was vaguely defined at the end of the colonial period.[287] Furthermore, as a society of ranchers and community farmers, Honduras lacked a powerful landed elite in any sense of the word. Perhaps today it is hard to think of Honduras as a country that could have eventually performed well on human-development indicators. But at the moment of independence, the region was more egalitarian than most areas of Spanish America and no poorer than its neighbors Nicaragua and Costa Rica. Honduras's place as a backwater and eventual banana republic was a result of its failure to grow during the mid- and late nineteenth century.

Nicaragua

Mostly ignored during the Habsburg period, Nicaragua remained a humble colonial region under the Bourbons, with late colonial reforms causing barely a ripple. León won the intendancy capital, but its late-eighteenth-century population was only about a thousand Spaniards and less than ten thousand people altogether. Other urban areas, such as the towns of Granada and Nicaragua, had even smaller Spanish populations. During the late colonial period, a majority of Spaniards actually lived in indigenous villages or on landholdings in the countryside, not in Spanish-style towns. Individuals considered indigenous probably still accounted for around half of the region's estimated 150,000 people, but ladinoization was steadily occurring, especially as encroaching Spaniards and ladinos came into frequent interaction with indigenous communities.[288] With no fresh mineral discoveries and few possibilities for harnessing labor for commercial production, Nicaragua held little interest for colonial authorities and settlers.

One can construct scenarios in which export-driven development might have occurred. Like Honduras, Nicaragua was nicely suited for livestock raising; its ranches provided the majority of cattle sold at the audiencia's annual fairs.[289] In addition, modest quantities of good-quality indigo were produced here. There were thus some possibilities. Yet if overseas commerce were to have taken hold, Nicaragua would have needed an alternative to the obligatory, costly, and circuitous trade route that ran via Guatemala City to the Honduran port of Omoa. Local actors would have had to overcome the same Guatemalan merchants who controlled profits and hobbled the economies in El Salvador and Honduras. Local merchants and landlords were well aware of the sources of their troubles. They explicitly sought royal support for the development of a water route across the province that would provide access to the Atlantic and its markets. One group of notables, for instance, argued the following in a 1798 petition: "This miserable and abandoned kingdom would be reborn and flourish . . . if overseas commerce could be conducted through the San Juan River and Lake Nicaragua."[290] Perhaps this is true. Certainly, indigo and livestock products could have been more cheaply shipped to the Caribbean and Europe. And the transit route would have brought commerce from many other parts of the empire.

But even if technologically feasible, a canal connecting the Atlantic and Pacific oceans was not going to be constructed in Nicaragua by the Bourbons. For the entire Central American region was never promising enough as a source of commercial wealth for the Crown to mount a serious challenge to the Guatemalan merchants. And this was a necessary precondition for any radical rearrangement of commercial routes in the isthmus. Moreover, given that the Spanish did not even secure the Pacific side of Nicaragua, including the region around the San Juan River, how could the Crown even contemplate a large-scale construction operation there? Spain failed to entice settlers to inhabit this tropical region even when the Treaty of Versailles in 1783 and the associated Mosquito Convention in 1786 obligated the English to evacuate the Mosquito Coast. The commerce that did exist remained in private British hands; an overstretched Spain had to look away and pay attention to more pressing matters elsewhere. Nicaragua was left to fend for itself.

Costa Rica

Diego de la Haya Fernández, in his report to the king in 1719, characterized the Costa Rican province that he oversaw as "the most poor and miserable in all of America."[291] Other eighteenth-century observers tended to agree – and not without some justification. For toward the end of the colonial period, the entire province was home to only about fifty thousand people, concentrated in nucleated villages surrounding the capital at Cartago and at nearby Heredia and San José. A large majority of these residents were poor ladino farmers not far beyond subsistence and barter; few indigenous settlements remained.[292] Life for most Costa Ricans revolved around their village. Here they grew staples such as corn and beans, and here they bought and sold food and handicrafts in daily local markets. In many villages, some individuals were artisans, and a few others were merchants. The largest merchants in the Central Valley amassed wealth by controlling the overland trade between Nicaragua and Panama. But the extent of this trade was always so limited that the wealthy Costa Ricans were really no more than village notables.[293] Cattle and cacao were the main exports, though they were never significant, and they declined at the end of the colonial period. A royal tobacco monopoly was also established in San José during the late colonial period, but this industry, too, tended toward stagnation and did not enrich Costa Ricans.[294]

Historical observers have long linked the poverty and relative isolation of Costa Rica during the colonial period with its later developmental success. The typical reasons given for this link, however, require one to embrace an unsustainable "rural democracy" interpretation of colonial Costa Rica. This interpretation casts the region as a homogenous, egalitarian society of individualist yeoman farmers living in isolation from one another.[295] Such equality and self-focused individualism are viewed as having provided the sociocultural foundations for later success. Yet in fact, as Lowell Gudmundson has shown, the colonial period left a social structure that was quite incongruous with this imagery. Late colonial Costa Rica was really a society in which

> access to agricultural land was not based primarily on private appropriation of isolated smallholdings, but rather on a mixture of nonprivate cultivation of common lands by village members, smallholding on the outskirts by villagers not resident on their plots, and estate ownership by the wealthy... Clear differences of wealth and status existed within older villages, not only between elite and commoner, but also within the latter group.[296]

Similar conclusions are obtained by Iván Molina Jiménez, who also suggests that village group solidarity and a collective mentality – not any special peasant individualism – were basic features of Costa Rican culture, much as elsewhere in Spanish America.[297]

There are other reasons why Costa Rica's peripheral status might have provided advantages for development. For example, according to José Antonio Fernández Molina, "the relative isolation of Costa Rica... became a benefit because provincial merchants, who had been marginal and therefore had built no rigid trading system, were able to adapt to the new trade opportunities beyond the Kingdom of Guatemala."[298] Yet while Costa Rica did reap some of these benefits, its overall colonial heritage was not dramatically different from that of several other peripheral countries, some of which – notably Nicaragua, Honduras, and El Salvador – did not develop nearly as much. Neither an institutional nor a geographic perspective provides any real reason to believe that at the time of independence, Costa Rica should have suddenly out-competed these other areas. The full answer to the puzzle of Costa Rican success will require us to move past the colonial period and consider events during the nineteenth century – events that advantaged this area in ways not true elsewhere in Central America.

CONCLUSION

Under the late Bourbon monarchy, there were two distinct paths to higher levels of colonial settlement and institutional implantation. In one, a previously marginal territory obtained the status of colonial center or semiperiphery because of its comparatively sparse indigenous population and strategically located port city. This pathway – that of the rising periphery – was exemplified by Argentina, but it also applied in diminished form to Uruguay and Venezuela. In another path, a territory received substantial colonial attention (including settlers and institutions) because it had been a core Habsburg colonial region and continued to provide wealth via the extraction of precious metals. This mercantilist-carryover pathway had Mexico as its exemplar and Peru and Colombia as its diminished examples. All other territories lacked the causal combinations that lay behind these pathways, and their status under the Bourbons was one of colonial periphery.

We can formally specify the aggregate logic of this argument with the tools of set-theoretic analysis (as in Chapter 3). At the most macroscopic level, as Table 4.2 shows, four main causal factors are in play: (A) small indigenous and African population; (B) strategic port; (C) mercantilist colonial center; and (D) new mineral wealth. The columns code the extent to which cases are members of each of these factors, with 0.0 representing little or no membership, 0.5 standing for partial membership, and 1.0 corresponding to full or nearly full membership. The last column (Y) summarizes the degree to which cases are members of the category liberal colonial center, where 1.0 represents a colonial center, 0.5 indicates a semiperiphery, and 0.0 stands for a periphery. Generally, the coding for "small indigenous and African population" is based on the size of these groups during the late colonial period, as discussed above. "Strategic port" captures the extent to which a territory featured a shipping port that was appropriate for overseas trade and that was linked to a viable internal market. "Mercantilist colonial center" codes cases according to whether they were centers, semiperipheries, or peripheries in the mercantilist era. And the scores for "new mineral wealth" are based on the extent to which silver and/or gold deposits were discovered in and exported from a territory during the Bourbon period.

The evidence supports the interpretation that a small indigenous population and a strategic port (i.e., A & B) *or* a mercantilist-center status and the presence of substantial mineral wealth (C & D) were each sufficient for

Table 4.2. Determinants of center, semiperipheral, and peripheral colonies: Liberal era

Country	(A) Small indigenous and African population	(B) Strategic port	(C) Mercantilist colonial center	(D) New mineral wealth	(A & B) v (C & D)	(Y) Liberal colonial center
Argentina	1.0	1.0	0.0	0.0	1.0	1.0
Bolivia	0.0	0.0	1.0	0.0	0.0	0.0
Chile	1.0	0.0	0.0	0.5	0.0	0.0
Colombia	0.5	0.5	0.5	0.5	0.5	0.5
Costa Rica	1.0	0.0	0.0	0.0	0.0	0.0
Ecuador	0.0	0.5	0.5	0.0	0.0	0.0
El Salvador	0.5	0.0	0.0	0.0	0.0	0.0
Guatemala	0.0	0.5	0.5	0.0	0.0	0.0
Honduras	1.0	0.0	0.0	0.5	0.0	0.0
Mexico	0.0	1.0	1.0	1.0	1.0	1.0
Nicaragua	1.0	0.0	0.0	0.0	0.0	0.0
Paraguay	1.0	0.0	0.0	0.0	0.0	0.0
Peru	0.0	0.5	1.0	0.5	0.5	0.5
Uruguay	1.0	0.5	0.0	0.0	0.5	0.5
Venezuela	0.5	1.0	0.0	0.0	0.5	0.5

Note: 1.0 = full or nearly full membership; 0.5 = partial membership; 0.0 = little or no membership. The "&" symbol stands for the logical AND, and the "v" symbol stands for the logical OR.

colonial-center status during the Bourbon phase. We can see this by looking at the perfect matching between the codes for the overall expression (A & B) v (C & D) and the codes for liberal colonial center (Y). While the claims in this chapter must stand or fall primarily on the far richer supporting evidence embodied in the narratives for each case, it nevertheless increases confidence to show that the argument holds up as logically coherent when summarized in this aggregate way.

From this perspective, Argentina and Mexico are the region's only full-blown liberal centers, because these are the only cases with a coding of 1.0 for both small indigenous population and strategic port (Argentina) or both mercantilist colonial center and mineral wealth (Mexico). Uruguay and Venezuela are diminished versions of Argentina because either the indigenous/African population was not particularly small (Venezuela) or the region's relevant port city was less economically strategic (Uruguay). Peru became a diminished version of Mexico because its mineral wealth was less extensive, and Colombia was a diminished version of Mexico not only because of its less impressive mineral wealth, but also because it was not previously a full-blown colonial center.[299]

Concerning the peripheral regions, each of these cases possessed one or more relevant causal factors in a full or partial form. Chile, Costa Rica, and Paraguay had very small indigenous populations (and this was partially true in El Salvador, Honduras, and Nicaragua as well); Chile further had some mineral wealth; Bolivia was a former colonial center; and Ecuador and Guatemala had moderately important ports. Yet each of these cases also *lacked completely* other relevant causal variables – in particular, entirely missing was the causal factor that had to combine with the partially or fully present one for a nonperipheral pathway to consummate. For instance, while Chile was like Argentina in its absence of a large indigenous population, it lacked the strategic port found in Buenos Aires – not only because of its isolated Pacific coast location, but also because it had no internal market to stimulate trade. As a result, Chile remained suspended as a periphery, whereas Argentina rose up to become a center. With Bolivia, a comparison with Mexico is useful: both Bolivia and Mexico had been Habsburg centers, but the mining economy totally busted in the former, while it boomed in the latter. As a result, Mexico remained a colonial heartland, while Bolivia faded into oblivion. Clearly, the full explanatory story for these cases is much more complicated than this, and many of those complexities are entertained in the presentation above. These summary tables and concluding remarks are intended to highlight only aggregate, general patterns.

With this analysis of levels of liberal colonialism, we are furthermore in a position to summarize the determinants of long-run economic and social development. We can now, finally, consider how different levels of mercantilist colonialism (the focus of Chapter 3) and liberal colonialism (the focus of this chapter) themselves combined to produce particular levels of

Table 4.3. *Pathway to higher economic development*

Country	(A) Mercantilist periphery	(B) Liberal center or semiperiphery	A & B	(Y) Higher level of economic development
Argentina	1.0	1.0	1.0	1.0
Uruguay	1.0	1.0	1.0	1.0
Venezuela[a]	1.0	1.0	1.0	1.0

Note: 1.0 = full or nearly full membership; 0.5 = partial membership; 0.0 = little or no membership. The "&" symbol stands for the logical AND.
[a] Venezuela could alternatively be coded as 0.5 for mercantilist periphery (A) and 0.5 for level of economic development (Y). See the analysis of Venezuela in the text.

development. Let us therefore close the discussion by spelling out the general causal logic for those nine countries that were not peripheries during both phases of colonialism. In the next chapter, we will return to the six other countries – the sustained peripheries – and the special issues that they raise.

Of this set of nine, the three countries that achieved the highest levels of long-run economic development were Argentina, Uruguay, and Venezuela. As Table 4.3 summarizes, these cases were all peripheries during the mercantilist period. But they acquired the status of center or semiperiphery during the liberal period. And it was this combination of mercantilist marginality and liberal centrality that produced their higher levels of economic performance. Because Argentina and Uruguay were ignored by the Habsburgs, they never received the institutions that created obstructionist mercantilist elites. Their primary colonial institutional heritage came from the late Bourbons, and it was characterized by institutions conducive to the creation of market-oriented actors – including a late colonial commercial bourgeoisie. Venezuela, for its part, inherited more considerable mercantilist institutions and actors. During the last decades of the Bourbon period, nevertheless, Venezuela attracted substantial liberal colonial attention, and it was the institutions and actors thereby forged that gave the newly independent country a growing economy and an intermediary level of prosperity.

The colonial pathway to the lowest levels of economic performance ran in the opposite direction: it involved mercantilist centrality and liberal peripheralization. This was the trajectory of Bolivia, Ecuador, and Guatemala, the three fallen cores (see Table 4.4). These cases acquired, so to speak, the worst of what Spanish colonialism had to offer: embedded mercantilist institutions and actors and little in the line of liberal institutions and actors. Bolivia was the exemplar of this pattern, for it inherited from the Habsburgs quite backward-looking landlords and uncompetitive local merchants who continued to dominate the economy during the Bourbon period. Any growth opportunities in Bolivia went unexploited for want of

Table 4.4. Pathway to lower economic development

Country	(A) Mercantilist center or semiperiphery	(B) Liberal periphery	A & B	(Y) Lower level of economic development
Bolivia	1.0	1.0	1.0	1.0
Ecuador	1.0	1.0	1.0	1.0
Guatemala	1.0	1.0	1.0	1.0

Note: 1.0 = full or nearly full membership; 0.5 = partial membership; 0.0 = little or no membership. The "&" symbol stands for the logical AND.

an entrepreneurial commercial class. Ecuador and Guatemala, which were somewhat less important mercantilist colonies, nevertheless ended up in much the same position. The prior establishment of mercantilist elites in these regions undercut commercial actors who otherwise could have spurred broader development.

A third pattern of economic development is represented by Colombia, Mexico, and Peru, all of which achieved intermediate levels. These mercantilist-carryover cases were semiperipheral or center territories during both the Habsburg and Bourbon phases (see Table 4.5). Their colonial heritage was a *hybrid* one, witnessing the implantation of significant mercantilist institutions *and* significant liberal institutions. The latter institutions fostered actors who spearheaded some export-oriented growth in the late colonial period, but groups associated with the former effectively limited the extent of this development. In Mexico, the superimposition of more-competitive institutions on top of the preexisting mineral and locally oriented agrarian economy was fraught with contradictions, limiting economic dynamism and export success. In Peru and Colombia, powerful actors from the Habsburg era also could not be fully dislodged during the Bourbon period, putting the brakes on late colonial growth and long-run economic performance.

Finally, relative levels of *social* development had their own determinants (see Table 4.6). To be sure, higher levels of economic development were

Table 4.5. Pathway to intermediate economic development

Country	(A) Mercantilist center or semiperiphery	(B) Liberal center or semiperiphery	A & B	(Y) Intermediate level of economic development
Colombia	1.0	1.0	1.0	1.0
Mexico	1.0	1.0	1.0	1.0
Peru	1.0	1.0	1.0	1.0

Note: 1.0 = full or nearly full membership; 0.5 = partial membership; 0.0 = little or no membership. The "&" symbol stands for the logical AND.

Table 4.6. *Determinants of levels of social development for the nonperipheral colonial regions*

Country	(A) Small indigenous and African population	(B) Higher level of economic development	A & B	(Y) Higher level of social development
Argentina	1.0	1.0	1.0	1.0
Bolivia	0.0	0.0	0.0	0.0
Colombia	0.5	0.5	0.5	0.5
Ecuador	0.0	0.0	0.0	0.0
Guatemala	0.0	0.0	0.0	0.0
Mexico[a]	0.0	0.5	0.0	0.5
Peru	0.0	0.5	0.0	0.0
Uruguay	1.0	1.0	1.0	1.0
Venezuela	0.5	1.0	0.5	0.5

Note: 1.0 = full or nearly full membership; 0.5 = partial membership; 0.0 = little or no membership. The "&" symbol stands for the logical AND.

[a] Mexico's level of social development at the conclusion of the colonial period and during the nineteenth century was 0.0. The score of 0.5 reported here corresponds to its average performance for the twentieth century. For a discussion, see Chapter 6.

associated with higher levels of social development. Yet the relationship was partial, with exceptions to the overall pattern. More exactly, the presence of a higher level of economic development (average or better) was necessary for a high level of social development. But it was not sufficient. For example, among the nine countries that were not sustained peripheries during the colonial period, Peru, Venezuela, and pre-revolutionary Mexico all underperformed in the area of social development relative to economic development – they all had higher levels of economic development than social development. In order for economic development to actually promote social development, it had to be combined with another necessary cause: a small indigenous and African population. The size of the indigenous and African population was consequential for initial levels of social development because this population was invariably an oppressed and/or exploited stratum of society, not entitled to whatever fruits might be disseminated from available economic resources and trickle down to promote general health and well-being. These benefits were indeed potentially more considerable in a context of higher economic development, but this mattered little if a large portion of the society was defined in a way that precluded citizenship. Thus, at the time of independence, territories such as Mexico, Peru, and Bolivia were not destined to perform well on social indicators, for resources could not reach societal majorities.

5

Warfare and Postcolonial Development

Independence was a powerful yet finite force, which tore through Spanish America like a great storm, sweeping away the lines of attachment to Spain and the fabric of colonial government, but leaving intact the deeply rooted bases of colonial society.
– John Lynch

War did have some of the expected results in Latin America. As in Europe, it often led to the destruction of the losing side... Among winners... [war] provided the expected economic stimulus.
– Miguel Angel Centeno

Colonial history was not destiny for the six territories that were peripheries under both the Habsburg and Bourbon monarchies. Chile, Costa Rica, El Salvador, Honduras, Nicaragua, and Paraguay emerged from colonialism as extremely poor new nations. This initial backwardness was, to be sure, a direct outgrowth of their colonial experience as sustained peripheries. Yet colonial institutions and actors were so weakly implanted in these countries that it remained possible for them to improve their situation in the decades immediately following independence. Less strongly imprinted than the colonial centers and semiperipheries, the sustained peripheries were capable of reinventing themselves.

Successful reinvention of economies and societies in the immediate aftermath of colonialism was hardly guaranteed, however. Of the six sustained peripheries, only two managed to rise from the bottom of the region's economic hierarchy. It was specifically Chile and Costa Rica where postcolonial actors established competitive economies and sustained real growth via primary exports during the decades that followed independence. Once takeoff occurred, these two held their status as good performers within the region across all the ensuing decades. In the other cases, outcomes were different. El Salvador, Honduras, and Nicaragua experienced no economic takeoff. And any development that perhaps initially occurred in Paraguay was soon undone. These nations have ever since endured lower levels of development.

The central purpose of this chapter is to identify the factors that allowed Chile and Costa Rica to capitalize on the "advantages" of having been permanent colonial backwaters in ways that El Salvador, Honduras, Nicaragua, and Paraguay could not. In this inquiry, institutions and geography are not irrelevant, but they are also not the most important considerations. The influence of colonial institutions is secondary because they did not vary in critical ways across these countries. The sustained peripheries were, speaking in the broadest terms, fundamentally alike by virtue of the relative absence of entrenched institutional orders upheld by the typical (mercantilist or liberal) stakeholders. Colonialism is thus critical only in the sense that its limited expression is what allowed development to remain contingent on postcolonial events.

Nor can geographical endowments help us much in accounting for the different outcomes. In Central America, all countries had ecologies with basically similar potentials for export agriculture, including especially coffee and/or banana exportation. Costa Rica's success derived not from any palpable geographic advantage it held over its neighbors. Rather, it succeeded because actors exploited, early on, an export potential that also existed – but was not realized – in the other Central American countries. Even landlocked Paraguay was not so disadvantaged by geography that postcolonial development was impossible; growth occurred there in the mid-nineteenth century, and for a time Paraguay functioned as a regional power.

Instead of colonial institutions or geography, attention in the search for causes must gravitate toward interstate warfare. For what really gave Chile and Costa Rica an advantage over the other four nations was their ability to elude the adverse consequences of international war – consequences that fell upon Paraguay, Honduras, Nicaragua, and El Salvador quite tragically. The point is not that development outcomes are generally dependent on the results of international war. When countries are thoroughly institutionally imprinted, those imprints usually reappear in the aftermath of war, returning the country to its prior developmental trajectory. The sustained peripheries are exceptions precisely because they lacked well-defined institutions. The form of their institutions could therefore be redirected by the contingencies of warfare and the resource shifts that it might bring.

THE EFFECT OF WARFARE ON DEVELOPMENT

The consequences of warfare for long-run development can be seen most basically in the fact that wars in part create the very states that experience (or do not experience) development. "War made the state, and the state made war," as Charles Tilly famously declared.[1] Although Tilly and most others have Europe in mind when calling attention to the state-making effects of wars,[2] it is certainly true that warfare helped carve out the country borders in Spanish America.[3] The wars of independence, in particular, played a leading role in constituting or at least reinforcing the territorial boundaries that define the units of analysis in this study. If the outcome of this warfare had been different, it is possible, for instance, that Uruguay and Bolivia never would have existed as independent states at all, or that departments such as Guayaquil and Tucumán would have become countries of their own.

Wars also shape development in ways that go beyond their role in state constitution.[4] Obviously, the human toll, the destruction of property, and the territorial shifts that war fighting may bring can have a dramatic impact on immediate growth rates. These economic effects sometimes cause a fundamental shift in a country's level of development. This is especially likely if wars undermine prevailing state institutions and trigger basic transformations in the societal distribution of power. The new institutions and actors that emerge out of such realignments may then foster exceptionally high (or low) growth rates over long periods of time. Conversely, the absence of warfare can promote long-run development if it allows a new country without well-defined institutions to forge effective ones that otherwise would not have come into being.

"Latin American states have only rarely fought one another," Miguel Angel Centeno points out.[5] And the few international wars that have occurred are, by historical standards, fairly simple affairs motivated by basic territorial competition. During the nineteenth century, approximately fifteen international wars occurred in Latin America.[6] Several of these, however, were simply battles that continued over time with the same countries involved. And some of them included the sustained peripheries – episodes of war fighting that are discussed below. If one leaves aside these cases, only two major wars stand out as potential candidates for redirecting development trajectories: the wars of independence (1808–26) and the Mexican–American War (1846–8). Solid evidence suggests that these two did not redirect development trajectories or overturn the colonial legacy. Let us briefly examine this evidence.

The wars of independence were violent and destructive; they saw the collapse of the colonial fiscal system, the disruption of the mineral economies, and the elimination of the colonial political order.[7] But for all their upheavals, these wars are remarkable in that over the long run, they actually changed little besides political institutions. "Spanish America slowly rebuilt itself," notes George Reid Andrews, "along lines not greatly dissimilar to what existed before."[8] Though infused with popular mobilization, the independence movements were really elite-led affairs, and they served to protect preexisting landed and commercial interests in the new nation-states that formed. These elites were, in the end, the ones best positioned to take advantage of any new economic opportunities that developed or to save themselves from the worst effects of dwindling economic possibilities.[9] In fact, because independence entailed the end of many "inefficient" colonial practices, the consequences of this period for long-run economic development in the region as a whole were actually quite mixed. It is hard to claim that the wars of independence were a cause of economic depression, much less the underdevelopment of Spanish America.[10]

Nor do variations in the location and extent of the violence during the early nineteenth century explain why some Spanish American countries were more prosperous than others following independence. Areas that were relatively peaceful did not tend to rise up in the regional hierarchy; areas that suffered the worst violence did not tend to plunge downward. In Central America, for example, independence from Spain came without violence, but this region remained quite impoverished. The same was true for Paraguay. By contrast, enormous upheavals shook Uruguay. Yet old and new cattle ranchers and sheep farmers still prospered in the midst of the wars; and toward the end of the nineteenth century, Uruguay was still one of the richer countries in the region. Remarkably, even for Mexico and Peru, where the violence associated with independence exacted its greatest toll, there was little movement in their economic positions within the regional hierarchy (as we shall see in Chapter 6). In an explanation of different trajectories of national-level development in Spanish America, in short, the independence period was not a decisive turning point.

Mexico's subsequent total defeat in war with the United States was also not an occasion for a fundamental shift in its relative level of development. Doubtless the loss of all territory above the Rio Grande, as well as California, undercut enormous future development possibilities, including the capacities of northern states to fully exploit the changes brought about by the Mexican Revolution (as we shall see).[11] But at the time, regions usurped by the United States were still wide-open territories. Their seizure did not immediately depress the economy at all. "As these vast provinces which amounted to almost half of Mexico's territory were almost entirely uninhabited and had few known resources," Jan Bazant points out, "their loss as such did not have a disruptive effect on the Mexican economy."[12] We also need to remember that Mexico was not stable or making any particular progress in the period before the war. "From 1821 to 1850, Mexico was in a state of constant turmoil. In thirty years there were fifty governments, almost all the result of military coups and eleven of them presided over by General Santa Ana."[13] The United States provoked Mexico in the first place because it knew that its feeble neighbor could not put up much of a fight. Against this backdrop, the violence of the war does not stand out as any redirecting occurrence that broke up some prior period of peace and prosperity. At the end of the war, the economy had the same basic strengths and weaknesses as before.

Among the countries that were not sustained peripheries, then, no wars during the nineteenth century tore asunder institutional orders and channeled countries toward radically new positions within the regional hierarchy. Only in the sustained peripheries were postcolonial wars of such great consequence. And only in Chile and Costa Rica did warfare (or its avoidance) actually help postcolonial actors to forge new institutions and improve the country's level of development from a starting point of backwardness. To understand why this is true, we need to look at these cases more closely.

COSTA RICAN EXCEPTIONALISM IN CENTRAL AMERICA

After independence, all of Central America was soon united as a single, sovereign entity known as the Federation of Central America (1823–38). Within this federation, the province of Costa Rica was at first the most isolated and unappealing part. Yet seclusion was actually an advantage. For while all of the other provinces quickly became engulfed in warfare and political chaos, Costa Rica escaped such devastation and made tentative economic strides forward. Then, when the federation broke apart into sovereign countries, Costa Rica's autonomy enabled it to avoid the conservative resurgence that bolstered colonial heritages and blocked liberal progress among all the other Central American countries. By the mid-nineteenth century, Costa Rica had achieved rudimentary state centralization, initiated significant land privatization, and begun exporting substantial quantities of coffee. All of this happened while the rest of the region languished in economic depression.

Comparative evidence from Central America leaves few doubts that Costa Rica's exceptionalism is found with this remarkable turn of events in the decades right after independence from Spain. As early as the 1820s, Costa Rica was converting communal lands into private lands, whereas that process was not initiated until after midcentury in Guatemala, El Salvador, Nicaragua, and Honduras.[14] Then, under the administration of Braulio Carrillo (1838–42), Costa Rica experienced an early "liberal reform" whereby state-centralization measures were enacted and civil and criminal laws were codified to guarantee the protection of persons and property and the enforcement of contracts. Similar liberal reform epochs also occurred in the other countries, but not until the 1870s and 1880s.[15] By midcentury, Costa Rica's coffee exports were sizable, and the country became the first in the region to establish a commercial bank and a land registry. Meanwhile, Honduras remained dependent on traditional products destined for local consumption, obtaining only modest revenues from mineral exports. And while El Salvador and Nicaragua were to become major coffee exporters, this advancement had to await reforms in the 1870s and 1880s. When coffee economies were peaking in El Salvador and Nicaragua, in fact, the total value of Costa Rica's per capita exports in pesos was still many times greater. By 1892, according to Lowell Gudmundson and Héctor Lindo-Fuentes, "Costa Rican per capita exports were approximately five times greater than in El Salvador, six times greater than in Honduras, and more than ten times greater than in Guatemala and Nicaragua."[16] Unsurprisingly, travelers to Central America during the late nineteenth and early twentieth centuries remarked upon the comparative industriousness and prosperity of the Costa Ricans.[17]

Not only did Costa Rica become more economically dynamic than the rest of the region, it also demonstrably outperformed its neighbors on human development as measured by education and working conditions. Here the organization of the early coffee economy is of great explanatory import. Coffee production in Costa Rica was overwhelmingly in the hands of small growers who used mostly family labor. During the entire period from 1840 to 1935, according to Ciro F. S. Cardoso, "there was an absolute predominance of small farms, in terms both of numbers and of the total area of land occupied."[18] No entrenched landed elite of any kind was featured in this economy. Nor was there ever in Costa Rica a large subservient labor force that functioned under highly coercive controls. The smallholder economy was instead built around nucleated villages where "landholding per se was not the defining characteristic or basis for power."[19] The elite that did exist instead derived its wealth from the commercial aspects of coffee production, specifically the financing, processing, and marketing of the crop. In such a context, the extension of public goods could be viewed in positive-sum terms. Costa Rican elites, for example, introduced the late-nineteenth-century education reforms that made this nation a regional leader in literacy. These elites also showed tolerance for other state activities that served broad sections of society, including providing access to credit for small farmers, infrastructure projects, and systems of justice that applied the rule of law broadly.[20]

One might suppose, as many in fact do, that the egalitarianism of Costa Rica's coffee economy was ultimately rooted in the small size of the indigenous population inherited from the colonial period. This idea is sometimes combined with the notion – discussed earlier – that Costa Rica had a special colonial inheritance of "rural democracy," one that featured a homogenous social structure of yeoman-type peasants.[21] But in truth, all of the Central American countries – except Guatemala – came out of colonialism with demographic and natural-resource endowments that offered broadly similar chances for development. In terms of ethnic composition, all of them were already overwhelmingly ladino nations (again excluding Guatemala and possibly, to a lesser degree, El Salvador). The idea that early-nineteenth-century Costa Ricans were substantially less indigenous and more European than Nicaraguans or Hondurans has never been linked to any evidence; it may be simply one of several nation-building myths that Costa Rican leaders invented after significant developmental success had already occurred and the country had become "the Switzerland of Central America." One might insist, nevertheless, that the small size of the Costa Rican population (regardless of its ethnic composition) during the nineteenth century made it very unlikely that this nation would develop labor-intensive plantations. On this point, we need to note that Costa Rica was no less densely populated (in terms of persons per unit of land) than Nicaragua and was actually more densely settled than Honduras.[22] Furthermore, Costa Rica's coffee was grown in the Central Valley, exactly the area where most Costa Ricans already lived, so that drafted labor would have been feasible during the nineteenth century. Costa Rica avoided severe land concentration and the use of coerced labor not because of its sparse population, but because its national and local governments early on promoted the small farmers, actively undermined the land grabbers, and refused to build up the military in ways that would have encouraged coercive labor systems. By contrast, in the other coffee-producing countries of Central America, state actors enacted land and labor laws that fostered inequality and economic polarization, and they encouraged the state militarization necessary for the intensely repressive agrarian orders that were consolidated.[23]

El Salvador, Honduras, and Nicaragua emerged independent with key elites eager to enact liberal-oriented changes, including by stimulating export agriculture. And these elites presided over territories that were well endowed for such agriculture (especially coffee and bananas). During the Federation of Central America, furthermore, early liberal reform legislation was passed to promote export agriculture in each of the provinces. Yet in sharp contrast to Costa Rica, these reforms were never implemented in the other provinces. For how could they have been? The rest of the region was immediately thrown into devastating warfare that precluded making any changes at all on the ground. Dozens of battles with many hundreds of deaths marred the histories of El Salvador, Honduras, and Nicaragua during the federation period.[24] The political effect was to bring conservative administrations back to power in El Salvador, Honduras, and Nicaragua, delaying the onset of liberal-oriented changes until the late nineteenth century. As Rafael Obregón Loría suggests, the Federation of Central America was "little more than a series of wars and struggles, internal revolutions . . . and localist pretensions" that destroyed early liberal reform efforts. What stands out is that "only Costa Rica had been able to avoid for the most part these maladies."[25] As crippling warfare befell Central America, Costa Rica remained neutral in federation matters and avoided bloody engagements with its more powerful neighbors.[26] Then, after the federation collapsed, Costa Rica's isolation and the fact that President Carrillo was opposed to the unionist cause helped this country escape the invasions from Guatemala that purged liberals and reinstalled conservatives everywhere else.

The critical difference in Costa Rica, then, was not so much that its immediate post-independence leadership was more farsighted or commercially oriented than elsewhere in Central America. Rather, the main difference was that in Costa Rica, liberal leaders were able to consolidate power and enact enduring reforms without being supplanted by conservatives. And they were able to accomplish this feat only because they did not become embroiled in the warfare that wreaked havoc in the rest of the region.

CONTRASTING PATHS: CHILE AND PARAGUAY

From the isthmus of Central America, we move now to explore the sharply diverging postcolonial paths followed by the two sustained peripheries of South America, Chile and Paraguay. The Chilean case illustrates that warfare could be a boon for development if it provided leaders with extraordinary new resources for growing the economy. The Paraguayan case, by contrast, shows that massive defeat in warfare was devastating for prosperity even if a country was not heavily dependent on the world market for its development.

Chile

"Sixty years after independence Chile was an altogether more prosperous land than would have seemed likely in 1810," writes Simon Collier.[27] Indeed, during the course of the nineteenth century, Chile evolved impressively, from a marginal colonial periphery into a regional economic leader. To understand why, comparisons and contrasts with Costa Rica prove enlightening.

As in Costa Rica, liberals in Chile were immediately politically dominant. And they moved quickly and successfully to promote growth via trade, including by ending commercial restrictions for Chile's four ports and lowering and simplifying tariffs.[28] Chilean elites were able to enact these liberalizing reforms because, like their counterparts in Costa Rica, they enjoyed remarkable political stability. Crucial in this respect was the victorious outcome in the war with the Peru-Bolivia Confederation (1836–9). Chilean colonial settlers had been battle-tested during their wars with the Mapuche. Now, when the military challenges of the postcolonial period presented themselves, Chile was well equipped to defeat its northern rivals and force them to split their threatening alliance. The effect of the war was, above all else, to stabilize things politically.[29] Liberals in Chile subsequently ruled mostly unchallenged by conservative actors seeking to restore the previous colonial order.[30]

Chile also enjoyed an advantage not found in Costa Rica: substantial mineral resources. The country's northern mines were largely unaffected by warfare, and, with new discoveries, gold, silver, and copper all became leading exports. Valparaíso, long a sleepy port town lacking strategic links to a profitable interior, suddenly became a bustling city, "the emporium of the Pacific." Merchants arrived there in significant numbers and furthered trade relations with Europe, especially Britain, from where many of them hailed. Then, after 1849, the California gold rush opened up whole new markets for Chilean wheat. In conjunction with the mineral exports, wheat and flour exports fueled an unprecedented economic boom:

The number of ships calling at Chilean ports rose to about 4,000 per year by 1870, a more than tenfold increase since 1840. The value of foreign trade showed a fivefold increase between the mid-1840s and the mid-1870s, from roughly 15 million pesos to 75 million per annum...The government was thus confident that it could rely on a generally buoyant source of income. Revenues did indeed rise, from around 3 million pesos in the early 1840s to over 16 million in 1875.[31]

Still, with the international depression of the mid-1870s, this economy faced serious problems as the world price for copper plummeted. In addition, the booming export market once enjoyed by Chilean grain evaporated when the United States became self-sufficient.[32] The inevitable consequence was a balance-of-payments crisis and a near collapse of the financial sector.

Renewed war fighting, instigated by Chilean political leaders, provided not only a solution to the downturn but also a guarantee that the Chilean nation would enter the next century as one of Spanish America's wealthiest. The War of the Pacific (1879–83) pitted Chile against its rivals Bolivia and Peru once more. At stake this time were disputed borderlands rich in lucrative nitrates. Although Chile was renowned as "the Prussia of the Pacific," in fact its army was no longer very impressive. Instead, its prowess rested with a strong navy and a comparatively developed economy that could support prolonged warfare. And these superiorities proved decisive: Chile eventually overwhelmed the Bolivian-Peruvian forces and made them pay a huge price. The terms of settlement expanded Chile's territory by one-third, including control over the nitrate mines. And the booming exports that followed erased the depression and stimulated huge returns well into the twentieth century:

Much as the victory in the early nineteenth-century war against the Peru-Bolivia confederation had helped to consolidate the Chilean polity, another war against the same adversaries...now provide[d] Chile with a new "golden goose" – the nitrate fields of the Atacama desert. The nitrate boom... allow[ed] the hard economic realities of export-dependent development to be put off for another four decades.[33]

Meanwhile, for Peru and Bolivia, the war put an exclamation point on their status as fallen cores.

A final contrast needs to be made in order to understand why Chile, despite its comparatively high level of economic development, would not surpass Costa Rica in the arena of social development. Ethnic composition is not the difference. For even more than Costa Rica, Chile was prone to understand itself as a nation of European immigrants, given that, at the end of the colonial period, the Mapuche and other native groups had already been reduced to less than 10 percent of the population and then lost all autonomy and most of their lands by the 1870s.[34] More causally important was the pronouncedly inegalitarian pattern of landholding in Chile during the nineteenth century. The basic problem was the persistence of large haciendas whose resident *inquilinos* faced heavy burdens and marginal life chances. "During the years following 1860," Arnold J. Bauer explains, "the institution of *inquilinaje* was extended and by 1930 had hardened into a conservative symbiosis with the hacienda system."[35] The countryside in late-nineteenth-century Chile indeed resembled Mexico more than Costa Rica in its relations between landowners and producers. Thus, while Chile's lucrative minerals and its forcibly acquired nitrates ensured it an even higher level of economic development than Costa Rica would enjoy, its land-tenure relations did not feature and empower small producers, as was the case with Costa Rica's small coffee farms. Chile could therefore not turn its substantial wealth into an equal measure of social development.

Paraguay

In both Costa Rica and Chile, nascent liberal actors capitalized on available natural resources and inaugurated prosperous export economies. But what would have happened if, even in the absence of warfare, these nascent liberals had not existed or had been too weak to seize the reins of state power in the immediate decades after independence? Would development have been possible without a liberal elite leading the way? Paraguay during the nineteenth century gives us a lens for deciding.

Paraguay's initial postcolonial development prospects were in some ways even more promising than Costa Rica's. For whereas Costa Rica started with no export base, Paraguay had seen notable yerba exports and the creation of an emergent merchant class during the late colonial period. According to Thomas Whigham, this was "a region of real potential ... for a thriving export economy."[36] Furthermore, as in Costa Rica, the usual block to social progress was absent: Paraguay had an ethnically homogenous population that "consisted almost wholly of (bilingual) assimilated mestizos, Creoles, and Indians, with Spanish and Guaraní characteristics. Peninsulares, other foreigners and blacks were so few in number that they scarcely affected the picture."[37] Any resources that were generated from exports might therefore disseminate broadly here, as they did in Costa Rica.

But the resources never fully materialized in Paraguay – the potential was not realized. At first, the trouble was political-economic conflict with Argentina. Buenos Aires strangled landlocked Paraguay's foreign trade by imposing heavy taxes or banning outright the use of river routes, which made Paraguay's exports completely uncompetitive. José Gaspar de Francia, who infamously ruled Paraguay with an iron fist from 1814 until his death in 1840, dealt with the situation by restricting contact with Buenos Aires and imposing self-sufficiency on the new nation. Francia permitted only bare-minimum levels of commerce with Argentina and Brazil (and no other direct trade) through the Pilar and Itapúa ports. The result was the stifling of exports: "Exports fell from 391,233 pesos in 1816 ... to a mere 57,498 pesos in 1820."[38] Under Francia, the value of total exports never reached even half of what it had been during the late colonial period.[39]

Until midcentury, then, Paraguay was an isolated and quite underdeveloped country, though self-sufficient and relatively egalitarian. Francia had imprisoned or executed the small commercially oriented elite, eliminating those most poised to promote trade and economic growth.[40] The state became the nation's leading landowner when it seized ecclesiastical properties and forced rural residents to show proof of ownership or relinquish their property.[41] National identity as encompassing a mixture of Spanish and Guaraní traits was cemented through policies that prohibited whites from marrying other whites and otherwise discouraged the presence of any European elite. "The Negroes and mulattoes rapidly lost their group identity ... The Indians ... became increasingly indistinguishable in their way of life from the majority of the ordinary – mestizo – rural population."[42] When Francia died, most citizens were poor mestizo subsistence farmers who owned small patches of land or worked as tenants on state properties.

Paraguay's unusual start was hardly auspicious, but it still left open some possibilities. The next president, Carlos Antonio López, "was far more liberal in outlook than the dictator Francia," and he sought to promote the trade of yerba and tobacco. The timing was good, because Argentine trade restrictions were loosened in the 1840s, and free river navigation returned after 1852. Better economic times followed. Yerba exports reached pre-Francia levels by the 1860s, and they were supplemented with additional income from the export of tobacco and hides.[43] The new model of growth was market-oriented but also state-led. Thus, yerba and tobacco were actively promoted as exports while still being held under state monopolies. Likewise, Paraguay's railway, telegraph, shipyard, and iron facilities – impressive by the regional standards of the time – were sponsored by the state, often as part of its defense industry but also with development in mind.[44] Private investors were not prohibited, even though they had to operate under the watchful eye of the state.

It was ultimately a devastating defeat in war that closed the door on long-run progress. The War of the Triple Alliance (1864–70), fought between Paraguay and the allied countries of Brazil, Uruguay, and Argentina, was the bloodiest conflict in all of Latin American history.[45] Paraguay entered the war with perhaps the largest military of any Spanish American country – thousands of troops, extensive artillery, and a large naval squadron. But Paraguay was no match for the combined forces of Brazil and Argentina.[46] By its end, the war had exacted an unprecedented toll: it reduced Paraguay's prewar population of 300,000–450,000 to 220,000–240,000. Depending on one's estimate, 50–90 percent of the male population perished from the fighting, disease, and hardship of the conflict.[47] Postwar treaties with occupying Brazil and Argentina then diminished the size of Paraguay. Asunción was left as a chaotic and lawless haven for criminals. The overall consequences for the economy were profound: "Agricultural production had practically ceased by 1869; a once thriving cattle industry disappeared; the short railway was wrecked and its rolling stock was unusable; vacant farmsteads fell into decay; and scores of villages were ghostly reminders of more prosperous days."[48] Paraguay did eventually rebalance its population and reassert itself in the international market. But it did so now as one of the poorer countries in Spanish America. Defeat in the War of the Triple Alliance undid the state-led export development that had briefly made the nation a regional power and a threat in the first place.

CONCLUSION

For most countries of Spanish America, colonialism left its mark by setting initial levels of postcolonial development and congealing patterns of power within the state and society that reproduced those initial levels over time. Only when Spanish colonialism imparted ephemeral institutions and feebly endowed elite colonial actors were there exceptions. It was specifically the six sustained peripheries – Chile, Costa Rica, El Salvador, Honduras, Nicaragua, and Paraguay – where colonial institutions were so weakly rooted that initially poor countries had the chance to remake themselves in the decades after independence.

Whether these countries actually did remake themselves and then prosper, however, depended heavily on the contingencies and eventualities of warfare. In nearly all cases, to be sure, there were postcolonial actors who sought to enrich themselves and their nations through liberal reforms and export agriculture (Paraguay during the Francia years is the exception). But only if countries either avoided warfare almost entirely (Costa Rica) or emerged victorious from fighting on their own terms (Chile) did these actors enact the reforms that allowed for considerable growth and at least intermediate levels of long-run economic development. If countries became entangled in destructive military conflicts and ended up on the losing side, institutional building to promote development either never got off the ground (as in Honduras, Nicaragua, and El Salvador) or was destroyed in the course of the fighting (as in Paraguay). One can thus conclude that, for the sustained peripheries, development required either (1) the presence of liberals who became hegemonic early on and enjoyed enough peace for their reforms to take hold (Costa Rica); or (2) massive victories in wars that brought in fresh resources to governments with regional power designs (Chile and nearly Paraguay).

Having now analyzed the sustained peripheries in some depth, we can finally summarize overall causal patterns that pertain to all fifteen countries. From Chapter 3, we will recall that the causes of mercantilist centrality under the Habsburgs can be expressed as

$$A \mathbin{\&} (B \mathbin{v} C) \rightarrow M, \tag{1}$$

where A is complex indigenous society, B is substantial mineral wealth, C is close proximity to an empire capital, and M is mercantilist colonial center. The "&" symbol stands for the logical AND, the "v" symbol stands for the logical OR, and the "→" symbol stands for causal sufficiency. The presence of a state-like indigenous society in combination with either abundant mineral resources or close proximity to the capital of the Aztec or Inca Empire was sufficient for mercantilist colonial centrality.

During the liberal phase, by contrast, we saw that there were two different paths to colonial centrality. These paths were summarized as

$$(D \ \& \ E) \ v \ (F \ \& \ G) \ \rightarrow \ L, \tag{2}$$

where D is small indigenous and African population, E is strategic trading port, F is mercantilist colonial center, G is new mineral wealth, and L is liberal colonial center. Liberal centrality was caused by either the combination of a sparse indigenous population and a strategic trading port or the combination of prior mercantilist centrality and significant new mineral wealth.

Putting the periods together, we see that the main colonial route to the outcome of higher level of economic development was the combination exemplified by Argentina: significant liberal colonialism built on top of minimal mercantilist colonialism. This pathway can be stated succinctly as

$$\sim M \ \& \ L \rightarrow Y, \tag{3}$$

where M is mercantilist center, L is liberal center, Y is higher level of economic development, and the "$\sim$" symbol is the logical negation sign. The absence of mercantilist colonial centrality and the presence of liberal colonial centrality were sufficient for a higher level of economic development. We can also state this finding by substituting in the causes of mercantilist centrality and liberal centrality, as follows:

$$\sim [A \ \& \ (B \ v \ C)] \ \& \ [(D \ \& \ E) \ v \ (F \ \& \ G)] \ \rightarrow \ Y. \tag{4}$$

This formulation simply makes clear that the standard way to achieve higher economic development was to lack the causes of mercantilist centrality and to possess the causes of liberal centrality.

Finally, Costa Rica and Chile demonstrate that it was possible for a country to have been a periphery during the entire colonial epoch and still achieve a higher level of economic and/or social development. These countries managed this feat only because they avoided costly engagements and defeats in postcolonial warfare. Thus, their pathway to progress was as follows:

$$\sim M \ \& \ \sim L \ \& \ \sim W \ \rightarrow \ Y, \tag{5}$$

where M is mercantilist center, L is liberal center, W is costly warfare during the nineteenth century, and Y is higher level of development.

The other sustained peripheries (El Salvador, Honduras, Nicaragua, and Paraguay) followed a pathway where costly warfare did prevent them from advancing beyond economic backwardness. Their road to underdevelopment was as follows:

$$\sim M \ \& \ \sim L \ \& \ W \rightarrow \sim Y. \tag{6}$$

These last formulations make it clear that the relative absence of both mercantilist and liberal colonialism left development outcomes contingent upon the occurrence and results of war fighting.

6

Postcolonial Levels of Development

Some set of causes once determined a social pattern . . . Then ever since, what existed in one year produced the same thing the next year. We will call such theories "historicist explanations."
                                                                    – Arthur L. Stinchcombe

Latin America has not escaped its heritage of colonialism.
                                    – Stanley J. Stein and Barbara H. Stein

Colonialism not only helped to create the countries of Spanish America; it also sorted them into different positions in the world hierarchy of development. And once these positions were occupied, most countries did not achieve significant improvements or suffer major setbacks in their relative standing. Instead, they tended to maintain their relative levels of development vis-à-vis one another.

Persistence is an old theme in work on Latin America. "More than in any other region," writes Jeremy Adelman, "the formulation of the past as persistence has shaped regional and national narratives of Latin American societies."[1] This quotation comes from a substantial anthology entitled *Colonial Legacies: The Problem of Persistence in Latin American History*. In it, contributors assess the extent to which social formations created during the colonial period have persisted (or not) into the present. My concern here, however, is different. My argument is *not* that colonial institutions themselves persisted into the present; rather, most of the colonial institutions analyzed here – and their affiliated actors – were gradually rearranged or even abolished in the first decades that followed independence from Spain. It was the *positions* of the countries in the world hierarchy of development that persisted over the long run. The basic socioeconomic legacy of Spanish colonialism was precisely stable cross-national differences in levels of development.

Colonialism is thus what Arthur Stinchcombe calls a "historical cause" – a cause that produces an outcome that then persists in the absence of this cause.[2] Historical causes contrast with "constant causes"; the latter explain persistence by reference to factors that are continuously present. With historical causation, as Stinchcombe points out, "the problem of explanation breaks down into two causal components. The first is the particular circumstances which caused [outcomes] to be started. The second is the general process by which [the outcomes] reproduce themselves."[3] Clearly, this is mostly a book about Stinchcombe's first component of explanation – the original causes of outcomes. In this chapter, however, attention will center on the outcomes as they were sustained during the postcolonial period. For reasons explored at length in Chapter 1, we should *expect* over-time stability in relative levels of development. Countries with institutions that are advantageous at one point in time will tend to have different but still advantageous institutions at a later point. Effective institutions beget other effective institutions; ineffective ones foster other ineffective ones.[4]

If stability in relative levels of development is the expected norm, then periods of discontinuity and change are what really need to be explained. Following Adelman, we can call these episodes of discontinuity in Spanish American history "ruptures" – that is, "moments when the continuous time lines were irrevocably snapped."[5] Analysts of path dependence often urge attention to precisely such breaking points and routes out of lock-in.[6] From the perspective of this study, ruptures occur when a country significantly shifts its relative level of development over a long period of time. When this happens, there is a break with the colonial heritage. In Spanish America, as we shall see, ruptures that have improved a country's relative economic standing have occurred either because of the discovery of massive petroleum reserves (in Venezuela) or in the context of social revolutionary transformations (in Mexico). Ruptures that generate long-run declines possibly have also taken place during episodes of civil war and counter-revolutionary violence (in Nicaragua and El Salvador).

To some, it may seem unimaginative or perhaps romantic to suggest that events such as social revolutions or the upheavals of war are what really change national trajectories of development. But it stands as a fact for Spanish America, and in marked contrast to the limited impact that other factors have had in changing the ordering of countries. For instance, macroeconomic policy decisions may well be associated with short-run fluctuations in performance, but they probably have not to date been consequential enough to dramatically alter a country's relative level of development, one way or the other, over the long run (including in cases such as twentieth-century Argentina, as we shall see). Likewise, with the obvious exception of oil in Venezuela, particular export commodities and other geographically driven endowments have not fundamentally reorganized the countries of this region. To claim such limited efficaciousness for policy orientation and natural-resource endowment in Spanish America may strike some as improbable. Certainly the point needs to be made empirically, by looking at each individual case in some depth, rather than arguing in the abstract.

The finding that, with a few important exceptions, relative levels of development inherited from the colonial period have persisted until our time also raises intriguing practical and normative questions. For one thing, because the focus of this study is on aggregate, long-run patterns, smaller and less enduring changes are naturally passed over. Yet in the lives of real people, such changes may be enormously consequential. It matters a great deal, for example, if there is a ten-year decline in growth rates, even if a subsequent growth spurt makes up all of the lost ground. Temporary fluctuations in economic and social performance affect life conditions and are worthy of analysis and explanation in their own right – especially when set against the background of a longer-run analysis sensitive to underlying stability, such as this one.

From some normative perspectives, it should be further noted, an emphasis on stability is discouraging, showcasing as it does just how rare major changes have been. Some might insist that, worse still, calling attention to stability serves only to reinforce that stability. Political leaders and activists may have compelling reasons to characterize change as being more readily accomplishable than it has been so far; doing so may, for instance, help them win popular support for agendas that would otherwise be seen as too improbable to garner large numbers of supporters. Yet objective information on the real challenges of transformation, even when this information generates pessimistic conclusions, can still be useful for those committed to transformation. This is especially true for an audience – such as the readers of this book – who already know that enduring macrolevel transformations have not to date been frequently or easily accomplished. Let us then proceed by describing things as they actually are – including assessing objective possibilities for change, as opposed to presenting evidence in ways that spotlight only the most optimistic possibilities for the future.

POSTCOLONIAL ECONOMIC DEVELOPMENT

The magnitude of differences in levels of economic development within Spanish America roughly parallels what we find for the full universe of non-OECD countries. Spanish America has always been a mix of some of the richest non-OECD countries (e.g., Argentina and Uruguay), some of the poorest ones (e.g., Honduras and Bolivia), and some middling ones (e.g., Peru and Colombia). Likewise, as John H. Coatsworth has shown, the extent of inequality across the Latin American countries since their independence has roughly corresponded to the extent of inequality in the world economy as a whole.[7] In focusing on this region, therefore, we obtain a sample that is fairly representative of the full range of variation in levels of development for non-OECD countries. In addition, despite their reputation for economic volatility, these countries illustrate well the long-run stability of relative

Panel A: Thorp Data

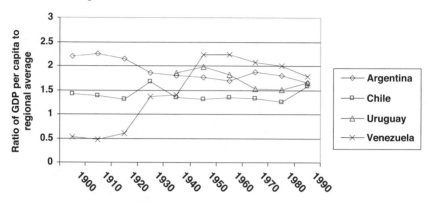

Panel B: Penn World Table Data

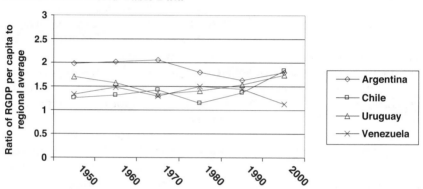

Panel C: World Bank Data

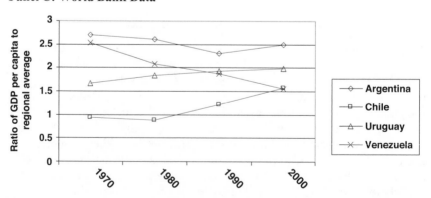

FIGURE 6.1. Levels of Economic Development: Wealthier Countries

levels of national development. We can see this by comparing time-series data on economic performance across countries.

Datasets on Long-Run Economic Development

Gross domestic product per capita is often regarded as the single best indicator of level of *economic* development. Statistical data for this indicator in Spanish America are available, but they mostly focus on the twentieth century, especially the period after 1950. The few available estimates of GDP per capita for the nineteenth century (or before) cover only a small and unrepresentative set of the region's countries.[8] For recent decades, the three most important datasets that cover all fifteen mainland Spanish American countries are (1) Rosemary Thorp's decadal index of national GDP for twentieth-century Latin America; (2) the Penn World Table's annual RGDP (real gross domestic product) per capita data for the 1950–2005 period; and (3) the World Bank's annual GDP per capita data for the 1965–2005 period.[9] These are not the only indices available, but they are the ones with the most comprehensive over-time data for the statistic (GDP per capita) that is now conventionally used as a measure of economic development.

Unsurprisingly, the datasets do not always agree with one another. Two especially important problems that arise from these differences should be noted. First, the datasets are not directly comparable when measuring *absolute* levels of GDP per capita. Their understandings of the size of GDP per capita for any given country-year often diverge sharply. Consider, for example, their estimates of average national GDP per capita in 1990 for the fifteen Spanish American countries: $4,375 according to the Penn World Table (PWT), $2,562 according to the World Bank (WB), and $697 according to Thorp. These large divergences suggest that it is better to use the datasets to evaluate *relative differences* among countries, rather than depending on them as measures of actual levels of GDP per capita. Second, the three datasets sometimes differ in their understandings of relative levels of development for particular countries. For example, while the PWT codes Nicaragua as above average in wealth in the region before the 1970s, the Thorp and WB indices say it is a quite poor country during these years. Such discrepancies do not warrant dismissing the indices as hopelessly idiosyncratic; they are in fact very highly correlated with one another for the years they have in common.[10] What these differences really suggest is that one should avoid treating the data and trends from any one index as being definitive. Strong claims about intertemporal stability or change in a country's level of development based on data points from a single index are potentially very misleading.

In order to focus squarely on *relative* levels of development, it is useful to compute how well a given Spanish American country performs over time in comparison to the average performance of the full population of fifteen Spanish American countries. Figures 6.1, 6.2, and 6.3 present the ratio of

Panel A: Thorp Data

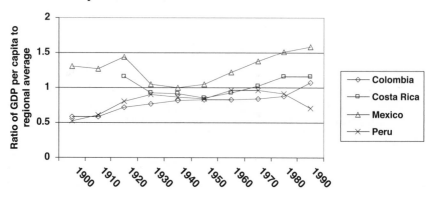

Panel B: Penn World Table Data

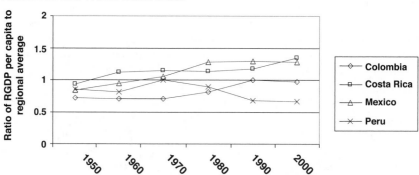

Panel C: World Bank Data

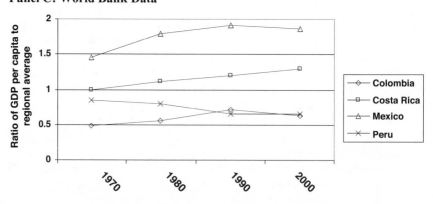

FIGURE 6.2. Levels of Economic Development: Intermediate Countries

Panel A: Thorp Data

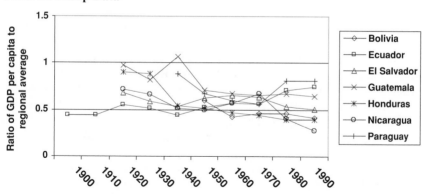

Panel B: Penn World Table Data

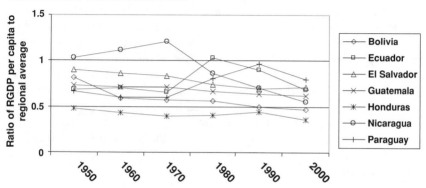

Panel C: World Bank Data

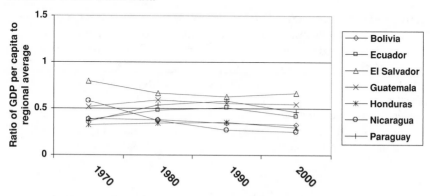

FIGURE 6.3. Levels of Economic Development: Poorer Countries

national GDP per capita to the regional-average GDP per capita. For the wealthier countries (Figure 6.1), intermediate countries (Figure 6.2), and poorer countries (Figure 6.3), information is presented in separate panels corresponding to the three datasets (Thorp, PWT, and WB). A score of 1 on the vertical axis indicates that the GDP for that country-year equals the average GDP per capita for the region (i.e., the fifteen countries); a score of 2 means a country-year is twice as wealthy as the regional average; and a score of 0.5 indicates that a country-year is only half as wealthy as the regional average. Countries at the top of the Spanish American hierarchy are among the wealthier non-OECD countries in the world; those at the bottom are among the poorest countries in the world.

As even a cursory inspection of the figures reveals, while countries exhibit substantial over-time stability in their relative positioning, there is also over-time change. To what extent do the changes represent enduring shifts in relative levels of development, as opposed to fluctuations produced perhaps by measurement error or transitory processes? Needless to say, if a country dramatically shifts its relative position during a given period in one of the three datasets but not the other two, then the apparent change could be an artifact of measurement error. Likewise, some shifts may result from temporary situations (e.g., a coup or a slump in international demand) that are soon "corrected" when the country returns to the level of development that existed prior to the "abnormal" circumstances.

In the remaining parts of this section, the postcolonial economic trajectories of the Spanish American countries are discussed not only in light of the data from these indices, but also with reference to the broader work of economic historians and case experts.

Trajectories for Wealthier Countries

At the end of the colonial period, as we have learned, Argentina and Uruguay were already the wealthiest territories of mainland Spanish America. Upon achieving independence, they instantly joined some of the wealthier nations of the world – at least in terms of per capita GDP. Argentina's GDP per capita during the mid- and late nineteenth century was fairly close to the average for western Europe, just behind countries such as Germany, the Netherlands, and Belgium.[11] During Argentina's "golden age" from 1870 to 1913, its GDP per capita was approximately the same as France's and well ahead of the output of fallen powers in Europe such as Spain, Portugal, Italy, and Austria – although Argentina started to decline relative to a skyrocketing United States.[12]

Although fewer data exist for Uruguay, its level of wealth in the late nineteenth and early twentieth centuries was probably similar to Argentina's. Angus Maddison's dataset actually puts Uruguay ahead of Argentina for 1870 in terms of GDP per capita and on par with the average for the western

European countries.[13] Estimates by others of Uruguay's GDP per capita for 1929 and 1940 have the country about equal to Argentina.[14] Montevideo was a less active port than Buenos Aires, and Uruguay's extreme dependency on livestock products made it very susceptible to market fluctuations, including during the crisis of 1890. On the other hand, Uruguay was the most urban country in Latin America, lacking the densely populated, poor rural towns that were common in northwestern Argentina (the part of Argentina whose colonial heritage was least favorable to development). Whether it exactly equaled Argentina or not, Uruguay was a quite rich nation by the simple standard of GDP per capita.[15]

Argentina's failure to become an advanced industrial nation raises what Carlos H. Waisman has called the "Argentine question."[16] By the mid-twentieth century, Argentina's wealth was no longer on par with the European average; and by the end of the century, its GDP per capita was only about half that of Spain, Italy, and Austria – nations it had once outstripped. In one sense, the Argentine question is even more puzzling than most economic historians suggest. For whereas they usually assume that Argentina only briefly rose toward the top of the world hierarchy during its golden age, in fact it held this lofty position for roughly the first hundred years of its history – from its independence until the Great Depression of the 1930s.

For at least two other reasons, however, the question of Argentine "failure" is much less of a mystery than has been implied. First, when compared to other so-called new countries (what Adam Smith called "new colonies"), Argentina has always been relatively poor. In 1913, its per capita GDP was only about half that of Canada, Australia, and probably also New Zealand.[17] Argentina was, from the beginning, the least able to capitalize on the presumed advantages of being a new country (e.g., heavy European migration, livestock, and temperate agriculture) and the least successful at achieving an industrial breakthrough. Although this fact is puzzling for scholars of new countries,[18] it is not surprising in light of the framework of this study. In all likelihood, Canada, Australia, and New Zealand started out at higher levels of economic prosperity than Argentina. They were, indeed, probably the richest countries in the world (strictly from a per capita GDP standpoint) shortly after their independence.[19] Their advantages relative to Argentina rested in part with the fact that they, unlike Argentina, were never colonized by a mercantilist power at all. Instead, they experienced an undiluted form of intensive liberal colonialism (see Chapter 7). This colonial heritage was highly advantageous for long-run economic development. After 1930, these countries declined some relative to Europe, as Argentina did. But because Canada, Australia, and New Zealand *started out* well ahead of Argentina and then maintained their relative advantage until 1930, they were poised to sustain industrial growth even in the aftermath of the Great Depression. Hence, while they declined from being the richest countries in the world, they nevertheless remained on par with the typical western

European country. As for Argentina, when it experienced its relative decline after 1930, the consequences were much graver. It remained wealthy in comparison to most countries in Africa, Asia, and Latin America. But its industrialization was distorted and incomplete, and its per capita GDP remained only roughly half that of Canada, Australia, and New Zealand, much as it always has been.

Second, data from the indices concerning GDP per capita in the twentieth century (see Figure 6.1) suggest another reason why the Argentine question is less intriguing than some have led us to believe: Argentina did *not* decline much relative to the rest of Spanish America during the period since 1930. Hence, any Argentine reversal of development was mostly an artifact of poor performance *throughout* Spanish America (compared to western Europe). The question of why Argentina declined in the mid-twentieth century is thus really a question of why Spanish America in general performed poorly relative to richer countries during this time.[20] There are various possible answers to this question (e.g., high population growth, international dependency, and poor macroeconomic policy), but for our purposes it is sufficient to note that the weak economic performance of the Spanish American region vis-à-vis Europe follows a three-hundred-year trend in which the upper-income countries pull away from the rest of the world in absolute levels of development (as discussed in Chapter 1).

During the second half of the twentieth century, Argentina was consistently 1.7 to 2.7 times wealthier than Spanish America as a whole, depending on which index one uses (see Figure 6.1). It lost some of its absolute advantage during the 1970–90 period, though it remained near the very top of the regional hierarchy. In the fifteen years after 1990, the country recaptured most of the ground that it had lost. Thus, little of lasting consequence changed with respect to Argentina's position in the regional hierarchy in the second half of the twentieth century. The same is true for Uruguay. It has consistently been a rich Spanish American country, though not quite as rich as Argentina. Uruguay experienced poor growth relative to the rest of the region in the two decades after World War II, but its growth after 1970 was higher than the regional average. Overall, the two trends were slight in magnitude and ultimately counterbalanced each other; Uruguay held steady as Spanish America's second or third wealthiest country – always around 1.5 to 2 times better than the Spanish American average.

Turning now to Chile, we find that estimates of per capita GDP by Victor Bulmer-Thomas and Angus Maddison put it as the third-richest country in Spanish America during the first decades of the twentieth century.[21] This placement is consistent with other indicators of modernization – urbanization, factory employment, and the density of railroads, telephones, electrical energy, and motorcars before 1930.[22] According to the Thorp index (Figure 6.1), Chile declines somewhat from 1930 to 1940, moving from a ratio of 1.7 times the regional average to approximately 1.4 times the regional average. It then maintains this 1.4 ratio until 1980, when it declines slightly, only to rise to 1.6 in 1990. The PWT closely parallels the Thorp index for the period since 1950. That dataset, however, continues to 2000, showing Chile rising to the very top of the regional hierarchy. The WB index also suggests a large relative gain for Chile at the end of the twentieth century.[23]

Chile's economic growth since the 1980s has, of course, attracted considerable attention.[24] Some analysts suggest that this growth signals a fundamental shift in the country's position in the world hierarchy. From a longer-run perspective, however, the recent growth appears to represent Chile's return to the position it held in the region before the Great Depression, when the country was near the top of the Spanish American hierarchy. Chile has regained all of the ground it lost after 1930. To be sure, this nation will surpass even its earlier position if it emerges as Spanish America's richest country and then holds that top spot for a prolonged period during the twenty-first century. But at the beginning of this century, the existing indices disagreed about whether Chile had gained the top spot. While the PWT indicates that during 2001–3 Chile was the wealthiest nation in the region, the WB index still has Chile behind Argentina, Mexico, and Uruguay. It remains to be seen whether Chile's recent growth has caused the country to assume an even higher position in the hierarchy than it has traditionally occupied.

Venezuela improved its level of economic development more than any other country in the region during the twentieth century. Its dramatic and enduring upward shift happened after 1920, when the oil industry was consolidated.[25] By 1950, Venezuela was suddenly among the richest countries in the region – and it maintained this position over the next five decades, though it eventually experienced a decline from its height (see Figure 6.1). The datasets differ considerably on the specifics, including exactly how rich Venezuela was at its height, when this high point occurred, and how much and when the country declined during the second half of the twentieth century. Obviously, these differences are partly an artifact of the challenges of validly assessing GDP per capita in what Terry Lynn Karl calls a "petrostate" – a capital-deficient country whose GDP per capita is largely dependent on oil exports.[26] Yet the basic trend of a rapid and dramatic rise for Venezuela after 1920, followed by abrupt fluctuations in annual growth rates, is not disputed. Nor is the claim that the world price for petroleum largely dictated fluctuating growth rates.

To ascertain the full extent to which oil exports produced a relative gain in Venezuela, however, we need to ask about the country's level of economic development *before* 1920. The evidence suggests that pre-oil Venezuela was at an intermediate level of development – a position that it likely maintained from the late colonial period. Maddison's early-twentieth-century data, for example, have Venezuela's GDP per capita about equal to that of Peru and Colombia, other average-level regional performers.[27] Historian John

V. Lombardi suggests that the coffee boom beginning in the 1830s, driven by production in the valleys of Caracas and Aragua, allowed the country to achieve a reasonable measure of postcolonial prosperity, even though it was heavily dependent on the international market.[28] Thorp notes that "Venezuela was a coffee economy of some importance in the late 19th century. It was the second largest coffee producer in the world after 1881."[29] On the basis of all these observations, we can conclude that Venezuela had an intermediate regional level of development for approximately the first century of its existence as a country. The basic effect of petroleum was to cause the country to rise from this middling position to the upper ranks of economic prosperity.

Trajectories for Intermediate-Level Countries

We saw that Mexico's pattern of development during the nineteenth century was erratic, to say the least. Despite the independence wars and the costly outcome of the war with the United States, however, Mexico recovered lost ground toward the end of the nineteenth century, if not well before.[30] Then, under the Porfirio Díaz government (1876–1911), an export boom was initiated, with both minerals and agriculture playing important roles. Growth was led by the northern region, precisely the area where the colonial heritage was most favorable for development. As Alan Knight stresses:

In general, northern Mexico – economically dynamic, underpopulated, mestizo, and more closely tied to the US economy – benefited from Porfirian growth. The mines of Sonora and Chihuahua flourished, attracting US capital... Commercial agriculture... sprang up in the Laguna, the Sonora river valleys, and the lower Río Grande valley... Monterrey became the preeminent industrial city of the north, producing steel, glass and beer, to the advantage of its dynamic entrepreneurial elite.[31]

By contrast, in central Mexico, heartland of the Habsburg colonial project, the growth was much less impressive. Landlords here sought to cash in on the new market opportunities, but "'feudal' relations acted as a brake on commercialization and a focus for subaltern resistance."[32] Central and southern Mexico in fact put the brakes on the Mexican economy as a whole. The northern regions had become rich (by regional standards) in the early twentieth century, but the densely populated central and southern regions dragged the country down to a regionally intermediate level of economic development.[33]

The upheavals of the revolution initially changed Mexico's economic performance very little. But once the revolution was consolidated, its structural transformations probably contributed to an episode of sustained economic prosperity. The prosperity itself seems undeniable. Both the Maddison and Thorp datasets show that, on average, Mexico had high growth rates relative to the rest of the region during the period after 1940.[34] With only brief set-backs, the growth occurred across the entire twentieth century. We can also glimpse this trend in the PWT and WB datasets, which show a steady rise for Mexico during the years they cover (see Figure 6.2). Led by its northern states, Mexico was, by the early twenty-first century, one of the more developed countries of the region. The PWT places it as the fifth-richest nation in the region for 2003, while the WB has it second only to Argentina. Mexico's colonial legacy of an intermediate level of economic development was thus partially eroded by the early twenty-first century. The country overperformed relative to what its immediate postcolonial positioning would lead us to expect.

Although proximity to U.S. markets surely helped northern Mexico, we need to remember that this part of Mexico was already performing at a comparatively high level in the early twentieth century. And northern Mexico's dynamism had deep colonial roots. What really seems to have changed after and as a consequence of the revolution was the performance of central and southern Mexico, those regions where colonialism had significantly hindered development. It was here, more than anywhere else, that the revolution

destroyed the power of the large landowners and succeeded in its goal of eliminating or at least significantly reducing "feudal" relations of production. In the process, it eliminated an important obstacle to increased agricultural production. In contrast to Latin American countries in which traditional forms of agriculture have persisted into the 1960's and 1970's, Mexico was self-sufficient in agricultural production... and agricultural exports supported the growth of industry by providing income for the import of industrial machinery and other industrial inputs.[35]

In central Mexico, revolutionary reforms modernized agriculture, which allowed this part of the country to contribute to industrialization in the north. The modernizing changes were not as extensive in southern Mexico, which still remains vastly impoverished. But the overall effect of the revolution was to erase important colonial legacies in the Habsburg core and lift Mexico toward the top of the hierarchy in Spanish America.

No similar social revolution occurred in Peru to wipe away this country's colonial legacy. Peru stayed at more or less the middle of the regional hierarchy throughout the postcolonial period. It did so despite all of the upheavals associated with many export booms and busts.[36] The first of these booms, and surely the most infamous, was the remarkable guano exports of the mid-nineteenth century.[37] Whereas this bonanza might have enabled another country (e.g., Chile) to harness foreign capital and rise to the top of the regional hierarchy, in Peru it generated dependence on British bondholders, public-sector debt, and little investment toward sustainable, long-run growth. Peru's challenges can thus hardly be seen as a matter of paltry natural resources; guano in the nineteenth century was nearly equivalent to oil in the twentieth century. Moreover, Peru's inability to capitalize on strategic resources is a theme that repeats itself across this nation's history. For Peruvian exports also rose to spectacular heights during the late nineteenth and early twentieth centuries, this time through a series of regionally profitable commodities (wool, rubber, oil, sugar, cotton, and metals), only to collapse by 1930.[38] Exports surged again during the 1950s and early 1960s – and once more were followed by stagnation.[39]

Statistical data reveal Peru's intermediate level of economic development, far behind Argentina and Chile but still well ahead of others such as Ecuador and El Salvador. Estimates of early-twentieth-century GDP per capita place Peru about equal to Colombia, another long-term average-level performer.[40] In the Thorp dataset, Peru holds steady as Spanish America's seventh- or eighth-richest country during the mid-twentieth century. The PWT and WB indices show the same for the years they cover. All of these sources, however, suggest that Peru experienced a nontrivial relative decline during the 1980s, slipping to about ninth place in the hierarchy (from a ratio of a little more than 0.8 of the regional average to a little less than 0.7). On the other hand, the PWT and WB indices point toward a possible recovery during the first few years of the twenty-first century. Overall, Peru still ranked in the middle of both the Spanish American and world economic hierarchies.

Colombia has usually been about tied with Peru on GDP per capita measures, though one or the other country has periodically held a lead (subject to the usual disagreements across datasets). Thorp's data show remarkably similar trajectories of economic development from 1900 all the way to 1980–90, when Colombia briefly grew and Peru declined. For 2003, the WB index has Peru barely ahead of Colombia, while the PWT awards Colombia a recently earned but significant advantage.

Whatever the exact ordering, Colombia's history – like Peru's – is dotted with episodes of export expansion and then export contraction that ultimately moved the nation neither toward the very top nor toward the very bottom.[41] During the first half of the nineteenth century, gold was still the main export, though tobacco gained importance when the monopoly over this product was finally broken. Further export-led growth occurred from the 1850s to the 1880s, with the opening up of regional markets for some of Colombia's agricultural and livestock products. Large annual fluctuations characterized exports during the last decades of the nineteenth century, though the trend was upward, with coffee now leading the way. After a brief crisis at the beginning of the twentieth century, exports of coffee, grown especially by medium-size producers in the western part of the country, dominated the economy for several decades. Then, after World War II, they gradually stagnated, only to recover during the coffee bonanza after 1975. Drug trafficking and oil, of course, have more recently boosted the economy, even during times of intense political violence. But none of this has made Colombia substantially richer or poorer relative to the Spanish American average.

Isolated in the isthmus, Costa Rica avoided regional warfare and launched coffee exportation during the early and mid-nineteenth century, well before its Central American neighbors to the north. By the late nineteenth and early twentieth centuries, it was an intermediate-level economic performer, easily the richest country in Central America on a per capita basis.[42] Commentators who traveled in Central America during this period were already remarking on Costa Rican exceptionalism. For example, Dana Munro considered Costa Rica "a nation which is entirely different from any of the other Central American republics." He argued that its relative political stability "enabled her to attain a prosperity which has entirely transformed the backward and poverty-stricken community of colonial days."[43]

Costa Rican history includes a further upward economic shift in the mid-twentieth century, when the country improved its relative standing to roughly 1.3 times the regional average and became the fifth-wealthiest nation in the region (see Figure 6.2). The immediate impetus for change was the conclusion of the civil war of 1948, whose settlement most famously gave birth to Latin America's longest-lasting democratic regime. This celebrated period of Costa Rican history also triggered a vast expansion of the public sector and helped to consolidate a national commitment to the provision of social-welfare services.[44] With the country's above-average growth since 1950, on top of its nineteenth-century advancement from colonial isolation, it is hard to deny that Costa Rica, more than any other country in Spanish America, has risen up in the economic hierarchy across the nearly two centuries since the end of colonialism. Costa Rica is Spanish America's great postcolonial improver.

Trajectories for Poorer Countries

Bolivia's economic crisis at the conclusion of the colonial period proved to be no passing moment; it did not abate until the silver-mining industry was finally modernized during the last decades of the nineteenth century. Only then did the nation again become a top exporter of refined silver. Yet the revenues thereby acquired were not seeds for development. "Bolivia remained a rural and Indian peasant nation . . . despite the growth of a modern export sector."[45] The same was true when, in the decades after 1900, tin became the country's main export; tin exports flourished while Bolivia languished as an overwhelmingly rural and impoverished country. When prices for tin crashed in the late 1920s and 1930s, the economy returned to crisis.[46]

Bolivia, then, stands as a good example of a country that started out very poor and remained very poor despite plentiful export-appropriate resources and some lengthy export booms. But the Bolivian story does not end there, of course, for this country was also the site of the massive upheavals and transformations associated with a full-blown social revolution. Indeed, the extraordinary events after 1952

fundamentally and permanently transformed Bolivian society in one of the more sweeping and profound revolutions to occur in the twentieth century... Land, the crucial resource in this predominately agrarian society, was effectively redistributed, ending in one stroke a system of feudal exploitation that had endured for the four centuries following the Spanish conquest of the Inca empire. The mining industry... was nationalized. Miners and workers were armed and their militias became the dominant military force in urban areas, rivaled in the national arena only by the might of the newly aroused peasantry. Education and welfare were massively supported.[47]

If the Bolivian Revolution encompassed these changes – in some respects similar to those of the Mexican Revolution, including the destruction of the old landed class – then what were the implications of the revolution for long-run economic development? All data suggest that social revolution in Bolivia did not yield over-time improvements for GDP per capita (or other macro indicators of national economic development). Once the hyper-inflation and depression generated by the revolution had been contained, growth did occur, but it was not sustained and thus never brought Bolivia to a higher position in the regional economic hierarchy. Compared to other countries, Bolivia remained about as poor as it had been before the revolution, with a GDP per capita around half the regional average (see Figure 6.3). If we focus strictly on the growth of the economy, it is hard to argue that the Bolivian Revolution had much of a long-term impact one way or the other.

Such limited effects, when compared to those of the Mexican Revolution, raise the question of why social revolution inaugurated structural changes that promoted long-run economic development in Mexico but not in Bolivia. We must remember that in Mexico, sustained high growth was driven by the rapidly industrializing north, the part of the country that had been marginal under the Habsburgs but of increasing importance during the Bourbon period. In a sense, the accomplishment of the Mexican Revolution was to sweep away the colonial heritage in the Central Valley and thereby remove the fetters that had been preventing growth from fully taking off in the country as a whole. The Bolivian Revolution also did away with many colonial legacies in the highland areas that had been the focus of Habsburg colonialism. But Bolivia lacked a region that could play the role that northern Mexico did for Mexico. The closest equivalent to northern Mexico was the Department of Santa Cruz in the east. Santa Cruz was, after all, a marginal territory under the Habsburgs; and after the Bolivian Revolution, the modernization in that area was noteworthy. Yet in contrast to northern Mexico, the Santa Cruz region did not receive any late colonial attention from the Bourbons. It consequently remained an isolated and impoverished region right up to the revolution. For Santa Cruz to have brought the Bolivian nation as a whole to a higher level of development, it would have needed to start from a much stronger base – which may have required a different colonial experience. The crucial difference between the Mexican and Bolivian revolutions, then, is not so much variations in the transformation of structures in those areas that had been the core parts of the colonial project (i.e., central Mexico and western Bolivia). Rather, the difference may lie in the contrasting ways in which late Bourbon colonialism had prepared key outlying areas to seize upon new possibilities that emerged in the aftermath of social revolution. Late colonial modernization left northern Mexico poised to drive nationwide economic prosperity in a way that was not true for eastern Bolivia.

Ecuador might have been able to better capitalize on a similar reworking of its institutional configurations. For, as we have seen, the littoral region around Guayaquil *was* ready to launch an economic takeoff in the late colonial period, but it was suffocated by a politically dominant interior region configured in ways that sustained poverty. It is certainly feasible that, had the Ecuadorian interior been fundamentally transformed during the postcolonial period – including through the destruction of its landed class – Guayaquil would have played the same role as northern Mexico in promoting a breakthrough to a higher level of economic development. In Ecuador, however, there was no revolutionary break to remake the interior. The heartland of the old Audiencia of Quito remained backward and dependent on the coast for wealth generation, dragging down national-level economic performance.

During the entire first 150 years following colonialism, consequently, Ecuador held steady as a poor country. Export production was monopolized by the coastal region – whether through cacao production, which flourished from the 1860s until the 1920s, or with coffee and bananas in the more recent period. For 1900, Thorp's data put Ecuador's GDP per capita behind that of all other Spanish American countries for which information is available, including Colombia, Peru, and Venezuela.[48] From 1950 to 1970, Ecuador was probably the second- or third-poorest country in the region, with a GDP per capita around half the regional average (see Figure 6.3). The brief upsurge after 1970, driven by the discovery of significant petroleum deposits in the deserted Oriente basin, stimulated government spending and the growth of GDP, especially in the Quito area. Yet even this bonanza could not elevate Ecuador in the development hierarchy, as oil had done for Venezuela. For by the 1980s, the volume of oil production had already started to decline, ending the magnificent export earnings.[49] Since 1990, Ecuador has returned to more or less the same position in the regional hierarchy that it held before petroleum was discovered.

Paraguay's economic history since the War of the Triple Alliance (1864–70) is not much more heartening. To alleviate the huge foreign debts that accumulated during the war, governments in the late nineteenth century

sold off portions of the remaining country to foreign investors, often Argentines, who sometimes oversaw labor-repressive fiefdoms on the estates they
thereby acquired. Paraguay's new outward-oriented governments rejected
José Gaspar de Francia's state-led approach and embraced the same liberal
approaches of the other countries in late-nineteenth-century Latin America.
But Paraguay witnessed no significant export boom during the late nineteenth and early twentieth centuries. International trade remained modest,
despite substantial policy changes and a favorable world economy.[50]

Still, in the early and mid-twentieth century, sparsely populated Paraguay
was not the poorest country in the region; it was only a little below average.
Small amounts of yerba, tobacco, and tannin exports, in conjunction with
a small and homogenous population, allowed Paraguay to reach a higher
level of GDP per capita than more populous countries such as Peru and
Bolivia. And the country's isolation meant that the Great Depression had
little effect here, though the Chaco War with Bolivia (1932–5) was quite
destructive. When the civil war of 1947 occurred, therefore, Paraguay was
in fact not that far behind the eventually successful country of Costa Rica
(see Figure 6.3), which experienced its own civil war at about the same time.
But Paraguay's civil war, of course, occurred in a very different historical
context. The war in Costa Rica was but a brief aberration in a generally
peaceful and prosperous history. By contrast, the 1947 civil war in Paraguay
was just one more episode in a long series of violent transfers of power.[51]
Surely the contrast between Costa Rica's generally peaceful and competitive
history and Paraguay's violent and authoritarian history – as opposed to
any events during the civil wars themselves – is what mainly explains why
Costa Rica's conflict soon yielded a social democracy and sustained high
growth, whereas Paraguay's quickly devolved into an old-fashioned military
coup and inaugurated a backward, personalistic dictatorship. Under the
long rule of General Alfredo Stroessner, in any event, Paraguay remained
a lower-middle-income economic performer. Its GDP per capita perhaps
declined some until 1970, shot up briefly in the 1970s in response to the
construction of the Itaipu Dam and surging cotton and soybean exports,
and then fell back down after 1980.[52] At the beginning of the twenty-first
century, Paraguay still ranked a little below average in the regional economic
hierarchy.

Finally, the remaining four Central American countries – Guatemala, El
Salvador, Honduras, and Nicaragua – have all been poor within the region
since the late colonial period. Coffee and banana exports during the liberal
period stimulated some growth in the decades before the Great Depression.
But these countries were below average on most economic indicators of
prosperity.[53] They suffered mightily with the Depression, and – notwithstanding an occasional outlying piece of data – they have never recovered.[54]
The one big economic shift occurred with the Nicaraguan Revolution (1979–
90). Beginning in the 1970s, Nicaragua declined and became perhaps the

poorest country in the region. The sources of tragedy are easy to locate: violence and disruptions associated with the overthrow of the Somoza government, the tumultuous upheavals under the Sandinistas, and the civil war that accompanied the U.S.-sponsored counterinsurgency. El Salvador had its own revolutionary violence during the 1970s and 1980s, and it too declined temporarily during this period, though less dramatically than Nicaragua. While Guatemala and Honduras did not experience major falls, they also did not rise from near the bottom of the hierarchy. Central America in the late twentieth century saw economic maladies, as well as new exports (beef, cotton, and sugar) that provided significant new revenues but also kept countries extremely dependent on agrarian products whose prices fluctuated in a sometimes crashing world market.[55]

U.S. intervention in Central America during the late twentieth century most likely made economic conditions worse; a strong case can be made that it helped fuel atrocious violence and contributed to great human suffering in the short term.[56] It is possible that, in the absence of this intervention, these countries would have risen some in the economic hierarchy. This possibility derives from the fact that a social revolutionary government in Nicaragua and social revolutionary movements in El Salvador and Guatemala sought basic changes in class and state structures that might have rearranged power constellations in ways permitting greater economic output. Yet one could also argue that the Central American economies stood to benefit economically no more than Bolivia did from radical revolutionary transformation. Lacking potentially dynamic regions poised to drive nationwide development, they were perhaps destined to remain highly dependent agrarian economies even under the best of international circumstances.

The real long-term gains that were truncated by U.S. intervention may have been in the arena of social development. For progress in social development can occur in the midst of economic backwardness.[57] And social revolutions *may* foster precisely improvements in human welfare. Let us therefore turn to postcolonial trajectories of social development in Spanish America, with an eye to noting any ruptures that occurred, perhaps without concomitant changes in economic development.

POSTCOLONIAL SOCIAL DEVELOPMENT

Stability is also the main story line in relative levels of social development in Spanish America. Countries that perform better on indicators of human well-being almost always do so year after year without interruption; the same is true for countries that perform poorly relative to the rest of the region. Moreover, the ordering of countries on one indicator of social development is positively correlated with the ordering on others. As a consequence, it is possible and useful to generalize broadly about overall levels of social development for the Spanish American countries during the postcolonial period.

Data on Long-Run Social Development

GDP per capita is widely accepted as the single best summary statistic for level of economic development. No similar overarching statistic exists for level of social development. Perhaps the closest is the United Nations' Human Development Index (HDI), which is an aggregate measure of overall national socioeconomic development. But the HDI includes GDP per capita as one of its composite indicators. In order to focus on social development independently of economic development, we need to bracket out the HDI's other indicators. Of these, we have good over-time data for Spanish America on adult literacy and life expectancy at birth.

Relative national levels of literacy in Spanish America have been quite stable. The correlation between levels of literacy from one decade to the next during the last century is usually above 0.9.[58] Stability also characterizes relative levels of life expectancy at birth, with few or no large shifts within the hierarchy. Another possible measure for assessing social development is child mortality, which is an excellent indicator of overall human welfare in a nation.[59] It, too, exhibits stability in the sense that countries do not change their relative positions. Table 6.1 illustrates the point by showing comparative data for each indicator from the earliest time when it was broadly available to a recent year.

Other important measures of social development look at equality across different categorical groups, including men and women. Although there are almost no truly historical statistics on gender inequality in Spanish America, those for the current period suggest that countries that do well on literacy and life expectancy also achieve higher levels of gender-related development.[60] The same is true for infant survival rates and gross school enrollment.[61] The fact that the same countries repeatedly do well (or poorly) on various social indicators across time suggests that "social development" can be treated as an aggregate whole that is subject to much stability.

National Trajectories

Uruguay, Argentina, Costa Rica, and Chile always appear among the regional leaders on the major indicators of social development. They lead in literacy and life expectancy going back to the early twentieth century, as surely as they lead in child mortality and gender equality for the early twenty-first century. Uruguay has been the best in the region for many years on many indicators; it is almost never lower than third on a given indicator for a given year. Argentina's rankings are similar, often just beneath Uruguay. More volatile is Chile, a country that historically falls below Uruguay and Argentina but that has improved over the last two decades to become the region's leader on child mortality and life expectancy. Costa Rica has ranked very high on literacy and life expectancy as far back as the early twentieth

Table 6.1. Levels of social development for Spanish American countries

	Literacy rate (% population)		Life expectancy at birth (years)		Under-five mortality rate (per 1,000 live births)	
	1900	2005	1950	2005	1975	2004
Uruguay	59.4 (1)	97.7 (1)	n.a.	75 (3) (tie)	57 (1)	17 (3)
Argentina	51.3 (2)	97.2 (2)	61 (1)	74 (5) (tie)	71 (3)	18 (4)
Costa Rica	35.1 (4)	94.9 (4)	56 (2)	78 (1) (tie)	83 (5)	13 (2)
Chile	43.5 (3)	95.7 (3)	49 (4) (tie)	78 (1) (tie)	98 (6)	8 (1)
Paraguay	31.4 (7)	93.0 (5) (tie)	48 (6) (tie)	71 (9) (tie)	78 (4)	24 (7)
Colombia	34 (5)	92.8 (7)	49 (4) (tie)	72 (8)	108 (7)	21 (6)
Venezuela	27.8 (9)	93.0 (5) (tie)	51 (3)	73 (7)	61 (2)	19 (5)
Mexico	24.4 (11)	91.0 (8) (tie)	48 (6) (tie)	75 (3) (tie)	110 (8)	28 (9) (tie)
Ecuador	33.1 (6)	91.0 (8) (tie)	48 (6) (tie)	74 (5) (tie)	140 (9)	26 (8)
Peru	24.3 (12)	87.7 (10)	40 (10) (tie)	70 (11)	178 (14)	29 (11)
Honduras	28.3 (8)	80.0 (13)	39 (12) (tie)	68 (13)	170 (13)	41 (13)
El Salvador	26.3 (10)	79.7 (14)	44 (9)	71 (9) (tie)	162 (10)	28 (9) (tie)
Nicaragua	n.a.	86.7 (11)	39 (12) (tie)	69 (12)	165 (11)	38 (12)
Bolivia	18.5 (13)	82.7 (12)	40 (10) (tie)	64 (15)	243 (15)	69 (15)
Guatemala	11.9 (14)	69.1 (15)	38 (14)	67 (14)	168 (12)	45 (14)

Note: The country's ranking within the region is provided in parentheses.
Sources: Rosemary Thorp, *Progress, Poverty and Exclusion: An Economic History of Latin America in the 20th Century* (New York: Inter-American Development Bank, 1998), 354, 356; United Nations, *Human Development Report, 2006* (New York: United Nations, 2006).

century, well before it experienced the political changes that followed the 1948 civil war. Overall, these four countries are in a class of their own; on average, they clearly outperform the rest of the region in the arena of social development.[62]

These four are also the places where, beginning in the late colonial and early independence periods, national myths were most effectively constructed to portray the population as a single homogenous and mostly European group. A necessary condition for such a mythology (as we have seen) was the near-complete disappearance of the indigenous population as a large, spatially concentrated, and systematically subordinated stratum of society. This disappearance facilitated the cultural creation of the nation as overwhelmingly white, in explicit contrast to neighboring countries to the north that were seen as racially mixed and racially inferior. In Argentina, Chile, Costa Rica, and Uruguay, in short, the legacy of the colonial period was societies that could be and would be imagined as ethnically pure and of elite stock. Investments in education would go forward at early stages and become part of the nation's obligation to its homogenous citizens, to a greater extent than elsewhere. Hospitals and doctors would be more widely available, eventually even in rural areas – where populations were conceptualized as noble gauchos and independent farmers, rather than uncultured campesinos (though Chile is a partial exception). No sizable groups of people were to be barred on ethnic grounds from enjoying the fruits of economic progress.

Intermediate levels of social development marked four other countries: Venezuela, Paraguay, Colombia, and Mexico. Before the oil bonanza, Venezuela was probably already in the middle of the region's social hierarchy. Benefits that derived from oil rents took the country to only a slightly higher level. Performance on life expectancy from 1930 to 1950 and on literacy from 1950 to 1990 seems to have improved (see Table 6.1). By the end of the twentieth century, however, Venezuela usually ranked between fifth and seventh on leading social indicators – still in the middle, roughly the same place where it was earlier. Petroleum may have permitted Venezuela to rise to the top of Spanish America's economic hierarchy, but it did not allow it to do the same with social development.

Given its relatively low level of economic development, Paraguay is more surprising as an intermediate performer in the social arena. But its intermediate position is quite clear from the data. Paraguay rarely, if ever, shows up in the bottom third of the region's hierarchy, and it often makes very respectable showings (relative to regional and global standards). Paraguay and Colombia consistently place between fifth and eighth in the hierarchy. They have been roughly equal on literacy, life expectancy, and child mortality. This intermediate ranking is expected for Colombia, because the country is a regionally intermediate economic performer. But it is not expected for Paraguay, which never recovered economically after the War of the Triple Alliance. What accounts for Paraguay's overperformance on social indicators? Again, one critical ingredient is surely ethnic homogeneity – in particular, the unique way in which indigenous ancestry was embraced and incorporated into national culture. Perhaps to a greater degree than in any other Spanish American country, Paraguay's indigenous past has been celebrated as an integral component of national identity.

In Mexico, the revolution may have slightly improved social development, though the evidence is not clear-cut. From 1900 to 1930, Mexico ranked about tenth on literacy and slightly below average on life expectancy. But from 1940 to 2005, it usually ranked about eighth for literacy and about sixth or seventh for life expectancy. Certainly, since the revolution, leaders have sought to forge a national identity that conceived Mexicans as a singular people of mixed racial ancestry (the "cosmic race").[63] Yet in practice, post-revolutionary Mexico has remained deeply bifurcated into indigenous and non-indigenous peoples. And the continued hardship and discrimination that the former have faced is a considerable blockage that prevents gains in economic development from translating into improvements in human welfare across the whole country.

The final seven countries – Bolivia, Ecuador, El Salvador, Guatemala, Honduras, Nicaragua, and Peru – have below-average levels of social development. Guatemala has had the region's lowest literacy rate and nearly its lowest life expectancy for as long as we have data; it currently has the worst gender-related performance in the region. As Jim Handy writes, "Guatemalan society is a logical expression of the country's history. Its modern history was founded in the bitter injustice of the colonial conquest; followed by protracted years of dispossession and racial and class oppression . . . It is this history which has created a deeply polarized, essentially unjust and violent society."[64] This sad past does include one near rupture point, the famous period of 1944 to 1954, when progressive governments pursued reforms to improve the lot of workers and peasants. But the tragic failure of this episode reveals just how hard it is to break with the past, for the period ended up giving way to one of the region's most repressive military regimes.[65]

As for Bolivia, it has historically fared only a little better than Guatemala on social indicators – Guatemala and Bolivia have probably had the worst life conditions in Spanish America for more than a century. And the Bolivian Revolution did not lift the country from the bottom of the social-development hierarchy. Still, it did have a demonstrable effect in the area of education and perhaps in social welfare more generally. According to Herbert S. Klein, "Although Bolivia still ranks as one of the poorest nations of the hemisphere, there has been major improvement in literacy and quality of life of its population. This was due to the heavy investments in education, health, and welfare that the governments of Bolivia had undertaken since the National Revolution of 1952."[66] Again, though, the social indicators show that these efforts have not pulled Bolivia up from the very bottom of the hierarchy.

The Central American countries of Honduras, El Salvador, and Nicaragua are more ethnically homogenous than Bolivia and Guatemala and achieve slightly higher positions on the various rankings of human well-being. According to the data in Table 6.1, Honduras and Nicaragua performed a little better during the early part of the twentieth century. This was, however, a period of intense U.S. imperialism for these nations.[67] Foreign investments may have briefly made more resources available for social expenditures, but their final legacy was not one of enhanced human well-being. Since the mid-twentieth century, these countries have consistently ranked with El Salvador in the bottom third of the social-development hierarchy. The Nicaraguan Revolution also did not represent a rupture for social development: any gains generated by the progressive social policies of the 1980s were canceled out by the violence that accompanied the counterrevolution.

Peru and Ecuador round out the lower-level social performers in the region. Although Peru manages an intermediate level of economic development, it performs poorly on social indicators, rarely ranking above tenth and often worse. Interestingly, the "revolution from above" during the 1968 juncture does not appear to have had any lasting effect on Peru's standing; nor does the dramatic violence associated with guerrilla warfare during the 1980s. Ecuador actually performs better than Peru on various social indicators; Ecuador is, indeed, the best of the low-level social performers, usually ranking between seventh and ninth in the hierarchy. Its social performance is higher than one would expect on the basis of its economy and ethnic composition alone.

Even from such a brief consideration, we can readily see that the social-development hierarchy in Spanish America is as firmly set as the region's economic hierarchy. There are few relative improvements or declines; no case has, for instance, moved from poor performance to good performance (or vice versa). Rarely does a country shift more than three or four places. Whatever historically caused countries to assume their initial positioning in the hierarchy is also what ultimately explains their current positioning.

And we need not guess about those historical causes. For we have learned how, during the late colonial period, economic wealth and ethnic homogeneity lay behind initial levels of social development. The secret to superior social performance was to avoid abject poverty and to build an understanding of the nation as a singular, cohesive ethnoracial community. In Argentina, Chile, Costa Rica, and Uruguay, nearly the entire population was understood to be European, a notion rooted in the presumed ethnic homogeneity from the late colonial period. In Paraguay, an ethnically homogenous nation was also invented, but the poverty of this territory prevented it from rising to the top tier in the social-development hierarchy. By contrast, Colombia, Venezuela, and Mexico had sufficient wealth, but they lacked the requisite ethnic homogeneity. In these cases, societies were understood to have multiple ethnic groups, with clear differences between them in status and entitlements. The situation was even worse in the remaining seven countries (Bolivia, Ecuador, El Salvador, Guatemala, Honduras, Nicaragua, and Peru). Either they lacked the economic resources to achieve any measurable level of social development, despite being constructed as relatively homogenous mestizo nations (El Salvador, Honduras, and Nicaragua), or their colonial period left a highly bifurcated racial order that separated indigenous people from whites (culturally defined) in a way that made substantial accomplishments in social development extremely unlikely (Bolivia, Ecuador, Guatemala, and Peru). In these last cases, mestizos were often lumped with indigenous people, reducing the spectrum of citizens eligible for true citizenship rights to a minority of inhabitants.

CONCLUSION

Differences in cross-national levels of development that originated in the colonial period have persisted, with some exceptions, throughout the post-colonial period in Spanish America. To explain this remarkable fact, it is tempting to assume that the persistence is rooted in the perpetuation of colonial institutions themselves: "The notion that bad political and legal institutions, created in the historical past to support an exploitative model of production, survive into the present to explain underdevelopment is implicit in much recent work."[68] Yet most political and legal institutions from the colonial period, including those causally relevant for situating countries into particular levels of development in the first place, have been superseded. Institutions that have ceased to exist cannot be what are driving over-time stability; the sustaining forces involve other mechanisms. Another temptation is to assume that constant levels of natural-resource endowments hold the key to adequate explanation. But the world market has varyingly rewarded particular export products over time, with many countries having had the chance to partake in export bonanzas that privileged their endowments. Profitable export commodities rarely changed anything over the long run. In the midst of spectacular export booms, countries with lower levels of development remained extremely poor and unable to translate their resource advantage into sustained growth. The only unambiguous exception is what oil did for Venezuela, lifting this country from a regionally intermediate level to a regionally high level of economic development.

The real mechanisms of perpetuation lay elsewhere. They will be found, most generally, with the varying power configurations that were originally put in place during colonialism. It is these configurations – the basic constellations of power in state and society – that persist in Spanish American countries in spite of changing economic opportunities and actors, evolving cultural practices, and fluctuating political conditions. This analysis, focused as it is on the historical causes of levels of development, must leave to future work the task of identifying the specific forms that these mechanisms have assumed across time and place. As this research proceeds, though, a basic lesson from this chapter is worth bearing in mind: routine episodes of continuity may not be the best place to look for perpetuating mechanisms. Instead, these mechanisms may be most visible during those rare periods of rupture, when countries shift their level of development. During the Mexican Revolution, for example, existing social and economic arrangements were overturned in ways that exposed the specific power constellations that had previously held back development possibilities.

In time, more and more countries may experience internal ruptures that change their level of development. Eventually, the ordering of nations in the regional development hierarchy inherited from the colonial period may only vaguely resemble their current positions. But at the beginning of the twenty-first century, it still made sense to argue that most differences in levels of development in Spanish America were a legacy of Spanish colonialism. For most countries had not broken out of the relative positions that they acquired during the colonial period.

7

British and Portuguese Colonialism

The policy of Great Britain with regard to the trade of her colonies has been dictated by the same mercantile spirit as that of other nations, it has, however, upon the whole, been less illiberal . . . than that of any of them . . . The absolutist governments of Spain, Portugal, and France, on the contrary, take place in their colonies . . . The administration of the French colonies, however, has always been conducted with more gentleness and moderation than that of the Spanish and Portuguese.

– Adam Smith

Spain was but one of several European powers that embarked on overseas colonization projects. Belgium, Britain, France, Germany, Italy, the Netherlands, and Portugal all controlled their own colonies in Africa, Asia, or the Americas. No one denies that different colonizing nations left distinctive legacies in their subject territories, such as their own European language. But recently, influential work on colonialism tells us that which European power colonized a particular territory did not matter in other critical ways.[1] Any institutional differences among the European nations did not, according to these arguments, affect the political-economic institutions that were established in the colonies. Nor did differences across the European powers have any discernable impact on long-run development outcomes. Instead, variations in development outcomes are explained solely on the basis of differences in the precolonial territories themselves.

Yet such arguments about the irrelevance of colonizer identity cannot be sustained. In the keynote passage for this chapter, Adam Smith provides one set of reasons why. He correctly notes that colonial policy was substantially shaped by the degree to which an illiberal "mercantile spirit" reigned in European economies. Writing in 1776, he points out that illiberal tendencies were least present in Britain, most strongly present in Portugal and Spain, and somewhere in the middle in France. In turn, such differences affected, among other things, the extent to which the rule of law was imposed in colonies. As Smith anticipated, it was only among the British colonies – never the Spanish, Portuguese, or even French colonies – where the rule of law fully took hold, allowing for remarkable postcolonial development in the United States, Canada, Australia, and New Zealand.

Despite its virtues, however, Smith's argument is not without its shortcomings. He assumed that a given colonizer laid down more or less analogous institutions in all of its colonies. On this view, all British colonies inherited more favorable institutions than their Spanish and Portuguese counterparts. Of course, such notions are much too simplistic. As proof, we need only remember that British colonialism left in its wake not only some of the richest countries in the world, but also some of the poorest. What Smith failed to appreciate is that the institutional heritage a colony acquired was also affected by the organization of the indigenous population (as currently prevalent social science paradigms do suggest). Adequate explanation thus demands that we explicitly take into account the institutional identity of the colonizer *and* the organization of the indigenous population, because they *interacted* to produce colonial and postcolonial outcomes.

The present chapter reaches beyond Spain and considers evidence from two quite different European colonizers: Britain and Portugal. These colonial powers are especially useful to examine because, in the first place, their institutional identities correspond closely with the two ideal types of colonizers. Britain matches well the characteristics of a liberal colonizer, whereas Portugal (especially before the late eighteenth century) corresponds nicely with those of a mercantilist colonizer. For any given territory that these nations colonized, therefore, the framework developed in this book will have clear predictions about the level of colonialism and the level of postcolonial development that should theoretically have transpired.

In the second place, differences in the nature of the British and Portuguese colonial projects make them good choices for analysis. The British colonized more countries than any other European nation; no fewer than fifty contemporary countries are former British colonies. There are, consequently, plenty of opportunities to study variations across cases within British colonialism – even more so than in Spanish colonialism (Spain being the second most prolific colonizer). For its part, the Portuguese Empire was comparatively small, and the analysis of variation across Portuguese colonies is therefore problematic. However, Portugal is of special interest because it colonized Brazil, a huge Latin American country about which this analysis has so far been mostly silent. Given that the Spanish and Portuguese colonial projects in the Americas overlapped substantially in time, and given that Portuguese colonialism in Brazil exhibits its own over-time and cross-regional variations, much can potentially be learned from an analysis of the colonial project in Brazil.

The British and Portuguese colonial experiences thus offer, in their own ways, leverage for assessing the arguments of this book. In looking at British colonialism, the goal will be to determine whether the general model of colonialism and development, as presented in Chapter 1, works "on average" for the full range of British colonies. With respect to Portuguese colonialism, by contrast, I present a historically grounded explanation of the colonial situations and long-run development patterns across diverse regions of Brazil.

Given the scope of British colonialism, we must focus here on only the most highly aggregated patterns, examining whether evidence broadly conforms to theoretical expectations. This requires looking briefly at a large number of cases. But let us start by considering the institutional identity of Britain when its colonial project began in the seventeenth century.

The Liberal Political Economy

Certainly by the end of the seventeenth century, England's political economy was much more liberal than that of Habsburg Spain. This is not to deny that England was still statist and far removed from a laissez-faire ideal. But we must give appropriate weight to the revolutionary liberalizing changes that had occurred in the English political economy.

Royal power was reduced dramatically by the English Revolution. The decision of Charles I to convene a parliament in 1640, the ensuing Civil War, and the "Glorious Revolution" of 1688–9 forever thwarted the monarchy's local economic and political power. Henceforth, the king would rule only with the confidence and legislative approval of Parliament. English society itself remained "gentlemanly" and probably more deeply stratified than ever along class lines (all radical efforts during the revolution to achieve social leveling had failed).[2] But notions of popular sovereignty, religious toleration, and economic and personal freedom were now part of the culture. As one advocate of the "social interpretation" of the English Revolution puts it:

After 1660, the temper of the age was radically different. An intensely pragmatic and utilitarian outlook came to prevail, and with it the wholesale and explicit pursuit of economic ends. The mystique of kingship, shattered in the 1640s, ceased to fascinate, while the doctrines of popular sovereignty and the contract of government were driven deep into the general consciousness.[3]

In turn, capitalist development was aided by the long-term political security of market-oriented actors – especially landlords engaged in commercial agriculture and profit-seeking merchants not directly tied to the monarchy. These actors probably had little or nothing to do with actually causing the revolution.[4] Yet they ended up as beneficiaries of the changes, ones that were never designed to help them but that wound up liberalizing Britain more than any other nation of the era except for perhaps the Netherlands (the world's first great commercial power).

The changes were a series of uncoordinated institutional rearrangements that also facilitated England's "commercial revolution" of the middle and later seventeenth century. Old-style commercial monopolies were weakened or abolished, and membership in merchant organizations became accessible to individual entrepreneurs. According to the distinguished historian C. G. A. Clay, "By 1700, the only branch of English overseas trade in which the monopoly of a regulated company was still effective was that with the Ottoman territories of the eastern Mediterranean."[5] The creation of the Bank of England provided entrepreneurs and merchants with new access to low-interest credit. Parliament itself became a political lever through which commercial actors could affect state policy. The merchants were freed from the bonds that had made them mere appendages of state monopolies. They had independent sources of capital and political autonomy. They still relied on the British state, to be sure, but this state was now also dependent on them (in marked contrast to the situation in Spain).

Given the powerful position of merchants (and capitalist landlords) within England, it is not surprising that British colonial policy would be favorable to commercial interests. As D. K. Fieldhouse argues, "In principle, the British commercial system resembled that of Spain and other colonial powers; but its effects were much less damaging to colonial prosperity. The British never restricted colonial trade to one or more specified ports, organized ships into annual fleets, or imposed restrictions on inter-colonial trade."[6] Moreover, the fact that England had undergone liberalizing changes in the seventeenth century meant that British colonialism carried the *potential* to leave in its wake institutions and actors congruent with such liberalism. The same could not be said of Habsburg Spain, which could only bequeath mercantilist legacies. The real question is thus, Under what circumstances *would* British colonialism leave behind a more liberal economic legacy?

Aggregate Cross-National Patterns

We can answer this question by considering, first, the relationship between the precolonial population and the extent of British colonialism and, second, the relationship between the level of British colonialism and level of postcolonial development. Exactly opposite to the pattern for Habsburg Spain, the British tended to settle heavily in territories that were relatively unpopulated at the onset of colonialism; conversely, they tended to sparsely settle territories with a dense precolonial population. The result is clearly evident in Figure 7.1, which plots, for thirty-nine former British colonies, the logarithm of precolonial population density (in persons per square kilometer) against the logarithm of the percentage of the population that was European at the end of the colonial period. The figure shows a strong negative relationship. A similarly negative, though slightly weaker, relationship emerges if one uses alternative measures, such as absolute precolonial population numbers (thus not holding constant land area) and absolute number of Europeans present (instead of their percentage of the total population).

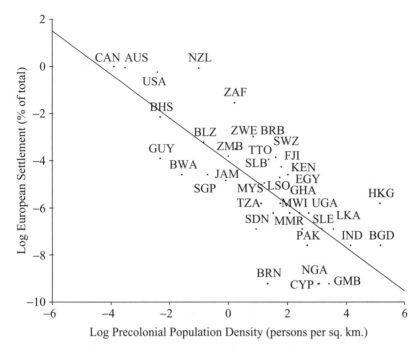

FIGURE 7.1. Relationship between Precolonial Population and Colonial Settlement for British Colonies

Note: Precolonial population density is measured as the number of inhabitants at the start of British colonialism divided by land area. European settlement is measured as the percentage of the total population that is European at the end of British colonialism. Precolonial population data are from Matthew Lange, James Mahoney, and Matthias vom Hau, "Colonialism and Development: A Comparative Analysis of Spanish and British Colonies," *American Journal of Sociology* 111, no. 5 (March 2006): 1434–5. European settlement data are from Matthew Lange, *Lineages of Despotism and Development: British Colonialism and State Power* (Chicago: University of Chicago Press, 2009).

In turn, more extensive British colonialism was associated with greater postcolonial development, again exactly the opposite of the pattern for Habsburg Spain. Figure 7.2 plots the logarithm of the percentage of the population that was European at the end of the colonial period against scores on the United Nations' Human Development Index (averaged from 1975 to 2005) for the former British colonies. A strong positive relationship is quite apparent. This association is even stronger if one measures level of colonialism using the number of Europeans present divided by land area.

These simple bivariate correlations do not by themselves make a convincing case for inferring causality. From a statistical standpoint, one would

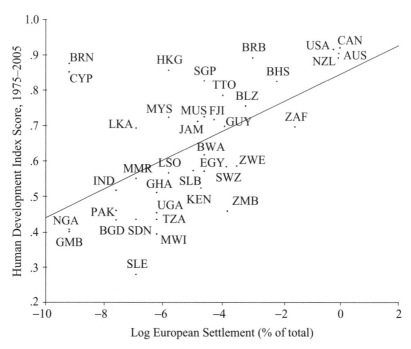

FIGURE 7.2. Relationship between Colonial Settlement and Postcolonial Development for British Colonies
Note: European settlement is measured as the percentage of the total population that is European at the end of British colonialism, as reported in Matthew Lange, *Lineages of Despotism and Development: British Colonialism and State Power* (Chicago: University of Chicago Press, 2009). The Human Development Index scores are derived from five-year averages across the 1975–2005 period.

want to assess the relationships when controlling for various potential confounders, especially geographic variables. This is essentially the tack taken by Daron Acemoglu, Simon Johnson, and James A. Robinson, as well as their critics, in an ongoing debate.[7] Alternatively, and perhaps with more conclusive results, one could try to move from correlation to causation by carrying out systematic case studies of the former British colonies, much as I have done for the Spanish American cases. But the sheer number of British colonies makes this strategy daunting, and certainly not feasible in the present context. A sensible alternative is to combine basic statistical findings with carefully selected case studies. Matthew Lange uses just such a strategy in his fine new book *Lineages of Despotism and Development: British Colonialism and State Power.*[8] Lange shows that the positive relationship between level of British colonialism and level of postcolonial development holds up in multivariate models. He also demonstrates with case studies that British institutions (especially state institutions) transmitted causal effects in ways suggested by the models. In examining cases, he is careful to pay attention to both colonial regions that became developmental success stories and those that became failures. He thus avoids the celebration of British colonialism that is present in some recent works.[9]

Building on Lange, the following discussion provides snapshots of four types of British colonialism, each corresponding with a particular level of colonial influence. First is *settler colonialism*, the most extensive form, in which permanent residents transplanted a broad range of institutions from Britain into the colonies without preserving precolonial arrangements. Second is *indirect colonialism*, the least extensive form of institutional implantation, in which the British did not settle and colonial authorities allowed precolonial leaders to maintain political and legal power over their subjects. Between these extremes were two intermediary types: *direct colonialism* and *hybrid colonialism*. With the former, the British installed a colonial state that was unified, bureaucratically organized, and of extensive territorial reach, but they did not pursue large-scale settlement. The hybrid colonies combined indirect colonialism with either settler colonialism (i.e., indirect settler colonialism) or direct colonialism (i.e., separate spheres of direct and indirect rule in the same territory).

Settlement Colonies

Four of the richest countries in the world – the United States, Canada, Australia, and New Zealand – were full-blown British settlement colonies and became, in effect, "neo-Britains." They showcase the most positive long-run developmental effects of undiluted and intensive liberal colonialism.

Before colonialism, these territories were sparsely populated by small societies without state-like forms of organization: various chiefdom societies in North America, aboriginal groups in Australia, and the Maoris in New Zealand.[10] Through their diseases and warfare, the British decimated the native populations, and the remaining indigenous people were systematically isolated and oppressed whenever they came into contact with frontier settlers. In turn, the removal of indigenous people allowed for the wholesale introduction of British institutions; the settlement colonies evolved into "clones" of Britain, albeit with a more rugged character and without a powerful landed aristocracy. Because of the lack of a landed aristocracy, the colonies tended to have active, participatory political institutions and egalitarian economies, and in this sense they were more liberal than the metropolis itself.

British settler colonialism laid the basis for future economic prosperity in part by setting up an effective legal system. Court systems and local policing institutions that could enforce contracts came into being, underpinning the stable property rights that Douglass C. North and others emphasize.[11]

Though biased toward business interests, the common-law system protected colonists from arbitrary state action and acted as a barrier to the instrumental use of colonial government for the enrichment of elite segments. Merchants and entrepreneurs thereby prospered. Land policies further promoted smallholders and facilitated economic transactions among farmers and planters.[12] Successful small farms undercut the formation of powerful landed elites in most places and helped the settlement colonies (with exceptions such as the U.S. South) to avoid the fate of the main Spanish settlement zones in Latin America.

Mostly homogenous white populations remained once the indigenous people were pushed aside or eliminated. With economic prosperity and continuing European migration, state actors sought to provide their white citizens with public goods such as education, health care, sanitation, and poverty relief – all of which had their own reciprocal spillover effects on economic development. In the United States, for example, agricultural productivity and later industrialization stimulated investment in primary education and enhanced the population's social well-being through nutrition and basic health care. Australia also saw substantial investments in social facilities after decades of vigorous growth.[13] Working at cross-purposes, however, were colonial legacies of ethnoracial discrimination and exploitation that severely tarnished the accomplishments of these societies. In Australia, racist policies deprived Aborigines of their tribal lands and excluded them from legally encoded rights. In the United States, colonists pursued slave-based plantation agriculture in the South, leaving behind racist ideologies and race-based deprivation and inequality. Ever since, the life chances for Aborigines and African Americans have been compromised. The consequences for social development have been especially grave in the United States, since African Americans constitute a sizable portion of the overall population.

Even with these gross defects, however, the British settler colonies are, from any comparative perspective, exceptional cases, in which colonialism erased preexisting societies and laid down institutions that catapulted the new nations to the highest levels of economic performance in the world system. Under no circumstances could a mercantilist colonizer have done the same. Mercantilist colonizers might destroy indigenous societies as readily as liberal colonizers, but they could never have put in their place the institutions and actors needed to support successful capitalist economies.

Indirectly Ruled Colonies

British colonialism fostered only a few of these "success" stories. For when the British colonized complex and densely populated societies, they usually did so by implanting or upholding rules that empowered preexisting actors that were quite incongruous with capitalist production. Nowhere can this be seen more clearly and tragically than in sub-Saharan Africa.

Many of the regions of sub-Saharan Africa that were colonized by the British had previously been home to relatively complex and populated societies.[14] These included polities such as the Ashanti Kingdom in Ghana, the Sokoto Caliphate and the Yoruba Empire in Nigeria, and the Buganda and Yoa societies in the Great Lakes region. Though complex, the institutions of these societies could not be easily refashioned and made to service British capitalism. This reality, more than anything else, discouraged British migration and the introduction of British institutions. The Crown was not prepared or willing to commit the resources necessary to establish real governments in Africa. Instead, it chose a process of conquest, cooptation, and indirect colonial rule through local elites – a pattern repeated throughout Africa as a low-cost means of ruling the vast territories.[15]

Under the mode of indirect rule thereby introduced, traditional leaders maintained political and legal power over their subjects, while reporting to and paying taxes to the colonial administration.[16] A small number of British authorities in each colony (usually only a few hundred) ruled through customary institutions and used existing political structures, courts, and landholding patterns. At the local level, chiefdoms' authority and control – legitimated on the grounds of ethnicity and common cultural heritage – were upheld by colonial officials under nearly all circumstances.[17] Through the chiefs, ethnic identity became linked to the provisioning of communal goods and land; the chiefs demanded political loyalty and ethnic solidarity in return. Thus, even when not pursuing an explicit divide-and-rule strategy, British colonial authorities helped to politicize ethnoracial identities and forge patron-client systems.

The patrimonial and fragmented states of British Africa, so regularly implicated in explanations of Africa's development problems, have roots in this colonial history.[18] Political actors, whether traditional chiefs at the local level or Western-style politicians at the pinnacle of national government, have followed colonial precedents by using their positions to extract resources and dominate subjects. No politically independent and viable commercial classes have been present to launch competitive investment activity. Instead, the leading political actors have themselves acted as the economic elite, and the feeble states under their control have often assumed the role of investor class. In the struggle to maintain (or gain) power, chiefs and other political entrepreneurs have found it expedient to use the ethnic divisions created or reinforced by the British as a basis for mobilizing support. Needless to say, political instability has become common; violent civil war and state collapse loom as ever-present possibilities and occasionally became realities.

In these fundamental ways, indirect British rule amounted to a formula for long-run economic and social disaster in Africa. Postcolonial actors who sought to right the course had to do much more than create effective institutions from scratch; they also had to tear down all of the colonial obstacles that had been put into place and that were staunchly supported by their powerful beneficiaries.

Directly Ruled Colonies

Colonial rule was direct when Britain dismantled preexisting political institutions and imposed centralized, bureaucratic legal-administrative institutions in their place. As Lange points out, "Direct rule depended on an integrated state apparatus and resembled the form of state domination developed in Western Europe over the previous five centuries... [It was] both transformative and intensive, being the British colonial version of Hobbes' *Leviathan.*"[19] The crucial contrast with indirect rule is that, under direct rule, centralized legal-administrative institutions were implanted not only in the colonial capital, but also in more peripheral regions, where indigenous elites had previously held sway. And the key difference from the settlement colonies is that Europeans did not become the overwhelming majority of the population.

In the West Indies, the British explored the possibility of creating full-blown settler colonies but ended up using systems of direct rule. These islands lacked complex precolonial societies because of either the absence of indigenous peoples or their speedy demise after the arrival of Europeans. Large numbers of British settlers migrated to the islands, especially Barbados and Jamaica, but high white mortality rates and low white fertility rates eventually more than offset the inflows.[20] Africans soon became the majority of the West Indies population, and white planters imposed slavery to exploit their labor. Even with the slave-based plantation economy that materialized, colonial forms consistent with direct rule were used for governance: the British installed policing and court systems to protect property rights and uphold the rights of nonslave citizens. Moreover, emancipation and liberalizing reforms beginning in the 1830s promoted participatory political institutions and erased some of the worst social legacies of slavery.[21] By the time independence was finally achieved in the 1960s and 1970s, the British West Indies had experienced a quite intensive form of British colonialism. And they came out of the experience with intermediate to high levels of socioeconomic development.

Hong Kong and Singapore experienced the most thorough colonial institutional transfer within Asia – indeed, within the whole British Empire – other than in the settler colonies. Before colonialism, these tiny city-states were fishing villages and small trading ports.[22] Although precolonial Hong Kong was quite densely populated in terms of persons per unit of land (see Figure 7.1), neither it nor sparsely populated Singapore housed an institutionally complex society. Rather, these were little towns that could be easily torn down and replaced with something brand-new. And the British were motivated to pursue such replacement because Hong Kong and

Singapore had obvious value as ports for securing the free passage of goods from Asia. Consequently, colonial authorities laid down here an "unusually sophisticated and pervasive set of property rights institutions."[23] Extensive legal systems based on common law, clear rules for selling and registering private property, and enforcement and policing apparatuses – these institutions were thoroughly implanted in Hong Kong and Singapore. Non-British immigrants settled heavily here precisely to take advantage of the stable business climate and economic opportunities. Soon, a Chinese bourgeoisie was investing heavily in real estate and industry. By the twentieth century, the two city-states had secured their role as open ports, regional trade leaders, and investment centers. At the time of their formal independence (1965 for Singapore and 1999 for Hong Kong), they were already two of the richest places in the world.

Levels of institutional transfer by the British were driven by their assessments of material opportunities. In general, populous and complex pre-colonial societies presented little in the line of such opportunities and thus dissuaded British authorities from pursuing direct rule. But there were exceptions. For instance, Great Britain pursued direct colonialism in Ceylon (Sri Lanka) even though it was ruled by the powerful and centralized (albeit weakening) Kandyan Kingdom.[24] Ceylon's commercial potential and strategic location enticed the British to insert centralized administrations and transfer legal-administrative institutions into this densely populated land. In turn, direct rule brought with it legal protections against domination by landed elites, which stimulated vibrant communities of small landholders. From these communities came movements that successfully pressured state officials to extend social-welfare policy during the late colonial and post-colonial periods. As a result, Sri Lanka was an impressive developer in the period immediately following independence in 1948, especially in terms of providing its citizens with social services.[25] More recently, of course, Sri Lanka has suffered from ethnic divisions and economic troubles. But as of the early twenty-first century, its citizens still enjoy widespread access to schools and health facilities that are well above average.

Hybrid Colonies

One mode of hybrid colonialism that was common in Asia and the Pacific combined direct and indirect rule. Perhaps most notably, colonial India contained within it both directly and indirectly ruled lands. Although the British may have preferred a single bureaucratic system for all of India, they were unwilling (or unable) to dominate this vast and highly populated territory through direct means. For in the aftermath of the Mughal Empire, sophisticated kingdoms, such as Bengal and Hyderabad, still remained.[26] As the East India Company came to exercise quasi-colonial control in the eighteenth and early nineteenth centuries, therefore, it did so in the presence of an agrarian-bureaucratic system that continued to have centralized administration, permanent armed forces, and relatively efficient tax collection. British colonial authorities gradually learned, through painful lessons such as the Great Rebellion of 1857, that they could hardly expect to simply abolish or even ignore local institutions without costly consequences. They resolved to formally colonize India but to do so by strengthening alliances with traditional elites and deploying those elites for collecting taxes and maintaining political order.

Thus was born a hybrid colony that combined indirect and direct forms of colonialism. Some six hundred princely states, comprising approximately two-fifths of colonial India, were ruled indirectly. The remainder of the colony continued to be dominated by a direct form of administration that did not incorporate indigenous institutions into the overall system of governance.[27] Because of the minuscule size of the colonial administration, however, both directly and indirectly ruled areas experienced rather low levels of colonial influence. In 1881, in fact, there was only one colonial official for every 267,300 people![28] Obviously, the colonial state never extended down to the community level. In the indirectly ruled areas, the British actively protected oppressive local elites, who otherwise likely would have faced major rebellions from the rural producers they exploited. Even in the directly ruled areas, officials relied on indigenous elites for a number of functions because of the general absence of the colonial administration, especially in the countryside.[29] In many instances, local elites were also given rights to large tracts of land and were thereby able to control villages technically under British administration. In turn, the concentration of these duties and powers in elite hands made possible the hyper-exploitation of the peasantry, something that appears to have retarded agricultural production and stultified investment in public goods, even after the end of colonialism.[30]

Although similar in some ways, India's hybrid colonialism differed from indirect colonialism in key respects. The central administration in colonial India was more bureaucratically organized than its counterpart in indirectly ruled colonies. As a result, in postcolonial India, the central state sometimes could and sometimes did act more corporately and effectively in policy implementation, especially when state action did not require complex linkages with societal groups. For instance, the Indian state had important successes in promoting information-technology industries, an outcome that required neither active state intervention at the local level nor the transformation of local power relations.[31]

Hybrid forms of rule left mixed legacies in other colonies as well. In Malaya, for example, British colonizers maintained very powerful legal-administrative institutions in the Straits Settlements and the Federated Malay States, while imposing weaker institutions in the Unfederated Malay States, where indirect forms of rule were used.[32] Predictably, economic development has been mostly limited to formerly directly ruled areas on the Malay Peninsula.[33]

In a few African cases, most notably in South Africa but also to a lesser extent in Zimbabwe, Kenya, and Zambia, the British established a hybrid mode of colonialism that combined indirect rule with considerable colonial settlement (i.e., indirect settler colonialism). The white settler and indigenous populations lived under separate institutions – the settlers in direct systems of colonialism, the Africans in indirect systems. The arrangement worked well (for the colonizers) because they depended so heavily on the local population for labor. In South Africa, for example, white territories featured effective legal-administrative institutions and a superb economic infrastructure, while the black areas were neglected and under the control of powerful chiefs who eventually collaborated with the apartheid regime.[34] Even today, South Africa is a relatively industrialized country that does poorly on most dimensions of social development.

To step back now and briefly summarize, it is evident that a wide variety of colonial forms existed within the British Empire. These forms are captured with the illuminating categories suggested by Lange: settlement colonies, indirectly ruled colonies, directly ruled colonies, and hybrid colonies. These categories pinpoint the differences in levels of colonial influence within the British Empire that were most consequential for long-run development.

Territories became particular kinds of British colonies in part because of variations in their precolonial institutional complexity. Those British colonies with the greatest levels of colonial influence – the settlement colonies and the directly ruled colonies – were usually populated by chiefdoms and/or hunter-gatherer groups before colonialism. By contrast, colonialism via indirect rule was generally imposed when the British encountered densely populated and institutionally differentiated societies. The contrast with Habsburg Spain is striking. The British chose not to absorb the costs of heavily populating and colonizing any major parts of an institutionally complex territory such as India, whereas the Spanish showed no similar reluctance in the indigenous heartlands of the New World. And while the British were attracted to the smallholding possibilities of North America (e.g., in Canada), Habsburg Spain found the same opportunities in the Southern Cone (e.g., in Argentina) uninteresting.

The different potentials for development carried by the different kinds of British colonies are consistent with the idea of a positive relationship between level of liberal colonialism and level of postcolonial development. Clearly, the British settlement colonies bear out the idea that intensive British colonialism promoted postcolonial prosperity. But even in statistical models that exclude the settlement colonies, levels of British colonialism are still positively associated with development: the former directly ruled colonies outperform the indirectly ruled ones.[35] For their part, the hybrid colonies tend to exhibit intermediate or mixed developmental outcomes. Subnational variations in these cases also often bear out the broader finding that direct rule leaves in its wake far superior chances for subsequent development than does indirect rule.

PORTUGUESE AMERICA

Portugal, the world's first modern colonizer, was mercantilist in its internal organization when it expanded overseas. Since the late fourteenth century, the state had been politically unified under absolute monarchy.[36] Much as in Spain, the king granted special legal privileges to various corporate bodies, especially the Roman Catholic Church, and he recognized three estates – clergy, nobility, and commoner – that served to rigidly stratify society. Monarchical policies promoting overseas expansion followed naturally from Portugal's long maritime tradition. Lisbon merchants engaged in exploration and made contact with new lands. They then received royal permissions to initiate trade, which in turn obligated them to pay dues to the Crown. The monarchy worked hard to limit economic opportunities to its selected and subordinate merchants, excluding foreigners and in some cases assuming political sovereignty over new territories. Most colonial occupations were, indeed, simply outgrowths of maneuvers to monopolize trade relations and ensure the monarchy and its representatives special access to spices, sugar, gold, and slaves. When colonial controls were imposed, the king's goal was always resource extraction. For he needed money desperately and immediately if Portugal was to sustain its position and sovereignty within the ever-threatening European states system.

Thus, starting in the fifteenth century with Atlantic islands and ports along the West African coast, a Portuguese colonial project was born. Sparsely populated Portugal was in no position to pursue large-scale settlement in most areas. Consequently, despite much Portuguese interference in various parts of Africa and Asia, the only sizable settlements that developed outside of the Americas were fairly small ones in Angola and Mozambique. In Angola, where Creole merchants had long been interlocutors for slave-trade operations, the Portuguese gradually occupied Luanda and a few other urban coastal areas. These locations were near complex indigenous kingdoms (e.g., the Kongo people) that settlers pacified through warfare. Nevertheless, because the goal was to extract slaves that could be exported (rather than to exploit the labor locally), the Portuguese did not significantly settle the kingdoms themselves; the interior remained almost entirely African.[37] In East Central Africa (Mozambique), Portuguese merchants established trade relations with Islamic towns on the coast, and eventually Afro-Portuguese settlers penetrated inland in quest of gold fields, though the dispersion of the gold and the resistance of the indigenous population meant that European settlement was scattered and relatively sparse here as well.[38]

It was ultimately the New World that became the whole foundation of the Portuguese Empire. The region of modern Brazil – which encompasses nearly half of the land area of South America and stands as the fifth most populous country in the world – was a colonial system unto itself. To grasp this system, we must apprehend subnational variations and be attentive to

Table 7.1. Development indicators for major regions of Brazil, 2005

	Northeast	North	Southeast	South	Central-West
Population (millions)	51.6	14.7	78.0	26.9	13.0
GDP per Capita ($)	5,498	7,247[a]	15,468	13,208[a]	14,604[a]
Human Development Index Score	.725	.790	.857	.860	.848
Life Expectancy (years)	69.0	71.0	73.5	74.2	73.0
Infant Mortality[b] (per 1000)	36.9	25.8	18.3	16.7	19.5
Literacy (% of population)	79.3[b]	88.7[b]	94.0[a]	94.3[b]	91.7[b]

[a] Data for 2004.
[b] Data for 2006.

Source: Instituto Brasileiro de Geografia e Estatística, *Contas regionais do Brasil, 2003–2006* (Rio de Janeiro: IBGE, 2008).

fluctuations over time. Comparative-historical analysis is ideally suited for this task.

Postcolonial Levels of Development

The five major regions that are conventionally understood to compose Brazil – the Northeast, North, Southeast, South, and Central-West – vary greatly across leading economic and social indicators (see Table 7.1). The Northeast and to a lesser extent the sparsely populated North stand out as extremely underdeveloped regions, whereas the Southeast and the South are more developed. The Central-West region is an intermediary case. By way of comparison with Spanish America, one can say that northern Brazil (i.e., the Northeast and North) is similar on major indicators to a poorer country, such as El Salvador, while southern Brazil (the Southeast and South) is similar to a richer country, such as Argentina. Central-West Brazil is more like an intermediate case, such as Colombia. Brazil as a whole is a product of the two halves: it has an intermediate level of economic and social development. Its GDP per capita and Human Development Index scores for the early twenty-first century place it as the sixth or seventh most developed country in Latin America, behind Argentina, Chile, Costa Rica, Mexico, Uruguay, and possibly Venezuela.

Large differences in wealth and human welfare across the northern and southern halves of Brazil are not new; quantitative indicators from the early twentieth century tell the same story.[39] Economic histories going back much further also underscore this difference. The really big change for the country as a whole was the economic "miracle" of the 1960s and 1970s, which boosted overall performance in Brazil. And the growth in this period appears to have had lasting consequences. Thus, in the mid-twentieth century, Brazil was at best an intermediate-low performer within Latin America, probably poorer than Colombia or Peru and possibly even among the poorest countries in all of Latin America.[40] The miracle years brought the country to its current intermediate level of development, well above Colombia and Peru. Yet the Brazilian miracle and subsequent years did not much change the long-standing relative difference between the North and the South. Both halves of Brazil experienced growth: the North moved from the "major underdeveloped region in the Western Hemisphere"[41] to a still-poor but more promising developing area, while the South experienced impressive industrialization and social advancement.

From a long-run historical perspective, then, the critical question is why the South became more developed than the North in the first place (the opposite of what happened in the United States). The contention here is that this difference can be explained by variations in the form of Portuguese colonialism. And the explanation focused on these variations conforms broadly to the general framework and theoretical principles outlined in Chapter 1.

An Early Colonial Periphery

As James Lockhart and Stuart B. Schwartz point out, "The patterns of Brazil's early colonization are in many ways parallel to those encountered in the peripheries of Spanish America."[42] Portuguese explorers in Brazil encountered indigenous communities very much like those in the original Spanish peripheries: scattered, nonsedentary or semi-sedentary communities without precious metals or any other forms of readily exploitable wealth. Estimates of the total size of Brazil's native population vary widely, though most observers suggest it was only 1 to 3 million for the entire vast territory when Pedro Álvares Cabral arrived in 1500.[43] Moreover, they all agree that no societies were more complex than, for example, the Guaraní peoples of the South or the Tupinambá peoples who lived on the coast and who encountered the early Portuguese explorers. These were modest chiefdoms of several hundred individuals who practiced slash-and-burn agriculture; they were completely unaccustomed to providing labor services or tribute to a state-like polity. Also very common in the interior of Brazil were even less complex hunter-gatherer societies, such as the Bororo tribes.[44]

For the better part of a hundred years, no large-scale colonial operation took place in Brazil. Although the Treaty of Tordesillas assigned Portugal sovereignty over enormous interior lands, the Crown exploited the region much as it had Africa, focusing only on the coast, leasing land to merchants, and creating trading stations to ship a few profitable commodities (notably dyewood) to Lisbon. Royal government was left in the hands of proprietary captains, who were granted essentially lordships in the fifteen original lots that were demarked to divide the colony. By 1585, there were about thirty thousand white settlers in all of Brazil, concentrated in the Pernambuco and Bahia captaincies of Northeast Brazil.[45] Here and elsewhere, securing native labor proved problematic and often unsuccessful – partly because the indigenous population had shrunk in size and partly because it so steadfastly resisted bondage.[46]

Portugal's marginal early colonization of Brazil corresponds well with theoretical expectations. Mercantilist Portugal was not much interested in Brazil because the region lacked the kind of population and riches that would have enabled quick wealth generation. So instead of focusing its energies on the New World, Portugal concentrated its sixteenth-century project on the colonies of Africa, where slaves could be taken, and on the plantation islands of the Atlantic, where those slaves could be put to work to harvest lucrative export crops.

Colonial Centrality and the Roots of Underdevelopment in the Northeast

By the late sixteenth century, major changes in colonial patterns were brewing in Brazil's Northeast. As it became fully apparent to settlers and the Crown just how profitably sugar could be exported to Lisbon, they moved to massively import African slaves and construct a plantation economy. The slaves, once relocated in the Northeast, in effect substituted for the "missing" state-like indigenous societies in Brazil. Settlers soon flocked to the Northeast, where the labor was concentrated, and mostly ignored the rest of Brazil.[47] There is no gainsaying that slaves were concentrated in the Northeast in the first place for primarily geographic reasons: this was a region with soils, rainfall, inland waterways, and ports conducive to sugar production and exportation. In that sense, geography was a "first mover" in determining the part of Brazil that became most central in the colonial project. However, variations in resistance by the indigenous population also mattered in shaping Portuguese assessments of the feasibility of producing sugar.[48] Once geography and indigenous reactions together determined which areas received the African slave laborers, colonial settlement and institutional implantation followed closely the location of this labor.

The captaincies of Pernambuco and Bahia became the centers of settlement and colonial activity. Already in the late sixteenth century, Pernambuco housed more than sixty *engenhos* (sugar mills and their surrounding operations) and was responsible for more than half of the gross product of colonial Brazil.[49] Colonial Bahia always had fewer engenhos, but it gradually caught up in total sugar production during the seventeenth century (its engenhos were more productive on average) and surpassed Pernambuco by the beginning of the eighteenth century.[50] Between them, these two captaincies were home to the vast majority of Brazil's European population, which grew to fifty thousand in 1614 and to one hundred thousand by the late seventeenth century.[51] They also received nearly all of the estimated 560,000 African slaves that were brought to Brazil during the seventeenth century.[52] The city of Salvador on the Bay of All Saints became the capital of Brazil in 1549, and soon only Lisbon itself was of more importance within the Portuguese Empire.[53] All of colonialism's great spectacles were here – the seat of the High Court, the most powerful viceroys, and the magnificent convents, churches, and mansions – as well as all manner of vice, earning Salvador the nickname "The Bay of All Saints and of Nearly All Sins."[54]

Economic institutions revolved around the plantation economy, and slavery cast its shadow over everything. Although there have long been suggestions by some analysts that slavery in Brazil was comparatively "humanitarian," contemporary historians soundly reject this thesis.[55] Work in the cane fields and at the mills was blatantly inhumane; the plight of slaves here was as traumatic as in the U.S. South. The Brazilian planters, by contrast, were notorious for their lavish spending and elite lifestyles. They were "essentially an aristocracy of wealth and power who performed and assumed many of the traditional roles of the Portuguese nobility... By drawing the line as sharply as possible between themselves and the rest of the population, the senhores de engenho [sugar mill owners] sought also to emphasize their racial and religious purity."[56] Within this racial order, mulattos and free blacks were subject to intense discrimination and were systematically shut out from the higher echelons of colonial society. As in the Andean regions of South America, society became bifurcated by race such that people of mixed heritage were regarded as fully part of the denigrated group.[57]

The heavy dependence of the planter class on slavery and other colonial institutions shielded it from market dynamics and left it ill equipped to adjust from plantation-based agriculture to other pursuits.[58] Because slave labor was available at fairly constant prices (which, however, increased some over time) and because the Crown oversaw land sales, sugar plantations would spread during boom periods, but they would not adapt – or necessarily fail – during periods of stagnation.[59] Planters did not have to improve their operations or make structural changes; production methods in the Northeast remained nearly the same from the early 1600s through the late 1800s.[60] Furthermore, the planters were fused (via economic and marriage or familial ties) with a small class of rich import-export merchants, based partly in Lisbon, who were not much different than the monopolists running trade through Mexico and Peru in the sixteenth and seventeenth centuries.[61] After 1649, the colonial activity of this elite was organized into the Brazil Company (Companhia Geral do Estado do Brasil), which functioned as the monopoly controlling the regulated fleet system and the prices for major import commodities.[62] By the end of the century, the Brazil Company was absorbed into the Portuguese government, ensuring the political subordination of the planter-merchant elite. "One of the great paradoxes of seventeenth-century Portuguese history is the fact that though commerce was the lifeblood of the nation's economy, the great merchants never wielded political power nearly commensurate with their economic importance."[63] Brazil really was "the king's plantation" – the Crown itself made the land grants, fixed the price of sugar, set the costs of imports, and controlled the fleet system.

Furthermore, the sugar industry was never able to generate any spillover development beyond plantation agriculture (except cattle in the vast northeastern *sertão*, or desert region). In his book *Sugar and the Underdevelopment of Northeastern Brazil*, Kit Sims Taylor pinpoints important reasons why:

> The extreme concentration of income, combined with the high propensity to import during the investment phase, explains the lack of development outside the sugar sector. Satellite economies could have been generated only if they produced something too perishable or bulky to import. Even payments made by the sugar sector to domestic factors of production were highly concentrated... There was little opportunity, then, for the senhor do engenho or the financier to invest his profits outside of the sugar sector; the profits had to be spent on imported luxury goods or reinvested in the sugar industry.[64]

At most, senhores de engenho could increase their competitiveness by expanding into other plantation crops (e.g., tobacco in Bahia).[65] But the production of these crops was equally dependent on slavery and colonial supports, and thus merely reproduced all of the problems with sugar production.

Brazil's plantation agriculture went into a century-long decline when Caribbean sugar producers entered the market in the late seventeenth century (the Caribbean was closer to Europe and thus enjoyed a shipping advantage over Brazil).[66] By the time the market finally improved during the late colonial period, the center of the colonial economy had shifted decisively to southern Brazil. The Northeast had now fallen irreversibly behind the more economically dynamic Southeast. This gap was only reinforced by Brazil's relatively seamless transition to nationhood, which left both slavery and the traditional planter class intact – the very things that had put the Northeast in its terrible predicament in the first place.

The Central Interior as a Semiperiphery

Gold rushes in the contemporary state of Minas Gerais in the early eighteenth century and then to a lesser degree in the states of Mato Grosso and Goiás fundamentally changed the shape of Portuguese colonialism. Suddenly, the secluded interior of central Brazil was the Crown's main resource base and the magnet for colonial settlement. Successive strikes stimulated both intracolony migration from the Northeast and exploding immigration from Portugal. A sizable portion of these newcomers arrived in and around

Minas Gerais.[67] Slave imports also reached shocking new heights, as miners flush with cash purchased their labor forces and towns grew up around the mines.[68] By the mid-eighteenth century, the Crown had created new captaincies at Minas Gerais, Mato Grosso, and Goiás to reflect the changed balance. As of 1776, the Captaincy at Minas Gerais was the most populous one in all of Brazil, housing almost 320,000 people (in comparison, Bahia had about 290,000 people and Pernambuco about 240,000).[69]

The flood of settlers and slaves to Minas Gerais and the surrounding interior regions certainly left an institutional legacy in central Brazil. In comparison to the Northeast, however, this legacy was less detrimental for long-run development. Three observations support this point. First, despite the massive migration, the colonial state in and around Minas Gerais was never very well implanted. Bewildering efforts by the Crown to impose order in the rambunctious mining towns never really worked, even when it came to enforcing the *quinto* (the tribute of one-fifth of all gold extracted).[70] Bureaucracy was coherent only on the coasts; "the crown had little authority in the mining zones."[71]

Second, racial bifurcation was less pronounced here. The virtual absence of white women and the huge slave population fostered high rates of racial mixing – much higher than in the Northeast. "Miscegenation also occurred in Bahia, of course, but there the white elite jealously guarded the privileges their presumed racial purity conferred . . . In disordered Minas Gerais, however, wealthy miners successfully passed on their estates and status to their mulatto offspring; some mulattoes even held seats on the municipal councils."[72] In addition, although the labor conditions in the mines here were terrible, slaves were more likely to enjoy some autonomy and had a better chance at manumission than in the Northeast.[73]

Finally, we need to remember that the real boom period of mining was relatively brief. Beginning in the 1760s, gold production went into a sharp decline as alluvial deposits were exhausted. By the end of the century, output was only about one-quarter of what it had been in midcentury, and it declined further still over the next twenty years.[74] For all of these reasons, Minas Gerais and the mineral zones are best understood as a kind of intermediary colonial region – a mercantilist semiperiphery – with its attendant unfavorable but not always utterly disastrous consequences for development.

Rising Peripheral Zones in the Late Colonial Southeast

Meanwhile, the metropolis of Portugal itself underwent institutional changes during the late eighteenth century – changes of rationalization and entrepreneurial promotion that shaped late colonial policy. During his rule in Portugal from 1750 to 1777, Sebastião José de Carvalho e Mello – the Marquis of Pombal – oversaw a series of reforms that often paralleled and even preceded the Bourbon reforms of late colonial Spanish America.[75] Pombal expelled the Jesuits from Brazil in 1759, expanded and modernized the colonial bureaucracy, and above all worked to enhance trade between Portugal and Brazil. To achieve the last, he reformed and then abolished the fleet system, which opened the way for any licensed vessel to sail to Brazil's major ports and for coastal trade to commence among the Brazilian ports themselves. Pombal also created new monopoly trading companies that targeted the most isolated regions of Brazil. These economic changes promoted the Lisbon merchants, who finally gained political influence by the end of the eighteenth century.[76]

Taken together, the mineral boom and the Pombaline reforms lifted up Brazil's Southeast, in particular Rio de Janeiro and to a lesser degree São Paulo. Rio de Janeiro achieved its prominence as the main port for shipping Minas Gerais gold and for receiving slaves and manufactured European goods. By 1760, when the mines started to decline, the city already had thirty thousand people; São Paulo to the south was a little smaller, with about twenty thousand. Rio de Janeiro soon replaced Salvador as the capital of Brazil and continued to grow considerably thereafter.[77] And a great demographic explosion occurred when the Portuguese king and court were relocated to Rio de Janeiro during the Napoleonic invasions. Thus, the population of the Captaincy of Rio de Janeiro increased from about 215,000 in 1776 to 250,000 in 1800 and to about 510,000 by 1819. The Captaincy of São Paulo also grew significantly during this period, from about 117,000 in 1776 to 160,000 in 1800 and to about 240,000 by 1819.[78]

In one way, Rio de Janeiro's late colonial prominence resembles the take-off of Buenos Aires at about the same time.[79] Both of these cities had originally become important as port towns moving massive quantities of mineral riches. They soon attracted the most prominent merchants of the late colonial era, ones with political autonomy and entrepreneurial inclinations that far exceeded those of their counterparts of the sixteenth and seventeenth centuries. Urban investments and sustained emigration fostered bustling late colonial cities with complex social and economic structures. Moreover, investments were soon made to promote commercial agriculture. Lands outside of Rio de Janeiro, like those near Buenos Aires, became dedicated to the agrarian products that could be most profitably exported.

Yet in another way, of course, Rio de Janeiro was quite unlike Buenos Aires and more similar to a region such as Caracas in Venezuela. For Rio de Janeiro was the slave capital of the world. Population growth here and in the Southeast more generally was tied to the massive importation of slaves, even though Rio de Janeiro and São Paulo probably had a higher percentage of citizens identified as white than did the Northeast.[80] At the end of the colonial period, furthermore, the countryside was dotted not with estancias but with sugar plantations – the very kind of estate that had caused irreparable harm in the Northeast. And the sugar plantations in the

Southeast were not much different from those of the Northeast in their use of labor and their agricultural practices.[81]

Despite some similarities to Buenos Aires, then, the "rising peripheries" in the Southeast of colonial Brazil were actually rather poorly prepared for postcolonial prosperity. Unlike in Argentina and Uruguay, labor-repressive planters were the fundamental dominant class in the Southeast (much as in Venezuela). It is true that merchants and investors in the Southeast were able to shift to coffee production in the provinces of Rio de Janeiro, São Paulo, and Minas Gerais during the nineteenth century. But in doing so, they remained completely dependent on slave labor. Thus, the Southeast emerged as certainly the most prosperous part of Brazil during the late colonial period. But its prosperity was more like the intermediate performance of Venezuela than the full-blown takeoff that occurred in Argentina and Uruguay.

At the time of independence, we must then conclude, there was no region within Brazil that was highly prosperous by Spanish American standards. The Northeast was extremely poor and destined to remain that way until the late twentieth century. The Central-West was by this time a fallen mining region and also quite poor. And the Southeast had achieved at best an intermediate level of development. It is thus not surprising that estimates of the GDP per capita for Brazil around 1800 suggest that it was less wealthy than Mexico.[82]

Of course, Brazil has undergone enormous economic and social changes since the nineteenth century, including the rapid growth of the late twentieth century that made the country one of Latin America's most industrialized. We cannot understand Brazil's current economic situation without taking these changes into account. But it is equally true that the pronounced differences between the Northeast and the Southeast, whose origins we have traced, have never been wiped away. When the Portuguese made the Northeast into their colonial center at the height of their mercantilist project, only to then let it sink, they ensured that this region would face long-term development problems. And when they shifted their attention to the Southeast during a somewhat more enlightened phase of colonialism, they did not foster any immediate prosperity – but they at least established this region as one where such prosperity would be possible in the future.

CONCLUSION

Our examination of the British and Portuguese colonial experiences points to the broad utility of the theoretical framework already employed to make sense of Spanish America. The discussion of British colonialism demonstrated that the general theory holds up well when applied to a large number of additional cases that may be similar to one another only by virtue of being recipients of British colonialism. And the discussion of Portuguese America revealed how the theoretical framework can guide the historically grounded explanation of subnational variations within an alternative colonial system that exhibited many broad parallels to the Spanish Empire. Let us accordingly conclude with some reflections on how both the British and Portuguese colonial experiences compare to those of Spanish America.

British patterns of settlement were strikingly different from those of Habsburg Spain: the British most heavily settled and most completely transformed precolonial territories with sparse populations that were not institutionally complex. Likewise, the legacies of heavy British colonialism were remarkably distinct from Habsburg Spanish colonialism: the most intensively settled and colonized British territories became rich countries. What can explain these differences? Certainly *not* geographic endowments, for British and Spanish regions with similar endowments often experienced essentially opposite levels of colonialism – as suggested by the comparison of Canada and Argentina. And geography cannot tell us why Canada is now richer than Argentina. Instead, institutional differences in the political economy of different colonizers hold the key to explanation. Canada was of considerable interest to Britain, and Argentina was *not* of interest to Habsburg Spain, because Britain was a liberal power and Habsburg Spain was a mercantilist one. These same institutional differences also explain why the privileged British colonies tended to do well after colonialism, whereas the favored Habsburg Spanish colonies did not. If a region was heavily settled and colonized, its chances of later becoming a wealthy country were simply much better if that settlement and colonization were led by a rising capitalist hegemon instead of a falling mercantilist one.

Portuguese America is similar to Spanish America in the basic sense that it was a single colonial system in which different regions occupied distinct roles. Even though a relatively seamless transition to independence yielded only one country out of Portuguese America, subnational regions had undergone different colonial experiences and emerged independent with contrasting levels of development. The overall logic was broadly similar to the explanations for Habsburg Spanish colonialism. Most basically, Brazil's Northeast became a mercantilist center and suffered gravely as a result; the Southeast was closer to being a colonial periphery and thus evaded much of the mercantilist colonial legacy. Insofar as one considers the Pombaline reforms to be a true liberal reorientation in Portugal, the parallels with Spanish colonialism are even more striking. For the Northeast can be understood as a fallen-core region, like Bolivia, while the Southeast approximates a rising peripheral region, like Argentina. Colonial patterns thus expose the original causes of why traveling today from Brazil's Northeast to its Southeast is like traveling from a quite poor country to a relatively rich one.

Finally, it needs to be said that colonies besides those controlled by Spain, Britain, and Portugal deserve analysis in their own right. While Belgium, France, Germany, Italy, and the Netherlands did not oversee vast empires, their individual colonies nevertheless can be analyzed through historically grounded case studies. In such research, I believe, a good starting point would be to ask about the (potentially evolving) political economy of the colonizing power and its "fit" with the institutions of the precolonial society. For out of this fit is likely to come a given level of settlement and institutional establishment. And this level of colonialism, in turn, is likely to be a driver of postcolonial development.

8

Conclusion

"There is no doubt that a large number of structural features of economic underdevelopment have historical roots going back to European colonization," writes Paul Bairoch in *Economics and World History*.[1] The view that colonialism left behind an underdeveloped periphery is widely held among theorists of world capitalism. Notwithstanding the patently objectionable purposes of colonialism, however, the countries that were born out of this traumatic experience now have remarkably diverse levels of development; they include some of the richest countries in the world as well as some of the poorest. Efforts aimed at explaining how colonialism universally led to the underdevelopment (or development) of its recipients seem ill conceived. The more appropriately targeted task is to adequately conceptualize *variations* in colonization, and then identify the causes and consequences of those variations in ways that can stand up against fine-grained evidence from the historical record.

This book has sought to carry out this task. It has argued that one must pay attention to, as an orienting centerpiece, variations in *levels of colonialism*, defined as the extent to which people and institutions from a colonizing nation are implanted in a colonized area. Differences in levels of colonialism are worthy of explanation in their own right, for they capture crucial contrasts in colonialism itself as a historical phenomenon. They also command attention by virtue of their role as causes of long-run development. Variations in level of colonialism, in conjunction with knowledge of the institutional organization of the colonizing nation itself, are essential to the explanation of persistent differences in development among postcolonial countries.

Let us then review what we have learned about the causes and consequences of levels of colonialism, both in broad strokes and for the Spanish American countries in particular. Then we can reflect more broadly, and perhaps also more boldly, about lessons that follow from these findings.

SUMMATION

This book has presented and assessed both a general historical-institutional model of colonialism, designed to apply to all formerly colonial cases, and a set of theoretical principles derived from both geographic and institutional approaches, intended to supplement the general theory in the examination of individual cases. The general theory set basic parameters for analysis; insights from the theoretical principles enriched the general theory in the actual explanation of specific cases.

The General Model

European colonizers differed fundamentally according to the dominant institutions that characterized their political economies. Some colonizing nations at some points in time, especially before 1700, featured a *mercantilist political economy*, whereby institutions were arranged to promote immediate wealth acquisition through statist protections that supported favorable trade balances, the accumulation of precious resources, and corporatist societal arrangements. Other nations at other points in time, especially after 1700, featured a *liberal political economy*, whereby institutions were designed to stimulate long-run accumulation through investment and trade for profit in competitive markets. In this study, Spain before 1700 and Portugal throughout most of its colonial history approximated the ideal-typical mercantilist colonizer, whereas Spain after 1700 (especially after 1770) and Britain throughout most of its colonial history more closely approximated the liberal type.

Institutional differences profoundly shaped both the *extent* to which a colonizing nation implanted its people and institutions in a territory, and the *kinds* of people and institutions it implanted. Regarding the latter, mercantilist and liberal colonizers brought authorities and settlers whose dispositions and mandates reflected in part the institutions of the societies from which they came. The colonial rules that they laid down or otherwise enforced were broadly congruent with the kinds of codes that prevailed in the metropolis. Habsburg Spain and Portugal were thus generally disseminators and enforcers of mercantilist economic institutions in their overseas territories, whereas Bourbon Spain and Britain transmitted and upheld more liberal ones. Colonies certainly did not become "clones" of their metropolises, but it is equally false that their colonial heritages were not influenced by the organization of the metropolises.

The extent to which a given colonizer brought its people and institutions to a particular territory – that is, the level of colonialism – was driven by the *interaction* of the institutional identity of the colonizing nation and the institutions present in the colonized territory (see Figure 8.1). Habsburg Spain and Portugal, the mercantilist colonizers, significantly settled and reproduced their institutions in polities with highly differentiated pre-existing institutions and state-like political formations. Thus, it was central Mexico around the capital of the Aztec Empire, the Andean regions where the Inca Empire had prevailed, and seventeenth-century Northeast Brazil

a. Mercantilist Colonialism: Habsburg Spain and Portugal

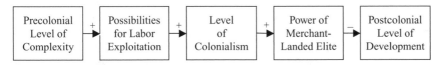

b. Liberal Colonialism: Bourbon Spain and Britain

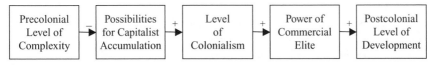

FIGURE 8.1. Elaborated Models of Colonialism and Development

with its slave-based plantation economy that were most thoroughly populated and transformed by settlers and authorities. Mercantilist colonizers gravitated to these places because they offered the best promise of economic returns under the mercantilist mode of accumulation – especially via the exploitation of native (or recently imported) labor. Areas without complex state-like societies, such as the Southern Cone of South America and, initially, the whole of Brazil, were of much less interest to these colonizers; the economic returns they promised were small and not soon forthcoming. Intermediate areas where various chiefdoms held sway either were mostly ignored, as happened in much of Central America, or saw middling levels of settlement and institutional implantation, as in Colombia and Angola, where the presence of readily exploitable resources (human slaves or precious metals) piqued colonial interest.

Settlement and institutional transfers followed a different path for the liberal colonizers, as exemplified by Britain but also including late Bourbon Spain. These colonizers mainly occupied, and most thoroughly brought their institutions to, the more sparsely populated areas featuring pre-state societies with less differentiated institutions. The British settler colonies – Australia, Canada, New Zealand, and the United States – are the leading examples: they were occupied by less complex polities at the time of colonization and then received massive settlement and a sweeping institutional reworking. But the pattern also generally holds for late colonial Spanish America, given that underpopulated areas in the Southern Cone experienced substantial colonization in the late eighteenth and early nineteenth centuries. These territories were vulnerable to extensive liberal colonialism precisely because their indigenous inhabitants and institutions could be ignored, pushed aside, or eliminated, any of which in turn made possible the full-blown implantation of liberal institutions that (broadly) supported long-run, market-oriented accumulation. Territories that housed complex, populous, state-like indigenous societies, as in much of late-nineteenth-century Africa and parts of Asia, did not usually see much settlement or market-oriented institutional implantation from the liberal colonizers. The populations and economic arrangements in these regions could not be readily reconfigured or undermined in ways that would allow for such accumulation; they thus merited less attention. Instead, especially under the British, these regions generally saw indirect rule, limited settlement, and the imposition of extractive institutions that were enforced without a substantial colonial presence or investment.

The kinds of institutions (mercantilist or liberal) that were imposed in colonized territories interacted with the extent to which they were imposed (level of colonialism) to produce different elite and subordinate actors, who in turn shaped long-run levels of development. Under mercantilist colonialism, there was an inverse relationship between level of colonialism and level of postcolonial development. Countries (or major subnational regions) with relatively superior postcolonial development, such as Argentina, Chile, Costa Rica, southern Brazil, and Uruguay, were all marginal colonies while ruled by a mercantilist power. By contrast, those countries or regions that became relatively poor after colonialism were often among the more important mercantilist colonial territories, such as Angola, Bolivia, Mexico, Northeast Brazil, and Peru. Level of mercantilist colonialism was inversely related to postcolonial development because the distributional effects of extensive mercantilist institutions brought into being elite actors who were a severe liability for future prosperity. Substantial mercantilist colonization usually entailed coercive labor systems, monopolistic guilds, and polarized ethnoracial hierarchies. Out of these arrangements came powerful merchant-landed coalitions that fettered successful development in an increasingly capitalist-oriented world economy. Countries heavily endowed with such actors fell behind and, with very few exceptions, would not catch up during the postcolonial period. By contrast, mercantilist colonies that avoided the intensive implantation of these institutions and actors were more capable of fashioning effective states and societies, either during the colonial period itself or shortly thereafter, and thus they could embark on a comparatively propitious trajectory of development.

Under a liberal colonizing power, by contrast, level of colonialism was positively related to postcolonial development. Indeed, an undiluted and intense form of liberal colonialism was the only way in which a colonial territory could reach the top of the worldwide economic hierarchy. It was thus the four British settler colonies and two other British city-states (Hong Kong and Singapore) that saw the complete reworking of their indigenous political economies in ways that enabled commercial elites to blossom and compete with the metropolis itself in the aftermath of colonialism. No Spanish colonial region could do the same, for none of the Spanish American countries had an undiluted liberal colonial experience. Even those countries that had been heavily colonized during the late Bourbon period (e.g., Argentina) still carried problems left over from the Habsburg mercantilist period.

Intensive liberal colonialism could produce exceptional levels of postcolonial development. But low levels of liberal colonialism resulted in some of the world's most disheartening developmental stories, as recent history in Africa well illustrates. The institutions that were established in indirectly ruled British colonies were designed to ensure political stability and revenue streams with as little cost as possible. Indirect British rule sponsored hierarchical patron-client systems and enforced quasi-market institutions that channeled sought-after resources to allied individuals (often representing a particular ethnic group) in strategic political positions, without creating or strengthening commercial business people. When colonialism ended, the new countries lacked functioning markets and integrated societies, and they were thus poised to disintegrate into developmental disasters.

The general model offered – as it was intended to do – insight about *typical* patterns of colonization and postcolonial development. As with any such model, however, this one could not and did not serve as a *complete* explanation for particular cases. To attempt this feat, it was necessary to supplement the general theory with additional insights suggested by other theoretical approaches. Doing so helped sidestep the characteristic pitfall associated with employing a general theory in historical research: arbitrarily selecting only facts that are in line with the model while ignoring those that are not.[2] Instead of mechanically "applying" the general theory, I considered a broad range of potentially relevant historical information and alternative hypotheses not suggested by the general model at each point in the analysis.

We can see just how the case analyses did and did not draw on the general theory as we now turn to the country-specific findings for Spanish America, beginning with the causes of levels of colonialism and then reviewing the consequences of levels of colonialism for long-run development. Since the colonial experience in Spanish America combined mercantilist and liberal colonialism, the operative model for these cases was the mercantilist-liberal one. Figure 8.2 presents an extended summary version of this model. Its predictions, to be sure, are more complicated than for situations when only a single type of colonizer is involved. Variations in both mercantilist and liberal colonialism become important, even as they work in opposite directions. Cases that experience high levels of both kinds of colonialism, or low levels of both, are especially complex and require special clarification.

Causes of Levels of Colonialism in Spanish America

Differences in levels of colonialism for the fifteen Spanish American cases are productively conceptualized with the categories of center, semiperiphery, and periphery. For Spain's empire was a single *system* within which different territories assumed particular roles and positions vis-à-vis the flow of people

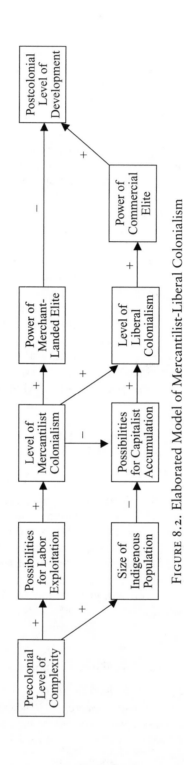

FIGURE 8.2. Elaborated Model of Mercantilist-Liberal Colonialism

and resources. During the mercantilist phase, Mexico, Peru, and Bolivia were colonial centers; Guatemala, Colombia, and Ecuador held a semiperipheral status. All other territories (Argentina, Chile, Costa Rica, El Salvador, Honduras, Nicaragua, Paraguay, Uruguay, and Venezuela) were peripheries. By contrast, for the liberal phase, the colonial centers were Argentina and Mexico, while Colombia, Peru, Uruguay, and Venezuela were semiperipheries. The remaining territories (Bolivia, Chile, Costa Rica, Ecuador, El Salvador, Honduras, Guatemala, Nicaragua, and Paraguay) were peripheries.

To explain why cases became mercantilist centers, semiperipheries, or peripheries, the general model provided much insight, but it had to be supplemented with insights from geographically oriented approaches. Thus, the presence of a bureaucratic, state-like indigenous empire was a necessary but not sufficient cause of mercantilist center status. Causal sufficiency was achieved only when a state-like indigenous empire combined with either abundant mineral wealth or close proximity to the capital of the Aztec or Inca Empire. Mexico and Peru had all three of these conditions fully present, overdetermining their status as colonial centers under the Habsburgs. Bolivia featured a state-like indigenous society and also stunning mineral resources, which ensured its center status. The mercantilist semiperipheries (Guatemala, Colombia, and Ecuador) had state-like indigenous civilizations, but they did not have the other geographic ingredients, at least not fully, and thus they attracted fewer settlers and less institutional transformation. And the colonial peripheries entirely lacked either highly differentiated indigenous societies or the relevant geographic factors (or both), which left them unimportant as sites of settlement and objects of royal attention.

During the subsequent liberal phase, especially under Charles III, two separate routes to center status were followed. In one, the combination of a sparse indigenous population and a strategic commercial port brought settlers and liberal institutions into relatively wide-open territories. This was the route of the *rising peripheries*, and it was exemplified by the liberal center Argentina but was also applicable to semiperipheral Uruguay and Venezuela. The second pattern characterized territories that had a large Spanish population and at least moderate mineral wealth. As exemplified by the center Mexico but also relevant for semiperipheral Peru and Colombia, *mercantilist carryovers* remained important colonial territories during the late Bourbon era because of their notable Spanish populations and still-vibrant mineral economies. The remaining territories lacked the conditions needed to become either a rising periphery or a mercantilist carryover; their fate was liberal colonial peripheralization.

Consequences of Levels of Colonialism in Spanish America

Because of Spanish America's dual colonial heritage, a *layered* explanation of postcolonial development was required, one that assessed the

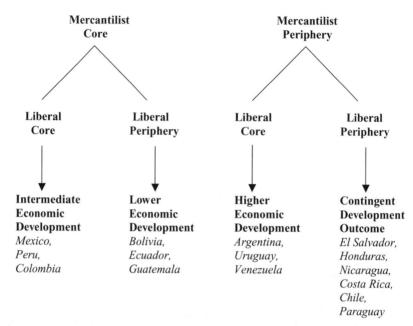

FIGURE 8.3. Colonial Paths to Development Outcomes in Spanish America

combined effects of institutions and actors acquired at different points in world-historical time.[3] Figure 8.3 offers a summary of this layered explanation. In the figure, the categories of colonial center and colonial semiperiphery are collapsed into a single concept – colonial core – and differences in levels of postcolonial economic development are summarized as higher, intermediate, and lower. The approach yields four pathways to postcolonial outcomes, which we will review in turn.

Three countries – Mexico, Peru, and Colombia – were center or semiperipheral regions (i.e., colonial cores) during *both* phases of Spanish colonialism. The substantial mercantilist and liberal institutions that they thereby acquired were the instruments through which powerful and ultimately contradictory colonial actors were built. In Mexico, Peru, and Colombia alike, the Habsburg era put into place legal and de facto rules that yielded powerful mercantilist actors. The great wealthy merchants of the era were born out of Spanish trade restrictions and monopolistic guild structures. They were often tied via investment and family to large estate owners, who arose in response to colonial institutions regulating the control of land and labor. The antithesis of a farsighted bourgeoisie, this merchant-landed elite trapped capital, stifled investment and entrepreneurial activity, and thus blocked development. By the late colonial period, however, the elites of Mexico, Peru, and Colombia were confronted with more liberal-oriented administrators and merchants who sought to make their own inroads, including through the promotion of commercial agriculture. New merchants in Veracruz challenged the hegemony of the old Mexico City elite; new peninsular traders gained a foothold at Lima and Arequipa; and liberal commercial actors from Barcelona and Cádiz encouraged export agriculture in New Granada. Yet in each case, actors associated with the old order were sufficiently powerful to block or temper the market-oriented directions undertaken by the Bourbon actors. And in each case, the final product was a colonial heritage in which the resulting country was an uneasy combination of the old and the new, allowing it to reach no higher than the middle of the regional economic hierarchy.

Liberal colonial reforms in Mexico, Peru, and Colombia nevertheless helped save these countries from a much worse destiny. This becomes clear when we consider the three countries – Bolivia, Ecuador, and Guatemala – that had intensive mercantilist colonialism without subsequent liberal changes during the Bourbon period. The combination bred extreme economic underdevelopment. During the sixteenth and seventeenth centuries, merchant moneylenders and commodity traders prospered under tight Spanish regulations in Bolivia, Ecuador, and Guatemala. They were often closely linked to the owners of large agricultural estates that specialized in foodstuffs and/or textile production. When the Spanish ignored or failed to transform these regions during the late eighteenth and early nineteenth centuries, the territories descended into economic oblivion: the decline of the mines in Bolivia put large landowners in control of what became a nearly subsistence economy; the collapse of the textile industry in Ecuador detached the region from the rest of Spanish America and left the economy in the hands of the food-producing estates; and the late colonial crisis of indigo exports in Guatemala ensured that the dominant merchant monopoly there controlled nothing more than an impoverished agricultural economy with only the most tenuous links to nonlocal markets.

The more satisfactory outcome – a regionally high level of economic development – involved precisely the opposite combination: mercantilist peripheral status combined with liberal core status. This was the trajectory of Argentina, Uruguay, and, with qualifications, Venezuela. Ignored under the Habsburgs, the Argentine littoral and Uruguay entered the mid-eighteenth century free from the obstacles imposed elsewhere by deeply entrenched merchant-landed elites. Then, under the late Bourbons, trade and tax reforms, new settlement patterns, and political realignments encouraged the development of commercial economies led by nascent bourgeois classes in Buenos Aires and Montevideo – classes that were tied to both inland and overseas markets and capable of steering successful export economies. Venezuela was a partial contrast because its slave-based cacao economy saw the introduction of more considerable mercantilist institutions and actors. Yet by the end of the Bourbon period, the region nevertheless was the site of new settlement patterns and was the beneficiary of trade reforms that stimulated commercial development and a late colonial efflorescence. Consequently, Argentina, Uruguay, and Venezuela alike were already regional economic overperformers when they won their independence from Spain.

In nine countries, then (Mexico, Peru, Colombia, Bolivia, Ecuador, Guatemala, Argentina, Uruguay, and Venezuela), colonialism left behind institutions and actors that were determinate of initial relative levels of economic development. Once acquired, these initial levels were maintained, with few exceptions, throughout the postcolonial period. When speaking in terms of long-run development, we can say that Argentina and Uruguay are richer now because they started richer; Bolivia, Ecuador, and Guatemala are poorer now because they have always been poorer; and Mexico, Colombia, and Peru are middling because that is how they were positioned at the beginning (though Mexico rose up some after the revolution). Colonialism brought most countries to their positions in the regional economic hierarchy.

For the six other countries where colonialism entailed less institutional imprinting – El Salvador, Honduras, Nicaragua, Costa Rica, Chile, and Paraguay – developmental outcomes were left open to the contingencies of the nineteenth century. These countries were the *sustained peripheries* – that is, marginal colonial areas during both the mercantilist and liberal periods. Precisely because they underwent considerably less intensive forms of Spanish colonialism, they could reinvent themselves during the postcolonial period. How successful they were depended, nevertheless, on the outcomes of interstate warfare in the decades following independence. Those former peripheral colonies that became entangled in and eventually losers of destructive military conflicts either failed to start the institution building that might have promoted development (Honduras, Nicaragua, El Salvador) or saw developmental projects destroyed in the course of the fighting (Paraguay). It was only when peripheral countries avoided warfare (Costa Rica) or emerged victorious from the fighting (Chile) that institutions fostering considerable growth were built during the nineteenth century. While these outcomes were firmly rooted in nineteenth-century occurrences, they were not unrelated to Spanish colonialism: Chile gained its military prowess under colonialism, and Costa Rica's isolation from the rest of Central America was a by-product of colonial settlement patterns. Colonialism thus helps explain both why some countries *could* change course in the nineteenth century and whether they actually succeeded in doing so.

Finally, this book considered the consequences of Spanish colonialism for long-run *social* development. To be sure, the ability of a country to maximize social well-being – as measured by indicators such as literacy, life expectancy, and education – is affected by level of economic development. No Spanish American country with a low level of economic development now enjoys a high level of social development. Intermediate or better economic development has been necessary for higher social development. Yet in order for economic development to promote social development, it has also been necessary for the available resources to reach a broad spectrum of society. When societies suffer from intense patterns of inequality, which are nearly always rooted in institutions that uphold asymmetrical power relations between categorical groups, the fruits of prosperity will not likely be enjoyed by large portions of society.[4] And the pernicious effects will show up on the indicators of social development. Social development therefore depends as much on patterns of categorical inequality as on absolute wealth.

In Spanish America, colonial institutions were implicated in new patterns of stratification, none of which were more consequential for enduring inequality than those that regulated indigenous people and other non-European ethnoracial groups. From diverse societies, the Spanish sought to create – and were partially successful in creating – a vast servile population. Land, labor, and governance institutions were used to systematically extract surplus from indigenous and African people. Spanish religious and sociocultural institutions were wielded as instruments to control their ways of life. Especially in those future countries where the precolonial population was large and concentrated – Bolivia, Peru, Ecuador, Guatemala, and Mexico – colonial institutions traumatized native communities, with tragic effects for social development. Societal majorities were prevented from partaking in whatever benefits and possibilities economic wealth may have created. Most people were left in abject poverty and outside of the benefits of citizenship. Only when native populations were initially sparse or soon became sparse, as in Argentina, Costa Rica, Chile, and Uruguay, did elites come to view a substantial range of the population as being entitled to the fruits of economic development. Only in these cases was it possible to reach comparatively high levels of education, health, and longevity.

There were thus two necessary causes of higher social development: intermediate or better levels of economic development and a sparse indigenous population. These were, of course, historical causes that generated only *initial* levels of social development. Yet once countries arrived at their initial relative level of social development – by the late colonial period, or earlier – subsequent shifts were rare. The reason is hardly that the situations of the non-European populations remained constant. Rather, even with changing ethnic composition, perhaps due to cultural-political shifts, patterns of stratification persisted. Ultimately, the colonial size of the indigenous population mattered as a long-run cause because it nearly irrevocably set broader levels of socioeconomic inequality. Societies that had first been built around the exclusion of the majority could not be easily reconfigured to provide collective goods later on. Only in countries that had been originally built in ways that allowed most citizens to enjoy broad entitlements could one hope to see higher levels of social development, unless the society was somehow upended.

If the comparative-historical findings just discussed are valid, we need to rethink some of the received wisdom about the onset and legacies of colonialism. In this final section, let us reflect on these new ways of thinking and consider, if only speculatively, what they might mean for development trajectories in the future.

Rethinking Colonialism and Its Legacies

In currently prominent work on colonialism, three types of causal variables – population size, disease/mortality environment, and natural-resource endowment – are often called upon to explain differences in levels of colonial settlement and institution building. In marshaling these factors, leading explanations stress the role of *conditions within the colonies*. By contrast, the approach of this book has been to simultaneously consider conditions in the colonies and conditions in the colonizing nation. I have contended that only by analyzing the "fit" between institutional realities in colonial areas and the institutional arrangements of the colonizing nation can we validly explain patterns of colonialism. We can make the point for each of the three causal variables highlighted in recent work.

First, by bringing colonizer institutions back into the picture, it is possible to clarify disagreements about the relationship between precolonial population size and colonial settlement. On the one hand, some theorists presume that population size is negatively associated with colonial settlement. Daron Acemoglu, Simon Johnson, and James A. Robinson contend that "relatively poor regions were sparsely populated, and this enabled or induced Europeans to settle in large numbers."[5] The reasoning behind this argument is that sparsely inhabited regions allowed Europeans to lay down the institutions of private property and, in effect, create neo-Europes via settlement. Yet on the other hand, we have seen – simply by codifying what historians already know – that Spanish colonizers preferred to settle in densely populated areas. And the Spanish (as well as the Portuguese) hardly created prosperous little neo-Europes in these areas of settlement. The apparent anomaly loses its mystery when we reflect on the fundamental problem with frameworks such as those of Acemoglu, Johnson, and Robinson: they treat all European colonizers as similar to liberal Britain in their institutional identity and colonizing orientation. Only with this assumption can they hypothesize that all European colonizers preferred to settle poor, sparsely inhabited areas. In point of fact, though, mercantilist colonizers chose to settle and build institutions mainly in densely populated lands. Indeed, if we accept – as we must – that there were major institutional differences among the European colonizing states, then we can reach a simple conclusion about when the settlement pattern assumed by Acemoglu, Johnson, and Robinson will apply and when it will not. The institutional identity of the colonizer provides the answer: Acemoglu, Johnson, and Robinson's hypothesis works for liberal colonizers but not for mercantilist colonizers.[6]

Second, attention to colonizer differences sheds new light on debates about whether or not colonial settlers preferred to inhabit low-mortality environments. Some findings – again, notably those of Acemoglu, Johnson, and Robinson – show a net effect for mortality environment on colonial settlement when averaged across those colonies for which statistical proxies are available.[7] Yet as Stanley L. Engerman and Kenneth L. Sokoloff point out, Europeans in the New World colonies often settled more heavily in areas with adverse mortality environments. They conclude that "the choices that European migrants made about where to locate – even controlling for returns to Europe – seem to be inconsistent with the argument of Acemoglu, Johnson, and Robinson about the importance of mortality conditions in Europeans' deciding where to settle."[8] Settlers from Habsburg Spain favored areas with high mortality rates because mineral wealth and indigenous civilizations were located there, and even the British were initially drawn to high-mortality plantation colonies in the New World. In the mercantilist era of colonialism, we must conclude, disease environment was at most a very minor consideration. The implication here is that one needs to take into consideration the *interaction* between disease environment and the institutional identity of the colonizer when explaining colonial settlement. Mortality environment exhibits greater effects on settlement levels under liberal colonialism than under mercantilist colonialism.

Third, a concern with colonizer identity helps make sense of over-time differences in the way natural-resource endowments historically shaped levels of colonization. To be sure, some natural resources had fairly constant effects – mineral wealth, profitable export agriculture, and strategic port locations, for example, generally induced colonial attention. Yet the consequences of natural resources for colonizing patterns also varied depending on the economic organization of the colonizing nation – a point not well recognized by those analysts who most strongly emphasize factor endowments.[9] We have seen, for instance, that the liberal settlement colonies had soils and climates favorable not to export agriculture, but rather to independent homesteads. Settlers from liberal colonizers seem to have preferred geographies conducive to small-scale farming. But these settings were precisely what the mercantilist settlers avoided. For whereas the liberal settlers originated in societies in which the most rigid and hierarchical systems of stratification had been checked, the mercantilist settlers hailed from a metropolis with a state-sponsored, hierarchical estate system still intact. Mercantilist settlers were more prone to regard small-scale farming as an unbecoming way of life. Liberal settlers, by contrast, were more apt to see that lifestyle as rewarding and possibly even dignified. Hence, analysts are correct to stress the importance of endowments such as climate and soil for settlement patterns – but once again, these factors differentially influence colonial settlement across mercantilist and liberal powers.

Some further broad implications that follow from the findings of this book concern the consequences of colonialism for long-run development. The argument that colonial institutions were basic determinants of long-run development outcomes is, of course, nothing new. More novel is the claim that colonial institutions exerted their effects by allocating resources in systematically uneven ways and thereby constituting the collective actors that subsequently drove development outcomes. Colonial institutions brought into being differentially endowed and differentially motivated groups, and these collective agents then carried out the behaviors (sometimes including conflict with one another) that established long-run trajectories of development. Approaches that see institutions as coordinating mechanisms for individuals are relevant here insofar as they help explain cohesive action (or lack of it) among the individuals who compose particular collective agents. But these approaches must be subsumed within an overarching framework that treats institutions as distributional instruments that create the collective actors in the first place.

Obviously, the very institution of colonialism always produces colonizing and colonized groups – the "citizens and subjects" of which Mahmood Mamdani writes.[10] What was investigated here were the *specific institutions* that constitute *certain kinds* of dominant and subordinate collectivities that were then positioned to shape, for better or worse, developmental paths. We found that land and labor institutions were nearly always implicated in the construction of colonized people. In Spanish America, such institutions had homogenizing effects, for they tended to define all native inhabitants of the Americas as simply Indians (though within the native communities, of course, diverse cultural practices were continued). But other colonizers found it more expedient to use land and labor regulations to exacerbate prior ethnic divisions or create de novo contentious ethnic groups as part of a divide-and-rule strategy (and the Spanish did the same during the conquest phase of colonialism). Either way, the resulting ethnic composition of society had momentous consequences for social development. If a substantial European settler population was left behind after colonialism, exorbitant inequality was bound to be a problem – unless the indigenous population had disappeared or become a tiny minority. In turn, categorical inequality drove down the level of social development, for economic gains could not touch substantial portions of society. By contrast, if few or no European people remained after colonialism, the extent of ethnic divisions that had been maintained or promoted during the colonial period was decisive. In most cases, ethnic polarization carried over from colonialism and meant intense inequality, with all of the attendant negative consequences. In rare circumstances, however, precolonial ethnic homogeneity was present and persisted during colonialism – a most favorable result for future social outcomes.

Crucial, too, were the ways in which institutions constructed elite actors by putting selected individuals in advantageous positions vis-à-vis resource flows. The groups thereby forged could steer the mode of accumulation within society as a whole. Full-blown mercantilist colonialism entailed the imposition of severe trade regulations and taxes, monopoly or near-monopoly rights to selected organizations and actors, and coercive labor systems of one kind or another. Such institutions not only stunted investment opportunities in the short run, they also created dominant mercantilist actors – especially monopolistic merchants and affiliated estate owners – who were motivated to trap capital and stifle investment and entrepreneurial activity throughout the colonial period. By the time independence arrived, economies had been driven into underdevelopment, and the new nations were consigned to the lowest rungs of the international hierarchy of wealth.

When liberal colonial institutions were thoroughly implanted, by contrast, elite actors were more adept at overseeing market-oriented development. Granted, even under the most intensive kind of liberal colonialism, the resulting elite was far from possessing the characteristics of a genuine bourgeoisie fully oriented toward investing profits in unconstrained markets. But something approximating a market-oriented commercial class was born out of institutions that channeled resources toward enterprising behavior for at least some selected groups, or that directed state actors to support commercial activities, or that promoted exchanges and linkages among merchants serving different markets. When these institutions were present, the legacy was a commercial class that stimulated growth via export-led economies and that positioned the newly independent countries onto higher tiers of the worldwide development hierarchy.

Collective actors forged by institutions are thus what we need to look at when explaining the potentially enduring influence of institutions. Future analysts of large-scale institutions must avoid the temptations – to which many have so far succumbed – of viewing the effects of institutional rules only or mainly in terms of how they define incentive structures and shape the strategic calculations of rationally behaving individuals. A basic reorientation is called for: macro-institutional analysts must turn their attention to the impact of societal rules for the distribution of power and the creation of collective groups. For these groups are the agents through which the long-run effects of institutions are transmitted at the macroscopic level.

Lessons from the Colonial Past

Momentously consequential though it was, formal colonialism has come to an end as an encompassing world phenomenon. And the process is not likely to soon, or ever, repeat itself. Still, colonialism and its legacies offer lessons for development in the future. By way of closing, let us consider these lessons.

Colonial history affirms the basic insight that the "best" institutions for achieving international success vary depending on the prevailing world system and world economy.[11] Tempting as it may be, one cannot conclude from the colonial experience that market-oriented institutions have been singularly effective tools for promoting development. Instead, the kinds of institutions that have stimulated prosperity have changed in response to evolving world-economic and international-political circumstances. Before the modern era, intensive mercantilist colonialism might have allowed regions to become militarily and economically successful. For the world system at that time rewarded polities with self-sufficient and hierarchical states fundamentally designed to extract resources and engage in conquest. Even in the modern epoch, colonial territories that received undiluted market-oriented institutions enjoyed decisive advantages mainly only during the period from the late seventeenth century to the early nineteenth century, when commercial classes in Europe struggled to win autonomy from overbearing monarchical states. Out of this period and its contests came the original free-market doctrines emphasizing the benevolence of liberal capitalism and the inherent deficiencies of statist economic arrangements.

Yet by the late nineteenth and twentieth centuries, successful economic performance increasingly required the state to play a leading role. All forms of capitalism, even in the advanced industrial countries, have come to depend quite heavily on state services that run through nonmarket channels (e.g., the provision of education, mass transportation, and public and social security). In developing countries, effective participation in the world economy has occurred largely only when the state actively stimulates and directs – and perhaps even creates do novo – commercial and entrepreneurial classes. This state role bears little resemblance to either the ideal-typical mercantilist or liberal-capitalist political economies. The new "developmental states" are, instead, founded on an active partnership between the state and private capital, one in which state actors enjoy relative autonomy from entrepreneurial classes even as they are deeply tied to those classes through social networks. This kind of state-society model, which perhaps has Japan as its exemplar, has proven most effective at achieving sustained high growth since the late nineteenth century.[12] It was, in fact, Japan that endowed its two most important and heavily settled colonial possessions – Korea and Taiwan – with institutions and actors congruent with a developmental state and a state-led industrial model. Korea and Taiwan are the postcolonial countries that have most impressively risen toward the top of the world economic hierarchy since the mid-twentieth century.[13]

The institutions and actors associated with developmental success have thus varied over time, in tandem with shifts in the world economy. Whereas the full-blown colonial implantation of liberal, market-oriented institutions and actors might have spurred development in the eighteenth century, identical institutions and actors could not do the same in the twentieth century. By this time, the forms of colonialism that led to successful industrializers and high-growth economies were the ones that left behind state organizations capable of managing entrepreneurial groups and guiding overall national economic activity. Those less fortunate developing countries that did not receive this favorable colonial heritage might still, under unusual conditions, experience an upward shift in their positioning in the world economy. But again, this required that dominant societal actors and state institutions be upended in ways that allowed for the blossoming of developmental states and state-society partnerships.

These last observations remind us that colonialism usually brought countries to relative levels of development that have been remarkably enduring. And one lesson to be drawn from this study is that the international hierarchy created from colonialism will not be easily rearranged. No simple change in policy, for example, will permit a broad range of poor countries with low levels of human welfare to become rich countries whose citizens live long and healthy lives. Nor can citizens with even the best intentions create at will the kind of sweeping transformation in the distribution of societal power that might trigger sustained development. Analyzing relative levels of development over the long run suggests some sobering conclusions about the likelihood of change in our world.

Yet not all lessons from colonialism point in such pessimistic directions. We need to remember that the colonial legacy has not prohibited gradual but cumulatively highly consequential changes in absolute levels of development. These incremental gains have occurred almost continuously: even as countries have maintained their *relative* levels of development, they have generally enjoyed increasing *absolute* levels of development.[14] The positive lesson is that poorer countries have often been able to derive some benefits from overall growth and expansion in the world economy. History suggests that if the world economy continues to grow over the long run, poorer regions should achieve slowly unfolding gains in absolute levels of development.

Even more-encouraging lessons can be gleaned from the colonial experience. For the very fact that colonialism occurred shows that a basic, worldwide transforming process is at least historically possible. European colonialism accomplished nothing short of fundamentally reversing levels of wealth in the vast territories of Africa, Asia, and Latin America that were subjected to this intervention. In the future, of course, colonialism cannot be expected to again act as the motor force that remakes the world hierarchy of development. But perhaps some new, alternative global process might one day achieve a similar feat. And perhaps such a transformation might avoid the pernicious consequences of past colonialism. Colonialism "reversed fortunes," but it did so by simply substituting one pattern of extreme global inequality for another. No humanly worthwhile process of global transformation in the future could do the same.

If some worldwide process were to ever again fundamentally rearrange territorial levels of development, *and* do so in an egalitarian form, it would have to emerge from very different motivations and circumstances than the colonialism of the past. European nations historically initiated their imperialist ventures in competition with one another and in quest of ever more extensive domination of territory and people. And they dismantled indigenous collectivities in the process. But in the future, I can only imagine, the pursuit of global egalitarianism would have to be directed by a supernational organization approximating a "world state."[15] For only if territorial states and territorial competition were at least in part superseded could far-reaching global redistribution take hold. And only if more citizens came to believe that their own personal capabilities and freedoms depend at least in part on the ever-broader expansion of collective capabilities and freedoms could the initiative hope to succeed.[16] Any future process of transformation directed at and destined to eliminate the most crippling expressions of maldevelopment on a worldwide scale would, in short, have to take a form that is nearly the antithesis of past colonialism.

Notes

Chapter 1. Explaining Levels of Colonialism and Postcolonial Development

1. Karl Marx and Frederick Engels, *The Communist Manifesto* (New York: International, 1948), 10.
2. David B. Abernethy, *The Dynamics of Global Dominance: European Overseas Empires, 1415–1980* (New Haven, CT: Yale University Press, 2000), 20–2. For other definitions of colonialism, see Jürgen Osterhammel, *Colonialism: A Theoretical Overview*, trans. Shelley L. Frisch (Princeton, NJ: Markus Wiener, 2005), 15–17; Ronald J. Horvath, "A Definition of Colonialism," *Current Anthropology* 13, no. 1 (February 1972): 45–57.
3. Abernethy, *Dynamics of Global Dominance*, 6, 409.
4. See ibid., pt. 3; Winfried Baumgart, *Imperialism: The Idea and Reality of British and French Colonial Expansion, 1880–1914* (New York: Oxford University Press, 1982); Niall Ferguson, *Empire: The Rise and Demise of the British World Order and the Lessons for Global Power* (New York: Basic Books, 2002).
5. See, for example, Andre Gunder Frank, *Lumpenbourgeoisie/Lumpendevelopment: Dependence, Class, and Politics in Latin America* (New York: Monthly Review, 1972); Mahmood Mamdani, *Citizen and Subject: Contemporary Africa and the Legacy of Late Colonialism* (Princeton, NJ: Princeton University Press, 1996); Walter Rodney, *How Europe Underdeveloped Africa*, rev. ed. (Washington, DC: Howard University Press, 1982); Crawford Young, *The African Colonial State in Comparative Perspective* (New Haven, CT: Yale University Press, 1994); Immanuel Wallerstein, "The Rise and Future Demise of the World Capitalist System: Concepts for Comparative Analysis," *Comparative Studies in Society and History* 16, no. 4 (September 1974): 387–415.
6. The two components of the framework correspond with different approaches to comparative-historical investigation. My "principles of analysis" are guidelines for conducting what Skocpol and Somers call "macro-causal analysis"; my "general theory" is consistent with their "parallel demonstration of theory" approach. See Theda Skocpol and Margaret Somers, "The Uses of Comparative History in Macrosocial Inquiry," *Comparative Studies in Society and History* 22, no. 2 (April 1980): 174–97.
7. Amartya Sen, *Development as Freedom* (New York: Knopf, 1999), 18.
8. Peter Evans, "Collective Capabilities, Culture, and Amartya Sen's *Development as Freedom*," *Studies in Comparative International Development* 37, no. 2 (Summer 2002): 54–60; Dietrich Rueschemeyer, Evelyne Huber Stephens, and

John D. Stephens, *Capitalist Development and Democracy* (Chicago: University of Chicago Press, 1992).

9. For arguments that link Korean development with colonialism, see Atul Kohli, *State-Directed Development: Political Power and Industrialization in the Global Periphery* (Cambridge: Cambridge University Press, 2004); Gi Wook-Shin and Michael Robinson, eds., *Colonial Modernity in Korea* (Cambridge, MA: Harvard University Press, 1999). For a more skeptical view on the extent to which Korea radically shifted its relative level of development after 1950, see Giovanni Arrighi and Jessica Drangel, "The Stratification of the World Economy: An Exploration of the Semiperipheral Zone," *Review* 10, no. 1 (1986): 9–74. For the view that the sources of Korean development may rest in the distant past before colonialism, see Bruce Cummings, "State Building in Korea: Continuity and Crisis," in Matthew Lange and Dietrich Rueschemeyer, eds., *States and Development: Historical Antecedents of Stagnation and Advance* (New York: Palgrave Macmillan, 2005), 211–35.

10. Explaining Europe's breakthrough was central to the work of classical theorists such as Adam Smith, Karl Marx, and Max Weber. For more contemporary work on the origins of capitalism in Europe, see T. H. Aston and C. H. E. Philipin, eds., *The Brenner Debate: Agrarian Class Structure and Economic Development in Pre-industrial Europe* (Cambridge: Cambridge University Press, 1985); Jack Goldstone, *Why Europe? The Rise of the West in World History, 1500–1850* (New York: McGraw-Hill, 2008); Richard Lachmann, *Capitalists in Spite of Themselves: Elite Conflict and Economic Transitions in Early Modern Europe* (Oxford: Oxford University Press, 2000); Douglass C. North and Robert P. Thomas, *The Rise of the Western World: A New Economic History* (Cambridge: Cambridge University Press, 1973); Immanuel Wallerstein, *The Modern World-System*, vols. 1–3 (New York: Academic Press, 1974–89). For a review of both the classical literature and contemporary studies, see Richard Lachmann, "Origins of Capitalism in Western Europe: Economic and Political Aspects," *Annual Review of Sociology* 15 (1989): 47–72.

11. In particular, attention has focused on the origins of different levels of social development among countries of the Organization for Economic Cooperation and Development (OECD). For literature reviews, see Edwin Amenta, "What We Know about the Development of Social Policy: Comparative and Historical Research in Comparative and Historical Perspective," in James Mahoney and Dietrich Rueschemeyer, eds., *Comparative Historical Analysis in the Social Sciences* (Cambridge: Cambridge University Press, 2003), 91–130; Paul Pierson, "Three Worlds of Welfare State Research," *Comparative Political Studies* 33, nos. 6–7 (August–September 2000): 822–44.

12. The literature on this topic now ranges from different strands of modernization theory to variants of dependency theory to older and newer political economy perspectives. For a sympathetic review of these strands, see, respectively, Samuel P. Huntington, "The Change to Change: Modernization, Development, and Politics," *Comparative Politics* 3, no. 3 (April 1971): 283–322; Gabriel Palma, "Dependency: A Formal Theory of Underdevelopment or a Methodology for the Analysis of Concrete Situations of Underdevelopment?" *World Development* 6, nos. 7–8 (July–August 1978): 881–924; Peter Evans and John D. Stephens, "Studying Development since the Sixties: The Emergence of a New

Comparative Political Economy," *Theory and Society* 17, no. 5 (September 1998): 13–45.

13. See, for example, Deon Filmer and Lant Pritchett, "The Impact of Public Spending on Health: Does Money Matter?" *Social Science and Medicine* 49, no. 10 (November 1999): 1309–23; Glenn Firebaugh and Frank D. Beck, "Does Economic Growth Benefit the Masses? Growth, Dependence, and Welfare in the Third World," *American Sociological Review* 59, no. 5 (October 1994): 631–53. For a more qualified view, see David Brady, Yunus Kaya, and Jason Beckfield, "Reassessing the Effect of Economic Growth on Well-Being in Less-Developed Countries," *Studies in Comparative International Development* 42, nos. 1–2 (Spring 2007): 1–35.

14. William Easterly et al., "Good Policy or Good Luck? Country Growth Performance and Temporary Shocks," *Journal of Monetary Economics* 32, no. 3 (December 1993): 460.

15. Jonathan Temple, "The New Growth Evidence," *Journal of Economic Literature* 37, no. 1 (March 1999): 116–17.

16. Danny T. Quah, "Convergence Empirics across Economies with (Some) Capital Mobility," *Journal of Economic Growth* 1, no. 1 (March 1996): 95–124; Charles I. Jones, "Convergence Revisited," *Journal of Economic Growth* 2, no. 2 (June 1997): 131–53; Robert Wade, "Should We Worry about Income Inequality?" in David Held and Ayse Kaya, eds., *Global Inequality* (Cambridge: Polity Press, 2007), 104–31.

17. Firebaugh finds that if population controls are introduced, global income distribution is stable in recent periods (due mostly to China). By contrast, Korzeniewicz and Moran find that distribution has been diverging since the 1980s, even when population weights are introduced. These divergent findings are linked to the specific way in which income is measured: Firebaugh adjusts income for purchasing-power parity, while Korzeniewicz and Moran use income estimates that are based on the foreign exchange method. See Glenn Firebaugh, "Empirics of World Income Inequality," *American Journal of Sociology* 104, no. 6 (May 1999): 1597–1630; Roberto P. Korzeniewicz and Timothy P. Moran, "World Economic Trends in the Distribution of Income, 1965–1992," *American Journal of Sociology* 102, no. 3 (November 1997): 1000–39.

18. The new growth literature generally supports the hypothesis of *conditional* convergence – that is, poorer countries tend to grow faster than richer countries when other factors are held constant. See, for example, Robert J. Barro, "Economic Growth in a Cross-Section of Countries," *Quarterly Journal of Economics* 106, no. 2 (May 1991): 407–43; Robert J. Barro and Xavier Sala-i-Martin, "Convergence," *Journal of Political Economy* 100, no. 2 (April 1992): 223–51; Gregory N. Mankiw, David Romer, and David N. Weil, "A Contribution to the Empirics of Economic Growth," *Quarterly Journal of Economics* 107, no. 2 (May 1992): 407–37. The neoclassical growth model explains this tendency in terms of diminishing returns to capital. See Robert M. Solow, "A Contribution to the Theory of Economic Growth," *Quarterly Journal of Economics* 70, no. 1 (February 1956): 65–94. Endogenous growth theory is designed to explore the variables that allow nations to overcome these diminishing returns. See Paul Romer, "Increasing Returns and Long-Run Growth," *Journal of Political Economy* 94, no. 5 (October 1986): 1002–37.

19. Ross Levine and David Renelt, "A Sensitivity Analysis of Cross-Country Growth Regressions," *American Economic Review* 82, no. 4 (September 1992): 942–63.

20. Ibid.; North and Thomas, *Rise of the Western World*, 2. Findings such as these contribute to a general sense among growth economists that "the most interesting findings are rarely convincing, while the more reliable ones hold few surprises." Temple, "The New Growth Evidence," 151. For other skeptical views, see William Russell Easterly, *The Elusive Quest for Growth: Economists' Adventures and Misadventures in the Tropics* (Cambridge, MA: MIT Press, 2001); Dani Rodrik, ed., *In Search of Prosperity: Analytic Narratives on Economic Growth* (Princeton, NJ: Princeton University Press, 2003).

21. Alice Amsden, *Asia's Next Giant: South Korea and Late Industrialization* (New York: Oxford University Press, 1989); Peter B. Evans, *Embedded Autonomy: States and Industrial Transformation* (Princeton, NJ: Princeton University Press, 1995); Dietrich Rueschemeyer and Peter Evans, "The State and Economic Transformation: Toward an Analysis of the Conditions Underlying Effective Intervention," in Peter Evans, Theda Skocpol, and Dietrich Rueschemeyer, eds., *Bringing the State Back In* (Princeton, NJ: Princeton University Press, 1985), 44–78; Robert Wade, *Governing the Market: Economic Theory and the Role of Government in East Asian Industrialization* (Princeton, NJ: Princeton University Press, 1990).

22. Joel S. Migdal, *Strong Societies and Weak States: State-Society Relations and State Capabilities in the Third World* (Princeton, NJ: Princeton University Press, 1988); Robert D. Putnam, *Making Democracy Work: Civic Traditions in Modern Italy* (Princeton, NJ: Princeton University Press, 1993); Sen, *Development as Freedom.*

23. A nice synthetic treatment of the Korean case with appropriate citations is James W. McGuire, "Development Policy and Its Determinants in East Asia and Latin America," *Journal of Public Policy* 14, no. 2 (1994): 205–42. On Kerala, see Jean Drèze and Amartya Sen, *Hunger and Public Action* (Oxford: Oxford University Press, 1989); Patrick Heller, *The Labor of Development: Workers and the Transformation of Capitalism in Kerala, India* (Ithaca, NY: Cornell University Press, 1999).

24. Richard Sandbrook, Marc Edelman, Patrick Heller, and Judith Teichman, *Social Democracy in the Global Periphery: Origins, Challenges, Prospects* (Cambridge: Cambridge University Press, 2006).

25. I draw these conclusions mostly from work on the origins of the developmental state. See, for example, Vivek Chibber, *Locked in Place: State Building and Late Industrialization in India* (Princeton, NJ: Princeton University Press, 2003); Richard Doner, Bryan Ritchie, and Dan Slater, "Systemic Vulnerability and the Origins of Developmental States: Northeast and Southeast Asia in Comparative Perspective," *International Organization* 59, no. 2 (Spring 2005): 327–61; Peter Evans, "Class, State, and Dependence in East Asia: Lessons for Latin Americanists," in Frederic C. Deyo, ed., *The Political Economy of the New Asian Industrialism* (Ithaca, NY: Cornell University Press, 1987), 203–26; Hagen Koo, "The Interplay of State, Social Class, and World System in East Asian Development: The Cases of South Korea and Taiwan," in Deyo, *Political Economy of the New Asian Industrialism*, 165–81.

26. Niccolò Machiavelli, *Discourses on Livy* (1519; repr., New York: Oxford University Press, 1987); Charles de Secondat Montesquieu, *The Spirit of the Laws* (1748; repr., New York: Cambridge University Press, 1989); Arnold J. Toynbee, *A Study of History*, 12 vols. (Oxford: Oxford University Press, 1934–61).

27. Jared Diamond, *Guns, Germs, and Steel: The Fates of Human Societies* (New York: Norton, 1997); John Luke Gallup, Jeffrey D. Sachs, and Andrew D. Mellinger, "Geography and Economic Development," *International Regional Science Review* 22, no. 2 (1999): 179–232; David Landes, *The Wealth and Poverty of Nations* (New York: Norton, 1998); Jeffrey D. Sachs, "Tropical Underdevelopment" (National Bureau of Economic Research, Working Paper No. 8119, 2001); Jeffrey D. Sachs and A. Warner, "Fundamental Sources of Long-Run Growth," *American Economic Review* 87, no. 2 (May 1997): 184–8.

28. Dani Rodrik, Arvind Subramanian, and Francesco Trebbi, "Institutions Rule: The Primacy of Institutions over Geography and Integration in Economic Development," *Journal of Economic Growth* 9, no. 2 (June 2004): 135. For a critique of this article from a geography perspective, see Jeffrey D. Sachs, "Institutions Don't Rule: Direct Effects of Geography on Per Capita Income" (National Bureau of Economic Research, Working Paper No. 9490, February 2003).

29. William Easterly and Ross Levine, "Tropics, Germs, and Crops: How Endowments Influence Economic Development," *Journal of Monetary Economics* 50, no. 1 (January 2003): 32. Similar conclusions appear in Daron Acemoglu, Simon Johnson, and James A. Robinson, "The Colonial Origins of Comparative Development: An Empirical Investigation," *American Economic Review* 91, no. 5 (December 2001): 1369–1401; Stanley L. Engerman and Kenneth L. Sokoloff, "Factor Endowments, Inequality, and Paths of Development among New World Economies," *Economia* 3 (Fall 2002): 41–88; Robert E. Hall and Charles L. Jones, "Why Do Some Countries Produce So Much More Output per Worker than Others?" *Quarterly Journal of Economics* 114, no. 1 (February 1999): 83–116.

30. Gallup, Sachs, and Mellinger, "Geography and Economic Development," 186.

31. See, for example, the classic studies of technology and economic prosperity during medieval times in Marc Bloch, *Land and Work in Medieval Europe* (New York: Harper & Row, 1966); Lynn White Jr., *Medieval Technology and Social Change* (London: Oxford University Press, 1962).

32. For a good review of theories and literature concerning the Dutch disease, see Michael L. Ross, "The Political Economy of the Resource Curse," *World Politics* 51, no. 2 (January 1999): 297–322. Statistical studies in particular suggest that the correlation between resource wealth and slow growth exists even when appropriate controls are introduced. See, for example, Jeffrey D. Sachs and Andrew M. Warner, "Natural Resource Abundance and Economic Growth" (Development Discussion Paper no. 517a, Harvard Institute for International Development, 1995).

33. This institutional explanation is discussed by Ross, "Political Economy of the Resource Curse," 319–20, who also provides various citations to the existing literature on the topic.

34. For a discussion, see John Luke Gallup, Alejandro Gaviria, and Eduardo Lora, *Is Geography Destiny? Lessons from Latin America* (Washington, DC: Inter-American Development Bank, 2003), 31–6.

35. Ibid., 10–11. See also Celso Furtado, *Economic Development of Latin America: Historical Background and Contemporary Problems*, trans. Suzette Macedo, 2nd ed. (New York: Cambridge University Press, 1976), 47–9.
36. Engerman and Sokoloff, "Factor Endowments, Inequality, and Paths of Development," 87.
37. See especially the models in Daron Acemoglu, Simon Johnson, and James A. Robinson, "Reversal of Fortune: Geography and Institutions in the Making of the Modern World Income Distribution," *Quarterly Journal of Economics* 117, no. 4 (November 2002): 1250–1.
38. Acemoglu, Johnson, and Robinson, "Colonial Origins"; Philip D. Curtin, *Death by Migration: Europe's Encounter with the Tropical World in the 19th Century* (New York: Cambridge University Press, 1989); Curtin, *Disease and Empire: The Health of European Troops in the Conquest of Africa* (New York: Cambridge University Press, 1998).
39. Engerman and Sokoloff, "Factor Endowments, Inequality, and Paths of Development," 51.
40. Acemoglu, Johnson, and Robinson, "Reversal of Fortune."
41. Historical institutionalism was first formally defined and contrasted with rational choice institutionalism in Kathleen Thelen and Sven Steinmo, "Historical Institutionalism in Comparative Politics," in Sven Steinmo, Kathleen Thelen, and Frank Longstreth, eds., *Structuring Politics: Historical Institutionalism in Comparative Analysis* (New York: Cambridge University Press, 1992), 1–32. Since then, a number of overviews of the two approaches have been presented, sometimes also including "sociological institutionalism" as a third approach. See Peter A. Hall and Rosemary C. R. Taylor, "Political Science and the Three New Institutionalisms," *Political Studies* 44, no. 5 (December 1996): 936–57; Ellen M. Immergut, "The Theoretical Core of the New Institutionalism," *Politics and Society* 26, no. 1 (March 1998): 5–34; Ira Katznelson, "Structure and Configuration in Comparative Politics," in Mark Irving Lichbach and Alan Zuckerman, eds., *Comparative Politics: Rationality, Culture, and Structure* (New York: Cambridge University Press, 1997), 81–112; James Mahoney and Kathleen Thelen, "A Theory of Gradual Institutional Change," in James Mahoney and Kathleen Thelen, eds., *Explaining Institutional Change: Ambiguity, Agency, and Power* (New York: Cambridge University Press, 2010); Paul Pierson and Theda Skocpol, "Historical Institutionalism in Contemporary Political Science," in Ira Katznelson and Helen V. Milner, eds., *Political Science: State of the Discipline* (New York: Norton, 2002), 693–721; Kathleen Thelen, "Historical Institutionalism in Comparative Politics," *Annual Review of Political Science* 2 (1999): 369–404. On the affinities between historical institutionalism and comparative-historical analysis, see James Mahoney and Dietrich Rueschemeyer, "Comparative Historical Analysis: Achievements and Agendas," in Mahoney and Rueschemeyer, *Comparative Historical Analysis in the Social Sciences*, 11, 15.
42. According to North, "institutions are the rules of the game in a society or, more formally, are the humanly devised constraints that shape human interaction." According to Hall and Taylor, historical institutionalists define institutions as "the formal or informal procedures, routines, norms and conventions embedded in the organizational structure of the polity or political economy." Douglass C. North, *Institutions, Institutional Change, and Economic Performance*

(New York: Cambridge University Press, 1990), 3; Hall and Taylor, "Political Science and the Three New Institutionalisms," 938. For similar definitions, see Peter Hall, *Governing the Economy: The Politics of State Intervention in Britain and France* (New York: Oxford University Press, 1986), 101–2; G. John Ikenberry, "Conclusion: An Institutional Approach to American Foreign Economic Policy," in G. John Ikenberry, David A. Lake, and Michael Mastanduno, eds., *The State and American Foreign Economic Policy* (Ithaca, NY: Cornell University Press, 1988), 222–3; Thelen and Steinmo, "Historical Institutionalism," 2.

43. Robert H. Bates, Avner Greif, Margaret Levi, Jean-Laurent Rosenthal, and Barry R. Weingast, *Analytic Narratives* (Princeton, NJ: Princeton University Press, 1998), 8–9; Margaret Levi, "A Model, a Method and a Map: Rational Choice in Comparative and Historical Analysis," in Lichbach and Zuckerman, *Comparative Politics*, 27; Kenneth A. Shepsle, "Studying Institutions: Some Lessons from the Rational Choice Approach," *Journal of Theoretical Politics* 1, no. 2 (1989): 145; Barry R. Weingast, "Rational-Choice Institutionalism," in Katznelson and Milner, *Political Science*, 661–9.

44. Hall and Taylor, "Political Science and the Three New Institutionalisms," 938; Immergut, "Theoretical Core," 16–17; Pierson and Skocpol, "Historical Institutionalism," 706; Thelen, "Historical Institutionalism," 379, 394. Although the view of institutions as distributional instruments is common in historical institutionalism and associated with that tradition, some "dissenters" within rational choice theory are critical of that theory's reigning consensual views and call for more attention to the power-distributional aspects of institutions. Most notable among these dissenters is Jack Knight in *Institutions and Social Conflict* (Cambridge: Cambridge University Press, 1992). But we also must include here Daron Acemoglu, Simon Johnson, and James A. Robinson, whose approach is summarized in "Institutions as the Fundamental Cause of Long-Run Growth," in Philippe Aghion and Steve Durlauf, eds., *Handbook of Economic Growth*, vol. 1A (Amsterdam: Elsevier, 2005), 385–472. As Moe emphasizes, rational choice institutionalists may invoke power and distributional considerations in their analyses, but these concerns are subordinated to the fundamental orientations of the approach: "Power is a peripheral component of the theory. The rational choice theory of political institutions is really a theory of cooperation that, with elaboration, can be used to say something about power." Terry M. Moe, "Power and Political Institutions," *Perspectives on Politics* 3, no. 2 (June 2005): 215. See also Margaret Levi, "Reconsiderations of Rational Choice in Comparative and Historical Analysis," in Mark Lichbach and Alan Zuckerman, eds., *Comparative Politics: Rationality, Culture, and Structure*, 2nd ed. (Cambridge: Cambridge University Press, 2008), 117–33, on the problem of theorizing power in rational choice institutionalism.

45. The most notable exceptions are institutions that do not require sanctions because they are so taken for granted that they become reified. See Peter L. Berger and Thomas Luckman, *The Social Construction of Reality: A Treatise in the Sociology of Knowledge* (New York: Doubleday, 1966), 89. For a good discussion of the connection between institutions and sanctions, see Robin Stryker, "Rules, Resources, and Legitimacy Processes: Some Implications for Social Conflict, Order, and Change," *American Journal of Sociology* 99, no. 4 (January 1994): 847–910.

46. This point is made nicely in the literature on path dependence, especially in Paul Pierson, "Increasing Returns, Path Dependence, and the Study of Politics," *American Political Science Review* 94, no. 2 (June 2000): 251–67.

47. Knight, *Institutions and Social Conflict*, 40.

48. Mahoney and Thelen, "A Theory of Gradual Institutional Change." Change remains possible because actors are embedded in a multiplicity of institutions whose intersection may allow for gradual or rapid shifts in the ongoing distribution of resources. See William H. Sewell Jr., "A Theory of Structure: Duality, Agency, and Transformation," *American Journal of Sociology* 98, no. 1 (July 1992): 1–29.

49. Knight, *Institutions and Social Conflict*, 126.

50. Hall, *Governing the Economy*, 19; Elisabeth S. Clemens and James M. Cook, "Politics and Institutionalism: Explaining Durability and Change," *Annual Review of Sociology* 25 (1999): 454–5.

51. Acemoglu, Johnson, and Robinson, "Colonial Origins"; Acemoglu, Johnson, and Robinson, "Reversal of Fortune."

52. D. K. Fieldhouse, *The Colonial Empires: A Comparative Survey from the Eighteenth Century* (New York: Dell, 1966); Young, *African Colonial State*; Kohli, *State-Directed Development*; Jonathan Krieckhaus, *Dictating Development: How Europe Shaped the Global Periphery* (Pittsburgh, PA: University of Pittsburgh Press, 2006).

53. For discussions, see Edward L. Glaeser, Rafael La Porta, Florencio Lopez-de-Silanes, and Andrei Shleifer, "Do Institutions Cause Growth?" *Journal of Economic Growth* 9, no. 3 (September 2004): 271–303; Adam Przeworski, "Economic History and Political Science," *The Political Economist* (newsletter of the section on political economy, American Political Science Association) 12, no. 2 (Fall 2004): 1–13; Raghuram G. Rajan and Luigi Zingales, "The Persistence of Underdevelopment: Institutions, Human Capital, or Constituencies?" (Centre for Economic Policy Research, Discussion Paper No. 5867, October 2006), 2. The more qualitative work of North and Thomas suggests that courts and police are the key institutions that sustain property rights. See North and Thomas, *Rise of the Western World*. To be sure, courts and police do sometimes serve to enforce contracts, guarantee investments, and uphold private ownership. But courts and police can just as easily be used in the service of extractive institutions that privilege rent-seeking elites. Moreover, the kinds of property-protecting courts and police that North and others have in mind may emerge *after* successful development has begun and thus could be partly a symptom or consequence of development itself.

54. Adam Przeworski, "The Last Instance: Are Institutions the Primary Cause of Economic Development?" *European Journal of Sociology* 45, no. 2 (2004): 173.

55. Acemoglu, Johnson, and Robinson, "Colonial Origins," 1373. See also James Robinson and Kenneth Sokoloff, "Historical Roots of Inequality in Latin America and the Caribbean," in David de Ferranti, ed., *Inequality in Latin America and the Caribbean: Breaking with History?* (Washington, DC: World Bank, 2003), 174.

56. Daron Acemoglu, Simon Johnson, and James A. Robinson, "The Rise of Europe: Atlantic Trade, Institutional Change, and Economic Growth," *American Economic Review* 95, no. 3 (June 2005): 546–79.

57. José Antonio Alonso, "Inequality, Institutions and Progress: A Debate between History and the Present," *CEPAL Review* 93 (December 2007): 65.

58. Ibid., 65–6.

59. Engerman and Sokoloff adopt a distributional approach to institutions and emphasize the inequality-enhancing effects of institutions. However, they do not explicitly link inequality to ethnoracial group formation, as I do here. See Engerman and Sokoloff, "Factor Endowments, Inequality, and Paths of Development"; Engerman and Sokoloff, "Factor Endowments, Institutions, and Differential Paths of Growth among New World Economies: A View from Economic Historians of the United States," in Stephen Haber, ed., *How Latin America Fell Behind: Essays on the Economic Histories of Brazil and Mexico, 1800–1914* (Stanford, CA: Stanford University Press, 1997), 260–304; Engerman and Sokoloff, "History Lessons: Institutions, Factor Endowments, and Paths of Development in the New World," *Journal of Economic Perspectives* 14, no. 3 (Summer 2000): 217–32. For a perspective more similar to mine on this point, see William Glade, "Institutions and Inequality in Latin America: Text and Subtext," *Journal of Interamerican Studies and World Affairs* 38, nos. 2–3 (Summer–Autumn 1996): 159–79.

60. Albert O. Hirschman, *The Strategy of Economic Development* (New Haven, CT: Yale University Press, 1958), 35.

61. On the distinction between institutions that coordinate investment and those that protect against expropriation, see Przeworski, "Economic History."

62. These features are stressed in classic works on mercantilism, especially Eli F. Heckscher, *Mercantilism*, 2 vols. (London: George Allen & Unwin, 1935). See also D. C. Coleman, "Eli Heckscher and the Idea of Mercantilism," *Scandinavian Economic History Review* 5, no. 1 (1957): 3–25.

63. This aspect of mercantilism is emphasized in Robert B. Ekelund and Robert D. Tollison, *Mercantilism as a Rent-Seeking Society: Economic Regulation in Historical Perspective* (College Station: Texas A&M University Press, 1981).

64. These aspects of liberal political economy have been emphasized since Adam Smith, *The Wealth of Nations* (1776; repr., New York: Modern Library, 2000).

65. Statistical studies that find that the timing of the colonial experience (e.g., before 1700 versus after 1700) influences long-run development may be picking up the effects of changes in the institutional identity of the European colonizers. See James Feyrer and Bruce Sacerdote, "Colonialism and Modern Income: Islands as Natural Experiments" (National Bureau of Economic Research, Working Paper No. 12546, September 2006); Ola Olsson, "On the Institutional Legacy of Mercantilist and Imperialist Colonialism" (Working Papers in Economics No. 247, School of Business, Economics, and Law, Göteborg University, March 2007).

66. J. A. Hobson, *Imperialism: A Study* (London: Archibald Constable, 1905), 5.

67. Matthew Lange, "British Colonial State Legacies and Development Trajectories: A Statistical Analysis of Direct and Indirect Rule," in Lange and Rueschemeyer, *States and Development*, 117–39.

68. Acemoglu, Johnson, and Robinson, "Colonial Origins."

69. James Lockhart and Stuart B. Schwartz, *Early Latin America: A History of Colonial Spanish America and Brazil* (Cambridge: Cambridge University Press,

1983), 254–5, 377; Christine Daniels and Michael V. Kennedy, eds., *Negotiated Empires: Centers and Peripheries in the Americas, 1500–1820* (New York: Routledge, 2002).

70. See, for example, Kent V. Flannery, "The Cultural Evolution of Civilizations," *Annual Review of Ecology and Systematics* 3 (November 1972): 399–426; Elman R. Service, *Primitive Social Organization: An Evolutionary Perspective* (New York: Random House, 1962).

71. Flannery, "Cultural Evolution"; Henry Wright, "Recent Research on the Origin of the State," *Annual Review of Anthropology* 6 (1977): 379–97; S. N. Eisenstadt, *The Political Systems of Empires: The Rise and Fall of the Historical Bureaucratic Societies* (New York: Free Press, 1963).

72. Flannery, "Cultural Evolution"; Wright, "Recent Research"; Gerhard Lenski, Patrick Nolan, and Jean Lenski, *Human Societies: An Introduction to Macrosociology*, 7th ed. (New York: McGraw-Hill, 1995).

73. The role of economic considerations was famously emphasized by Hobson, *Imperialism*; V. I. Lenin, *Imperialism: The Highest Stage of Capitalism* (1916; repr., New York: International Publishers, 1939). On the role of non-economic factors, see E. J. Hobsbawm, *Nations and Nationalism since 1780* (New York: Cambridge University Press, 1980); Hendrik Spruyt, *Ending Empire: Contested Sovereignty and Territorial Partition* (Ithaca, NY: Cornell University Press, 2005), chap. 2.

74. As Service put it, "The more alike the conquerors and conquered, the more simple and easy the adjustment will be, other things being equal." Elman R. Service, "Indian–European Relations in Colonial Latin America," *American Anthropologist* 57, no. 3 (June 1955): 416.

75. Acemoglu, Johnson, and Robinson, "Reversal of Fortune."

76. The transition from hunter-gatherer society to chiefdom and then to state did not, as anthropologists once supposed, allow for greater longevity, better health, and more security and leisure. Rather, as revisionist scholars in the field of paleopathology have shown, these transitions caused an increase in inequality, a rise in malnutrition, and the spread of infectious diseases. For an example of the early anthropological view, see R. J. Braidwood, "The Agricultural Revolution," *Scientific American* 203, no. 3 (1960): 130–48. On the more recent work in paleopathology, see Mark Cohen and George Armelagos, "Paleopathology at the Origins of Agriculture: Editors' Summation," in Mark Cohen and George Armelagos, eds., *Paleopathology at the Origins of Agriculture* (Orlando, FL: Academic Press, 1984), 585–601; Jared Diamond, *The Third Chimpanzee: The Evolution and Future of the Human Animal* (New York: HarperCollins, 1993); Clark Spencer Larsen, "Biological Changes in Human Populations with Agriculture," *Annual Review of Anthropology* 24 (1995): 185–213; Richard H. Steckel and Jerome C. Rose, "Patterns of Health in the Western Hemisphere," in Richard H. Steckel and Jerome C. Rose, eds., *The Backbone of History: Health and Nutrition in the Western Hemisphere* (Cambridge: Cambridge University Press, 2002), 563–79.

77. The strengths and weaknesses of small-*N* research are now the subject of a large methodological literature. For recent contributions, see Henry E. Brady and David Collier, eds., *Rethinking Social Inquiry: Diverse Tools, Shared Methods* (Lanham, MD: Rowman & Littlefield, 2004); Alexander L. George and

Andrew Bennett, *Case Studies and Theory Development in the Social Sciences* (Cambridge, MA: MIT Press, 2005); Mahoney and Rueschemeyer, *Comparative Historical Analysis in the Social Sciences.*

78. Robert Adcock and David Collier, "Measurement Validity: A Shared Standard for Qualitative and Quantitative Research," *American Political Science Review* 95, no. 3 (September 2001): 529–46.

79. James Mahoney, Erin Kimball, and Kendra Koivu, "The Logic of Historical Explanation in the Social Sciences," *Comparative Political Studies* 42, no. 1 (January 2009): 114–46.

80. Panama, Cuba, and the Dominican Republic did not achieve independence in the same way or at the same time as the rest of Spanish America. And when they did gain independence, their sovereignty was more equivocal. As a result, their inclusion in the analysis would unduly complicate the presentation and undercut the advantages of focusing on a small group of cases that exhibit homogeneity along key dimensions.

Chapter 2. Spain and Its Colonial Empire in the Americas

1. For basic background on Spain at the onset of the colonial project, see J. H. Elliott, *Imperial Spain, 1469–1716*, reprinted with a revised foreword (London: Penguin, 2002); Henry Kamen, *Spain, 1469–1714: A Society of Conflict*, 2nd ed. (London: Longman, 1991); John Lynch, *Spain under the Habsburgs: Empire and Absolutism, 1516–1598* (Oxford: Basil Blackwell, 1964); Antonio Domínguez Ortiz, *The Golden Age of Spain, 1516–1659* (London: Weidenfeld & Nicolson, 1971); William D. Phillips Jr. and Carla Rahn Phillips, "Spain in the Fifteenth Century," in Kenneth J. Andrien and Rolena Adorno, eds., *Transatlantic Encounters: Europeans and Andeans in the Sixteenth Century* (Berkeley: University of California Press, 1991), 11–39.

2. "Each component part of [the] empire had a separate administration as well as its own laws, institutions, and taxation, and no part was constitutionally subordinate to the other." Lynch, *Spain under the Habsburgs*, 46.

3. Elliott, *Imperial Spain*, 199.

4. J. H. Elliott, "Self-Perception and Decline in Early Seventeenth-Century Spain," *Past and Present* 74 (February 1977): 46. See also J. H. Elliott, "The Decline of Spain," *Past and Present* 20 (November 1961): 52–75; Henry Kamen, "The Decline of Spain: A Historical Myth?" *Past and Present* 81 (November 1978): 24–50.

5. José Larraz López, *La época del mercantilismo en Castilla, 1500–1700* (Madrid: Aguilar, 1963), 18.

6. Robert Sidney Smith, *The Spanish Merchant Guild: A History of the Consulado, 1250–1700* (Durham, NC: Duke University Press, 1940), 68.

7. Jaime Vicens Vives, *An Economic History of Spain*, trans. Frances M. López-Morillas (Princeton, NJ: Princeton University Press, 1969), 303–4; Lynch, *Spain under the Habsburgs*, 17.

8. Lynch, *Spain under the Habsburgs*, 18. To make matters worse, high textile prices were just one component of an overall price revolution in sixteenth-century Spain that undercut the accumulation of capital needed to finance a commercial takeoff.

Though scholars debate the exact workings and causes of Spain's sustained price inflation, and not all accept Hamilton's thesis proposing influxes of American silver as its source, few deny that a century of inflation inhibited a commercial takeoff. See Earl J. Hamilton, *American Treasure and Price Revolution in Spain, 1501–1650* (Cambridge, MA: Harvard University Press, 1934).

9. See Immanuel Wallerstein, *The Modern World-System: Capitalist Agriculture and the Origins of the European World-Economy in the Sixteenth Century* (San Diego, CA: Academic Press, 1974). According to Wallerstein (p. 191), "the cause [of the decline of Spain] seems to be that Spain did not erect (probably because she could not erect) the kind of state machinery which would enable the dominant classes in Spain to profit from the creation of a European world-economy."

10. Smith, *The Spanish Merchant Guild*, esp. chap. 6; Geoffrey J. Walker, *Spanish Politics and Imperial Trade, 1700–1789* (Bloomington: Indiana University Press, 1979), 10.

11. Vicens Vives, *Economic History of Spain*, 429–31.

12. Larraz López, *La época del mercantilismo*, 18–20.

13. An earlier generation of work often viewed Castilian sociocultural institutions in organic terms, such that Spanish society was "like the human body, its several parts [being] structurally and functionally interrelated and interdependent. The health of the body depended on the vigor and proper functioning of the constituent organs." L. N. McAlister, "Social Structure and Social Change in New Spain," *Hispanic American Historical Review* 43, no. 3 (August 1963): 350. We need not accept such imageries, though certainly many members of Castilian society did at the time. See also Richard M. Morse, "The Heritage of Latin America," in Louis Hartz, ed., *The Founding of New Societies* (New York: Harcourt, Brace, & World, 1964), 123–77; Howard J. Wiarda, "Toward a Framework for the Study of Political Change in the Iberic-Latin Tradition: The Corporative Model," *World Politics* 25, no. 2 (January 1973): 206–35.

14. James Casey, *Early Modern Spain: A Social History* (London: Routledge, 1999); Teofilo F. Ruiz, *Spanish Society: 1400–1600* (Harlow, UK: Pearson Education, 2001), chaps. 2–4; David E. Vassberg, *Land and Society in Golden Age Castile* (Cambridge: Cambridge University Press, 1984).

15. Walker, *Spanish Politics*, 8. Lynch notes that the monopolization of this trade is hardly surprising: "Spain was already a protectionist country, barricaded with customs, and a government which theoretically controlled everything entering and leaving its frontiers was unlikely to allow the new-found treasure to escape its grasp." Lynch, *Spain under the Habsburgs*, 122.

16. Classic works on Spanish colonialism provide good discussions of political organization and bureaucracy in the Americas. See, for example, Charles Gibson, *Spain in America* (New York: Harper & Row, 1966); C. H. Haring, *The Spanish Empire in America* (New York: Oxford University Press, 1947); Curtis A. Wilgus, *The Development of Hispanic America* (New York: Farrar & Rinehart, 1941).

17. An audiencia might also be designated as a special military area known as a captaincy general *(capitanía general)*.

18. "Castile, the conqueror of America, thought the Indies as the exclusive patrimony of the country's collective wealth . . . America was set up to be a greater Castile,

with all Castile's virtues and defects." Vicens Vives, *Economic History of Spain*, 316.

19. Ricardo Levene, *Las Indias no eran colonias* (Buenos Aires: Cía. Editora Espasa-Calpe Argentina, 1951). See also Víctor Tau Anzoátegui, "La monarquía: Poder central y poderes locales," in Academia Nacional de la Historia, *Nueva historia de la nación Argentina*, vol. 2, *Período español (1600–1800)* (Buenos Aires: Academia Nacional de la Historia, 1989), 216–17.

20. See Woodrow Borah, "The Mixing of Populations," in Fredi Chiappelli (with Michael J. B. Allen and Robert L. Benson), ed., *First Images of America: The Impact of the New World on the Old*, vol. 2 (Berkeley: University of California Press, 1976), 708; Peter Boyd-Bowman, *Indice geobiográfico de cuarenta mil pobladores españoles de América en el siglo XVI*, vol. 1, *1493–1519* (Bogotá: Instituto Caro y Cuervo, 1964), ix; José Luis Martínez, *Pasajeros de Indias: Viajes transatlánticos en el siglo XVI* (Madrid: Alianza Editorial, 1983), 156–9; Magnus Mörner, "Spanish Migration to the New World prior to 1810: A Report on the State of Research," in Chiappelli, *First Images of America*, 2:741–3, 767.

21. Martínez, *Pasajeros de Indias*, 31–3; Haring, *Spanish Empire*, 214, 222–3.

22. Mary M. Kirtz, "The British and Spanish Migration Systems in the Colonial Era: A Policy Framework," in Mercedes Pedrero Nieto, ed., *The Peopling of the Americas*, vol. 1 (Veracruz, Mexico: International Union for the Scientific Study of Population, 1992), 269–70. Kirtz appears to follow the work of Moses. However, my reading of Moses is that royal restrictions were primarily designed to exclude Jews, Muslims, and foreigners; the intention was not to limit Catholic Spanish men from migrating. See Bernard Moses, *The Establishment of Spanish Rule in America: An Introduction to the History and Politics of Spanish America* (New York: G. P. Putnam's Sons, 1907), 55–61. Engerman and Sokoloff in part reproduce (what I see as) the errors of Kirtz by relying heavily on her study. See Stanley L. Engerman and Kenneth L. Sokoloff, "Factor Endowments, Inequality, and Paths of Development among New World Economies," *Economia* 3 (Fall 2002): 50, 54.

23. Here I follow Mörner, "Spanish Migration," 738, 750, quite closely. Mörner's work draws on (in part critically) the studies of Richard Konetzke.

24. Peter Boyd-Bowman's work is still the main source for understanding the regional origins of Spanish emigrants during the sixteenth century. See the summary of his findings in "Patterns of Spanish Emigration to the Indies until 1600," *Hispanic American Historical Review* 56, no. 4 (November 1976): 580–604. See also Mörner, "Spanish Migration," 745, 751–2, 769. On the people who left Extremadura in the sixteenth century, see Ida Altman, *Emigrants and Society: Extremadura and America in the Sixteenth Century* (Berkeley: University of California Press, 1989).

25. Mörner, "Spanish Migration," 755.

26. Boyd-Bowman, "Patterns of Spanish Emigration," 583.

27. Historical overviews can be found in Antonio Domínguez Ortiz, *Sociedad y estado en el siglo XVIII español* (Barcelona: Editorial Ariel, 1976); John Lynch, *Bourbon Spain, 1700–1808* (Oxford: Basil Blackwell, 1989); Felipe Nieto and Gabino Mendoza, *Los Borbones del siglo XVIII*, vol. 12, *Historia de España* (Madrid: Círculo de Amigos de la Historia, 1979); Vicente Palacio Atard, *La*

España del siglo XVIII: El siglo de las reformas (Madrid: U.N.E.D., 1978). I rely especially on Domínguez Ortiz and Lynch.

28. On the (later) emergence of the Enlightenment in Spain, see Richard Herr, *The Eighteenth-Century Revolution in Spain* (Princeton, NJ: Princeton University Press, 1958).

29. Domínguez Ortiz, *Sociedad y estado*, 84–5; Lynch, *Bourbon Spain*, 115–16; James Lang, *Conquest and Commerce: Spain and England in the Americas* (New York: Academic Press, 1975), chap. 4; Vicens Vives, *Economic History of Spain*, 476–7.

30. Jacques A. Barbier, "The Culmination of the Bourbon Reforms," *Hispanic American Historical Review* 57, no. 1 (February 1977): 51–68. For the basic details of these reforms, see also Nieto and Mendoza, *Los Borbones*, 127–8.

31. John Lynch, *Spanish Colonial Administration, 1782–1810: The Intendant System in the Viceroyalty of the Río de la Plata* (London: Athlone Press, 1958), 7.

32. "Charles III... practiced an extremely liberal economic policy," yet "the economic mentality of the 18th century manifested itself in Spain as a conflict between protectionism and economic liberalism." Vicens Vives, *Economic History of Spain*, 561, 566.

33. Ibid., 515–16, 570–1.

34. Domínguez Ortiz, *Sociedad y estado*, 395–400; Lynch, *Bourbon Spain*, 244–5, 351–3; Vicens Vives, *Economic History of Spain*, 497–8, 517–18.

35. Domínguez Ortiz, *Sociedad y estado*, chaps. 19, 23; Lynch, *Bourbon Spain*, 226–33; Nieto and Mendoza, *Los Borbones*, 189; Palacio Atard, *La España del siglo XVIII*, chap. 6.

36. Lynch, *Bourbon Spain*, 269–90.

37. Mark A. Burkholder and D. S. Chandler, *From Impotence to Authority: The Spanish Crown and the American Audiencias, 1687–1808* (Columbia: University of Missouri Press, 1977).

38. Ibid., 124–30.

39. Lynch, *Spanish Colonial Administration*, chap. 3.

40. The main sources for this paragraph are Lynch, *Bourbon Spain*, 350–70; Lynch, *Spanish Colonial Administration*, chap. 1; Vicens Vives, *Economic History of Spain*, chap. 36; Walker, *Spanish Politics*, chap. 1.

41. Trade with other European nations remained officially prohibited except when approved by the Crown, as with the African slave trade between the Americas and mostly Portuguese companies.

42. John Fisher, "Commerce and Imperial Decline: Spanish Trade with Spanish America, 1797–1820," *Journal of Latin American Studies* 30, no. 3 (October 1998): 460–1.

43. Walker, *Spanish Politics*, 1–3.

44. Mark A. Burkholder and Lyman L. Johnson, *Colonial Latin America*, 4th ed. (New York: Oxford University Press, 2001), 285–6; James Mahoney, "Long-Run Development and the Legacy of Colonialism in Spanish America," *American Journal of Sociology* 109, no. 1 (July 2003): 50–106.

45. Magnus Mörner (with Harold Sims), *Adventurers and Proletarians: The Story of Migrants in Latin America* (Pittsburgh, PA: University of Pittsburgh Press,

1985), 14. An estimate of fifty thousand is also offered in Vicens Vives, *Economic History of Spain*, 541.

46. Eltis arrives at this figure by multiplying Mörner's estimate of migration from 1580 to 1640 (minus 20 percent for return migration) by the ratio of America's silver production, 1700–60/1580–1640. The dubious assumption is that migration is simply a function of New World silver production. See David Eltis, "Slavery and Freedom in the Early Modern World," in Stanley L. Engerman, ed., *Terms of Labor: Slavery, Serfdom and Free Labor* (Stanford, CA: Stanford University Press, 1999), 28–9.

47. Burkholder and Johnson, *Colonial Latin America*, 289–90.

48. Ibid., 290.

49. Lynch, *Bourbon Spain*, 353–4; Vicens Vives, *Economic History of Spain*, 497–8. According to Floyd, approximately eight thousand merchants (including many from Cádiz) immigrated to Spanish America during the eighteenth century. Troy S. Floyd, "The Indigo Merchant: Promoter of Central American Economic Development, 1750–1808," *Business History Review* 39, no. 4 (Winter 1965): 467.

50. Lynch, *Bourbon Spain*, 365; Burkholder and Johnson, *Colonial Latin America*, 291.

Chapter 3. Mercantilist Colonialism

1. Linda A. Newson, "Indian Population Patterns in Colonial Spanish America," *Latin American Research Review* 20, no. 3 (1985): 50.

2. Ibid.

3. Eric Olin Wright, *Class Counts: Comparative Studies in Class Analysis* (Cambridge: Cambridge University Press, 1997), 9–13.

4. Ibid., 10–11.

5. In researching the Aztec Empire, I consulted the following books: Burr Cartwright Brundage, *A Rain of Darts: The Mexican Aztecs* (Austin: University of Texas Press, 1972); Nigel Davies, *The Aztecs: A History* (Norman: University of Oklahoma Press, 1980); Ross Hassig, *Aztec Warfare: Imperial Expansion and Political Control* (Norman: University of Oklahoma Press, 1988); Alan Knight, *Mexico: From the Beginning to the Spanish Conquest* (Cambridge: Cambridge University Press, 2002), pt. 3; Michael E. Smith, *The Aztecs* (Cambridge, MA: Blackwell, 1996); Richard F. Townsend, *The Aztecs*, rev. ed. (New York: Thames & Hudson, 2000).

6. For coverage of the different groups within the Aztec Empire, see Robert Wauchope, ed., *Handbook of Middle American Indians: Ethnology*, vols. 7 and 8 (Austin: University of Texas Press, 1969). See esp. pt. 1, sec. 2 of vol. 7 and pt. 2, sec. 5 of vol. 8.

7. See Ralph L. Beals, "The Tarascans," in Wauchope, *Handbook of Middle American Indians*, vol. 8, pt. 2, pp. 725–73; Ulíses Beltrán, "Estado y sociedad tarascos," in Pedro Carrasco, ed., *La sociedad indígena en el centro y occidente de México* (Zamora, Mexico: El Colegio de Michoacán, 1986), 21–46; Helen Perlstein Pollard, *Taríacuri's Legacy: The Prehispanic Tarascan State* (Norman: University of Oklahoma Press, 1993).

8. See François Chevalier, "Estudio preliminar," in Domingo Lázaro de Arregui, ed., *Descripción de la Nueva Galicia* (Seville: Escuela de Estudios Hispano-Americanos, 1946), xxv; P. J. Bakewell, *Silver Mining and Society in Colonial Mexico: Zacatecas, 1546–1700* (Cambridge: Cambridge University Press, 1971), 266; Robert Carmack, "Mesoamerica at Spanish Contact," in Robert M. Carmack, Janine Gasco, and Gary H. Grossen, eds., *The Legacy of Mesoamerica: History and Culture of a Native American Civilization* (Upper Saddle River, NJ: Prentice Hall, 1996), 80–122; Philip Wayne Powell, *Soldiers, Indians, and Silver: The Northward Advance of New Spain, 1550–1600* (Berkeley: University of California Press, 1952), chap. 3; Edward H. Spicer, "Northwest Mexico: Introduction," in Wauchope, *Handbook of Middle American Indians*, vol. 8, pt. 2, 777–91.

9. Alan Knight, *Mexico: The Colonial Era* (Cambridge: Cambridge University Press, 2002), 63.

10. Charles Gibson, *Tlaxcala in the Sixteenth Century* (Stanford, CA: Stanford University Press, 1967), 1–15; Nancy M. Farriss, *Maya Society under Colonial Rule: The Collective Enterprise of Survival* (Princeton, NJ: Princeton University Press, 1984); Inga Clendinnen, *Ambivalent Conquests: Maya and Spaniard in Yucatán, 1517–1570*, 2nd ed. (Cambridge: Cambridge University Press, 2003).

11. For information regarding the Spanish conquest, I rely especially on Hugh Thomas, *Conquest: Montezuma, Cortés, and the Fall of Old Mexico* (New York: Simon & Schuster, 1993). See also Bernal Díaz del Castillo, *The Bernal Díaz Chronicles: The True Story of the Conquest of Mexico*, trans. and ed. Albert Idell (Garden City, NY: Doubleday, 1956); William H. Prescott, *History of the Conquest of Mexico, with a Preliminary View of the Ancient Mexican Civilization, and the Life of the Conqueror Hernando Cortez* (Philadelphia: J. B. Lippincott & Co., 1867).

12. Inga Clendinnen, "'Fierce and Unnatural Cruelty': Cortés and the Conquest of Mexico," in "The New World," special issue, *Representations* 33 (Winter 1991): 65.

13. Thomas, *Conquest*, 308–9.

14. "It was the intense hatred provoked by the Aztecs among their vassal states which made possible the conquest of an empire by a mere handful of Spaniards." Lesley Byrd Simpson, *The Encomienda in New Spain* (Berkeley: University of California Press, 1950), viii. See also J. H. Elliott, "The Spanish Conquest and Settlement of America," in Leslie Bethell, ed., *The Cambridge History of Latin America*, vol. 1, *Colonial Latin America* (Cambridge: Cambridge University Press, 1984), 174; Nathan Wachtel, "The Indian and the Spanish Conquest," in Bethell, *Cambridge History of Latin America*, 1:210–11.

15. See the fine analysis by John F. Guilmartin Jr., "The Cutting Edge: An Analysis of the Spanish Invasion and Overthrow of the Inca Empire, 1532–1539," in Kenneth J. Andrien and Rolena Adorno, eds., *Transatlantic Encounters: Europeans and Andeans in the Sixteenth Century* (Berkeley: University of California Press, 1991), 40–69.

16. Farriss, *Maya Society*, 12. See also Robert S. Chamberlain, *The Conquest and Colonization of Yucatan, 1517–1550* (Washington, DC: Carnegie Institution, 1948); Clendinnen, *Ambivalent Conquests*, chap. 2; Grant D. Jones, *Maya*

Resistance to Spanish Rule: Time and History on a Colonial Frontier (Albuquerque: University of New Mexico Press, 1989), chap. 2.

17. Peter Gerhard, *The North Frontier of New Spain*, rev. ed. (Norman: University of Oklahoma Press, 1993), 5–7.

18. J. Benedict Warren, *The Conquest of Michoacán: The Spanish Domination of the Tarascan Kingdom in Western Mexico, 1521–1530* (Norman: University of Oklahoma Press, 1985).

19. Peter Boyd-Bowman, "Patterns of Spanish Emigration to the Indies until 1600," *Hispanic American Historical Review* 56, no. 4 (November 1976): 602. This estimate excludes the northern frontier and Yucatán.

20. Sherburne F. Cook and Woodrow Borah, *Essays in Population History: Mexico and the Caribbean*, vol. 2 (Berkeley: University of California Press, 1974), 180, 197–8.

21. J. I. Israel, *Race, Class and Politics in Colonial Mexico* (Oxford: Oxford University Press, 1975), 1–2. Slightly smaller Spanish population figures are reported for 1570 in B. H. Slicher van Bath, "Dos modelos referidos a la relación entre población y economía en Nueva España y Perú durante la época colonial," in Arij Ouweneel and Cristina Torales Pacheco, eds., *Empresarios, indios y estado: Perfil de la economía mexicana (siglo XVIII)* (Amsterdam: CEDLA, 1988), 20.

22. For Mexico City population estimates circa 1630, see Louisa Hoberman, "Bureaucracy and Disaster: Mexico City and the Flood of 1629," *Journal of Latin American Studies* 6, no. 2 (1974): 214.

23. Richard Boyer, "Mexico in the Seventeenth Century: Transition of a Colonial Society," *Hispanic American Historical Review* 57, no. 3 (August 1977): 456.

24. This paragraph draws on Woodrow Borah, *Early Colonial Trade and Navigation between Mexico and Peru* (Berkeley: University of California Press, 1954); Ross Hassig, *Trade, Tribute, and Transportation: The Sixteenth-Century Political Economy of the Valley of Mexico* (Norman: University of Oklahoma Press, 1985), chap. 10.

25. See Colin A. Palmer, *Slaves of the White God: Blacks in Mexico, 1570–1630* (Cambridge, MA: Harvard University Press, 1976), 43. For data on the size of the slave population in Mexico City, see p. 46.

26. John Frederick Schwaller, *Origins of Church Wealth in Mexico: Ecclesiastical Revenues and Church Finances, 1523–1600* (Albuquerque: University of New Mexico Press, 1985).

27. Estimates of Puebla's Spanish population in the 1630–40 period range from one thousand to three thousand households. For sources and a discussion, see Boyer, "Mexico in the Seventeenth Century," 464 n. 32.

28. Guadalupe Albi Romero, "La sociedad de Puebla de los Angeles en el siglo XVI," *Jahrbuch für Geschichte von Staat, Wirtschaft und Gesellschaft Lateinamerikas* 7 (1970): 73–145 (quotation is on p. 93; unless otherwise noted, all translations throughout the book are my own). On Puebla's economy, see Julia Hirschberg, "Social Experiment in New Spain: A Prosopographical Study of the Early Settlement at Puebla de los Angeles," *Hispanic American Historical Review* 59, no. 1 (February 1979): 1–33.

29. On the indigenous population of Oaxaca, see John K. Chance, *The Conquest of the Sierra: Spaniards and Indians in Colonial Oaxaca* (Norman: University

of Oklahoma Press, 1989), esp. xiii–xv and chap. 1. On its Spanish population, see Nicolás Sánchez-Albornoz, *The Population of Latin America: A History* (Berkeley: University of California Press, 1974), 99; Woodrow Borah, *New
Spain's Century of Depression* (Berkeley: University of California Press, 1951),
7, 14.

30. Peter Gerhard, *The Southeast Frontier of New Spain*, rev. ed. (Norman: University of Oklahoma Press, 1993), 42–6, 158–62; Farriss, *Maya Society*, chap. 2;
Jones, *Maya Resistance*, chap. 2.

31. The Spanish population in 1646 in Acapulco and Veracruz has been estimated
at 150 and 500 households, respectively. See Sánchez-Albornoz, *Population of
Latin America*, 99.

32. This is the major theme of Powell, *Soldiers, Indians and Silver*. See also Bakewell,
Silver Mining, chaps. 1–2.

33. Richard L. Garner, "Long-Term Silver Mining Trends in Spanish America: A
Comparative Analysis of Peru and Mexico," *American Historical Review* 93,
no. 4 (October 1988): 905. Garner's research, along with the work of Bakewell on
Zacatecas and of TePaske and Klein on silver taxes from all mining treasuries in
colonial Mexico, effectively undercuts to my satisfaction the notion of long-term
declining silver production in seventeenth-century Mexico, a position originally
advocated by Hamilton and popularized by Borah. See Bakewell, *Silver Mining*;
John J. TePaske and Herbert S. Klein, "The Seventeenth-Century Crisis in New
Spain: Myth or Reality?" *Past and Present* 90 (February 1981): 116–35; Earl
J. Hamilton, *American Treasure and Price Revolution in Spain, 1501–1650*
(Cambridge, MA: Harvard University Press, 1934); Borah, *New Spain's Century
of Depression*. See also the debate of Henry Kamen and Jonathan Israel versus
TePaske and Klein in *Past and Present* 97 (November 1982): 144–61.

34. D. A. Brading and Harry E. Cross, "Colonial Silver Mining: Mexico and Peru,"
Hispanic American Historical Review 52, no. 4 (November 1972): 573; Peter
Bakewell, "Mining in Colonial Spanish America," in Bethell, *Cambridge History
of Latin America*, 2:138–45.

35. For estimates of the Spanish population in Zacatecas, see Bakewell, *Silver Mining*,
268; Gerhard, *North Frontier*, 159; Israel, *Race, Class and Politics*, 2–3.

36. For Guadalajara's Spanish population, see Eric Van Young, *Hacienda and Market in Eighteenth-Century Mexico: The Rural Economy of the Guadalajara
Region, 1675–1820* (Berkeley: University of California Press, 1981), 30–1. Van
Young also describes the marginality of Guadalajara during this period; see, for
example, chap. 2 and p. 343.

37. François Chevalier, *Land and Society in Colonial Mexico: The Great Hacienda*
(Berkeley: University of California Press, 1963), chap. 2; Knight, *Mexico: The
Colonial Era*, 24, 78.

38. Sugarcane was also cultivated using African slaves in southern New Galicia and
the warm valleys of Michoacán, Huatusco, and Oaxaca. Palmer, *Slaves of the
White God*, 66–7.

39. Chevalier, *Land and Society*. The early literature on hacienda agriculture also
includes James Lockhart, "Encomienda and Hacienda: The Evolution of the
Great Estate in the Spanish Indies," *Hispanic American Historical Review* 49,
no. 3 (August 1969): 411–29; Robert G. Keith, "Encomienda, Hacienda and
Corregimiento in Spanish America: A Structural Analysis," *Hispanic American*

Historical Review 51, no. 3 (August 1971): 431–46; Magnus Mörner, "The Spanish American Hacienda: A Survey of Recent Research and Debate," *Hispanic American Historical Review* 53, no. 2 (May 1973): 183–216. See also Eric Van Young, "Mexican Rural History since Chevalier: The Historiography of the Colonial Hacienda," *Latin American Research Review* 18 (1983): 3–61; John Frederick Schwaller, "Mexico City Market Structures and the Formation of the Hacienda," in Richard Herr, ed., *Themes in Rural History of the Western World* (Ames: Iowa State University Press, 1993), 249–62.

40. Enrique Florescano, "The Formation and Economic Structure of the Hacienda in New Spain," in Bethell, *Cambridge History of Latin America*, 2:153.

41. The size of the preconquest population is the subject of great debate in the historiography of central Mexico. Cook and Simpson originally calculated a population of 11 million. This was subsequently revised by Borah and Cook to be about 25 million. Some physical anthropologists believe that the region could have sustained a population of only 5–10 million. Still other scholars argue in favor of an even lower estimate, such as 4–8 million. The figure of 10 million reported in the text is my approximate average of these various estimates. My argument does not depend on this particular estimate. See Sherburne F. Cook and Lesley B. Simpson, *The Population of Central Mexico in the Sixteenth Century* (Berkeley: University of California Press, 1948); Sherburne F. Cook and Woodrow Borah, *The Indian Population of Central Mexico, 1531* (Berkeley: University of California Press, 1960); Woodrow Borah and Sherburne F. Cook, *The Aboriginal Population of Central Mexico on the Eve of the Spanish Conquest* (Berkeley: University of California Press, 1963); Rudolph Zambardino, "Mexico's Population in the Sixteenth Century: Demographic Anomaly or Mathematical Illusion?" *Journal of Interdisciplinary History* 11 (1980): 1–27; William M. Denevan, "Native American Populations in 1492: Recent Research and a Revised Hemispheric Estimate," in William M. Denevan, ed., *The Native Population of the Americas in 1492*, 2nd ed. (Madison: University of Wisconsin Press, 1992), xxi–xxii; Francis J. Brooks, "Revising the Conquest of Mexico: Smallpox, Sources, and Populations," *Journal of Interdisciplinary History* 24, no. 1 (Summer 1993): 1–29; Nicolás Sánchez-Albornoz, "The Population of Colonial Spanish America," in Bethell, *Cambridge History of Latin America*, 2:4–5. The over-time population estimates reported in the text are from Cook and Borah, *Indian Population*, 1.

42. Farriss, *Maya Society*, 57–8; Gerhard, *Southeast Frontier*, 25.

43. Gerhard, *North Frontier*, 24.

44. Knight, *Mexico: The Colonial Era*, 21. On the role of disease and conquest in the demographic collapse, see above all Noble David Cook, *Born to Die: Disease and the New World Conquest, 1492–1650* (Cambridge: Cambridge University Press, 1998), esp. the concluding chapter.

45. On the timing of specific diseases, see Hassig, *Trade, Tribute, and Transportation*, 156; Cook, *Born to Die*, 139.

46. Indian slavery was practiced fairly extensively before being abolished in 1548. African slavery persisted for much longer. By the mid-seventeenth century, more than one hundred thousand slaves had been brought to New Spain. See Florescano, "Formation and Economic Structure of the Hacienda," 165. However, after the mid-seventeenth century, the slave trade halted, and slave numbers

plummeted to ten thousand for the late eighteenth century. Knight, *Mexico: The Colonial Era*, 82 n. 297.

47. See Charles Gibson, *The Aztecs under Spanish Rule: A History of the Indians of the Valley of Mexico, 1519–1810* (Stanford, CA: Stanford University Press, 1964), 61. For data on the first 506 encomenderos of Mexico, see Robert Himmerich y Valencia, *The Encomenderos of New Spain, 1521–1555* (Austin: University of Texas Press, 1991).

48. On encomiendas in Yucatán, see Farriss, *Maya Society*, 87–8; Clendinnen, *Ambivalent Conquests*, 42.

49. In fact, the Spanish conquerors did not use Montezuma's tribute collectors, instead working more directly through native caciques who exchanged loyalty for various privileges. See Gibson, *Aztecs*, 155, 194–7, 221–2.

50. Irene Silverblatt, "Becoming Indian in the Central Andes of Seventeenth-Century Peru," in Gyan Prakash, ed., *After Colonialism: Imperial Histories and Postcolonial Displacements* (Princeton, NJ: Princeton University Press, 1994), 281.

51. Peter Gerhard, "Congregaciones de Indios en la Nueva España antes de 1570," *Historia Mexicana* 103, no. 3 (January–March 1977): 347–95.

52. For three different regions, see Farriss, *Maya Society*, chap. 5; Cheryl English Martin, *Rural Society in Colonial Morelos* (Albuquerque: University of New Mexico Press, 1985), 28, 60; William B. Taylor, *Landlord and Peasant in Colonial Oaxaca* (Stanford, CA: Stanford University Press, 1972). Taylor writes that "congregaciones in the Valley of Oaxaca were remarkably short lived. Most had broken down into their constituent communities by the end of the seventeenth century" (p. 27). Farriss and Martin suggest that they were more consequential in Yucatán and Morelos, respectively, though even here they appear to have broken down considerably. See also the cross-regional analysis in Gerhard, "Congregaciones de Indios."

53. Howard F. Cline, "Civil Congregations of the Indians in New Spain, 1598–1606," *Hispanic American Historical Review* 29, no. 3 (August 1949): 365–6.

54. Gibson, *Aztecs*, 285.

55. James Lockhart, *The Nahuas after the Conquest: A Social and Cultural History of the Indians of Central Mexico, Sixteenth through Eighteenth Centuries* (Stanford, CA: Stanford University Press, 1992), 163–5. More generally, Lockhart shows, using Nahuatl sources, that "indigenous structures and patterns survived the conquest on a much more massive scale and for a longer period of time than had seemed to be the case when we had to judge by the reports of Spaniards alone. The indigenous world retained much social and cultural as well as jurisdictional autonomy, maintaining its center of balance to a surprising extent, concerned above all with its own affairs." Lockhart, *Nahuas and Spaniards: Postconquest Central Mexican History and Philology* (Stanford, CA: Stanford University Press, 1991), 20.

56. On these fluctuating Spanish land laws, see Taylor, *Landlord and Peasant*, 67.

57. Simpson, *The Encomienda*, chaps. 1–2; Gibson, *Aztecs*, 63, 81.

58. On the repartimiento, see Borah, *New Spain's Century of Depression*, 35–6; Florescano, "Formation and Economic Structure of the Hacienda," esp. 164–8; Gibson, *Aztecs*, 27, 224–36; Knight, *Mexico: The Colonial Era*, 82–7. For a close look at labor policy in Oaxaca, in many ways an instructive comparison

with central Mexico, see John K. Chance, *Race and Class in Colonial Oaxaca* (Stanford, CA: Stanford University Press, 1978), 42–3, 78–9, 108–10; Taylor, *Landlord and Peasant*, 143–7.

59. Borah, *New Spain's Century of Depression*, 37–44; Boyer, "Mexico in the Seventeenth Century," 459–60; Florescano, "Formation and Economic Structure of the Hacienda," 165; Gibson, *Aztecs*, 236–42; Clendinnen, *Ambivalent Conquests*, 42. For an account that emphasizes more the role of coercion on haciendas, see Enrique Semo, *The History of Capitalism in Mexico: Its Origins, 1521–1763*, trans. Lidia Lozano (Austin: University of Texas Press, 1993), 133.

60. Bakewell, *Silver Mining*, 121–2. See also Garner, "Long-Term Silver Mining Trends," 927–9; Brading and Cross, "Colonial Silver Mining," 557.

61. See esp. Bakewell, *Silver Mining*, 122–9.

62. Louisa Schell Hoberman, *Mexico's Merchant Elite, 1590–1660* (Durham, NC: Duke University Press, 1991), esp. chap. 2.

63. See, for example, Hassig, *Trade, Tribute, and Transportation*.

64. J. H. Parry, *The Sale of Public Office in the Spanish Indies under the Hapsburgs* (Berkeley: University of California Press, 1953).

65. Hoberman, *Mexico's Merchant Elite*, chaps. 3–4. Periodically, the Mexico City consulado clashed with the Crown over the direction of imperial policy, especially regarding the Crown's prohibitions on Mexico's contraband trade with Manila. See Louisa Schell Hoberman, "Merchants in Seventeenth-Century Mexico City: A Preliminary Report," *Hispanic American Historical Review* 57, no. 3 (August 1977): 490–4; Israel, *Race, Class and Politics*, 99–100.

66. On the sale of regimientos, see Parry, *The Sale of Public Office*, 33–47. On the politics of the Mexico City town council in the sixteenth century, including its relationship to the merchants, see Israel, *Race, Class and Politics*, 96–102.

67. Stuart Schwartz, "The Landed Elite," in Louisa Schell Hoberman and Susan Migden Socolow, eds., *The Countryside in Colonial Latin America* (Albuquerque: University of New Mexico Press, 1997), 120.

68. Bakewell, *Silver Mining*, 115–18; Chevalier, *Land and Society*, 165–78.

69. Schwaller, *Origins of Church Wealth*, 146–7; Victoria Hennessey Cummins, "The Church and Business Practices in Late Sixteenth Century Mexico," *The Americas* 44, no. 4 (April 1988): 421–40.

70. Terence N. D'Altroy, *The Incas* (Malden, MA: Blackwell, 2002), xiii. For a lower estimate of the size of the Inca Empire, see John V. Murra, "Andean Societies before 1532," in Bethell, *Cambridge History of Latin America*, 1:64. In addition to D'Altroy's book, works on the Incas include Nigel Davies, *The Incas* (Niwot: University Press of Colorado, 1995); Craig Morris, "The Infrastructure of Inka Control in the Peruvian Central Highlands," in George A. Collier, Renato I. Rosaldo, and John D. Wirth, eds., *The Inca and Aztec States, 1400–1800: Anthropology and History* (New York: Academic Press, 1982), 153–71; John Victor Murra, *The Economic Organization of the Inka State* (Greenwich, CT: JAI Press, 1980); María Rostworowski de Diez Canseco, *History of the Inca Realm*, trans. Harry Iceland (Cambridge: Cambridge University Press, 1999); John Howland Rowe, "Inca Culture at the Time of the Spanish Conquest," in Julian H. Steward, ed., *Handbook of South American Indians*, vol. 2, *The Andean Civilizations* (Washington, DC: U.S. Government Printing Office, 1946), 183–330.

71. The original and subsequent meanings of *mit'a* are discussed in John Howland Rowe, "The Incas under Spanish Colonial Institutions," *Hispanic American Historical Review* 37, no. 2 (May 1957): 155–99, at 170.

72. Rowe, "Inca Culture," 184–92; D'Altroy, *The Incas*, 42–3; Robert G. Keith, *Conquest and Agrarian Change: The Emergence of the Hacienda System on the Peruvian Coast* (Cambridge, MA: Harvard University Press, 1976), chap. 1.

73. See, for example, Davies, *The Incas*, 87.

74. Guilmartin, "The Cutting Edge."

75. On the conquest, see John Hemming, *The Conquest of the Incas* (New York: Harcourt Brace Jovanovich, 1970); Philip Ainsworth Means, *Fall of the Inca Empire and the Spanish Rule in Peru, 1530–1780* (New York: Gordian Press, 1971), chaps. 1–5; William H. Prescott, *History of the Conquest of Peru* (London: J. M. Dent & Co., 1908).

76. An especially good analysis of Spanish-indigenous alliances is Steve J. Stern, "The Rise and Fall of Indian-White Alliances: A Regional View of 'Conquest' History," *Hispanic American Historical Review* 61, no. 3 (August 1981): 461–91. Perhaps also working to the advantage of the Spanish was the fact that the Inca vertical archipelago system and its associated institutions were in the midst of profound changes by 1532. See esp. the conclusion of John V. Murra, "El control vertical de un máximo de pesos ecológicos en la economía de las sociedades andinas," in Murra's *El mundo andino: Población, medio ambiente y economía* (Lima: IEP/Pontificia Universidad Católica del Perú, 2002), 85–125.

77. The historical events of this paragraph are described in many sources, including Hemming, *The Conquest of the Incas*, chaps. 5–12.

78. Peter Flindell Klarén, *Peru: Society and Nationhood in the Andes* (New York: Oxford University Press, 2000), 39. See also Karen Spalding, *Huarochirí: An Andean Society under Inca and Spanish Rule* (Stanford, CA: Stanford University Press, 1984), 118–19.

79. James Lockhart, *Spanish Peru, 1532–1560: A Social History*, 2nd ed. (Madison: University of Wisconsin Press, 1994), 12–13.

80. Pierre L. van de Berghe and George P. Primov, *Inequality in the Peruvian Andes: Class and Ethnicity in Cuzco* (Columbia: University of Missouri Press, 1977), 37–51; Spalding, *Huarochirí*, 117–18; Keith, *Conquest and Agrarian Change*, 13.

81. Keith, *Conquest and Agrarian Change*, 23–4; Noble David Cook, *Demographic Collapse: Indian Peru, 1520–1620* (Cambridge: Cambridge University Press, 1981), 159–60; Paul Charney, *Indian Society in the Valley of Lima, Peru, 1532–1824* (Lanham, MD: University Press of America, 2001), 1–2.

82. Magnus Mörner, "The Rural Economy and Society of Colonial Spanish America," in Bethell, *Cambridge History of Latin America*, 2:195; Mark A. Burkholder, *Politics of a Colonial Career: José Baquíjano and the Audiencia of Lima* (Albuquerque: University of New Mexico Press, 1980), 4.

83. Frederick P. Bowser, *The African Slave in Colonial Peru, 1524–1650* (Stanford, CA: Stanford University Press, 1974), 75.

84. Lockhart, *Spanish Peru*, 6.

85. Keith A. Davies, *Landowners in Colonial Peru* (Austin: University of Texas Press, 1984), 5, 10, 115. See chap. 5 generally on the wine economy. See also Cook, *Demographic Collapse*, 171–6. The early history of Arequipa is covered

in Guillermo Galdos Rodríguez, *Una ciudad para la historia, una historia para la ciudad: Arequipa en el siglo XVI* (Arequipa, Peru: Editorial Universidad de San Agustín, 1997).

86. Copious information on the *obrajes* (textile mills) of this area can be found in Mirian Salas de Coloma's massive work *Estructura colonial del poder español en el Perú: Huamanga (Ayacucho) a través de sus obrajes, siglos XVI–XVIII*, vol. 1 (Lima: Pontificia Universidad Católica del Perú, 1998).

87. Jorge E. Hardoy and Carmen Aranovich, "Urban Scales and Functions in Spanish America toward the Year 1600: First Conclusions," *Latin American Research Review* 5, no. 3 (Autumn 1970): 67.

88. J. R. Fisher, *Silver Mines and Silver Miners in Colonial Peru, 1776–1824* (Liverpool, England: Centre for Latin-American Studies, University of Liverpool, 1977), chap. 1 and p. 141; Cook, *Demographic Collapse*, 209.

89. Two excellent works on mercury mining in Huancavelica are Guillermo Lohmann Villena, *Las minas de Huancavelica en los siglos XVI y XVII* (Seville: Escuela de Estudios Hispano-Americanos, 1949); Arthur Preston Whitaker, *The Huancavelica Mercury Mine: A Contribution to the History of the Bourbon Renaissance in the Spanish Empire* (Cambridge, MA: Harvard University Press, 1941). The role of Huancavelica in the overall colonial mineral economy is covered in Brading and Cross, "Colonial Silver Mining"; Bakewell, "Mining in Colonial Spanish America." On the transportation of mercury, see Alvaro Jara, *Tres ensayos sobre economía minera hispanoamericana* (Santiago: Centro de Investigaciones de Historia Americana, 1966), chap. 6.

90. Carlos Contreras, *La ciudad de mercurio: Huancavelica, 1570–1700* (Lima: Instituto de Estudios Peruanos, 1982), 62; Lohmann Villena, *Las minas de Huancavelica*, 97–8.

91. Cook, *Demographic Collapse*, 114. See also Cook, *Born to Die*; Sánchez-Albornoz, "The Population of Colonial Spanish America," 6–7. The nadir for the Peruvian indigenous population was reached after an epidemic in 1719.

92. For the specific provinces from which *mitayos* were taken, see Luis Millones, *Perú colonial: De Pizarro a Tupac Amaru II* (Lima: Industrial Gráfica, 1995), 92.

93. Charney, *Indian Society*, 9; Bowser, *The African Slave*, 11, 75.

94. Cook, *Demographic Collapse*, 253.

95. On the encomiendas in Peru, see Lockhart, *Spanish Peru*; Manuel Belaunde Guinassi, *La encomienda en el Perú* (Lima: Mercurio Peruano, 1945). Belaunde Guinassi covers the entire history of the institution in Peru.

96. Spalding, *Huarochirí*, 127; see also Steve J. Stern, *Peru's Indian Peoples and the Challenge of Spanish Conquest: Huamanga to 1640* (Madison: University of Wisconsin Press, 1982), 40–4.

97. Silverblatt, "Becoming Indian," 280.

98. Key features of the mita are ably covered in Rowe, "The Incas under Spanish Colonial Institutions"; Spalding, *Huarochirí*, 164–7; Stern, *Peru's Indian Peoples*, 82–9.

99. Stern, *Peru's Indian Peoples*, 89.

100. Kenneth J. Andrien, *Andean Worlds: Indigenous History, Culture, and Consciousness under Spanish Rule, 1532–1825* (Albuquerque: University of New Mexico Press, 2001), 50.

101. Ann M. Wightman, *Indigenous Migration and Social Change: The Forasteros of Cuzco, 1570–1720* (Durham, NC: Duke University Press, 1990), 20.

102. "Technically, forasteros were individuals living outside their reducciones who were exempt from mita service but still legally members of their home community. In practice, forastero migrants and their descendants negotiated a wide range of relationships with established indigenous communities and assumed a variety of tasks." Wightman, *Indigenous Migration*, 19.

103. Ibid., 18.

104. Susan Elizabeth Ramírez, *The World Upside Down: Cross-Cultural Contact and Conflict in Sixteenth-Century Peru* (Stanford, CA: Stanford University Press, 1996), 40. See also Spalding, *Huarochirí*, chap. 7; Stern, *Peru's Indian Peoples*, 92–3.

105. This corruption by indigenous kurakas might better be called resistance. See, for example, Wightman's description of the tendency of Cuzco-area kurakas to hide the presence of forasteros. Wightman, *Indigenous Migration*, 130. On corruption by Spanish officials, see Javier Tord and Carlos Lazo, *Hacienda, comercio, fiscalidad y luchas sociales (Perú colonial)* (Lima: Pontificia Universidad Católica del Perú, 1981), chap. 4.

106. Karen Spalding, "Social Climbers: Changing Patterns of Mobility among the Indians of Colonial Peru," *Hispanic American Historical Review* 50, no. 4 (November 1970): 647. As Spalding emphasizes, indigenous people often had their own criteria – separate from the Spanish norms – for evaluating social status.

107. Burkholder, *Politics of a Colonial Career*, 6. On the merchants generally, see also Lockhart, *Spanish Peru*, chap. 5.

108. Furthermore, the Peruvian merchants benefited from the Crown's decision to privilege Peru over Mexico in the distribution of mercury. Brading and Cross, "Colonial Silver Mining," 573–4. See also D. A. Brading, *Miners and Merchants in Bourbon Mexico, 1763–1810* (Cambridge: Cambridge University Press, 1971), 9–12; Boyer, "Mexico in the Seventeenth Century," 473.

109. L. A. Clayton, "Trade and Navigation in the Seventeenth-Century Viceroyalty of Peru," *Journal of Latin American Studies* 7, no. 1 (May 1975): 10.

110. María Encarnación Rodríguez Vicente, *El Tribunal del Consulado de Lima en la primera mitad del siglo XVII* (Madrid: Ediciones Cultura Hispánica, 1960). On the conflict with the town council, see pp. 32–4; on the size of the merchant class, see p. 69.

111. Ibid., chap. 11; Kenneth J. Andrien, *Crisis and Decline: The Viceroyalty of Peru in the Seventeenth Century* (Albuquerque: University of New Mexico Press, 1985), 36–9.

112. Fred Bronner, "Church, Crown, and Commerce in Seventeenth-Century Lima: A Synoptic Interpretation," *Jahrbuch für Geschichte von Staat, Wirtschaft und Gesellschaft Lateinamerikas* 29 (1992): 82–3; Rodríguez Vicente, *El Tribunal del Consulado de Lima*, 99–101; Lockhart, *Spanish Peru*, 103.

113. This paragraph and the next one rely on the following sources: Carlos Sempat Assadourian, "The Colonial Economy: The Transfer of the European System of Production to New Spain and Peru," *Journal of Latin American Studies*, Quincentenary Supplement, 24 (1992): 55–68; Fred Bronner, "Peruvian

Encomenderos in 1630: Elite Circulation and Consolidation," *Hispanic American Historical Review* 57, no. 4 (November 1977): 633–59; Nicholas P. Cushner, *Lords of the Land: Sugar, Wine, and Jesuit Estates of Coastal Peru, 1600–1767* (Albany: State University of New York Press, 1980); Davies, *Landowners in Colonial Peru*; Lockhart, "Encomienda and Hacienda"; Keith, "Encomienda, Hacienda and Corregimiento"; Keith, *Conquest and Agrarian Change*; Mörner, "Rural Economy and Society"; Mörner, "The Spanish American Hacienda"; Susan E. Ramírez, *Provincial Patriarchs: Land Tenure and the Economics of Power in Colonial Peru* (Albuquerque: University of New Mexico Press, 1986).

114. Of course, the Spanish state supported the church with tax exemptions and land grants, and it openly encouraged the practice of using clerical organizations as key lending institutions. Fernando de Armas Medina, *Cristianización de Perú (1532–1600)* (Seville: Escuela de Estudios Hispano-Americanos, 1953), esp. chap. 15.

115. Andrien, *Crisis and Decline*, chap. 5; Mark A. Burkholder and D. S. Chandler, *From Impotence to Authority: The Spanish Crown and the American Audiencias, 1687–1808* (Columbia: University of Missouri Press, 1997), appendix 5.

116. The discussion of the Aymaras in this paragraph draws on Herbert S. Klein, *A Concise History of Bolivia* (Cambridge: Cambridge University Press, 2003), 13–22; Brooke Larson, *Cochabamba, 1550–1900: Colonialism and Agrarian Transformation in Bolivia*, expanded ed. (Durham, NC: Duke University Press, 1998), 17–31; John V. Murra, "An Aymara Kingdom in 1567," *Ethnohistory* 15, no. 2 (Spring 1968): 115–51; Harry Tschopik, "The Aymara," in Steward, *Handbook of South American Indians*, vol. 2, *The Andean Civilizations*, 501–73.

117. William M. Denevan, "Introduction to Part IV: South America," in Denevan, *Native Population of the Americas*, 153; Davies, *The Incas*, 129.

118. William M. Denevan, "The Aboriginal Cultural Geography of the Llanos de Mojos of Bolivia," *Ibero-Americana* 48 (1966): 40–57.

119. Julian H. Steward and Louis C. Faron, *Native Peoples of South America* (New York: McGraw-Hill, 1959), 413–24.

120. For basic details of the Spanish conquest of Bolivia, see Eduardo Arze Quiroga, *Historia de Bolivia: Fases del proceso hispano-americano: Orígenes de la sociedad boliviana en el siglo XVI* (La Paz: Editorial "Los Amigos del Libro," 1969), 149–221.

121. Hardoy and Aranovich, "Urban Scales," 73; Sánchez-Albornoz, *Population of Latin America*, 83.

122. Julio Díaz Arguedas, *Síntesis histórica de la ciudad La Paz, 1548–1948* (La Paz: Litografías e Imprentas Unidas, 1978), 411–12. On early industry in La Paz, see pp. 100–3. See also Laura Escobari de Querejazu, *Producción y comercio en el espacio sur andino en el siglo XVII: Cuzco-Potosí, 1650–1700* (La Paz: Industrias Offset Color, 1985), 108–9.

123. Sánchez-Albornoz, *Population of Latin America*, 83. See also Oscar Cornblit, *Power and Violence in the Colonial City: Oruro from the Mining Renaissance to the Rebellion of Tupac Amaru (1740–1782)*, trans. Elizabeth Ladd Glick (Cambridge: Cambridge University Press, 1995), 5–7; Laura Escobari

de Querejazu, *Caciques, yanaconas y extravagantes: La sociedad colonial en Charcas, s. XVI–XVIII* (La Paz: Plural Editores, 2001), 53–9.

124. Peter Bakewell, *Miners of the Red Mountain: Indian Labor in Potosí, 1545–1650* (Albuquerque: University of New Mexico Press, 1984), 34–7; Jeffrey A. Cole, *The Potosí Mita, 1573–1700: Compulsory Indian Labor in the Andes* (Stanford, CA: Stanford University Press, 1985), 3.

125. Bakewell, *Miners of the Red Mountain*, 46.

126. Ibid., chap. 1; Brading and Cross, "Colonial Silver Mining," 553–4.

127. Brading and Cross, "Colonial Silver Mining," 571.

128. Bakewell, "Mining in Colonial Spanish America," 144. See also Brading and Cross, "Colonial Silver Mining," 571. For data on mineral production, see Bakewell, *Miners of the Red Mountain*, 28–9. For comparisons with Mexican production, see Clara López Beltrán, *Estructura económica de una sociedad colonial: Charcas en el siglo XVII* (La Paz: Escuela Profesional "Don Bosco," 1988), 67; and esp. Garner's excellent "Long-Term Silver Mining Trends."

129. By one estimate – exaggerated, in my view – seventeenth-century Potosí contained thirty-five thousand Spanish people who had migrated from other provinces in the New World and another forty thousand who had come from Spanish territories in Europe. See Escobari de Querejazu, *Producción y comercio*, 39. For other estimates, see note 130.

130. Population data are from Carlos Sempat Assadourian, "La producción de la mercancía dinero en la formación del mercado interno colonial: El caso del espacio peruano, siglo XVI," in Enrique Florescano, ed., *Ensayos sobre el desarrollo económico de México y América Latina (1500–1975)* (Mexico City: Fondo de Cultura Económica, 1979), 229–30; Peter Bakewell, *Silver and Entrepreneurship in Seventeenth-Century Potosí: The Life and Times of Antonio López de Quiroga* (Albuquerque: University of New Mexico Press, 1988), 22–3, 191; Gwendolin Ballantine Cobb, *Potosí y Huancavelica: Bases económicas del Perú, 1545–1640* (La Paz: Biblioteca "BAMIN," 1977), 143; Cole, *The Potosí Mita*, 15; Lewis Hanke, *Bartolomé Arzáns de Orsúa y Vela's History of Potosí* (Providence, RI: Brown University Press, 1965), 15, 36.

131. Bakewell, *Silver and Entrepreneurship*, 24–36; Cobb, *Potosí y Huancavelica*, 148–55; Gwendolin B. Cobb, "Supply and Transportation for the Potosí Mines, 1545–1640," *Hispanic American Historical Review* 29, no. 1 (February 1949): 25–45. For a detailed look at Potosí's imports, see Escobari de Querejazu, *Producción y comercio*, 39–47, 100–6.

132. Escobari de Querejazu, *Producción y comercio*, 119.

133. Klein, *Concise History of Bolivia*, 40. To be sure, beginning around 1615, production at Potosí began a decline that would continue throughout the colonial period. Because of this, one could reasonably argue that Bolivia became a semiperiphery of the empire at some point in the mid-seventeenth century. Even so, when we consider the boom period between the mid- to late sixteenth century and the early to mid-seventeenth century, it makes sense to view Bolivia as a center region during the first phase of Spanish colonialism. The advantages of doing so are clear when we note Bolivia's similarities with Mexico and Peru in the configuration of actors that were constituted by early colonial institutions.

134. Bakewell, *Miners of the Red Mountain*; López Beltrán, *Estructura económica*. For information on the evolution of the number of mita draftees, see Enrique

Tandeter, *Coercion and Market: Silver Mining in Colonial Potosí, 1692–1826* (Albuquerque: University of New Mexico Press, 1993), 24–36.

135. Cole, *The Potosí Mita*, 68–70; see also chaps. 4–5 more generally.

136. Ibid., 36, 42, 124; Tandeter, *Coercion and Market*, 29.

137. Bakewell, *Miners of the Red Mountain*, 181; López Beltrán, *Estructura económica*, 201.

138. Brading and Cross, "Colonial Silver Mining," 558.

139. Bakewell, *Miners of the Red Mountain*, 182–3. As Brading and Cross point out, the use of the mita represented a massive input of cheap labor in Potosí that was not available in Mexico, and "it was the *mita* which permitted production at Potosí alone to soar far beyond the contemporary total for all of New Spain." Brading and Cross, "Colonial Silver Mining," 560. See also Garner, "Long-Term Silver Mining Trends," 923–4; Tandeter, *Coercion and Market*, 52–61.

140. For a case study of the social networks underpinning the encomienda in La Plata, see Ana María Presta, *Los encomenderos de La Plata, 1550–1600* (Lima: Instituto de Estudios Peruanos, 2000); for data on the extent of encomiendas in La Plata, see esp. 257–8. On the encomienda more generally, see Josep M. Barnadas, *Charcas: Orígenes históricos de una sociedad colonial* (La Paz: Empresa Editora Universo, 1973), 215–60.

141. This paragraph draws on Nicolás Sánchez-Albornoz, *Indios y tributos en el Alto Perú* (Lima: Instituto de Estudios Peruanos, 1978), chaps. 2–3; Larson, *Cochabamba*, 94–100; Herbert S. Klein, "The State and the Labor Market in Rural Bolivia in the Colonial and Early Republican Periods," in Karen Spalding, ed., *Essays in the Political, Economic and Social History of Colonial Latin America* (Newark, NJ: University of Delaware, Latin American Studies Program, 1982), 95–106; Thierry Saignes, "Indian Migration and Social Change in Seventeenth-Century Charcas," in Brooke Larson and Olivia Harris (with Enrique Tandeter), eds., *Ethnicity, Markets, and Migration in the Andes: At the Crossroads of History and Anthropology* (Durham, NC: Duke University Press, 1995), 167–95.

142. Cornblit, *Power and Violence*, 7, 97. For comparative data on silver production in Oruro and Potosí, see pp. 99–101.

143. Bakewell, *Miners of the Red Mountain*, 110.

144. Cook, *Demographic Collapse*, 118; Sánchez-Albornoz, *Indios y tributos*, 32–4.

145. Cole, *The Potosí Mita*, 47.

146. Bakewell, *Silver and Entrepreneurship*, 47.

147. Cole, *The Potosí Mita*, 124.

148. See Bakewell, *Silver and Entrepreneurship*, 36–47.

149. Barnadas, *Charcas*, 348–53, 377–86; Larson, *Cochabamba*, 74–91.

150. Klein, *Concise History of Bolivia*, 49.

151. Jorge Hidalgo, "The Indians of Southern South America in the Middle of the Sixteenth Century," in Bethell, *Cambridge History of Latin America*, 1:92–103; Samuel K. Lothrop, "The Diaguita of Chile," in Steward, *Handbook of South American Indians*, vol. 2, *The Andean Civilizations*, 633–6; Fernando Márquez Miranda, "The Diaguita of Argentina," in Steward, *Handbook of South American Indians*, vol. 2, *The Andean Civilizations*, 637–54.

152. Renzo Pi Hugarte, *Los indios del Uruguay* (Montevideo: Ediciones de la Banda Oriental, 1998), esp. 73–111. See also Washington Reyes Abadie and Andrés

Vázquez Romero, *Crónica general del Uruguay*, vol. 1, *Los orígenes* (Montevideo: Ediciones de la Banda Oriental, 1998), 121–7; Salvador Canals Frau, *Las poblaciones indígenas de la Argentina: Su origen, su pasado, su presente* (Buenos Aires: Editorial Sudamericana, 1953), 235–54; Antonio Serrano, "The Charrua," in Steward, *Handbook of South American Indians*, vol. 1, *The Marginal Tribes*, 191–6.

153. There were other hunter-gatherer groups even farther to the south, in Patagonia. In learning about indigenous societies in Argentina, I benefited especially from the following works: Osvaldo Barsky and Jorge Gelman, *Historia del agro argentino: Desde la conquista hasta fines del siglo XX* (Buenos Aires: Grijalbo, 2001), esp. 21–3; John M. Cooper, "The Patagonian and Pampean Hunters," in Steward, *Handbook of South American Indians*, vol. 1, *The Marginal Tribes*, 127–68; Canals Frau, *Las poblaciones indígenas*, esp. 188–234; Hidalgo, "Indians of Southern South America"; Kristine L. Jones, "Warfare, Reorganization, and Readaptation at the Margins of Spanish Rule: The Southern Margin (1573–1882)," in Frank Salomon and Stuart B. Schwartz, eds., *The Cambridge History of the Native Peoples of the Americas*, vol. 3, *South America*, pt. 2 (Cambridge: Cambridge University Press, 1999), 138–87; S. K. Lothrop, "Indians of the Paraná Delta and La Plata Littoral," in Steward, *Handbook of South American Indians*, vol. 1, *The Marginal Tribes*, 177–90.

154. Ulderico Schmidel, quoted in Jones, "Warfare, Reorganization, and Readaptation," 149.

155. Cooper, "The Patagonian and Pampean Hunters," 163.

156. Jones, "Warfare, Reorganization, and Readaptation," 152.

157. The Mapuche and other Chilean indigenous groups became known as the Araucanians to the Spanish. On the Mapuche before the Spanish arrived, see esp. José Bengoa, *Historia de los antiguos mapuches del sur: Desde antes de la llegada de los españoles hasta las paces de Quilín* (Santiago: Catalonia, 2003), esp. 5–6; Bengoa, *Historia del pueblo mapuche (siglo XIX y XX)* (Santiago: Biblioteca Bicentenario, 2000), esp. 21–33. Traditional accounts are John M. Cooper, "The Araucanians," in Steward, *Handbook of South American Indians*, vol. 2, *The Andean Civilizations*, 687–760; Luis Galdames, *A History of Chile*, trans. Isaac Joslin Cox (Chapel Hill: University of North Carolina Press, 1941), chap. 1. On the Picunches, see also René León Echaiz, *Prehistoria de Chile Central* (Buenos Aires: Editorial Francisco de Aguirre, 1976), chap. 4.

158. Bengoa, *Historia del pueblo mapuche*, 27.

159. Ibid., 25.

160. On the history of Uruguay from 1500 to 1700, see Juan José Arteaga, *Uruguay: Breve historia contemporánea* (Mexico City: Fondo de Cultura Económica, 2000), 7–26; Reyes Abadie and Vázquez Romero, *Crónica general del Uruguay*, vol. 1, *Los orígenes*, chaps. 9–11; Jan M. G. Kleinpenning, *Peopling the Purple Land: A Historical Geography of Rural Uruguay, 1500–1915* (Amsterdam: CEDLA, 1995), chap. 1; John Street, *Artigas and the Emancipation of Uruguay* (Cambridge: Cambridge University Press, 1959), 1–20; Alberto Zum Felde, *Proceso histórico del Uruguay*, 11th ed. (Montevideo: ARCA Editorial, 1991), 10–18.

161. Zum Felde, *Proceso histórico del Uruguay*, 10–11.

162. On the number of cattle in the region, see Marvin Alisky, *Uruguay: A Contemporary Survey* (New York: Praeger, 1969), 6; Julio Millot and Magdalena Bertino, *Historia económica del Uruguay*, vol. 1 (Montevideo: Fundación de Cultura Universitaria, 1991), 51.

163. For the basic details on the founding of this settlement, see Pedro Santos Martínez, "Política de España en Europa: Conflictos con Portugal e Inglaterra," in Academia Nacional de la Historia, *Nueva historia de la nación Argentina*, vol. 2, *Período español (1600–1800)* (Buenos Aires: Editorial Planeta, 1999), 319–50. For a more detailed history of the formation of Montevideo, see Luis Enrique Azarola Gil, *Los orígenes de Montevideo, 1607–1749* (Buenos Aires: Librería y Editorial "La Facultad," 1933).

164. Mendoza's expedition is described in reasonable detail in Julian M. Rubio, *Exploración y conquista del Río de la Plata: Siglos XVI y XVII* (Barcelona–Buenos Aires: Salvat Editores, 1942), chap. 2.

165. See Hugo Humberto Beck, "Distribución territorial de la conquista: Red de urbanización y vías de comunicación," in Academia Nacional de la Historia, *Nueva historia de la nación Argentina*, vol. 2, *Período español (1600–1800)*, 21–3; David Rock, *Argentina, 1516–1987: From Spanish Colonization to Alfonsín*, rev. ed. (Berkeley: University of California Press, 1987), 15.

166. Jorge Comadrán Ruiz, *Evolución demográfica argentina durante el período hispano (1535–1810)* (Buenos Aires: Editorial Universitaria de Buenos Aires, 1969), 48. On the founding of the towns, see chap. 1.

167. Ibid., 31. These numbers are broadly consistent with other estimates for Tucumán as a whole. For example, in 1582, the number of indigenous people held in encomiendas in Tucumán was calculated at twenty-seven thousand or twenty-eight thousand; "fourteen years later that figure rises to 56,000, according to calculations made by Governor Ramírez de Velazco." Ricardo Zorraquín Becú, *La organización política argentina en el período hispánico*, 2nd ed. (Buenos Aires: Editorial Perrot, 1962), 109–10. See also Barsky and Gelman, *Historia del agro argentino*, 46–7.

168. Zorraquín Becú, *La organización política argentina*, 105–6.

169. Carlos Sempat Assadourian, *El sistema de la economía colonial: Mercado interno, regiones y espacio económico* (Lima: Instituto de Estudios Peruanos, 1982), chap. 1. See also Barsky and Gelman, *Historia del agro argentino*, 54–9; Laura Randall, *A Comparative Economic History of Latin America, 1500–1914*, vol. 2, *Argentina* (Ann Arbor, MI: University Microfilms International for Institute of Latin American Studies, Columbia University, 1977), chap. 6.

170. Zorraquín Becú, *La organización política argentina*, 95–6.

171. Rubio, *Exploración y conquista del Río de la Plata*, 682.

172. Mario Rodríguez, "The Genesis of Economic Attitudes in the Rio de la Plata," *Hispanic American Historical Review* 36, no. 2 (May 1956): 189.

173. Rock, *Argentina*, 27.

174. Susana R. Frías, "La expansión de la población," in Academia Nacional de la Historia, *Nueva historia de la nación Argentina*, vol. 2, *Período español (1600–1800)*, 110.

175. Rodríguez, "Genesis of Economic Attitudes," 173–5, offers a good discussion of the Portuguese merchants.

176. Ibid., 182. On the Argentine elite in the seventeenth century, see esp. César A. García Belsunce, "La sociedad hispano-criolla," in Academia Nacional de la Historia, *Nueva historia de la nación Argentina*, vol. 2, *Período español (1600–1800)*, 158–9.

177. Rock, *Argentina*, 27–8; Rodríguez, "Genesis of Economic Attitudes," 177–9.

178. This slowdown was also likely related to the decline in silver production at Potosí. Warfare with indigenous groups may have further contributed. On the latter, see Alfred J. Tapson, "Indian Warfare on the Pampa during the Colonial Period," *Hispanic American Historical Review* 42, no. 1 (February 1962): 1–28.

179. Pedro de Valdivia, the leader of an early settler expedition, extolled the area: "This land is such that for living in, and for settling, there is none better in the world." He estimated that Chile "had been deliberately created by God in order to have everything close at hand." Quoted in, respectively, Simon Collier and William F. Sater, *A History of Chile, 1808–1994* (Cambridge: Cambridge University Press, 1996), 3; Arnold J. Bauer, *Chilean Rural Society: From the Spanish Conquest to 1930* (Cambridge: Cambridge University Press, 1975), 3.

180. Collier and Sater, *A History of Chile*, 3.

181. Eugene H. Korth, *Spanish Policy in Colonial Chile: The Struggle for Social Justice, 1535–1700* (Stanford, CA: Stanford University Press, 1968), 22.

182. Brian Loveman, *Chile: The Legacy of Hispanic Capitalism*, 2nd ed. (New York: Oxford University Press, 1988), 40.

183. On this history, see Louis de Armond, "Frontier Warfare in Colonial Chile," *Pacific Historical Review* 23, no. 2 (May 1954): 125–32; G. F. Scott Elliot, *Chile: Its History and Development, Natural Features, Products, Commerce and Present Conditions* (New York: Charles Scribner's Sons, 1907); Francisco Antonio Encina, *Historia de Chile: Desde la prehistoria hasta 1891*, vols. 1 and 2 (Santiago: Editorial Nascimento, 1941); Galdames, *A History of Chile*; John L. Rector, *The History of Chile* (New York: Palgrave Macmillan, 2003). There are also various accounts written by participants in the conflict. See, for example, Alonso de Góngora Marmolejo, *Historia de Chile desde su descubrimiento hasta el año 1575* (Santiago: Editorial Universitaria, 1969).

184. Loveman, *Chile*, 58. See also pp. 87–8.

185. Population and other numerical estimates in this paragraph are from Encina, *Historia de Chile*, 2:246–8. For various other (and widely differing) population estimates, see Bauer, *Chilean Rural Society*, 7; Marcello Carmagnani, "Colonial Latin American Demography: Growth of the Chilean Population, 1700–1830," *Journal of Social History* 1, no. 2 (Winter 1967): 185, 190; Galdames, *A History of Chile*, 97; Loveman, *Chile*, 70.

186. Thomas Chapin Braman, "Land and Society in Early Colonial Santiago de Chile, 1540–1575" (PhD diss., Department of History, University of Florida, 1975), 158–9.

187. Admittedly, it is difficult to know whether Chile actually possessed substantial mineral deposits that were realistically accessible to the Spanish in the sixteenth and seventeenth centuries (as was the case in Colombia) or whether minerals could not be easily taken, even with more adequate labor (as in Honduras). The definitive work on gold and silver mining in Chile during the sixteenth and seventeenth centuries has yet to be written. However, Mackenna argues strongly that the war with the indigenous population, not the withering of

mineral resources, explains the mineral decline during this period. See Benjamín Vicuña Mackenna, *La edad del oro de Chile* (Buenos Aires: Editorial Francisco de Aguirre, 1969), 80, and chap. 3 more generally. See also Marcello Carmagnani, *El salariado minero en Chile colonial: Su desarrollo en una sociedad provincial, el Norte Chico, 1690–1800* (Santiago: Editorial Universitaria, 1963); Bernhard Neumann, "Historia de la amalgamación de la plata," *Revista Chilena de Historia y Geografía* 102 (January–June 1943): 158–259; Armando de Ramón and José Manuel Larraín, *Orígenes de la vida económica chilena, 1659–1808* (Santiago: Imprenta Calderón, 1982), chap. 2. Basic data on gold production in different areas are provided in Ramón and Larraín, *Orígenes de la vida económica chilena*, 47–9.

188. The agricultural economy and its labor system are discussed in Mario Góngora, *Encomenderos y estancieros: Estudios acerca de la constitución social aristocrática de Chile después de la conquista, 1580–1660* (Santiago: Editorial Universitaria, 1971); Góngora, *Origen de los inquilinos de Chile central* (Santiago: ICIRA, 1974), chaps. 3–4; Loveman, *Chile*, chap. 3; Ramón and Larraín, *Orígenes de la vida económica chilena*.

189. Mario Gongora, "Urban Social Stratification in Colonial Chile," *Hispanic American Historical Review* 55, no. 3 (August 1975): 440.

190. Galdames, *A History of Chile*, 71.

191. Accounts of the Guaraní are provided by P. Pedro Francisco Javier de Charlevoix, *Historia de Paraguay*, vol. 1 (Madrid: Librería General de Victoriano Suárez, 1910), 49–70; Jan M. G. Kleinpenning, *Paraguay, 1515–1870: A Thematic Geography of Its Development*, vol. 1 (Madrid: Iberoamericana, 2003), 109–22; H. Sánchez Quell, *Estructura y función del Paraguay colonial* (Buenos Aires: Editorial Kraft, 1964), chaps. 4–6; Elman R. Service, *Spanish-Guarani Relations in Early Colonial Paraguay* (Westport, CT: Greenwood Press, 1954), chap. 1.

192. Kleinpenning, *Paraguay*, 129. Some of the Chaco indigenous groups were more complex than others, occasionally leading a semi-sedentary lifestyle, not unlike the Guaraní. See, for example, Alfred Métraux, "Ethnography of the Chaco," in Steward, *Handbook of South American Indians*, vol. 1, *The Marginal Tribes*, 197–370; James Saeger, "Warfare, Reorganization, and Readaptation at the Margins of the Spanish Rule – The Chaco and Paraguay (1573–1882)," in Salomon and Schwartz, *Cambridge History of the Native Peoples of the Americas*, vol. 3, *South America*, pt. 2, p. 258.

193. Efraim Cardozo, *El Paraguay colonial: Las raíces de la nacionalidad* (Buenos Aires: Ediciones Nizza, 1959), 68; Kleinpenning, *Paraguay*, 593–604. Susnik attributes myths about the Guaraní to the mission communities that subsequently developed (discussed below). See Branislava Susnik, *El indio colonial del Paraguay*, vol. 2, *Los trece pueblos guaraníes de las misiones (1767–1803)* (Asunción: Museo Etnográfico "Andres Barbero," 1966), 9. Nevertheless, some observers believe that the Guaraní much more readily adapted to Spanish culture than did other indigenous groups in Latin America. See José Luis Mora Merida, *Historia social de Paraguay, 1600–1650* (Seville: EEHA, 1973), 21.

194. Kleinpenning, *Paraguay*, 609–10, 673.

195. See esp. Branislava Susnik, *El indio colonial del Paraguay*, vol. 1, *El guaraní colonial* (Asunción: Museo Etnográfico "Andres Barbero," 1965), chap. 1;

Juan Carlos Garavaglia, *Mercado interno y economía colonial* (Mexico City: Editorial Grijalbo, 1983), 262–81.

196. Garavaglia, *Mercado interno*, 164–76. The fact that mestizo children born from liaisons between Spanish men and Guaraní women were considered Spanish also contributed to the decline. Mora Merida, *Historia social de Paraguay*, 27.

197. Kleinpenning, *Paraguay*, 674.

198. Garavaglia, *Mercado interno*, 201; Kleinpenning, *Paraguay*, 682, 702–3.

199. Kleinpenning, *Paraguay*, 917.

200. On yerba production, see Garavaglia, *Mercado interno*, chap. 2; Cardozo, *El Paraguay colonial*, 93–6; Kleinpenning, *Paraguay*, chaps. 25 and 26.

201. "During all of the seventeenth century, Santa Fe was indisputably the most important center of the redistribution of yerba." Garavaglia, *Mercado interno*, 89.

202. Mora Merida, *Historia social de Paraguay*, 107–8; Kleinpenning, *Paraguay*, 1212, 1223.

203. Kleinpenning, *Paraguay*, 539.

204. Garavaglia, *Mercado interno*, 204–11.

205. Kleinpenning, *Paraguay*, 543.

206. Despite some efforts, the Jesuits were not successful at creating settlements for the Chaco indigenous people in western Paraguay.

207. Elman R. Service, "Indian-European Relations in Colonial Latin America," *American Anthropologist* 57, no. 3 (June 1955): 415.

208. Kleinpenning's coverage of the Jesuits is extensive. See Kleinpenning, *Paraguay*, 352–63, 464–93, 732–40, 946–63, 1463–84, 1600–4.

209. Leading works on the indigenous societies of Venezuela include Miguel Acosta Saignes, *Estudios de etnología antigua de Venezuela* (Caracas: Universidad Central de Venezuela, 1961); Marc de Civrieux, "Los Cumanagoto y sus vecinos," in Audrey Butt Colson, ed., *Los aborígenes de Venezuela* (Caracas: Instituto Caribe de Antropología y Sociología, 1980); Gregorio Hernández de Alba, "Tribes of Northwestern Venezuela," in Julian H. Steward, ed., *Handbook of South American Indians*, vol. 4, *The Circum-Caribbean Tribes* (Washington, DC: U.S. Government Printing Office, 1948), 469–79; Alfred Kidder II, "The Archeology of Venezuela," in Steward, *Handbook of South American Indians*, vol. 4, *The Circum-Caribbean Tribes*, 413–38; Paul Kirchhoff, "The Otomac," "Food-Gathering Tribes of the Venezuelan Llanos," and "The Tribes North of the Orinoco River," in Steward, *Handbook of South American Indians*, vol. 4, *The Circum-Caribbean Tribes*, 439–44, 445–68, 481–93; Steward and Faron, *Native Peoples of South America*, 241–5; Steward, "The Circum-Caribbean Tribes: An Introduction," in Steward, *Handbook of South American Indians*, vol. 4, *The Circum-Caribbean Tribes*, 1–41; Neil Whitehead, "Native Peoples Confront Colonial Regimes in Northeastern South America (1500–1900)," in Salomon and Schwartz, *Cambridge History of the Native Peoples of the Americas*, vol. 3, *South America*, pt. 2, pp. 382–442.

210. Kirchhoff, "Tribes North of the Orinoco River," 481.

211. Denevan, "Native American Populations in 1492," xxviii.

212. Federico Brito Figueroa, *La estructura económica de Venezuela colonial*, 3rd ed. (Caracas: Universidad Central de Venezuela, 1983), chaps. 2–3.

213. On these expeditions, see John Hemming, *The Search for El Dorado* (London: Michael Joseph, 1978), esp. chap. 2; José de Oviedo y Baños, *The Conquest and Settlement of Venezuela*, trans. Jeannette Johnson Varner (Berkeley: University of California Press, 1987), esp. book 2.

214. John V. Lombardi, *Venezuela: The Search for Order, the Dream of Progress* (New York: Oxford University Press, 1982), 69.

215. To be sure, a version of the encomienda was practiced, and, as late as the 1660s, inspectors still found thousands of indigenous people incorporated into encomiendas. Eduardo Arcila Farías, *El régimen de la encomienda en Venezuela* (Seville: Escuela de Estudios Hispano-Americanos, 1957), 5, 191–7.

216. Eduardo Arcila Farías, *Economía colonial de Venezuela* (Mexico City: Fondo de Cultura Económica, 1946), 125. See also Brito Figueroa, *La estructura económica*, 73–81, for details on the value of gold production.

217. John V. Lombardi, *People and Places in Colonial Venezuela* (Bloomington: Indiana University Press, 1976), 24. On the formation of the provinces of colonial Venezuela, see Guillermo Morón, *Breve historia contemporánea de Venezuela* (Mexico City: Fondo de Cultura Económica, 1994), pt. 2.

218. See Federico Brito Figueroa, *Historia económica y social de Venezuela*, vol. 1 (Caracas: Universidad Central de Venezuela, 1966), 124. Salcedo-Bastardo estimates that five thousand Spanish had entered Venezuela by the end of the sixteenth century. J. L. Salcedo-Bastardo, *Historia fundamental de Venezuela*, 8th ed. (Caracas: Universidad Central de Venezuela, 1979), 79.

219. Robert J. Ferry, *The Colonial Elite of Early Caracas: Formation and Crisis, 1567–1767* (Berkeley: University of California Press, 1989), 15–20, 48–9.

220. About fifty thousand black slaves were shipped to Venezuela from 1500 to 1700; another seventy thousand arrived between 1700 and 1810. Altogether, Venezuela received about 12 percent of all black slaves legally imported into the Spanish American colonies. See Brito Figueroa, *La estructura económica*, 120, 124.

221. Lombardi, *Venezuela*, 76–7. See also Brito Figueroa, *La estructura económica*, 209–15.

222. William R. Fowler Jr., *The Cultural Evolution of Ancient Nahua Civilizations: The Pipil-Nicarao of Central America* (Norman: University of Oklahoma Press, 1989), 131. Fowler's quotation draws on Carl O. Sauer, *The Early Spanish Main* (Berkeley: University of California Press, 1966), 65.

223. This paragraph is based on Fowler, *Cultural Evolution*, 151 (on population size), 140–1, 224, 226 (on political organization), and 112–13, 190, 213 (on the economy).

224. For a good discussion of the subgroups within the Lenca population, see Linda Newson, *The Cost of Conquest: Indian Decline in Honduras under Spanish Rule* (Boulder, CO: Westview Press, 1986), 20–5. More generally on the Lenca, see Gloria Lara Pinto, "Sociopolitical Organization in Central and Southwest Honduras at the Time of the Conquest: A Model for the Formation of Complex Society," in William R. Fowler Jr., ed., *The Formation of Complex Society in Southeastern Mesoamerica* (Boca Raton, FL: CRC Press, 1991), 215–35; Doris Stone, "The Northern Highland Tribes: The Lenca," in Steward, *Handbook of South American Indians*, vol. 4, *The Circum-Caribbean Tribes*, 205–17; Anne

Chapman, *Los lencas de Honduras en el siglo XVI* (Tegucigalpa: Instituto Hondureño de Antropología e Historia, 1978).

225. On the Chorotega, see Anne M. Chapman, *Los nicarao y los chorotega según las fuentes históricas*, Serie Historia y Geografía, no. 4 (San José: Universidad de Costa Rica, 1960).

226. Carmack estimates the population of the various chiefdoms of eastern El Salvador, central and western Honduras, and northern Nicaragua at 1 million. See Robert M. Carmack, "Perspectivas sobre la historia antigua de Centroamérica," in Robert M. Carmack, ed., *Historia general de Centroamérica*, vol. 1, *Historia antigua* (Madrid: Sociedad Estatal Quinto Centenario, 1993), 302. See also Newson, *The Cost of Conquest*, chap. 5.

227. Here I follow William R. Fowler Jr., "The Formation of Complex Society among the Nahua Groups of Southeastern Mesoamerica: A Comparison of Two Approaches," in Fowler, *Formation of Complex Society*, 193–213. See also Linda A. Newson, *Indian Survival in Colonial Nicaragua* (Norman: University of Oklahoma Press, 1987), chap. 3; Frederick Johnson, "The Meso-American Indians," in Steward, *Handbook of South American Indians*, vol. 4, *The Circum-Caribbean Tribes*, 202–3. For a dissenting view that holds that the Nicarao were a state-like society, see Carmack, "Perspectivas," 321 n. 21.

228. Fowler, *Cultural Evolution*, 219. My description of Nicarao society draws from this work.

229. There are several different estimates of the precolonial populations of these areas. See, for example, Carmack, "Perspectivas," 299–300; Denevan, "Native American Populations in 1492," xxviii; Newson, *Indian Survival*, 88.

230. On the chiefdoms of Costa Rica and Panama, see Carmack, "Perspectivas," 299–301; Mary W. Helms, *Ancient Panama: Chiefs in Search of Power* (Austin: University of Texas Press, 1979); Eugenia Ibarra Rojas, *Las sociedades cicicales de Costa Rica (siglo XVI)* (San José: Editorial de la Universidad de Costa Rica, 1990); Frederick Johnson, "Central American Cultures: An Introduction," in Steward, *Handbook of South American Indians*, vol. 4, *The Circum-Caribbean Tribes*, 43–68; Frederick Johnson, "The Caribbean Lowland Tribes: The Talamanca Division," in Steward, *Handbook of South American Indians*, vol. 4, *The Circum-Caribbean Tribes*, 231–51.

231. Information for this paragraph comes from Johnson, "Central American Cultures"; Paul Kirchhoff, "The Caribbean Lowland Tribes: The Mosquito, Sumo, Paya, and Jicaque," in Steward, *Handbook of South American Indians*, vol. 4, *The Circum-Caribbean Tribes*, 219–29; Newson, *The Cost of Conquest*, 34–45, 67–85; Newson, *Indian Survival*, chap. 4; Mary W. Helms, *Middle America: A Culture History of Heartland and Frontiers* (Englewood Cliffs, NJ: Prentice Hall, 1975), chap. 7; Tomás Ayón, *Historia de Nicaragua: Desde los tiempos más remotos hasta el año 1852* (Managua: Fondo de Promoción Cultural, BANIC, 1993), chap. 1.

232. David Browning, *El Salvador: Landscape and Society* (Oxford: Clarendon Press, 1971), 31; Robert Chamberlain, "The Early Years of San Miguel de la Frontera," *Hispanic American Historical Review* 27, no. 4 (November 1947): 623–47; William R. Fowler Jr., "The Political Economy of Indian Survival in Sixteenth-Century Izalco, El Salvador," in David Hurst Thomas, ed.,

Columbian Consequences, vol. 3, *The Spanish Borderlands in Pan-American Perspective* (Washington, DC: Smithsonian Institution Press, 1991), 187–204; Jorge Lardé y Larín, *El Salvador: Descubrimiento, conquista y colonización*, 2nd ed. (San Salvador: Dirección de Publicaciones e Impresos, 2000), 66–8.

233. Murdo J. MacLeod, *Spanish Central America: A Socioeconomic History, 1520–1720* (Berkeley: University of California Press, 1973), chap. 5; Fowler, "Political Economy of Indian Survival," 193–6; William R. Fowler Jr., "Cacao, Indigo, and Coffee: Cash Crops in the History of El Salvador," *Research in Economic Anthropology* 8 (1987): 144–7; Lardé y Larín, *El Salvador*, 551–2; Browning, *El Salvador*, 58.

234. Jorge Lardé y Larín, *El Salvador: Historia de sus pueblos, villas y ciudades*, 2nd ed. (San Salvador: Dirección de Publicaciones e Impresos, 2000), 549; Alastair White, *El Salvador* (London: Ernest Benn, 1973), 30.

235. MacLeod, *Spanish Central America*, 98–100, nicely summarizes the epidemics in Central America from 1520 to 1700. Rough population estimates are in Rodolfo Barón Castro, *La población de El Salvador: Estudio acerca de su desenvolvimiento desde la época prehispánica hasta nuestros días* (Madrid: Consejo Superior de Investigaciones Científicas, 1942), chap. 10. See also Fowler, "Political Economy of Indian Survival," 192–3.

236. MacLeod, *Spanish Central America*, 87. Spanish policy forced indigenous persons to pay tribute in cacao, even when they did not live in a cacao-producing area. Hence, many people were forced from the highlands to the cacao estates in order to be able to pay their tribute.

237. Ibid., 191.

238. Ibid., 177–203, 382–4.

239. See William L. Sherman, *Forced Native Labor in Sixteenth-Century Central America* (Lincoln: University of Nebraska Press, 1979), 360–2; Browning, *El Salvador*, 111–12.

240. On the early conquest of Honduras, see Rómulo E. Durón, *Bosquejo histórico de Honduras, 1502 a 1921* (San Pedro Sula, Honduras: Tip. del Comercio, 1927), 3–11; Newson, *The Cost of Conquest*, 96–9; Elizabeth Fonseca Corrales, "Economía y sociedad en Centroamérica (1540–1680)," in Julio César Pinto Soria, ed., *Historia general de Centroamérica: El régimen colonial (1524–1750)* (Madrid: Sociedad Estatal Quinto Centenario, 1993), 128.

241. At least a few thousand people were shipped out of the region as slaves, and many more were used locally as slaves before 1550. See Sherman, *Forced Native Labor*, 74. For a much higher estimate, see Newson, *The Cost of Conquest*, 127.

242. Newson, *The Cost of Conquest*, 330.

243. MacLeod, *Spanish Central America*, 55.

244. This paragraph draws on Linda Newson, "Labour in the Colonial Mining Industry of Honduras," *The Americas* 39, no. 2 (October 1982): 186–203; Robert C. West, "The Mining Economy of Honduras during the Colonial Period," *Actas del XXXIII Congreso Internacional de Americanistas* 2 (1959): 767–77; MacLeod, *Spanish Central America*, 56–61, 148–51, 253–63.

245. MacLeod, *Spanish Central America*, 263.

246. Sherman, *Forced Native Labor*.

247. Newson, *The Cost of Conquest*, 322–3.

248. David Richard Radell, "A Historical Geography of Western Nicaragua: The Spheres of Influence of León, Granada, and Managua, 1519–1965" (PhD diss., Department of Geography, University of California, Berkeley, 1969), 63–4.

249. MacLeod, *Spanish Central America*, 50–5; Sherman, *Forced Native Labor*, chap. 4; Newson, *Indian Survival*, 101–6; Radell, "A Historical Geography," chap. 4.

250. Newson, *Indian Survival*, 118.

251. Radell estimates that between 450,000 and 500,000 slaves were exported from Nicaragua. MacLeod suggests that 200,000 is a conservative estimate for Nicaragua. Newson estimates that between 200,000 and 500,000 were exported from all of Central America. Sherman estimates that 50,000 slaves were exported from Central America between 1524 and 1549. Radell, "A Historical Geography," 66, 76, 78; MacLeod, *Spanish Central America*, 52; Newson, *Indian Survival*, 105; Sherman, *Forced Native Labor*, 82. For additional estimates, see Pablo Kraudy Medina, *Historia social de las ideas en Nicaragua: El pensamiento de la conquista* (Managua: Banco Central de Nicaragua, 2001), 111.

252. Dan Stanislawski, *The Transformation of Nicaragua: 1519–1548* (Berkeley: University of California Press, 1983); Newson, *Indian Survival*, 150–67.

253. Newson, *Indian Survival*, 106–7, 146–7.

254. Radell, "A Historical Geography," 108; Newson, *Indian Survival*, 147–9.

255. Radell, "A Historical Geography," 167.

256. Newson, *Indian Survival*, 143. Surprisingly little is known about early indigo production in Nicaragua. But see Radell, "A Historical Geography," 171–4; MacLeod, *Spanish Central America*, 177–8.

257. Newson, *Indian Survival*, 244, 130, 129.

258. Elizabeth Fonseca, *Costa Rica colonial: La tierra y el hombre*, 2nd ed. (San José: EDUCA, 1984), 40. This view is common. Hall writes, for example, "Far from the major administrative centers of the empire, Costa Rica was one of the most neglected provinces in Spanish America." Carolyn Hall, *Costa Rica: A Geographical Interpretation in Historical Perspective* (Boulder, CO: Westview Press, 1985), 92.

259. Fonseca, *Costa Rica colonial*, 41.

260. A brief account of the conquest of Costa Rica can be found in Paulino González Villalobos, "La coyuntura de la conquista," in Paulino González Villalobos, ed., *Desarrollo institucional de Costa Rica (1523–1914)* (San José: SECASA, 1983), 19–46. For a longer version, see Ricardo Fernández Guardia, *Historia de Costa Rica: El descubrimiento y la conquista*, 4th ed. (San José: Librería Lehmann y Cía., 1941). The changing political jurisdictions in Central America are beautifully illustrated in Carolyn Hall and Héctor Pérez Brignoli, *Historical Atlas of Central America* (Norman: University of Oklahoma Press, 2003), 32–3.

261. MacLeod, *Spanish Central America*, 205–6.

262. Claudia Quirós, *La era de la encomienda* (San José: EDUCR, 1998), 129–31; Elizet Payne Iglesias, *Origen y crisis de una colonia marginal: El siglo XVII en Costa Rica* (San José: EUNED, 1992), chap. 3.

263. Fonseca, *Costa Rica colonial*, 66. On the early colonial economy, see also Payne Iglesias, *Origen y crisis*, chap. 2.

264. Fonseca, *Costa Rica colonial*, chap. 5; MacLeod, *Spanish Central America*, chap. 18.
265. Fonseca, *Costa Rica colonial*, 48; Hall and Pérez Brignoli, *Historical Atlas of Central America*, 82–3, 89.
266. MacLeod, *Spanish Central America*, 337.
267. Luis Guillermo Brenes Quesada et al., *Historia de Costa Rica*, vol. 1 (San José: Editorial EIDOS, 1997), 566, 570–1.
268. MacLeod, *Spanish Central America*, 228. According to Fonseca, Cartago was populated by "511 individuals who were Spanish or mestizos of very white skin." Fonseca, *Costa Rica colonial*, 76.
269. Brenes Quesada et al., *Historia de Costa Rica*, 569.
270. See W. George Lovell and William Swezey, "The Population of Southern Guatemala at Spanish Contact," *Canadian Journal of Anthropology* 3, no. 1 (Fall 1982): 81; Denevan, "Native American Populations in 1492," xxii, xxviii; Jorge Arias de Blois, "Evolución demográfica hasta 1700," in Jorge Luján Muñoz, ed., *Historia general de Guatemala*, vol. 2, *Dominación española: Desde la conquista hasta 1700* (Guatemala City: Fundación para la Cultura y el Desarrollo, 1994), 318–19. For a summary of estimates of precolonial population sizes, see W. George Lovell, "Surviving Conquest: The Maya of Guatemala in Historical Perspective," *Latin American Research Review* 23, no. 2 (1988): 29.
271. The description of precolonial Guatemala in this paragraph and the next one relies heavily on Robert M. Carmack, *The Quiché Mayas of Utatlán: The Evolution of a Highland Guatemala Kingdom* (Norman: University of Oklahoma Press, 1981). However, I also consulted the following works: W. George Lovell, *A Historical Geography of the Cuchumatán Highlands, 1500–1821* (Montreal: McGill-Queen's University Press, 2005), chap. 3; MacLeod, *Spanish Central America*, 33–7; Elias Zamora Acosta, *Los Mayas de las tierras altas en el siglo XVI* (Seville: Gráficas del Sur, 1985), esp. chaps. 1, 4.
272. Carmack highlights the following traits of the Quiché Maya, which also characterize the other major Maya groups of precolonial Guatemala: "a preoccupation with military conquest, commoner-aristocrat social ranking, human sacrifice, segmentary lineage organization, quadripartite political rule, a variant of Mixteca-Puebla arts and crafts, dualism and cardinal-point orientation in religious symbolism, ritual calendrics, heroic history." Carmack, *The Quiché Mayas*, 6.
273. On the precious minerals of colonial Guatemala, see Ernesto Chinchilla Aguilar, "Lavaderos de oro y la minería," in Luján Muñoz, *Historia general de Guatemala*, vol. 2, *Dominación española*, 443–50.
274. On the varying difficulty of conquering different kinds of societies in Guatemala, see Jorge Luján Muñoz, "Características, consecuencias, y alcances de la conquista," in Luján Muñoz, *Historia general de Guatemala*, vol. 2, *Dominación española*, 76. Alvarado's path of conquest is well described (and illustrated with excellent maps) in Jorge Luján Muñoz and Horacio Cabezas Carcache, "La conquista," in Luján Muñoz, *Historia general de Guatemala*, vol. 2, *Dominación española*, 47–74. More generally on Alvarado, see John E. Kelly, *Pedro de Alvarado, Conquistador* (1934; repr., Port Washington, NY:

Kennikat Press, 1967); Pedro de Alvarado, *An Account of the Conquest of Guatemala in 1524*, ed. Sedley J. Mackie (New York: Cortés Society, 1924).

275. Beatriz Suñe Blanco, "La ciudad de Santiago de Guatemala," in Luján Muñoz, *Historia general de Guatemala*, vol. 2, *Dominación española*, 187–205.

276. Ibid., 192; Christopher H. Lutz, "Evolución demográfica de la población no indígena," in Luján Muñoz, *Historia general de Guatemala*, vol. 2, *Dominación española*, 251–2; Lutz, *Santiago de Guatemala, 1541–1773: City, Caste, and the Colonial Experience* (Norman: University of Oklahoma Press, 1994), 110.

277. Jorge Luján Muñoz, "Política fundacional en los siglos XVI y XVII," in Luján Muñoz, *Historia general de Guatemala*, vol. 2, *Dominación española*, 135. Lutz's data suggest that Santiago grew from 33,400 in the 1650s to 38,900 in the 1680s. Lutz, *Santiago de Guatemala*, 110.

278. Luján Muñoz, "Política fundacional," 135. Likewise, as Jones suggests, "Guatemala emerged as the most important province [in Central America] and was also the social and economic center of the kingdom." Oakah L. Jones Jr., *Guatemala in the Spanish Colonial Period* (Norman: University of Oklahoma Press, 1994), 38.

279. Except for a brief period from 1564 to 1570, the province of Guatemala controlled the capital of the audiencia. After 1570, the Central American region became known as the Audiencia of Guatemala (often later called the Kingdom of Guatemala). See Hall and Pérez Brignoli, *Historical Atlas of Central America*, 32.

280. Jones, *Guatemala*, 42.

281. Stephen Andrew Webre, "The Social and Economic Bases of Cabildo Membership in Seventeenth-Century Santiago de Guatemala" (PhD diss., University of Tulane, 1980). Webre's argument is summarized in part in Stephen Webre, "Antecedentes económicos de los regidores de Santiago de Guatemala, siglos XVI y XVII: Una élite colonial," in Stephen Webre, ed., *La sociedad colonial en Guatemala: Estudios regionales y locales* (Antigua, Guatemala: Centro de Investigaciones Regionales de Mesoamérica, 1989), 189–219.

282. Valentín Solórzano F., *Evolución económica de Guatemala* (Guatemala City: Centro Editorial "José de Pineda Ibarra," 1963), 109–17.

283. Zamora Acosta, *Los Mayas*, provides a nice account of the different kinds of tribute collection in Guatemala and their relationship to traditional Maya practices. Key works on the early phase of encomiendas are Wendy Kramer, *Encomienda Politics in Early Colonial Guatemala, 1524–1544* (Boulder, CO: Westview Press, 1994); Salvador Rodríguez Becerra, *Encomienda y conquista: Los inicios de la colonización en Guatemala* (Seville: Universidad de Sevilla, 1977). Kramer argues that the process of forming encomiendas was started in Guatemala much earlier than most histories acknowledge, though Rodríguez Becerra also discusses early encomiendas in the region.

284. See Zamora Acosta, *Los Mayas*, chap. 6.

285. Horacio Cabezas Carcache, "Régimen regulador del trabajo indígena," in Luján Muñoz, *Historia general de Guatemala*, vol. 2, *Dominación española*, 392.

286. Horacio Cabezas Carcache, "Las encomiendas," in Luján Muñoz, *Historia general de Guatemala*, vol. 2, *Dominación española*, 384.

287. These data are reported in appendix 3 of Rodríguez Becerra, *Encomienda y conquista*, 168–70.
288. W. George Lovell, Christopher H. Lutz, and William R. Swezey, "The Indian Population of Southern Guatemala, 1549–1551: An Analysis of López de Cerrato's *Tasaciones de Tributos,*" *The Americas* 40, no. 4 (April 1984): 459–77. See p. 471 for the estimate of more than eighty-five thousand.
289. Ibid., 472. For a similar estimate and a broader discussion of the literature, see Arias de Blois, "Evolución demográfica hasta 1700," 318–19. Arias de Blois believes the late-seventeenth-century population to have been no less than four hundred thousand (p. 325).
290. W. George Lovell and Christopher H. Lutz, *Demography and Empire: A Guide to the Population History of Spanish Central America, 1500–1821* (Boulder, CO: Westview Press, 1995), 9.
291. Jones, *Guatemala*, 89. On the link between congregaciones and encomiendas, see esp. W. George Lovell and William R. Swezey, "Indian Migration and Community Formation: An Analysis of 'Congregación' in Colonial Guatemala," in David J. Robinson, ed., *Migration in Colonial Spanish America* (Cambridge: Cambridge University Press, 1990), 18–40.
292. MacLeod, *Spanish Central America*, 207–9.
293. Cabezas Carcache, "Las encomiendas," 384–5.
294. Lutz, *Santiago de Guatemala*, 162; Michel Bertrand, "La tierra y los hombres: La sociedad rural en Baja Verapaz durante los siglos XVI al XIX," in Webre, *La sociedad colonial*, 141–87.
295. See Jorge Luján Muñoz and Horacio Cabezas Carcache, "Comercio," in Luján Muñoz, *Historia general de Guatemala*, vol. 2, *Dominación española*, 466.
296. Ibid.; Troy S. Floyd, "The Guatemalan Merchants, the Government, and the *Provincianos*, 1750–1800," *Hispanic American Historical Review* 41, no. 1 (February 1961): 92–8.
297. Webre, "Social and Economic Bases," 180–1.
298. Ibid.; Webre, "Antecedentes económicos."
299. Luján Muñoz and Cabezas Carcache, "Comercio," 466.
300. Horacio Cabezas Carcache, "Agricultura," in Luján Muñoz, *Historia general de Guatemala*, vol. 2, *Dominación española*, 421–42.
301. The population estimate of 3 million is from Denevan, "Native American Populations in 1492," xxviii. For various other estimates, ranging from less than a million to 4 or 5 million, see Germán Colmenares, *Historia económica y social de Colombia*, vol. 1, *1537–1719*, 5th ed. (Bogotá: Tercer Mundo Editores, 1997), 101; Jorge Orlando Melo, *Historia de Colombia*, vol. 1, *El establecimiento de la dominación española* (Medellin, Colombia: Editorial La Carreta, 1977), 107–16; Hermes Tovar Pinzón, "Estado actual de los estudios de demografía histórica en Colombia," *Anuario Colombiano de Historia Social y de la Cultura* 5 (1970): 65–103; Jaime Jaramillo Uribe, *Ensayos de historia social* (Bogotá: Tercer Mundo Editores, 1989), 145.
302. For similar estimates of the size of the Muisca, see A. L. Kroeber, "The Chibcha," in Steward, *Handbook of South American Indians*, vol. 2, *The Andean Civilizations*, 892–3; Melo, *Historia de Colombia*, 1:100; Guillermo Hernández Rodríguez, *De los chibchas a la colonia y la República: Del clan a la encomienda y al latifundio en Colombia* (Bogotá: Ediciones Internacionales, 1978), 22–4. In the mid-1940s, Kroeber lamented that "the sources on the

Chibcha [Muisca] are not only limited but poor in quality" ("The Chibcha," 898). Since that time, the situation has dramatically improved: there are now several good studies on the Muiscas. For this paragraph, I consulted especially Sylvia M. Broadbent, *Los Chibchas: Organización socio-política* (Bogotá: Imprenta Nacional, 1964); Hernández Rodríguez, *De los chibchas.*

303. Melo, *Historia de Colombia*, 1:86–91.
304. Gerardo Reichel-Dolmatoff, "Colombia indígena, período prehispánico," in Jaime Jaramillo Uribe, ed., *Nueva historia de Colombia* (Bogotá: Planeta Colombiana Editorial, 1989), 54–7.
305. Melo, *Historia de Colombia*, 1:72–9.
306. Luis F. Calero, *Chiefdoms under Siege: Spain's Rule and Native Adaptation in the Southern Colombian Andes, 1535–1700* (Albuquerque: University of New Mexico Press, 1997), 35–46; Gregorio Hernández de Alba, "The Highland Tribes of Southern Colombia," in Steward, *Handbook of South American Indians*, vol. 2, *The Andean Civilizations*, 915–60.
307. For example, see Rausch's description of the indigenous societies in the western llanos near Venezuela. Jane M. Rausch, *A Tropical Plains Frontier: The Llanos of Colombia, 1531–1831* (Albuquerque: University of New Mexico Press, 1984), 12–21.
308. For a powerful demonstration of the relationship between the size of indigenous populations and the location of Spanish urban centers in early colonial Colombia, see the map on p. 427 in Melo, *Historia de Colombia*, vol. 1. For good discussions of the various expeditions that explored and conquered Colombia, see Juan Friede, "La conquista del territorio y el poblamiento," in Jaramillo Uribe, *Nueva historia de Colombia*, 69–115; Friede, *Los Chibchas bajo la dominación española* (Bogotá: La Carreta, 1974); Melo, *Historia de Colombia*, vol. 1, chaps. 4–8; José Ignacio Avellaneda, *The Conquerors of the New Kingdom of Granada* (Albuquerque: University of New Mexico Press, 1995); Juan A. Villamarín, "Encomenderos and Indians in the Formation of Colonial Society in the Sabana de Bogota, Colombia, 1537 to 1740" (PhD diss., Department of Anthropology, Brandeis University, 1972), chap. 1.
309. Hardoy and Aranovich, "Urban Scales," 72.
310. However, the subsequent creation of a separate audiencia in Quito brought the southwest region around Popayán under partially separate authority. Colmenares, *Historia económica y social*, 1:23. Popayán always had an autonomous existence: it was originally the province where Sebastián de Belalcázar ruled as governor after he failed to control Quito and the eastern highlands of Colombia. See Peter Marzahl, *Town in the Empire: Government, Politics, and Society in Seventeenth-Century Popayán* (Austin: University of Texas Press, 1978), 3.
311. Jaramillo Uribe, *Ensayos de historia social*, 196–8; Julián Vargas Lesmes, *La sociedad de Santa Fe colonial* (Bogotá: CINEP, 1990), 299–341.
312. Julián B. Ruiz Rivera, *Encomienda y mita en Nueva Granada en el siglo XVII* (Seville: Escuela de Estudios Hispano-Americanos, 1975), 45, 95–7, 207–9; Melo, *Historia de Colombia*, 1:297; Colmenares, *Historia económica y social*, 1:123.
313. Frank Safford and Marco Palacios, *Colombia: Fragmented Land, Divided Society* (Oxford: Oxford University Press, 2002), 44–8.

314. Ibid., 36; Calero, *Chiefdoms under Siege*, x–xi; Marzahl, *Town in the Empire*, 5.
315. Anthony McFarlane, *Colombia before Independence: Economy, Society, and Politics under Bourbon Rule* (Cambridge: Cambridge University Press, 1993), 17.
316. A succinct treatment of the mineral economy is Robert C. West, *Colonial Placer Mining in Colombia* (Baton Rouge: Louisiana State University Press, 1952).
317. See esp. Jaramillo Uribe, *Ensayos de historia social*, chap. 3.
318. For various discussions of diseases and the decline of the indigenous population across different regions, see Calero, *Chiefdoms under Siege*, 81–7 (for southern regions); Colmenares, *Historia económica y social*, vol. 1, chap. 2 (for comparison of regions); Friede, *Los Chibchas*, chap. 18 (for the eastern highlands); Safford and Palacios, *Colombia*, 25–6 (for comparison of regions); Juan A. Villamarín and Judith E. Villamarín, "Epidemic and Disease in the Sabana of Bogotá," in Noble David Cook and W. George Lovell, eds., *Secret Judgments of God: Old World Disease in Colonial Spanish America* (Norman: University of Oklahoma Press, 1992) (for the eastern highland region near Bogotá).
319. Colmenares, *Historia económica y social*, 1:90.
320. Ibid., 91–103. See also Orlando Fals-Borda, "Indian Congregations in the New Kingdom of Granada: Land Tenure Aspects, 1595–1850," *The Americas* 13, no. 4 (April 1957): 331–51.
321. Ruiz Rivera, *Encomienda y mita*, 95. See also Villamarín, "Encomenderos and Indians"; Hernández Rodríguez, *De los chibchas*, 201–75.
322. Villamarín, "Encomenderos and Indians," 128–30.
323. Jorge Palacios Preciado, "La esclavitud y la sociedad esclavista," in Jaramillo Uribe, *Nueva historia de Colombia*, 160–1.
324. Colmenares, *Historia económica y social*, 1:347–8. See also West, *Colonial Placer Mining*, 83–90.
325. On the use of slave labor in the Chocó, see William Frederick Sharp, *Slavery on the Spanish Frontier: The Colombian Chocó, 1680–1810* (Norman: University of Oklahoma Press, 1976). As Sharp makes clear, the need for black slaves was related to the "rebellious nature of the Indians" (p. 21).
326. West, *Colonial Placer Mining*, 102; Sharp, *Slavery on the Spanish Frontier*, 46.
327. On the rise of haciendas in the sixteenth century, see Juan Friede, "Proceso de formación de la propiedad territorial en la América intertropical," *Jahrbuch für Geschichte von Staat, Wirtschaft und Gesellschaft Lateinamerikas* 2 (1965): 75–87; McFarlane, *Colombia before Independence*, 19–20.
328. By contrast, the literature does make clear the important role of the church in the everyday lives of Spanish and indigenous citizens in particular regions. On its role among the Spanish in Popayán, see Marzahl, *Town in the Empire*, chap. 9; on the relationship of the church to the indigenous people in the eastern llanos, see Rausch, *A Tropical Plains Frontier*, chap. 3.
329. Colmenares, *Historia económica y social*, 1:421.
330. This paragraph draws especially on Colmenares, *Historia económica y social*, 1:413–24; María Cristina Navarrete, *Historia social del negro en la colonia: Cartagena, siglo XVII* (Cali, Colombia: Talleres de la Editorial de la Facultad de Humanidades de la Universidad del Valle, 1995); Sharp, *Slavery on the Spanish Frontier*, chap. 5; West, *Colonial Placer Mining*, 122–3.

331. Sharp, *Slavery on the Spanish Frontier*, 37.

332. Newson estimates the aboriginal population of the sierra region at 838,600; her estimates for the coastal and Oriente regions are 546,828–571,828 and 230,000–251,000, respectively. Linda A. Newson, *Life and Death in Early Colonial Ecuador* (Norman: University of Oklahoma Press, 1995), 341.

333. Suzanne Austin Alchon, *Native Society and Disease in Colonial Ecuador* (Cambridge: Cambridge University Press, 1991), 5–6.

334. Background for this paragraph is from Newson, *Life and Death*, chaps. 2–4; Alchon, *Native Society and Disease*, chap. 1; John Murra, "The Historic Tribes of Ecuador," in Steward, *Handbook of South American Indians*, vol. 2, *The Andean Civilizations*, 785–821; Frank Salomon, "Vertical Politics on the Inka Frontier," in John V. Murra, Nathan Wachtel, and Jacques Revel, eds., *Anthropological History of Andean Politics* (Cambridge: Cambridge University Press, 1986), 89–117; Frank Salomon, *Native Lords of Quito in the Age of the Incas: The Political Economy of North Andean Chiefdoms* (Cambridge: Cambridge University Press, 1986), esp. chap. 7.

335. This paragraph draws especially on Newson, *Life and Death*, chaps. 3–4.

336. The conquest episode is described in many sources, including C. Reginald Enock's traditional account, *Ecuador: Its Ancient and Modern History* (New York: Charles Scribner's Sons, 1914), chaps. 4–5.

337. Gabriel Cevallos García, *Historia del Ecuador* (Cuenca, Ecuador: Editorial "Don Bosco," 1964), 132–5.

338. Hardoy and Aranovich, "Urban Scales," 73.

339. Javier Ortiz de la Tabla Ducasse, *Los encomenderos de Quito, 1534–1660: Origen y evolución de una elite colonial* (Seville: Escuela de Estudios Hispano-Americanos, 1993), 13. On the dominance of Quito, see his chap. 1 more generally.

340. John Leddy Phelan, *The Kingdom of Quito in the Seventeenth Century: Bureaucratic Politics in the Spanish Empire* (Madison: University of Wisconsin Press, 1967), chaps. 1–2.

341. Nicholas P. Cushner, *Farm and Factory: The Jesuits and the Development of Agrarian Capitalism in Colonial Quito, 1600–1767* (Albany: State University of New York Press, 1982); Cevallos García, *Historia del Ecuador*, chap. 4.

342. Hardoy and Aranovich, "Urban Scales," 67. Quito's population in 1577 was one thousand Spanish men and three hundred Spanish women. See Newson, *Life and Death*, 185.

343. For discussions of the mining sector, see José María Vargas, *La economía política del Ecuador durante la colonia* (Quito: Banco Central del Ecuador, 1980), pt. 2; Kris Lane, *Quito 1599: City and Colony in Transition* (Albuquerque: University of New Mexico Press, 2002), chap. 4. For data on mineral exports, see the tables in Aquiles R. Pérez, *Las mitas en la Real Audiencia de Quito* (Quito: Ministerio del Tesoro, 1947), 251–2; Lane, *Quito 1599*, 133–5.

344. Phelan, *Kingdom of Quito*, 66–7.

345. Linda A. Newson, "Highland-Lowland Contrasts in the Impact of Old World Diseases in Early Colonial Ecuador," *Social Science Medicine* 36, no. 9 (1993): 1187–95.

346. Adam Szaszdi, "The Economic History of the Diocese of Quito, 1616–1787," *Latin American Research Review* 21, no. 2 (1986): 270. However, the

organization of work in Inca textile production was quite different from that used by the Spanish. These differences are described in Manuel Miño Grijalva, "Estudio introductorio," in Manuel Miño Grijalva, ed., *La economía colonial: Relaciones socioeconómicas de La Real Audiencia de Quito* (Quito: Corporación Editora Nacional, 1984), 44. See also Murra, *Economic Organization of the Inka State*, chap. 4.

347. Miño Grijalva, "Estudio introductorio," 52–64; Phelan, *Kingdom of Quito*, 69–70; Robson Brines Tyrer, "The Demographic and Economic History of the Audiencia of Quito: Indian Population and the Textile Industry" (PhD diss., University of California, Berkeley, 1976), 162–3.

348. Tyrer, "Demographic and Economic History," 149–51; Phelan, *Kingdom of Quito*, 68; Newson, *Life and Death*, 207–13.

349. Hardoy and Aranovich, "Urban Scales," 73.

350. John C. Super, "Partnership and Profit in the Early Andean Trade: The Experiences of Quito Merchants, 1580–1610," *Journal of Latin American Studies* 11, no. 2 (November 1979): 280. According to Minchom, "the exceptional place occupied by the church in Quito society is beyond question, and few observers, whether contemporaries or historians, have failed to comment on it." Martin Minchom, *The People of Quito, 1690–1810: Change and Unrest in the Underclass* (Boulder, CO: Westview Press, 1994), 94.

351. Szaszdi, "Economic History," 267. See also Ortiz de la Tabla Ducasse, *Los encomenderos de Quito*, 150–1.

352. Ortiz de la Tabla Ducasse, *Los encomenderos de Quito*, 130–8.

353. Ibid., 9. See also Lane, *Quito 1599*, for many descriptive details on life and culture in Quito at the end of the sixteenth century.

354. Lawrence Anthony Clayton, "The Guayaquil Shipyards in the Seventeenth Century: History of a Colonial Industry" (PhD diss., Tulane University, 1972).

355. Newson, *Life and Death*, chap. 12, p. 341.

356. As Contreras C. summarizes, "Before the middle of the eighteenth century, the Ecuadoran coast was a periphery region, little populated and poorly urbanized, and whose principal function was to serve as a link between the dynamic sierra region and the Peruvian market." Carlos Contreras C., *El sector exportador de una economía colonial: La costa del Ecuador entre 1760 y 1820* (Quito: Flacso, 1990), 27. See also Michael L. Conniff, "Guayaquil through Independence: Urban Development in a Colonial System," *The Americas* 33, no. 3 (January 1977): 392; Miño Grijalva, "Estudio introductorio," 69.

357. Newson, *Life and Death*, 342.

358. Ibid., 165. This paragraph and the next one also draw on pp. 165, 178–9, 350–1.

359. Ibid., 342. See also Tyrer, "Demographic and Economic History," 106.

360. See, for example, Phelan, *Kingdom of Quito*, chap. 4.

361. Newson, *Life and Death*, 350–1.

362. For a breakdown of these diseases, see Alchon, *Native Society and Disease*, 37, 59.

363. Newson, *Life and Death*, 196–201; Karen Vieira Powers, *Andean Journeys: Migration, Ethnogenesis, and the State in Colonial Quito* (Albuquerque: University of New Mexico Press, 1995). Powers especially suggests that "the seventeenth-century rise exhibited in Quito's demographic curve was not the

result of natural growth, but rather of sixteenth-century migrations from marginal areas to the center of the audiencia" (p. 8).

364. This paragraph draws especially on Super, "Partnership and Profit."

365. Ibid., 279.

366. Ortiz de la Tabla Ducasse, *Los encomenderos de Quito.*

367. Miño Grijalva, "Estudio introductorio," 52–60; Ortiz de la Tabla Ducasse, *Los encomenderos de Quito,* 209–15; Tyrer, "Demographic and Economic History," chap. 3.

368. Tyrer, "Demographic and Economic History," 151.

369. See Miño Grijalva, "Estudio introductorio," 60–6; Ortiz de la Tabla Ducasse, *Los encomenderos de Quito,* 217–26; Tyrer, "Demographic and Economic History," chap. 4.

370. Ortiz de la Tabla Ducasse, *Los encomenderos de Quito,* chap. 4.

371. Newson, *Life and Death,* 180–1, 207.

372. See, for example, the data in Vargas, *La economía política de Ecuador,* 137–42.

373. See Charles C. Ragin, *Fuzzy-Set Social Science* (Chicago: University of Chicago Press, 2000).

374. With the logical AND, the researcher codes cases using the *minimum* value of the causal factors being considered. For example, if a case's values on three causal factors are 1.00, 0.50, and 0.25, then the case is coded as 0.25 for the combination of these three factors. By contrast, with the logical OR, the researcher codes cases using the *maximum* value of the causal factors being considered. For a discussion, see ibid.

375. This is true because the values for a necessary cause will be greater than or equal to the values for an outcome across all cases in a set-theoretic analysis. Ibid.

Chapter 4. Liberal Colonialism

1. Vilma Milletich, "El Río de la Plata en la economía colonial," in Enrique Tandeter, ed., *Nueva Historia Argentina: La sociedad colonial* (Buenos Aires: Sudamericana, 2000), 225. For similar population estimates for Buenos Aires during the eighteenth century, see Jonathan C. Brown, *A Socioeconomic History of Argentina, 1776–1860* (Cambridge: Cambridge University Press, 1979), 22; David Rock, *Argentina, 1516–1987: From Spanish Colonization to Alfonsín,* rev. ed. (Berkeley: University of California Press, 1987), 64.

2. Jorge Comadrán Ruiz, *Evolución demográfica argentina durante el período hispano (1535–1810)* (Buenos Aires: Editorial Universitaria de Buenos Aires, 1969), 80–1.

3. These population estimates are from Comadrán Ruiz, *Evolución demográfica argentina,* 80–1, and chap. 4 more generally.

4. Brown, *Socioeconomic History,* 72.

5. Aldo Ferrer, *The Argentine Economy,* trans. Marjory M. Urquidi (Berkeley: University of California Press, 1967), 41.

6. John Lynch, *Spanish Colonial Administration, 1782–1810: The Intendant System in the Viceroyalty of the Río de la Plata* (London: Athlone Press, 1958), 33.

7. Rock, *Argentina,* 62.

8. Lynch, *Spanish Colonial Administration*, 43–4.

9. For different perspectives on the founding of the viceroyalty, see the contributions to Enrique M. Barba, ed., *Bicentenario del Virreinato del Río de la Plata*, vol. 1 (Buenos Aires: Academia Nacional de la Historia, 1977). See also the massive chapter by Emilio Ravignani, "El Virreinato del Río de la Plata (1776–1810)," in Ricardo Levene, ed., *Historia de la nación Argentina*, vol. 4, *El momento histórico del Virreinato del Río de la Plata* (Buenos Aires: Imprenta de la Universidad, 1938), 27–332.

10. Lynch, *Spanish Colonial Administration*, chap. 4.

11. Susan Migden Socolow, *The Bureaucrats of Buenos Aires, 1769–1810: Amor al Real Servicio* (Durham, NC: Duke University Press, 1987); Lynch, *Spanish Colonial Administration*, chap. 6.

12. Susan Migden Socolow, *The Merchants of Buenos Aires, 1778–1810: Family and Commerce* (Cambridge: Cambridge University Press, 1978), 169; Tulio Halperín-Donghi, *Politics, Economics, and Society in Argentina in the Revolutionary Period*, trans. Richard Southern (Cambridge: Cambridge University Press, 1975), 30. This paragraph draws especially on Socolow, *Merchants of Buenos Aires*.

13. Juan Carlos Nicolau, *Antecedentes para la historia de la industria Argentina* (Buenos Aires: Talleres Gráficos Lumen, 1968). See esp. chap. 10 on the lack of an industrial orientation among the merchants. See also Jeremy Adelman, *Sovereignty and Revolution in the Iberian Atlantic* (Princeton, NJ: Princeton University Press, 2006), 48–9.

14. John Lynch, "The River Plate Republics," in Leslie Bethell, ed., *Spanish America after Independence, c. 1820–c. 1870* (Cambridge: Cambridge University Press, 1987), 314; Halperín-Donghi, *Politics, Economics, and Society*, 36. See also Brown, *Socioeconomic History*, 30. The 80 percent figure is also reported in Miguel A. Rosal and Roberto Schmit, "Las exportaciones pecuarias bonaerenses y el espacio mercantile rioplatense (1768–1854)," in Raúl O. Fradkin and Juan Carlos Garavaglia, eds., *En busca de un tiempo perdido: La economía de Buenos Aires en el país de la abundancia, 1750–1865* (Buenos Aires: Prometeo Libros, 2004), 159. For specific data on the dramatic rise of precious-metal exports after the Bourbon reforms, see Zacharías Moutoukias, "El crecimiento en una economía colonial de antiguo régimen: Reformismo y sector externo en el Río de la Plata (1760–1796)," *Arquivos do Centro Cultural Calouste Gulbenkian* 34 (1995): 782. Moutoukias's analysis also contains good information on the continued role of contraband in the economy.

15. In pursuing this trade, the merchants were not a particularly farsighted or entrepreneurial group. Indeed, they created artificial scarcity to keep prices high. See Socolow, *Merchants of Buenos Aires*, 8–9; Halperín-Donghi, *Politics, Economics, and Society*, 33.

16. Socolow, *Merchants of Buenos Aires*, 65. When British merchants later became dominant in the Argentine economy, many Buenos Aires merchants did begin to invest in land (in the mid-nineteenth century). However, they never practiced labor-repressive agriculture. On the divisions between the merchants and the landed classes, see also Eduardo Azcuy Ameghino, *La otra historia: Economía, estado y sociedad en el Río de la Plata* (Buenos Aires: Imago Mundi, 2002), esp. chap. 2.

17. Samuel Amaral, "Rural Production and Labour in Late Colonial Buenos Aires," *Journal of Latin American Studies* 19, no. 2 (November 1987): 235–78. On the wages of seasonal workers, see, for example, Jonathan C. Brown, "Revival of the Rural Economy and Society in Buenos Aires," in Mark D. Szuchman and Jonathan C. Brown, eds., *Revolution and Restoration: The Rearrangement of Power in Argentina, 1776–1860* (Lincoln: University of Nebraska Press, 1994), 258.

18. Carlos A. Mayo, "Landed but Not Powerful: The Colonial Estancieros of Buenos Aires," *Hispanic American Historical Review* 71, no. 4 (November 1991): 761–79. The situation does not appear to have radically changed during the 1816–52 period. See Juan Carlos Garavaglia, "Patrones de inversión y 'elite económica dominante': Los empresarios rurales en la pampa bonaerense a mediados del siglo XIX," in Jorge Gelman, Juan Carlos Garavaglia, and Blanca Zeberio, eds., *Expansión capitalista y transformaciones regionales: Relaciones sociales y empresas agrarias en la Argentina del siglo XIX* (Buenos Aires: Editorial La Colmena, 1999), 121–43.

19. On the political power of merchants in Buenos Aires, see Socolow, *Merchants of Buenos Aires*, chap. 6 and p. 171.

20. On the banking role of merchants during the colonial period, see Socolow, *Merchants of Buenos Aires*, 66; for the mid-nineteenth century, see Hilda Sábato, *Agrarian Capitalism and the World Market: Buenos Aires in the Pastoral Age, 1840–1890* (Albuquerque: University of New Mexico Press, 1990), 217–21.

21. Samuel Amaral, *The Rise of Capitalism on the Pampas: The Estancias of Buenos Aires, 1785–1870* (Cambridge: Cambridge University Press, 1998), 17.

22. Brown, *Socioeconomic History*, 29. A classic statement on this period is Carlos F. Díaz Alejandro, *Essays on the Economic History of the Argentine Republic* (New Haven, CT: Yale University Press, 1970), chap. 1.

23. Amaral, *Rise of Capitalism*, 253.

24. Brown, *Socioeconomic History*, 81.

25. Amaral, *Rise of Capitalism*, 271; Sábato, *Agrarian Capitalism*, 30–2. There are numerous other works analyzing the export composition of mid-nineteenth-century Argentina.

26. Jeremy Adelman, *Frontier Development: Land, Labour, and Capital on the Wheatlands of Argentina and Canada, 1890–1914* (Oxford: Clarendon Press, 1994), 80–1.

27. John H. Coatsworth, "Economic and Institutional Trajectories in Nineteenth-Century Latin America," in John H. Coatsworth and Alan M. Taylor, eds., *Latin America and the World Economy since 1800* (Cambridge, MA: Harvard University Press, 1998), 29.

28. Ibid., 26; John H. Coatsworth, "Notes on the Comparative Economic History of Latin America and the United States," in Walther L. Bernecker and Hans Werner Tobler, eds., *Development and Underdevelopment in America: Contrasts of Economic Growth in North and Latin America in Historical Perspective* (Berlin: Walter de Gruyter, 1993), 10–30. If one incorporates Maddison's data, it is clear that the decline of Argentina relative to the United States began during the nineteenth century, especially the period before 1870, when the whole region of Latin America fell far behind the United States. See Angus Maddison, "A Comparison of Levels of GDP Per Capita in the Developed and Developing

Countries, 1700–1980," *Journal of Economic History* 43, no. 1 (March 1983): 30. See also Adam Przeworski (with Carolina Curvale), "Does Politics Explain the Economic Gap between the United States and Latin America?" in Francis Fukuyama, ed., *Falling Behind: Explaining the Development Gap between Latin America and the United States* (Oxford: Oxford University Press, 2008), 104–5.

29. Celso Furtado, *Economic Development of Latin America: Historical Background and Contemporary Problems*, trans. Suzette Macedo, 2nd ed. (New York: Cambridge University Press, 1976), 45.

30. Jorge Gelman, Juan Carlos Garavaglia, and Blanca Zeberio, "Introducción," in Gelman, Garavaglia, and Zeberio, *Expansión capitalista*, 1. A famous work that emphasizes late-nineteenth-century growth is Díaz Alejandro, *Economic History*.

31. Argentina's nineteenth-century rate of growth was actually slower than Mexico's and Chile's and about the same as that of Peru. See Coatsworth, "Economic and Institutional Trajectories," 26; Coatsworth, "Notes on the Comparative Economic History," 25. On the twentieth century, see Chapter 5.

32. This fact has led observers to see Argentina as a "new country." See, for example, Carter Goodrich, "Argentina as a New Country," *Comparative Studies in Society and History* 7 (1964–5): 70–88.

33. Carlos A. Mayo and Amalia Latrubesse, *Terratenientes, soldados y cautivos: La frontera, 1736–1815*, 2nd ed. (Buenos Aires: Editorial Biblos, 1998); Roberto H. Marfany, "La lucha con los indios en la época colonial" and "Los pueblos fronterizos en la época colonial," in Ricardo Levene, ed., *Historia de la Provincia de Buenos Aires y formación de sus pueblos*, vol. 1 (La Plata, Argentina: Taller de Impresiones Oficiales, 1940), 121–35, 137–46; Alfred J. Tapson, "Indian Warfare on the Pampa during the Colonial Period," *Hispanic American Historical Review* 42, no. 1 (February 1962): 1–28.

34. Halperín-Donghi, *Politics, Economics, and Society*, 40.

35. "Buenos Aires did not have a university, a strong clerical establishment, a strong *hacendado* group, or titled nobility, all natural foci of creole power. The only elite in Buenos Aires was a commercial one, and this group benefited greatly from the economic and commercial features of the [Bourbon] reform package." Socolow, *Bureaucrats of Buenos Aires*, 263.

36. Halperín-Donghi, *Politics, Economics, and Society*, 48.

37. Brown, "Revival of the Rural Economy," 257.

38. Comadrán Ruiz, *Evolución demográfica argentina*, 80–1.

39. Brown, *Socioeconomic History*, 114.

40. Carlos Newland, "Economic Development and Population Change: Argentina, 1810–1870," in Coatsworth and Taylor, *Latin America*, 215.

41. This conclusion is consistent with "the florescence in the city of liberal professionals, in which jurists predominated, followed by doctors and some military engineers." César A. García Belsunce, "La sociedad hispano-criolla," in Academia Nacional de la Historia, *Nueva historia de la nación Argentina*, vol. 2, *Período español (1600–1800)* (Buenos Aires: Editorial Planeta, 1999), 175. For details, see generally Levene, *Historia de la nación Argentina*, vol. 4, *El momento histórico del Virreinato del Río de la Plata*.

42. Tulio Halperín-Donghi, "Argentina: Liberalism in a Country Born Liberal," in Joseph Love and Nils Jacobsen, eds., *Guiding the Invisible Hand: Economic Liberalism and the State in Latin America* (New York: Praeger, 1988), 99–116.

On intellectual life in the late nineteenth century, see also Ricardo Levene, *A History of Argentina*, trans. and ed. William Spence Robertson (Chapel Hill: University of North Carolina Press, 1937), 157–72.

43. J. D. Gould, "European Inter-continental Emigration, 1815–1914: Patterns and Causes," *Journal of European Economic History* 8, no. 3 (Winter 1979): 619.

44. Herbert S. Klein, "The Integration of Immigrants into the United States and Argentina: A Comparative Analysis," *American Historical Review* 88, no. 2 (April 1983): 306–29. For raw data on migration for 1857–1924, see República Argentina, *Resumen estadístico del movimiento migratorio en la República Argentina, años 1857–1924* (Buenos Aires: Ministerio de Agricultura de la Nación, 1925). The table "Movimiento Migratorio de Ultramar, 1857–1924" (on p. 3) summarizes the trends over time.

45. Newland, "Economic Development," 216–17.

46. Lucía Sala de Touron, Nelson de la Torre, and Julio C. Rodríguez, *Estructura económico-social de la colonia* (Montevideo: Ediciones Pueblos Unidos, 1967), 28–9; José O. Barrán and Benjamín Nahum, *Bases económicas de la revolución artiguista* (Montevideo: Ediciones de la Banda Oriental, 1963), 48–51.

47. Julio Millot and Magdalena Bertino, *Historia económica del Uruguay*, vol. 1 (Montevideo: Fundación de Cultura Universitaria, 1991), 75–6.

48. Rock, *Argentina*, 65.

49. Jan M. G. Kleinpenning, *Peopling the Purple Land: A Historical Geography of Rural Uruguay, 1500–1915* (Amsterdam: CEDLA, 1995), 33. On this point, see also Washington Reyes Abadie and Andrés Vázquez Romero, *Crónica general del Uruguay*, vol. 2, *El siglo XVIII* (Montevideo: Ediciones de la Banda Oriental, 1998), 29; Brown, *Socioeconomic History*, 35; José L. Buzzetti, *Historia económica y financiera del Uruguay* (Montevideo: Talleres Gráficos "La Paz," 1969), 19; Pablo Blanco Acevedo, *El gobierno colonial en el Uruguay y los orígenes de la nacionalidad* (Montevideo: Casa A. Barreiro y Ramos, 1944), chap. 12.

50. Halperín-Donghi, *Politics, Economics, and Society*, 26.

51. Russell H. Fitzgibbon, *Uruguay: Portrait of a Democracy* (New York: Russell & Russell, 1966), 8.

52. Jaime Klaczko and Juan Rial, *Uruguay: El país urbano* (Montevideo: Ediciones de la Banda Oriental, 1981), 16–26; Kleinpenning, *Peopling the Purple Land*, 65–73; Reyes Abadie and Vázquez Romero, *Crónica general del Uruguay*, vol. 2, *El siglo XVIII*, 135–45.

53. Klaczko and Rial, *Uruguay*, 20.

54. These population data are from Reyes Abadie and Vázquez Romero, *Crónica general del Uruguay*, vol. 2, *El siglo XVIII*, 78–80.

55. Ibid., 81.

56. Ibid., chap. 14.

57. The key work on the Uruguayan merchants is Sala de Touron, de la Torre, and Rodríguez, *Estructura económico-social*, esp. chaps. 3 and 8. See also Reyes Abadie and Vázquez Romero, *Crónica general del Uruguay*, vol. 2, *El siglo XVIII*, 85–89; Kleinpenning, *Peopling the Purple Land*, 34–5; Millot and Bertino, *Historia económica del Uruguay*, 75–84.

58. Sala de Touron, de la Torre, and Rodríguez, *Estructura económico-social*, 96.

59. Amaral, "Rural Production," 237–8; Kleinpenning, *Peopling the Purple Land*, 34; Javier Cuenca Esteban, "Statistics of Spain's Colonial Trade, 1792–1820: Consular Duties, Cargo Inventories, and Balances of Trade," *Hispanic American Historical Review* 61, no. 3 (August 1981): 418.

60. Millot and Bertino, *Historia económica del Uruguay*, 64; Sala de Touron, de la Torre, and Rodríguez, *Estructura económico-social*, 28.

61. Millot and Bertino, *Historia económica del Uruguay*, 32.

62. This could explain why estancieros appear to have had considerable influence within the cabildo in Montevideo. Sala de Touron, de la Torre, and Rodríguez, *Estructura económico-social*, 119–24.

63. My interpretation in this paragraph is a synthesis of points of agreement in Ricardo Salvatore and Jonathan Brown, "Trade and Proletarianization in Late Colonial Banda Oriental: Evidence from the Estancia de las Vacas, 1791–1805," *Hispanic American Historical Review* 67, no. 3 (August 1987): 431–59; Jorge Gelman, "New Perspectives on an Old Problem and the Same Source: The Gaucho and the Rural History of the Colonial Río de la Plata," *Hispanic American Historical Review* 69, no. 4 (November 1989): 715–31; Ricardo Salvatore and Jonathan Brown, "The Old Problem of Gauchos and Rural Society," *Hispanic American Historical Review* 69, no. 4 (November 1989): 733–45.

64. Coatsworth, "Notes on Comparative Economic History," 12.

65. Kleinpenning, *Peopling the Purple Land*, 34.

66. Lucía Sala de Touron and Rosa Alonso Eloy, *El Uruguay comercial, pastoral y caudillesco*, vol. 1, *Economía* (Montevideo: Ediciones de la Banda Oriental, 1986), 72–3.

67. Millot and Bertino, *Historia económica del Uruguay*, 77.

68. Ibid., 25.

69. Information in this paragraph is from Renzo Pi Hugarte, *Los indios del Uruguay* (Montevideo: Ediciones de la Banda Oriental, 1998), chaps. 5–6; W. H. Koebel, *Uruguay* (London: T. Fisher Unwin, 1911), 43, 50; Reyes Abadie and Vázquez Romero, *Crónica general del Uruguay*, vol. 2, *El siglo XVIII*, 80.

70. Millot and Bertino, *Historia económica del Uruguay*, 27; Reyes Abadie and Vázquez Romero, *Crónica general del Uruguay*, vol. 2, *El siglo XVIII*, 80.

71. On this migration, see Millot and Bertino, *Historia económica del Uruguay*, 123–31.

72. Ibid., 101.

73. Roland Dennis Hussey, *The Caracas Company, 1728–1784: A Study in the History of Spanish Monopolistic Trade* (Cambridge, MA: Harvard University Press, 1934), 58.

74. Eugenio Piñero, "The Cacao Economy of the Eighteenth-Century Province of Caracas and the Spanish Cacao Market," *Hispanic American Historical Review* 68, no. 1 (February 1988): 77.

75. The seminal work is Hussey, *The Caracas Company*. See also Jules Humbert, *Los orígenes venezolanos (ensayo sobre la colonización española en Venezuela)* (Caracas: Academia Nacional de la Historia, 1976), 57–120.

76. Piñero, "Cacao Economy," 86–8, 91, 98–9; John V. Lombardi, *Venezuela: The Search for Order, the Dream of Progress* (New York: Oxford University Press, 1982), 98.

77. Federico Brito Figueroa, *La estructura económica de Venezuela colonial* (Caracas: Universidad Central de Venezuela, 1983), 118, 120.
78. Miguel Acosta Saignes, *Vida de los esclavos negros en Venezuela* (Caracas: Hesperides, 1967), esp. the map following p. 138; Angelina Pollak-Eltz, *La esclavitud en Venezuela: Un estudio histórico-cultural* (Caracas: Universidad Católica Andres Bello, 2000), 64–5.
79. Brito Figueroa, *La estructura económica*, 121.
80. Hussey, *The Caracas Company*, 95.
81. P. Michael McKinley, *Pre-revolutionary Caracas: Politics, Economics, and Society, 1777–1811* (Cambridge: Cambridge University Press, 1985), 4.
82. Ibid., 37.
83. Ibid., 36.
84. Eduardo Arcila Farías, *Economía colonial de Venezuela* (Mexico City: Fondo de Cultura Económica, 1946), 290; Lombardi, *Venezuela*, 100.
85. McKinley, *Pre-revolutionary Caracas*, 40. Other information in this paragraph is from pp. 39–41; Arcila Farías, *Economía colonial de Venezuela*, 357–61.
86. Guillermo Morón, *A History of Venezuela*, trans. John Street (New York: Roy Publishers, 1963), 66.
87. Federico Brito Figueroa, *Historia económica y social de Venezuela: Una estructura para su estudio*, 4th ed., vol. 1 (Caracas: Universidad de Venezuela, Ediciones de la Biblioteca, 1974), 154. For discussions of the estimate of more than forty thousand for the late colonial period, see also John V. Lombardi, *People and Places in Colonial Venezuela* (Bloomington: Indiana University Press, 1976), 62; Manuel Lucena Salmoral, "La sociedad de la provincia de Caracas a comienzos del siglo XIX," *Anuario de Estudios Americanos* 37 (1980): 159–60; Robert McCaa, "Figures, Facts and Fallacies: The Population of Colonial Venezuela," *Latin American Research Review* 13, no. 1 (1978): 198.
88. All of Venezuela had a population of approximately nine hundred thousand inhabitants in 1800, of which, roughly speaking, 45 percent were *pardo* (nonslave of partial African ancestry), 20 percent white, 15 percent indigenous, 10 percent slave, and 10 percent free black. Brito Figueroa, *Historia económica y social* (1974), 160. See also Lucena Salmoral, "La sociedad de la provincia de Caracas," 163–5.
89. McKinley, *Pre-revolutionary Caracas*, 14.
90. Ibid., 1. For similar views from another leading authority, see Lombardi, *Venezuela*, 85, 107–10.
91. McKinley, *Pre-revolutionary Caracas*, chap. 4.
92. Ibid., 63.
93. Ibid., 73.
94. Ibid., chap. 4.
95. Lucena Salmoral, "La sociedad de la provincia de Caracas," 188–9.
96. The reasons for the decline in slave imports in the 1780s are not well understood. For a discussion, see McKinley, *Pre-revolutionary Caracas*, 24. See also Pollak-Eltz, *La esclavitud en Venezuela*, 119–24.
97. See, for example, Lombardi, *Venezuela*, 176–7.
98. D. A. Brading, *Miners and Merchants in Bourbon Mexico, 1763–1810* (Cambridge: Cambridge University Press, 1971), 14. For more detailed data, see Enrique Florescano and Isabel Gil Sánchez, "La época de las reformas borbónicas

y el crecimiento económico, 1750–1808," in Daniel Cosío Villegas, ed., *Historia general de México*, vol. 1 (Mexico City: El Colegio de México, 1976), 520–3.

99. Eric Van Young, *Hacienda and Market in Eighteenth-Century Mexico: The Rural Economy of the Guadalajara Region, 1675–1820* (Berkeley: University of California Press, 1981), chap. 2.

100. Brading, *Miners and Merchants*, 106–7.

101. John E. Kicza, *Colonial Entrepreneurs: Families and Businesses in Bourbon Mexico City* (Albuquerque: University of New Mexico Press, 1983), xiii.

102. Ibid., 2–3.

103. Mark A. Burkholder and Lyman L. Johnson, *Colonial Latin America*, 4th ed. (New York: Oxford University Press, 2001), 277.

104. Alan Knight, *Mexico: The Colonial Era* (Cambridge: Cambridge University Press, 2002), 209.

105. John Kicza, "Migration to Major Metropoles in Colonial Mexico," in David J. Robinson, ed., *Migration in Colonial Spanish America* (Cambridge: Cambridge University Press, 1990), 198.

106. Kicza, *Colonial Entrepreneurs*. On occupations, see D. A. Brading, "Government and Elite in Late Colonial Mexico," *Hispanic American Historical Review* 53, no. 3 (August 1973): 395.

107. Richard L. Garner, "Silver Production and Entrepreneurial Structure in 18th-Century Mexico," *Jahrbuch für Geschichte von Staat, Wirtschaft und Gesellschaft Lateinamerikas* 17 (1980): 162; John H. Coatsworth, "The Mexican Mining Industry in the Eighteenth Century," in Nils Jacobsen and Hans-Jürgen Puhle, eds., *The Economies of Mexico and Peru during the Late Colonial Period, 1760–1810* (Berlin: Colloquium-Verlag, 1986), 26–46; Knight, *Mexico: The Colonial Era*, 212–13.

108. Richard L. Garner (with Spiro E. Setanou), *Economic Growth and Change in Bourbon Mexico* (Gainesville: University of Florida Press, 1993), 112–17.

109. Alan Knight, "The Peculiarities of Mexican History: Mexico Compared to Latin America, 1821–1992," *Journal of Latin American Studies*, Quincentenary Supplement, 24 (1992): 99.

110. "The Bourbon 'revolution from above'…could not succeed…Society remained too backward, introverted and particularist – in a word, glib but suggestive, too 'feudal.' In taking upon themselves the tasks of a bourgeois revolution…the Bourbons assumed tasks beyond their dynastic capacity. They failed, and bequeathed to their republican successor of the nineteenth century the same contradictory, conflict-ridden project." Knight, *Mexico: The Colonial Era*, 242.

111. Linda Arnold, *Bureaucracy and Bureaucrats in Mexico City, 1742–1835* (Tucson: University of Arizona Press, 1988), chap. 3; Colin M. MacLachlan and Jaime E. Rodríguez O., *The Forging of the Cosmic Race: A Reinterpretation of Colonial Mexico* (Berkeley: University of California Press, 1980), 268–70; Mark A. Burkholder and D. S. Chandler, *From Impotence to Authority: The Spanish Crown and the American Audiencias, 1687–1808* (Columbia: University of Missouri Press, 1977), 97–8 and appendix 7. In addition, a new professional army was created; see Christon I. Archer, *The Army in Bourbon Mexico, 1760–1810* (Albuquerque: University of New Mexico Press, 1977).

112. Brading, "Government and Elite," 390; Van Young, *Hacienda and Market*, 173–5.

113. Barbara A. Tenenbaum, *The Politics of Penury: Debts and Taxes in Mexico, 1821–1856* (Albuquerque: University of New Mexico Press, 1986), chap. 1; Doris M. Ladd, *The Mexican Nobility at Independence, 1780–1826* (Austin: University of Texas Press, 1976), chap. 5; John H. Coatsworth, "The Limits of Colonial Absolutism: The State in Eighteenth Century Mexico," in Karen Spalding, ed., *Essays in the Political, Economic and Social History of Colonial Latin America* (Newark: University of Delaware, Latin American Studies Program, 1982), 25–51.

114. Florescano and Sánchez, "La época de las reformas borbónicas," 501–3; Charles Gibson, *The Aztecs under Spanish Rule: A History of the Indians of the Valley of Mexico, 1519–1810* (Stanford, CA: Stanford University Press, 1964), 206–8. In the north, hostile indigenous groups thwarted these most recent efforts at Spanish centralization. See MacLachlan and Rodríguez, *Forging of the Cosmic Race*, 270.

115. Florescano and Sánchez, "La época de las reformas borbónicas," 510–11; MacLachlan and Rodríguez, *Forging of the Cosmic Race*, 273.

116. Brading, *Miners and Merchants*, 115. See also Garner, *Economic Growth*, 160–4, 189–94, 254.

117. MacLachlan and Rodríguez, *Forging of the Cosmic Race*, 273.

118. Garner, *Economic Growth*, 190, 257.

119. Kicza, *Colonial Entrepreneurs*, 63–4.

120. Ibid., 19–25; Van Young, *Hacienda and Market*, chap. 8. On Oaxaca, see William B. Taylor, *Landlord and Peasant in Colonial Oaxaca* (Stanford, CA: Stanford University Press, 1972), 160–1.

121. Late colonial ecclesiastical reform and the reaction of the clergy is the subject of N. M. Farriss, *Crown and Clergy in Colonial Mexico, 1759–1821: The Crisis of Ecclesiastical Privilege* (London: Athlone Press, 1968). Chapter 1 of Taylor's massive book summarizes the Bourbon reforms that affected the parish clergy. See William B. Taylor, *Magistrates of the Sacred: Priests and Parishioners in Eighteenth-Century Mexico* (Stanford, CA: Stanford University Press, 1996).

122. However, land values did increase over time. Van Young, *Hacienda and Market*, chap. 7; Brading, "Government and Elite," 392–3; Taylor, *Landlord and Peasant*, 140–2.

123. Garner, *Economic Growth*, 161–3; Brading, *Miners and Merchants*, 96; Brian R. Hamnett, *Politics and Trade in Southern Mexico, 1750–1821* (Cambridge: Cambridge University Press, 1971), chap. 1.

124. Van Young, *Hacienda and Market*, chap. 11; Gibson, *Aztecs*, 253–6.

125. Van Young, *Hacienda and Market*, 268. See also David A. Brading, *Haciendas and Ranchos in the Mexican Bajío: León, 1700–1860* (Cambridge: Cambridge University Press, 1978); Florescano and Sánchez, "La época de las reformas borbónicas," 570; Knight, *Mexico: The Colonial Era*, 228–30; Arij Ouweneel, *Shadows over Anáhuac: An Ecological Interpretation of Crisis and Development in Central Mexico, 1730–1800* (Albuquerque: University of New Mexico Press, 1996), 8.

126. Coatsworth, "Economic and Institutional Trajectories," 35. Coatsworth's estimate of GDP for Mexico is on a par with those offered by Fernando Rosenwieg and by John TePaske. For a discussion of these estimates, see Richard J. Salvucci, "Mexican National Income in the Era of Independence, 1800–40," in Stephen Haber, ed., *How Latin America Fell Behind: Essays on the Economic Histories of Brazil and Mexico, 1800–1914* (Stanford, CA: Stanford University Press, 1997), 217–20.

127. Richard L. Garner, "Exportaciones de circulante en el siglo XVIII (1750–1810)," *Historia Mexicana* 31, no. 4 (1982): 577–88; Coatsworth, "Limits of Colonial Absolutism," 29; Salvucci, "Mexican National Income," 232–3; Knight, *Mexico: The Colonial Era*, 231–4; John Jay TePaske, "The Financial Disintegration of the Royal Government of Mexico during the Epoch of Independence," in Jaime E. Rodríguez, ed., *The Independence of Mexico and the Creation of the New Nation* (Los Angeles: UCLA Latin American Center Publications, University of California, 1989), 63.

128. See Richard J. Salvucci, *Textiles and Capitalism in Mexico: An Economic History of the Obrajes, 1539–1840* (Princeton, NJ: Princeton University Press, 1987).

129. Enrique Cárdenas, "A Macroeconomic Interpretation of Nineteenth-Century Mexico," in Haber, *How Latin America Fell Behind*, 65–92; John H. Coatsworth, "Obstacles to Economic Growth in Nineteenth-Century Mexico," *American Historical Review* 83, no. 1 (February 1978): 80–100. See also the discussion of various works in Salvucci, "Mexican National Income." The collapse of the mining industry is the subject of Hira de Gortari Rabiela, "La minería durante la Guerra de Independencia y los primeros años del Mexico independiente, 1810–1824," in Rodríguez, *The Independence of Mexico*, 129–61.

130. For cautions about such exaggerations, see Salvucci, "Mexican National Income," 234; Knight, *Mexico: The Colonial Era*, 313; Garner, *Economic Growth*, 178; Coatsworth, "Mexican Mining Industry," 26–7, 43. See also Ladd, *Mexican Nobility*, 148.

131. Coatsworth, "Comparative Economic History," 21, 25; Coatsworth, "Economic and Institutional Trajectories," 26, 29.

132. Coatsworth, "Obstacles to Economic Growth," 91–2. See also Garner, *Economic Growth*, 180–4.

133. For example: "Most of Mexico's greatly varying ecological regions offered propitious conditions for livestock ... The lush piedmont of the eastern and western Sierra Madre, falling off to the Gulf of Mexico and the Pacific Ocean, offered rich grazing lands." Nils Jacobsen, "Livestock Complexes in Late Colonial Peru and New Spain: An Attempt at Comparison," in Jacobsen and Puhle, *Economies of Mexico and Peru*, 114.

134. Coatsworth, "Obstacles to Economic Growth," 95.

135. Garner notes, "Although other commodities might have been more fully developed for export – cochineal, sugar, grain, wool – in the eighteenth century, only cochineal among the potentially exportable raw materials played any role." Garner, *Economic Growth*, 258. For the points in the remainder of the paragraph, I draw on pp. 64, 67, 255–8.

136. Knight, *Mexico: The Colonial Era*, 230–1.

137. Salvucci, *Textiles and Capitalism*, 124–7.
138. On the continuing importance of phenotype with special reference to Oaxaca, see John K. Chance, *Race and Class in Colonial Oaxaca* (Stanford, CA: Stanford University Press, 1978), chap. 6.
139. Florescano and Sánchez, "La época de las reformas borbónicas," 537, 524.
140. Salvucci, *Textiles and Capitalism*, 18; Van Young, *Hacienda and Market*, 264.
141. Florescano and Sánchez, "La época de las reformas borbónicas," 538. See also Taylor, *Landlord and Peasant*, 196–8; Gibson, *Aztecs*, 298–9; Ouweneel, *Shadows over Anáhuac*, chap. 3.
142. For vivid accounts focused on the Mayas, see Nancy M. Farriss, *Maya Society under Colonial Rule: The Collective Enterprise of Survival* (Princeton, NJ: Princeton University Press, 1984), 375–86; Robert W. Patch, *Maya and Spaniard in Yucatan, 1648–1812* (Stanford, CA: Stanford University Press, 1993), 230–2.
143. Data in this paragraph are from John R. Fisher, *Bourbon Peru, 1750–1824* (Liverpool, England: Liverpool University Press, 2003), 55–7; John R. Fisher, *Government and Society in Colonial Peru: The Intendant System, 1784–1814* (London: Athlone Press, 1970), 6–7; Alberto Flores Galindo, *Aristocracia y plebe: Lima, 1760–1830* (Lima: Mosca Azul Editores, 1984), 15–16; Scarlett O'Phelan Godoy, *Rebellions and Revolts in Eighteenth Century Peru and Upper Peru* (Cologne: Böhlau, 1985), 47; Paul Gootenberg, "Population and Ethnicity in Early Republican Peru: Some Revisions," *Latin American Research Review* 26, no. 3 (1991): 140; Marcel Manuel Haitin, "Late Colonial Lima: Economy and Society in an Era of Reform and Revolution" (PhD diss., University of California, Berkeley, 1983), 199–202, 279.
144. Burkholder and Johnson, *Colonial Latin America*, 278.
145. The changes described in this paragraph are reported by Fisher in *Government and Society*. For further analysis, see Mark A. Burkholder, "From Creole to Peninsular: The Transformation of the Audiencia of Lima," *Hispanic American Historical Review* 52, no. 3 (August 1972): 395–415; Burkholder and Chandler, *From Impotence to Authority*, 125–6 and appendixes 5–8; Leon G. Campbell, "A Colonial Establishment: Creole Domination of the Audiencia of Lima during the Late Eighteenth Century," *Hispanic American Historical Review* 52, no. 1 (February 1972): 19–20.
146. "The problem of the subdelegates . . . showed above all that neither the crown nor the intendants had solved the problem of enforcing decisions detrimental to the private interests of those entrusted with their application at a local level. The attempt merely caused administrative confusion and disputes in Peru, which underlined the weaknesses of the peninsular authorities." Fisher, *Government and Society*, 99. The immediate source of the trouble was inadequate salaries, which pushed the subdelegates into the same corrupt practices of the corregidores. See Nils Jacobsen, *Mirages of Transition: The Peruvian Altiplano, 1780–1930* (Berkeley: University of California Press, 1993), 95–6; Haitin, "Late Colonial Lima," 66.
147. John Fisher, "Mining and the Peruvian Economy in the Late Colonial Period," in Jacobsen and Puhle, *Economies of Mexico and Peru*, 46–60; Fisher, *Bourbon Peru*, 51, 63–4.
148. O'Phelan Godoy, *Rebellions and Revolts*, 48–9, 162–73.

149. Their arguments that these changes would and then did produce economic stagnation strongly influenced later historians, who initially overstated the extent to which the late colonial viceroyalty was economically depressed. The classic historical work to this effect is Guillermo Céspedes del Castillo's "Lima y Buenos Aires: Repercusiones económicas y políticas de la creación del virreinato del Plata," *Anuario de Estudios Americanos* 3 (1946): 669–874. See also Alberto Flores Galindo, "Aristocracia en vilo: Los mercaderes de Lima en el siglo XVIII," in Jacobsen and Puhle, *Economies of Mexico and Peru*, 252–80.

150. Patricia H. Marks, "Confronting a Mercantile Elite: Bourbon Reformers and the Merchants of Lima, 1765–1796," *The Americas* 60, no. 4 (April 2004): 519. See also Marks, "Power and Authority in Late Colonial Peru: Viceroys, Merchants, and the Military, 1775–1821" (PhD diss., Princeton University, 2003), esp. chap. 2.

151. Marks, "Confronting a Mercantile Elite."

152. Marcel Haitin, "Urban Market and Agrarian Hinterland: Lima in the Late Colonial Period," in Jacobsen and Puhle, *Economies of Mexico and Peru*, 284. See also Haitin, "Late Colonial Lima," 81.

153. Kendall W. Brown, *Bourbons and Brandy: Imperial Reform in Eighteenth-Century Arequipa* (Albuquerque: University of New Mexico Press, 1986), 168–9.

154. Haitin, "Urban Market," 286.

155. Flores Galindo, "Aristocracia en vilo," esp. 274–7. See also Flores Galindo, *Aristocracia y plebe*, chap. 3.

156. Nils Jacobsen, "Commerce in Late Colonial Peru and Mexico: A Comment and Some Comparative Suggestions," in Jacobsen and Puhle, *Economies of Mexico and Peru*, 306–7; Marks, "Power and Authority," 58–9.

157. J. R. Fisher, *Silver Mines and Silver Miners in Colonial Peru, 1776–1824* (Liverpool, England: Centre for Latin-American Studies, University of Liverpool, 1977), 97–102; Richard L. Garner, "Long-Term Silver Mining Trends in Spanish America: A Comparative Analysis of Peru and Mexico," *American Historical Review* 93, no. 4 (October 1988): 929–30.

158. Magnus Mörner, "The Rural Economy and Society of Colonial Spanish America," in Leslie Bethell, ed., *The Cambridge History of Latin America*, vol. 2, *Colonial Latin America* (Cambridge: Cambridge University Press, 1984), 196–7. For an in-depth look at haciendas in the valleys of Lima, see Ileana Vegas de Cáceres, *Economía rural y estructura social en las haciendas de Lima durante el siglo XVIII* (Lima: Fondo Editorial, 1996). See also Haitin, "Late Colonial Lima," chap. 4.

159. Ileana Vegas de Cáceres, "Una imagen distorsionada: Las haciendas de Lima hacia del siglo XVIII," in Scarlett O'Phelan Godoy, ed., *El Perú en el siglo XVIII: La era borbónica* (Lima: Pontificia Universidad Católica del Perú, 1999), 97–125.

160. Less than a third of the population consumed imported goods. Haitin, "Late Colonial Lima," 59.

161. Peru's two most important intercontinental agricultural exports – cascarilla and cacao – were completely dwarfed by mineral exports.

162. This paragraph draws on Brown, *Bourbons and Brandy*, chap. 2; Fisher, *Government and Society*, 134–5; Fisher, *Bourbon Peru*, 63; Flores Galindo,

Aristocracia y plebe, chap. 2; O'Phelan Godoy, *Rebellions and Revolts*, 28–38; Jacobsen, "Livestock Complexes," 119–20.

163. Fisher, *Bourbon Peru*, 52.

164. Marks, "Confronting a Mercantile Elite," 522.

165. Fisher, *Government and Society*, 155.

166. See Coatsworth, "Economic and Institutional Trajectories," 29, for the comparison with South America. According to Coatsworth's data, the GDP per capita of Peru also lagged behind that of Mexico at the end of the colonial period. During a visit to Lima in 1802, Humboldt also remarked on "the enormous difference in wealth apparent in Peru and Mexico." Quoted in Marks, "Confronting a Mercantile Elite," 557.

167. See José Deustua, *La minería peruana y la iniciación de la república, 1820–1840* (Lima: Instituto de Estudios Peruanos, 1986), 34.

168. See, for example, Paul Gootenberg, *Between Silver and Guano: Commercial Policy and the State in Postindependence Peru* (Princeton, NJ: Princeton University Press, 1989); Gootenberg, *Imagining Development: Economic Ideas in Peru's 'Fictitious Prosperity' of Guano, 1840–1880* (Berkeley: University of California Press, 1993).

169. Charles F. Walker, *Smoldering Ashes: Cuzco and the Creation of Republican Peru, 1780–1840* (Durham, NC: Duke University Press, 1999), 11. See also Walker, "Civilize or Control? The Lingering Impact of the Bourbon Urban Reforms," in Nils Jacobsen and Cristóbal Aljovín de Losada, eds., *Political Cultures in the Andes, 1750–1950* (Durham, NC: Duke University Press, 2005), 82; Haitin, "Late Colonial Lima," chap. 6.

170. George Kubler, *The Indian Caste of Peru, 1795–1940: A Population Study Based upon Tax Records and Census Reports* (Westport, CT: Greenwood Press, 1973), 38–40; O'Phelan Godoy, *Rebellions and Revolts*, 46.

171. Florencia E. Mallon, "Indian Communities, Political Cultures, and the State in Latin America, 1780–1990," *Journal of Latin American Studies*, Quincentenary Supplement, 24 (1992): 43.

172. For representative discussions, see Jacobsen, *Mirages of Transition*, 95–106; O'Phelan Godoy, *Rebellions and Revolts*, 46–51.

173. O'Phelan Godoy, *Rebellions and Revolts*. There is a huge literature on the Great Rebellion of 1780–1; for an entry into it, see the bibliography in Peter Flindell Klarén, *Peru: Society and Nationhood in the Andes* (New York: Oxford University Press, 2000), 450–2.

174. John R. Fisher, "The Effects of Comercio Libre on the Economies of New Granada and Peru: A Comparison," in John R. Fisher, Allan J. Kuethe, and Anthony McFarlane, eds., *Reform and Insurrection in Bourbon New Granada and Peru* (Baton Rouge: Louisiana State University Press, 1990), 157.

175. Germán Colmenares, *Historia económica y social de Colombia*, vol. 2, *Popayán: Una sociedad esclavista, 1680–1800*, 2nd ed. (Bogotá: Tercer Mundo Editores, 1997), pts. 1, 2; Anthony McFarlane, *Colombia before Independence: Economy, Society, and Politics under Bourbon Rule* (Cambridge: Cambridge University Press, 1993), chap. 3; Frank Safford and Marco Palacios, *Colombia: Fragmented Land, Divided Society* (Oxford: Oxford University Press, 2002), 44–50; Ann Twinam, *Miners, Merchants, and Farmers in Colonial Colombia* (Austin: University of Texas Press, 1982), chap. 1.

176. McFarlane, *Colombia before Independence*, 32.
177. John Leddy Phelan, *The People and the King: The Comunero Revolution in Colombia, 1781* (Madison: University of Wisconsin Press, 1978).
178. McFarlane, *Colombia before Independence*, 218.
179. Ibid., 129.
180. Fisher, "Effects of Comercio Libre," 157.
181. Lance R. Grahn, "An Irresoluble Dilemma: Smuggling in New Granada, 1713–1763," in Fisher, Kuethe, and McFarlane, *Reform and Insurrection*, 123–46.
182. Safford and Palacios, *Colombia*, 61.
183. McFarlane, *Colombia before Independence*, 151.
184. Ibid., 120, 152.
185. Safford and Palacios, *Colombia*, 60.
186. William Paul McGreevey, *An Economic History of Colombia, 1845–1930* (Cambridge: Cambridge University Press, 1971), 25.
187. McFarlane, *Colombia before Independence*, 143–4.
188. Safford and Palacios, *Colombia*, 59.
189. McFarlane, *Colombia before Independence*, 163.
190. Salomón Kalmanovitz, *Economía y nación: Una breve historia de Colombia* (Bogotá: Grupo Editorial Norma, 2003), 61.
191. David Bushnell, *The Making of Modern Colombia: A Nation in Spite of Itself* (Berkeley: University of California Press, 1993), 14.
192. McFarlane, *Colombia before Independence*, 34.
193. Safford and Palacios, *Colombia*, 183. For data on the decline of slave importation, see Jorge Palacios Preciado, "La esclavitud y la sociedad esclavista," in Jaime Jaramillo Uribe, ed., *Nueva historia de Colombia* (Bogotá: Planeta Colombiana Editorial, 1989), 164.
194. William Frederick Sharp, *Slavery on the Spanish Frontier: The Colombian Chocó, 1680–1810* (Norman: University of Oklahoma Press, 1976), 151.
195. Ibid., 154.
196. Juan A. Villamarín and Judith E. Villamarín, "The Concept of Nobility in Colonial Santa Fe de Bogotá," in Spalding, *Political, Economic and Social History*, 125–53. On the Creole basis of this elite, see Joseph Pérez, "El nuevo reino de Granada en vísperas de la independencia (1781–1809)," in Inge Buisson, Günter Kahle, Hans-Joachim König, and Horst Pietschmann, eds., *Problemas de la formación del estado y de la nación en hispanoamérica* (Cologne: Böhlau, 1984), 93–106.
197. Burkholder and Chandler, *From Impotence to Authority*, 221–7.
198. This paragraph draws on Enrique Tandeter, *Coercion and Market: Silver Mining in Colonial Potosí, 1692–1826* (Albuquerque: University of New Mexico Press, 1993), esp. chap. 1; Brooke Larson, *Cochabamba, 1550–1900: Colonialism and Agrarian Transformation in Bolivia*, expanded ed. (Durham, NC: Duke University Press, 1998), 102–8; Herbert S. Klein, *A Concise History of Bolivia* (Cambridge: Cambridge University Press, 2003), 60–1, 67–70; Peter Bakewell, "Mining in Colonial Spanish America," in Bethell, *Cambridge History of Latin America*, 2:144, 147–8; Ann Zulawski, *They Eat from Their Labor: Work and Social Change in Colonial Bolivia* (Pittsburgh, PA: University of Pittsburgh Press, 1995), chaps. 4–5.

199. Tandeter also suggests that the implementation of work quotas at Potosí was critical for the increase in silver output. See Enrique Tandeter, "Forced and Free Labour in Late Colonial Potosí," *Past and Present* 93 (November 1981): 98–136.
200. Larson, *Cochabamba*, 272. See also Tandeter, "Forced and Free Labour," 99–100.
201. Tandeter, "Forced and Free Labour," 100. For eighteenth-century silver-production totals, see Oscar Cornblit, *Power and Violence in the Colonial City: Oruro from the Mining Renaissance to the Rebellion of Tupac Amaru (1740–1782)*, trans. Elizabeth Ladd Glick (Cambridge: Cambridge University Press, 1995), 99–100.
202. Klein, *Concise History of Bolivia*, 61. The one urban area that did experience population growth was La Paz.
203. Tandeter, *Coercion and Market*, chap. 5.
204. Larson, *Cochabamba*, 258.
205. Lynch, *Spanish Colonial Administration*, 135–45.
206. Larson, *Cochabamba*, 253.
207. Ibid., 257. This paragraph draws on Larson's book more generally.
208. Ibid., 257–8.
209. On these landlords and hacienda agriculture, see Herbert S. Klein, *Haciendas and Ayllus: Rural Society in the Bolivian Andes in the Eighteenth and Nineteenth Centuries* (Stanford, CA: Stanford University Press, 1993), chaps. 1–2; Klein, "The State and the Labor Market in Rural Bolivia in the Colonial and Early Republican Periods," in Spalding, *Political, Economic and Social History*, 100–3; Larson, *Cochabamba*, chaps. 5–6. For regional coverage, see Olivia Harris, Brooke Larson, and Enrique Tandeter, eds., *La participación indígena en los mercados surandinos: Estrategias y reproducción social, siglos XVI a XX* (La Paz: Centro de Estudios de la Realidad Económica y Social, 1987).
210. Tandeter, *Coercion and Market*, esp. chap. 4.
211. Ibid., 162. This paragraph also draws on pp. 115–25.
212. Klein, *Haciendas and Ayllus*, 8; Klein, *Concise History of Bolivia*, 104. The presentation of subsequent data in this paragraph also draws on p. 9 of Klein, *Haciendas and Ayllus*.
213. Larson, *Cochabamba*, 375–6.
214. Nicolás Sánchez-Albornoz, *Indios y tributos en el Alto Perú* (Lima: Instituto de Estudios Peruanos, 1978), 107.
215. This paragraph draws on Klein, *Haciendas and Ayllus*, chap. 3; Larson, *Cochabamba*, chaps. 4–6; Sánchez-Albornoz, *Indios y tributos*, chap. 2; Ann Zulawski, "Frontier Workers and Social Change: Pilaya y Paspara (Bolivia) in the Early Eighteenth Century," in Robinson, *Migration in Colonial Spanish America*, 112–27; Erwin P. Grieshaber, "Survival of Indian Communities in Nineteenth-Century Bolivia: A Regional Comparison," *Journal of Latin American Studies* 12, no. 2 (November 1980): 223–69.
216. Robson Brines Tyrer, "The Demographic and Economic History of the Audiencia of Quito: Indian Population and the Textile Industry" (PhD diss., University of California, Berkeley, 1976), 323, 314; see also chap. 5.
217. Kenneth J. Andrien, *The Kingdom of Quito, 1690–1830: The State and Regional Development* (Cambridge: Cambridge University Press, 1995), 29.

218. Ibid., 59. For similar arguments, see Tyrer, "Demographic and Economic History," 225.

219. Andrien, *The Kingdom of Quito*, 39–40.

220. Martin Minchom, *The People of Quito, 1690–1810: Change and Unrest in the Underclass* (Boulder, CO: Westview Press, 1994), chap. 6; Suzanne Austin Alchon, *Native Society and Disease in Colonial Ecuador* (Cambridge: Cambridge University Press, 1991), 113–24.

221. Andrien, *The Kingdom of Quito*, 97–8. "Guayaquil benefited most directly from royal efforts to stimulate colonial export economies; the lifting of restrictions on colonial trade, beginning in 1778, led to the rapid growth of plantation agriculture, particularly cacao production." Ibid., 54. Contreras agrees that "the decade of the 1770s was key," but he cautions that some prior progress had occurred. Carlos Contreras C., *El sector exportador de una economía colonial: La costa del Ecuador entre 1760 y 1820* (Quito: Flacso, 1990), 31; see also the summary remarks on p. 39. See also the excellent discussion in Carlos Marchán Romero, "Economía y sociedad durante el siglo XVIII," *Cultura: Revista del Banco Central del Ecuador* 8, no. 24 (April 1986): 60–3.

222. Andrien, *The Kingdom of Quito*, 43. The population figure is from p. 39. This paragraph also draws on pp. 51–3.

223. Douglas Alan Washburn, "The Bourbon Reforms: A Social and Economic History of the Audiencia of Quito, 1760–1810" (PhD diss., University of Texas at Austin, 1984), 107; Kenneth J. Andrien, "Economic Crisis, Taxes and the Quito Insurrection of 1765," *Past and Present* 129 (November 1990): 110.

224. Contreras, *El sector exportador*, 69–78, 130; Andrien, *The Kingdom of Quito*, 54, 100, 110, 148, 161–2.

225. Andrien, *The Kingdom of Quito*, 53. See also the discussion in Manuel Miño Grijalva, "Estudio introductorio," in Manuel Miño Grijalva, ed., *La economía colonial: Relaciones socioeconómicas de La Real Audiencia de Quito* (Quito: Corporación Editora Nacional, 1984), 79–84.

226. This paragraph and the next one draw generally on Tyrer, "Demographic and Economic History."

227. Washburn, "The Bourbon Reforms," 10–13; Miño Grijalva, "Estudio introductorio," 72; Andrien, "Economic Crisis," 111.

228. Andrien, *The Kingdom of Quito*, chap. 4.

229. Tyrer, "Demographic and Economic History," 327. This paragraph draws on pp. 324–33 more generally; and on the discussions of rural labor in Nicholas P. Cushner, *Farm and Factory: The Jesuits and the Development of Agrarian Capitalism in Colonial Quito, 1600–1767* (Albany: State University of New York Press, 1982), chap. 6; Christiana Borchart de Moreno, "Capital comercial y producción agricola: Nueva España y la Audiencia de Quito en el siglo XVIII," *Anuario de Estudios Americanos* 46 (1989): 131–72.

230. Contrasting arguments about the effect of the obraje crisis on indigenous people appear in Tyrer, "Demographic and Economic History," 324; and Andrien, *The Kingdom of Quito*, 111–12. On overall hardship, see Gabriel Cevallos García, *Historia del Ecuador* (Cuenca, Ecuador: Editorial "Don Bosco," 1964), 195–6.

231. Kenneth J. Andrien, "The State and Dependency in Late Colonial and Early Republican Ecuador," in Kenneth J. Andrien and Lyman L. Johnson, eds., *The*

Political Economy of Spanish America in the Age of Revolution, 1750–1850 (Albuquerque: University of New Mexico Press, 1994), 169–95.

232. See, for example, Tyrer, "Demographic and Economic History," 334; Andrien, "Economic Crisis."

233. Mark Van Aken, "The Lingering Death of Tribute in Ecuador," *Hispanic American Historical Review* 61, no. 3 (August 1981): 429–59.

234. José Manuel Santos Pérez, *Élites, poder local y régimen colonial: El cabildo y los regidores de Santiago de Guatemala, 1700–1787* (South Woodstock, VT: Plumstock Mesoamerican Studies, 1999), 34–5.

235. José Antonio Fernández Molina, "Colouring the World in Blue: The Indigo Boom and the Central American Market, 1750–1810" (PhD diss., University of Texas at Austin, 1992); Robert Smith, "Indigo Production and Trade in Colonial Guatemala," *Hispanic American Historical Review* 39, no. 2 (May 1959): 181–211.

236. Fernández Molina, "Colouring the World in Blue," 81, 84, 103–4; Smith, "Indigo Production," 186; Troy S. Floyd, "The Guatemalan Merchants, the Government, and the Provincianos, 1750–1800," *Hispanic American Historical Review* 41, no. 1 (February 1961): 100.

237. Miles L. Wortman, *Government and Society in Central America, 1680–1840* (New York: Columbia University Press, 1982), 193.

238. On the merchants, see Fernández Molina, "Colouring the World in Blue," chap. 5; Floyd, "Guatemalan Merchants"; Troy S. Floyd, "The Indigo Merchant: Promoter of Central American Economic Development, 1750–1808," *Business History Review* 39, no. 4 (Winter 1965): 466–88.

239. Ralph Lee Woodward Jr., "Economic and Social Origins of the Guatemalan Political Parties (1773–1823)," *Hispanic American Historical Review* 45, no. 4 (November 1965): 552.

240. Floyd, "Guatemalan Merchants," 90.

241. Ibid., 98.

242. Ibid., 103–4, chap. 5; Smith, "Indigo Production," 203–4.

243. Santos Pérez, *Élites, poder local y régimen colonial,* 20–2.

244. María Lorena Castellanos Rodríguez, "La minería," in Jorge Luján Muñoz, ed., *Historia general de Guatemala,* vol. 3, *Siglo XVIII hasta la independencia* (Guatemala City: Fundación para la Cultura y el Desarrollo, 1995), 323–33.

245. Jorge Arias de Blois, "Demografía," in Luján Muñoz, *Historia general de Guatemala,* vol. 3, *Siglo XVIII hasta la independencia,* 111.

246. Woodward, "Economic and Social Origins," 545.

247. Miles Wortman, "Government Revenue and Economic Trends in Central America, 1787–1819," *Hispanic American Historical Review* 55, no. 2 (May 1975): 256–9; Wortman, *Government and Society,* 165; Fernández Molina, "Colouring the World in Blue," 358–60.

248. "It was mainly the burden of taxes, in the opinion of many producers and exporters, that weakened the competitive position of Guatemalan indigo." Smith, "Indigo Production," 209. See also Wortman, *Government and Society,* 186.

249. Christopher H. Lutz, "Evolución demográfica de la población ladina," in Luján Muñoz, *Historia general de Guatemala,* vol. 3, *Siglo XVIII hasta la independencia,* 119–33.

250. Santos Pérez, *Élites, poder local y régimen colonial*, 183–4.
251. Horacio Cabezas Carcache, "Los Indios," in Luján Muñoz, *Historia general de Guatemala*, vol. 3, *Siglo XVIII hasta la independencia*, 154–6; Wilbur Eugene Meneray, "The Kingdom of Guatemala during the Reign of Charles III" (PhD diss., University of North Carolina at Chapel Hill, 1975), 6.
252. Murdo J. MacLeod, "Ethnic Relations and Indian Society in the Province of Guatemala, ca. 1620–ca. 1800," in Murdo J. MacLeod and Robert Wasserstrom, eds., *Spaniards and Indians in Southeastern Mesoamerica: Essays on the History of Ethnic Relations* (Lincoln: University of Nebraska Press, 1983), 196–7; Julio César Pinto Soria, "Apuntes históricos sobre la estructura agrarian y asentamiento en la Capitanía General de Guatemala," in Stephen Webre, ed., *La sociedad colonial de Guatemala: Estudios regionales y locales* (Antigua, Guatemala: Centro de Investigaciones Regionales de Mesoamérica, 1989), 112–15.
253. John L. Rector, *The History of Chile* (New York: Palgrave Macmillan, 2003), 56.
254. Bakewell, "Mining in Colonial Spanish America," 142–3.
255. See, for example, Eduardo Cavieres, *El comercio chileno en la economía colonial* (Valparaíso, Chile: Ediciones Universitarias de Valparaíso, 1996).
256. Arnold J. Bauer, "Expansión económica en una sociedad tradicional: Chile central en el siglo XIX," *Historia* 9 (1970): 144.
257. Jacques A. Barbier, *Reform and Politics in Bourbon Chile, 1755–1796* (Ottawa: University of Ottawa Press, 1980), 158–9; Jay Kinsbruner, *Chile: A Historical Interpretation* (New York: Harper & Row, 1973), 37–8; Sergio Villalobos R., *Comercio y contrabando en el Río de la Plata y Chile* (Buenos Aires: Editorial Universitaria de Buenos Aires, 1965), 129. For an opposing view, see Cavieres, *El comercio chileno*, 53. Despite Cavieres's thesis that the Bourbon reforms triggered a dynamic late colonial economy, I do not believe he presents convincing data to support the argument. Rather, his own analysis points to a hugely indebted economy that lacked a significant export sector (see, e.g., table 3 on p. 59).
258. Fernando Silva Vargas, "Peru y Chile: Notas sobre sus vinculaciones administrativas y fiscales (1785–1800)," *Historia* 7 (1968): 166–70.
259. Barbier, *Reform and Politics*, 160.
260. Brian Loveman, *Chile: The Legacy of Hispanic Capitalism*, 2nd ed. (New York: Oxford University Press, 1988), 98; Rector, *The History of Chile*, 52; Barbier, *Reform and Politics*, 32.
261. Marcello Carmagnani, "Colonial Latin American Demography: Growth of the Chilean Population, 1700–1830," *Journal of Social History* 1, no. 2 (Winter 1967): 185; Barbier, *Reform and Politics*, 189.
262. Charles G. Pregger-Román, "The Origin and Development of the Bourgeoisie in Nineteenth-Century Chile," *Latin American Perspectives* 10 (1983): 41.
263. John L. Rector, "El impacto económico de la independencia en América Latina: El caso de Chile," *Historia* 20 (1985): 297. See also Robert M. Will, "The Introduction of Classical Economics into Chile," *Hispanic American Historical Review* 44, no. 1 (February 1964): 1–21.
264. Carmagnani, "Colonial Latin American Demography," 190.

265. Loveman, *Chile*, 92. See also Bauer, "Expansión económica."
266. John Hoyt Williams, *The Rise and Fall of the Paraguayan Republic, 1800–1870* (Austin: Institute of Latin American Studies, University of Texas at Austin, 1979), 3.
267. Ibid., 12.
268. Jan M. G. Kleinpenning, *Paraguay, 1515–1870: A Thematic Geography of Its Development*, vol. 2 (Madrid: Iberoamericana, 2003), 919–24.
269. Ibid., chap. 26.
270. Ibid., 924–45, 1060–70. For data on exports in the late colonial period, see also Thomas Whigham, *The Politics of River Trade: Tradition and Development in the Upper Plata, 1780–1870* (Albuquerque: University of New Mexico Press, 1991), 17–18.
271. Williams, *Rise and Fall*, 4–7.
272. Ibid., 13; Kleinpenning, *Paraguay*, 1:847–52, 2:964–6, 1071–8, and chaps. 26, 34.
273. Héctor Lindo-Fuentes, *Weak Foundations: The Economy of El Salvador in the Nineteenth Century, 1821–1898* (Berkeley: University of California Press, 1990), chap. 1.
274. David Browning, *El Salvador: Landscape and Society* (Oxford: Clarendon Press, 1971), 112.
275. Rodolfo Barón Castro, *La población de El Salvador: Estudio acerca de su desenvolvimiento desde la época prehispánica hasta nuestros días* (Madrid: Consejo Superior de Investigaciones Científicas, 1942), 273.
276. Wortman, *Government and Society*, 162–3; Fernández Molina, "Colouring the World in Blue," 81, 103–4, 125–6.
277. Wortman, "Government Revenue," 261.
278. Floyd, "The Indigo Merchant," 475–9.
279. Aldo A. Lauria-Santiago, *An Agrarian Republic: Commercial Agriculture and the Politics of Peasant Communities in El Salvador, 1823–1914* (Pittsburgh, PA: University of Pittsburgh Press, 1999), 24; Fernández Molina, "Colouring the World in Blue," 90–104. For a Marxist view that haciendas played a larger role in land concentration and depopulation, see Mario Flores Macal, *Origen, desarrollo y crisis de las formas de dominación en El Salvador* (San José: SECASA, 1983), 22–37.
280. Browning, *El Salvador*, 65, 77, 115–33; Fernández Molina, "Colouring the World in Blue," 91.
281. Lauria-Santiago, *An Agrarian Republic*, 32.
282. Linda Newson, "Labour in the Colonial Mining Industry of Honduras," *The Americas* 39, no. 2 (October 1982): 198.
283. Bernabé Fernández Hernández, *El gobierno del Intendente Anguiano en Honduras (1796–1812)* (Seville: Universidad de Sevilla, 1997), 73–88; Juan Carlos Solórzano Fonseca, "Los años finales de la dominación española (1750–1821)," in Héctor Pérez Brignoli, ed., *Historia general de centroamérica*, vol. 3, *De la ilustración al liberalismo (1750–1870)* (Madrid: Sociedad Estatal Quinto Centenario, 1993), 27.
284. This paragraph draws generally on Newson, "Labour in the Colonial Mining Industry."

285. Linda Newson, *The Cost of Conquest: Indian Decline in Honduras under Spanish Rule* (Boulder, CO: Westview Press, 1986), 141–3; Floyd, "Guatemalan Merchants," 96.

286. Fernández Hernández, *El gobierno del Intendente Anguiano,* 66; Floyd, "Guatemalan Merchants," 93.

287. Fernández Hernández, *El gobierno del Intendente Anguiano,* 90–3.

288. Linda A. Newson, *Indian Survival in Colonial Nicaragua* (Norman: University of Oklahoma Press, 1987), 259, 318–19, 285–7; Germán Romero Vargas, *Las estructuras sociales de Nicaragua en el siglo XVIII* (Managua: Vanguardia, 1987), 173–82, 296–360; Solórzano Fonseca, "Los años finales," 25–6.

289. David Richard Radell, "A Historical Geography of Western Nicaragua: The Spheres of Influence of León, Granada, and Managua, 1519–1965" (PhD diss., Department of Geography, University of California, Berkeley, 1969), 156–8; Newson, *Indian Survival,* 265–6. On the nineteenth-century economy generally, see Romero Vargas, *Las estructuras sociales,* 223–46.

290. Quoted in E. Bradford Burns, *Patriarch and Folk: The Emergence of Nicaragua, 1798–1858* (Cambridge, MA: Harvard University Press, 1991), 5.

291. Quoted in Víctor Hugo Acuña Ortega and Iván Molina Jiménez, *Historia económica y social de Costa Rica (1750–1950)* (San José: Editorial Porvenir, 1991), 21.

292. Iván Molina Jiménez, *Costa Rica (1800–1850): El legado colonial y la génesis del capitalismo* (San José: Editorial de la Universidad de Costa Rica, 1991), 60; Lowell Gudmundson, *Costa Rica before Coffee: Society and Economy on the Eve of the Export Boom* (Baton Rouge: Louisiana State University Press, 1986), 1–2.

293. Molina Jiménez, *Costa Rica,* 48–65; Gudmundson, *Costa Rica before Coffee,* chap. 1.

294. On the late colonial economy generally, see Fernández Molina, "Colouring the World in Blue," 425–59. On cacao, see Carlos Rosés Alvarado, "El ciclo del cacao en la economía colonial de Costa Rica, 1650–1794," *Mesoamérica* 3, no. 4 (December 1982): 247–78; on cattle, see Lowell Gudmundson, *Estratificación socio-racial y económica de Costa Rica, 1700–1850* (San José: Editorial Universidad Estatal a Distancia, 1978), 81–105; and on tobacco, see Víctor Hugo Acuña Ortega, "Historia económica del tabaco: Época colonial," *Anuario de Estudios Centroamericanos* 4 (1979): 279–392.

295. The classic work from this perspective is Carlos Monge Alfaro, *Historia de Costa Rica,* 14th ed. (San José: Librería Trejos, 1976). In his characterization of landholding structures, Monge Alfaro drew on Rodrigo Facio, *Estudio sobre economía costarricense,* reprinted in *Obras de Rodrigo Facio,* vol. 1 (San José: Editorial Costa Rica, 1972). The idea of yeomanry in colonial Costa Rica was later developed most carefully in Mitchell A. Seligson, *Peasants of Costa Rica and the Development of Agrarian Capitalism* (Madison: University of Wisconsin Press, 1980).

296. Gudmundson, *Costa Rica before Coffee,* 22.

297. Molina Jiménez, *Costa Rica,* chaps. 2–3.

298. Fernández Molina, "Colouring the World in Blue," 457.

299. Colombia's status as a semiperiphery region is thus overdetermined, given the data in Table 4.2.

Chapter 5. Warfare and Postcolonial Development

1. Charles Tilly, "Reflections on the History of European State-Making," in Charles Tilly, ed., *The Formation of National States in Western Europe* (Princeton, NJ: Princeton University Press, 1975), 42.
2. See, for example, Brian M. Downing, *The Military Revolution and Political Change: Origins of Democracy and Autocracy in Early Modern Europe* (Princeton, NJ: Princeton University Press, 1992); Thomas Ertman, *Birth of the Leviathan: Building States and Regimes in Medieval and Early Modern Europe* (Cambridge: Cambridge University Press, 1997); Charles Tilly, *Coercion, Capital, and European States, A.D. 990–1990* (Cambridge: Basil Blackwell, 1990).
3. On early state building in Latin America, see Miguel Angel Centeno, "Blood and Debt: War and Taxation in Nineteenth-Century Latin America," *American Journal of Sociology* 102, no. 6 (May 1997): 1565–1605; Miguel Angel Centeno, *Blood and Debt: War and the Nation-State in Latin America* (University Park: Pennsylvania State University Press, 2002); Fernando López-Alves, *State Formation and Democracy in Latin America, 1810–1900* (Durham, NC: Duke University Press, 2000).
4. The effect of wars on economic development is quite understudied. As Stubbs writes, "Despite the evident importance of wars to the course of history, they have had little impact on analysts interested in economic development beyond Europe and the major powers." Richard Stubbs, "War and Economic Development: Export-Oriented Industrialization in East and Southeast Asia," *Comparative Politics* 31, no. 3 (April 1999): 337.
5. Centeno, *Blood and Debt*, 37.
6. Ibid., 44. On twentieth-century wars, see Cameron G. Thies, "War, Rivalry, and State Building in Latin America," *American Journal of Political Science* 49, no. 3 (July 2005): 451–65.
7. With the disruptions of the independence period, Spanish America as a region grew little, if at all, and thus fell further behind the United States and western Europe (though not other regions). See Victor Bulmer-Thomas, *The Economic History of Latin America since Independence* (Cambridge: Cambridge University Press, 1994), 28–31; Stanley L. Engerman and Kenneth L. Sokoloff, "Factor Endowments, Institutions, and Differential Paths of Growth among New World Economies: A View from Economic Historians of the United States," in Stephen Haber, ed., *How Latin America Fell Behind: Essays on the Economic Histories of Brazil and Mexico, 1800–1914* (Stanford, CA: Stanford University Press, 1997), 260–304; Leandro Prados de la Escosura, "Colonial Independence and Economic Backwardness in Latin America" (Working Paper No. 10/05, Department of Economic History, London School of Economics, February 2005).

    For general background on the independence period, see Jorge I. Domínguez, *Insurrection or Loyalty: The Breakdown of the Spanish American Empire* (Cambridge, MA: Harvard University Press, 1980); Richard Graham, *Independence in Latin America: A Comparative Approach* (New York: Knopf, 1972);

Brian R. Hamnett, "Process and Pattern: A Re-examination of the Ibero-American Independence Movements, 1808–1826," *Journal of Latin American Studies* 29, no. 2 (May 1997): 279–328; Jay Kinsbruner, *Independence in Spanish America: Civil Wars, Revolutions, and Underdevelopment,* rev. ed. (Albuquerque: University of New Mexico Press, 2000); John Lynch, *The Spanish American Revolutions, 1808–1826,* 2nd ed. (New York: Norton, 1986); Jaime E. Rodríguez O., *The Independence of Spanish America* (Cambridge: Cambridge University Press, 1998). For explicit discussions of the extent to which the independence years were a break with the colonial past, see the essays in Victor M. Uribe-Uran, ed., *State and Society in Spanish America during the Age of Revolution* (Wilmington, DE: Scholarly Resources, 2001).

 8. George Reid Andrews, "Spanish American Independence: A Structural Analysis," *Latin American Perspectives* 12, no. 1 (Winter 1985): 105.

 9. Kinsbruner, *Independence in Spanish America,* 156; John H. Coatsworth, "La independencia latinoamericana: Hipótesis sobre sus costes y beneficios," in Leandro Prados de la Escosura and Samuel Amaral, eds., *La independencia americana: Consecuencias económicas* (Madrid: Alianza Editorial, 1993), 19.

10. Coatsworth, "La independencia latinoamericana," 17–27.

11. For basic historical background, see David S. Heidler and Jeanne T. Heidler, *The Mexican War* (Westport, CT: Greenwood Press, 2006).

12. Jan Bazant, *A Concise History of Mexico: From Hidalgo to Cárdenas, 1805–1940* (Cambridge: Cambridge University Press, 1977), 57.

13. Luis González y González, "The Period of Formation," in Daniel Cosío Villegas, Ignacio Bernal, Alejandra Moreno Toscano, Luis González, and Eduardo Blanquel, *A Compact History of Mexico,* trans. Marjory Mattingly Urquidi (Los Angeles: UCLA Latin American Center, 1975), 97–8.

14. Robert G. Williams, *States and Social Evolution: Coffee and the Rise of National Governments in Central America* (Chapel Hill: University of North Carolina Press, 1994).

15. James Mahoney, *The Legacies of Liberalism: Path Dependence and Political Regimes in Central America* (Baltimore: Johns Hopkins University Press, 2001).

16. Lowell Gudmundson and Héctor Lindo-Fuentes, *Central America, 1821–1871: Liberalism before Liberal Reform* (Tuscaloosa: University of Alabama Press, 1995), 61.

17. Hubert Howe Bancroft, *History of Central America,* vol. 3 (San Francisco: The History Company, 1887), 596–9; Dana G. Munro, *The Five Republics of Central America: Their Political and Economic Development and Their Relations with the United States* (New York: Oxford University Press, 1918), 159.

18. Ciro F. S. Cardoso, "The Formation of the Coffee Estate in Nineteenth-Century Costa Rica," in Kenneth Duncan and Ian Rutledge (with Collin Harding), eds., *Land and Labour in Latin America* (Cambridge: Cambridge University Press, 1977), 176.

19. Lowell Gudmundson, *Costa Rica before Coffee: Society and Economy on the Eve of the Export Boom* (Baton Rouge: Louisiana State University Press, 1986), 68.

20. Astrid Fischel, *Consenso y represión: Una interpretación socio-política de la educación costarricense* (San José: Editorial Costa Rica, 1990); Iván Molina

Jiménez, *Costa Rica (1800–1850): El legado colonial y la génesis del capitalismo* (San José: Editorial de la Universidad de Costa Rica, 1991).

21. See Gudmundson, *Costa Rica before Coffee*, for an extensive literature review and discussion. I also address the relevant literature in Mahoney, *Legacies of Liberalism*, 75–7.

22. See the data in Ralph Lee Woodward Jr., "The Aftermath of Independence, 1821–c. 1870," in Leslie Bethell, ed., *Central America since Independence* (Cambridge: Cambridge University Press, 1991), 8.

23. Mahoney, *Legacies of Liberalism*, 143–6.

24. Thomas L. Karnes, in *The Failure of Union: Central America, 1824–1960* (Chapel Hill: University of North Carolina Press, 1961), 94, compiled the following statistics for conflicts between 1824 and 1842 from Alejandro Marure, *Efemérides de los hechos notables acaecidos en la república de Centro América* (Guatemala: Tipografía Nacional, 1895), 141, 154:

	Number of battles	Number killed	Number of men wielding executive power
Guatemala	51	2,291	18
El Salvador	40	2,546	23
Honduras	27	682	20
Nicaragua	17	1,203	18
Costa Rica	5	144	11

25. Rafael Obregón Loría, *Costa Rica en la independencia y en la federación*, 2nd ed. (San José: Editorial Costa Rica, 1979), 224.

26. See, for example, Karnes, *The Failure of Union*, 34–5; Alberto Herrate, *La unión de Centroamérica: Tragedia y esperanza* (Guatemala City: Editorial del Ministerio de Educación Pública, 1955), 166.

27. Simon Collier, "Chile," in Leslie Bethell, ed., *Spanish America after Independence, c. 1820–c. 1870* (Cambridge: Cambridge University Press, 1987), 303.

28. John L. Rector, "El impacto económico de la independencia en América Latina: El caso de Chile," *Historia* 20 (1985): 297–8. However, free-market economics were not fully embraced until after the 1830s. See Robert M. Will, "The Introduction of Classical Economics into Chile," *Hispanic American Historical Review* 44, no. 1 (February 1964): 1–21.

29. Simon Collier and William F. Sater, *A History of Chile, 1808–1994* (Cambridge: Cambridge University Press, 1996), 68–9; John L. Rector, *The History of Chile* (New York: Palgrave Macmillan, 2003), 90–1.

30. Carmen Cariola Sutter and Osvaldo Sunkel, *La historia económica de Chile, 1830 y 1930: Dos ensayos y una bibliografía* (Madrid: Ediciones Cultura Hispánica del Instituto de Cooperación Iberoamericana, 1982), 32–3 and pt. 1 more generally.

31. Collier and Sater, *A History of Chile*, 75–6.

32. Arnold J. Bauer, *Chilean Rural Society: From the Spanish Conquest to 1930* (Cambridge: Cambridge University Press, 1975), 63–6; William F. Sater, "Chile

and the World Depression of the 1870s," *Journal of Latin American Studies* 11, no. 1 (May 1979): 67–99; Cariola Sutter and Sunkel, *La historia económica*, 33–9.

33. Brian Loveman, *Chile: The Legacy of Hispanic Capitalism*, 2nd ed. (New York: Oxford University Press, 1988), 153. There are many works analyzing the effect of the nitrate industry on Chile's growth after the 1870s. See, for example, Thomas F. O'Brien, *The Nitrate Industry and Chile's Crucial Transition, 1870–1891* (New York: New York University Press, 1982).

34. Marcello Carmagnani, "Colonial Latin American Demography: Growth of the Chilean Population, 1700–1830," *Journal of Social History* 1, no. 2 (Winter 1967): 190.

35. Bauer, *Chilean Rural Society*, 159.

36. Thomas Whigham, *The Politics of River Trade: Tradition and Development in the Upper Plata, 1780–1870* (Albuquerque: University of New Mexico Press, 1991), xviii.

37. Jan M. G. Kleinpenning, *Paraguay, 1515–1870: A Thematic Geography of Its Development*, vol. 2 (Madrid: Iberoamericana, 2003), 1571.

38. Richard Alan White, *Paraguay's Autonomous Revolution, 1810–1840* (Albuquerque: University of New Mexico Press, 1978), 82.

39. Kleinpenning, *Paraguay*, 2:1412.

40. White, *Paraguay's Autonomous Revolution*, 62–3; Kleinpenning, *Paraguay*, 2:1388–9; John Hoyt Williams, *The Rise and Fall of the Paraguayan Republic, 1800–1870* (Austin: Institute of Latin American Studies, University of Texas at Austin, 1979), chap. 3.

41. White, *Paraguay's Autonomous Revolution*, 69–71, 81; Kleinpenning, *Paraguay*, vol. 1, chap. 18.

42. Kleinpenning, *Paraguay*, 2:1571–2.

43. Ibid., 1247.

44. Thomas Lyle Whigham, "The Iron Works of Ybycui: Paraguayan Industrial Development in the Mid-nineteenth Century," *The Americas* 35, no. 2 (October 1978): 201–18; Kleinpenning, *Paraguay*, 2:1308–20. For reservations about the extent of state-led development in Paraguay, see Mario Pastore, "State-Led Industrialization: The Evidence on Paraguay, 1852–1870," *Journal of Latin American Studies* 26, no. 2 (May 1994): 295–324.

45. See Thomas L. Whigham, *The Paraguayan War*, vol. 1, *Causes and Consequences* (Lincoln: University of Nebraska Press, 2002); Hendrik Kraay and Thomas L. Whigham, eds., *I Die with My Country: Perspectives on the Paraguayan War, 1864–1870* (Lincoln: University of Nebraska Press, 2004).

46. Williams, *Rise and Fall*, 203–5.

47. Kleinpenning's analysis of the debate over the extent of population loss is excellent. See his *Paraguay*, 2:1573–81. For two different estimates, see Vera Blinn Reber, "The Demographics of Paraguay: A Reinterpretation of the Great War, 1864–1870," *Hispanic American Historical Review* 86, no. 2 (May 1988): 289–319; Thomas Lyle Whigham and Barbara Potthast, "The Paraguayan Rosetta Stone: New Insights into the Demographics of the Paraguayan War, 1864–1870," *Latin American Research Review* 34, no. 1 (1999): 174–86.

48. Harris Gaylord Warren (with the assistance of Katherine F. Warren), *Rebirth of the Paraguayan Republic: The First Colorado Era, 1878–1904* (Pittsburgh,

PA: University of Pittsburgh Press, 1985), 3. See also Harris Gaylord Warren (with the assistance of Katherine F. Warren), *Paraguay and the Triple Alliance: The Postwar Decade, 1869–1878* (Austin: Institute of Latin American Studies, University of Texas at Austin, 1978).

Chapter 6. Postcolonial Levels of Development

1. Jeremy Adelman, "Preface," in Jeremy Adelman, ed., *Colonial Legacies: The Problem of Persistence in Latin American History* (New York: Routledge, 1999), ix.
2. Arthur L. Stinchcombe, *Constructing Social Theories* (New York: Harcourt, Brace, & World, 1968), 103–4. Such continuity in relative levels of development could be considered, under many definitions, a form of "path-dependent" stability. On path dependence, see Paul Pierson, *Politics in Time: History, Institutions, and Social Analysis* (Princeton, NJ: Princeton University Press, 2004); James Mahoney, "Path Dependence in Historical Sociology," *Theory and Society* 29, no. 4 (August 2000): 507–48.
3. Stinchcombe, *Constructing Social Theories*, 102–3.
4. Institutional persistence is linked to the reproduction of power asymmetries. For an interesting recent discussion, see Daron Acemoglu and James A. Robinson, "Persistence of Power, Elites, and Institutions," *American Economic Review* 98, no. 1 (March 2008): 267–93.
5. Jeremy Adelman, "Introduction: The Problem of Persistence in Latin American History," in Adelman, *Colonial Legacies*, 11.
6. See, for example, Ronald Aminzade, "Historical Sociology and Time," *Sociological Methods and Research* 20, no. 4 (May 1992): 456–80; Kathleen Thelen, "Historical Institutionalism in Comparative Politics," *Annual Review of Political Science* 2 (1999): 369–404; Jill Quadagno and Stan J. Knapp, "Have Historical Sociologists Forsaken Theory?" *Sociological Methods and Research* 20, no. 4 (May 1992): 481–507.
7. John H. Coatsworth, "Notes on the Comparative Economic History of Latin America and the United States," in Walther L. Bernecker and Hans Werner Tobler, eds., *Development and Underdevelopment in America: Contrasts of Economic Growth in North and Latin America in Historical Perspective* (Berlin: Walter de Gruyter, 1993), 25–6.
8. Coatsworth and Maddison estimate GDP per capita for select years or periods during the nineteenth century for Argentina, Chile, Colombia, Mexico, Peru, and Venezuela. John H. Coatsworth, "Economic and Institutional Trajectories in Nineteenth-Century Latin America," in John H. Coatsworth and Alan M. Taylor, eds., *Latin America and the World Economy since 1800* (Cambridge, MA: Harvard University Press, 1998), 23–54; Coatsworth, "Comparative Economic History"; Angus Maddison, *The World Economy: A Millennial Perspective* (Paris: Organization for Economic Cooperation and Development, 2001), 195.
9. Rosemary Thorp, *Progress, Poverty and Exclusion: An Economic History of Latin America in the 20th Century* (New York: Inter-American Development Bank, 1998); Alan Heston, Robert Summers, and Bettina Aten, "Penn World Table Version 6.2" (Center for International Comparisons of Production, Income

and Prices at the University of Pennsylvania, September 2006); World Bank, *World Development Report* (Washington, DC: World Bank, various years). World Bank data can be downloaded from www.worldbank.org.

10. The simple correlation coefficient among the datasets for the years they have in common for the Spanish American cases is never less than 0.9.

11. The key source here is Alfred Maizels, *Industrial Growth and World Trade* (Cambridge: Cambridge University Press, 1963), table E2, p. 533.

12. Angus Maddison, "A Comparison of Levels of GDP Per Capita in the Developed and Developing Countries, 1700–1980," *Journal of Economic History* 43, no. 1 (March 1983): 30.

13. Maddison, *The World Economy*, 185, 195.

14. Victor Bulmer-Thomas, *The Economic History of Latin America since Independence* (Cambridge: Cambridge University Press, 1994), 444; Thorp, *Progress, Poverty and Exclusion*, 353. Bulmer-Thomas also reports Uruguay's GDP per capita as about equal to Argentina's in 1913, but this estimate is derived from data for 1928–9. I believe the same is probably true of the 1913 GDP per capita estimate for Uruguay that can be calculated from data in Michael J. Twomey, "Patterns of Foreign Investment in Latin America in the Twentieth Century," in Coatsworth and Taylor, *Latin America*, 173.

15. On Uruguay's economy, see Enrique Méndez Vives, *Historia Uruguaya*, vol. 5, *El Uruguay de la modernización, 1876–1904* (Montevideo: Ediciones de la Banda Oriental, 1975), 24–9, 51–66, 96–106; Benjamín Nahum, *Historia Uruguaya*, vol. 6, *La época batllista, 1905–1929* (Montevideo: Ediciones de la Banda Oriental, 1975); Nahum, *Manual de historia del Uruguay*, vol. 1, *1830–1903* (Montevideo: Ediciones de la Banda Oriental, 2004), 228–45; M. H. J. Finch, *A Political Economy of Uruguay since 1870* (New York: St. Martin's Press, 1981). For comparative national statistics on the size of the urban population in Latin America, see Ruth Berins Collier and David Collier, *Shaping the Political Arena: Critical Junctures, the Labor Movement, and Regime Dynamics in Latin America* (Princeton, NJ: Princeton University Press, 1991), 66–7.

16. Carlos H. Waisman, *Reversal of Development in Argentina: Postwar Counterrevolutionary Policies and Their Structural Consequences* (Princeton, NJ: Princeton University Press, 1987), 3–11.

17. Ibid., 6; Maddison, "A Comparison of Levels of GDP Per Capita," 30. According to the Penn World Table, New Zealand's GDP per capita in 1950 was well above Argentina's.

18. This puzzle is discussed at length, with many citations, in Waisman, *Reversal of Development*, chaps. 1–2.

19. See, for example, the data in Waisman, *Reversal of Development*, 6, which indicate that Canada and Australia were slightly richer than Britain in 1913 and 1929.

20. However, Latin America may have performed better than the United States from 1870 to 1970. See Adam Przeworski (with Carolina Curvale), "Does Politics Explain the Economic Gap between the United States and Latin America?" in Francis Fukuyama, ed., *Falling Behind: Explaining the Development Gap between Latin America and the United States* (Oxford: Oxford University Press, 2008), 104–5. Przeworski and Curvale apparently derive their finding from Coatsworth, "Comparative Economic History," 10.

21. Bulmer-Thomas, *Economic History*, 444; Angus Maddison, *Monitoring the World Economy, 1820–1992* (Paris: Organization for Economic Cooperation and Development, 1995), 202.

22. Collier and Collier, *Shaping the Political Arena*, 66–7; Thorp, *Progress, Poverty and Exclusion*, 362–5.

23. The World Bank index is an outlier for the 1970–80 period in suggesting that Chile's level of development was at the regional average (and slightly lower than Costa Rica's). Given that on all other indicators of modernization Chile was much richer than the regional average, the World Bank estimates for this period seem much too low.

24. For an overview, see the essays in Guillermo Perry and Danny M. Leipziger, eds., *Chile: Recent Policy Lessons and Emerging Challenges* (Washington, DC: World Bank, 1999).

25. Thorp, *Progress, Poverty and Exclusion*, 75, 353; Maddison, *Monitoring the World Economy*, 202–3. For the history of oil revenues and development in Venezuela, see Jorge Salazar-Carrillo and Bernadette West, *Oil and Development in Venezuela during the 20th Century* (Westport, CT: Praeger, 2004).

26. Terry Lynn Karl, *The Paradox of Plenty: Oil Booms and Petro-States* (Berkeley: University of California Press, 1997).

27. Maddison, *Monitoring the World Economy*, 202.

28. John V. Lombardi, *Venezuela: The Search for Order, the Dream of Progress* (New York: Oxford University Press, 1982), 176–8.

29. Thorp, *Progress, Poverty and Exclusion*, 76.

30. Richard J. Salvucci and Linda K. Salvucci, "Las consecuencias económicas de la independencia Mexicana," in Leandro Prados de la Escosura and Samuel Amaral, eds., *La independencia americana: Consecuencias económicas* (Madrid: Alianza Editorial, 1993), 31–53.

31. Alan Knight, "Export-Led Growth in Mexico, c. 1900–30," in Enrique Cárdenas, José Antonio Ocampo, and Rosemary Thorp, eds., *An Economic History of Twentieth-Century Latin America*, vol. 1 (New York: Palgrave, 2000), 128.

32. Ibid., 129.

33. For example, estimates of early-twentieth-century levels of GDP per capita place Mexico above Peru and Colombia, but well below Argentina and Chile. See Bulmer-Thomas, *Economic History*, 444; Maddison, *Monitoring the World Economy*, 202; Thorp, *Progress, Poverty and Exclusion*, 353.

34. Maddison, *Monitoring the World Economy*, 202; Thorp, *Progress, Poverty and Exclusion*, 353.

35. Nora Hamilton, *The Limits of State Autonomy: Post-revolutionary Mexico* (Princeton, NJ: Princeton University Press, 1982), 178.

36. Rosemary Thorp and Geoffrey Bertram, *Peru, 1890–1977: Growth and Policy in an Open Economy* (London: Macmillan Press, 1978).

37. A seminal analysis is Paul Gootenberg, *Between Silver and Guano: Commercial Policy and the State in Postindependence Peru* (Princeton, NJ: Princeton University Press, 1989).

38. Paulo Drinot, "Peru, 1884–1930: A Beggar Sitting on a Bench of Gold?" in Cárdenas, Ocampo, and Thorp, *Economic History*, 1:152–87.

39. Thorp and Bertram, *Peru*.

40. Maddison, *Monitoring the World Economy*, 202; Thorp, *Progress, Poverty and Exclusion*, 353; André A. Hofman and Nanno Mulder, "The Comparative Productivity Performance of Brazil and Mexico," in Coatsworth and Taylor, *Latin America*, 88.

41. Historical background for this paragraph comes from José Antonio Ocampo, *Colombia y la economía mundial, 1830–1910* (Bogotá: Siglo XXI–Fedesarrollo, 1984); Jorge Orlando Melo, "La evolución de Colombia, 1830–1900," in Jaime Jaramillo Uribe, ed., *Manual de historia de Colombia*, vol. 2 (Bogotá: Tercer Mundo Editores, 1999), 135–207; David Bushnell, *The Making of Modern Colombia: A Nation in Spite of Itself* (Berkeley: University of California Press, 1993); Marco Palacios, *Coffee in Colombia, 1850–1970: An Economic, Social and Political History* (Cambridge: Cambridge University Press, 1980).

42. Victor Bulmer-Thomas, *The Political Economy of Central America since 1920* (Cambridge: Cambridge University Press, 1987), 10.

43. Dana G. Munro, *The Five Republics of Central America: Their Political and Economic Development and Their Relations with the United States* (New York: Oxford University Press, 1918), 139, 159.

44. John Patrick Bell, *Crisis in Costa Rica: The 1948 Revolution* (Austin: Institute of Latin American Studies, University of Texas Press, 1971); Ana Sojo, *Estado empresario y lucha política en Costa Rica* (San José: EDUCA, 1984); Jorge Mas Rovira, *Estado y política económica en Costa Rica, 1948–1970* (San José: Editorial Porvenir, 1988); Anthony Winson, "One Road to Democracy with Development: José Figueres and the Social Democratic Project after 1948," in John M. Kirk and George W. Schuler, eds., *Central America: Democracy, Development, and Change* (New York: Praeger, 1988), 89–100.

45. Herbert S. Klein, *A Concise History of Bolivia* (Cambridge: Cambridge University Press, 2003), 148.

46. Background for this paragraph is from ibid.; Manuel E. Contreras, "Bolivia, 1900–39: Mining, Railways and Education," in Cárdenas, Ocampo, and Thorp, *Economic History*, 1:188–216.

47. Jonathan Kelley and Herbert S. Klein, *Revolution and the Rebirth of Inequality: A Theory Applied to the National Revolution in Bolivia* (Berkeley: University of California Press, 1981), 103–4.

48. Thorp, *Progress, Poverty and Exclusion*, 353.

49. Allen Gerlach, *Indians, Oil, and Politics: A Recent History of Ecuador* (Wilmington, DE: Scholarly Resources, 2003); David W. Schodt, *Ecuador: An Andean Enigma* (Boulder, CO: Westview Press, 1987), chap. 5.

50. Harris Gaylord Warren (with the assistance of Katherine F. Warren), *Paraguay and the Triple Alliance: The Postwar Decade, 1869–1878* (Austin: Institute of Latin American Studies, University of Texas at Austin, 1978); Joseph Pincus, *The Economy of Paraguay* (New York: Praeger, 1968), chap. 1; Daniel Seyler, "Growth and Structure of the Economy," in Sandra W. Meditz and Dennis M. Hanratty, eds., *Paraguay: A Country Study* (Washington, DC: U.S. Government Printing Office, 1990).

51. Paul H. Lewis, *Paraguay under Stroessner* (Chapel Hill: University of North Carolina Press, 1980).

52. Werner Baer and Melissa H. Birch, "Expansion of the Economic Frontier: Paraguayan Growth in the 1970s," *World Development* 12, no. 8 (1984):

783–98; Werner Baer and Luis Breuer, "From Inward- to Outward-Oriented Growth: Paraguay in the 1980s," *Journal of Interamerican Studies and World Affairs* 28, no. 3 (Autumn 1986): 125–40.

53. Compare, for example, Thorp's data for GDP per capita with her data for infrastructure per capita. Thorp, *Progress, Poverty and Exclusion*, 353, 362–5. I explore the liberal reform period in James Mahoney, *The Legacies of Liberalism: Path Dependence and Political Regimes in Central America* (Baltimore: Johns Hopkins University Press, 2001).

54. Bulmer-Thomas, *Political Economy*.

55. Robert G. Williams, *Export Agriculture and the Crisis in Central America* (Chapel Hill: University of North Carolina Press, 1994).

56. The literature on U.S. intervention and the Central American crisis is vast. For an entry into it, see Mahoney, *Legacies of Liberalism*, 345–6 n. 65.

57. For a recent work on the topic, with many other references, see Richard Sandbrook, Marc Edelman, Patrick Heller, and Judith Teichman, *Social Democracy in the Global Periphery: Origins, Challenges, Prospects* (Cambridge: Cambridge University Press, 2006).

58. James Mahoney, "Long-Run Development and the Legacy of Colonialism in Spanish America," *American Journal of Sociology* 109, no. 1 (July 2003): 59–61.

59. John Gerring, "Global Justice as an Empirical Question," *PS: Political Science and Politics* 40, no. 1 (January 2007): 67–78.

60. The Gender-Related Development Index from the United Nations' *Human Development Report* is a composite indicator that measures the average achievement of a population in the same dimensions as the HDI while adjusting for gender inequalities. It thus uses the same variables as the HDI, disaggregated by gender. The ranking and scores for the Spanish American countries for this index in 2004 are as follows:

1. Argentina (.859)
2. Chile (.850)
3. Uruguay (.847)
4. Costa Rica (.831)
5. Mexico (.812)
6. Colombia (.787)
7. Venezuela (.780)
8. Peru (.759)
9. El Salvador (.725)
10. Bolivia (.687)
11. Nicaragua (.684)
12. Honduras (.676)
13. Guatemala (.659)

There are no data for Ecuador and Paraguay. See United Nations, *Human Development Report, 2006* (New York: United Nations, 2006).

61. Ibid.

62. The discussion in this section draws generally on Thorp, *Progress, Poverty and Exclusion*; United Nations, *Human Development Report*.

63. Colin M. MacLachlan and Jaime E. Rodríguez O., *The Forging of the Cosmic Race: A Reinterpretation of Colonial Mexico* (Berkeley: University of California Press, 1980).

64. Jim Handy, *Gift of the Devil: A History of Guatemala* (Boston: South End Press, 1984), 278.

65. I discuss this period and reasons for its failure in Mahoney, *Legacies of Liberalism*, 212–16.

66. Klein, *Concise History of Bolivia*, 250.

67. Mahoney, *Legacies of Liberalism*, chap. 7.

68. Raghuram G. Rajan and Luigi Zingales, "The Persistence of Underdevelopment: Institutions, Human Capital, or Constituencies?" (Centre for Economic Policy Research, Discussion Paper No. 5867, October 2006), 2.

Chapter 7. British and Portuguese Colonialism

1. Daron Acemoglu, Simon Johnson, and James A. Robinson, "The Colonial Origins of Comparative Development: An Empirical Investigation," *American Economic Review* 91, no. 5 (December 2001): 1369–1401; Stanley L. Engerman and Kenneth L. Sokoloff, "Factor Endowments, Inequality, and Paths of Development among New World Economies," *Economia* 3 (Fall 2002): 41–88; Daron Acemoglu, Simon Johnson, and James A. Robinson, "Reversal of Fortune: Geography and Institutions in the Making of the Modern World Income Distribution," *Quarterly Journal of Economics* 117, no. 4 (November 2002): 1231–94.

2. In their influential book *British Imperialism, 1688–2000* (London: Longman, 1993), P. J. Cain and A. G. Hopkins link "gentlemanly capitalism" to British imperial expansion. But for a telling critique of Cain and Hopkins, see Geoffrey Ingham, "British Capitalism: Empire, Merchants and Decline," *Social History* 20, no. 3 (October 1995): 339–54.

3. Peter Zagorin, "The Social Interpretation of the English Revolution," *Journal of Economic History* 19, no. 3 (September 1959): 401. On this interpretation, see also Lawrence Stone, *The Causes of the English Revolution, 1529–1642* (London: Routledge & Kegan Paul, 1972), 146–7. For a more recent look at cultural changes in Britain in the late seventeenth century, see Alan Houston and Steve Pincus, eds., *A Nation Transformed: England after the Restoration* (Cambridge: Cambridge University Press, 2001).

4. Here is not the place to engage the theoretical controversies in the huge literature on the causes of the English Revolution. I have sought to report points of agreement between earlier Marxist writers, such as Christopher Hill in *The Century of Revolution* (New York: Norton, 1961), and their "Whig" critics, such as Lawrence Stone in *Causes of the English Revolution*. I have also tried to be sensitive to the concerns of scholars who argue that there were only minimal changes, such as G. R. Elton in *England under the Tudors*, 3rd ed. (London: Routledge, 1991). Although now slightly dated, Goldstone's coverage and discussion of the broader literature remain excellent. See Jack A. Goldstone, *Revolution and Rebellion in the Early Modern World* (Berkeley: University of California Press, 1991), chap. 2.

5. C. G. A. Clay, *Economic Expansion and Social Change: England, 1500–1700*, vol. 2 (Cambridge: Cambridge University Press, 1984), 200.

6. D. K. Fieldhouse, *The Colonial Empires: A Comparative Survey from the Eighteenth Century* (New York: Dell, 1966), 67–8.

7. Acemoglu, Johnson, and Robinson, "Colonial Origins"; Jeffrey D. Sachs, "Tropical Underdevelopment" (National Bureau of Economic Research, Working Paper No. 8119, 2001); Edward L. Glaeser, Rafael La Porta, Florencio Lopez-de-Silanes, and Andrei Shleifer, "Do Institutions Cause Growth?" *Journal of Economic Growth* 9, no. 3 (September 2004): 271–303; Matthew D. Fails and Jonathan Krieckhaus, "Constitutive British Colonialism and the Modern World Income Distribution" (manuscript, June 2007); Ola Olsson, "On the Institutional Legacy of Mercantilist and Imperialist Colonialism" (Working Papers in Economics No. 247, School of Business, Economics, and Law, Göteborg University, March 2007).

8. Matthew Lange, *Lineages of Despotism and Development: British Colonialism and State Power* (Chicago: University of Chicago Press, 2009).

9. An example is Niall Ferguson, *Empire: The Rise and Demise of the British World Order and the Lessons for Global Power* (New York: Basic Books, 2002).

10. Donald Denoon, *Settler Capitalism: The Dynamics of Dependent Development in the Southern Hemisphere* (Oxford: Oxford University Press, 1983).

11. Douglass C. North, *Institutions, Institutional Change, and Economic Performance* (New York: Cambridge University Press, 1990). See also Morton Horwitz, *The Transformation of American Law, 1780–1860* (Cambridge, MA: Harvard University Press, 1977).

12. Jeremy Adelman, *Frontier Development: Land, Labour, and Capital on the Wheatlands of Argentina and Canada, 1890–1914* (Oxford: Clarendon Press, 1994); Carl E. Solberg, *The Prairies and the Pampas: Agrarian Policy in Canada and Argentina, 1880–1930* (Stanford, CA: Stanford University Press, 1987).

13. Donald Denoon and Philippa Mein-Smith, *A History of Australia, New Zealand, and the Pacific* (Oxford: Blackwell, 2000); Douglas Pike, *Australia: The Quiet Continent* (Cambridge: Cambridge University Press, 1970).

14. The British colonies in Africa correspond closely with areas that Oliver and Atmore identify as having been African states in 1884. See Roland Anthony Oliver and Anthony Atmore, *Africa since 1800*, 2nd ed. (Cambridge: Cambridge University Press, 1972), 106–7. See also Robert O. Collins, James McDonald Burns, and Erik Kristofer Ching, eds., *Historical Problems of Imperial Africa* (Princeton, NJ: Markus Wiener, 1994), 6D. More generally, I judge African societies to have been complex and populous in light of other precolonial societies, including those of Latin America in roughly 1500. Given this frame of comparison, precolonial Africa was actually more populated than precolonial Latin America. For example, sub-Saharan Africa in 1900 had 4.4 persons per square kilometer, whereas Latin America in 1500 had only 2.2 persons. See Jeffrey Herbst, *States and Power in Africa: Comparative Lessons in Authority and Control* (Princeton, NJ: Princeton University Press, 2000), 16.

15. See, for example, Edward A. Alpers, *Ivory and Slaves: Changing Pattern of International Trade in East Central Africa to the Later Nineteenth Century* (Berkeley: University of California Press, 1975); Michael Crowder, *West Africa under Colonial Rule* (London: Hutchinson, 1968); H. A. Ibrahim, "African Initiatives and Resistance in North-East Africa," in A. Adu Boahen, ed., *General History of*

Africa, vol. 7, *Africa under Colonial Domination, 1880–1935* (Berkeley: University of California Press, 1985), 63–86; M. H. Y. Kaniki, "The Colonial Economy: The Former British Zones," in Boahen, *General History of Africa*, vol. 7, *Africa under Colonial Domination, 1880–1935*, 382–419; Oliver and Atmore, *Africa since 1800*; Richard D. Wolff, *The Economics of Colonialism: Britain and Kenya, 1870–1930* (New Haven, CT: Yale University Press, 1974); Christopher Wrigley, *Kingship and State: The Buganda Dynasty* (New York: Cambridge University Press, 1996).

16. Lange, *Lineages of Despotism*, makes this argument, building on especially Mahmood Mamdani, *Citizen and Subject: Contemporary Africa and the Legacy of Late Colonialism* (Princeton, NJ: Princeton University Press, 1996). On indirect rule in Africa, see also J. D. Fage, *A History of Africa*, 4th ed. (New York: Routledge, 2002); Robert W. July, *A History of the African People*, 5th ed. (Prospect Heights, IL: Waveland Press, 1998); Irving Leonard Markovitz, *Power and Class in Africa* (Englewood Cliffs, NJ: Prentice Hall, 1977).

17. David Laitin, *Hegemony and Culture: Politics and Religious Change among the Yoruba* (Chicago: University of Chicago Press, 1986); Ann Stoler and Frederick Cooper, "Between Metropole and Colony: Rethinking a Research Agenda," in Frederick Cooper and Ann Stoler, eds., *Tensions of Empire: Colonial Cultures in a Bourgeois World* (Berkeley: University of California Press, 1997), 1–58; LeRoy Vail, ed., *The Creation of Tribalism in Southern Africa* (Berkeley: University of California Press, 1989).

18. Mamdani, *Citizen and Subject*; Robert H. Bates, *Markets and States in Tropical Africa: The Political Basis of Agricultural Policies* (Berkeley: University of California Press, 1981); Catherine Boone, "States and Ruling Classes in Postcolonial Africa: The Enduring Contradictions of Power," in Joel Migdal, Atul Kohli, and Vivienne Shue, eds., *State Power and Social Forces: Domination and Transformation in the Third World* (New York: Cambridge University Press, 1994), 108–40; Joel S. Migdal, *Strong Societies and Weak States: State-Society Relations and State Capabilities in the Third World* (Princeton, NJ: Princeton University Press, 1988); Crawford Young, *The African Colonial State in Comparative Perspective* (New Haven, CT: Yale University Press, 1994).

19. Lange, *Lineages of Despotism*, 4.

20. David W. Galenson, "The Settlement and Growth of the Colonies: Population, Labor, and Economic Development," in Stanley L. Engerman and Robert E. Gallman, eds., *The Cambridge Economic History of the United States* (Cambridge: Cambridge University Press, 1996), 135–207.

21. Gordon K. Lewis, *The Growth of the Modern West Indies* (New York: Monthly Review, 1968).

22. Background for this paragraph is from Barbara Leitch LePoer, ed., *Singapore: A Country Study* (Washington, DC: Library of Congress, 1991); Tak-Wing Ngo, ed., *Hong Kong's History: State and Society under Colonial Rule* (New York: Routledge, 1999); Elfred Roberts, Sum Ngai Ling, and Peter Bradshaw, *Historical Dictionary of Hong Kong and Macau* (Metuchen, NJ: Scarecrow Press, 1992); N. J. Ryan, *A History of Malaysia and Singapore* (New York: Oxford University Press, 1976).

23. Fails and Krieckhaus, "Constitutive British Colonialism," 14.

24. On this case, see Chandra Richard de Silva, *Sri Lanka: A History* (New Delhi: Vikas, 1997); Charles Jeffries, *Ceylon: The Path to Independence* (London: Pall Mall Press, 1962); Richard Nyrop, Beryl Benderly, Ann Cort, Newton Parker, James Perlmutter, Rinn-Sup Shinn, and Mary Shivanandan, *Area Handbook for Ceylon* (Washington, DC: U.S. Government Printing Office, 1971).

25. A classic comparative discussion of Sri Lankan social development is John C. Caldwell, "Routes to Low Mortality in Poor Countries," *Population and Development Review* 12, no. 2 (June 1986): 171–220.

26. Historical background for this paragraph is from C. A. Bayly, *The New Cambridge History of India: Indian Society and the Making of the British Empire* (Cambridge: Cambridge University Press, 1988); Hermann Kulke and Dietmar Rothermund, *A History of India* (New York: Routledge, 1998); R. P. Masani, *Britain in India* (London: Oxford University Press, 1960); Eric Stokes, "The First Century of British Colonial Rule in India: Social Revolution or Social Stagnation?" *Past and Present* 58, no. 1 (1973): 136–60.

27. Atul Kohli, *State-Directed Development: Political Power and Industrialization in the Global Periphery* (Cambridge: Cambridge University Press, 2004), 225–7; Dharma Kumar, *Colonialism, Property and the State* (Delhi: Oxford University Press, 1998); P. J. Marshall, *Problems of Empire: Britain and India, 1757–1813* (New York: Barnes & Noble, 1968).

28. By contrast, Nigeria – which had the fewest officials per capita in British Africa – had a ratio of 1:51,800 in the 1930s. Michael Fisher, *Indirect Rule in India: Residents and the Residency System* (Delhi: Oxford University Press, 1991), 8.

29. Michael Edwardes, *British India, 1772–1947: A Survey of the Nature and Effects of Alien Rule* (London: Sidgwick & Jackson, 1967), 75–9; Ram Gopal, *British Rule in India: An Assessment* (New York: Asia Publishing House, 1963); V. B. Kulkarni, *British Dominion in India and After* (Bombay: Bharatiya Vidya Bhavan, 1964), 153; Kumar, *Colonialism, Property and the State.*

30. Abhijit Banerjee and Lakshmi Iyer, "History, Institutions and Economic Performance: The Legacy of Colonial Land Tenure Systems in India" (Bureau for Research and Economic Analysis of Development, Working Paper No. 003, 2003).

31. Peter B. Evans, *Embedded Autonomy: States and Industrial Transformation* (Princeton, NJ: Princeton University Press, 1995). See also Vivek Chibber, *Locked in Place: State Building and Late Industrialization in India* (Princeton, NJ: Princeton University Press, 2003).

32. On the colonial history of Malaya, see Ian Brown and Rajeswary Ampalavanar, *Malaysia* (Denver, CO: Clio Press, 1986); Robert Heussler, *British Rule in Malaya: The Malayan Civil Service and Its Predecessors, 1867–1942* (Westport, CT: Greenwood Press, 1981); Zawawi Ibrahim, *The Malay Labourer: By the Window of Capitalism* (Singapore: Stamford Press, 1998); Ryan, *History of Malaysia and Singapore.*

33. T. A. Harper, *The End of Empire and the Making of Malaya* (Cambridge: Cambridge University Press, 1999); K. S. Jomo, ed., *Industrializing Malaysia: Policy, Performance, Prospects* (New York: Routledge, 1993).

34. Mamdani, *Citizen and Subject.*

35. Lange, *Lineages of Despotism*, 55–62.

36. For background on Portugal during the fifteenth and sixteenth centuries, I consulted A. H. de Oliveira Marques, *History of Portugal*, vol. 1, *From Lusitania to Empire* (New York: Columbia University Press, 1972); Stanley G. Payne, *A History of Spain and Portugal*, vol. 1 (Madison: University of Wisconsin Press, 1973). On Portugal's overall colonial project at this time, see C. R. Boxer, *The Portuguese Seaborne Empire, 1415–1825* (New York: Knopf, 1969), chaps. 1–3; Bailey W. Diffie and George D. Winius, *Foundations of the Portuguese Empire, 1415–1580* (Minneapolis: University of Minnesota Press, 1977).

37. David Birmingham, *The Portuguese Conquest of Angola* (London: Oxford University Press, 1965); Gerald Bender, *Angola under the Portuguese: The Myth and the Reality* (Berkeley: University of California Press, 1978).

38. James Duffy, *Portugal in Africa* (Cambridge, MA: Harvard University Press, 1962), chap. 3.

39. See the data in Instituto Brasileiro de Geografia e Estatística, *Estatísticas do século XX* (Rio de Janeiro: IBGE, 2003).

40. For three different estimates of Brazil's midcentury GDP per capita, see Angus Maddison, "A Comparison of Levels of GDP Per Capita in the Developed and Developing Countries, 1700–1980," *Journal of Economic History* 43 (1983): 30; Alan Heston, Robert Summers, and Bettina Aten, "Penn World Table Version 6.2" (Center for International Comparisons of Production, Income and Prices at the University of Pennsylvania, September 2006); Rosemary Thorp, *Progress, Poverty and Exclusion: An Economic History of Latin America in the 20th Century* (New York: Inter-American Development Bank, 1998), 353.

41. Stefan H. Robock, *Brazil's Developing Northeast* (Washington, DC: Brookings Institution, 1963), 1.

42. James Lockhart and Stuart B. Schwartz, *Early Latin America: A History of Colonial Spanish America and Brazil* (Cambridge: Cambridge University Press, 1983), 181.

43. For a discussion of various population estimates, see John Hemming, *Red Gold: The Conquest of the Brazilian Indians* (London: Macmillan, 1978), 487–92. Hemming's own estimate is 2,431,000 (p. 492).

44. For descriptions of several different indigenous groups in precolonial Brazil, see Julian H. Steward, ed., *Handbook of South American Indians*, vol. 1, *The Marginal Tribes* (Washington, DC: U.S. Government Printing Office, 1946), pt. 3, "The Indians of Eastern Brazil," pp. 381–574.

45. H. B. Johnson, "Portuguese Settlement, 1500–1580," in Leslie Bethell, ed., *Colonial Brazil* (Cambridge: Cambridge University Press, 1987), 31. For a good comparison with Spanish America at this time, see Stuart B. Schwartz, "Cities of Empire: Mexico and Bahia in the Sixteenth Century," *Journal of Inter-American Studies* 11, no. 4 (October 1969): 616–37.

46. Stuart B. Schwartz, "Indian Labor and New World Plantations: European Demands and Indian Responses in Northeastern Brazil," *American Historical Review* 83, no. 1 (February 1978): 43–79.

47. "In the first two centuries of colonization, the Northeast, with its two sugar ports of Bahia and Recife, was Brazil's economic and social center." Kit Sims Taylor, *Sugar and the Underdevelopment of Northeastern Brazil, 1500–1970* (Gainesville: University Presses of Florida, 1978), 7.

48. On the reasons why certain regions succeeded or failed at sugarcane cultivation, see Stuart B. Schwartz, *Sugar Plantations in the Formation of Brazilian Society: Bahia, 1550–1835* (Cambridge: Cambridge University Press, 1985), 17–22; Schwartz, "Plantations and Peripheries, c. 1580–c. 1750," in Bethell, *Colonial Brazil*, 69–71.

49. Johnson, "Portuguese Settlement," 31, 37; Schwartz, *Sugar Plantations*, 165, 168.

50. Schwartz, *Sugar Plantations*, 168.

51. Maria Luiza Marcílio, "The Population of Colonial Brazil," in Leslie Bethell, ed., *The Cambridge History of Latin America*, vol. 2, *Colonial Latin America* (Cambridge: Cambridge University Press, 1984), 45–7; James Lang, *Portuguese Brazil: The King's Plantation* (New York: Academic Press, 1979), 56.

52. Philip D. Curtin, *The Atlantic Slave Trade: A Census* (Madison: University of Wisconsin Press, 1969), 119. For a discussion of alternative (and even higher) estimates, see Robert Edgar Conrad, *World of Sorrow: The African Slave Trade to Brazil* (Baton Rouge: Louisiana State University Press, 1986), 28–9.

53. By 1724, Salvador had a population of twenty-five thousand, and it grew to forty thousand by 1750. Schwartz, "Plantations and Peripheries," 128; see also A. J. R. Russell-Wood, "Ports of Colonial Brazil," in Franklin W. Knight and Peggy K. Liss, eds., *Atlantic Port Cities: Economy, Culture, and Society in the Atlantic World, 1650–1850* (Knoxville: University of Tennessee Press, 1991), 222.

54. A vivid description of colonial Salvador is found in C. R. Boxer, *The Golden Age of Brazil, 1695–1750: Growing Pains of a Colonial Society* (Berkeley: University of California Press, 1962), chap. 6.

55. Schwartz, *Sugar Plantations*, chap. 6. A discussion of much of the relevant secondary literature can also be found in Anthony W. Marx, *Making Race and Nation: A Comparison of the United States, South Africa, and Brazil* (Cambridge: Cambridge University Press, 1998), 48–55.

56. Schwartz, *Sugar Plantations*, 272–4.

57. A. J. R. Russell-Wood, "Class, Creed and Colour in Colonial Bahia: A Study in Prejudice," *Race* 9, no. 2 (October 1967): 149.

58. "From the beginning, the Portuguese crown monopolized and controlled the Brazilian commodity export trade." John R. Hall, "The Patrimonial Dynamic in Colonial Brazil," in Richard Graham, ed., *Brazil and the World System* (Austin: University of Texas Press, 1991), 77.

59. Taylor, *Sugar*, 39–40; Schwartz, "Plantations and Peripheries," 93–5.

60. Taylor, *Sugar*, 67–8.

61. David Grant Smith, "The Mercantile Class of Portugal and Brazil in the Seventeenth Century: A Socio-economic Study of the Merchants of Lisbon and Bahia, 1620–1690" (PhD diss., University of Texas at Austin, 1975), chap. 10; Rae Flory and David Grant Smith, "Bahian Merchants and Planters in the Seventeenth and Eighteenth Centuries," *Hispanic American Historical Review* 58, no. 4 (November 1978): 571–94.

62. Smith, "Mercantile Class," chap. 5; Lang, *Portuguese Brazil*, 31–3, 101–2, 105–6.

63. Smith, "Mercantile Class," 161. In his concluding chapter, Smith also discusses reasons why Lisbon merchants were notoriously anti-entrepreneurial.

64. Taylor, *Sugar*, 38.

65. Dauril Alden, "Late Colonial Brazil, 1750–1808," in Bethell, *Colonial Brazil*, 314–16.

66. "There is every indication that during the long period between the last quarter of the seventeenth and the beginning of the nineteenth century, the economy of the Northeast underwent a slow process of atrophy, in the sense that the real per capita income of the population declined steadily with the passing of time." Celso Furtado, *The Economic Growth of Brazil: A Survey from Colonial to Modern Times*, trans. Ricardo W. de Aguiar and Eric Charles Drysdale (Berkeley: University of California Press, 1963), 69.

67. The white population there reached over seventy-five thousand by 1776 (starting from almost nothing at the beginning of the century). Laird W. Bergad, *Slavery and the Demographic and Economic History of Minas Gerais, Brazil, 1720–1888* (Cambridge: Cambridge University Press, 1999), 82, 91.

68. In the period from 1735 to 1760, an estimated 160,000 slaves entered Minas Gerais. Marcílio, "Population of Colonial Brazil," 53. See also Bergad, *Slavery*, 83–92.

69. Alden, "Late Colonial Brazil," 286. A slightly different population estimate is given in Bergad, *Slavery*, 91.

70. A. J. R. Russell-Wood, "The Gold Cycle, c. 1690–1750," in Bethell, *Colonial Brazil*, 203–13, 227–31.

71. Lang, *Portuguese Brazil*, 125.

72. Ibid., 132.

73. A. J. R. Russell-Wood, "Colonial Brazil," in David W. Cohen and Jack P. Greene, eds., *Neither Slave nor Free: The Freedman of African Descent in the Slave Societies of the New World* (Baltimore: Johns Hopkins University Press, 1972), 85–98. On manumission specifically in Bahia, see also Stuart B. Schwartz, "The Manumission of Slaves in Colonial Brazil: Bahia, 1684–1745," *Hispanic American Historical Review* 54, no. 4 (November 1974): 603–35.

74. Lockhart and Schwartz, *Early Latin America*, 376; Bergad, *Slavery*, 4.

75. Background for this paragraph is from Kenneth Maxwell, *Pombal: Paradox of the Enlightenment* (Cambridge: Cambridge University Press, 1995); Maxwell, *Conflicts and Conspiracies: Brazil and Portugal, 1750–1808* (New York: Routledge, 2004); Payne, *History of Spain and Portugal*, 405–14; Andrée Mansuy-Diniz Silvia, "Imperial Re-organization, 1750–1808," in Bethell, *Colonial Brazil*, 244–83.

76. de Oliveira Marques, *History of Portugal*, 1:403–4.

77. Alden, "Late Colonial Brazil," 288.

78. Ibid., 286–7; Marcílio, "Population of Colonial Brazil," 63. A good feel for life in Rio de Janeiro during the 1808–21 period can be gained from Kirsten Schultz, *Tropical Versailles: Empire, Monarchy, and the Portuguese Royal Court in Rio de Janeiro, 1808–1821* (New York: Routledge, 2001).

79. For comparisons of Rio de Janeiro and Buenos Aires, see Jeremy Adelman, *Sovereignty and Revolution in the Iberian Atlantic* (Princeton, NJ: Princeton University Press, 2006), esp. chap. 6; Harold B. Johnson Jr., "A Preliminary Inquiry into Money, Prices, and Wages in Rio de Janeiro, 1763–1823," in Dauril Alden, ed., *Colonial Roots of Modern Brazil* (Berkeley: University of California Press, 1973), 260–7.

80. For data on the racial composition of the urban population of Brazil in 1872, see Thomas W. Merrick and Douglas H. Graham, *Population and Economic Development in Brazil: 1800 to the Present* (Baltimore: Johns Hopkins University Press, 1979), 70.

81. Caio Prado Jr., *The Colonial Background of Modern Brazil*, trans. Suzette Macedo (Berkeley: University of California Press, 1967), 154–5. On agriculture in these regions, see pp. 148–79 more generally; see also Alden, "Late Colonial Brazil," 310–36.

82. John H. Coatsworth, "Economic and Institutional Trajectories in Nineteenth-Century Latin America," in John H. Coatsworth and Alan M. Taylor, eds., *Latin America and the World Economy since 1800* (Cambridge, MA: Harvard University Press, 1998), 29; Angus Maddison, *Monitoring the World Economy, 1820–1992* (Paris: Organization for Economic Cooperation and Development, 1995), 202.

Chapter 8. Conclusion

1. Paul Bairoch, *Economics and World History: Myths and Paradoxes* (New York: Harvester, 1993), 88.

2. As Skocpol notes, the use of general theory is inherently "subject to charges of tailoring historical presentations to fit a preconceived theory." Theda Skocpol, "Emerging Agendas and Recurrent Strategies in Historical Sociology," in Theda Skocpol, ed., *Vision and Method in Historical Sociology* (Cambridge: Cambridge University Press, 1984), 366.

3. This approach to thinking about causal combinations as "layers" brings together the work of Charles Ragin with recent methodological writings on temporal analysis by scholars such as Ruth Berins Collier and David Collier, Paul Pierson, and Kathleen Thelen. See Charles Ragin, *The Comparative Method: Moving beyond Qualitative and Quantitative Strategies* (Berkeley: University of California Press, 1987); Ruth Berins Collier and David Collier, *Shaping the Political Arena: Critical Junctures, the Labor Movement, and Regime Dynamics in Latin America* (Princeton, NJ: Princeton University Press, 1991); Paul Pierson, *Politics in Time: History, Institutions, and Social Analysis* (Princeton, NJ: Princeton University Press, 2004); Kathleen Thelen, *How Institutions Evolve: The Political Economy of Skills in Germany, Britain, the United States, and Japan* (Cambridge: Cambridge University Press, 2004).

4. Charles Tilly, *Durable Inequality* (Berkeley: University of California Press, 1998).

5. Daron Acemoglu, Simon Johnson, and James A. Robinson, "Reversal of Fortune: Geography and Institutions in the Making of the Modern World Income Distribution," *Quarterly Journal of Economics* 117, no. 4 (November 2002): 1235.

6. This also explains why statistical models find that results change when one controls for the timing of the colonial experience (e.g., before 1700 vs. after 1700). See James Feyrer and Bruce Sacerdote, "Colonialism and Modern Income: Islands as Natural Experiments" (National Bureau of Economic Research, Working Paper No. 12546, September 2006); Ola Olsson, "On the Institutional Legacy of Mercantilist and Imperialist Colonialism" (Working Papers in Economics No. 247, School of Business, Economics, and Law, Göteborg University, March 2007).

7. Daron Acemoglu, Simon Johnson, and James A. Robinson, "The Colonial Origins of Comparative Development: An Empirical Investigation," *American Economic Review* 91, no. 5 (December 2001): 1369–1401.

8. Stanley L. Engerman and Kenneth L. Sokoloff, "Factor Endowments, Inequality, and Paths of Development among New World Economies," *Economia* 3 (Fall 2002): 51.

9. Ibid.

10. Mahmood Mamdani, *Citizen and Subject: Contemporary Africa and the Legacy of Late Colonialism* (Princeton, NJ: Princeton University Press, 1996).

11. This insight comes from Alexander Gerschenkron, *Economic Backwardness in Historical Perspective* (Cambridge, MA: Belknap Press of Harvard University Press, 1962).

12. On the Japanese industrial model, see Chalmers Johnson, *MITI and the Japanese Miracle: The Growth of Industrial Policy, 1925–1975* (Stanford, CA: Stanford University Press, 1982); Daniel I. Okimoto, *Between MITI and the Market: Japanese Industrial Policy for High Technology* (Stanford, CA: Stanford University Press, 1989). On this model and its variants as engines of growth, see the classic works in the "state-centric" literature on development, including Peter B. Evans, *Embedded Autonomy: States and Industrial Transformation* (Princeton, NJ: Princeton University Press, 1995); Peter J. Katzenstein, *Small States in World Markets: Industrial Policy in Europe* (Ithaca, NY: Cornell University Press, 1985); Dietrich Rueschemeyer and Peter Evans, "The State and Economic Transformation: Toward an Analysis of the Conditions Underlying Effective Intervention," in Peter Evans, Theda Skocpol, and Dietrich Rueschemeyer, eds., *Bringing the State Back In* (Princeton, NJ: Princeton University Press, 1985), 44–78.

13. Alice Amsden, *Asia's Next Giant: South Korea and Late Industrialization* (New York: Oxford University Press, 1989); Thomas B. Gold, *State and Society in the Taiwan Miracle* (Armonk, NY: M. E. Sharpe, 1985); Atul Kohli, *State-Directed Development: Political Power and Industrialization in the Global Periphery* (Cambridge: Cambridge University Press, 2004); Robert Wade, *Governing the Market: Economic Theory and the Role of Government in East Asian Industrialization* (Princeton, NJ: Princeton University Press, 1990).

14. These changes in absolute levels of development occur because institutions are subject to gradual transformation over time. For a general framework aimed at explaining this gradual institutional change, see James Mahoney and Kathleen Thelen, "A Theory of Gradual Institutional Change," in James Mahoney and Kathleen Thelen, eds., *Explaining Institutional Change: Ambiguity, Agency, and Power* (New York: Cambridge University Press, 2010).

15. For two different, provocative arguments on the "inevitability" of a world state, see Alexander Wendt, "Why a World State Is Inevitable: Teleology and the Logic of Anarchy," *European Journal of International Relations* 9, no. 4 (December 2003): 491–542; Robert Wright, *Nonzero: The Logic of Human Destiny* (New York: Random House, 2000).

16. Peter Evans, "Collective Capabilities, Culture, and Amartya Sen's *Development as Freedom*," *Studies in Comparative International Development* 37, no. 2 (Summer 2002): 54–60.

Glossary

The following glossary provides a short definition for the Spanish, Portuguese, and indigenous-language terms that appear in the text.

aguardiente: alcohol derived from sugarcane

alcabala: sales tax

alcalde mayor: official appointed to oversee Spanish and indigenous towns

alcaldía mayor: administrative district

almojarifazgo: customs duty

audiencia: territory of a judicial body charged with broad governance tasks (and the judicial body itself)

aviador: silver merchant

ayllu: familial and kinship group

ayuntamiento: town council

azoguero: owner of a silver mine and refinery

bandeirante: leader of an expedition to acquire indigenous slaves

cabildo: town council

cacao: plant used to make chocolate

cacique: indigenous community leader

cazonci: king

coca: narcotic plant used recreationally in the Andes

concierto: resident hacienda worker

congregación: town of resettled indigenous people

consulado: merchant guild

corregidor: official appointed to oversee Spanish and indigenous towns

corregimiento: administrative district

Creole: Spaniard born in the New World

diezmo: tax of one-tenth on gold and silver mined in the New World

encomendero: holder of an encomienda

encomienda: grant providing the right to tribute and/or labor from a group of indigenous people

encomienda originaria: grant providing the right to use indigenous people as personal servants

engenho: sugar mill

estancia: large cattle estate

estanciero: owner of an estancia

flota: fleet that sailed between Seville and Veracruz

forastero: indigenous person living outside his or her home community

fuero: special privilege or exemption for the church

galeones: fleet that sailed beween Seville and Cartagena and between Seville and Panama

gaucho: cowboy in Argentina, Uruguay, or southern Brazil

gobierno: governship within an audiencia

guano: fertilizer derived from bird droppings

hacendado: owner of a hacienda

hacienda: large agricultural estate

hidalgo: untitled gentleman

inquilino: agricultural tenant who pays rent with labor

kuraka: indigenous community leader

ladino: individual of mixed Spanish and indigenous ancestry

limeño: resident of Lima

llanos: plains of southern Venezuela

mayordomo: resident boss on a hacienda

mazamorrero: independent mining prospector

merced: land grant

minga: wage laborer in mines of Potosí

mita: forced-labor draft system applied to indigenous people

mitayo: indigenous person subject to the mita

mulato: individual of African and European ancestry

Nahuatl: dominant language of the Aztecs

obraje: textile mill

obraje de comunidad: textile mill on indigenous land

palenque: village of runaway slaves

pampas: plains of Argentina

paño azul: indigo-dyed fabric

pardo: individual of African and European ancestry

peninsular: Spaniard born in Iberia

plata: silver

porteño: resident of Buenos Aires

provincia: province within an audiencia

pueblo: indigenous town

Quechua: dominant language of the Inca Empire

quinto: tax of one-fifth on gold and silver mined in the New World

reducción: town of resettled indigenous people

regimiento: seat on the town council

repartimiento: forced-labor draft applied to indigenous people

senhor de engenho: owner of a sugar mill

sertão: desert region of Northeast Brazil

tevií: familial and kinship group

tithe: tax of one-tenth on agricultural production, to support the church

yanacona: individual who serves under a yanaconazgo; sometimes applied to indigenous workers more generally

yanaconazgo: grant providing the right to use indigenous people as servants

yerba: plant used to make an herbal tea

zambo: individual of African and indigenous ancestry

Select Bibliography of Works on Colonial Spanish America

The following bibliography lists the historical studies of colonial Spanish America that are cited primarily in Chapters 2, 3, and 4. References to the various works on theory and method, postcolonial Spanish America, and British and Portuguese colonialism from the other chapters are found in the endnotes.

Acosta Saignes, Miguel. *Vida de los esclavos negros en Venezuela*. Caracas: Hesperides, 1967.

_____. *Estudios de etnología antigua de Venezuela*. Caracas: Universidad Central de Venezuela, 1961.

Acuña Ortega, Víctor Hugo. "Historia económica del tabaco: Época colonial." *Anuario de Estudios Centroamericanos* 4 (1979): 279–392.

Acuña Ortega, Víctor Hugo, and Iván Molina Jiménez. *Historia económica y social de Costa Rica (1750–1950)*. San José: Editorial Porvenir, 1991.

Adelman, Jeremy. *Sovereignty and Revolution in the Iberian Atlantic*. Princeton, NJ: Princeton University Press, 2006.

_____. *Frontier Development: Land, Labour, and Capital on the Wheatlands of Argentina and Canada, 1890–1914*. Oxford: Clarendon Press, 1994.

Albi Romero, Guadalupe. "La sociedad de Puebla de los Angeles en el siglo XVI." *Jahrbuch für Geschichte von Staat, Wirtschaft und Gesellschaft Lateinamerikas* 7 (1970): 73–145.

Alchon, Suzanne Austin. *Native Society and Disease in Colonial Ecuador*. Cambridge: Cambridge University Press, 1991.

Alisky, Marvin. *Uruguay: A Contemporary Survey*. New York: Praeger, 1969.

Altman, Ida. *Emigrants and Society: Extremadura and America in the Sixteenth Century*. Berkeley: University of California Press, 1989.

Alvarado, Pedro de. *An Account of the Conquest of Guatemala in 1524*. Edited by Sedley J. Mackie. New York: Cortés Society, 1924.

Amaral, Samuel. *The Rise of Capitalism on the Pampas: The Estancias of Buenos Aires, 1785–1870*. Cambridge: Cambridge University Press, 1998.

_____. "Rural Production and Labour in Late Colonial Buenos Aires." *Journal of Latin American Studies* 19, no. 2 (November 1987): 235–78.

Andrien, Kenneth J. *Andean Worlds: Indigenous History, Culture, and Consciousness under Spanish Rule, 1532–1825*. Albuquerque: University of New Mexico Press, 2001.

_____. *The Kingdom of Quito, 1690–1830: The State and Regional Development*. Cambridge: Cambridge University Press, 1995.

_____. "The State and Dependency in Late Colonial and Early Republican Ecuador." In Kenneth J. Andrien and Lyman L. Johnson, eds., *The Political Economy of Spanish America in the Age of Revolution, 1750–1850*, 169–95. Albuquerque: University of New Mexico Press, 1994.

_____. "Economic Crisis, Taxes and the Quito Insurrection of 1765." *Past and Present* 129 (November 1990): 104–31.

———. *Crisis and Decline: The Viceroyalty of Peru in the Seventeenth Century.* Albuquerque: University of New Mexico Press, 1985.

Archer, Christon I. *The Army in Bourbon Mexico, 1760–1810.* Albuquerque: University of New Mexico Press, 1977.

Arcila Farías, Eduardo. *El régimen de la encomienda en Venezuela.* Seville: Escuela de Estudios Hispano-Americanos, 1957.

———. *Economía colonial de Venezuela.* Mexico City: Fondo de Cultura Económica, 1946.

Arias de Blois, Jorge. "Demografía." In Jorge Luján Muñoz, ed., *Historia general de Guatemala,* vol. 3, *Siglo XVIII hasta la independencia,* 103–18. Guatemala City: Fundación para la Cultura y el Desarrollo, 1995.

———. "Evolución demográfica hasta 1700." In Jorge Luján Muñoz, ed., *Historia general de Guatemala,* vol. 2, *Dominación española: Desde la conquista hasta 1700,* 313–26. Guatemala City: Fundación para la Cultura y el Desarrollo, 1994.

Armas Medina, Fernando de. *Cristianización de Perú (1532–1600).* Seville: Escuela de Estudios Hispano-Americanos, 1953.

Armond, Louis de. "Frontier Warfare in Colonial Chile." *Pacific Historical Review* 23, no. 2 (May 1954): 125–32.

Arnold, Linda. *Bureaucracy and Bureaucrats in Mexico City, 1742–1835.* Tucson: University of Arizona Press, 1988.

Arteaga, Juan José. *Uruguay: Breve historia contemporánea.* Mexico City: Fondo de Cultura Económica, 2000.

Arze Quiroga, Eduardo. *Historia de Bolivia: Fases del proceso hispano-americano: Orígenes de la sociedad boliviana en el siglo XVI.* La Paz: Editorial "Los Amigos del Libro," 1969.

Avellaneda, José Ignacio. *The Conquerors of the New Kingdom of Granada.* Albuquerque: University of New Mexico Press, 1995.

Ayón, Tomás. *Historia de Nicaragua: Desde los tiempos más remotos hasta el año 1852.* Managua: Fondo de Promoción Cultural, BANIC, 1993.

Azarola Gil, Luis Enrique. *Los orígenes de Montevideo, 1607–1749.* Buenos Aires: Librería y Editorial "La Facultad," 1933.

Azcuy Ameghino, Eduardo. *La otra historia: Economía, estado y sociedad en el Río de la Plata.* Buenos Aires: Imago Mundi, 2002.

Bakewell, Peter. *Silver and Entrepreneurship in Seventeenth-Century Potosí: The Life and Times of Antonio López de Quiroga.* Albuquerque: University of New Mexico Press, 1988.

———. *Miners of the Red Mountain: Indian Labor in Potosí, 1545–1650.* Albuquerque: University of New Mexico Press, 1984.

———. "Mining in Colonial Spanish America." In Leslie Bethell, ed., *The Cambridge History of Latin America,* vol. 2, *Colonial Latin America,* 105–51. Cambridge: Cambridge University Press, 1984.

———. *Silver Mining and Society in Colonial Mexico: Zacatecas, 1546–1700.* Cambridge: Cambridge University Press, 1971.

Barba, Enrique M., ed. *Bicentenario del Virreinato del Río de la Plata,* vol. 1. Buenos Aires: Academia Nacional de la Historia, 1977.

Barbier, Jacques A. *Reform and Politics in Bourbon Chile, 1755–1796.* Ottawa: University of Ottawa Press, 1980.

———. "The Culmination of the Bourbon Reforms." *Hispanic American Historical Review* 57, no. 1 (February 1977): 51–68.

Barnadas, Josep M. *Charcas: Orígenes históricos de una sociedad colonial.* La Paz: Empresa Editora Universo, 1973.

Barón Castro, Rodolfo. *La población de El Salvador: Estudio acerca de su desenvolvimiento desde la época prehispánica hasta nuestros días.* Madrid: Consejo Superior de Investigaciones Científicas, 1942.

Barrán, José O., and Benjamín Nahum. *Bases económicas de la revolución artiguista.* Montevideo: Ediciones de la Banda Oriental, 1963.

Barsky, Osvaldo, and Jorge Gelman. *Historia del agro argentino: Desde la conquista hasta fines del siglo XX.* Buenos Aires: Grijalbo, 2001.

Bauer, Arnold J. *Chilean Rural Society: From the Spanish Conquest to 1930.* Cambridge: Cambridge University Press, 1975.

———. "Expansión económica en una sociedad tradicional: Chile central en el siglo XIX." *Historia* 9 (1970): 137–235.

Beals, Ralph L. "The Tarascans." In Wauchope, *Handbook of Middle American Indians,* vol. 8, pt. 2, pp. 725–73.

Beck, Hugo Humberto. "Distribución territorial de la conquista: Red de urbanización y vías de comunicación." In Academia Nacional de la Historia, *Nueva historia de la nación Argentina,* vol. 2, *Período español (1600–1800),* 21–46. Buenos Aires: Editorial Planeta, 1999.

Belaunde Guinassi, Manuel. *La encomienda en el Perú.* Lima: Mercurio Peruano, 1945.

Beltrán, Ulíses. "Estado y sociedad tarascos." In Pedro Carrasco, ed., *La sociedad indígena en el centro y occidente de México,* 45–62. Zamora, Mexico: El Colegio de Michoacán, 1986.

Bengoa, José. *Historia de los antiguos mapuches del sur: Desde antes de la llegada de los españoles hasta las paces de Quilín.* Santiago: Catalonia, 2003.

———. *Historia del pueblo mapuche (siglo XIX y XX).* Santiago: Biblioteca Bicentenario, 2000.

Bertrand, Michel. "La tierra y los hombres: La sociedad rural en Baja Verapaz durante los siglos XVI al XIX." In Stephen Webre, ed., *La sociedad colonial en Guatemala: Estudios regionales y locales,* 141–87. Antigua, Guatemala: Centro de Investigaciones Regionales de Mesoamérica, 1989.

Blanco Acevedo, Pablo. *El gobierno colonial en el Uruguay y los orígenes de la nacionalidad.* Montevideo: Casa A. Barreiro y Ramos, 1944.

Borah, Woodrow. "The Mixing of Populations." In Fredi Chiappelli (with Michael J. B. Allen and Robert L. Benson), ed., *First Images of America: The Impact of the New World on the Old,* 2:707–22. Berkeley: University of California Press, 1976.

———. *Early Colonial Trade and Navigation between Mexico and Peru.* Berkeley: University of California Press, 1954.

———. *New Spain's Century of Depression.* Berkeley: University of California Press, 1951.

Borah, Woodrow, and Sherburne F. Cook. *The Aboriginal Population of Central Mexico on the Eve of the Spanish Conquest.* Berkeley: University of California Press, 1963.

Borchart de Moreno, Christiana. "Capital comercial y producción agricola: Nueva España y la Audiencia de Quito en el siglo XVIII." *Anuario de Estudios Americanos* 46 (1989): 131–72.

Bowser, Frederick P. *The African Slave in Colonial Peru, 1524–1650.* Stanford, CA: Stanford University Press, 1974.

Boyd-Bowman, Peter. "Patterns of Spanish Emigration to the Indies until 1600." *Hispanic American Historical Review* 56, no. 4 (November 1976): 580–604.

———. *Indice geobiográfico de cuarenta mil pobladores españoles de América en el siglo XVI,* vol. 1, *1493–1519.* Bogotá: Instituto Caro y Cuervo, 1964.

Boyer, Richard. "Mexico in the Seventeenth Century: Transition of a Colonial Society." *Hispanic American Historical Review* 57, no. 3 (August 1977): 455–78.

Brading, David A. *Haciendas and Ranchos in the Mexican Bajío: León, 1700–1860.* Cambridge: Cambridge University Press, 1978.

———. "Government and Elite in Late Colonial Mexico." *Hispanic American Historical Review* 53, no. 3 (August 1973): 389–414.

———. *Miners and Merchants in Bourbon Mexico, 1763–1810.* Cambridge: Cambridge University Press, 1971.

Brading, D. A., and Harry E. Cross. "Colonial Silver Mining: Mexico and Peru." *Hispanic American Historical Review* 52, no. 4 (November 1972): 545–79.

Braman, Thomas Chapin. "Land and Society in Early Colonial Santiago de Chile, 1540–1575." PhD diss., Department of History, University of Florida, 1975.

Brenes Quesada, Luis Guillermo, et al. *Historia de Costa Rica*, vol. 1. San José: Editorial EIDOS, 1997.

Brito Figueroa, Federico. *La estructura económica de Venezuela colonial.* 3rd ed. Caracas: Universidad Central de Venezuela, 1983.

———. *Historia económica y social de Venezuela: Una estructura para su estudio.* 4th ed. Vol. 1. Caracas: Universidad de Venezuela, Ediciones de la Biblioteca, 1974.

———. *Historia económica y social de Venezuela*, vol. 1. Caracas: Universidad Central de Venezuela, 1966.

Broadbent, Sylvia M. *Los Chibchas: Organización socio-política.* Bogotá: Imprenta Nacional, 1964.

Bronner, Fred. "Church, Crown, and Commerce in Seventeenth-Century Lima: A Synoptic Interpretation." *Jahrbuch für Geschichte von Staat, Wirtschaft und Gesellschaft Lateinamerikas* 29 (1992): 75–89.

———. "Peruvian Encomenderos in 1630: Elite Circulation and Consolidation." *Hispanic American Historical Review* 57, no. 4 (1977): 633–59.

Brooks, Francis J. "Revising the Conquest of Mexico: Smallpox, Sources, and Populations." *Journal of Interdisciplinary History* 24, no. 1 (Summer 1993): 1–29.

Brown, Jonathan C. "Revival of the Rural Economy and Society in Buenos Aires." In Mark D. Szuchman and Jonathan C. Brown, eds., *Revolution and Restoration: The Rearrangement of Power in Argentina, 1776–1860*, 240–72. Lincoln: University of Nebraska Press, 1994.

———. *A Socioeconomic History of Argentina, 1776–1860.* Cambridge: Cambridge University Press, 1979.

Brown, Kendall W. *Bourbons and Brandy: Imperial Reform in Eighteenth-Century Arequipa.* Albuquerque: University of New Mexico Press, 1986.

Browning, David. *El Salvador: Landscape and Society.* Oxford: Clarendon Press, 1971.

Brundage, Burr Cartwright. *A Rain of Darts: The Mexican Aztecs.* Austin: University of Texas Press, 1972.

Burkholder, Mark A. *Politics of a Colonial Career: José Baquíjano and the Audiencia of Lima.* Albuquerque: University of New Mexico Press, 1980.

———. "From Creole to Peninsular: The Transformation of the Audiencia of Lima." *Hispanic American Historical Review* 52, no. 3 (August 1972): 395–415.

Burkholder, Mark A., and D. S. Chandler. *From Impotence to Authority: The Spanish Crown and the American Audiencias, 1687–1808.* Columbia: University of Missouri Press, 1977.

Burkholder, Mark A., and Lyman L. Johnson. *Colonial Latin America.* 4th ed. New York: Oxford University Press, 2001.

Burns, E. Bradford. *Patriarch and Folk: The Emergence of Nicaragua, 1798–1858.* Cambridge, MA: Harvard University Press, 1991.

Bushnell, David. *The Making of Modern Colombia: A Nation in Spite of Itself.* Berkeley: University of California Press, 1993.

Buzzetti, José L. *Historia económica y financiera del Uruguay.* Montevideo: Talleres Gráficos "La Paz," 1969.

Cabezas Carcache, Horacio. "Los Indios." In Jorge Luján Muñoz, ed., *Historia general de Guatemala*, vol. 3, *Siglo XVIII hasta la independencia*, 149–62. Guatemala City: Fundación para la Cultura y el Desarrollo, 1995.

———. "Agricultura." In Jorge Luján Muñoz, ed., *Historia general de Guatemala*, vol. 2, *Dominación española: Desde la conquista hasta 1700*, 421–42. Guatemala City: Fundación para la Cultura y el Desarrollo, 1994.

———. "Las encomiendas." In Jorge Luján Muñoz, ed., *Historia general de Guatemala*, vol. 2, *Dominación española: Desde la conquista hasta 1700*, 373–85. Guatemala City: Fundación para la Cultura y el Desarrollo, 1994.

———. "Régimen regulador del trabajo indígena." In Jorge Luján Muñoz, ed., *Historia general de Guatemala*, vol. 2, *Dominación española: Desde la conquista hasta 1700*, 387–97. Guatemala City: Fundación para la Cultura y el Desarrollo, 1994.

Calero, Luis F. *Chiefdoms under Siege: Spain's Rule and Native Adaptation in the Southern Colombian Andes, 1535–1700*. Albuquerque: University of New Mexico Press, 1997.

Campbell, Leon G. "A Colonial Establishment: Creole Domination of the Audiencia of Lima during the Late Eighteenth Century." *Hispanic American Historical Review* 52, no. 1 (February 1972): 1–25.

Canals Frau, Salvador. *Las poblaciones indígenas de la Argentina: Su origen, su pasado, su presente*. Buenos Aires: Editorial Sudamericana, 1953.

Cárdenas, Enrique. "A Macroeconomic Interpretation of Nineteenth-Century Mexico." In Stephen Haber, ed., *How Latin America Fell Behind: Essays on the Economic Histories of Brazil and Mexico, 1800–1914*, 65–92. Stanford, CA: Stanford University Press, 1997.

Cardozo, Efraim. *El Paraguay colonial: Las raíces de la nacionalidad*. Buenos Aires: Ediciones Nizza, 1959.

Carmack, Robert M. "Mesoamerica at Spanish Contact." In Robert M. Carmack, Janine Gasco, and Gary H. Gossen, eds., *The Legacy of Mesoamerica: History and Culture of a Native American Civilization*, 80–122. Upper Saddle River, NJ: Prentice Hall, 1996.

———. "Perspectivas sobre la historia antigua de Centroamérica." In Robert M. Carmack, ed., *Historia general de Centroamérica*, vol. 1, *Historia antigua*, 283–326. Madrid: Sociedad Estatal Quinto Centenario, 1993.

———. *The Quiché Mayas of Utatlán: The Evolution of a Highland Guatemala Kingdom*. Norman: University of Oklahoma Press, 1981.

Carmagnani, Marcello. "Colonial Latin American Demography: Growth of the Chilean Population, 1700–1830." *Journal of Social History* 1, no. 2 (Winter 1967): 179–91.

———. *El salariado minero en Chile colonial: Su desarrollo en una sociedad provincial, el Norte Chico, 1690–1800*. Santiago: Editorial Universitaria, 1963.

Casey, James. *Early Modern Spain: A Social History*. London: Routledge, 1999.

Castellanos Rodríguez, María Lorena. "La minería." In Jorge Luján Muñoz, ed., *Historia general de Guatemala*, vol. 3, *Siglo XVIII hasta la independencia*, 323–33. Guatemala City: Fundación para la Cultura y el Desarrollo, 1995.

Cavieres, Eduardo. *El comercio chileno en la economía colonial*. Valparaíso, Chile: Ediciones Universitarias de Valparaíso, 1996.

Céspedes del Castillo, Guillermo. "Lima y Buenos Aires: Repercusiones económicas y políticas de la creación del virreinato del Plata." *Anuario de Estudios Americanos* 3 (1946): 669–874.

Cevallos García, Gabriel. *Historia del Ecuador*. Cuenca, Ecuador: Editorial "Don Bosco," 1964.

Chamberlain, Robert S. *The Conquest and Colonization of Yucatan, 1517–1550*. Washington, DC: Carnegie Institution, 1948.

———. "The Early Years of San Miguel de la Frontera." *Hispanic American Historical Review* 27, no. 4 (November 1947): 623–47.

Chance, John K. *The Conquest of the Sierra: Spaniards and Indians in Colonial Oaxaca*. Norman: University of Oklahoma Press, 1989.

———. *Race and Class in Colonial Oaxaca*. Stanford, CA: Stanford University Press, 1978.

Chapman, Anne M. *Los lencas de Honduras en el siglo XVI*. Tegucigalpa: Instituto Hondureño de Antropología e Historia, 1978.

———. *Los nicarao y los chorotega según las fuentes históricas*. Serie Historia y Geografía, no. 4. San José: Universidad de Costa Rica, 1960.

Charlevoix, P. Pedro Francisco Javier de. *Historia de Paraguay*, vol. 1. Madrid: Librería General de Victoriano Suárez, 1910.

Charney, Paul. *Indian Society in the Valley of Lima, Peru, 1532–1824*. Lanham, MD: University Press of America, 2001.

Chevalier, François. *Land and Society in Colonial Mexico: The Great Hacienda*. Berkeley: University of California Press, 1963.

————. "Estudio preliminar." In Domingo Lázaro de Arregui, ed., *Descripción de la Nueva Galicia*, xiii–lxxi. Seville: Escuela de Estudios Hispano-Americanos, 1946.

Chinchilla Aguilar, Ernesto. "Lavaderos de oro y la minería." In Jorge Luján Muñoz, ed., *Historia general de Guatemala*, vol. 2, *Dominación española: Desde la conquista hasta 1700*, 443–50. Guatemala City: Fundación para la Cultura y el Desarrollo, 1994.

Clayton, Lawrence Anthony. "Trade and Navigation in the Seventeenth-Century Viceroyalty of Peru." *Journal of Latin American Studies* 7, no. 1 (May 1975): 1–21.

————. "The Guayaquil Shipyards in the Seventeenth Century: History of a Colonial Industry." PhD diss., Tulane University, 1972.

Clendinnen, Inga. *Ambivalent Conquests: Maya and Spaniard in Yucatán, 1517–1570*. 2nd ed. Cambridge: Cambridge University Press, 2003.

————. "'Fierce and Unnatural Cruelty': Cortés and the Conquest of Mexico." In "The New World," special issue, *Representations* 33 (Winter 1991): 65–100.

Cline, Howard F. "Civil Congregations of the Indians in New Spain, 1598–1606." *Hispanic American Historical Review* 29, no. 3 (August 1949): 349–69.

Coatsworth, John H. "Economic and Institutional Trajectories in Nineteenth-Century Latin America." In John H. Coatsworth and Alan M. Taylor, eds., *Latin America and the World Economy since 1800*, 23–54. Cambridge, MA: Harvard University Press, 1998.

————. "Notes on the Comparative Economic History of Latin America and the United States." In Walther L. Bernecker and Hans Werner Tobler, eds., *Development and Underdevelopment in America: Contrasts of Economic Growth in North and Latin America in Historical Perspective*, 10–30. Berlin: Walter de Gruyter, 1993.

————. "The Mexican Mining Industry in the Eighteenth Century." In Nils Jacobsen and Hans-Jürgen Puhle, eds., *The Economies of Mexico and Peru during the Late Colonial Period, 1760–1810*, 26–46. Berlin: Colloquium-Verlag, 1986.

————. "The Limits of Colonial Absolutism: The State in Eighteenth Century Mexico." In Karen Spalding, ed., *Essays in the Political, Economic and Social History of Colonial Latin America*, 25–51. Newark: University of Delaware, Latin American Studies Program, 1982.

————. "Obstacles to Economic Growth in Nineteenth-Century Mexico." *American Historical Review* 83, no. 1 (February 1978): 80–100.

Cobb, Gwendolin Ballantine. *Potosí y Huancavelica: Bases económicas del Perú, 1545–1640*. La Paz: Biblioteca "BAMIN," 1977.

————. "Supply and Transportation for the Potosí Mines, 1545–1640." *Hispanic American Historical Review* 29, no. 1 (February 1949): 25–45.

Cole, Jeffrey A. *The Potosí Mita, 1573–1700: Compulsory Indian Labor in the Andes*. Stanford, CA: Stanford University Press, 1985.

Collier, Simon, and William F. Sater. *A History of Chile, 1808–1994*. Cambridge: Cambridge University Press, 1996.

Colmenares, Germán. *Historia económica y social de Colombia*, vol. 1, *1537–1719*. 5th ed. Bogotá: Tercer Mundo Editores, 1997.

————. *Historia económica y social de Colombia*, vol. 2, *Popayán: Una sociedad esclavista, 1680–1800*. 2nd ed. Bogotá: Tercer Mundo Editores, 1997.

Comadrán Ruiz, Jorge. *Evolución demográfica argentina durante el período hispano (1535–1810)*. Buenos Aires: Editorial Universitaria de Buenos Aires, 1969.

Conniff, Michael L. "Guayaquil through Independence: Urban Development in a Colonial System." *The Americas* 33, no. 3 (January 1977): 385–410.

Contreras C., Carlos. *El sector exportador de una economía colonial: La costa del Ecuador entre 1760 y 1820*. Quito: Flacso, 1990.

————. *La ciudad de mercurio: Huancavelica, 1570–1700*. Lima: Instituto de Estudios Peruanos, 1982.

Cook, Noble David. *Born to Die: Disease and the New World Conquest, 1492–1650*. Cambridge: Cambridge University Press, 1998.
_____. *Demographic Collapse: Indian Peru, 1520–1620*. Cambridge: Cambridge University Press, 1981.
Cook, Sherburne F., and Woodrow Borah. *Essays in Population History: Mexico and the Caribbean*, vol. 2. Berkeley: University of California Press, 1974.
_____. *The Indian Population of Central Mexico, 1531*. Berkeley: University of California Press, 1960.
Cook, Sherburne F., and Lesley B. Simpson. *The Population of Central Mexico in the Sixteenth Century*. Berkeley: University of California Press, 1948.
Cooper, John M. "The Araucanians." In Julian H. Steward, ed., *Handbook of South American Indians*, vol. 2, *The Andean Civilizations*, 687–760. Washington, DC: U.S. Government Printing Office, 1946.
_____. "The Patagonian and Pampean Hunters." In Julian H. Steward, ed., *Handbook of South American Indians*, vol. 1, *The Marginal Tribes*, 127–68. Washington, DC: U.S. Government Printing Office, 1946.
_____. "The Southern Hunters." In Julian H. Steward, ed., *Handbook of South American Indians*, vol. 1, *The Marginal Tribes*, 13–15. Washington, DC: U.S. Government Printing Office, 1946.
Cornblit, Oscar. *Power and Violence in the Colonial City: Oruro from the Mining Renaissance to the Rebellion of Tupac Amaru (1740–1782)*. Translated by Elizabeth Ladd Glick. Cambridge: Cambridge University Press, 1995.
Cuenca Esteban, Javier. "Statistics of Spain's Colonial Trade, 1792–1820: Consular Duties, Cargo Inventories, and Balances of Trade." *Hispanic American Historical Review* 61, no. 3 (August 1981): 381–428.
Cushner, Nicholas P. *Farm and Factory: The Jesuits and the Development of Agrarian Capitalism in Colonial Quito, 1600–1767*. Albany: State University of New York Press, 1982.
_____. *Lords of the Land: Sugar, Wine, and Jesuit Estates of Coastal Peru, 1600–1767*. Albany: State University of New York Press, 1980.
D'Altroy, Terence N. *The Incas*. Malden, MA: Blackwell, 2002.
Daniels, Christine, and Michael V. Kennedy, eds. *Negotiated Empires: Centers and Peripheries in the Americas, 1500–1820*. New York: Routledge, 2002.
Davies, Keith A. *Landowners in Colonial Peru*. Austin: University of Texas Press, 1984.
Davies, Nigel. *The Incas*. Niwot: University Press of Colorado, 1995.
_____. *The Aztecs: A History*. Norman: University of Oklahoma Press, 1980.
de Civrieux, Marc. "Los Cumanagoto y sus vecinos." In Audrey Butt Colson, ed., *Los aborígenes de Venezuela*, 27–239. Caracas: Instituto Caribe de Antropología y Sociología, 1980.
de Gortari Rabiela, Hira. "La minería durante la Guerra de Independencia y los primeros años del México independiente, 1810–1824." In Jaime E. Rodríguez, ed., *The Independence of Mexico and the Creation of the New Nation*, 129–61. Los Angeles: UCLA Latin American Center Publications, University of California, 1989.
Denevan, William M. "Introduction to Part IV: South America." In William M. Denevan, ed., *The Native Population of the Americas in 1492*, 2nd ed., 151–5. Madison: University of Wisconsin Press, 1992.
_____. "Native American Populations in 1492: Recent Research and a Revised Hemispheric Estimate." In William M. Denevan, ed., *The Native Population of the Americas in 1492*, 2nd ed., xvii–xxix. Madison: University of Wisconsin Press, 1992.
_____. "The Aboriginal Cultural Geography of the Llanos de Mojos of Bolivia." *Ibero-Americana* 48 (1966): 40–57.
de Ramón, Armando, and José Manuel Larraín. *Orígenes de la vida económica chilena, 1659–1808*. Santiago: Imprenta Calderón, 1982.

Deustua, José. *La minería peruana y la iniciación de la república, 1820–1840.* Lima: Instituto de Estudios Peruanos, 1986.

Diamond, Jared. *Guns, Germs, and Steel: The Fates of Human Societies.* New York: Norton, 1997.

Díaz Alejandro, Carlos F. *Essays on the Economic History of the Argentine Republic.* New Haven, CT: Yale University Press, 1970.

Díaz Arguedas, Julio. *Síntesis histórica de la ciudad La Paz, 1548–1948.* La Paz: Litografías e Imprentas Unidas, 1978.

Díaz del Castillo, Bernal. *The Bernal Díaz Chronicles: The True Story of the Conquest of Mexico.* Translated and edited by Albert Idell. Garden City, NY: Doubleday, 1956.

Domínguez Ortiz, Antonio. *Sociedad y estado en el siglo XVIII español.* Barcelona: Editorial Ariel, 1976.

———. *The Golden Age of Spain, 1516–1659.* London: Weidenfeld & Nicolson, 1971.

Durón, Rómulo E. *Bosquejo histórico de Honduras, 1502 a 1921.* San Pedro Sula, Honduras: Tip. del Comercio, 1927.

Echaiz, René León. *Prehistoria de Chile Central.* Buenos Aires: Editorial Francisco de Aguirre, 1976.

Elliot, G. F. Scott. *Chile: Its History and Development, Natural Features, Products, Commerce and Present Conditions.* New York: Charles Scribner's Sons, 1907.

Elliott, J. H. *Imperial Spain, 1469–1716.* Reprinted with a revised foreword. London: Penguin, 2002.

———. "The Spanish Conquest and Settlement of America." In Leslie Bethell, ed., *The Cambridge History of Latin America,* vol. 1, *Colonial Latin America,* 149–206. Cambridge: Cambridge University Press, 1984.

———. "Self-Perception and Decline in Early Seventeenth-Century Spain." *Past and Present* 74 (February 1977): 41–61.

———. "The Decline of Spain." *Past and Present* 20 (November 1961): 52–75.

Eltis, David. "Slavery and Freedom in the Early Modern World." In Stanley L. Engerman, ed., *Terms of Labor: Slavery, Serfdom and Free Labor,* 25–49. Stanford, CA: Stanford University Press, 1999.

Encina, Francisco Antonio. *Historia de Chile: Desde la prehistoria hasta 1891,* vols. 1 and 2. Santiago: Editorial Nascimento, 1941.

Enock, C. Reginald. *Ecuador: Its Ancient and Modern History.* New York: Charles Scribner's Sons, 1914.

Escobari de Querejazu, Laura. *Caciques, yanaconas y extravagantes: La sociedad colonial en Charcas, s. XVI–XVIII.* La Paz: Plural Editores, 2001.

———. *Producción y comercio en el espacio sur andino en el siglo XVII: Cuzco-Potosí, 1650–1700.* La Paz: Industrias Offset Color, 1985.

Facio, Rodrigo. *Estudio sobre economía costarricense.* Reprinted in *Obras de Rodrigo Facio,* vol. 1. San José: Editorial Costa Rica, 1972.

Fals-Borda, Orlando. "Indian Congregations in the New Kingdom of Granada: Land Tenure Aspects, 1595–1850." *The Americas* 13, no. 4 (April 1957): 331–51.

Farriss, Nancy M. *Maya Society under Colonial Rule: The Collective Enterprise of Survival.* Princeton, NJ: Princeton University Press, 1984.

———. *Crown and Clergy in Colonial Mexico, 1759–1821: The Crisis of Ecclesiastical Privilege.* London: Athlone Press, 1968.

Fernández Guardia, Ricardo. *Historia de Costa Rica: El descubrimiento y la conquista.* 4th ed. San José: Librería Lehmann y Cía., 1941.

Fernández Hernández, Bernabé. *El gobierno del Intendente Anguiano en Honduras (1796–1812).* Seville: Universidad de Sevilla, 1997.

Fernández Molina, José Antonio. "Colouring the World in Blue: The Indigo Boom and the Central American Market, 1750–1810." PhD diss., University of Texas at Austin, 1992.

Ferrer, Aldo. *The Argentine Economy.* Translated by Marjory M. Urquidi. Berkeley: University of California Press, 1967.

Ferry, Robert J. *The Colonial Elite of Early Caracas: Formation and Crisis, 1567–1767.* Berkeley: University of California Press, 1989.

Fisher, John R. *Bourbon Peru, 1750–1824.* Liverpool, England: Liverpool University Press, 2003.

_____. "Commerce and Imperial Decline: Spanish Trade with Spanish America, 1797–1820." *Journal of Latin American Studies* 30, no. 3 (October 1998): 459–79.

_____. "The Effects of Comercio Libre on the Economies of New Granada and Peru: A Comparison." In John R. Fisher, Allan J. Kuethe, and Anthony McFarlane, eds., *Reform and Insurrection in Bourbon New Granada and Peru,* 147–63. Baton Rouge: Louisiana State University Press, 1990.

_____. "Mining and the Peruvian Economy in the Late Colonial Period." In Nils Jacobsen and Hans-Jürgen Puhle, eds., *The Economies of Mexico and Peru during the Late Colonial Period, 1760–1810,* 46–60. Berlin: Colloquium-Verlag, 1986.

_____. *Silver Mines and Silver Miners in Colonial Peru, 1776–1824.* Liverpool, England: Centre for Latin-American Studies, University of Liverpool, 1977.

_____. *Government and Society in Colonial Peru: The Intendant System, 1784–1814.* London: Athlone Press, 1970.

Fitzgibbon, Russell H. *Uruguay: Portrait of a Democracy.* New York: Russell & Russell, 1966.

Florescano, Enrique. "The Formation and Economic Structure of the Hacienda in New Spain." In Leslie Bethell, ed., *The Cambridge History of Latin America,* vol. 2, *Colonial Latin America,* 153–88. Cambridge: Cambridge University Press, 1984.

Florescano, Enrique, and Isabel Gil Sánchez. "La época de las reformas borbónicas y el crecimiento económico, 1750–1808." In Daniel Cosío Villegas, ed., *Historia general de México,* 1:471–589. Mexico City: El Colegio de México, 1976.

Flores Galindo, Alberto. "Aristocracia en vilo: Los mercaderes de Lima en el siglo XVIII." In Nils Jacobsen and Hans-Jürgen Puhle, eds., *The Economies of Mexico and Peru during the Late Colonial Period, 1760–1810,* 252–80. Berlin: Colloquium-Verlag, 1986.

_____. *Aristocracia y plebe: Lima, 1760–1830.* Lima: Mosca Azul Editores, 1984.

Flores Macal, Mario. *Origen, desarrollo y crisis de las formas de dominación en El Salvador.* San José: SECASA, 1983.

Floyd, Troy S. "The Indigo Merchant: Promoter of Central American Economic Development, 1750–1808." *Business History Review* 39, no. 4 (Winter 1965): 466–88.

_____. "The Guatemalan Merchants, the Government, and the Provincianos, 1750–1800." *Hispanic American Historical Review* 41, no. 1 (February 1961): 90–110.

Fonseca Corrales, Elizabeth. "Economía y sociedad en Centroamérica (1540–1680)." In Julio César Pinto Soria, ed., *Historia general de Centroamérica: El régimen colonial (1524–1750),* 95–150. Madrid: Sociedad Estatal Quinto Centenario, 1993.

_____. *Costa Rica colonial: La tierra y el hombre.* 2nd ed. San José: EDUCA, 1984.

Fowler, William R., Jr. "The Formation of Complex Society among the Nahua Groups of Southeastern Mesoamerica: A Comparison of Two Approaches." In William R. Fowler Jr., ed., *The Formation of Complex Society in Southeastern Mesoamerica,* 193–213. Boca Raton, FL: CRC Press, 1991.

_____. "The Political Economy of Indian Survival in Sixteenth-Century Izalco, El Salvador." In David Hurst Thomas, ed., *Columbian Consequences,* vol. 3, *The Spanish Borderlands in Pan-American Perspective,* 187–204. Washington, DC: Smithsonian Institution Press, 1991.

_____. *The Cultural Evolution of Ancient Nahua Civilizations: The Pipil-Nicarao of Central America.* Norman: University of Oklahoma Press, 1989.

_____. "Cacao, Indigo, and Coffee: Cash Crops in the History of El Salvador." *Research in Economic Anthropology* 8 (1987): 144–7.

Frías, Susana R. "La expansión de la población." In Academia Nacional de la Historia, *Nueva historia de la nación Argentina*, vol. 2, *Período español (1600–1800)*. Buenos Aires: Editorial Planeta, 1999.

Friede, Juan. "La conquista del territorio y el poblamiento." In Jaime Jaramillo Uribe, ed., *Nueva historia de Colombia*, 69–115. Bogotá: Planeta Colombiana Editorial, 1989.

———. *Los Chibchas bajo la dominación española*. Bogotá: La Carreta, 1974.

———. "Proceso de formación de la propiedad territorial en la América intertropical." *Jahrbuch für Geschichte von Staat, Wirtschaft und Gesellschaft Lateinamerikas* 2 (1965): 75–87.

Furtado, Celso. *Economic Development of Latin America: Historical Background and Contemporary Problems*. Translated by Suzette Macedo. 2nd ed. New York: Cambridge University Press, 1976.

Galdames, Luis. *A History of Chile*. Translated by Isaac Joslin Cox. Chapel Hill: University of North Carolina Press, 1941.

Galdos Rodríguez, Guillermo. *Una ciudad para la historia, una historia para la ciudad: Arequipa en el siglo XVI*. Arequipa, Peru: Editorial Universidad de San Agustín, 1997.

Garavaglia, Juan Carlos. "Patrones de inversión y 'elite económica dominante': Los empresarios rurales en la pampa bonaerense a mediados del siglo XIX." In Jorge Gelman, Juan Carlos Garavaglia, and Blanca Zeberio, eds., *Expansión capitalista y transformaciones regionales: Relaciones sociales y empresas agrarias en la Argentina del siglo XIX*, 121–43. Buenos Aires: Editorial La Colmena, 1999.

———. *Mercado interno y economía colonial*. Mexico City: Editorial Grijalbo, 1983.

García Añoveros, Jesús María. "La iglesia en el Reino de Guatemala." In Jorge Luján Muñoz, ed., *Historia general de Guatemala*, vol. 2, *Dominación española: Desde la conquista hasta 1700*, 155–82. Guatemala City: Fundación para la Cultura y el Desarrollo, 1994.

García Belsunce, César A. "La sociedad hispano-criolla." In Academia Nacional de la Historia, *Nueva historia de la nación Argentina*, vol. 2, *Período español (1600–1800)*, 149–81. Buenos Aires: Editorial Planeta, 1999.

Garner, Richard L. "Long-Term Silver Mining Trends in Spanish America: A Comparative Analysis of Peru and Mexico." *American Historical Review* 93, no. 4 (October 1988): 898–935.

———. "Exportaciones de circulante en el siglo XVIII (1750–1810)." *Historia Mexicana* 31, no. 4 (1982): 544–98.

———. "Silver Production and Entrepreneurial Structure in 18th-Century Mexico." *Jahrbuch für Geschichte von Staat, Wirtschaft und Gesellschaft Lateinamerikas* 17 (1980): 157–85.

Garner, Richard L. (with Spiro E. Setanou). *Economic Growth and Change in Bourbon Mexico*. Gainesville: University of Florida Press, 1993.

Gelman, Jorge. "New Perspectives on an Old Problem and the Same Source: The Gaucho and the Rural History of the Colonial Río de la Plata." *Hispanic American Historical Review* 69, no. 4 (November 1989): 715–31.

Gelman, Jorge, Juan Carlos Garavaglia, and Blanca Zeberio. "Introducción." In Jorge Gelman, Juan Carlos Garavaglia, and Blanca Zeberio, eds., *Expansión capitalista y transformaciones regionales: Relaciones sociales y empresas agrarias en la Argentina del siglo XIX*, 1–6. Buenos Aires: Editorial La Colmena, 1999.

Gerhard, Peter. *The North Frontier of New Spain*. Rev. ed. Norman: University of Oklahoma Press, 1993.

———. *The Southeast Frontier of New Spain*. Rev. ed. Norman: University of Oklahoma Press, 1993.

———. "Congregaciones de Indios en la Nueva España antes de 1570." *Historia Mexicana* 103, no. 3 (January–March 1977): 347–95.

Gibson, Charles. *Tlaxcala in the Sixteenth Century*. Stanford, CA: Stanford University Press, 1967.

_____. *Spain in America*. New York: Harper & Row, 1966.

_____. *The Aztecs under Spanish Rule: A History of the Indians of the Valley of Mexico, 1519–1810*. Stanford, CA: Stanford University Press, 1964.

Glade, William. "Institutions and Inequality in Latin America: Text and Subtext." *Journal of Interamerican Studies and World Affairs* 38, nos. 2–3 (Summer–Autumn 1996): 159–79.

Góngora, Mario. "Urban Social Stratification in Colonial Chile." *Hispanic American Historical Review* 55, no. 3 (August 1975): 421–48.

_____. *Origen de los inquilinos de Chile central*. Santiago: ICIRA, 1974.

_____. *Encomenderos y estancieros: Estudios acerca de la constitución social aristocrática de Chile después de la conquista, 1580–1660*. Santiago: Editorial Universitaria, 1971.

Góngora Marmolejo, Alonso de. *Historia de Chile desde su descubrimiento hasta el año 1575*. Santiago: Editorial Universitaria, 1969.

González Villalobos, Paulino. "La coyuntura de la conquista." In Paulino González Villalobos, ed., *Desarrollo institucional de Costa Rica (1523–1914)*, 19–46. San José: SECASA, 1983.

Goodrich, Carter. "Argentina as a New Country." *Comparative Studies in Society and History* 7 (1964–5): 70–88.

Gootenberg, Paul. *Imagining Development: Economic Ideas in Peru's 'Fictitious Prosperity' of Guano, 1840–1880*. Berkeley: University of California Press, 1993.

_____. "Population and Ethnicity in Early Republican Peru: Some Revisions." *Latin American Research Review* 26, no. 3 (1991): 109–57.

_____. *Between Silver and Guano: Commercial Policy and the State in Postindependence Peru*. Princeton, NJ: Princeton University Press, 1989.

Gould, J. D. "European Inter-Continental Emigration, 1815–1914: Patterns and Causes." *Journal of European Economic History* 8, no. 3 (Winter 1979): 593–639.

Grahn, Lance R. "An Irresoluble Dilemma: Smuggling in New Granada, 1713–1763." In John R. Fisher, Allan J. Kuethe, and Anthony McFarlane, eds., *Reform and Insurrection in Bourbon New Granada and Peru*, 123–46. Baton Rouge: Louisiana State University Press, 1990.

Grieshaber, Erwin P. "Survival of Indian Communities in Nineteenth-Century Bolivia: A Regional Comparison." *Journal of Latin American Studies* 12, no. 2 (November 1980): 223–69.

Gudmundson, Lowell. *Costa Rica before Coffee: Society and Economy on the Eve of the Export Boom*. Baton Rouge: Louisiana State University Press, 1986.

_____. *Estratificación socio-racial y económica de Costa Rica, 1700–1850*. San José: Editorial Universidad Estatal a Distancia, 1978.

Guilmartin, John F., Jr. "The Cutting Edge: An Analysis of the Spanish Invasion and Overthrow of the Inca Empire, 1532–1539." In Kenneth J. Andrien and Rolena Adorno, eds., *Transatlantic Encounters: Europeans and Andeans in the Sixteenth Century*, 40–69. Berkeley: University of California Press, 1991.

Haitin, Marcel Manuel. "Urban Market and Agrarian Hinterland: Lima in the Late Colonial Period." In Nils Jacobsen and Hans-Jürgen Puhle, eds., *The Economies of Mexico and Peru during the Late Colonial Period, 1760–1810*, 281–98. Berlin: Colloquium-Verlag, 1986.

_____. "Late Colonial Lima: Economy and Society in an Era of Reform and Revolution." PhD diss., University of California, Berkeley, 1983.

Hall, Carolyn. *Costa Rica: A Geographical Interpretation in Historical Perspective*. Boulder, CO: Westview Press, 1985.

Hall, Carolyn, and Héctor Pérez Brignoli. *Historical Atlas of Central America*. Norman: University of Oklahoma Press, 2003.

Halperín-Donghi, Tulio. "Argentina: Liberalism in a Country Born Liberal." In Joseph Love and Nils Jacobsen, eds., *Guiding the Invisible Hand: Economic Liberalism and the State in Latin America*, 99–116. New York: Praeger, 1988.

————. *Politics, Economics, and Society in Argentina in the Revolutionary Period.* Translated by Richard Southern. Cambridge: Cambridge University Press, 1975.

Hamilton, Earl J. *American Treasure and Price Revolution in Spain, 1501–1650.* Cambridge, MA: Harvard University Press, 1934.

Hamnett, Brian R. *Politics and Trade in Southern Mexico, 1750–1821.* Cambridge: Cambridge University Press, 1971.

Hanke, Lewis. *Bartolomé Arzáns de Orsúa y Vela's History of Potosí.* Providence, RI: Brown University Press, 1965.

Hardoy, Jorge E., and Carmen Aranovich. "Urban Scales and Functions in Spanish America toward the Year 1600: First Conclusions." *Latin American Research Review* 5, no. 3 (Autumn 1970): 57–91.

Haring, C. H. *The Spanish Empire in America.* New York: Oxford University Press, 1947.

Harris, Olivia, Brooke Larson, and Enrique Tandeter, eds. *La participación indígena en los mercados surandinos: Estrategias y reproducción social, siglos XVI a XX.* La Paz: Centro de Estudios de la Realidad Económica y Social, 1987.

Hassig, Ross. *Aztec Warfare: Imperial Expansion and Political Control.* Norman: University of Oklahoma Press, 1988.

————. *Trade, Tribute, and Transportation: The Sixteenth-Century Political Economy of the Valley of Mexico.* Norman: University of Oklahoma Press, 1985.

Helms, Mary W. "The Indians of the Caribbean and Circum-Caribbean at the End of the Fifteenth Century." In Leslie Bethell, ed., *The Cambridge History of Latin America*, vol. 1, *Colonial Latin America*, 37–58. Cambridge: Cambridge University Press, 1984.

————. *Ancient Panama: Chiefs in Search of Power.* Austin: University of Texas Press, 1979.

————. *Middle America: A Culture History of Heartland and Frontiers.* Englewood Cliffs, NJ: Prentice Hall, 1975.

Hemming, John. *The Search for El Dorado.* London: Michael Joseph, 1978.

————. *The Conquest of the Incas.* New York: Harcourt Brace Jovanovich, 1970.

Hennessey Cummins, Victoria. "The Church and Business Practices in Late Sixteenth Century Mexico." *The Americas* 44, no. 4 (April 1988): 421–40.

Hernández de Alba, Gregorio. "Tribes of Northwestern Venezuela." In Julian H. Steward, ed., *Handbook of South American Indians*, vol. 4, *The Circum-Caribbean Tribes*, 469–79. Washington, DC: U.S. Government Printing Office, 1948.

————. "The Highland Tribes of Southern Colombia." In Julian H. Steward, ed., *Handbook of South American Indians*, vol. 2, *The Andean Civilizations*, 915–60. Washington, DC: U.S. Government Printing Office, 1946.

Hernández Rodríguez, Guillermo. *De los chibchas a la colonia y la República: Del clan a la encomienda y al latifundio en Colombia.* Bogotá: Ediciones Internacionales, 1978.

Herr, Richard. *The Eighteenth-Century Revolution in Spain.* Princeton, NJ: Princeton University Press, 1958.

Hidalgo, Jorge. "The Indians of Southern South America in the Middle of the Sixteenth Century." In Leslie Bethell, ed., *The Cambridge History of Latin America*, vol. 1, *Colonial Latin America*, 91–117. Cambridge: Cambridge University Press, 1984.

Himmerich y Valencia, Robert. *The Encomenderos of New Spain, 1521–1555.* Austin: University of Texas Press, 1991.

Hirschberg, Julia. "Social Experiment in New Spain: A Prosopographical Study of the Early Settlement at Puebla de los Angeles." *Hispanic American Historical Review* 59, no. 1 (February 1979): 1–33.

Hoberman, Louisa Schell. *Mexico's Merchant Elite, 1590–1660.* Durham, NC: Duke University Press, 1991.

————. "Merchants in Seventeenth-Century Mexico City: A Preliminary Report." *Hispanic American Historical Review* 57, no. 3 (August 1977): 479–503.

————. "Bureaucracy and Disaster: Mexico City and the Flood of 1629." *Journal of Latin American Studies* 6, no. 2 (1974): 211–30.

Humbert, Jules. *Los orígenes venezolanos (ensayo sobre la colonización española en Venezuela)*. Caracas: Academia Nacional de la Historia, 1976.

Hussey, Roland Dennis. *The Caracas Company, 1728–1784: A Study in the History of Spanish Monopolistic Trade*. Cambridge, MA: Harvard University Press, 1934.

Ibarra Rojas, Eugenia. *Las sociedades cicicales de Costa Rica (siglo XVI)*. San José: Editorial de la Universidad de Costa Rica, 1990.

Israel, J. I. *Race, Class and Politics in Colonial Mexico*. Oxford: Oxford University Press, 1975.

Jacobsen, Nils. *Mirages of Transition: The Peruvian Altiplano, 1780–1930*. Berkeley: University of California Press, 1993.

———. "Commerce in Late Colonial Peru and Mexico: A Comment and Some Comparative Suggestions." In Nils Jacobsen and Hans-Jürgen Puhle, eds., *The Economies of Mexico and Peru during the Late Colonial Period, 1760–1810*, 299–315. Berlin: Colloquium-Verlag, 1986.

———. "Livestock Complexes in Late Colonial Peru and New Spain: An Attempt at Comparison." In Nils Jacobsen and Hans-Jürgen Puhle, eds., *The Economies of Mexico and Peru during the Late Colonial Period, 1760–1810*, 113–42. Berlin: Colloquium-Verlag, 1986.

Jara, Alvaro. *Tres ensayos sobre economía minera hispanoamericana*. Santiago: Centro de Investigaciones de Historia Americana, 1966.

Jaramillo Uribe, Jaime. *Ensayos de historia social*. Bogotá: Tercer Mundo Editores, 1989.

Johnson, Frederick. "The Caribbean Lowland Tribes: The Talamanca Division." In Julian H. Steward, ed., *Handbook of South American Indians*, vol. 4, *The Circum-Caribbean Tribes*, 231–51. Washington, DC: U.S. Government Printing Office, 1948.

———. "Central American Cultures: An Introduction." In Julian H. Steward, ed., *Handbook of South American Indians*, vol. 4, *The Circum-Caribbean Tribes*, 43–68. Washington, DC: U.S. Government Printing Office, 1948.

———. "The Meso-American Indians." In Julian H. Steward, ed., *Handbook of South American Indians*, vol. 4, *The Circum-Caribbean Tribes*, 199–204. Washington, DC: U.S. Government Printing Office, 1948.

Jones, Grant D. *Maya Resistance to Spanish Rule: Time and History on a Colonial Frontier*. Albuquerque: University of New Mexico Press, 1989.

Jones, Kristine L. "Warfare, Reorganization, and Readaptation at the Margins of Spanish Rule: The Southern Margin (1573–1882)." In Frank Salomon and Stuart B. Schwartz, eds., *The Cambridge History of the Native Peoples of the Americas*, vol. 3, *South America*, pt. 2, pp. 138–87. Cambridge: Cambridge University Press, 1999.

Jones, Oakah L., Jr. *Guatemala in the Spanish Colonial Period*. Norman: University of Oklahoma Press, 1994.

Kalmanovitz, Salomón. *Economía y nación: Una breve historia de Colombia*. Bogotá: Grupo Editorial Norma, 2003.

Kamen, Henry. *Spain, 1469–1714: A Society of Conflict*. 2nd ed. London: Longman, 1991.

———. "The Decline of Spain: A Historical Myth?" *Past and Present* 81 (November 1978): 24–50.

Keith, Robert G. *Conquest and Agrarian Change: The Emergence of the Hacienda System on the Peruvian Coast*. Cambridge, MA: Harvard University Press, 1976.

———. "Encomienda, Hacienda and Corregimiento in Spanish America: A Structural Analysis." *Hispanic American Historical Review* 51, no. 3 (August 1971): 431–46.

Kelly, John E. *Pedro de Alvarado, Conquistador*. 1934. Reprint, Port Washington, NY: Kennikat Press, 1967.

Kicza, John E. "Migration to Major Metropoles in Colonial Mexico." In David J. Robinson, ed., *Migration in Colonial Spanish America*, 193–211. Cambridge: Cambridge University Press, 1990.

———. *Colonial Entrepreneurs: Families and Businesses in Bourbon Mexico City*. Albuquerque: University of New Mexico Press, 1983.

Kidder, Alfred II. "The Archeology of Venezuela." In Julian H. Steward, ed., *Handbook of South American Indians*, vol. 4, *The Circum-Caribbean Tribes*, 413–38. Washington, DC: U.S. Government Printing Office, 1948.

Kinsbruner, Jay. *Chile: A Historical Interpretation*. New York: Harper & Row, 1973.

Kirchhoff, Paul. "The Caribbean Lowland Tribes: The Mosquito, Sumo, Paya, and Jicaque," "The Otomac," "Food-Gathering Tribes of the Venezuelan Llanos," and "The Tribes North of the Orinoco River." In Julian H. Steward, ed., *Handbook of South American Indians*, vol. 4, *The Circum-Caribbean Tribes*, 219–29, 439–44, 445–68, 481–93. Washington, DC: U.S. Government Printing Office, 1948.

Kirtz, Mary M. "The British and Spanish Migration Systems in the Colonial Era: A Policy Framework." In Mercedes Pedrero Nieto, ed., *The Peopling of the Americas*, 1:263–81. Veracruz, Mexico: International Union for the Scientific Study of Population, 1992.

Klaczko, Jaime, and Juan Rial. *Uruguay: El país urbano*. Montevideo: Ediciones de la Banda Oriental, 1981.

Klarén, Peter Flindell. *Peru: Society and Nationhood in the Andes*. New York: Oxford University Press, 2000.

Klein, Herbert S. *A Concise History of Bolivia*. Cambridge: Cambridge University Press, 2003.

———. *Haciendas and Ayllus: Rural Society in the Bolivian Andes in the Eighteenth and Nineteenth Centuries*. Stanford, CA: Stanford University Press, 1993.

———. "The Integration of Immigrants into the United States and Argentina: A Comparative Analysis." *American Historical Review* 88, no. 2 (April 1983): 306–29.

———. "The State and the Labor Market in Rural Bolivia in the Colonial and Early Republican Periods." In Karen Spalding, ed., *Essays in the Political, Economic and Social History of Colonial Latin America*, 95–106. Newark: University of Delaware, Latin American Studies Program, 1982.

Kleinpenning, Jan M. G. *Paraguay, 1515–1870: A Thematic Geography of Its Development*, vols. 1 and 2. Madrid: Iberoamericana, 2003.

———. *Peopling the Purple Land: A Historical Geography of Rural Uruguay, 1500–1915*. Amsterdam: CEDLA, 1995.

Knight, Alan. *Mexico: From the Beginning to the Spanish Conquest*. Cambridge: Cambridge University Press, 2002.

———. *Mexico: The Colonial Era*. Cambridge: Cambridge University Press, 2002.

———. "The Peculiarities of Mexican History: Mexico Compared to Latin America, 1821–1992." *Journal of Latin American Studies*, Quincentenary Supplement, 24 (1992): 99–144.

Koebel, W. H. *Uruguay*. London: T. Fisher Unwin, 1911.

Korth, Eugene H. *Spanish Policy in Colonial Chile: The Struggle for Social Justice, 1535–1700*. Stanford, CA: Stanford University Press, 1968.

Kramer, Wendy. *Encomienda Politics in Early Colonial Guatemala, 1524–1544*. Boulder, CO: Westview Press, 1994.

Kraudy Medina, Pablo. *Historia social de las ideas en Nicaragua: El pensamiento de la conquista*. Managua: Banco Central de Nicaragua, 2001.

Kroeber, A. L. "The Chibcha." In Julian H. Steward, ed., *Handbook of South American Indians*, vol. 2, *The Andean Civilizations*, 887–909. Washington, DC: U.S. Government Printing Office, 1946.

Kubler, George. *The Indian Caste of Peru, 1795–1940: A Population Study Based upon Tax Records and Census Reports*. Westport, CT: Greenwood Press, 1973.

Ladd, Doris M. *The Mexican Nobility at Independence, 1780–1826*. Austin: University of Texas Press, 1976.

Lane, Kris. *Quito 1599: City and Colony in Transition*. Albuquerque: University of New Mexico Press, 2002.

Lang, James. *Conquest and Commerce: Spain and England in the Americas*. New York: Academic Press, 1975.

Lara Pinto, Gloria. "Sociopolitical Organization in Central and Southwest Honduras at the Time of the Conquest: A Model for the Formation of Complex Society." In William R. Fowler Jr., ed., *The Formation of Complex Society in Southeastern Mesoamerica*, 215–35. Boca Raton, FL: CRC Press, 1991.

Lardé y Larín, Jorge. *El Salvador: Descubrimiento, conquista y colonización.* 2nd ed. San Salvador: Dirección de Publicaciones e Impresos, 2000.

———. *El Salvador: Historia de sus pueblos, villas y ciudades.* 2nd ed. San Salvador: Dirección de Publicaciones e Impresos, 2000.

Larraz López, José. *La época del mercantilismo en Castilla, 1500–1700.* Madrid: Aguilar, 1963.

Larson, Brooke. *Cochabamba, 1550–1900: Colonialism and Agrarian Transformation in Bolivia.* Expanded ed. Durham, NC: Duke University Press, 1998.

Lauria-Santiago, Aldo A. *An Agrarian Republic: Commercial Agriculture and the Politics of Peasant Communities in El Salvador, 1823–1914.* Pittsburgh, PA: University of Pittsburgh Press, 1999.

Levene, Ricardo. *Las Indias no eran colonias.* Buenos Aires: Cía. Editora Espasa-Calpe Argentina, 1951.

———, ed. *Historia de la nación Argentina*, vol. 4, *El momento histórico del Virreinato del Río de la Plata.* Buenos Aires: Imprenta de la Universidad, 1938.

———. *A History of Argentina.* Translated and edited by William Spence Robertson. Chapel Hill: University of North Carolina Press, 1937.

Lindo-Fuentes, Héctor. *Weak Foundations: The Economy of El Salvador in the Nineteenth Century, 1821–1898.* Berkeley: University of California Press, 1990.

Lockhart, James. *Spanish Peru, 1532–1560: A Social History.* 2nd ed. Madison: University of Wisconsin Press, 1994.

———. *The Nahuas after the Conquest: A Social and Cultural History of the Indians of Central Mexico, Sixteenth through Eighteenth Centuries.* Stanford, CA: Stanford University Press, 1992.

———. *Nahuas and Spaniards: Postconquest Central Mexican History and Philology.* Stanford, CA: Stanford University Press, 1991.

———. "Encomienda and Hacienda: The Evolution of the Great Estate in the Spanish Indies." *Hispanic American Historical Review* 49, no. 3 (August 1969): 411–29.

Lockhart, James, and Stuart B. Schwartz. *Early Latin America: A History of Colonial Spanish America and Brazil.* Cambridge: Cambridge University Press, 1983.

Lohmann Villena, Guillermo. *Las minas de Huancavelica en los siglos XVI y XVII.* Seville: Escuela de Estudios Hispano-Americanos, 1949.

Lombardi, Cathryn L., and John V. Lombardi (with K. Lynn Stoner). *Latin American History: A Teaching Atlas.* Madison: University of Wisconsin Press, 1983.

Lombardi, John V. *Venezuela: The Search for Order, the Dream of Progress.* New York: Oxford University Press, 1982.

———. *People and Places in Colonial Venezuela.* Bloomington: Indiana University Press, 1976.

López Beltrán, Clara. *Estructura económica de una sociedad colonial: Charcas en el siglo XVII.* La Paz: Escuela Profesional "Don Bosco," 1988.

Lothrop, Samuel K. "The Diaguita of Chile." In Julian H. Steward, ed., *Handbook of South American Indians*, vol. 2, *The Andean Civilizations*, 633–6. Washington, DC: U.S. Government Printing Office, 1946.

———. "Indians of the Paraná Delta and La Plata Littoral." In Julian H. Steward, ed., *Handbook of South American Indians*, vol. 1, *The Marginal Tribes*, 177–90. Washington, DC: U.S. Government Printing Office, 1946.

Lovell, W. George. *A Historical Geography of the Cuchumatán Highlands, 1500–1821.* Montreal: McGill-Queen's University Press, 2005.

———. "Surviving Conquest: The Maya of Guatemala in Historical Perspective." *Latin American Research Review* 23, no. 2 (1988): 25–57.

Lovell, W. George, and Christopher H. Lutz. *Demography and Empire: A Guide to the Population History of Spanish Central America, 1500–1821.* Boulder, CO: Westview Press, 1995.

Lovell, W. George, Christopher H. Lutz, and William R. Swezey. "The Indian Population of Southern Guatemala, 1549–1551: An Analysis of López de Cerrato's *Tasaciones de Tributos.*" *The Americas* 40, no. 4 (April 1984): 459–77.

Lovell, W. George, and William R. Swezey. "Indian Migration and Community Formation: An Analysis of 'Congregación' in Colonial Guatemala." In David J. Robinson, ed., *Migration in Colonial Spanish America*, 18–40. Cambridge: Cambridge University Press, 1990.

———. "The Population of Southern Guatemala at Spanish Contact." *Canadian Journal of Anthropology* 3, no. 1 (Fall 1982): 71–84.

Loveman, Brian. *Chile: The Legacy of Hispanic Capitalism.* 2nd ed. New York: Oxford University Press, 1988.

Lucena Salmoral, Manuel. "La sociedad de la provincia de Caracas a comienzos del siglo XIX." *Anuario de Estudios Americanos* 37 (1980): 157–89.

Luján Muñoz, Jorge. "Características, consecuencias, y alcances de la conquista." In Jorge Luján Muñoz, ed., *Historia general de Guatemala*, vol. 2, *Dominación española: Desde la conquista hasta 1700*, 75–84. Guatemala City: Fundación para la Cultura y el Desarrollo, 1994.

———. "Política fundacional en los siglos XVI y XVII." In Jorge Luján Muñoz, ed., *Historia general de Guatemala*, vol. 2, *Dominación española: Desde la conquista hasta 1700*, 131–42. Guatemala City: Fundación para la Cultura y el Desarrollo, 1994.

Luján Muñoz, Jorge, and Horacio Cabezas Carcache. "Comercio." In Jorge Luján Muñoz, ed., *Historia general de Guatemala*, vol. 2, *Dominación española: Desde la conquista hasta 1700*, 451–68. Guatemala City: Fundación para la Cultura y el Desarrollo, 1994.

———. "La conquista." In Jorge Luján Muñoz, ed., *Historia general de Guatemala*, vol. 2, *Dominación española: Desde la conquista hasta 1700*, 47–74. Guatemala City: Fundación para la Cultura y el Desarrollo, 1994.

Lutz, Christopher H. "Evolución demográfica de la población ladina." In Jorge Luján Muñoz, ed., *Historia general de Guatemala*, vol. 3, *Siglo XVIII hasta la independencia*, 110–33. Guatemala City: Fundación para la Cultura y el Desarrollo, 1995.

———. "Evolución demográfica de la población no indígena." In Jorge Luján Muñoz, ed., *Historia general de Guatemala*, vol. 2, *Dominación española: Desde la conquista hasta 1700*, 249–68. Guatemala City: Fundación para la Cultura y el Desarrollo, 1994.

———. *Santiago de Guatemala, 1541–1773: City, Caste, and the Colonial Experience.* Norman: University of Oklahoma Press, 1994.

Lynch, John. *Bourbon Spain, 1700–1808.* Oxford: Basil Blackwell, 1989.

———. "The River Plate Republics." In Leslie Bethell, ed., *Spanish America after Independence, c. 1820–c. 1870*, 314–75. Cambridge: Cambridge University Press, 1987.

———. *Spain under the Habsburgs: Empire and Absolutism, 1516–1598.* Oxford: Basil Blackwell, 1964.

———. *Spanish Colonial Administration, 1782–1810: The Intendant System in the Viceroyalty of the Río de la Plata.* London: Athlone Press, 1958.

MacLachlan, Colin M., and Jaime E. Rodríguez O. *The Forging of the Cosmic Race: A Reinterpretation of Colonial Mexico.* Berkeley: University of California Press, 1980.

MacLeod, Murdo J. "Ethnic Relations and Indian Society in the Province of Guatemala, ca. 1620–ca. 1800." In Murdo J. MacLeod and Robert Wasserstrom, eds., *Spaniards and Indians in Southeastern Mesoamerica: Essays on the History of Ethnic Relations*, 189–214. Lincoln: University of Nebraska Press, 1983.

———. *Spanish Central America: A Socioeconomic History, 1520–1720.* Berkeley: University of California Press, 1973.

Mahoney, James. "Long-Run Development and the Legacy of Colonialism in Spanish America." *American Journal of Sociology* 109, no. 1 (July 2003): 50–106.

Mallon, Florencia E. "Indian Communities, Political Cultures, and the State in Latin America, 1780–1990." *Journal of Latin American Studies*, Quincentenary Supplement, 24 (1992): 35–53.

Marchán Romero, Carlos. "Economía y sociedad durante el siglo XVIII." *Cultura: Revista del Banco Central del Ecuador* 8, no. 24 (April 1986): 55–76.

Marfany, Roberto H. "La lucha con los indios en la época colonial" and "Los pueblos fronterizos en la época colonial." In Ricardo Levene, ed., *Historia de la Provincia de Buenos Aires y formación de sus pueblos*, 1:121–35, 137–46. La Plata, Argentina: Taller de Impresiones Oficiales, 1940.

Marks, Patricia H. "Confronting a Mercantile Elite: Bourbon Reformers and the Merchants of Lima, 1765–1796." *The Americas* 60, no. 4 (April 2004): 519–58.

———. "Power and Authority in Late Colonial Peru: Viceroys, Merchants, and the Military, 1775–1821." PhD diss., Princeton University, 2003.

Márquez Miranda, Fernando. "The Diaguita of Argentina." In Julian H. Steward, ed., *Handbook of South American Indians,* vol. 2, *The Andean Civilizations*, 637–54. Washington, DC: U.S. Government Printing Office, 1946.

Martin, Cheryl English. *Rural Society in Colonial Morelos.* Albuquerque: University of New Mexico Press, 1985.

Martínez, José Luis. *Pasajeros de Indias: Viajes transatlánticos en el siglo XVI.* Madrid: Alianza Editorial, 1983.

Marzahl, Peter. *Town in the Empire: Government, Politics, and Society in Seventeenth-Century Popayán.* Austin: University of Texas Press, 1978.

Mayo, Carlos A. "Landed but Not Powerful: The Colonial Estancieros of Buenos Aires." *Hispanic American Historical Review* 71, no. 4 (November 1991): 761–79.

Mayo, Carlos A., and Amalia Latrubesse. *Terratenientes, soldados y cautivos: La frontera, 1736–1815.* 2nd ed. Buenos Aires: Editorial Biblos, 1998.

McAlister, L. N. "Social Structure and Social Change in New Spain." *Hispanic American Historical Review* 43, no. 3 (August 1963): 349–70.

McCaa, Robert. "Figures, Facts and Fallacies: The Population of Colonial Venezuela." *Latin American Research Review* 13, no. 1 (1978): 195–200.

McFarlane, Anthony. *Colombia before Independence: Economy, Society, and Politics under Bourbon Rule.* Cambridge: Cambridge University Press, 1993.

McGreevey, William Paul. *An Economic History of Colombia, 1845–1930.* Cambridge: Cambridge University Press, 1971.

McKinley, P. Michael. *Pre-revolutionary Caracas: Politics, Economics, and Society, 1777–1811.* Cambridge: Cambridge University Press, 1985.

Means, Philip Ainsworth. *Fall of the Inca Empire and the Spanish Rule in Peru, 1530–1780.* New York: Gordian Press, 1971.

Melo, Jorge Orlando. *Historia de Colombia*, vol. 1, *El establecimiento de la dominación española.* Medellin, Colombia: Editorial La Carreta, 1977.

Meneray, Wilbur Eugene. "The Kingdom of Guatemala during the Reign of Charles III." PhD diss., University of North Carolina at Chapel Hill, 1975.

Métraux, Alfred. "Ethnography of the Chaco." In Julian H. Steward, ed., *Handbook of South American Indians,* vol. 1, *The Marginal Tribes*, 197–370. Washington, DC: U.S. Government Printing Office, 1946.

Milletich, Vilma. "El Río de la Plata en la economía colonial." In Enrique Tandeter, ed., *Nueva Historia Argentina: La sociedad colonial*, 189–240. Buenos Aires: Sudamericana, 2000.

Millones, Luis. *Perú colonial: De Pizarro a Tupac Amaru II.* Lima: Industrial Gráfica, 1995.

Millot, Julio, and Magdalena Bertino. *Historia económica del Uruguay*, vol. 1. Montevideo: Fundación de Cultura Universitaria, 1991.

Mills, Kenneth. *Idolatry and Its Enemies: Colonial Andean Religion and Extirpation, 1640–1750.* Princeton, NJ: Princeton University Press, 1997.

Minchom, Martin. *The People of Quito, 1690–1810: Change and Unrest in the Underclass.* Boulder, CO: Westview Press, 1994.

Miño Grijalva, Manuel. "Estudio introductorio." In Manuel Miño Grijalva, ed., *La economía colonial: Relaciones socioeconómicas de La Real Audiencia de Quito,* 13–85. Quito: Corporación Editora Nacional, 1984.

Molina Jiménez, Iván. *Costa Rica (1800–1850): El legado colonial y la génesis del capitalismo.* San José: Editorial de la Universidad de Costa Rica, 1991.

Monge Alfaro, Carlos. *Historia de Costa Rica.* 14th ed. San José: Librería Trejos, 1976.

Mora Merida, José Luis. *Historia social de Paraguay, 1600–1650.* Seville: EEHA, 1973.

Mörner, Magnus (with Harold Sims). *Adventurers and Proletarians: The Story of Migrants in Latin America.* Pittsburgh, PA: University of Pittsburgh Press, 1985.

Mörner, Magnus. "The Rural Economy and Society of Colonial Spanish America." In Leslie Bethell, ed., *The Cambridge History of Latin America,* vol. 2, *Colonial Latin America,* 189–217. Cambridge: Cambridge University Press, 1984.

———. "Spanish Migration to the New World prior to 1810: A Report on the State of Research." In Fredi Chiappelli (with Michael J. B. Allen and Robert L. Benson), ed., *First Images of America: The Impact of the New World on the Old,* 2:737–82. Berkeley: University of California Press, 1976.

———. "The Spanish American Hacienda: A Survey of Recent Research and Debate." *Hispanic American Historical Review* 53, no. 2 (May 1973): 183–216.

Morón, Guillermo. *Breve historia contemporánea de Venezuela.* Mexico City: Fondo de Cultura Económica, 1994.

———. *A History of Venezuela.* Translated by John Street. New York: Roy, 1963.

Morris, Craig. "The Infrastructure of Inka Control in the Peruvian Central Highlands." In George A. Collier, Renato I. Rosaldo, and John D. Wirth, eds., *The Inca and Aztec States, 1400–1800: Anthropology and History,* 153–71. New York: Academic Press, 1982.

Morse, Richard M. "The Heritage of Latin America." In Louis Hartz, ed., *The Founding of New Societies,* 123–77. New York: Harcourt, Brace, & World, 1964.

Moses, Bernard. *The Establishment of Spanish Rule in America: An Introduction to the History and Politics of Spanish America.* New York: G. P. Putnam's Sons, 1907.

Moutoukias, Zacharías. "El crecimiento en una economía colonial de antiguo régimen: Reformismo y sector externo en el Río de la Plata (1760–1796)." *Arquivos do Centro Cultural Calouste Gulbenkian* 34 (1995): 763–813.

Murra, John V. "El control vertical de un máximo de pesos ecológicos en la economía de las sociedades andinas." In John V. Murra, *El mundo andino: Población, medio ambiente y economía,* 85–125. Lima: IEP/Pontificia Universidad Católica del Perú, 2002.

———. "Andean Societies before 1532." In Leslie Bethell, ed., *The Cambridge History of Latin America,* vol. 1, *Colonial Latin America,* 59–90. Cambridge: Cambridge University Press, 1984.

———. *The Economic Organization of the Inka State.* Greenwich, CT: JAI Press, 1980.

———. "An Aymara Kingdom in 1567." *Ethnohistory* 15, no. 2 (Spring 1968): 115–51.

———. "The Historic Tribes of Ecuador." In Julian H. Steward, ed., *Handbook of South American Indians,* vol. 2, *The Andean Civilizations,* 785–821. Washington, DC: U.S. Government Printing Office, 1946.

Navarrete, María Cristina. *Historia social del negro en la colonia: Cartagena, siglo XVII.* Cali, Colombia: Talleres de la Editorial de la Facultad de Humanidades de la Universidad del Valle, 1995.

Neumann, Bernhard. "Historia de la amalgamación de la plata." *Revista Chilena de Historia y Geografía* 102 (January–June 1943): 158–259.

Newland, Carlos. "Economic Development and Population Change: Argentina, 1810–1870." In John H. Coatsworth and Alan M. Taylor, eds., *Latin America and the World Economy since 1800,* 208–17. Cambridge, MA: Harvard University Press, 1998.

Newson, Linda A. *Life and Death in Early Colonial Ecuador.* Norman: University of Oklahoma Press, 1995.

———. "Highland-Lowland Contrasts in the Impact of Old World Diseases in Early Colonial Ecuador." *Social Science Medicine* 36, no. 9 (1993): 1187–95.

———. *Indian Survival in Colonial Nicaragua.* Norman: University of Oklahoma Press, 1987.

———. *The Cost of Conquest: Indian Decline in Honduras under Spanish Rule.* Boulder, CO: Westview Press, 1986.

———. "Indian Population Patterns in Colonial Spanish America." *Latin American Research Review* 20, no. 3 (1985): 41–74.

———. "Labour in the Colonial Mining Industry of Honduras." *The Americas* 39, no. 2 (October 1982): 186–203.

Nicolau, Juan Carlos. *Antecedentes para la historia de la industria Argentina.* Buenos Aires: Talleres Gráficos Lumen, 1968.

Nieto, Felipe, and Gabino Mendoza. *Historia de España,* vol. 12, *Los Borbones del siglo XVII.* Madrid: Círculo de Amigos de la Historia, 1979.

O'Phelan Godoy, Scarlett. *Rebellions and Revolts in Eighteenth Century Peru and Upper Peru.* Cologne: Böhlau, 1985.

Ortiz de la Tabla Ducasse, Javier. *Los encomenderos de Quito, 1534–1660: Origen y evolución de una elite colonial.* Seville: Escuela de Estudios Hispano-Americanos, 1993.

Ouweneel, Arij. *Shadows over Anáhuac: An Ecological Interpretation of Crisis and Development in Central Mexico, 1730–1800.* Albuquerque, University of New Mexico Press, 1996.

Oviedo y Baños, José de. *The Conquest and Settlement of Venezuela.* Translated by Jeannette Johnson Varner. Berkeley: University of California Press, 1987.

Palacio Atard, Vicente. *La España del siglo XVIII: El siglo de las reformas.* Madrid: U.N.E.D., 1978.

Palacios Preciado, Jorge. "La esclavitud y la sociedad esclavista." In Jaime Jaramillo Uribe, ed., *Nueva historia de Colombia,* 153–74. Bogotá: Planeta Colombiana Editorial, 1989.

Palmer, Colin A. *Slaves of the White God: Blacks in Mexico, 1570–1630.* Cambridge, MA: Harvard University Press, 1976.

Parry, J. H. *The Sale of Public Office in the Spanish Indies under the Hapsburgs.* Berkeley: University of California Press, 1953.

Patch, Robert W. *Maya and Spaniard in Yucatan, 1648–1812.* Stanford, CA: Stanford University Press, 1993.

Payne Iglesias, Elizet. *Origen y crisis de una colonia marginal: El siglo XVII en Costa Rica.* San José: EUNED, 1992.

Pérez, Aquiles R. *Las mitas en la Real Audiencia de Quito.* Quito: Ministerio del Tesoro, 1947.

Pérez, Joseph. "El nuevo reino de Granada en vísperas de la independencia (1781–1809)." In Inge Buisson, Günter Kahle, Hans-Joachim König, and Horst Pietschmann, eds., *Problemas de la formación del estado y de la nación en hispanoamérica,* 93–106. Cologne: Böhlau, 1984.

Pérez, Louis A. *Cuba: Between Reform and Revolution.* New York: Oxford University Press, 1988.

Perlstein Pollard, Helen. *Taríacuri's Legacy: The Prehispanic Tarascan State.* Norman: University of Oklahoma Press, 1993.

Phelan, John Leddy. *The People and the King: The Comunero Revolution in Colombia, 1781.* Madison: University of Wisconsin Press, 1978.

———. *The Kingdom of Quito in the Seventeenth Century: Bureaucratic Politics in the Spanish Empire.* Madison: University of Wisconsin Press, 1967.

Phillips, William D. Jr., and Carla Rahn Phillips. "Spain in the Fifteenth Century." In Kenneth J. Andrien and Rolena Adorno, eds., *Transatlantic Encounters: Europeans and Andeans in the Sixteenth Century,* 11–39. Berkeley: University of California Press, 1991.

Pi Hugarte, Renzo. *Los indios del Uruguay.* Montevideo: Ediciones de la Banda Oriental, 1998.

Piñero, Eugenio. "The Cacao Economy of the Eighteenth-Century Province of Caracas and the Spanish Cacao Market." *Hispanic American Historical Review* 68, no. 1 (February 1988): 75–100.

Pinto Soria, Julio César. "Apuntes históricos sobre la estructura agrarian y asentamiento en la Capitanía General de Guatemala." In Stephen Webre, ed., *La sociedad colonial de Guatemala: Estudios regionales y locales,* 109–40. Antigua, Guatemala: Centro de Investigaciones Regionales de Mesoamérica, 1989.

Pollak-Eltz, Angelina. *La esclavitud en Venezuela: Un estudio histórico-cultural.* Caracas: Universidad Católica Andres Bello, 2000.

Powell, Philip Wayne. *Soldiers, Indians, and Silver: The Northward Advance of New Spain, 1550–1600.* Berkeley: University of California Press, 1952.

Powers, Karen Vieira. *Andean Journeys: Migration, Ethnogenesis, and the State in Colonial Quito.* Albuquerque: University of New Mexico Press, 1995.

Pregger-Román, Charles G. "The Origin and Development of the Bourgeoisie in Nineteenth-Century Chile." *Latin American Perspectives* 10 (1983): 39–59.

Prescott, William H. *History of the Conquest of Peru.* London: J. M. Dent & Co., 1908.

———. *History of the Conquest of Mexico, with a Preliminary View of the Ancient Mexican Civilization, and the Life of the Conqueror Hernando Cortez.* Philadelphia: J. B. Lippincott & Co., 1867.

Presta, Ana María. *Los encomenderos de La Plata, 1550–1600.* Lima: Instituto de Estudios Peruanos, 2000.

Przeworski, Adam (with Carolina Curvale). "Does Politics Explain the Economic Gap between the United States and Latin America?" In Francis Fukuyama, ed. *Falling Behind: Explaining the Development Gap between Latin America and the United States,* 99–133. Oxford: Oxford University Press, 2008.

Quirós, Claudia. *La era de la encomienda.* San José: EDUCR, 1998.

Radell, David Richard. "A Historical Geography of Western Nicaragua: The Spheres of Influence of León, Granada, and Managua, 1519–1965." PhD diss., Department of Geography, University of California, Berkeley, 1969.

Ramírez, Susan Elizabeth. *The World Upside Down: Cross-Cultural Contact and Conflict in Sixteenth-Century Peru.* Stanford, CA: Stanford University Press, 1996.

———. *Provincial Patriarchs: Land Tenure and the Economics of Power in Colonial Peru.* Albuquerque: University of New Mexico Press, 1986.

Randall, Laura. *A Comparative Economic History of Latin America, 1500–1914,* vol. 2, *Argentina.* Ann Arbor, MI: University Microfilms International for Institute of Latin American Studies, Columbia University, 1977.

Rausch, Jane M. *A Tropical Plains Frontier: The Llanos of Colombia, 1531–1831.* Albuquerque: University of New Mexico Press, 1984.

Ravignani, Emilio. "El Virreinato del Río de la Plata (1776–1810)." In Richard Levene, ed., *Historia de la nación Argentina,* vol. 4, *El momento histórico del Virreinato del Río de la Plata,* 27–332. Buenos Aires: Imprenta de la Universidad, 1938.

Rector, John L. *The History of Chile.* New York: Palgrave Macmillan, 2003.

———. "El impacto económico de la independencia en América Latina: El caso de Chile." *Historia* 20 (1985): 295–318.

Reichel-Dolmatoff, Gerardo. "Colombia indígena, período prehispánico." In Jaime Jaramillo Uribe, ed., *Nueva historia de Colombia,* 27–68. Bogotá: Planeta Colombiana Editorial, 1989.

República Argentina. *Resumen estadístico del movimiento migratorio en la República Argentina, años 1857–1924.* Buenos Aires: Ministerio de Agricultura de la Nación, 1925.

Reyes Abadie, Washington, and Andrés Vázquez Romero. *Crónica general del Uruguay,* vol. 1, *Los orígenes.* Montevideo: Ediciones de la Banda Oriental, 1998.

———. *Crónica general del Uruguay,* vol. 2, *El siglo XVIII.* Montevideo: Ediciones de la Banda Oriental, 1998.

Rock, David. *Argentina, 1516–1987: From Spanish Colonization to Alfonsín.* Rev. ed. Berkeley: University of California Press, 1987.

Rodríguez, Mario. "The Genesis of Economic Attitudes in the Rio de la Plata." *Hispanic American Historical Review* 36, no. 2 (May 1956): 171–89.

Rodríguez Becerra, Salvador. *Encomienda y conquista: Los inicios de la colonización en Guatemala.* Seville: Universidad de Sevilla, 1977.

Rodríguez Vicente, María Encarnación. *El Tribunal del Consulado de Lima en la primera mitad del siglo XVII.* Madrid: Ediciones Cultura Hispánica, 1960.

Romero Vargas, Germán. *Las estructuras sociales de Nicaragua en el siglo XVIII.* Managua: Vanguardia, 1987.

Rosal, Miguel A., and Roberto Schmit. "Las exportaciones pecuarias bonaerenses y el espacio mercantile rioplatense (1768–1854)." In Raúl O. Fradkin and Juan Carlos Garavaglia, eds., *En busca de un tiempo perdido: La economía de Buenos Aires en el país de la abundancia, 1750–1865,* 159–89. Buenos Aires: Prometeo Libros, 2004.

Rosés Alvarado, Carlos. "El ciclo del cacao en la economía colonial de Costa Rica, 1650–1794." *Mesoamérica* 3, no. 4 (December 1982): 247–78.

Rostworowski de Diez Canseco, María. *History of the Inca Realm.* Translated by Harry Iceland. Cambridge: Cambridge University Press, 1999.

Rowe, John Howland. "The Incas under Spanish Colonial Institutions." *Hispanic American Historical Review* 37, no. 2 (May 1957): 155–99.

———. "Inca Culture at the Time of the Spanish Conquest." In Julian H. Steward, ed., *Handbook of South American Indians,* vol. 2, *The Andean Civilizations,* 183–330. Washington, DC: U.S. Government Printing Office, 1946.

Rubio, Julian M. *Exploración y conquista del Río de la Plata: Siglos XVI y XVII.* Barcelona–Buenos Aires: Salvat Editores, 1942.

Ruiz, Teofilo F. *Spanish Society: 1400–1600.* Harlow, England: Pearson Education, 2001.

Ruiz Rivera, Julián B. *Encomienda y mita en Nueva Granada en el siglo XVII.* Seville: Escuela de Estudios Hispano-Americanos, 1975.

Sábato, Hilda. *Agrarian Capitalism and the World Market: Buenos Aires in the Pastoral Age, 1840–1890.* Albuquerque: University of New Mexico Press, 1990.

Saeger, James. "Warfare, Reorganization, and Readaptation at the Margins of the Spanish Rule – The Chaco and Paraguay (1573–1882)." In Frank Salomon and Stuart B. Schwartz, eds., *The Cambridge History of the Native Peoples of the Americas,* vol. 3, *South America,* pt. 2, pp. 257–86. Cambridge: Cambridge University Press, 1999.

Safford, Frank, and Marco Palacios. *Colombia: Fragmented Land, Divided Society.* Oxford: Oxford University Press, 2002.

Saignes, Thierry. "Indian Migration and Social Change in Seventeenth-Century Charcas." In Brooke Larson and Olivia Harris (with Enrique Tandeter), eds., *Ethnicity, Markets, and Migration in the Andes: At the Crossroads of History and Anthropology,* 167–95. Durham, NC: Duke University Press, 1995.

Sala de Touron, Lucía, and Rosa Alonso Eloy. *El Uruguay comercial, pastoral y caudillesco,* vol. 1, *Economía.* Montevideo: Ediciones de la Banda Oriental, 1986.

Sala de Touron, Lucía, Nelson de la Torre, and Julio C. Rodríguez. *Estructura económico-social de la colonia.* Montevideo: Ediciones Pueblos Unidos, 1967.

Salas de Coloma, Mirian. *Estructura colonial del poder español en el Perú: Huamanga (Ayacucho) a través de sus obrajes, siglos XVI–XVIII,* vol. 1. Lima: Pontificia Universidad Católica del Perú, 1998.

Salcedo-Bastardo, J. L. *Historia fundamental de Venezuela.* 8th ed. Caracas: Universidad Central de Venezuela, 1979.

Salomon, Frank. *Native Lords of Quito in the Age of the Incas: The Political Economy of North Andean Chiefdoms.* Cambridge: Cambridge University Press, 1986.

_____. "Vertical Politics on the Inka Frontier." In John V. Murra, Nathan Wachtel, and Jacques Revel, eds., *Anthropological History of Andean Politics*, 89–117. Cambridge: Cambridge University Press, 1986.

Salvatore, Ricardo, and Jonathan Brown. "The Old Problem of Gauchos and Rural Society." *Hispanic American Historical Review* 69, no. 4 (November 1989): 733–45.

_____. "Trade and Proletarianization in Late Colonial Banda Oriental: Evidence from the Estancia de las Vacas, 1791–1805." *Hispanic American Historical Review* 67, no. 3 (August 1987): 431–59.

Salvucci, Richard J. "Mexican National Income in the Era of Independence, 1800–40." In Stephen Haber, ed., *How Latin America Fell Behind: Essays on the Economic Histories of Brazil and Mexico, 1800–1914*, 216–42. Stanford, CA: Stanford University Press, 1997.

_____. *Textiles and Capitalism in Mexico: An Economic History of the Obrajes, 1539–1840.* Princeton, NJ: Princeton University Press, 1987.

Sánchez-Albornoz, Nicolás. "The Population of Colonial Spanish America." In Leslie Bethell, ed., *The Cambridge History of Latin America*, vol. 2, *Colonial Latin America*, 3–35. Cambridge: Cambridge University Press, 1984.

_____. *Indios y tributos en el Alto Perú.* Lima: Instituto de Estudios Peruanos, 1978.

_____. *The Population of Latin America: A History.* Translated by W. A. R. Richardson. Berkeley: University of California Press, 1974.

Sánchez Quell, H. *Estructura y función del Paraguay colonial.* Buenos Aires: Editorial Kraft, 1964.

Santos Martínez, Pedro. "Política de España en Europa: Conflictos con Portugal e Inglaterra." In Academia Nacional de la Historia, *Nueva historia de la nación Argentina*, vol. 2, *Período español (1600–1800)*, 319–50. Buenos Aires: Editorial Planeta, 1999.

Santos Pérez, José Manuel. *Élites, poder local y régimen colonial: El cabildo y los regidores de Santiago de Guatemala, 1700–1787.* South Woodstock, VT: Plumstock Mesoamerican Studies, 1999.

Sauer, Carl O. *The Early Spanish Main.* Berkeley: University of California Press, 1966.

Schwaller, John Frederick. "Mexico City Market Structures and the Formation of the Hacienda." In Richard Herr, ed., *Themes in Rural History of the Western World*, 249–62. Ames: Iowa State University Press, 1993.

_____. *Origins of Church Wealth in Mexico: Ecclesiastical Revenues and Church Finances, 1523–1600.* Albuquerque: University of New Mexico Press, 1985.

Schwartz, Stuart. "The Landed Elite." In Louisa Schell Hoberman and Susan Migden Socolow, eds., *The Countryside in Colonial Latin America*, 97–121. Albuquerque: University of New Mexico Press, 1997.

Seligson, Mitchell A. *Peasants of Costa Rica and the Development of Agrarian Capitalism.* Madison: University of Wisconsin Press, 1980.

Semo, Enrique. *The History of Capitalism in Mexico: Its Origins, 1521–1763.* Translated by Lidia Lozano. Austin: University of Texas Press, 1993.

Sempat Assadourian, Carlos. "The Colonial Economy: The Transfer of the European System of Production to New Spain and Peru." *Journal of Latin American Studies*, Quincentenary Supplement, 24 (1992): 55–68.

_____. *El sistema de la economía colonial: Mercado interno, regiones y espacio económico.* Lima: Instituto de Estudios Peruanos, 1982.

_____. "La producción de la mercancía dinero en la formación del mercado interno colonial: El caso del espacio peruano, siglo XVI." In Enrique Florescano, ed., *Ensayos sobre el desarrollo económico de México y América Latina (1500–1975)*, 223–92. Mexico City: Fondo de Cultura Económica, 1979.

Serrano, Antonio. "The Charrua." In Julian H. Steward, ed., *Handbook of South American Indians*, vol. 1, *The Marginal Tribes*, 191–6. Washington, DC: U.S. Government Printing Office, 1946.

Service, Elman R. "Indian-European Relations in Colonial Latin America." *American Anthropologist* 57, no. 3 (June 1955): 411–25.

———. *Spanish-Guaraní Relations in Early Colonial Paraguay*. Westport, CT: Greenwood Press, 1954.

Sharp, William Frederick. *Slavery on the Spanish Frontier: The Colombian Chocó, 1680–1810*. Norman: University of Oklahoma Press, 1976.

Sherman, William L. *Forced Native Labor in Sixteenth-Century Central America*. Lincoln: University of Nebraska Press, 1979.

Silva Vargas, Fernando. "Peru y Chile: Notas sobre sus vinculaciones administrativas y fiscales (1785–1800)." *Historia* 7 (1968): 147–203.

Silverblatt, Irene. "Becoming Indian in the Central Andes of Seventeenth-Century Peru." In Gyan Prakash, ed., *After Colonialism: Imperial Histories and Postcolonial Displacements*, 279–98. Princeton, NJ: Princeton University Press, 1994.

Simpson, Lesley Byrd. *The Encomienda in New Spain*. Berkeley: University of California Press, 1950.

Slicher van Bath, B. H. "Dos modelos referidos a la relación entre población y economía en Nueva España y Perú durante la época colonial." In Arij Ouweneel and Cristina Torales Pacheco, eds., *Empresarios, indios y estado: Perfil de la economía mexicana (siglo XVIII)*, 15–44. Amsterdam: CEDLA, 1988.

Smith, Michael E. *The Aztecs*. Cambridge, MA: Blackwell, 1996.

Smith, Robert. "Indigo Production and Trade in Colonial Guatemala." *Hispanic American Historical Review* 39, no. 2 (May 1959): 181–211.

Smith, Robert Sidney. *The Spanish Merchant Guild: A History of the Consulado, 1250–1700*. Durham, NC: Duke University Press, 1940.

Socolow, Susan Migden. *The Bureaucrats of Buenos Aires, 1769–1810: Amor al Real Servicio*. Durham, NC: Duke University Press, 1987.

———. *The Merchants of Buenos Aires, 1778–1810: Family and Commerce*. Cambridge: Cambridge University Press, 1978.

Solórzano F., Valentín. *Evolución económica de Guatemala*. Guatemala City: Centro Editorial "José de Pineda Ibarra," 1963.

Solórzano Fonseca, Juan Carlos. "Los años finales de la dominación española (1750–1821)." In Héctor Pérez Brignoli, ed., *Historia general de centroamérica*, vol. 3, *De la ilustración al liberalismo (1750–1870)*, 13–71. Madrid: Sociedad Estatal Quinto Centenario, 1993.

Spalding, Karen. *Huarochirí: An Andean Society under Inca and Spanish Rule*. Stanford, CA: Stanford University Press, 1984.

———. "Social Climbers: Changing Patterns of Mobility among the Indians of Colonial Peru." *Hispanic American Historical Review* 50, no. 4 (November 1970): 645–64.

Spicer, Edward H. "Northwest Mexico: Introduction." In Wauchope, *Handbook of Middle American Indians*, vol. 8, pt. 2, pp. 725–73. Austin: University of Texas Press, 1969.

Stanislawski, Dan. *The Transformation of Nicaragua: 1519–1548*. Berkeley: University of California Press, 1983.

Stern, Steve J. *Peru's Indian Peoples and the Challenge of Spanish Conquest: Huamanga to 1640*. Madison: University of Wisconsin Press, 1982.

———. "The Rise and Fall of Indian-White Alliances: A Regional View of 'Conquest' History." *Hispanic American Historical Review* 61, no. 3 (August 1981): 461–91.

Steward, Julian H. "The Circum-Caribbean Tribes: An Introduction." In Julian H. Steward, ed., *Handbook of South American Indians*, vol. 4, *The Circum-Caribbean Tribes*, 1–41. Washington, DC: U.S. Government Printing Office, 1948.

Steward, Julian H., and Louis C. Faron. *Native Peoples of South America*. New York: McGraw-Hill, 1959.

Stone, Doris. "The Northern Highland Tribes: The Lenca." In Julian H. Steward, ed., *Handbook of South American Indians*, vol. 4, *The Circum-Caribbean Tribes*, 205–17. Washington, DC: U.S. Government Printing Office, 1948.

Street, John. *Artigas and the Emancipation of Uruguay.* Cambridge: Cambridge University Press, 1959.

Suñe Blanco, Beatriz. "La ciudad de Santiago de Guatemala." In Jorge Luján Muñoz, ed., *Historia general de Guatemala,* vol. 2, *Dominación española: Desde la conquista hasta 1700,* 187–205. Guatemala City: Fundación para la Cultura y el Desarrollo, 1994.

Super, John C. "Partnership and Profit in the Early Andean Trade: The Experiences of Quito Merchants, 1580–1610." *Journal of Latin American Studies* 11, no. 2 (November 1979): 265–81.

Susnik, Branislava. *El indio colonial del Paraguay,* vols. 1 and 2. Asunción: Museo Etnográfico "Andres Barbero," 1965–6.

Szaszdi, Adam. "The Economic History of the Diocese of Quito, 1616–1787." *Latin American Research Review* 21, no. 2 (1986): 266–77.

Tandeter, Enrique. *Coercion and Market: Silver Mining in Colonial Potosí, 1692–1826.* Albuquerque: University of New Mexico Press, 1993.

———. "Forced and Free Labour in Late Colonial Potosí." *Past and Present* 93 (November 1981): 98–136.

Tapson, Alfred J. "Indian Warfare on the Pampa during the Colonial Period." *Hispanic American Historical Review* 42, no. 1 (February 1962): 1–28.

Tau Anzoátegui, Víctor. "La monarquía: Poder central y poderes locales." In Academia Nacional de la Historia, *Nueva historia de la nación Argentina,* vol. 2, *Período español (1600–1800),* 211–50. Buenos Aires: Editorial Planeta, 1989.

Taylor, William B. *Magistrates of the Sacred: Priests and Parishioners in Eighteenth-Century Mexico.* Stanford, CA: Stanford University Press, 1996.

———. *Landlord and Peasant in Colonial Oaxaca.* Stanford, CA: Stanford University Press, 1972.

Tenenbaum, Barbara A. *The Politics of Penury: Debts and Taxes in Mexico, 1821–1856.* Albuquerque: University of New Mexico Press, 1986.

TePaske, John Jay. "The Financial Disintegration of the Royal Government of Mexico during the Epoch of Independence." In Jaime E. Rodríguez, ed., *The Independence of Mexico and the Creation of the New Nation,* 63–83. Los Angeles: UCLA Latin American Center Publications, University of California, 1989.

TePaske, John J., and Herbert S. Klein. "The Seventeenth-Century Crisis in New Spain: Myth or Reality?" *Past and Present* 90 (February 1981): 116–35.

Thomas, Hugh. *Conquest: Montezuma, Cortés, and the Fall of Old Mexico.* New York: Simon & Schuster, 1993.

Tord, Javier, and Carlos Lazo. *Hacienda, comercio, fiscalidad y luchas sociales (Perú colonial).* Lima: Pontificia Universidad Católica del Perú, 1981.

Tovar Pinzón, Hermes. "Estado actual de los estudios de demografía histórica en Colombia." *Anuario Colombiano de Historia Social y de la Cultura* 5 (1970): 65–103.

Townsend, Richard F. *The Aztecs.* Rev. ed. New York: Thames & Hudson, 2000.

Tschopik, Harry. "The Aymara." In Julian H. Steward, ed., *Handbook of South American Indians,* vol. 2, *The Andean Civilizations,* 501–73. Washington, DC: U.S. Government Printing Office, 1946.

Twinam, Ann. *Miners, Merchants, and Farmers in Colonial Colombia.* Austin: University of Texas Press, 1982.

Tyrer, Robson Brines. "The Demographic and Economic History of the Audiencia of Quito: Indian Population and the Textile Industry." PhD diss., University of California, Berkeley, 1976.

Uribe, Jaime Jaramillo. *Ensayos de historia social.* Bogotá: Tercer Mundo Editores, 1989.

Van Aken, Mark. "The Lingering Death of Tribute in Ecuador." *Hispanic American Historical Review* 61, no. 3 (August 1981): 429–59.

van de Berghe, Pierre L., and George P. Primov. *Inequality in the Peruvian Andes: Class and Ethnicity in Cuzco.* Columbia: University of Missouri Press, 1977.

Van Young, Eric. "Mexican Rural History since Chevalier: The Historiography of the Colonial Hacienda." *Latin American Research Review* 18 (1983): 3–61.

————. *Hacienda and Market in Eighteenth-Century Mexico: The Rural Economy of the Guadalajara Region, 1675–1820.* Berkeley: University of California Press, 1981.

Vargas, José María. *La economía política del Ecuador durante la colonia.* Quito: Banco Central del Ecuador, 1980.

Vargas Lesmes, Julián. *La sociedad de Santa Fe colonial.* Bogotá: CINEP, 1990.

Vassberg, David E. *Land and Society in Golden Age Castile.* Cambridge: Cambridge University Press, 1984.

Vegas de Cáceres, Ileana. "Una imagen distorsionada: Las haciendas de Lima hacia del siglo XVIII." In Scarlett O'Phelan Godoy, ed., *El Perú en el siglo XVIII: La era borbónica*, 97–125. Lima: Pontificia Universidad Católica del Perú, 1999.

————. *Economía rural y estructura social en las haciendas de Lima durante el siglo XVIII.* Lima: Fondo Editorial, 1996.

Vicens Vives, Jaime. *An Economic History of Spain.* Translated by Frances M. López-Morillas. Princeton, NJ: Princeton University Press, 1969.

Vicuña Mackenna, Benjamín. *La edad del oro de Chile.* Buenos Aires: Editorial Francisco de Aguirre, 1969.

Villalobos R., Sergio. *Comercio y contrabando en el Río de la Plata y Chile.* Buenos Aires: Editorial Universitaria de Buenos Aires, 1965.

Villamarín, Juan A. "Encomenderos and Indians in the Formation of Colonial Society in the Sabana de Bogota Colombia, 1537 to 1740." PhD diss., Department of Anthropology, Brandeis University, 1972.

Villamarín, Juan A., and Judith E. Villamarín. "Epidemic and Disease in the Sabana of Bogotá." In Noble David Cook and W. George Lovell, eds., *Secret Judgments of God: Old World Disease in Colonial Spanish America*, 113–41. Norman: University of Oklahoma Press, 1992.

————. "The Concept of Nobility in Colonial Santa Fe de Bogotá." In Karen Spalding, ed., *Essays in the Political, Economic and Social History of Colonial Latin America,* 125–53. Newark: University of Delaware, Latin American Studies Program, 1982.

Wachtel, Nathan. "The Indian and the Spanish Conquest." In Leslie Bethell, ed., *The Cambridge History of Latin America,* vol. 1, *Colonial Latin America*, 207–48. Cambridge: Cambridge University Press, 1984.

Walker, Charles F. "Civilize or Control? The Lingering Impact of the Bourbon Urban Reforms." In Nils Jacobsen and Cristóbal Aljovín de Losada, eds., *Political Cultures in the Andes, 1750–1950*, 74–95. Durham, NC: Duke University Press, 2005.

————. *Smoldering Ashes: Cuzco and the Creation of Republican Peru, 1780–1840.* Durham, NC: Duke University Press, 1999.

Walker, Geoffrey J. *Spanish Politics and Imperial Trade, 1700–1789.* Bloomington: Indiana University Press, 1979.

Warren, J. Benedict. *The Conquest of Michoacán: The Spanish Domination of the Tarascan Kingdom in Western Mexico, 1521–1530.* Norman: University of Oklahoma Press, 1985.

Washburn, Douglas Alan. "The Bourbon Reforms: A Social and Economic History of the Audiencia of Quito, 1760–1810." PhD diss., University of Texas at Austin, 1984.

Wauchope, Robert, ed. *Handbook of Middle American Indians: Ethnology,* vols. 7 and 8. Austin: University of Texas Press, 1969.

Webre, Stephen. "Antecedentes económicos de los regidores de Santiago de Guatemala, siglos XVI y XVII: Una élite colonial." In Stephen Webre, ed., *La sociedad colonial en Guatemala: Estudios regionales y locales,* 189–219. Antigua, Guatemala: Centro de Investigaciones Regionales de Mesoamérica, 1989.

————. "The Social and Economic Bases of Cabildo Membership in Seventeenth-Century Santiago de Guatemala." PhD diss., University of Tulane, 1980.

West, Robert C. "The Mining Economy of Honduras during the Colonial Period." *Actas del XXXIII Congreso Internacional de Americanistas* 2 (1959): 767–77.

———. *Colonial Placer Mining in Colombia*. Baton Rouge: Louisiana State University Press, 1952.

Whigham, Thomas. *The Politics of River Trade: Tradition and Development in the Upper Plata, 1780–1870*. Albuquerque: University of New Mexico Press, 1991.

Whitaker, Arthur Preston. *The Huancavelica Mercury Mine: A Contribution to the History of the Bourbon Renaissance in the Spanish Empire*. Cambridge, MA: Harvard University Press, 1941.

White, Alastair. *El Salvador*. London: Ernest Benn, 1973.

Whitehead, Neil. "Native Peoples Confront Colonial Regimes in Northeastern South America (1500–1900)." In Frank Salomon and Stuart B. Schwartz, eds., *The Cambridge History of the Native Peoples of the Americas*, vol. 3, *South America*, pt. 2, pp. 382–442. Cambridge: Cambridge University Press, 1999.

Wiarda, Howard J. "Toward a Framework for the Study of Political Change in the Iberic-Latin Tradition: The Corporative Model." *World Politics* 25, no. 2 (January 1973): 206–35.

Wightman, Ann M. *Indigenous Migration and Social Change: The Forasteros of Cuzco, 1570–1720*. Durham, NC: Duke University Press, 1990.

Wilgus, Curtis A. *The Development of Hispanic America*. New York: Farrar & Rinehart, 1941.

Will, Robert M. "The Introduction of Classical Economics into Chile." *Hispanic American Historical Review* 44, no. 1 (February 1964): 1–21.

Williams, John Hoyt. *The Rise and Fall of the Paraguayan Republic, 1800–1870*. Austin: Institute of Latin American Studies, University of Texas at Austin, 1979.

Woodward, Ralph Lee Jr. "Economic and Social Origins of the Guatemalan Political Parties (1773–1823)." *Hispanic American Historical Review* 45, no. 4 (November 1965): 544–66.

Wortman, Miles L. *Government and Society in Central America, 1680–1840*. New York: Columbia University Press, 1982.

———. "Government Revenue and Economic Trends in Central America, 1787–1819." *Hispanic American Historical Review* 55, no. 2 (May 1975): 251–86.

Zambardino, Rudolph. "Mexico's Population in the Sixteenth Century: Demographic Anomaly or Mathematical Illusion?" *Journal of Interdisciplinary History* 11 (1980): 1–27.

Zamora Acosta, Elias. *Los Mayas de las tierras altas en el siglo XVI*. Seville: Gráficas del Sur, 1985.

Zorraquín Becú, Ricardo. *La organización política argentina en el período hispánico*. 2nd ed. Buenos Aires: Editorial Perrot, 1962.

Zulawski, Ann. *They Eat from Their Labor: Work and Social Change in Colonial Bolivia*. Pittsburgh, PA: University of Pittsburgh Press, 1995.

———. "Frontier Workers and Social Change: Pilaya y Paspara (Bolivia) in the Early Eighteenth Century." In David J. Robinson, ed., *Migration in Colonial Spanish America*, 112–27. Cambridge: Cambridge University Press, 1990.

Zum Felde, Alberto. *Proceso histórico del Uruguay*. 11th ed. Montevideo: ARCA Editorial, 1991.

Index

Abad people, 106
Abernethy, David B., 2
Aborigines, 236
Acemoglu, Daron, 13–14, 17–19, 234, 264–5; quoted, 264
Adelman, Jeremy, 204; quoted, 203
Africa: British colonialism in, 236–7; economic and social disaster in, 237, 257; precolonial societies, 256
African population: as cause of liberal colonialism, 183, 201; in colonial Argentina, 125–6, 130; in colonial Brazil, 245–6; in colonial Colombia, 107–8, 160; in colonial El Salvador, 95; colonial exploitation of, 53; in colonial Mexico, 58, 60; in colonial Peru, 67–9, 71; in colonial Uruguay, 80; in United States, 236; in West Indies, 238; see also slavery
Alvarado, Pedro de, 94, 97
Amaral, Samuel, quoted, 128
Amsden, Alice, 9
Andrews, George Reid, quoted, 191
Andrien, Kenneth J., quoted, 329
Angola: as Portuguese colony, 242, 255–6
Argentina: administrative reforms in, 126; and the "Argentine question," 211; capitalism in, 127; classified as liberal colonial center, 120, 259; classified as mercantilist colonial periphery, 51, 256, 259; colonial settlement of, 81–2, 124–5; compared

to Canada, 251; and contrasting levels of development in interior vs. littoral, 132; and estancias, 127–8, 146; European migration to, 131, 211; and exploitation of indigenous population, 81; exports of, 128; financial institutions in, 126; and "free trade," 125–6; gaucho workers in, 127; GDP per capita of, 128, 210–12; "golden age" in, 128, 210, 211; intendant system in, 126; investments in education in, 224; lack of dominance of large estates in, 127; landed class of, 127; literacy and life expectancy in, 222–4; livestock industry of, 82, 126–7, 130, 211; merchants in, 82, 126–8; nation-building myths in, 224; precolonial societies in, 77–9; problems of industrialization in, 211, 212; reversal of development in, 212; silver exports of, 82–3; temperate agriculture of, 211; and timing of economic takeoff, 129; as "wealthier nation of the world," 210–12; see also Buenos Aires
Arias de Ávila, Pedro (also Pedrarias Dávila), 97
Armada, the Spanish Invincible, 36
Ashanti Kingdom, 237
Atahualpa, king of Inca Empire, 66
Australia: as British colony, 235–6, 255; as a "new country," 211–12; rule of law in, 229, 235
Austria: GDP per capita of, 210–11